“Strong Men of the Regiment Sobbed Like Children”:

John Reynolds’ I Corps at Gettysburg on July 1, 1863

The Savas Beatie

Essential Gettysburg Series

Mitchell Yokelson
Series Editor

1. Elwood W. Christ, *"Over a Wide, Hot . . . Crimson Plain": The Struggle for the Bliss Farm at Gettysburg, July 2nd and 3rd, 1863*

2. John Michael Priest, *"Strong Men of the Regiment Sobbed Like Children": John Reynolds' I Corps at Gettysburg on July 1, 1863*

John Michael Priest

"Strong Men of the Regiment Sobbed Like Children":

John Reynolds' I Corps at Gettysburg on July 1, 1863

Foreword
by Bradley M. Gottfried

Savas Beatie
California

Title: "Strong Men of the Regiment Sobbed Like Children":
John Reynolds' I Corps at Gettysburg on July 1, 1863 / by John Michael Priest.
Description: El Dorado Hills, CA: Savas Beatie LLC [2024] | Series: The Savas Beatie Essential Gettysburg Series | Includes bibliographical references and index. | Summary: "The fighting on the first day at Gettysburg, July 1, 1863, was heavy, confusing, and decisive. Much of it consisted of short and often separate simultaneous engagements or "firefights," a term the soldiers themselves often used to describe the close, vicious, and bloody combat. Several books have studied this important inaugural day of Gettysburg, but none have done so from the perspective of the rank and file of both armies. Priest's "Strong Men of the Regiment Sobbed Like Children": John Reynolds's I Corps at Gettysburg on July 1, 1863, rectifies this oversight"— Provided by publisher.
Identifiers: LCCN 2023023638 | ISBN 9781611216899 (hardcover) | ISBN 9781954547612 (ebook)
Subjects: LCSH: Gettysburg, Battle of, Gettysburg, Pa., 1863. | Reynolds, John Fulton, 1820-1863. | United States. Army. Corps, 1st (1862-1865) | United States—History—Civil War, 1861-1865—Campaigns. | Soldiers—Confederate States of America. | Soldiers—United States—History—19th century.
Classification: LCC E475.53 .P945 2023 | DDC 973.7/349—dc23/eng/20230606
LC record available at https://lccn.loc.gov/2023023638

First Trade Paperback Edition, First Printing, 2025
ISBN-13: 978-1-61121-750-6

SB
Savas Beatie
989 Governor Drive, Suite 101
El Dorado Hills, CA 95762
916-941-6896
www.savasbeatie.com
sales@savasbeatie.com

To Rhonda,
my wife and partner since 1969.
I could not survive without your love, support, and understanding.

Contents

List of Maps

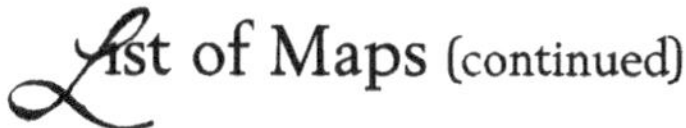

List of Maps (continued)

Photos have been placed throughout the book
for the benefit of the reader.

Acknowledgments

It has taken ten years to research and write this book. I could not have accomplished this without the assistance of some very gifted and generous historians and Civil War enthusiasts. In no particular order, I want to thank the following for their contributions.

Joyce Henry, a mounted artillery specialist/trainer, fox hunter, and movie consultant, graciously shared her expertise in helping me ascertain the capabilities of a cavalry horse.

Special thanks to Gettysburg author David G. Martin for permission to use his and John W. Busey's *Regimental Strengths and Losses at Gettysburg* in the Order of Battle. Both are superb researchers.

Tom Elmore, a major contributor to the online discussion group Civil War Talk, shared hard-to-find Confederate sources from his personal collection dealing with couriers, Iverson's Brigade, the capture of the 149th Pennsylvania's flags, and other sources dealing with Joe Davis's Brigade.

Phil Spaugy, whose passion is the study of the 19th Indiana, graciously provided me with valuable primary sources about the color guard of that Iron Brigade regiment as well as Hollon Richardson's speech at an Iron Brigade reunion in Indianapolis.

Mike Lavis of Buffalo, New York, is a devoted living historian with the 49th New York and a brother in Christ. He read the rough draft of the manuscript and offered some insightful suggestions. Bob Lehman, Mahoning Valley Civil War Round Table, accompanied by several of his close friends, trekked the rough terrain along Willoughby Run a couple of times. He also read and critiqued the manuscript. Former teaching colleague and avid miniature wargamer, Adam Perry also read the manuscript. He patiently listened to me bounce my reasoning behind many conclusions on how bits and pieces of this part of the battle was fought. I greatly appreciate his honest observations and excellent knowledge of Napoleonic tactics.

William T. Venner, the author of *Hoosiers' Honor*, *The Seventh Tennessee Infantry in the Civil War*, and *The 11th North Carolina Infantry in the Civil War*, also reviewed portions of the book. His well-documented regimentals provided me with a treasure of primary sources to hunt up and read.

Joseph Bilby, renowned Civil War weapons expert and the author of *Small Arms at Gettysburg*, *The Irish Brigade in the Civil War*, and other topics, introduced me to "patent cartridges," the Enfield cartridge, and the standard U. S. cartridge. He explained how the first two types of ammunition facilitated loading while on the march.

Lance Herdegen, the nationally recognized historian of the Iron Brigade, the author of many books on that unit, and my friend, gave his imprimatur to my description of the Westerners' role in the fighting, including the famous charge by the 6th Wisconsin against the railroad cut. Lance provided good suggestions that improved the writing. He is a great fellow. "You betcha!"

James McLean, former owner of the prestigious Butternut and Blue, is a true Gettysburg expert. Jim is the author of several studies and the renowned historian of Lysander Cutler's brigade. His classic on that outfit has just been revised and released by Savas Beatie as *"The Bullets Flew Like Hail": Cutler's Brigade at Gettysburg, from McPherson's Ridge to Culp's Hill*. Jim generously provided me with a copy of one of his sources involving the 76th New York's encounter with Alfred Iverson's men.

Fellow historian David Ward scrounged his exhaustive files and shared several primary sources with me.

Steve Stanley provided the excellent base maps upon which I placed troop movements specific to the various actions on the field.

Bradley Gottfried, fellow Antietam battlefield guide and the author, cartographer, and the man who came up with the idea of the Savas Baeatie Military Atlas Series (which includes *The Maps of Gettysburg*), was kind enough to pen the Foreword for this book. He also patiently listened to how I arrived at my conclusions of the fighting on July 1, some of which varies from traditional interpretations. Brad is extremely knowledgeable and a most affable fellow for whom I have the greatest respect.

I would be remiss if I did not thank John Heiser, former National Park Service archivist and historian at the Gettysburg National Military Park library.

John was a joy to work with and his encyclopedic knowledge of the campaign and battle provided me with a plethora of primary sources, published and unpublished, from the massive files and books stacks at the library. I shall miss not seeing him there. He is a national treasure.

I particularly want to thank James Pula, the recently retired editor of *Gettysburg Magazine*. Over the years Jim published several of my articles related to the research behind this book. His two-volume set *Under the Crescent Moon with the Eleventh Corps in the Civil War* (Savas Beatie) remains the best history of this oft- maligned corps in print.

To Theodore P. Savas of Savas Beatie, thank you for including this study in the Essential Gettysburg Series, and for working with me throughout the years. Your attention to detail and willingness to answer my questions about the intricacies of the publishing industry has made me a better author. I appreciate your straightforward and unpretentious frankness.

Mitchell "Mitch" Yokelson, an outstanding military historian and archivist at the National Archives, does incredible work as the series editor in finding and filtering manuscripts for publication. Ted assigned Joel Manuel to an early draft of the manuscript. Joel helped edit a rough draft and it was a pleasure working with him. His meticulous attention to detail has smoothed out the rough edges in the book and made it so much better. Thanks also to the wonderful SB ladies, including Sarah Closson and Lisa Murphy, for their hard work behind the scenes on this series.

I am particularly grateful. for my wife of 54 years, Rhonda. She has put up with the long hours of writing, research, and annoying but necessary map revisions. More importantly, she has shown me how to balance my time between my love of history and the family. She is the voice of common sense and truth in my life.

For those of you reading this book, I humbly thank you. History, not propaganda and mythology, is the lifeblood of a nation and its culture. Thank you for perpetuating the memory of those who preceded us.

Finally, any mistakes that made it into print, whether of fact, grammar, or interpretation, are mine alone. In a work of this magnitude, undoubtedly some crept in. I apologize in advance.

John M. Priest
April 2023

Foreword

When I ask battlefield guides and other folks who study Gettysburg about the most intriguing part of the engagement, I am always surprised by how many reply, "The events of July 1."

All three days of the battle were filled with action, drama, and seminal events, but July 1 may hold the most interest for the most people. Perhaps it was the "accident" that caused Maj. Gen. Henry Heth's Confederate division to collide with Brig. Gen. John Buford's Union cavalry outside of Gettysburg and the gallant stand made by the troopers until the infantry and artillery of Maj. Gen. John Reynolds's I Corps appeared.

The subsequent pendulum swings during the morning are the stuff of legend, when fate (and perhaps a bit of good luck) smiled on the Union troops. The Iron Brigade appeared at just the right moment to catch Brig. Gen. James Archer's brigade crossing Willoughby Run in front and flank, causing many Confederates to throw up their hands, including Archer himself—the first of Robert E. Lee's generals to turn over his sword during a battle. A short time later, Brig. Gen. Joseph Davis's Rebel brigade achieved success on the north side of the Chambersburg Pike, driving Brig. Gen. Lysander Cutler's brigade from its position on Seminary Ridge. A well-timed counterattack by two of Cutler's regiments and one of the Iron Brigade, however, caused Davis's men to seek refuge in an unfinished railroad cut, where scores were captured.

The ensuing lull allowed both armies to bring up reinforcements. Brigadier General John Robinson led his Second Division men north beyond the Chambersburg Pike to Oak Ridge. They wanted the more dominant Oak Hill farther north, but Maj. Gen. Robert Rodes's Confederate division beat them to it. Rodes, however, launched an uncoordinated attack. Robinson held his ground and inflicted heavy losses. The sudden and violent repulse of Brig. Gen. Alfred Iverson's exposed Tar Heels still brings chills to all of us.

While the I Corps was fighting west of town, Maj. Gen. Oliver Howard's XI Corps marched through Gettysburg and took up a position north of it. The terrain there was not optimal for a defensive action. Blocher's Knoll was used to anchor the right flank. A cloud of Confederates from Maj. Gen. Jubal Early's Division attacked the XI Corps from the north as part of Rodes's Division attacked from the north and west. This combined effort broke apart Howard's corps and drove Robinson's brigades from their positions.

To the south of the Chambersburg Pike, the Iron Brigade continued strengthening its position on McPherson's Ridge as the rest of Heth's Division appeared in its front about 3:00 p.m. Outnumbered and outflanked, the tough Westerners were driven from their positions on the ridge, as was Col. Chapman Biddle's brigade, which had formed in an open field behind it and to its left, without ever making contact.

Fresh Confederate troops from Maj. Gen. Dorsey Pender's Division replaced Heth's bloodied and exhausted men. Driving through the open fields leading to Seminary Ridge, Pender's infantry encountered what was left of the I Corps making its last stand. The gallant charge by Pender's men threw the Union troops off defensibly ground and into the streets of Gettysburg, where chaos ensued. What occurred next, or perhaps what did not happen, may have sealed the outcome of the battle: A. P. Hill, Lee's Third Corps commander, chose not to attack Cemetery Hill/Ridge, and Second Corps leader Richard Ewell decided to wait to assail Culp's Hill. The battle's first day drew to close.

The story of Gettysburg's inaugural day has been recounted in several very good books. That fact alone might cause some to throw up their hands and announce, "No! Not another book on Gettysburg!" For those of us who value the complexity and importance of the battle, however, Mike Priest's new study is a breath of fresh air.

There are many books on Gettysburg; this one is different. *"Strong Men of the Regiment Sobbed Like Children": John Reynolds' I Corps at Gettysburg on July 1, 1863* delves into the battle from the soldiers' point of view. Many fine works tell the story of Gettysburg via seminal events, while others concentrate on leaders, strategy, and tactics. This one puts readers in the shoes of the men who did the actual fighting.

Mike has made a career out of telling the story of the Civil War through the actions and words of the men who pulled the triggers, yanked the lanyards, and fired the carbines. What began with a pair of books on the Maryland Campaign moved on to two more on the Battle of the Wilderness. This is not Mike's first book on Gettysburg. In 2016, Savas Beatie published his best-selling *"Stand To It and Give Them Hell": Gettysburg as the Soldiers Experienced it From Cemetery Ridge to Little Round Top, July 2, 1863.*

I have always appreciated Mike's enthusiasm for research. He is especially interested in solving mysteries or correcting erroneous but widely accepted views on the battle. He regularly approaches me with new finds/interpretations on Gettysburg and his passion is contagious. This shows in his prose, which draws you in and makes you feel that you know the men he is writing about.

There are many things I like about this book. Yes, it covers the I Corps—John Reynolds's boys—in great detail, but it also adds context by fully covering the Confederates who eventually overwhelmed them. This helps to better understand what the I Corps and cavalrymen faced as they encountered overwhelming numbers of enemy while waiting for reinforcements. I also appreciate the time he took to assemble the statistics on the strengths and losses of both sides at the end of the book. His thoughtful analysis of the roles of terrain and man-made features is outstanding. Finally, the list of references and extensive footnotes make it clear that Mike spent considerable time researching the actions he describes. Not everyone will agree with all of his conclusions or analysis, but there is no doubt he will make you reflect more deeply on a wide range of issues.

No matter your level of interest and experience with the battle of Gettysburg, you will find this book fascinating and enlightening. I thank Mike for making the effort to share the story with all of us.

Bradley M. Gottfried
Fayetteville, Pennsylvania

Introduction

"Pray, that you may never know,
the Hell where youth and laughter go."

On Tuesday, August 11, 1863, 41-year-old hospital steward John N. Henry (Company I, 49th New York, Sedgwick's VI Corps, Army of the Potomac), who had barely recovered from sunstroke, scrawled the following in his diary:

> My general health is failing and my day of usefulness and improvement is nearly passed. My hair is turning gray and I am growing old. I have not seen my family for nearly two years and have but faint hope of ever seeing them again. The practice here in the army is to drag men along when they are of any use and then turn them out to die like a mule.[1]

Traditionally, many historians and the general reading public cited Gettysburg as the turning point of the Civil War—the infamous "High Water Mark of the Confederacy." John Henry, whose VI Corps saw limited action in the most written-about battle in history, emphasized the brutal reality of the effects of the battle on the men—both veteran and green—who fought it. Soldiers of all wars have felt the same way.

The effects of combat affected me because I grew up with them. My father, Ira Lee Priest, never left the Marine Corps, or, for that matter, Guadalcanal. Like many men who had seen too much combat, he seldom talked about the war.

1 John Michael Priest, ed., *Turn Them Out To Die Like A Mule* (Leesburg, VA, 1995), 258.

During the few time he did, his eyes reflected the deep trauma he had experienced during World War II. His pupils dilated and turned black as he spoke. The distant frightening "thousand-yard stare" overshadowed his face. The memories of his six months in the South Pacific haunted him for the rest of his life. It is no exaggeration to say those months siphoned the soul out of him and entombed him in a mental grave from which he was unable to extricate himself. His loneliness, anger, and nightmares affected the entire family.

Death lurked everywhere on Guadalcanal, which stank of decaying wildlife and vegetation. Dad was always worse at night, especially during lightning storms. When the weather turned noisy outdoors, he would pace the floor while vehemently cursing. Sometimes he cried. He often woke up suddenly, frightened and angry. We never approached him while he slept.

Death haunted him. He often cursed God for not letting him die like a large portion of his battalion at Peleliu. Crippled with malaria and weight loss, many Marines, my father among them, had to be evacuated on stretchers. Every summer after that the disease returned to knock him flat. I can still see him on the couch covered with quilts, saturated with sweat, delirious, and freezing.

Dad taught me the lessons of history rarely found in books. He taught me how fragile love and compassion are. He taught me never to forget the "little man." He showed me that emotional scars run deeper than the physical ones, and that many men like himself have carried and will carry bitter memories and broken spirits to the edge of eternity. In so many ways, these men died long before they grew old.

A navy doctor who examined the Marines after they left Guadalcanal concluded they suffered not so much from "a bloodstream infection nor gastrointestinal disease but from a disturbance of the whole organism—a disorder of thinking and living, or even wanting to live." It is no coincidence that Dad suffered from "survivors' guilt." He equated death in combat with sainthood. After the Canal he lived to die—to release himself from the bondage of his memories.[2]

Civil War veterans suffered every bit as much my father or other World War II survivors. Many never left the battlefields. Some drank to forget, but intoxication often intensified the clarity of their memories. Others self-medicated with opiates like morphine, sitting in the shadows remembering while feeling real pain in arms and legs they no longer had. Thousands helped

2 George McMillan, *The Old Breed* (Washington, D.C., 1949), 159.

monument the battlefields with cenotaphs to remember the dead and the mortally wounded. For far too many, the monuments also marked the places where their emotions had died.

"Strong Men of the Regiment Sobbed Like Children" describes what the men of both armies endured in vivid detail. Their memoirs, diaries, letters, books, and articles wrote this book. I merely clarified and corrected occasional mistaken recollections, and did my best to organize them into a cohesive storyline.

Few if any intentionally exaggerated what they experienced. Some made mistakes, all of them understandable; the fog and confusion and chaos of combat impacted everyone, and each man only witnessed a small slice of that sprawling battlefield. Each absorbed it through their own chaotic prism. It took some of these men many long years, and in some cases many decades, to talk or write about their personal trauma. The death, the maiming, and the horror of it all, left countless survivors empty and lost.

In his World War I poem "Suicide in the Trenches," English combat veteran Siegfried Sassoon aptly wrote, "Pray, that you may never know, the Hell where youth and laughter go." Erich Maria Remarque, a German veteran of that war, penned *All Quiet on the Western Front,* one of literature's all-time classics and a groundbreaking portrayal of trench warfare. Like Sassoon, Remarque spoke for all combat soldiers throughout the ages when he penned:

> This book is to be neither an accusation nor a confession, and least of all an adventure, for death is not an adventure to those who stand face to face with it. It will try simply to tell of a generation of men who, even though they may have survived its shells, were destroyed by the war.[3]

John Michael Priest

3 Erich Maria Remarque, *All Quiet on the Western Front* (New York, NY, 1930), 1.

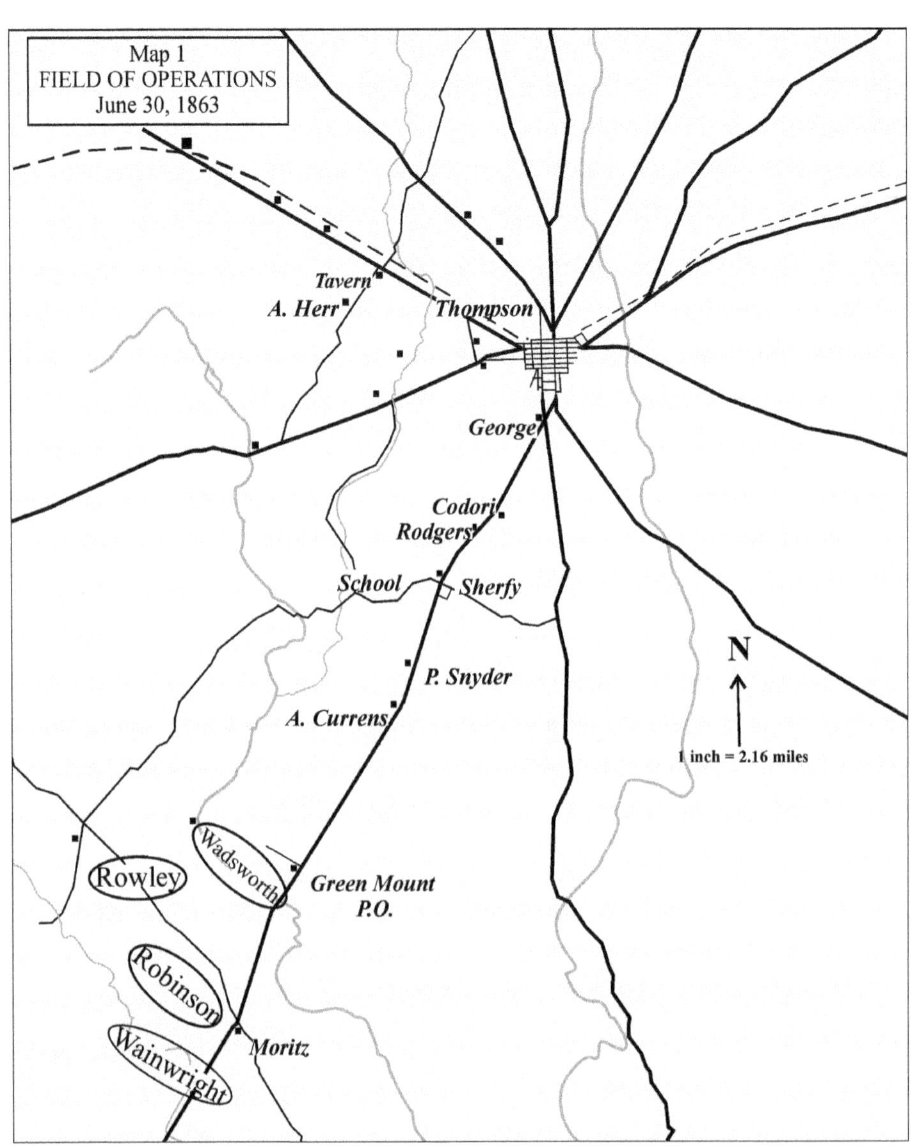
Map 1
FIELD OF OPERATIONS
June 30, 1863
Tavern
A. Herr
Thompson
George
Codori
Rodgers
School
Sherfy
P. Snyder
A. Currens
N
1 inch = 2.16 miles
Wadsworth
Rowley
Green Mount
P.O.
Robinson
Wainwright
Moritz

Chapter One

"Well, I guess some of us will be bait for the crows pretty soon."

— *Anonymous soldier, 2nd Wisconsin, June 29, 1863*

First Contact: June 29 to 30, 1863

Brigadier General John Buford's Union cavalry division, comprised of Cols. William Gamble's and Thomas C. Devin's brigades, and Lt. John H. Calef's Battery A, 2nd U.S. Artillery, was on the last part of its arduous reconnaissance from Middletown, Maryland to Gettysburg, Pennsylvania. By crossing to the west side of South Mountain, Buford could quickly alert the Army of the Potomac of any Confederate movement that could threaten its advance north through Maryland.

The column rode west from Middletown on the National Pike across South Mountain to Boonsboro, then north along the western base of the mountain range into Pennsylvania. At Waterloo (now Rouzerville), Pennsylvania, it recrossed the mountain through Monterrey Pass and headed east toward Emmitsburg, Maryland, from which it was to ride north to Gettysburg. Buford had until the evening of June 30 to cover the 55 miles. The first leg of the march, 32 miles in 14 hours of essentially nonstop riding, ended at 10:00 p.m. on June 29 at Fountain Dale on the eastern base of the South Mountain range.[1]

1 *The War of the Rebellion: A Compilation of the Official Records of the Union and Confederate Armies*, 128 vols. (Washington, D.C., 1880-1901), Series 1, vol. 27, Part 3, p. 376, hereafter cited as *OR* 27/3:376; Abner Frank, Diary, June 29, 1863, USAHEC,

June 30, 1863

The second day's march began in an impenetrable fog at 4:00 a.m. when Buford, apparently to save time and unnecessary hardship for his saddle-sore men and spent horses, attempted to get to Gettysburg by way of the Fairfield (Hagerstown) Road, thereby bypassing the longer march to Emmitsburg. His lead regiment, the 8th Illinois Cavalry, stumbled into a Confederate picket outpost commanded by Lt. William E. Kyle (Company B, 52nd North Carolina) at the covered bridge on the Jacks Mountain Road. A brief but heated firefight ensued. Buford abruptly disengaged rather than bring on a general fight in the fog. The 8th countermarched, accidentally leaving a dismounted trooper, Pvt. Thomas Withrow (Company C), behind; Withrow's horse joined the column without him. Captain William L. Heermance's squadron (Companies B and C, 6th New York Cavalry) from Devin's brigade replaced the Hoosiers on the line to cover the division's escape. Heermance dismounted his men in skirmish order and put up a sporadic fight until the column slipped away.[2]

Carlisle, PA; Eric J. Wittenberg, *"The Devil's to Pay": John Buford at Gettysburg, A History and Walking Tour* (El Dorado Hills, CA, 2014). Wittenberg's groundbreaking study—the first dedicated to the role of the Federal cavalry during the battle—is an essential source and should be among the first consulted.

2 Abner Hard, *History of the Eighth Cavalry Regiment, Illinois Volunteers* (Aurora, IL, 1868), 255; Committee on Regimental History, *History of the Sixth New York Cavalry (Second Ira Harris Guard), Second Brigade, First Division, Cavalry Corps, Army of the Potomac, 1861-1865* (Worcester, MA, 1908), 133; Letters and Partial Diary of Capt. William L. Heermance, 91, Library, BV 487-01 ts, Fredericksburg and Spotsylvania National Military Park (FSNMP); Sarah Sites Thomas, Tim Smith, Gary Kross, & Dean S. Thomas, *Fairfield in the Civil War* (Gettysburg, PA, 2011), 42; Walter Clark, ed., *Histories of the Several Regiments and Battalions from North Carolina in the Great War*, 5 vols. (Goldsboro, NC, 1901), 3:236; "Account of Captain Benjamin F. Little, Co. E, 52nd North Carolina," Vertical Files, V7-NC52, Library, GNMP. The traditional story says the 6th New York Cavalry clashed with the Confederates on the Iron Springs Road (Maria Furnace Road), which paralleled the Jacks Mountain Road. Buford, however, made no mention of splitting his column before or after he reached Fountain Dale. Heermance specifically wrote, "I was sent to check them [the Confederates] with my squadron while the column took another road." Company B, 52nd North Carolina engaged some Federal cavalry (yet unidentified) on the night of June 29-30 on the road to Emmitsburg.

Emmitsburg, Maryland

8 miles southeast of Fairfield, Pennsylvania

The rainy morning of June 30 found this prosperous farming community occupied by the larger part of two Federal corps. Most of the I Corps, Maj. Gen. John F. Reynolds commanding, had arrived during the late afternoon and night of the previous day.[3]

Brigadier General James S. Wadsworth (First Division) placed four of Brig. Gen. Lysander Cutler's five regiments north of the town to cover the Emmitsburg Road to Gettysburg. The 56th Pennsylvania, stuck behind a lengthy wagon train as the rear guard, reached Emmitsburg sometime between midnight and 1:00 a.m. on June 30. Unable to catch up with the rest of the brigade, Col. John W. Hofmann ordered his weary men into a big clover field alongside the Emmitsburg Road just south of the town near St. Joseph's Academy. Except for his headquarters guard, Hofmann's thoroughly soaked soldiers spread their gum blankets over the equally wet grass and collapsed in a deep sleep.[4]

Brigadier General John C. Robinson posted his Second Division about half a mile west of town, north of the Fairfield Road. Having seen war's devastation before, the veterans took little note of the debris from a fire that had destroyed the square and eastern side of the town a little over two weeks earlier. Musician Samuel Webster (Company D, 13th Massachusetts) curtly noted in his diary that Emmitsburg was "half burnt." The Third Division (Maj. Gen. Abner Doubleday commanding) filled the gap between Robinson's men and Wadsworth's.[5]

The gray drizzly morning began with an irritating rain between 3:00 a.m. and 5:00 a.m. In Brig. Gen. Henry Baxter's brigade (Robinson's division), Pvt.

3 Ladd & Ladd, *Bachelder Papers*, 2:939. Lieutenant Colonel William W. Dudley said his 19th Indiana covered about 22 miles in 8.5 hours on June 29.

4 Benjamin F. Cook, *History of the Twelfth Massachusetts Volunteers (Webster Regiment)* (Boston, 1882), 100; J. W. Hofmann, "The Battle: Twenty-Three Years Ago," *Gettysburg Compiler*, June 29, 1886; John Nicholson, ed., *Pennsylvania at Gettysburg*, 3 vols. (Harrisburg, PA, 1893), 1:315; Samuel P. Bates, *History of Pennsylvania Volunteers*, 5 vols. (Harrisburg, PA, 1869), 2:220.

5 Samuel Webster, Diary, June 29, 1863, Huntington Library, San Marino, CA; Survivor's Association, *History of the 121st Regiment, Pennsylvania Volunteers: An Account From the Ranks* (Philadelphia, 1906), 51. I based Rowley's position on an account in the 121st Pennsylvania's history.

Robert S. Coburn (Company H, 83rd New York) groused in his diary, "Still raining for the last four days. Wet through all the time." Corporal Charles Smedley (Company G, 90th Pennsylvania), despite the rain, woke up refreshed around 5:00 and set about his morning routine.

Not long thereafter an elderly couple in their farm wagon rumbled into Companies B's and G's bivouacs. The gentleman and his wife surprised Capt. Jacob M. Davis by dismounting and handing out delicacies to his men in Company B. When Davis asked what they were doing, they calmly replied the obvious: they had food for his soldiers. Knowing that the "boys" would more than likely throng the couple and frighten them away, Davis started shouting at his men to form a line. Company G joined them.

Corporal Smedley waited his turn to get what he could of the biscuits, buttered bread, and donuts. He listened as one of the good Samaritans said, "Poor fellows, we'll give you all we have, if you drive the rebels off, and hope you'll not get killed." Smedley and Davis never forgot the old pair. Davis, noting their plain clothes and the beardless gentleman's cropped hair, mistook them for Quakers.[6]

XI Corps

Major General Oliver O. Howard's XI Corps wheezed into Emmitsburg and camped southwest of town around Mount St. Mary's Convent (the "White House") and St. Joseph's Academy between 4:00 pm. and 6:00 p.m. on June 29. The soldiers admired the convent's well-kept grounds and farm fields. Their beauty astounded Lt. William Ballentine (Company E, 82nd Ohio), who wrote, "The institution of the Sisters of Charity (whose grounds we are now on) farm and building (especially the latter) is the finest I ever saw." The white crosses on the grassy graves and the tiny chapel with its "saintly group of gentle worshippers" greatly impressed Ballentine's captain, Alfred E. Lee. A native of Lima, New York, Pvt. John T. McMahon (Company E, 136th New York)

6 Robert S. Coburn, Diary, June 30, 1863, *Civil War Times Illustrated* Collection, Manuscript Department, USAMHI, Carlisle, PA; The Ladies' and Gentlemen's Fulton Aid Society, *Life in Southern Prisons; from the Diary of Corporal Charles Smedley, of Company G, 90th Regiment Penn'a Volunteers* (Lancaster, PA, 1865), 54. Davis specifically said they were Quakers; they could have been Mennonites. While he did not describe their appearances, the one way to tell the two sects from the German Baptist Brethren and the Amish was that married men in the former two did not grow beards.

scrawled in his diary, "The country here is the best I have ever seen. It will beat our land at home."[7]

Between 3:00 a.m. and 5:00 a.m. on June 30, orders rippled through the XI Corps to Maj. Gen. Carl Schurz's Third Division to be ready to march at daybreak. The morning dawned gray, and a heavy rain pelted the soldiers as they struck their tents and squatted by their smoldering breakfast fires.

At 6:00 a.m., having moved not a yard, officers commanded the men to pitch their saturated tents again and wait. Nineteen-year-old drummer William R. Kiefer (Company F, 153rd Pennsylvania) awakened with a stiff knee and blistered feet, and felt particularly old that morning. His two "pards," Pvts. Stephen "Feldy" and Edwin "Chunky" Knecht, came in from picket duty and joined him for breakfast. The worn-out musician longed for smoking tobacco but had no money to pay for it. Out of nowhere, his extremely sick captain, Lucius Q. Stout, defied the surgeon's orders and showed up with the "insidious weed" and dry socks, both of which he gave to Kiefer. (The previous evening, he had told the boy that he had $79.00 on his person. By daylight he had spent the entire amount to provide his company with socks, tobacco, and other niceties.)[8]

Buford's cavalry reached Emmitsburg between 6:00 a.m. and 7:00 a.m. Without halting, the general directed his two brigades north on the Emmitsburg Road toward Gettysburg. Gamble's regiments took the lead, with the 8th New York holding the "post of honor" at the front of the column. On the way through town, one of Buford's aides stopped momentarily in Battery B, 4th U.S. Artillery's bivouac to inform Lt. James Stewart of their brush with a contingent

7 John W. Hand, "Gettysburg," *National Tribune*, July 24, 1890, 3, hereafter cited as *NT*; John Michael Priest, ed., *John T. McMahon's Diary of the 136th New York, 1861-1864* (Shippensburg, PA, 1993), 53; *OR* 27/:733; William R. Kiefer, *History of the One Hundred Fifty-third Regiment Pennsylvania Volunteer Infantry, Which Was Recruited in Northampton County, PA, 1862-1863* (Easton, PA, 1909), 207; Stephen A. Wallace, Diary, June 29, 1863, Diaries and Journals, Collection, Pennsylvania State Archives, Harrisburg, PA; "A Company Officer," "Reminiscences of the Battle of Gettysburg," *Lippincott's Magazine*, New Series (Philadelphia, 1883), 32:54; John A. Miller, "Monterrey Pass Battlefield Institute's 'When War Passed This Way,'" https://southmountaincw.wordpress.com/; D. G. Brinton Thompson, "From Chancellorsville to Gettysburg: A Doctor's Diary," https://journals.psu.edu/pmhb/article/viewFile/42056/41777. The officer in question was Capt. Alfred E. Lee, Company E, the only wounded and captured officer in the 82nd Ohio.

8 T. A. Dodge, Diary, June 30, 1863, Vertical Files, VF 6-NY119, Library, GNMP; Kiefer, *History of the One Hundred Fifty-third Regiment*, 207; Wallace diary, June 30, 1863.

of Lt. Gen. Ambrose P. Hill's Rebel corps, and that they expected to have a battle the next day.

Stewart, having mustered and inspected the battery that morning, found himself between the proverbial "rock and a hard place." With June 30 being the last day of the month, he, like every battery and regimental commander that morning, found himself preoccupied with filling out and comparing the unit's June returns with the payroll. Every number had to match. Additionally, he had to compile and reconcile the quartermaster, commissary, ordnance, and regimental returns, and have them in the mail no later than the following morning—in addition to preparing his battery for a possible engagement.[9]

Buford stopped briefly at headquarters to inform Reynolds that the Confederates occupied Fairfield. Reynolds immediately sent that information via courier to Maj. Gen. George G. Meade, Army of the Potomac, commanding, at Taneytown. Reynolds, whom Col. Charles S. Wainwright (Chief of Artillery, I Corps) described as "better at carrying out plans than at devising them," immediately issued orders for the corps to march. By the time the infantry divisions got under way, Buford was miles closer to Gettysburg.[10]

Reynolds's I Corps lurched northward at 8:00 a.m. Wadsworth's division, as the command closest to the Pennsylvania line and Marsh Creek, left its bivouac first, followed by Robinson's two brigades, then Doubleday's division.

9 James Stewart, "Battery B Fourth United States Artillery at Gettysburg," in *Sketches of War History, 1861-1865; Papers Prepared for the Ohio Commandery of the Military Order of the Loyal Legion of the United States, 1890-1896*, 8 vols. (Cincinnati, 1896), 4:183; J. William Hofmann, *"Remarks on the Battle of Gettysburg," Paper Read Before the Historical Society of Pennsylvania March 8th 1880* (Philadelphia, 1880), 3. General James Wadsworth's division drew pay that day.

10 Allan Nevins, ed., *A Diary of Battle: The Personal Journals of Colonel Charles S. Wainwright, 1861-1865* (Boston, 1998), 229; John Watts De Peyster, "The Death of Reynolds," *Army and Navy Journal*, June 22, 1867, 43, 4:694; Michael J. Riggleman, *Poinsett's Cavalry Tactics for Reenactors* (2nd U.S. Cavalry, Co. A/9th VA Cavalry, Co. D, Training Committee, 2005), 3 (https://tinyurl.com/3989uhf7, accessed Jan. 10, 2023); *OR* 27/1:926, 3:419; Abner Hard, *History of the Eighth Cavalry Regiment*, 255; John Watts De Peyster, *The Decisive Conflicts of the Late Civil War, or Slaveholders Rebellion*, No. 3 (New York, 1867), 27. *The Army and Navy Journal* began publication in 1863 and exists today as *The Armed Forces Journal*. Based upon Mr. Riggleman's interpretation of *Poinsett's Cavalry Tactics* and knowing that it would have taken about four hours for Buford to enter Gettysburg around 11:00 a.m., I estimated his departure from Emmitsburg to have occurred between the hours stated above. The Army of the Potomac's left wing consisted of the I, III, and XI Corps. Wainwright noted that the I Corps marched at 8:00 a.m.

Brigadier General John Buford's best day of the war was on July 1, 1863, where his stout defense gave time for the rest of the army to come up and possess the high ground below Gettysburg. LOC

The XI Corps received the orders at 8:30 a.m. but did not get under way on schedule.

General Schurz used the delay to find himself some suitable quarters. He called upon Sister Ann Simeon, Mother Superior of the Sisters of Charity, for permission to use one of the school's buildings for his headquarters. After he reassured her that his presence would ensure the school's safety better than a posted sentinel, she graciously agreed. She asked Father James F. Burlando, C.M., the school's chaplain, to take the officers on a tour of the main campus building. The reverend father permitted one of the staff to play the chapel organ.[11]

Emmitsburg Road, South of Gettysburg

A mile or so south of Gettysburg, a rotund farmer on an emaciated horse intercepted Lieutenant Calef's Battery A, 2nd U.S. Artillery, near the tail of Buford's column. Exhausted by the "long, hot dusty march," Calef and Lt. John W. Roder reined in on the roadside, broadly grinning at one another over the comedic-looking fellow's stout body and red face. "How you vas, Shentlemens?" the civilian blurted. Roder, being German, replied in Deutsch.

The "Dutchman," thinking they were grinning at his pathetic mount, said he had hidden his good horses in the "woots, and those damned rebels won't get

11 Carl Schurz, *The Reminiscences of Carl Schurz*, 3 vols. (New York, 1908), 3:3; *The Catholic Church in the United States of America*, 2 vols. (New York, 1914), 2:48. Saint Vincent de Paul founded the Congregation of the Mission (C.M.) in the 1600s.

them sometimes." Before the words had cleared his mouth, two cavalry stragglers with "captured" chickens slung over their saddles and sabers slashing the air stampeded past the three men, covering them in dust. Calef loudly ordered them to halt, knowing full well he was wasting his time. They stopped long enough for him to demand they identify their command and to reprimand their inappropriate behavior. Ignoring him, they "dug spurs" and clattered down the road, the officers' grins following them as they disappeared.

The farmer misinterpreted their response and yelled after them, "That's right, fellers: goes in and knocks down everything what comes before you." Roder and Calef choked back their laughter to tell the farmer that those men were the type who "lived to fight another day."[12]

Cashtown, Pennsylvania

7 miles northwest of Gettysburg

Brigadier General J. Johnston Pettigrew's Brigade, Heth's Division, A. P. Hill's Corps, Army of Northern Virginia

Dawn found musician Julius A. Leinbach and his comrades in the 26th North Carolina drenched from the evening rain. Before the men had stoked their morning fires, a disturbing command arrived from brigade headquarters for them to leave their knapsacks in camp along with anyone not able to endure a "forced march." To Leinbach's relief, his colonel, Henry K. Burgwyn, gave the regimental band the option to participate in the excursion or to remain behind. The band members, all Moravian pacifists, decided to stay with the knapsacks and their disabled comrades.[13]

McKnightstown, Pennsylvania

1.5 miles southeast of Cashtown

Colonel William S. Christian (55th Virginia, Heth's Division), who had not slept at all within the last 24 hours, was not in a good spirits. His misery had

12 John H. Calef, "Gettysburg Notes," *Journal of Military Service Institution of the United States*, 40:45-46.

13 Julius A. Lineback (Leinbach), Untitled Newspaper Article, "26th North Carolina Band," 55, Julius A. Lineback Papers, Southern Historical Collection, Library of the University of North Carolina, Chapel Hill, NC.

begun at sunset the previous evening when his men stacked their arms on a hill west of Cashtown. Hungry and looking for something edible other than army rations, he had started riding toward town to procure an edible meal when an orderly from his brigade commander, Col. John M. Brockenbrough, rode up to him with an urgent message. The colonel wanted Christian to uproot his regiment and head east on the Chambersburg Pike to establish a picket line at a suitable location. Miffed at not getting supper, the colonel heard the messenger blather something about not mistaking friends as foes, and that he would probably encounter troops from Richard Ewell's Second Corps, or perhaps some of General Stuart's cavalry. Christian blocked out whatever else the fellow droned on about.

The frustrated colonel rode to brigade headquarters and asked Brockenbrough to clarify how far out was he to establish his picket. Brockenbrough brushed him aside by saying that Christian knew no more than he did, and that it was an exact copy of an order from General Heth. Christian spurred to division headquarters, where Heth told him the order had come down from General Hill. No one seemed to know much of anything.

Christian returned to his regiment in the dark, formed his companies, and marched about a mile and a half east to the crossroads at McKnightstown. The colonel posted the bulk of his men in a cemetery in the southeastern section of the intersection and placed the rest of the regiment across both sides of the crossroads. Nothing of any importance occurred during the night except that someone "confiscated" several Pennsylvania chickens before daylight and had them cooking by sunup.[14]

Cashtown

General Heth ordered Brig. Gen. Johnston Pettigrew to proceed to Gettysburg with most of his brigade and requisition supplies, including shoes. Under no circumstances was he to bring on a general engagement should he encounter any organized force. Word rippled through the 11th, 26th and 47th North Carolina regiments to strip down for a quick advance. The men of the

14 https://tinyurl.com/rhbh4rx4, Map #22: Map of Adams County, Pennsylvania, 1858 (accessed Jan. 15, 2023), hereafter cited as Map #22; W. S. Christian to John W. Daniel, October 24, 1903, Vertical Files, V 7-VA 55, Library, GNMP. The McKnightstown crossroad consisted of the Lutheran and German Reformed Church (southwest), T. J. Cooker's store (northwest), a schoolhouse (northeast), and the cemetery (southeast).

Brigadier General J. Johnston Pettigrew, a scholar, author, and politician, performed well for his first time at the head of a brigade. He would be mortally wounded near the end of the campaign, and die on July 17, 1863. *Generals in Gray*

26th lost some time getting started to take roll so they could get paid later that day.[15]

Assembling the raiding party consumed a couple of hours of precious daylight. Pettigrew brought up 15 wagons to haul away whatever supplies they might find. Although he only anticipated minor annoyance from the local militia, Pettigrew beefed up the column with a trio of rifled guns from the Donaldsonville Artillery. The column, in the road at prescribed distances, occupied about 2,900 feet.[16]

The exhausted Colonel Christian (55th Virginia) was enjoying his freshly cooked Pennsylvania chicken when he saw Pettigrew's column heading down the pike toward his picket line. The general halted his regiments at the crossroads and asked one of the Virginians to summon his commanding officer. Pettigrew informed Christian that he was on a reconnaissance and wanted his

15 Clark, *Histories of the Several Regiments*, 5:115; *OR* 27/2:637. Heth made it a matter of record in his September 13, 1863, report that he sent Pettigrew to Gettysburg to find supplies, including shoes. Some writers have argued that Maj. Gen. Jubal Early (Ewell's Corps) had passed through the town a few days before and had found no shoes. Heth, who led a division in Hill's Corps, would not have known this.

16 Andrew R. Cross, *The War. Battle of Gettysburg and the Christian Commission* (Baltimore, 1865), 88; Michael Jacobs, *Notes on the Rebel Invasion of Maryland and Pennsylvania and the Battle of Gettysburg, Jul 1st, 2d and 3d, 1863* (Philadelphia, 1864), 21; Lineback, *26th North Carolina Band*, 55. According to Capt. John H. Thorp, Co. A, "Forty-Seventh Regiment," in Clark, *Histories of the Several Regiments*, 3:88-89, a civilian warned the column of an ambush. Given that no other regiment in the reconnaissance reported contact of any sort with Union forces, and the 26th North Carolina stayed at Cashtown to draw pay, the 47th must have led the column. According to Jacobs, "their line of march extended at least a mile and a half in length."

Virginia regiment to join the expedition. The Virginia colonel, who had just spent a sleepless night and had no orders from his brigade commander to go anywhere, predictably declined. Pettigrew acknowledged that he had no right to ask that Christian's 55th Virginia go along, but that his own regiment, the 26th North Carolina, despite being equipped well and well-drilled, had little combat experience, and he wanted a veteran regiment to come along. With that, Christian recalled, "I readily consented to go."[17]

9:30 a.m.
Outskirts of Gettysburg
7 Miles Southeast of Cashtown

Riding in advance of the column and behind a screen of skirmishers drawn from the 47th North Carolina, Pettigrew and his staff halted in the Chambersburg Pike on the crest of Seminary Ridge. The offficers scanned the town in the distance with their field glasses while skirmishers swarmed into the low ground toward Elias Sheads's house and orchard. Curious civilians clustered around the knot of mounted officers. The Confederates casually gleaned fragmentary military intelligence from them. The Carolinians were marching into the hollow between McPherson's Ridge and Seminary Ridge when one of Maj. Gen. James Longstreet's scouts, Henry T. Harrison, passed alongside the column. The scout continued east and briefed Pettigrew on his mission before descending the hill into town.[18]

Meanwhile, Companies F, H, and C of the 8th New York Cavalry, riding well in advance of Buford's column, entered Gettysburg from the south. Harrison spotted them and headed back to Pettigrew. A few minutes ahead of the New Yorkers, he halted long enough to tell Pettigrew that Yankee cavalry now occupied Gettysburg. Almost immediately a Knight of the Golden Circle approached the general and confirmed Harrison's report. Realizing that a larger force of unknown composition might not be far behind, Pettigrew dispatched a courier to Cashtown with orders to bring up the 26th and 52nd regiments and to

17 Christian to Daniel, October 24, 1903.

18 Clark, *Histories of the Several Regiments*, 5:115; Jacobs, *Notes On The Rebel Invasion*, 21. I believe the 47th North Carolina may have stopped on the western slope of Seminary Ridge, because the regiment would have stayed in supporting distance of the skirmishers, and Jacobs said "a portion of Hill's corps" had gotten that far, which implies it was a larger force than a skirmish line.

request further instructions from Heth. He also sent an aide along the column to deliver the command to turn about.[19]

"Halt! About face—quick time, march!" reverberated through the 47th North Carolina, recalled Capt. John H. Thorp (Company A). As the Carolinians reversed direction, shots, apparently from both sides of the road, reverberated over the ridges behind them. Unbeknownst to the captain, Company F, 8th New York Cavalry, in advance of the other two companies, had just chased the 47th's skirmishers away from the Sheads house. With scattered rounds snapping overhead, the Rebs withdrew without responding.[20]

The New Yorkers saw a couple of mounted officers on the top of the hill but did not approach them. What they did not know was that Pettigrew had left behind his aide-de-camp, Lt. Louis G. Young, and his ordnance officer, Lt. Walter G. Robertson, to observe the Federal cavalry. The general was reluctant to break off his scout because of the arrival of companies of Union cavalry, but prudence dictated that he do so. According to Young, "It was purely an affair of observation on both sides and the cavalry made no effort to molest us." Colonel William S. Christian (55th Virginia), having been informed by the orderly that Pettigrew "had found all that he came for," turned back toward McKnightstown.[21]

19 Clark, *Histories of the Several Regiments*, 5:115; Jacobs, *Notes On The Rebel Invasion*, 21; Cross, *The War*, 26; Robert E. L. Krick, *Staff Officers in Gray: A Biographical Register of The Staff Officers in the Army of Northern Virginia* (Chapel Hill, NC, 2003), 311. In 1901 Lt. Louis G. Young, Pettigrew's aide-de-camp, mistakenly recalled that Harrison reported that Buford's entire division was in the town. Harrison would not have been able to see the entire command, nor would he have known it was Buford's division. Young's postwar knowledge influenced his recollection. Pettigrew did not send back for the 52nd North Carolina (of his brigade) and the 42nd Mississippi (Davis's Brigade), as Lt. Young also later recalled, because he did not have the authority to call up the latter. He may have called up the 26th North Carolina, which had remained behind to muster for pay. Captain Benjamin F. Little (Co. E, 52nd North Carolina) said Pettigrew sent back for his regiment.

20 Cross, *The War*, 88-89; Walter B. Norton, "The Last Word About the First Shot," *NT*, April 24, 1884, 7; Frank E. Willett, "Another Gettysburg," *NT*, December 1, 1892, 4. Willett recalled firing at the Confederates while Norton remembered them falling back without any resistance. Captain Thorp claimed several long-range shots came in from both sides of the road as the regiment headed back toward Marsh Creek.

21 Clark, *Histories of the Several Regiments*, 5:116; Thomas J. Luttrell, Diary, June 30, 1863, Manuscript Department, William R. Perkins, Library, Duke University, Durham, NC; Christian to Daniel. Christian may have found the rest of his brigade in bivouac at the crossroad because it makes sense that Brockenbrough would have followed Pettigrew's two remaining regiments forward. Whether he did or not remains unclear.

Gettysburg, Pennsylvania

11:00 a.m. to Noon

While Pettigrew backpedaled, the rest of 8th New York (Gamble's brigade) led the division into Gettysburg on the Emmitsburg Road between 11:00 a.m. and noon. As the column crested the western side of Cemetery Hill the men, glancing to the northwest toward Seminary Ridge, noticed Lieutenants Young and Robertson watching them from the Fairfield Road and assumed they were Confederate cavalrymen. Private Andrew Foulds, Jr. (Company K, 8th New York) believed the Rebs were paying attention to the size of the column.

Turning to the left onto South Washington Street at the Taneytown Road intersection, the troopers rode into a wildly enthusiastic crowd of civilians. Foulds took note of the stark contrast between battle-scarred northern Virginia and Gettysburg. The ladies sang, waved their handkerchiefs, and blew kisses at the cavalrymen, fondly recalled Cpl. James M. Gardner (Company E, 12th Illinois).

Fifteen-year-old Tillie Pierce, along with her sister and other girls, ran down the "side street" from her home on Baltimore Street and clustered on the corner of Washington and High streets to greet the soldiers as they passed Catherine Foster's house. Her sister broke into the chorus of "Our Union Forever" and the other girls chimed in. Not knowing the rest of the song, they repeated the chorus ad nauseam until the last weary soldier passed.[22]

Women proudly wearing red, white, and blue badges and carrying U.S. flags thronged Company C, 6th New York Cavalry. The sounds of "Rally Round the Old Flag Once More" and "We Will Fight For the Union" inundated the street. When one of the ladies handed Capt. William L. Heermance flowers

22 James M. Gardner, "Union vs. Rebel Cavalry," *NT*, November 8, 1898, 8; Andrew Foulds, Jr. to Rev. R. S. McArthur, September 7, 1896, Vertical Files, V6-NY8 Cav, Library, GNMP; Norton, "The Last Word About the First Shot"; William Gamble to W. S. Church, March 10, 1864; Frank diary, June 30, 1863; *OR* 27/1:923-924; David A. Murdoch, "Catherine Mary White Foster's Eyewitness Account of the Battle of Gettysburg, with Background on the Foster Family Union Soldiers," *Adams County History*, no. 5 (1995), 1:49, https://cupola.gettysburg.edu/ach/vol1/iss1/5/ (accessed January 11, 2023); Tillie Pierce Alleman, *At Gettysburg, or What a Girl Saw and Heard of the Battle* (New York, 1889), 28-29; Edmund J. Raus, Jr., *A Generation on the March: The Union Army at Gettysburg* (Lynchburg, VA, 1993), 93. Foster stated the cavalry rode by her home on the corner of S. Washington and High streets. They did not reach the Eagle Hotel by way of Baltimore Street. Tillie Pierce Alleman also said the troopers passed by that corner.

and a flag, his eyes welled with tears. He bit his lips to stifle his surging emotions.[23]

Lieutenant Calef (Battery A, 2nd U.S.) stared at the schoolchildren decked out in white and carrying bunches of flowers and wreaths standing on the street corners and greeting the artillerymen with "The Battle Cry of Freedom." A young girl, in what the lieutenant described as a "very coy and diffident manner," boldly walked into the middle of the street and handed him a huge bouquet.[24]

Another child, about 10 years old, stepped off the sidewalk and tried to pin a corsage on a passing trooper of the 8th Illinois. Seeing she could not reach him, he dismounted. After fastening it on his uniform, she handed him a long purple ribbon, saying. "Soldier, I want you to wear this ribbon in the next fight you're in, the one you're going to have now." "Thank you, my little lady," he politely replied, "and I will, if there is a fight, but I don't think we will have one." "Oh, yes you will, soldier," she insisted. "There's thousands of rebels there, and you will surely have a fight!" "I hope not," he reassured her, "but I thank you very much, and if there is a fight, I will wear it."[25]

Riding alongside Company A, 8th Illinois, Lt. William C. Hazelton encountered a married couple at their front yard gate. They repeatedly asked him to come in and eat: "Can't we do something for you?" one of them pleaded. The lieutenant responded, "You will have an opportunity to do something for us to-morrow." "Why," the startled woman replied, "will there be a battle to-morrow?" The lieutenant rode on without replying.

As the cavalrymen walked their jaded horses through the town, civilians of all ages vied with one another to grasp their filthy hands. They passed beer, wine, cakes, and milk out to every cavalryman within reach. Hazelton sadly recollected, "The careless, happy lads of a few years before had been transformed into stern, resolute veteran soldiers." Bright-eyed women crowded open windows and doorways along the route, waving handkerchiefs at the

23 William L. Heermance to Susie Leeds, July 4, 1863, Vertical Files, VF 48701, FSNMP.

24 Calef, "Gettysburg Notes," 46-47. The 6th New York had only six companies in action on July 1, 1863. Companies D and K, being the II Corps' headquarters escort, did not join the regiment until the morning of July 2. Company A served as the III Corps' headquarters escort. Company L was the provost guard of the 2nd Brigade, First Cavalry Division, and Companies F and H were in Yorktown, Virginia, with the IV Corps.

25 Anonymous Veteran, 8th Illinois Cavalry, *New York Times*, July 1, 1913, Vertical Files, V6-Ill.8 Cav., Library, GNMP.

troopers. A matronly looking lady, who Hazelton assumed had a boy in the army, managed a doleful smile through tears that trickled down her cheeks.[26]

With Buford in the lead, the division worked its way through the throngs of joyous civilians to the Washington Street-Chambersburg Pike intersection. The general and his staff established headquarters at John L. Tate's Eagle Hotel on the northeast corner of the intersection. He ordered Colonel Gamble to proceed west, instructing him to identify the best lines for battle beyond the town, to find cover to shelter the brigade, to send one or two squadrons out to find the enemy, and to establish picket lines. Gamble ordered Maj. John L. Beveridge (8th Illinois Cavalry) to conduct the reconnaissance. Despite the run-down condition of his horses and men, Colonel Devin was tasked with scouting every road northwest and north of Gettysburg.[27]

The 8th New York broke to the southwest along the Fairfield Road where it forked from the Chambersburg Pike near the John Burns house. In passing the Lutheran Seminary on the crest of ridge, the men latched their eyes upon women sporting white dresses thronging the plaza and the balcony of the main building. The ladies, who seemed peculiarly angelic to many of the onlookers, burst into the "Star Spangled Banner" as the colors of the regiment came into view. The soldiers responded with "Three Huzzahs and a Tiger." Private Foulds could not tell who rejoiced more—the delivered or the deliverers. "Inside of five minutes we expected guns would be cracking and bullets singing a deadly tune to (the) rebels," he recalled.

Proceeding to the top of McPherson's Ridge, the New Yorkers halted. Below them lay Willoughby Run and, to the west, wooded Herr's Ridge. No Confederates were in sight. Just below the western crest of McPherson's Ridge they encountered John Horting, who rented the place from George Arnold. Horting told the New Yorkers that the Rebels had spotted the column's approach and vacated the premises not 10 minutes earlier.[28]

26 William C. Hazelton, "People of Gettysburg," *NT*, March 24, 1892, 4.

27 Hard, *History of the Eighth Cavalry*, 256; Gamble to Church; Frank diary, June 30, 1863; *OR* 27/1:923-924; Ladd & Ladd, *Bachelder Papers*, 1:201; Murdoch, "Catherine Mary White Foster's Eyewitness Account." Lieutenant Aaron B. Jerome's letter to Winfield Scott Hancock, Oct. 18, 1865, confirms Buford's headquarters were in a hotel on June 30, 1863.

28 Foulds to McArthur. Foulds erroneously identified the Horting residence as John Burns's house. According to a 1998 map by Thomas J. Desjardin, Horting was a tenant of George Arnold, who owned the property.

McPherson's Ridge

12:00 p.m.to 4:00 p.m.

Lieutenant Colonel William L. Markell (8th New York) ordered Companies B and F west to picket on both sides of the Fairfield Road. They deployed into the low ground on the east bank of Willoughby Run with some of the line extending north along the western face of Herbst Woods. Two mounted videttes from Company F ascended Herr's Ridge to the crossroad west of the Henry Meals house. Twelve "volunteers" from Company C headed down the road under orders to scout as far as Fairfield. Captain Charles D. Follett followed them with Company D and established a second picket line along the eastern base of Bream's Hill. He posted two videttes in the road cut toward the western crest of the hill within sight of the Black Horse Tavern on Marsh Creek.[29]

The rest of the regiment filed into the low ground just west of the Lutheran Seminary. Company K held the right of the line on the Chambersburg Pike. Leaving their horses saddled, the troopers dismounted to give their worn-out and underfed animals and themselves some respite. Within the hour, however, Colonel Gamble sent Companies H and M back into town with orders to proceed southeast on the Baltimore Pike to Littlestown, some 10 miles away. They were to patrol and picket the area, watching for signs that the Confederates had crossed the Federal lines between York, Pennsylvania, and Westminster, Maryland. The disgruntled saddle-stiff troopers mounted and walked back into town along the same route they had entered.[30]

Farther to the right front (northwest), Maj. John Beveridge halted the 8th Illinois in the Chambersburg Road on the crest of McPherson's Ridge. To the west he spotted what appeared to be troops (47th North Carolina) in the road moving away from the town. He dispatched Capt. Henry J. Hotopp's squadron

29 Frank E. Willett, "Another Gettysburg: A Comrade Who Says the 8th N. Y. Cav. Opened the Great Battle," *NT*, December 1, 1894, 4; Norton, "The Last Word About the First Shot"; Henry Norton, *Deeds of Daring or History of the Eighth N. Y. Volunteer Cavalry* (Norwich, NY, 1889), 147; George B. McClellan, *Regulations and Instructions for the Field Service of the U.S. Cavalry in Time of War* (Philadelphia,1862), 64, 65. Subsections 215 and 220, ibid., specifically state that videttes should occupy heights during the day to observe approaches to the field, and that pickets were to occupy crossroads. Based on this, I placed Company D and its forward videttes near and on Bream's Hill. Herbst Woods has traditionally been called McPherson's Woods.

30 Foulds to McArthur.

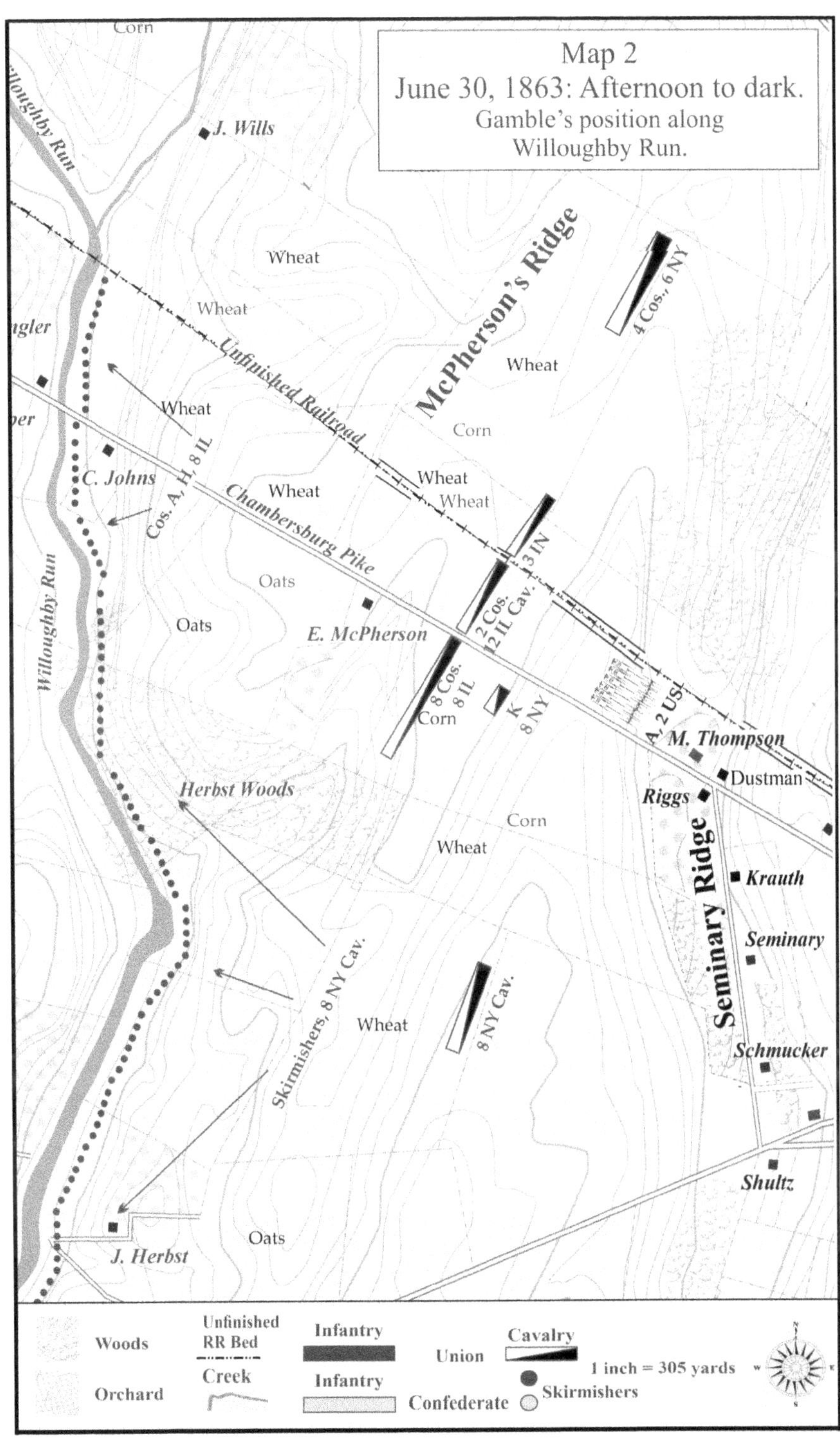
Map 2
June 30, 1863: Afternoon to dark.
Gamble's position along
Willoughby Run.
Corn
Willoughby Run
J. Wills
Wheat
Wheat
McPherson's Ridge
4 Cos., 6 NY
Unfinished Railroad
Wheat
Wheat
Corn
Wheat
Wheat
C. Johns
Cos. A, H, 8 IL
Wheat
Chambersburg Pike
3 IN
Oats
2 Cos. 12 IL Cav.
Willoughby Run
Oats
E. McPherson
8 Cos. 8 IL
Corn
K 8 NY
A, 2 US
M. Thompson
Dustman
Riggs
Herbst Woods
Corn
Wheat
Krauth
Seminary Ridge
Seminary
Skirmishers, 8 NY Cav.
8 NY Cav.
Wheat
Schmucker
Shultz
Oats
J. Herbst
Woods
Orchard
Unfinished RR Bed
Creek
Infantry
Infantry
Union
Confederate
Cavalry
Skirmishers
1 inch = 305 yards

(Companies D and F) to find out who they were. Hotopp reined in atop Knoxlyn Ridge. His men had lost sight of the enemy, who had crossed safely to the west side of Marsh Creek and disappeared over the next ridge. From his picket outpost on the Lohr Farm, Lt. John H. Moore (Company B, 7th Tennessee) spied a few of the distant Union troopers. Being so far away, and because Heth's Division had no cavalry with it, Moore automatically assumed they were Yankee scouts and nothing more. Nevertheless, he sent word of their presence back to Cashtown.[31]

Had the Hoosiers pursued the 47th North Carolina over the first ridge beyond the stone bridge over Marsh Creek, they would have run into the newly arrived 26th and 52nd North Carolina regiments in the small village of Seven Stars. The 26th bivouacked to the south side of the road in a well-kept grove while Colonel Burgwyn posted Lt. Col. John R. Lane with the pickets along the soggy bottom land west of Marsh Creek and south of the 52nd. With his brigade situated for the evening, Pettigrew and his aide, Lieutentant Young, rode back toward division headquarters at Cashtown.[32]

McPherson's Ridge

Hotopp's troopers returned with two black servants who had strayed from their officers in the North Carolina brigade. Major Beveridge ordered Capt. Daniel W. Buck with his Company E and Company H forward on the pike and

31 Marcellus E. Jones, *Journal*, Monday, June 29, 1863, Perrin-Wheaton Chapter, National Society of the Daughters of the American Revolution, Wheaton, IL, n.p.; John H. Moore, "Seventh Tennessee Infantry," in John Berrien Lindsley, ed., *The Military Annals of Tennessee, Confederate, First Series* (Nashville, 1886), 245; Jacobs, *The Rebel Invasion*, 22. Jacobs's description of the Confederates deploying two regiments on both sides of the Chambersburg Pike under the cover of a hill near Marsh Creek, while the third was sent a short distance forward (east) in the road to decoy the Union cavalry into pursuing them, dovetails with Young's account. "Whenever it [Hotopp's squadron, 8th Illinois] would come within three or four hundred yards of us we would make our appearance, mounted, when the column [47th North Carolina] would halt until we retired." Moore said he spotted the Federals around noon.

32 Clark, *Histories of the Several Regiments*, 2:342 and 5:116; Jones, *Journal*. Assistant Surgeon George C. Underwood (26th North Carolina) wrote that the regiment marched 3.5 miles during the afternoon, which would have placed it near the village. This is my conclusion based upon Jacobs's and Young's accounts. It substantiates Young's claim that Pettigrew was "willing to make an attack had not his orders forbidden it." Jacobs's assertion that two Confederate regiments covered the creek crossing included the 26th North Carolina, which came up later in the afternoon.

gave the officers the standard admonition to immediately report any enemy activity and not be taken by surprise. His second lieutenant, Marcellus E. Jones, sarcastically noted, "This advice, while good, was perfectly useless."[33]

Buck took his men into the low ground to the west, crossed the small bridge on Willoughby Run, and ascended to the crest of Herr's Ridge. He established his headquarters at the tavern south of the pike and placed his picket reserve under Lt. Amasa E. Dana in the Herr Ridge Road where it intersected the pike at the tavern. The command of the advance picket post devolved upon Lieutenant Jones: "It fell my lot to have charge of the picket line." Major Beveridge, meanwhile, dismounted Lt. William C. Hazelton's picket reserve along the eastern bank of sluggish Willoughby Run. Company G, the other half of the squadron, straddled the Chambersburg Pike just east of Isaac Leeper's house.[34]

Jones set off with 35 men from his company. About a mile farther to the west he dismounted all but six troopers below the eastern side of Knoxlyn Ridge. About 600 yards beyond them, near Ephraim Wisler's house at the crossroads on the crest of the hill, Jones posted Sgt. Levi S. Shaeffer and Pvts. George S. Sager, James O. Hale, T. Benton Kelley, George Heim, and Horace O. Dodge. Remaining mounted, they operated in pairs with instructions to keep within sight of each other. Kelley, who supposed it was around 4:00 p.m., recalled that he and Hale stayed in the road while the others spread out to either side. Dodge settled down for what would be a long and boring night. While the advanced part of Company E secured Knoxlyn Ridge, the rest of the regiment

33 Jones, *Journal*; Hard, *History of the Eighth Cavalry*, 167, 256; McClellan, *Regulations and Instructions*, 58, 63, 65. Based on Hard's early description of the regimental organization and including the changes occasioned by Gettysburg, the 8th Illinois Cavalry consisted of the following squadrons: K/B, F/D, L/C, M/I, H/E, A/G. The soldiers' descriptions of the picket posts clearly illustrate that they were implementing McClellan's instructions for posting pickets and videttes as described in Part II, Chapter I.

34 Jones, *Journal*; Hard, *History of the Eighth Cavalry*, 167, 256; Horace O. Dodge, "Opening the Battle: Lt. Jones, the 8th Ill. Cavalryman, Fired the First Shot at Gettysburg," *NT*, September 24, 1891, 3; Hazelton, "People of Gettysburg." Based on the available evidence, I believe Companies H and E occupied the western side of Herr's Ridge. Private Dodge (Company E) said the two companies were along the edge of the woods just east of Marsh Creek. I believe he was part of the advance picket that evening under Lt. Jones, which was very close to Marsh Creek. Company H and some of Company E, however, remained behind as the reserve picket line. Surgeon Hard (8th Illinois) said that during the fighting on July 1, he saw Lieutenant Dana, who commanded the picket line, falling back over the ridge with Company E. As the senior lieutenant, Dana would have stayed with the reserve picket and Lt. Jones would have been assigned to the forward picket line and the videttes, farther to the front.

halted in the swale between Seminary and McPherson's ridges, with its right flank near the Chambersburg Pike.[35]

Colonel George H. Chapman, commanding two small regiments (the 12th Illinois and his own 3rd Indiana) detached a squadron (two companies) from the 12th across Willoughby Run and up the hill into the farm lane from Herr's Tavern north to Michael Crist's home. The rest of the regiment bivouacked in the open field, between the pike and railroad cut. The 3rd Indiana (Companies A, B, C, D, E, and F) deployed north of the cut. Major Charles Lemon, the officer in charge of the pickets, led a squadron west in the roadbed down to the creek. The Hoosiers used the bridge to cross and continued uphill to the Crist house, where they dismounted and connected with the 12th Illinois' detachment.[36]

In the meantime, civilians inundated the regiment's bivouac, bringing plenty of decent food and showering the men with invitations to have supper in their homes. Not one to turn aside such an opportunity. Private Thomas G. Day (Company E) took his horse down to Willoughby Run and scrubbed it clean. After washing his hands and face, he headed back to town.[37]

35 Jones, *Journal*; T. Benton Kelley, "An Account of Who Opened the Battle By One Who Was There," *NT*, December 31, 1891, 4; Dodge, "Opening the Battle"; John L. Beveridge, "The First Gun at Gettysburg," in *Military Essays and Recollections: Papers Read Before the Commandery of the State of Illinois, Military Order of the Loyal Legion of the United States*, 8 vols. (Chicago, 1894), 2:90. Dodge, when naming the videttes, probably meant to write "George Heim" and "J. O. Hale" but inadvertently wrote "George Hale." It could also be a typesetting error. Company E had no "George Hale." It makes sense; there would have been six men on duty, not five.

36 Frank diary; Thomas G. Day, "Opening the Battle: A Cavalryman's Recollections of the First Day's Fight at Gettysburg," *NT*, July 30, 1903, 3. Though not stated by Frank or Day, I placed the pickets in the road because it complies with the instructions in McClellan's manual to occupy crossroads and lanes of access. The cavalry was deploying "by the book."

37 Bradley M. Gottfried, *The Maps of Gettysburg: An Atlas of the Gettysburg Campaign, June 3-July 13, 1863* (El Dorado Hills, CA, 2007), 61; Day, "Opening the Battle"; Frank diary, June 30, 1863. Based on casualty returns, the 12th Illinois had elements from six not four companies (233 officers and men) at Gettysburg. The two smallest companies likely merged with two larger ones but kept their company designations. John Bachelder's Map in the GNMP library clearly shows a substantial bridge spanning the creek where the proposed rail line crossed it.

Northeast, North, and Northwest of Gettysburg

Private Ashbel R. Mix (Company F) and another enlisted man from the 9th New York Cavalry, part of Devin's brigade's advance guard, trotted ahead of the regiment as it led the brigade past the Eagle Hotel. The horsemen continued on North Washington Street to the Mummasburg Road, and then followed that beyond Pennsylvania College and farther northwest. The mounted regiment finally halted in column of squadrons in the field on the north side of the road, below Oak Ridge.[38]

Devin placed two competent officers from the 9th in command of the brigade's pickets. Colonel William Sackett had the left of the picket and was assigned the section running across the Mummasburg Road to Oak Hill. Captain Wilber G. Bentley (Company H) supervised the coverage of the northern approaches—the Newville, Carlisle, Harrisburg, and Hunterstown roads, a distance of about 1.75 miles.[39]

The 3rd Squadron (D and L) and 5th Squadron (I and G), 9th New York Cavalry, remained on the north side of the Mummasburg Road northwest of the college. Sackett deployed the first squadron—Companies F and K—west to the Forney house on both sides of the Mummasburg Road as the picket reserve. A mounted vidette consisting of a corporal and three privates continued farther west to the stone bridge over Willoughby Run.

To the left, the exceedingly small 3rd West Virginia Cavalry (63 officers and men) and the six companies of the 6th New York moved into the big wheatfield on the eastern side of McPherson's Ridge north of the 3rd Indiana. The 3rd West Virginia crossed the run and climbed the ridge into the farm lane running from Christ's house to the Samuel Hartzell house on the Mummasburg Road. The 6th New York's 1st Squadron (Companies B and C) continued the picket line to the right. Captain Heermance spread his dismounted Company C at wide intervals to deceive the Rebels into overestimating their strength.

38 Newell Cheney, *History of the Ninth Regiment, New York Volunteer Cavalry* (Poland Center, NY, 1901), 102.

39 Cheney, *History of the Ninth Regiment*, 21; Wilber G. Bentley to the Illinois Commandery of the State of Illinois (Military Order of the Loyal Legion of the United States), n.d., Vertical Files, V6-NY9 Cav., Library, GNMP, 2; New York Monuments Commission, *New York at Gettysburg: Final Report of the Battlefield of Gettysburg*, 3 vols. (Albany, NY, 1902), 3:1153, hereafter cited as *NYAG*.

Lieutenant John E. Hofman (Company C, 3rd West Virginia) briefly noted, "Drizzling rain."[40]

Devin left two squadrons of the 17th Pennsylvania Cavalry (Companies E and L, and C and I) along the Mummasburg Road just northwest of the college. Colonel Josiah H. Kellogg (17th Pennsylvania) established his headquarters at the seminary and detailed his remaining five companies north and northeast to cover most of the approach roads into Gettysburg. Companies B, F, and M, under Maj. James Q. Anderson, advanced about a mile north beyond where the Newville Road split off from the Carlisle Road. With the picket reserve at the intersection, the videttes fanned out across both roads. Lieutenant John Sweeney took his squadron (Companies A and G) out on the Harrisburg Road northeast of the college.

Corporal John Mowry and Pvt. David H. Niblo of Company A, the advance guard, rode well ahead of the column. About three miles beyond the town they ran into a pair of Confederates. They captured one and the other escaped. Once the squadron caught up with Mowry and Niblo, the two videttes continued another half mile and stopped. In the distance they saw Confederate cavalry forming a column in the road, waiting for the Pennsylvanians to charge. Lieutenant Sweeney countermarched his two companies and raced back to the seminary to report their discovery to Colonel Kellogg, who in turn commanded Capt. Henry M. Donehoo (Company B) to picket the Harrisburg Road with Companies B and L. To Sweeney's right, Companies A and H, 9th New York, patrolled Rock Creek between the Hunterstown and the Harrisburg roads.

40 *OR* 27/1:185, 938; John E. Hoffman, Diary, Vertical Files, V6-WV3 Cav., Library, GNMP; Committee on Regimental History, *History of the Sixth New York*, 101, 136-137; Cheney, *History of the Ninth Regiment*, 102; Heermance to Leeds, July 4, 1863. The squadron (two companies) was the basic operational unit of the cavalry regiment. In his letter, Heermance wrote that his company lost two men wounded and four missing. The regimental history reported 14 lost for the entire regiment. Eight of those casualties occurred on July 2. The *Official Records* reported nine. The 9th New York's picket outpost was never along the Chambersburg Pike, despite the assertions of its veterans. Corporal Hodges did not know the name of the road he patrolled on July 1. He was pressured into saying it was the Willoughby Run bridge on the Chambersburg Pike, rather than the one on the Mummasburg Road that had been replaced. Chances are the bridges were of similar construction, much like those along the Antietam Creek in Washington County, Maryland. I placed the pickets in the farm road because Lieutenant Jones said his pickets connected with Devin's. I believe the pickets occupied the road because it would have given them a good view of the open valley below.

Companies B and E covered the area between the Hunterstown Road and the York Pike.[41]

Cashtown, Pennsylvania

General Pettigrew, meanwhile, reported to Harry Heth and informed him that he had not carried out his orders to secure supplies because Federal cavalry occupied Gettysburg. Further, some of his officers had heard drums in the distance south of the town. Third Corps commander A. P. Hill rode up and joined them. Heth repeated Pettigrew's report to Hill. "The only force in Gettysburg is cavalry," Hill dismissively replied, "probably a detachment of observation. I am just from General Lee, and the information he has from his scouts corroborates that [which] I have received from mine—that is, the enemy are still at Middleburg and have not yet struck their tents."

Heth reasserted his previous directive. "If there is no objection, I will take my division tomorrow and go to Gettysburg and get those shoes." "None in the world," Hill consented. Unable to let the matter go, Pettigrew insisted that Lieutenant Young be allowed to corroborate his report. The general believed that Hill might listen to Young, who had served on Hill's staff during the Seven Days' Battles.

Hill agreed, and asked Young about the size of the forces he had observed. The aide firmly explained that the cavalry maneuvered like veterans and not home guards. The general brushed the comments aside. He did not believe that any part of the Army of the Potomac was in proximity. Hill emphatically added that if it were in vicinity, this was the place where he wanted to engage it. James Archer's Brigade would rotate to the front and lead the column, followed by the brigades of Davis, Pettigrew, and Brockenbrough.

Pettigrew and Young left the meeting incredulous at the "blindness [which] in part seemed to have come over our commanders." Despite Heth's and Hill's assertions to the contrary, Pettigrew believed there was going to be a battle the

41 Henry P. Moyer, *History of the Seventeenth Regiment Pennsylvania Volunteer Cavalry* (Lebanon, PA, n.d.), 49, 56, 329, 381; Cheney, *History of the Ninth Regiment*, 103, 105; Raus, Jr., *A Generation on the March*, 93. The 17th Pennsylvania Cavalry had 12 companies divided into six squadrons of two companies each: A and G; B and H; C and I; D and K; E and L; F and M. At Gettysburg D and H served as the V Corps' headquarters guard and Company K was attached to the XI Corps' headquarters. Company B joined the Sixth Squadron, consisting of Companies F and M. The picket line would have stretched from the Cobean farm to the Yeatts farm to Rock Creek.

next day. He showed up at Archer's headquarters and prepared him for the advance by explaining in detail the terrain between Cashtown and Gettysburg. He warned Archer to watch out for a road on Herr's Ridge that intersected the pike at right angles from the south. The Yankees could use it to flank him. Pettigrew also told him that a ridge (McPherson's) west of Gettysburg would make an exceptionally good defensive position. Archer listened, but like the division and corps commanders, he may not have believed there would be any strong resistance.[42]

The Fairfield Road and Chambersburg Pike
4:00 p.m. to Dark

As Lt. William C. Hazelton (Company A, 8th Illinois Cavalry) supervised his skirmishers along Willoughby Run, Isaac Leeper invited the lieutenant and the enlisted man on duty in the road to supper. Hazelton politely declined, saying he could not leave his post, whereupon Leeper offered to walk the enlisted man's post so he could enjoy a good meal. The lieutenant replied again, "No." As it grew darker, the elderly Leeper joined the troopers on the picket line and chatted with them throughout the night. When the lieutenant finally bedded down, he dreamed of his sister waving her handkerchief at him as he left home. His thoughts also drifted to seeing another young woman, Frances A. Morill, standing under the maple tree in front of her cottage bidding him adieu. "God bless her," he said half aloud.[43]

The members of Battery A, 2nd U.S. Artillery tore down a section of a rotten post and rail fence along the north side of the Chambersburg Pike just west of Mary Thompson's house before filing onto her property. They parked their limbers and caissons on battery front in the field west of the orchard. The horses remained in their harnesses, facing west, with the guns still on the pintle

42 Clark, *Histories of the Several Regiments*, 5:116-117; Henry Heth to Rev. J. William Jones, June 1877, *SHSP*, 4:157.

43 Hazelton, "People of Gettysburg"; www.findagrave.com/memorial/112709060/william-cross-hazelton and www.findagrave. com/memorial 112709047/frances-amanda-hazelton, accessed Jan. 14, 2023. Hazelton said he had charge of the reserve picket that evening near a farmer's house along the Chambersburg Pike. With the picket line along Willoughby Run, Leeper's was the closest house. The 30-year-old officer had only one sister, Josephine, who was four years his junior. At the time of Gettysburg Frances was 22 years old.

hooks. The artillerists tied their animals to picket stakes and lay down in the wet freshly cut grass close to their teams. Lieutenant John H. Calef did not believe a battle would occur on the morrow. Farther west near the smithy on the east side of Marsh Creek, the videttes from the 8th Illinois observed Rebel campfires dancing in the night on a distant ridge, punctuated occasionally by a man walking in front of the lights. The Illinois troopers knew a hard day lay ahead.[44]

With his pickets posted along Willoughby Run, Maj. William F. Beardsley (8th New York Cavalry) allowed his reserve along McPherson's Ridge to wander into town by squads to buy victuals. They returned loaded with soft bread, biscuits, pies, cakes, meats, jellies, preserves, and fruits—gifts from the civilians. Toward evening, locals visited their bivouac with more delicacies to reward the troopers for liberating them from the Confederates.[45]

Littlestown, Pennsylvania
10 miles Southeast of Gettysburg

Companies H and M of the 8th New York Cavalry arrived at Littlestown sometime in the afternoon and relieved an infantry regiment on duty there belonging to Maj. Gen. Henry Slocum's XII Corps. To the troopers' surprise and relief, the local farmers overwhelmed them with butter, milk, and gigantic loaves of bread. Their generosity blunted any anger the New Yorkers may have harbored for having drawn the extra duty.[46]

44 Calef, "Gettysburg Notes," 47, 50; Dodge, "Opening the Battle"; Michael Hayes, "The 2d U.S. Art.," *NT*, December 29, 1892, 4. Hayes drove the wheel team on the left piece of Sergeant Pergel's section. They would have staked the horses to keep them in place during the night. Calef wrote that the battery passed to the next ridge in front of the command after the fences were torn down along his front. That implies the guns were north of the Chambersburg Pike behind a fence. That fence was on the west side of Thompson's orchard. Calef also noted the battery had camped in the low field east of the middle ridge. The Bachelder map clearly shows a rail fence along the north side of the road from Thompsons to Willoughby Run. As of October 23, 2019, a survey of Google maps shows a fenced field 470 feet west of the restored Mary Thompson house that does not appear on any of the previous maps, probably because it runs along a contour line south to north from the Chambersburg Pike to the railroad cut. The field runs west 270 feet from the fence along the western side of the orchard.

45 Moyer, *History of the Seventeenth Regiment*, 49.

46 "Genesee," "From the 8th Cavalry—List of Killed and wounded, Westminster, Md., July 4th, 1863," *Rochester Daily Union and Advertiser*, July 9, 1863.

Lutheran Seminary
Gettysburg, Pennsylvania

General Buford spent the late afternoon and early evening hours near the seminary gathering intelligence from Gamble's and Devin's patrols. One of them, an 18-man detachment from the 9th New York, bagged a prisoner on the road to Hunterstown. Buford spent a good deal of time with Devin, who had fewer men than Gamble but the largest area of the field to scout. Sometime before 10:00 p.m. Buford returned to the Eagle Hotel and ordered his lone signal officer, Lt. Aaron B. Jerome, to find the highest points from which he could observe "everything." He admonished the lieutenant to pay careful attention to campfires before daylight and for dust after that. "He seemed anxious, more so than I ever saw him," Jerome recollected. Jerome left headquarters, gathered his enlisted personnel, and headed west toward Seminary Ridge.[47]

Moritz Tavern
The Intersection of the Emmitsburg and Bull Frog Roads
1.7 miles Northeast of the Maryland-Pennsylvania Border

James S. Wadsworth's First Division led the army's advance that day, moving about one mile north on the Emmitsburg Road to a small covered bridge over Marsh Creek. It bivouacked there around noon on the northern and southern sides of the creek. Brigadier General Solomon Meredith's "Black Hat Brigade" (1st Brigade) bivouacked in the woods along the northern bank, leaving Lysander Cutler's 2nd Brigade on the opposite side to the east of the Emmitsburg Road.[48]

47 Cheney, *History of the Ninth Regiment*, 105; DePeyster, *Decisive Conflicts*, 152. I did not include the oft-quoted discussion Buford had with Devin about the Rebels attacking in the morning with "skirmishers three deep" because Jerome was not with the general when the alleged conversation occurred. It is hearsay and not corroborated.

48 *OR* 27/1:244; Gottfried, *The Maps of Gettysburg*, 38; A. P. Smith, *History of the Seventy-Sixth Regiment New York Volunteers; What It Endured And Accomplished* (Cortland, NY, 1867), 233; C. W. Cook, "A Day at Gettysburg," *NT*, April 7, 1898, 2; Hofmann, "The Battle"; Nathaniel Rollins, Journal, June 30, 1863, Wisconsin Historical Society, Madison, WI; Rufus G. Northup, "Going Into Gettysburg," *NT*, October 11, 1906, 6. Hofmann said the two brigades camped on the opposite sides of Marsh Creek. Northup (Co. A., 90th Pennsylvania) described the span as "a little covered bridge," which had a speed limit posted citing a $5.00 "penalty for driving faster than a walk!"

The 14th Brooklyn (Cutler, 318 officers and men) bivouacked in one of Joseph Creager's freshly tilled fields close to his house. At Creager's request, Col. Edward B. Fowler went to see him. The farmer demanded the colonel relocate his command. Fowler apologized for upsetting him, but insisted the regiment could not comply. When Creager shot back that he would hold Fowler responsible for any damages to his property, the colonel replied that he sincerely doubted his complaint would go very far. Fowler assured him that he would "endeavor" to keep his men in line, but he had some "in that crowd" that no human could restrain. Creager stormed away and the New Yorkers, using the dark as cover, promptly stole every chicken they could find. Soon, the aroma of cooking birds inundated the bivouac.[49]

Meredith sent Col. Samuel J. Williams's 19th Indiana forward on picket duty. Less than half a mile into the advance on the Emmitsburg Road, the residents of the small village of Green Mount thronged the Hoosiers as they marched by, overwhelming the soldiers with their hospitality. Adjutant George E. Finney relished the fresh milk and the abundance of home cooked food, including pies, the villagers gave out. Long before the Westerners reached the Alexander Currens house some two and a half miles north of Marsh Creek, their haversacks bulged with turkey, chicken, and soft bread. At Currens, Colonel Williams ordered Companies A, B, C, and E to establish picket outposts, which spread a mile to each side of the road to cover the flanks of the I Corps. The left reached almost to Willoughby Run, while the right curved around the southern base of Big Round Top. Back at the regimental reserve, the veterans mustered for pay, despite rain that started after dark.[50]

The I Corps averaged a leisurely one and a half miles per hour in its four-hour march north from Emmitsburg. General Reynolds established his

49 C. V. Tevis and D. R. Marquis, comp., *The History of the Fighting Fourteenth* (Brooklyn, NY, 1911), 81-82. According to Map #22, Joseph Creager's was the only farm on the south side of Marsh Creek and was the closest to the creek.

50 Ladd & Ladd, *Bachelder Papers*, 2:939; Michael Thompson, "In Their Own Words: 19th Indiana at Gettysburg, PA, 1863," Vertical Files, VF-IN19, Library, GNMP, 2, 6; William C. Barnes to W. W. Dudley, March 28, 1883, Vertical Files, VF-IN19, Library, GNMP; David Stevenson, *Indiana's Roll of Honor*, 2 vols. (Indianapolis, 1864), 1:374-375. Barnes erred when he said the regiment drew pay on the morning of July 1. Adjutant Finney noted in his pocket diary that they got paid the evening of June 30. Stevenson's account places the regimental reserve at Green Mount, which the regiment had to pass through en route to Gettysburg. I decided to go with Dudley's report. The reserve would not have been 2 miles behind the picket outposts.

headquarters at Moritz Tavern and placed Maj. Gen. Abner Doubleday's Third Division and Battery B, 1st Pennsylvania Artillery, along the Bull Frog Road northwest of the inn to protect the approach from Fairfield. In Brig. Gen. Thomas A. Rowley's 1st Brigade, the 121st Pennsylvania drew picket duty. Colonel Chapman Biddle commanded the right wing of the regiment, which anchored itself on the western side of Marsh Creek at the J. and J. Bingham place and stretched west to William Ross White's house on Bull Frog Road. From there, Maj. Alexander Biddle, the colonel's cousin, extended the left wing of the regiment to William C. Topper's potato patch along Middle Creek. The annoying intermittent rain sent the rest of the brigade into the woods west of the Emmitsburg Road.[51]

The veteran 20th New York State Militia (80th New York Volunteers) had just joined the brigade that afternoon. The New Yorkers were less than excited about being in a Pennsylvania brigade, much less one with the 151st Pennsylvania, a new nine-month regiment whose enlistment had almost run out. As Capt. John D. S. Cook (Company I) noted, "We very naturally were not pleased with the assignment, as we were by no means sure that we could depend on them for support in action."[52]

South Bank of Marsh Creek on the Emmitsburg Road

1st Brigade, Third Division, I Corps

Colonel Roy Stone's three Pennsylvania regiments, "The Second Bucktail Brigade," bivouacked along the wooded southern side of Marsh Creek, immediately west of the Emmitsburg Road. The men nestled down in the wet brush along the creek bank. It was a drizzly day, and Capt. Francis B. Jones (Company B, 149th Pennsylvania) decided to sleep off the ground to avoid waking to a bad case of rheumatism by using a lean-to of rails and slats from a nearby fence. The two top rails formed the sides of the frame. Four strategically spaced slats across the space between the rails became his "springs" and provided support for his head, shoulders, buttocks, and feet. His blanket spread over the frame served as his "mattress." The descending angle of the bed kept

51 *History of the 121st Regiment*, 51; *Pennsylvania at Gettysburg*, 2:730.

52 John D. S. Cook, "Personal Reminiscences of Gettysburg," *War Talks in Kansas; A Series of Papers Read Before the Kansas Commandery of the Military Order of the Loyal Legion of the United States* (Kansas City, MO, 1906), 322.

him out of the mud. Major Thomas Chamberlin (150th Pennsylvania) noted that the foliage protected his regiment from the sporadic showers that fell throughout the evening. Pursuant to Doubleday's orders, Stone had posted the brigade there to defend that portion of the line from any possible Confederate threat.[53]

It was the last day of the month, so Wadsworth's division was supposed to muster for pay that evening. In the 76th New York, acting Lt. Col. Andrew J. Grover dispatched one company out on picket and in the process failed to muster the regiment in time. The men bedded down that night without their money. The 56th Pennsylvania (2nd Brigade, First Division), having caught up with the brigade just after daylight, bivouacked near a mill dam in the creek. Crusty from marching in the daily rains of that week, the boys stripped down and bathed.[54]

Emmitsburg, Maryland

Brigadier General John C. Robinson's Second Division and three I Corps batteries marched into Emmitsburg from the west around 10:00 a.m. and immediately became ensnarled with Brig. Gen. Francis C. Barlow's First Division, Oliver Howard's XI Corps, as it attempted to cross through town to the northwest, or, as Pvt. Robert S. Coburn (Company H, 83rd New York) succinctly noted, "11th Corps agoing out the other way."[55]

Barlow's division pushed through to the fields northwest of Emmitsburg and went into camp behind some artillery lunettes. On the way through town, Pvt. Reuben Ruch (Company F, 153rd Pennsylvania) passed by a garden with a nice onion bed and vowed to visit it later. The traffic jam stalled Brig. Gen. Carl Schurz's division before it had moved several hundred yards, forcing it to bivouac south of town. Brigadier General Adolph von Steinwehr's division did not stir at all. At noon, with Emmitsburg cleared of troops, Col. Frederick Hecker (82nd Illinois) received orders to dispatch 100 men to Fairfield, some

53 *Pennsylvania at Gettysburg*, 2:730.

54 *OR* 27/1:244; Smith, *History of the Seventy-Sixth Regiment*, 233; Cook, "A Day at Gettysburg"; Hofmann, "The Battle"; Rollins journal. Grover was promoted to lieutenant colonel on June 25, 1863, but was never commissioned before his death on July 1. He died holding the rank of major, but was acting lieutenant colonel.

55 Coburn diary, June 30, 1863.

seven miles away, to see if the Rebs still occupied that place. The detail set out under the command of Lt. Col. Edward Salomon.[56]

Robinson's division (I Corps) passed through town and north along the Emmitsburg Road toward the Pennsylvania state line about two miles away. Civilians lined both sides of the burned-out square to enthusiastically cheer them on. When the 13th Massachusetts stepped by, one of them shouted, "There goes Sam Webster!" Webster (Company D), who was unable to fall out, ignored the catcall thinking that a member of his own company was guying him.[57]

As the 11th Pennsylvania drew near the state line, someone showed Chaplain William H. Locke the unimpressive old tree in a fence corner along the Emmitsburg Road marking the Mason-Dixon Line. Cheering, shouts of joy, and singing erupted in the 88th Pennsylvania (Baxter's brigade) when it stepped onto Pennsylvania soil. "Home Again," and "Home Sweet Home" reverberated overhead. Samuel G. Boone (Company B) somberly predicted that for many it would be "home forever." The 90th Pennsylvania delivered nine "manly cheers." A quarter mile above the state line, the brigade went into bivouac on both sides of the road on the James Wolford farm in the vicinity of Middle Creek. Orders went out to pitch tents. Corporal Charles Smedley (Company G, 90th Pennsylvania) pulled off his brogans to tend to his painfully blistered feet. Captain Jacob M. Davis (Company B), who had not eaten all day, detailed his partner to fill their canteens with water to cook coffee while he set to work getting a fire going. When his tent mate did not return, Davis sat down by the crackling flames and waited, getting angrier with each passing minute.[58]

56 Kiefer, *History of the One Hundred Fifty-third Regiment*, 207; Calvin S. Heller, Diary, June 30, 1863, Civil War Miscellaneous Collection, Manuscript Department, USAMHI; Wallace diary, June 30, 1863; *OR* 27/1:733.

57 Charles E. Davis, Jr., *Three Years in the Army: The Story of the Thirteenth Massachusetts Volunteers* (Boston, 1894), 223; Webster diary, June 30, 1863.

58 William Henry Locke, *The Story of the Regiment* (Philadelphia, PA, 1868), 224; Samuel G. Boone, "Personal Experiences," Michael Winey Collection, Manuscripts Department, USAHEC; Adjutant Cyrus S. Detre, "88th Penna. Regt. at Gettysburg," October 2, 1878, RG 04, War Records Office, Union Battle Reports, Vol. 27, boxes 48-52, National Archives and Records Administration, Washington, D.C., hereafter cited as NARA; *Life in Southern Prisons*, 54; Jacob M. Davis, "History of the 19th/90th Pennsylvania Volunteers," Unpublished Manuscript (copy), Archives of the Grand Army of the Potomac Museum and Library, Philadelphia, PA, 8, 9; *Annual Report of the Adjutant-General of the Commonwealth of Massachusetts, December 31, 1863* (Boston, 1864), 603.

Brigadier General Gabriel R. Paul's infantry brigade marched another two miles before stacking arms for the evening. Soon afterward, the colonels formed their regiments to read General Meade's circular encouraging the men to fight for their homeland. The last line instructed officers to instantly kill any soldier who shirked his duty. That irked the veterans in the 13th Massachusetts and generated a heated debate. The Bay State men wanted to reply in a blunt manifesto to Meade that he should have shown "more ability and judgment than his predecessors had shown when conducting a battle, and above all, avoid issuing appeals on circulars reflecting the slightest doubt on the courage of the men." Cooler heads prevailed, and no response was dispatched.[59]

Orders arrived at Moritz's Tavern sometime late in the day promoting Reynolds to command of the Army of the Potomac's left wing, which consisted of the I Corps, III Corps, and XI Corps. This change placed Doubleday in charge of the I Corps, gave Rowley control of the Third Division, and bumped Col. Chapman Biddle to command Rowley's brigade.[60]

Colonel Wainwright, who had begun his monthly returns, noted in his journal that Doubleday nominally commanded the I Corps, yet operated directly under Reynolds's supervision. Wainwright disapproved of the arrangement, noting that "he (Reynolds) looks as closely as ever after everything himself." The colonel also observed that the "Pennsylvanians did not give us an over-warm welcome." To him they seemed greedier than the Marylanders, peddling butter for an outrageous $.50 a pound and selling skimmed milk at $.25 a canteen. They complained to headquarters if anyone so much as burned a single fence rail.

Wainwright got into a loud argument with the farmer in whose clover field his artillerists camped. The man demanded half the value of the field to compensate for the destruction of what the gunner called a "poor crop of clover." When the colonel argued that the destroyed clover would not have

59 Davis, *Three Years in the Army*, 224; John D. Vautier, "At Gettysburg," *Philadelphia Weekly Press*, November 10, 1886; Boone, "Personal Experiences."

60 *OR* 27/2:244, 427; Jacob F. Slagle to Brother, September 13, 1863, Vertical Files, V6-149PA, Library, GNMP. General Seth Williams dispatched a message to Maj. Gen. Daniel Sickles, III Corps commanding, at 12:45 p.m. informing him of Reynolds's promotion. Lieutenant Slagle, who served as Doubleday's acting judge-advocate-general, wrote that during the evening of June 30, "We received orders to march early in the morning and at the same time General Doubleday, was notified that General Reynolds assumed command of the left wing, and that Gen'l. Doubleday should assume command of the 1st corps."

fetched $15.00 on the market, the farmer countered that his wife had been up all night baking bread for the troops, and that she "had guv" them all her milk and butter. Wainwright knew that "guv" translated into selling the delicacies to his soldiers at three to 10 times the going price, and bluntly told the civilian what he thought of him and Pennsylvanians in general. "They fully maintain their reputation for meanness," he concluded.[61]

Private B. Frank Noble (Company D, 7th Wisconsin), a detached volunteer with Battery B, 4th U.S. Artillery, ventured onto a neighboring farm with several canteens to get milk. When the farmer, who the men later referred to as an "Adams County Copperhead," demanded too much money for the milk, Noble stormed into the barnyard and milked one of the cows without permission. The farmer followed the private back to camp and filed a report.

Lieutenant James Stewart, in compliance to general orders against looting and fearing the repercussions of ignoring the complaint (which would inevitably travel up the chain of command), reluctantly sentenced Noble to "Field Punishment Number One," commonly referred to as "crucifixion." Stewart had Noble tied on his back, spread-eagled over the spare wheel on the back of a caisson with the hub tight against his crotch. The artillerymen swarmed around the prisoner and the lieutenant, openly protesting the punishment. Stewart, swearing, ordered them to disperse. The mob gradually faded away with epithets and angry complaints trailing behind them. Noble, who had just returned to the battery after being severely wounded at Antietam nine months earlier, stoically bore the "crucifixion" but never forgot or forgave the lieutenant for the incident.[62]

61 Stewart, "Battery B," 183; Nevins, *A Diary of Battle*, 229-230; *OR* 27/3:418,1:244. Wainwright was not the only one the locals failed to impress. Years later, Maj. Samuel H. Hurst (73rd Ohio), whose men camped northwest of Emmitsburg, wrote, "We expected to see them rising as one man, and rushing to arms to defend their homes. We only saw them rush to the fields with scythe, and reaper, and leave the work of driving back the foe all undivided to ourselves." Samuel H. Hurst, *Journal History of the Seventy-Third Ohio Volunteer Infantry* (Chillicothe, OH, 1866), 65.

62 Augustus C. Buell, *"The Cannoneer." Recollections of Service in the Army of the Potomac* (Washington, D.C., 1890), 62. *"The Cannoneer"* is a fictional history of Battery B, 4th U.S. Artillery, into which Buell inserted himself. To his credit, Buell filled the work with quotes from recollections that he acquired from many of the men in the battery. For instance, Horace Ripley's granddaughter has the letter Buell quoted on page 39 of the book. Anything Buell wrote about his actual participation with the battery and any of the quotes associated with "his personal" recollections, however, should be read with caution.

Colonel Lucius Fairchild (2nd Wisconsin) bedded his regiment down in what Pvt. Emanuel Markle (Company B) described as a "nice woods." The colonel personally inspected the men's cartridge boxes, checking to see if they had serviceable cartridges. One of the "boys" cynically quipped, "Well, I guess some of us will be bait for the crows pretty soon."[63]

Marsh Creek, Evening

Most of Baxter's brigade (Robinson's division) stacked arms and camped in a lush clover field alongside the Emmitsburg Road. The 88th Pennsylvania went on picket duty in a westerly facing line from the Two Fords Farm on Marsh Creek to across the Maryland state line, just north of Emmitsburg. As soon as the 90th Pennsylvania bivouacked in a peach orchard near the road, the enlisted men busied themselves scrounging the countryside for farmers' wives from whom to buy fresh wheat bread and hot cherry pies.

Sergeant Anson B. Barton (Company A, 12th Massachusetts) had just started filling his canteen from Marsh Creek when a slim boy who looked no older than 15 walked up to inquire about what was likely to result from the army's advance. The veteran replied that a battle was coming. The boy's face beamed. He asked to enlist and fight the Rebs. Barton took the youth back to the bivouac and handed him over to Capt. Erastus L. Clark: "Captain, here's a recruit for you." Clark listened to the boy and walked him over to Col. James L. Bates who, as the father of a teenage son, tried to dissuade him from enlisting. The lad told the colonel that he lived nearby, that he was willing to enlist, and insisted that Bates equip him to fight. "Well captain," relented the colonel, "you may take him into your company, if you wish, but we cannot muster him in now, as the books are back with the teams." The enlisted men scrounged up a uniform and accoutrements and took him in as one of the "boys." Thus did Charles F. Weakley, who was actually 21, become an unregistered volunteer in Company A.[64]

63 Emanuel Markle, "The Story of Battle Told By Survivor," *The La Crosse* [WI] *Chronicle*, Vertical Files, VF-WI2, Library, GNMP.

64 George Kimball, "A Young Hero of Gettysburg," *Century Magazine*, November 1886-April 1887, (New York, 1887), 33:133; Allan D. Gaff and Donald H. Gaff, eds., *A Corporal's Story: Civil War Recollections of the Twelfth Massachusetts* (Norman, OK, 2014), 211-214. In the magazine article, Kimball identified the young man as J. W. Weakley. Kimball noted his correct name and age in his memoirs. Years later, they learned

Captain Jacob M. Davis (Company B) accosted his long-absent messmate when the latter finally returned. The wayward comrade casually responded, "Well, I went for water, but when I got there, it looked too muddy, so I went further on and found better." He handed Davis his canteen. "Just taste this and see how you like it." The parched captain took a long swig only to discover it was not water, but corn liquor. His messmate had raided D. Rodes's still about half a mile northwest of their camp.

Several men of the 13th Massachusetts, despite a horrendous downpour that forced nearly everyone into their shelter halves, looted the distillery and quickly got "tight." General Reynolds found out about the boozing in the ranks and posted a detail around the still. Meanwhile, Sam Webster (Company D) learned the person who had called out his name while marching through town was a female. He snuck out of camp and returned to town to find her.[65]

Nearby, in the 104th New York, Pvt. Frank N. Bell (Company C) sat down alongside his best friend, English immigrant Sgt. G. Maurice Buckingham. Buckingham, who carried the national flag, turned to Bell and announced, "Frank, I have a proposition to make."

"Anything but popping the question," Bell quipped, "I ain't ready for that yet."

"I am in earnest," the sergeant replied.

"Very well, proceed," Bell said.

Buckingham knew that as a regimental clerk and orderly, his friend did not carry a weapon. "Since you can't use the musket, I'll let you carry the Colors and I'll use the musket in the next fight."

Bell knew he would not be allowed to comply but replied, "I'll do it."[66]

---

that the 21-year-old Charles F. Weakley of Carroll County, Maryland, had never mustered into the 12th Massachusetts, but following his stint with them at Gettysburg, enlisted in Company G, 13th Pennsylvania Cavalry. On November 23, 1864, his comrades found him drowned, the victim of an epileptic seizure.

65 Northup, "Going Into Gettysburg"; Report of Adjutant Cyrus S. Detre, 88th Pennsylvania Infantry, RG 94, War Records Office, Union Battle reports, Vol. 27, Boxes 48-52, NARA; Webster diary, June 30, 1863; Davis, "History of the 19th/90th Pennsylvania Volunteers," 8-9.

66 F. N. Bell to the State Historian, February 22, 1898, New York State Archives, GAR Surveys, B 1706-00.

South and West of Emmitsburg, Maryland

Lieutenant Colonel Salomon's reconnaissance from the 82nd Illinois (Schurz's division, XI Corps) reached Fairfield at 3:00 p.m. and discovered from the locals that some 2,000 Confederates had left the town about an hour before. After resting half an hour, Salomon headed back to Emmitsburg and reported his findings to Colonel Hecker by 8:00 p.m. Not knowing the whereabouts of the Rebels, a number of patrols sprayed west from all three divisions of the XI Corps. Around 10:00 p.m., the 55th Ohio (Brig. Gen. Adolph Von Steinwehr's Second Division), was roused from its tents, formed in column, and tramped into the rain-swept darkness. The regiment marched and counter marched, lost in the Stygian darkness, for an estimated two miles until it entered a wood, which the men thought was near a road of some sort.

Ordered to stay there all night, their officers prohibited them from making loud noises, sleeping, or moving about. They further instructed the men to listen for any unusual noises that might indicate enemy movement. Minutes after issuing the orders, most of the captains curled up in their ponchos and dozed off, leaving the companies under the command of the lieutenants and non-coms.[67]

While the Ohioans poked about in the dark, Schurz ordered Col. Wladimir Krzyzanowski (2nd Brigade) to send out another scouting party to the south toward Creagerstown. Captain Emil Koenig (Company E, 58th New York) and 100 men soon found themselves sloshing around in the gooey roads in a blinding rain searching for Rebel cavalry. Back near Emmitsburg, the rain, which drove the enlisted men into their soggy dog tents, also forced Lt. Louis Fischer and several of General Schurz's lower-ranking staff officers into a shed filled with straw that, unknown to them, had recently sheltered hogs. An hour into their sleep they found themselves blanketed with black ticks. Scurrying one by one through the narrow doorway, they escaped into the rain.[68]

In Barlow's division, acting Maj. George B. Fox led a detachment of 100 men from the 75th Ohio northwest on the road toward Fountain Dale and Monterey Springs atop of South Mountain. Fox's detachment had not yet

67 *OR* 27/1:733; Andrew F. Sweetland, "The 55th Ohio at Gettysburg," *NT*, September 9, 1909, 7.

68 *OR* 27/1:739-740; Memoirs of 1st Lt. Louis Fischer, Company K, 74th Pennsylvania Infantry, Vertical Files, VF-74PA, Library, GNMP; "Reminiscences of the Battle of Gettysburg," 54. Fischer had been promoted to the Pioneer Company, 3rd Division on June 29.

reached the halfway point when he learned Confederate cavalry was patrolling the immediate area. He detailed scouts to safely gather as much intelligence as they could before hunkering down in silence for the night.

Similarly, in the 153rd Pennsylvania, Lt. J. Clyde Miller (Company A), with part of his company and some men from Company F, went out on picket in the humid misty darkness. They had orders to fire on anyone appearing in front without demanding the countersign. After posting his men somewhere near a cornfield, he imagined something suspicious going on in front of his line. He advised his detachment that he was going on scout to see if any Rebs were out there and that he would softly whistle "Yankee Doodle" to identify himself on the way back. He had walked halfway into the cornfield when firing erupted on the left of the line. He heard something rushing through the corn that he believed to be Rebel cavalry. Knowing his men would not hesitate to cut loose into the corn, the lieutenant—without whistling—crashed through the field into his own line. He spent the rest of the night anxiously waiting to determine if they had dropped any Confederates.[69]

Just before dark, General Howard received a message at Mount St. Mary's College requesting him to meet General Reynolds at Moritz's Tavern. Taking two aides-de-camp, Frederick W. Gilbreth and his brother Maj. Charles H. Howard, the general started toward headquarters, which was about six miles to the north. When they reached the tavern about an hour later, the general dismounted and, leaving his aides behind, was escorted by one of Reynolds's aides to a back room on the south side of the house.

Reynolds rose from a chair next to a document-blanketed table and greeted Howard, handing him Meade's circular to the army (the same one that had offended members of the 13th Massachusetts). After Howard read it, the two pored over the material on the table. Reports both civilian and military, news dispatches, and communiqués from army headquarters indicated that Lt. Gen. James Longstreet's First Corps of the Army of Northern Virginia was at Chambersburg, and that Lt. Gen. A. P. Hill's Third Corps had crossed over South Mountain from Fayetteville to within about four miles of Gettysburg. For the next several hours the two generals studied what local maps they had on hand and agreed that some sort of encounter would take place the next day. Reynolds's apparent depression bothered Howard, who left headquarters around 11:00 p.m. On the way back to Mount St. Mary's, he expressed his

69 Kiefer, *History of the One Hundred Fifty-third Regiment*, 130.

personal confidence in Reynolds as an energetic and competent general as well as the feeling that there would likely be fighting on the morrow. Howard bedded down sometime after midnight and dropped off to sleep.[70]

Eagle Hotel, Gettysburg, Pennsylvania

Buford's Headquarters

At 10:30 p.m., Buford sat at his desk and penned a detailed report to Reynolds. A. P. Hill's Corps had gathered nine miles west of Gettysburg with pickets, including infantry and artillery, within four miles west of town on the Cashtown [Chambersburg Pike] Road. The patrols north, northeast, and northwest, having crossed and recrossed the road from Cashtown to Oxford, had seen no evidence of large bodies of enemy forces passing through the area. "However, the place is infested with prowling cavalry parties," Buford warned.

Buford added that a patrol had captured one of Lee's couriers who, while having nothing on his person of any value, did say that Ewell's Corps, with Rodes's Division in the advance at Petersburg, was crossing the mountains from Carlisle. Longstreet was probably behind Hill. Buford concluded that, after continually hearing rumors and reports of the Confederates advancing upon Gettysburg from York, he had to pay attention to them, thus overworking his already fatigued horses and men. He had neither forage for the horses nor rations for the soldiers. He added that civilians selling or giving the men food "generates dreadful straggling."[71]

Under such circumstances, the cavalry commander had reason to be unusually anxious.

70 *OR* 27/1:699; Oliver Otis Howard, *Autobiography of Oliver Otis Howard, Major General United States Army*, 2 vols. (New York, 1907), 1:402-403; Charles Henry Howard, "First Day at Gettysburg," Charles Henry Howard Collection, George J. Mitchell Department of Special Collections & Archives, Bowdoin College Library, Brunswick, ME, Box 1, Folder 55, M90.2, Articles and addresses, diaries, clippings, notes, etc., 1808-1957. In a draft of the address he later published in *Papers Read Before the Commandery of the State of Illinois*, vol. 4, Charles Howard never claimed he was the only aide who went with his brother to Reynolds's headquarters. His subsequent comment indicates that he was not inside at the meeting, either. More than likely the other aide also attended.

71 *OR* 27/1:923.

The Chambersburg Pike

1 mile east of the Samuel Lohr Farm

Brigadier General James J. Archer's undersized mixed brigade left Cashtown after dark and marched a couple of miles along the Chambersburg Pike before bivouacking along both sides of the road. It was not a pleasant march.

"It rained [an] almighty hard rain," recalled Col. John A. Fite (7th Tennessee), whose regiment camped close to a farmhouse and barn near the pike. Because the ground was so thoroughly soaked, he told some of his "boys" to search the barn for straw or anything that could be used for bedding. The party returned with the good news that the place was filled with straw. Taking a squad, Fite went to the farmhouse and told the woman living there that he wanted to get some for his men to use as ground cover to prevent sickness from lying in the mud. She adamantly refused, to which the determined colonel bluntly replied that he was going to take it anyway. The squad discovered large quantities of bacon stashed beneath the straw, which Colonel Fite reported to brigade headquarters. Archer dispatched wagons to the barn and the Tennesseans hastily loaded the contraband into them—without being allowed to take any of it for themselves.[72]

Near Seven Stars, Pennsylvania

Pettigrew's Brigade

During the evening, two frightened women wandered into the 26th North Carolina's picket line just east of Seven Stars. When they encountered Lt. Col. John R. Lane, they blurted out that their homes were between his pickets and the creek. The colonel assured them that the Confederates did not make war on women and children, and that it was his privilege and duty to protect them. To their amazement, he moved his men closer to the creek to allow the ladies safe return to their families.

The day ended quietly and rather drearily. On the summit of South Mountain west of Cashtown, Brig. Gen. Joseph Davis's Brigade bedded down in the mud under a torrential downpour. A soaking wet Lt. Joseph J. Hoyle

72 John A. Fite, "Memoirs of Colonel John A. Fite," Lebanon-Wilson County Library, Lebanon, TN, 99-100.

(Company F, 55th North Carolina) tersely summed up his experience in a letter to his wife: "We have remained in bivouac all day—Raining."[73]

73 Jeffrey M. Girvan, *"Deliver Us from This Cruel War": The Civil War Letters of Joseph J. Hoyle, 55th North Carolina Infantry* (Jefferson, NC, 2010), 128; Samuel W. Hankins, *Simple Story of a Soldier* (Nashville, TN, 1912), 43.

Chapter Two

"My God, you are not going to fire here, are you?"

— *Ephraim Wisler, civilian*

Skirmishers Open the Battle, July 1, 1863

Dawn to 8:30 a.m.

The Operations West of Gettysburg Before Daylight

Unfinished Rail Line, the Bridge on Willoughby Run

The previous days of high humidity, intermittent drizzles, and, at times, torrential downpours, combined with the gradually rising temperature to smother the muggy creek bottoms with a low-hanging fog. The mist blanketed the hollows between the ridges with an eerie pall. Through the ghost-like fog stepped Maj. William S. McClure of the 3rd Indiana Cavalry. Using the railroad bed to guide him, the trooper walked down the western side of McPherson's Ridge to inspect the picket line.

As he drew near the bridge, Maj. Charles Lemon called out to McClure, who found Lemon beneath a large tree. The major had just come in from the picket line and greeted McClure with a flask. "Come, Major, take a drink with me; it will be the last one we ever take together," Lemon explained, "as I will be a dead man before night."[1]

1 Day, "Opening the Battle"; "First Shot at Gettysburg"; E. M. Bradshaw, "That March to Gettysburg," *NT*, September 30, 1909, 7; Hofmann, "The Battle"; L. Cutler to Gov. Andrew

Fairfield Road on Bream's Hill

1.4 miles southwest of Seminary Ridge

Privates William Sholes and Albert S. Wetmore (Company D, 8th New York Cavalry), mounted near the brow of the hill, peered into the predawn darkness. Sholes was the chief vidette and had his carbine at the ready, while Wetmore, carbine slung, was several feet behind him. The 12-man patrol from Company C was returning from its reconnaissance to Fairfield and had just passed through on its way to report to headquarters at the seminary. Sholes noticed something in the fog at the bridge along Marsh Creek. Pursuant to instructions, he rapidly fired several shots from his breech-loading Sharps carbine to alert the picket reserve. He and Wetmore remained in the road to see what developed.[2]

The Crossroads at the Henry Meals House

About 1,200 yards east of Sholes, Pvts. Alfred W. Davies and William Rawlinson (Company F, 8th New York) had just relieved the outpost at the crossroad at 4:35 a.m. Davies, the chief vidette, was watching the two men walk their horses down to Willoughby Run to water them when he heard a pair of shots in quick succession. His carbine at the ready, Davies rode west on the Fairfield Road. He cleared the edge of the woods north of the road and spied two enemy foragers in the open field feverishly trying to reload their weapons. He yelled at them to surrender, which they did. Corporal George M. Matthews (Company B) and Pvt. Charles Isham (Company C), both from the 5th Alabama Battalion (Archer's Brigade), had slipped away from their bivouac to forage without permission. Davies was escorting his hungry captives toward the

---

Curtin, November 5, 1863, as cited in "What Our Veterans Have to Say About Their Old Campaigns," *NT*, March 30, 1884, 7.

2 John W. Busey & David G. Martin, *Regimental Strengths and Losses at Gettysburg*, 4th ed. (Hightstown, NJ, 2005), 158; Norton, "The Last Word About the First Shot"; McClellan, *Regulations and Instructions*, 59, 61-63; Willett, "Another Gettysburg." According to the manual, videttes were to fire their weapons in poor lighting conditions only if the enemy "approaches resolutely.... [T]o fire without necessity... would... create useless alarm." I think it is more likely than not that Sholes fired because he thought the enemy was somewhere to his immediate front. Norton erred when he wrote the pickets were along the Chambersburg Pike, that they were armed with Spencer carbines, and by referring to Sholes as "George."

vidette post when bugler Dennis Curran called for them in to rejoin the company along Willoughby Run. Davies turned the strays over to someone at the creek and returned to the picket line.[3]

4:35 a.m. to 6:00 a.m.
The Samuel Hartzell House
Intersection of the Herr Ridge Road and the Mummasburg Road, .92 miles northwest of the J. Forney House

Private John P. Robertson (Company I, 9th New York Cavalry) and the five other men on his picket post had been on duty at the crossroads for just over half an hour when the sun broke over the horizon. Robertson, who had posted himself under a fine cherry tree along the road, watched the sun evaporate the thin fog that had veiled the crest during the night. A small brook cut through the gently sloping ridge about 200 yards to the west. Robertson latched his gaze on the David Schriver farm some 400 yards away. In the early light he observed activity between the house on the south side of the Mummasburg Road and the barn north side of it.

A short time later, the 52-year-old Schriver, accompanied by a young boy, drove into the picket post and reined in alongside Robertson. His daughter Hannah, he explained, had spied a large Rebel column with a field glass from her upstairs room about a mile or so down the road. Schriver asked the private if he thought there was going to be a scrap and what should he do about it. Robertson did not think a major battle would occur nearby, but that a skirmish was likely. He told "the old man" that he had better take his family to a "secure place."[4]

3 Norton, *Deeds of Daring*, 147; John W. Busey and Travis W. Busey, *Confederate Casualties at Gettysburg: A Comprehensive Record*, 4 vols. (Jefferson, NC, 2017), 1:60, 62. Matthews is the only man listed as AWOL in the 5th Alabama Battalion, and Isham is the only man in the regiment listed specifically as captured on July 1. Their commanding officer did not list any captured for the action along Willoughby Run because he had no knowledge of their absence. Therefore, it is probable that they had left to forage and/or had deserted and accidentally ended up at the Union picket outpost.

4 John P. Robertson, "Opening the Battle. How I Saw the First Shot Fired at Gettysburg," *NT*, April 2, 1903, 3; www.findagrave.com/memorial/39383726/david-schriver; www.findagrave.com/memorial/18347356/hannah-catherine-spangler; www.findagrave.com/memorial/18347348/levi-spangler (all three accessed Jan. 13, 2023). Robertson did not know the name of the man and the boy (who apparently was not Schriver's son) because his sons were

As Schriver and the boy turned about, the private stepped his mount into the middle of the road where he could get a clearer view of the house and barn on the ridge to the west. About 6:00 a.m., just as he anticipated seeing the Rebs top the ridge at the Schriver place, Lt. Newel Cheney (Company C) approached him with the picket relief from Company F. As soon as he informed Cheney of the situation, the lieutenant, in his usual abrupt manner, turned to Alpheus Hodges and snapped, "Corporal, take two men and ride as far as the top of the hill. If you see anything suspicious, send one of the men back, and you go on and see if you can see anything of the column of Confederates."

Hodges and his men dug their spurs and galloped west to the Shriver place. Robertson and the rest of his outpost remained in the road while the lieutenant delivered instructions to Hodges's sergeant. Meanwhile, the balance of the party teased Robertson for imagining Rebs were anywhere in vicinity. Seconds after Hodges departed, a glint of steel bobbing in the sunlight from the distant hills attracted Robertson's attention. The erratic rhythm of the reflections convinced him it was infantry marching in route step. "Here they come!" he exclaimed.

Hodges's party reined to a halt about 200 yards beyond Shriver's place. In the distance, well beyond the Jacob Hankey farm, he spotted a cavalry detachment, with an infantry column behind it, top a rise of ground. Pursuant to orders forbidding him to open fire on any movement to the front, the corporal dispatched both of his men to the rear to notify the reserve at Hartzell's and the main reserve at the Forney house. As they departed, Hodges walked his horse west into the water pool on the north side of the bridge over Willoughby Run to let it drink. A minute later he spurred farther west to the next rise of ground at Hankey's to get a closer look in an attempt to verify the true identity of the approaching force.

They were Rebs. Robertson watched as Hodges stood in the stirrups and snapped off a round at the distant column. The corporal calmly turned his horse about, reloaded his carbine, turned about again, and squeezed off another shot. The Confederate point riders, who had cautiously reached the first rise of ground west of Hankey's, halted to return fire. Moving to the north side of the

---

all of military age. An examination of the family records in the immediate vicinity indicates he was the only "old man" living in the area with a daughter. Seventeen-year-old Hannah had been married for about a year to 21-year-old Levi Spangler, whose family owned Spangler's Spring; she was staying with her father on this particular day.

bridge, Hodges and the vidette, who had returned from Shriver's, remained mounted in the water and engaged in a brief and harmless long-range firefight.

Lieutenant Cheney turned to Hodges's non-commissioned officer and ordered, "Sergeant, take your men and report to Col. Sackett that there is a large column of Confederates coming down the road. I will try to hold them in check with my pickets, until relieved or reinforced." As Robertson rode east with his detachment toward Forney's, the sporadic slapping sound of Sharps carbine fire reverberated in the air behind them.[5]

Daylight (4:35 a.m.)
I Corps Bivouac Along Marsh Creek
About 6 miles south of Gettysburg, PA

Reveille sounded at 4:00 a.m., about half an hour before first light. The regiments on both sides of Marsh Creek breakfasted on coffee and hard crackers. The sun weakly squinted through the low-hanging rain clouds. John Reynolds, now in command of the army's left wing, had been up for a couple of hours when Capt. Craig W. Wadsworth arrived just after daylight with General Buford's last dispatch. Reynolds studied its contents before sending an orderly to fetch Brig. Gen. James Wadsworth.[6]

Farther up the road, the general's son, Capt. Craig Wadsworth, came upon Lt. James Stewart (Battery B, 4th U.S. Artillery). The lieutenant asked Wadsworth if he had eaten. When he replied "No," Stewart offered him food from his officers' mess. Wadsworth declined because of time constraints, but admitted he would love a cup of coffee. After hurriedly gulping it down, he

5 Cheney, *History of the Ninth Regiment*, 106; Wilber G. Bentley to the Illinois Commandery of the State of Illinois, n.d., Vertical Files, V6-NY9 Cav., Library, GNMP, 4, 6; Robertson, "Opening the Battle." This is my interpretation of the event, pending the discovery of new information that can verify whether Robertson actually saw a Confederate infantry column in the Mummasburg Road or not. Considering that it occurred at the end of the two-hour watch, it had to have been at least 6:00 a.m. rather than 5:30 a.m.

6 Eminel Potter Halstead, "The First Day of the Battle of Gettysburg," *A Paper Read Before the District of Columbia Commandery of the Military Order of the Loyal Legion of the United States*, 4 vols. (Washington, D.C., 1887), 1:3; Hofmann, "The Battle"; William H. Harries, "The Iron Brigade in the First Days' Battle at Gettysburg," *Glimpses of the Nation's Struggle; Papers Read Before the Minnesota Commandery of the Loyal Legion of the United States, 1892-1897*, 6 vols. (St. Paul, MN, 1898), 4:339.

asked Stewart to go with him to watch the cavalry fight. The Scotsman replied that he would go out after he had finished breakfast.[7]

On the north side of Marsh Creek, Sgt. James P. "Mickey" Sullivan (Company K, 6th Wisconsin) and the other Black Hat boys packed their "traps" in the somewhat cooler temperature that accompanied the rain. No one in the brigade seemed to be in a hurry. Along the opposite bank, the soaked men in the 76th New York pulled the wet cartridges from their weapons. Lieutenant James Volney Pierce (Company G, 147th New York, Cutler's brigade), his stomach less than full from two hard crackers and a tin of black coffee, recollected that the men received one day's rations from the commissary sergeant and 60 rounds of ammunition per man from the quartermaster. He knew that his brigade, having marched in the rear of the division the day before, would move to the head of the column as prescribed in the regulations.[8]

Meanwhile, General Wadsworth and his staff met Reynolds at the tavern, where Wadsworth learned of Reynolds's promotion to command the left wing. Reynolds explained, as best he could, the strategic and tactical situation at Gettysburg. When Wadsworth asked permission to forego protocol and allow him to lead the I Corps on the march, Reynolds readily agreed. The decision thrilled Wadsworth's provost-marshal, Lt. Clayton E. Rogers, who wanted to see his first cavalry action.[9]

Seven Stars, on the Chambersburg Pike

Colonel John A. Fite (7th Tennessee) left Cashtown and rode down to the Samuel Lohr house just after daylight to inspect his pickets from Company B.

7 Stewart, "Battery B at Gettysburg," 183. I concluded that Wadsworth was the staff officer sent by Buford to Reynolds. He is the only staff officer from Buford mentioned in the accounts about the start of the advance on July 1.

8 Mickey [Sullivan] of Company "K," "The Charge of the Iron Brigade at Gettysburg," *Mauston* [WI] *Star*, March 22, 1883; Hofmann, "The Battle"; J. V. Pierce, " Gettysburg: Last Words as to What Regiment Opened the Battle," *NT*, April 3, 1884, 7; Smith, *History of the Seventy-Sixth Regiment*, 235; *NYAG*, 3:990; Robert K. Beecham, "Adventures of an Iron Brigade Man," *NT*, October 30, 1902, 3. Hofmann said Cutler's brigade took the road ahead of Meredith's regiments, which were still in bivouac. In the roster, Pierce's name appears as Volney J. Pierce.

9 Clayton E. Rogers, "Gettysburg Scenes," *Milwaukee Sunday Telegraph*, May 13, 1887; Lance J. Herdegen, "The Lieutenant Who Arrested a General," *Gettysburg Magazine*, January 1, 1991, 25, hereafter cited as *GM*.

To his surprise, he found the men eating freshly cooked breakfasts. The women in the house insisted he have some food. Not one to decline such hospitality, particularly when it involved something other than army fare, the colonel happily agreed. Once seated, he cordially conversed with a young lady who shared the uncomfortable news that she had lost her beau the prior summer in the fighting around Richmond. Colonel Fite had hardly finished his meal when a courier from General Archer rushed in with orders for the pickets to return to the regiment.[10]

Cashtown

7 miles northwest of Gettysburg

Privates Samuel W. Bickley and William H. Bird (Archer's Brigade) arose well before daylight. Gathering up five canteens apiece and several haversacks from their friends in Company C, they stole away from the 13th Alabama's bivouac on an unauthorized foraging expedition. The skilled looters managed to "find" a farmer's stash of cherry wine, but no food. Their raid ended in an orchard with both men perched in separate trees gorging themselves on cherries. In the distance they heard drummers rattling out the "long roll." Skittering down to the ground, they snatched up the canteens and took off toward camp, leaving empty haversacks on the ground.[11]

Archer's Brigade started out from Cashtown at 5:00 a.m., about half an hour after daylight, just behind Joe Davis's Brigade. Captain Edward A. Marye's Fredericksburg Battery fell in behind Archer. The 5th Alabama Battalion (135 officers and men) led the column. A short distance out of the village, the two brigades passed through Colonel Brockenbrough's bivouac around the McKnightsville crossroads.[12]

10 Moore, "Seventh Tennessee Infantry," 245; Fite, "Memoirs," 100. In his memoirs, Fite wrote that he sent the picket out the evening before, which contradicts Moore's account. Because Moore commanded the pickets, I went with his statement.

11 W. H. Bird, *Stories of the Civil War, Company C, 13th Regiment Alabama Volunteers, The Army of Northern Virginia* (Columbia, SC, n.d.), 6.

12 William Frierson Fulton, Jr., *Family and War Reminiscences of William Frierson Fulton, Jr.* (Livingston, AL, 1919), 100; Busey & Martin, *Regimental Strengths and Losses*, 226; E. T. Boland, "Beginning of the Battle of Gettysburg," *CV*, 14:398; John L. Marye, "The First Gun at Gettysburg, 'With the Confederate Advance Guard,'" in Charles

Bird and Bickley returned to the camp to find it abandoned. Snatching up their rifles and knapsacks, they took off at a run to locate their regiment. The pair caught up with the 13th Alabama, returned the wine-filled canteens to their comrades, and fell in with the column.[13]

6:00 a.m. to 6:45 a.m.[14]
The Ephraim Wisler House
Chambersburg Pike, 2.2 miles West of Seminary Ridge

Lieutenant Marcellus Jones (Company E, 8th Illinois Cavalry) replaced his vidette outpost across the Chambersburg Pike and the Knoxlyn Road with the next watch, which consisted of Cpl. Levi S. Shaeffer and Pvts. Sager, Heim, Hale, Kelley, and Dodge. The lieutenant delivered the customary instructions required for posting videttes before riding back toward the picket reserve. A short distance away, he stopped at the Lewis Hoopee house south of the road and bought some bread for himself and a ration of oats for his famished mount.[15]

Barely 10 minutes after Jones's departure, Kelley and Hale, on duty in the road, spied a dust cloud trailing along the horizon about two and a half miles west and to the right of the pike. By 6:40 a.m. they surmised that an infantry column was kicking up the dust. A few minutes later they could make out the front of the column cresting the farthest ridge in front of them.[16]

Kelley glanced to the right and left along the picket line and could not see Cpl. Levi Shaeffer anywhere. "I am going for the reserve," he announced, "and if Shaeffer comes tell him I have gone for the reserves."[17]

H. Browning, ed., *The American Historical Register*, March-August 1895 (Philadelphia, 1895), 1228.

13 Bird, *Stories of the Civil War*, 6.

14 These times and the ones following that deal with the cavalry action through 8:00 a.m. are estimates at best, based upon the accounts of the various participants.

15 Dodge, "Opening the Battle"; Jones, *Journal*; T. Benton Kelley, "An Account of Who Opened the Battle," *NT*, December 31, 1891, 4. Dodge identified the men in the detachment. Kelley set the time at 6:00 a.m. The Hoopee place was just east of Wisler's.

16 T. Benton Kelley, "First Shot At Gettysburg. It Was Fired by Lt. E. M. Jones, 8th Ill. Cav.," *NT*, October 15, 1908, 7; Kelley, "An Account of Who Opened the Battle."

17 Marshall Krolick, Chicago CWRT, F. Tilberg copy, Vertical Files, V6-8 IL-Cav, Library, GNMP, np; Dodge, "Opening the Battle"; Jones, *Journal*; Kelley, "An Account of Who Opened the Battle"; Kelley, "First Shot At Gettysburg."

6:30 a.m.[18]
Advance Patrol, Devin's Brigade,
4th Squadron, 9th New York Cavalry
Hunterstown, Pennsylvania, 6 Miles Northeast of Gettysburg

Privates Thomas D. Smith and Marcus Hall (Company E), who had been on the road for about two hours, finally reached the outskirts of Hunterstown. Looking east into the distance, they spotted four mounted Rebels at the town square near the Jacob Grass hotel. Riding up to Mrs. Galbraith's house along the north side of the road, Hall asked the civilians on the front porch how many Confederates were in the area. "About three hundred," they replied. The troopers quietly turned toward Gettysburg and walked their mounts in the opposite direction.

The Rebels were a detachment from Company B, 35th Battalion, Virginia Cavalry, comprised of Pvts. Edward Simpson, John Monier, William T. Peters, and Albert C. Stotsenberger. They had seen Smith and Hall and were slowly moving after them. A short distance from the town, the two Yankees crested a hill and ran into a patrol from their regiment in the road. The patrol spurred over the crest and captured the unsuspecting Virgina Confederates as they ascended the opposite side. With their prisoners in hand, the New Yorkers returned to Gettysburg.[19]

6:00 a.m. to 7:00 a.m.[20]
Moritz Tavern, near Marsh Creek

Abner Doubleday reported to General Reynolds before 7:00 a.m. and officially learned of his own promotion to I Corps command. Together, the

18 This time is an estimate based upon the troopers' probable rate of march (the "walk") and how long it could have taken them to reach Hunterstown from Gettysburg.

19 Cheney, *History of the Ninth Regiment*, 105-106; Map #22; John E. Divine, *35th Battalion Virginia Cavalry* (Lynchburg, VA, 1985), 99, 101, 104; Tom Elmore, "Couriers at Gettysburg," Oct. 26, 2017, civilwartalk.com, accessed Jan. 11, 2023. Jacob Grass owned the hotel on the northwest side of the town square. I concluded they stopped at the Galbreath house because it was the only single dwelling on the same side of the road as the hotel and the troopers would have had a direct line of sight to the hotel from there.

20 Abner Doubleday, *Chancellorsville and Gettysburg* (New York, 1882), 124. Doubleday said he was at Moritz Tavern around 6:00 a.m.

generals reviewed Buford's messages from the previous evening. The Confederates had large bodies of men at Cashtown and Mummasburg and cavalry skirmishing had broken out along the two roads leading from those places to Gettysburg. Reynolds added that he had ordered Wadsworth to take Capt. James A. Hall's Battery B, 2nd Maine Artillery, and march at once. Reynolds himself would personally lead the advance. Doubleday would bring up the rest of the I Corps. Doubleday knew it would take at least an hour and a half, and possibly as much as two hours, to organize his corps and bring in the pickets. Around 8:00 a.m., he dispatched Lt. Jacob F. Slagle, his acting judge-advocate-general, toward Emmitsburg to bring forward Col. Charles S. Wainwright's three remaining batteries of the I Corps Artillery Brigade and to get Brig. Gen. John C. Robinson's Second Division on the road. As Doubleday would later write, "Wadsworth's division was, therefore, obliged to bear the brunt of the action alone for this amount of time."[21]

It was drizzling when the men of Robinson's division woke that morning, just as it had so often during the prior week. The boys from Company G, 83rd New York, found themselves in what Pvt. Robert S. Coburn described as a "Scottish mist," much like those that blanketed the moors of the "olde country." The men paid no heed as they set about fixing breakfast. For Corporal Smedley and the sergeant with whom he shared a tent in Company G of the 90th Pennsylvania, the morning fare turned out to be fresh beef. Around 8:00 a.m., they formed in the Emmitsburg Road. The troops who had preceded them had churned the small stones in the road into the mud beneath, which morphed the road into a thick sticky paste. Their smooth-soled shoes slipped on the wet gravel still on the surface, which in turn made marching that much more difficult. A few days later, Maj. Alfred Sellers (90th Pennsylvania) wrote that since crossing the Potomac he and his comrades were "used to being saturated and plodding through mud and over the mountains."[22]

21 Doubleday, *Chancellorsville and Gettysburg*, 125; *OR* 27/1:244; Lt. Jacob Slagle to Brother, September 13, 1863. Doubleday wrote that Reynolds told him to send Wadsworth forward. The *OR* account is the more accurate of the two.

22 Coburn diary, July 1, 1863; Thomas L. Hanna, "A Day at Gettysburg," *NT*, May 23, 1901, 6; John W. Jaques, *Three Years' Campaign of the Ninth, N. Y.S.M., During the Southern Rebellion* (New York, 1865), 154; William Todd, ed., *History of the Ninth Regiment N.Y.S.M. - N.G.S.N.Y (Eighty-Third N. Y. Volunteers)* (New York, 1889), 268; Letter, Major Alfred Sellers, 90th Pennsylvania, July 9, 1863, Vertical Files, VF 6-90PA, Library, GNMP; *Life in Southern Prisons*, 54-55.

Brigadier General Lysander Cutler led the first infantry brigade onto the field at Gettysburg and fought a long and bloody battle. LOC

The order to move disrupted what Colonel Wainwright thought was going to be a quiet day. He had just finished the artillery brigade's monthly returns and got his three batteries moving forward at a walk, with Battery L, 1st New York in the lead, followed by Battery B, 4th U.S., and the 5th Maine battery in the rear. He rode to headquarters at Moritz Tavern to confer with Reynolds, who told him that he did not expect a battle, and that the corps was moving forward to support Buford, who was expected to reconnoiter farther to the west.[23]

Marsh Creek

Lieutenant Clayton E. Rogers, acting under orders from Wadsworth, rode into Brig. Gen. Lysander Cutler's bivouac on the southern bank of Marsh Creek shortly after 6:00 a.m. and ordered the brigade to march toward Gettysburg. Cutler formed his 1,566 men in the Emmitsburg Road by 6:30 a.m. The 76th New York took the lead followed by the 56th Pennsylvania, 147th New York, 95th New York, and 14th Brooklyn. The 7th Indiana remained behind as the I Corps train and cattle guard, with the promise of being relieved by a green regiment in Brig. Gen. George J. Stannard's Vermont brigade.

23 Nevins, *A Diary of Battle*, 232. Cooper's Battery B, 1st Pennsylvania Artillery, served with Chapman Biddle's brigade at the intersection of the Bull Frog and Nunemaker Mill roads (Pumping Station Road). Hall's guns were detached with the Iron Brigade on Marsh Creek.

Twenty-five minutes later the column got under way, leaving Solomon Meredith's "Black Hats" and Captain Hall's Maine battery behind. Rogers crossed to the north side of Marsh Creek and repeated the order to General Meredith, who formed his brigade in the Emmitsburg Road around 7:00 a.m. The lieutenant rode forward to catch up with Cutler, assuming Meredith would immediately follow. He did not.[24]

As Meredith's men stood to arms, Company L, 1st Maine Cavalry (the headquarters guard), followed by Capt. James A. Hall and his 2nd Maine artillery, thundered up from behind and forced the Westerners to take to the either side of the pike. An irate private named Tommy Flynn (Company K, 6th Wisconsin) shouted at their backs in his thick brogue, "May the devil fly away with the roofs of yese jackets; yese going ahead now to get us into a scrape and thin walk off and let us fight it out like ye always do."

Once the rolling wheeled danger was past, the regiments slipped back into the roadbed. The 2nd Wisconsin took the lead, followed by the 7th Wisconsin and the 24th Michigan. Lieutenant Colonel Rufus Dawes's 6th Wisconsin, having rotated to the rear of the brigade, finished out the column. Lieutenant William N. Remington (Company K), who had been detached from his company to command a squad of six men from Company I, found himself at the back of the regiment rounding up stragglers. Remington was suffering from a bad summer cold and had wrapped his head and throat in cloth to protect himself from the morning drizzles. The 100-man brigade guard under Lt. L. Grayson Harris of Company C formed behind Remington. With the regiments in the

24 Lance J. Herdegen, "Old Soldiers And War Talk," *GM*, January 1, 1990, 20; Hoffman, "Remarks on the Battle of Gettysburg," 3; Orville Thompson, *Narrative of the Service of the Seventh Indiana Infantry in the War for the Union* (published by the author, n.d.), 161; *Pennsylvania at Gettysburg*, 1:316; George H. Otis, Diary, 2nd Wisconsin, Wisconsin Historical Society, Madison, WI; Earl Rogers, "The Second, or Fifty-Sixth, Which?" *Milwaukee Sunday Telegraph*, June 22, 1884; Robert K. Beecham, "The Second, or Fifty-Sixth, Which?" *Milwaukee Sunday Telegraph*, July 20, 1884. Captain Otis (Company I) said the regiment advanced at 7:00 a.m. Lieutenant Clayton E. Rogers told his brother, Earl, that Meredith did not advance with Cutler because "of a delay in giving orders." Beecham, in his rebuttal of Rogers' account, quoted Rogers by writing, "he [Wadsworth] directed his aide [Clayton Rogers] to move the division toward Gettysburg." It was Lieutenant Rogers, not Wadsworth, who led Cutler to Gettysburg. Lloyd Grayson Harris went by his middle name. According to Iron Brigade historian Lance Herdegen, the men in the "Black Hat Brigade" did not refer to themselves as members of the "Iron Brigade" at that time.

road, the order passed along the formation to lie down and await further orders.[25]

7:00 a.m. to 7:15 a.m.
Cupola, Lutheran Seminary

Lieutenant Aaron B. Jerome, General Buford's signal officer, observed Cpl. Levi Shaeffer's videttes (Company E, 8th Illinois) operating on Knoxlyn Ridge more than a mile away and mistook them for Confederate cavalry. As the only signal officer with the cavalry, and thus the only man who could decode incoming messages, he dispatched an enlisted man to convey the information to Buford.[26]

25 Sullivan, "The Charge of the Iron Brigade"; Bradford H. Tripp, "At Gettysburg: Substantiating the Claim That the Iron Brigade Opened the Battle," *NT*, September 24, 1892, 4; Lance J. Herdegen & William J. K. Beaudot, *In the Bloody Railroad Cut at Gettysburg: The 6th Wisconsin of the Iron Brigade and Its Famous Charge* (El Dorado Hills, CA, 2015), 157 (fn 34), 161-162, 166; Earl W. Hauer, *A Record of the Descendants of Levi Nelson Tongue and Adeline Sutton Morse* (privately printed, 1949), 2; *Index to the Reports of Committees of the House of Representatives for the First Session of the Forty-Ninth Congress, 1885-'86*, 12 vols. (Washington, D.C., 1886), 7:Report 2060. Sullivan did not record the events in chronological order. The cavalry and artillery (though not horse artillery) that passed through the ranks had to have been the headquarters cavalry and Hall's battery. Private Tripp (Company F, 7th Wisconsin) wrote that the men were lying in the road at 7:30 a.m. Confirmation of Remington's cold is from his pension record (fn 34). Herdegen's and Beaudot's statement that he commanded a squad from Company I (p. 166), while not supported by a specific footnote, probably came from the pension file. Based on my research, Remington commanded Sgt. Levi Legrand Tongue, Cpl. Francis Ashbury Wallar, and Pvts. Levi Stedman, Ed Lind, Samuel Wallar, and John Harland. A squad comprised 1/8 of a company, which would include a corporal and the men in his part of the line. In the rank and file, that would account for six men in the detachment. Levi Legrand Tongue was a private at the time of Gettysburg and is often confused with his father, Levi Nelson Tongue, who started at 1st sergeant in Company I, transferred to the band on October 1, 1861, and was discharged with the band on March 31, 1862.

26 DePeyster, *Decisive Conflicts*, 152; Ladd & Ladd, *Bachelder Papers*, 1:201. In his Oct. 18, 1865 letter to Hancock in *The Bachelder Papers*, Jerome said he spotted the Rebel advance. In his later story to DePeyster, he wrote, "I saw from the steeple of the Seminary a portion of their cavalry observing us from the Chambersburg Pike." I am unsure of the veracity of Jerome's account, which should be used with discretion. See, however, Wittenberg, *"The Devil's to Pay": Buford at Gettysburg*, 62-73, for another interpretation of Jerome's account, and refer to the excellent map of the entire vidette line west and north of Gettysburg.

Woodlot east of Ephraim Wisler's

Lieutenant Jones (8th Illinois Cavalry) had just dismounted and handed the bread and oats to his servant when he glanced up and saw T. Benton Kelley galloping toward him at full tilt. The private was shouting about a Rebel column. Without waiting for his servant to saddle his fresh horse, Jones climbed onto his regular mount while calling back to Kelley, "Tell Alex to get the reserve to the front." The lieutenant galloped west with his orderly, bugler Morgan Hughes. Kelley relayed the order to Sgt. Alexander Riddler before wheeling about and clattering after the lieutenant.[27]

7:15 a.m. to 7:30 a.m.
Seven Stars
About .5 miles west of Marsh Creek

The head of James Archer's small mixed infantry brigade passed through Seven Stars, a hamlet consisting of a several brick houses. What Pvt. Elijah T. Boland (Company F, 13th Alabama) described as a "misty rain" fell as the Confederates continued east into the wooded swamp area that sheltered Johnston Pettigrew's Brigade along the west bank of Marsh Creek. Archer halted his column in the road. Unaware the Yankee videttes across from them on Knoxlyn Ridge had seen them descending into the valley, Col. Birkett D. Fry (13th Alabama) rode to the colorbearer, Pvt. Thomas J. Grant (Company I), and told him to uncase the flag. The six-foot tall Grant, who had started his day with too much Pennsylvania wine, ripped the cover from the colors ready for a fight.[28]

27 Jones, *Journal*; Morgan Hughes, "Buford's Cavalry at Gettysburg," *NT*, Aug. 27, 1891, 3; Kelley, "First Shot At Gettysburg"; www.8thillinoiscavalry.org/home/gettysburg-june-30-july-1-1863, accessed Jan. 12, 2023. Jones mistakenly recollected the fellow who delivered the message as George Heim. The only "Alex" in the company was Sgt. Alexander McSwain S. Riddler.

28 Boland, "Beginning of the Battle of Gettysburg," *CV*, 14:398; W. H. Moon, "Beginning of the Battle at Gettysburg," *CV*, 33:449; John T. Reilly, *History and Directory of the Boroughs of Gettysburg, Oxford, Littlestown, York Springs, Berwick, and East Berlin, Adams County, Pa. with Historical Collections* (Gettysburg, PA, 1880), 150. Boland described a small village with several brick houses three to four miles from Gettysburg. Seven Stars, which was founded in 1840 with one brick dwelling, had at least four houses by 1880, most of which were likely there during the war. It is four miles from Gettysburg.

Private Boland knew trouble lay ahead. Glancing upward to the right front, he spotted a squad of dismounted videttes with reins in their hands in an old field atop Knoxlyn Ridge. William H. Moon, who was standing next to the colors, also saw them. Colonel Fry filed the regiment to the right into an apple orchard and commanded them to load at will. The lead regiment, the 5th Alabama Battalion, rushed across the bridge spanning Marsh Creek and fanned out into skirmish order. Lieutenant William H. Crawford (Company C), with Companies B, C, and G from the 13th Alabama, joined them, adding another 50 men to the line.[29]

7:15 a.m. to 7:30 a.m.
Ephraim Wisler House

Lieutenant Jones dismounted at the crest of the hill and handed the reins to Pvt. John O. Hale. He could see the Rebel infantry. Tearing a sheet from his memoranda book, he scrawled a message to Major Beveridge that a heavy column was headed toward them. He handed the note off to bugler Hughes, who galloped back toward Seminary Ridge while Jones and his men continued studying the Rebels. The approaching Rebels spotted the Union videttes when they reached the first ridge top. Skirmishers fanned out to both sides of the road while the main column, led by an officer on a light-colored horse, continued its slow but inexorable advance.

Jones ordered the horse holders and their assigned mounts to the rear while he and his seven remaining men waited for what looked to be an inevitable clash of arms. Kelley had just spurred up to the outpost when Jones asked for Shaeffer's carbine. "What condition is she in, Levi?" he inquired as he stepped up to the stake and rider fence and rested the weapon in the crotch of a pair of the stakes.

"Good," replied the corporal.

Kelley watched as Jones targeted a mounted officer in gray. The carbine cracked. Before the smoke cleared, Confederate skirmishers were rushing over the bridge into the field below the cavalrymen. Jones knew his detachment could not hold its position against such overwhelming numbers. Jones and his

29 Boland, "Beginning of the Battle of Gettysburg," 398; W. H. Moon, "Beginning of the Battle of Gettysburg," 449; Fulton, *Family Record and War Reminiscences*, 100. I am not convinced that Marye's Battery fired at the videttes from the Lohr house, which I will explain in a subsequent footnote.

men, with their horse holders in the lead, retired half a mile to a new position on the ridge at Charles Polley's house.[30]

Off to the south, the 5th Alabama Battalion and the skirmish detachment spread out to cover a front about 750 yards wide as they pushed east. The 13th Alabama crossed the bridge in the road. Lieutenant Colonel Newton J. George, whose 1st Tennessee was next in the column, detached Capt. Felix G. Buchanan (Company G) with the regimental sharpshooters to the right front to bolster the skirmish line farther to the south toward the Fairfield Road.[31]

7:45 a.m.
Herr's Ridge

When he reached the 8th Illinois' main reserve at Herr's Tavern, Private Dodge relayed the message to his captain, Daniel W. Buck. The officer sent a runner back to the regiment on Seminary Ridge and had his squadron mount and head west. Companies H and E reached the eight-man picket line at Polley's, dismounted, and sent the horse holders to the rear. The troopers spread out along the crest, using any available cover to stall the Confederate skirmishers. They did not stay long. When the Alabamians south of the Chambersburg Road crested Knoxlyn Ridge, followed by a large body of infantry, the cavalrymen mounted and skedaddled.[32]

30 Jones, *Journal*; Kelley, "An Account of Who Opened the Battle"; Beveridge, "The First Gun at Gettysburg," 2:92; Dodge, "Opening the Battle"; Kelley, "First Shot At Gettysburg." Dodge said Jones used George Sager's carbine, while Kelley claimed Jones used Shaeffer's weapon. All agree that Jones fired at a mounted officer and none say that he hit him, which is quite probable because carbines were not accurate beyond a few hundred yards. Kelley based his rendition on his wartime diary, which is why I used his account.

31 J. (Jacob) B. Turney, "The First Tennessee at Gettysburg," *CV*, 8:535; William J. Hardee, *Rifle and Light Infantry Tactics for the Exercise and Manoeuvres of Troops When Acting as Light Infantry or Riflemen*, 2 vols. (Philadelphia, 1861), 1:174-175. According to regulations, a skirmish detachment of the same strength as Archer's skirmishers, at the prescribed distances, would have covered a front of that length. This is my conclusion based upon Captain Turney's account, which said the sharpshooters encountered the Federals about three miles southwest of Gettysburg. Interestingly, that would have placed his men just about as far south as the bridge over Marsh Creek at Black Horse Tavern.

32 Jones, *Journal*; Moore, "Seventh Tennessee Infantry," 246; *OR* 27/2:646; June Kimble, "Tennesseans at Gettysburg—The Retreat," *CV*, 18:460; Moon, "Beginning of the Battle of Gettysburg," 449; Hankins, *Simple Story of a Soldier*, 43. Confederate accounts indicate that the brigades stayed in the road until going into line on the western side of Herr's Ridge.

Abraham Spangler House
East of Herr's Tavern

Private Thomas G. Day (Company E, 3rd Indiana Cavalry), whose horse refused to drink from Willoughby Run, urged his mount a short distance west to Abraham Spangler's water trough. Once there, the animal lowered his head and drank while Day looked east through the damp mist. The sun was rising above the high ground, piercing the cloud cover with brilliant shafts of light. His horse lifted its head upright from the trough and turned it side to side, apparently disturbed by something nearby. From over his right shoulder Day heard a rifle shot, followed by a slight pause, and then two more shots in close order. Looking west up the hill toward Herr's Tavern, he thought he saw a couple of men straggling over the high ground. Deeming it unwise to wait to verify whether they were Rebels, he dug his heels into his horse's flanks and raced back toward his regiment.[33]

8:00 a.m. to 8:30 a.m.
Ephraim Wisler House
Chambersburg-Knoxlyn Ridge Road Intersection

Archer's and Davis's brigades filed into the fields on opposite sides of the road just east of the Wisler house—Davis to the north and Archer to the south. The regiments "fronted," and Davis's skirmishers sprinted east to catch up with the left edge of Archer's line. Meanwhile, the bespectacled Maj. William "Willie" Pegram, accompanied by Capt. Edward A. Marye and the officers of his Fredericksburg Artillery, rode ahead of the battery and reined to a halt directly in front of the veranda-like front porch of the Ephraim Wisler home.

Pegram studied distant Herr's Ridge through his field glasses, trying to decide if the formation of men on the crest south of the road were Federals or Confederates. When he told his officers they were probably the enemy, they countered that they were more likely James Longstreet's men, who they believed were advancing east on a parallel road off to their right. One of Marye's sergeants, who had rejoined the battery the evening before, overheard

33 Day, "Opening the Battle." It takes a while to groom and feed a horse. Over the years, Day may have the timing of his event wrong. His description parallels Major Beveridge's account of the morning events. There were no Confederates in the vicinity at the time. He had to have seen Federal pickets and mistook them for Confederates.

them. The man interjected that he had passed Longstreet's Corps en route from Virginia, and it was some two days' march behind them. That was enough for Pegram, who ordered his lead gun, a 3-inch Ordnance Rifle, unlimbered in the road.[34]

Sergeant John L. Marye dropped the trail of his gun in front of the house. When Ephraim Wisler heard the command to "Load with shrapnel shell," he burst through his front door onto his porch. "My God, you are not going to fire here, are you?" he shouted. Before Marye could answer, Wisler frantically threw his hands in the air and disappeared. The sergeant, clearing the trail, gave the order "Fire!" The gun cracked and recoiled. The projectile screamed through the air and burst a couple seconds later high above Herr's Ridge. The round elicited no response. The crew fired several more rounds before limbering up and trundling east, with the infantry filing into the road behind them.[35]

Swale East of McPherson's Ridge

Major John L. Beveridge's men of the 8th Illinois Cavalry began their morning following the standard army routine. They groomed and fed their horses and then fed themselves before cleaning their equipment and weapons. With no threat of immediate trouble, Beveridge allowed some of his officers and men to meander into town. Captain Buck's messenger abruptly brought all of that to an end. With no superior officers present, the major ordered chief bugler George Bartholomew to sound "Boots and Saddles," followed by "To Horse."

34 *OR* 27/2:637; Marye, "The First Gun at Gettysburg," 1229; C. B. Fleet, "In the Three Days' Battle at Fredericksburg [Gettysburg], 1863," *SHSP*, 32:240; A. H. Belo, "The Battle of Gettysburg," *CV*, 8:165. In his after-action report, General Heth wrote that the gun fired from the crest of the second ridge west of Gettysburg. Fleet described the house as a brick structure that looked like "an old Virginia courthouse tavern." A 1900 photograph of the Wisler house shows its porch extending across the front of the entire house, much like one would see at a tavern. In the *SHSP* article the editor accidentally wrote "Fredericksburg" in the title when it should have been "Gettysburg."

35 Marye, "The First Gun at Gettysburg," 1229; Fleet, "In the Three Days' Battle," 240; *OR* 27/2:677. The National Park Service tablet at the site states that the battery had two 10-pounder Parrott Rifles. At this point in the advance Heth's artillery took the lead behind the skirmishers, with the infantry in the road behind it. The man on the gun would have accurately remembered whether he had a 3-inch Ordnance Rifle or a 10-pounder Parrott.

Bartholomew set off a chain reaction in the brigade, and the other buglers picked up the calls on both sides of the regiment. The troopers scrambled to saddle up and fall in alongside their mounts, with the reins in their hands. After forwarding the orderly to Colonel Gamble's headquarters at the Lutheran Seminary, Beveridge, on his own initiative, hurried another squadron forward to assist his skirmishers and sent orderlies into town to round up what men they could find there.[36]

Lieutenant William C. Hazelton (Company A) listened to the distant picket fire increase. He could clearly distinguish the louder reports of the Confederate rifles from the sharp cracks of the carbines. His veteran instincts told him "hard work" lay ahead.[37]

Private Day reached the 3rd Indiana about the same time and yelled for his company to saddle up—the Rebs were coming! Before anyone had time to respond, the bugler sounded "Boots and Saddles" and "To Horse." Company E mounted and clattered south toward the Chambersburg Pike. Crossing the creek, they swung into line north of the road at the Spangler house. The horse holders stayed in place while the rest of the men dismounted and hurried to the skirmish line atop Herr's Ridge.[38]

Lutheran Seminary

Colonel Gamble passed on the news from Captain Buck's dispatch from the 8th Illinois to John Buford, who in turn ordered Gamble to deploy his brigade. Simultaneously, Buford dispatched a rider to Lt. John H. Calef (Battery A, 2nd U.S.) to advance his guns. The orderly intercepted Calef in his return to the battery from his jaunt into town to purchase supplies for the officers' mess. He had no sooner ordered his drivers to unhitch their teams than Calef countermanded himself. The men hastily tore down the bivouac. Their baggage and the caissons pulled back to the seminary. Gamble, en route to the front, stopped and instructed Calef to select his own position upon which to unlimber

36 *OR* 27/2:677; Monument Commission, *Illinois Monuments at Gettysburg* (Springfield, IL, 1892), 17-18; Beveridge, "The First Gun at Gettysburg," 91. Major Beveridge noted that he received Buck's communiqué between 8:00 a.m. and 8:30 a.m.

37 Hazelton, "People of Gettysburg."

38 Day, "Opening the Battle."

Colonel William Gamble's cavalry brigade played a major role in slowing down the Rebel advance on the morning of July 1, 1863. *Civil War Library and Museum, Philadelphia, PA*

his guns. The artillerist latched his eyes on the open ridge 600 yards to the west.[39]

Gamble and Buford rode into the 1st Brigade. The regiments mounted and advanced through the wet ground fog toward the crest of McPherson's Ridge. The 8th Illinois anchored its right on the pike while the 8th New York continued the line to the south across the Fairfield Road. The 12th Illinois stood between the railroad cut and the Chambersburg Pike. With the regiments in position, Gamble deployed three more squadrons from the 8th Illinois to Herr's Ridge to reinforce the line north of the road. The two companies along Willoughby Run forded the creek and headed up the ridge while the four remaining companies spurred into the Chambersburg Pike.[40]

Orders went out for Colonel Devin to move his brigade to the right of Gamble's troopers. The three remaining companies of the 3rd Indiana held the

39 Calef, "Gettysburg Notes," 47; Hayes, "2d U.S. Art."; *OR* 27/1:1030. Calef wrote that Gamble ordered him to select his position around 8:00 a.m. Using Beveridge's time reference, it was closer to 8:30 a.m. Private Hayes mistakenly recalled that the ridge was about 300 yards west of the bivouac.

40 *Illinois Monuments at Gettysburg*, 18; *OR* 27/1:934. Gamble erred when he claimed his right rested on the railroad cut. One squadron of the 3rd Indiana extended the line beyond that point. The colonel sent three squadrons forward, some dismounted. Two companies from the 8th Illinois were along Willoughby Run, and six more companies were mounted along the Chambersburg Pike. As the largest regiment and so close to the road, it would have had quicker access to Herr's Ridge than the rest of the brigade. Gamble did not say which regiments supplied those two squadrons. The placement of the regiment is based upon my interpretation of the available data and differs somewhat from other writers.

ground on the north side of the cut, with the remaining four companies of the 6th New York extending the line northward. To their right rear, at the Forney place, a portion of Companies F and K of the 9th New York remained as the picket reserve, the balance of the two companies having gone down into the valley to the east to water their mounts in Rock Creek.[41]

Seminary Ridge
Chambersburg Pike

Calef waited patiently for his pioneers to clear the fence line along his front. With the rails down, he moved his battery forward in column of sections. Lieutenant Roder's two pieces took the lead, followed by sections under Sgt. Charles Pergel and Sgt. Joseph Newman. Each pair of guns wheeled successively into battery front once they topped the hill northwest of McPherson's house. Once freed from the guns, the drivers moved the limbers east into the hollow and circled around at the base of the hill to face the trails of their respective pieces.[42]

The skirmishers from Archer's and Davis's brigades, who had come under long-range carbine fire when they reached the Belmont School House, increased their pressure on the dismounted Union cavalry skirmishers along Herr's Ridge. Southern fire started taking effect in Company E, 3rd Indiana Cavalry, where both Cpl. William E. "Park" Story and Sgt. James Boyd suffered shots through their bodies. Private Thomas G. Day did not remember which man he and Pvt. John Hoagland boosted onto the saddle of Hoagland's white horse to get to the rear. Decades later, Day vividly remembered the man's

41 *OR* 27/1:938; Gottfried, *The Maps of Gettysburg*, 61; Moyer, *History of the Seventeenth Regiment*, 61, 381. The 17th's regimental history is a poorly constructed and often inaccurate account. Companies D and I, not D and H, were at V Corps Headquarters, and Company L was with XI headquarters. Companies E and L were not in the same squadron. Rather, B and L comprised a squadron and, with A and G, were on the Harrisburg Road. Colonel Josiah Kellogg had ensconced himself at brigade headquarters with Asst. Surg. J. Wilson De Witt.

42 Calef, "Gettysburg Notes," 47; http://wildcatbatterya2usarty.files.wordpress.com/2007/06/roster-officers-and-enlisted-men-light-company-a-second-artillery-1861-1865/, accessed Jan. 12, 2023. The roster shows Pergel as a sergeant and Newman as 1st sergeant until July 30, 1863, when the ranks were reversed. Calef makes no mention of the railroad cut on his right flank.

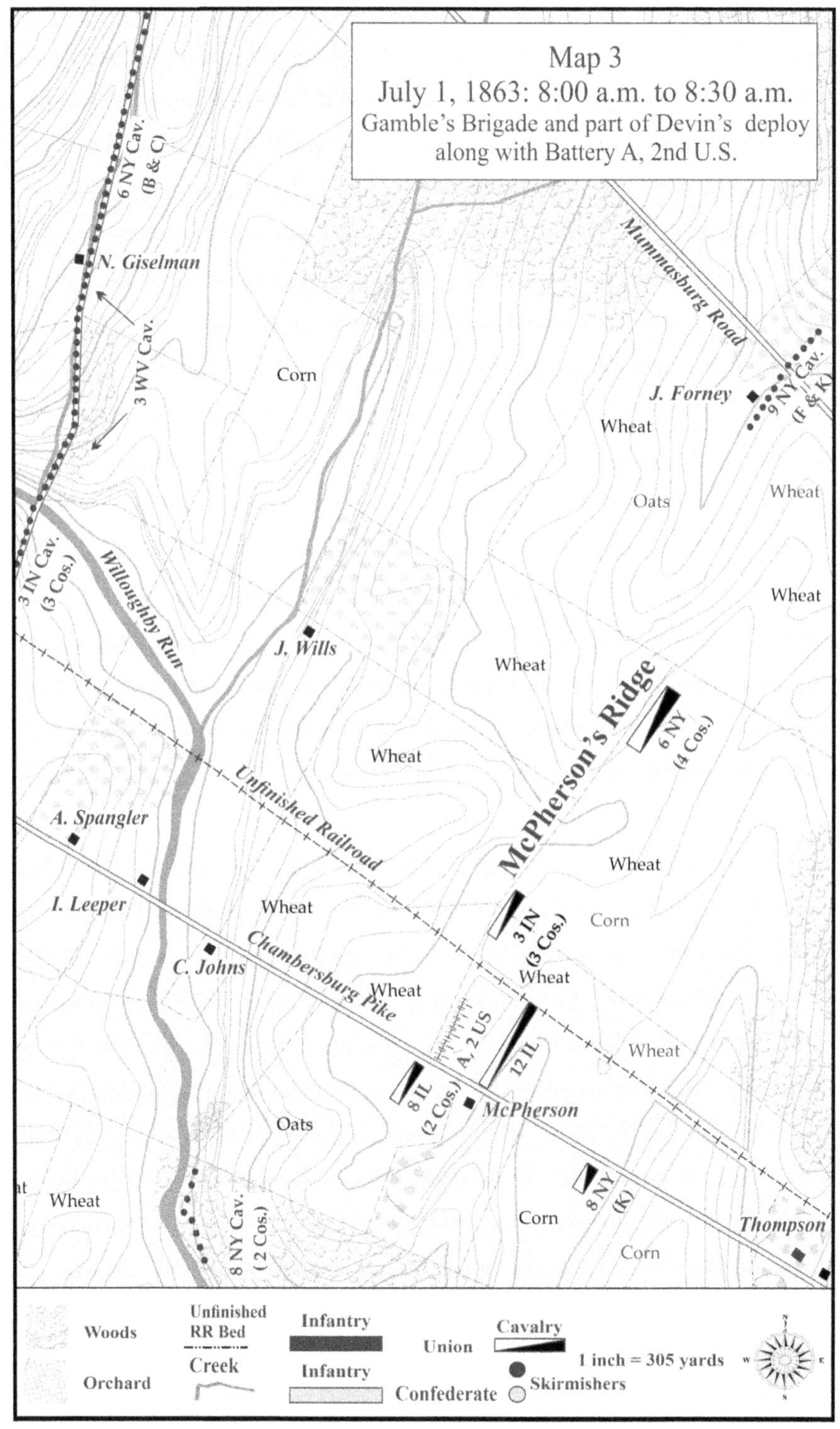
Map 3
July 1, 1863: 8:00 a.m. to 8:30 a.m.
Gamble's Brigade and part of Devin's deploy along with Battery A, 2nd U.S.
6 NY Cav. (B & C)
N. Giselman
3 WV Cav.
Corn
Mummasburg Road
J. Forney
9 NY Cav. (F & K)
Wheat
Oats
Wheat
Wheat
3 IN Cav. (3 Cos.)
Willoughby Run
J. Wills
Wheat
McPherson's Ridge
6 NY (4 Cos.)
Wheat
Unfinished Railroad
A. Spangler
I. Leeper
Wheat
Wheat
3 IN (3 Cos.)
Corn
C. Johns
Chambersburg Pike
Wheat
Wheat
A, 2 US
12 IL
Wheat
8 IL (2 Cos.)
McPherson
Oats
8 NY (K)
Wheat
8 NY Cav. (2 Cos.)
Corn
Thompson
Corn
Woods
Orchard
Unfinished RR Bed
Creek
Infantry
Infantry
Union
Confederate
Cavalry
Skirmishers
1 inch = 305 yards

blood pumping from the wound onto the horse, coloring its hide a dark crimson.[43]

Although it seemed to many like a "long time," but probably consumed just several minutes, the Rebel skirmishers herded the troopers off the Herr Ridge Road from the tavern to Giselman's toward McPherson's Ridge. As the right wing of the 8th Illinois sloshed through Willoughby Run near the railroad cut, Lt. Marcellus Jones (Company E) watched about 25 to 30 troopers take up positions in the cut on the eastern side of the bridge.[44]

Company E of the 3rd Indiana saddled up and crossed the Willoughby Run bridge to the crest of McPherson's Ridge, where the troopers found Calef's horseholders and their own regiment hugging the ground on both sides of the Chambersburg Pike. Private Day never forgot what he described as the "set look"—that countenance of resignation to fate—upon the faces of the cavalrymen as they awaited the inevitable clash of arms. Colonel George Chapman called for his troopers to mount. Leaving the artillerymen on their own, the 3rd Indiana troopers galloped south into the hollow on the eastern side of Herbst Woods.[45]

Captain William L. Heermance, commanding the 6th New York's squadron north of Giselman's, found his two companies stranded. "With unusual forethought our horses were called back and we [were] left to care for ourselves as best we could," he later recalled. His veterans, who were beyond the left front of Joe Davis's advancing brigade, hunkered down in the roadbed, as determined as Captain Heermance to harass the approaching enemy flank.[46]

43 Day, "Opening the Battle." John "Hoag" in his account is John Hoagland, who probably went by "Hoag." Story died from his wound on July 10, 1863.

44 Jones, *Journal.*

45 Day, "Opening the Battle."

46 Letters and Partial Diary of Capt. William L. Heermance, 91, hereafter cited as Heermance Letters/Diary; *NYAG*, 3:1134. This is my conclusion based upon the scanty information from the sources on the regiment. Heermance clearly indicated that his skirmishers were abandoned.

Chapter Three

"We did not suspect that the foe was within a few hours' march."

— Lt. William Harries, Company B, 2nd Wisconsin

The Confederate Advance Stalls

8:00 a.m. to 9:30 a.m.

8:00 a.m.
North Bank of Marsh Creek

While Generals Wadsworth, Reynolds, and their staffers cantered toward the front, "Long Sol" got his regiments to their feet. The 2nd Wisconsin led Brig. Gen. Solomon Meredith's brigade, followed by the 7th Wisconsin, 24th Michigan, and the 6th Wisconsin. The regiments moved out at a leisurely pace around 8:00 a.m. "We did not suspect that the foe was within a few hours' march," admitted Lt. William H. Harries (Company B, 2nd Wisconsin).[1]

Sergeant Cornelius Wheeler (Company I) echoed that sentiment. Although nearly everyone felt they were catching up with the Confederate army, no one believed a major battle was but hours away. Sergeant Joseph O. Williams (Company I), who had slipped away from his post near the rear of the column, shuffled alongside Sergeant Wheeler. Williams had seen action with the regiment from First Bull Run through Chancellorsville, and had never shirked

1 Harries, "The Iron Brigade in the First Days' Battle at Gettysburg," 339.

any duty. Something was different this day. The sergeant bluntly told his friend that he did not feel right, and that something was going to happen to him before the sun set. Wheeler laughed. Why was he so blue? It was a beautiful day and trouble was nowhere to be found. Should it occur, he assured him, he would come out of it unscathed, as he had every engagement. With nothing more to say, the tormented sergeant returned to his post in the column.[2]

Within a few minutes, Sgt. Maj. George Legate fell in beside Wheeler. "Corny," he announced, "we are going to have a fight to-day, and I will not come out alive." "Corny" laughed at the notion and informed Legate that he was the second man to come to him with a premonition of doom. It was "all nonsense," scoffed Wheeler. They were not going to have a fight that day. He also told the sergeant major to not go into battle if he felt that way. Besides, sergeant majors were "not of much account in a fight, anyway." Legate would have none of that. "No," he insisted, "I will stay with the regiment whatever happens." With that, he returned to his post at the rear of the regiment. Wheeler recalled looking at the bright blue sky through a break in the clouds. It was indeed a pretty day.[3]

In the 6th Wisconsin, the "United Turners" of Company F burst into a rousing marching tune. The rest of the regiment responded by switching from the "route step" into the "common time" to march with the music. "Mickey" Sullivan of Company K did not understand a word of German, but he recalled how the Western men broke into three resounding "Huzzahs" when they finished their song. His company also responded with several stanzas of "On the Distant Prairie Where the Heifer Wild," a ditty about a cabbage-stealing bovine. Sullivan recalled the "boys" in his company, officers included, "sang, without as much melody as a government mule." As the song brayed into silence, Pvt. Tommy Flynn killed off any further singing with his rendition of "Paddy's Wedding." "It seems odd for men to be marching towards their death singing,

2 Hofmann, "Remarks on the Battle of Gettysburg," 3; Bradshaw, "That March to Gettysburg"; O. B. Curtis, *History of the Twenty-Fourth Michigan of the Iron Brigade, Known as the Detroit And Wayne County Regiment* (Detroit, 1891), 156; Cornelius Wheeler, "Reminiscences of the Battle of Gettysburg," in *War Papers Read Before the Commandery of the State of Wisconsin, Military Order of the Loyal Legion of the United States*, 4 vols. (Milwaukee, 1896), 2:209. Elmer M. Bradshaw was a private in Company K, 56th Pennsylvania.

3 Wheeler, "Reminiscences of the Battle of Gettysburg," 209.

shouting and joking, as if it were a street parade or holiday show," Sullivan would later reflect.[4]

7:00 a.m. to 8:00 a.m.
The Bull Frog-Nunemaker Mill Roads Intersection
2.45 miles west of Moritz's Tavern[5]

Newly promoted to brigade command, Col. Chapman Biddle began what would be one of the longest days of his life at 4:00 a.m. Sometime before 7:00 a.m., General Doubleday's acting aide-de-camp, Capt. J. Harrison Lambdin (Company H), sought out Biddle's cousin, Maj. Alexander Biddle, who had been recently elevated to command the 121st Pennsylvania. Lambdin passed along an order to the major to recall his skirmishers before riding on to attach Capt. James H. Cooper's Battery B, 1st Pennsylvania Artillery, to the brigade. He also ordered the entire command north on detached service to cover the flank of the I Corps.[6]

The men cooked and ate their breakfasts like they had on any other morning. Once they finished, the regiments assembled and mustered for pay before dispersing to return to their camp fires and boiling coffee. In the veteran 20th New York State Militia (N.Y.S.M.), messmates Cpl. John Ovendorf (Company H) and 19-year-old Cpl. Enos B. Vail (Company E), being excused from all camp duties, decided to strip to their drawers and wash their clothes in a nearby stream. They had just shoved their uniforms into the water when the bugler sounded "Assembly."

The men wrung out their clothing as best as they could, raced back to the bivouac, and "saddled up." They hurried as they pulled on their socks and brogans, hoisted on their knapsacks, slung their canteens over their shoulders, and pulled their rifles from the color guard's stack, fully prepared to march in their drawers with their wet clothing dangling unceremoniously from the ends

4 Sullivan, "The Charge of the Iron Brigade."

5 Nunemaker Mill Road is now Pumping Station Road

6 *Pennsylvania at Gettysburg*, 2:746; *OR* 27/1:312. In his official report, Brig. Gen. Thomas Rowley specifically stated that Chapman Biddle's 1st Brigade was "detached and directed to take the advance with a battery of four pieces [Cooper's Battery B, 1st Pennsylvania Light Artillery]." Colonel Stone did not follow Biddle's brigade on the same road.

of the fixed bayonets. "Thus decorated, we made a fine looking pair," joked Vail decades later.[7]

By 7:00 a.m., Vail and Ovendorf had rejoined the regiment at the Bull Frog-Nunemaker Mill crossroads. The 151st Pennsylvania led the column, followed by the 142nd Pennsylvania, part of the 121st Pennsylvania, and the 20th N.Y.S.M. Cooper's Battery B, 1st Pennsylvania (four 3-inch rifles) brought up the rear. To the east, Brig. Gen. Thomas A. Rowley, now in command of the division, marched north with Col. Roy Stone's brigade on the Emmitsburg Road.[8]

An hour later, Biddle's column, without waiting for the rest of the 121st Pennsylvania to come in from picket duty, stepped out on the Nunemaker Mill Road and headed north. (Company B remained behind as part of the I Corps headquarters guard). The sharpshooters of Company K, 20th N.Y.S.M., under the command of Capt. Ambrose N. Baldwin, covered the front of the advance. The 142nd Pennsylvania deployed two companies forward on both sides of the road to screen the brigade's flanks. Private Edwin R. Gearhart (Company G) went out with the company to the left front of the regiment, armed only with his haversack and a recently purchased pound of butter in his tin cup. One of the walking sick with the regiment, he had turned in his musket, cartridge box, and accoutrements on the march toward Emmitsburg in exchange for light duty.[9]

The brigade stepped off at the "common time" (about 2.4 m.p.h.) for roughly three miles to Sachs Bridge on Marsh Creek, which the head of the column reached around 9:15 a.m. Biddle halted there to give his sweating men a

7 Enos B. Vail, *Recollections of a Boy in the Civil War* (Brooklyn, NY, 1915), 89, 116; *Pennsylvania at Gettysburg*, 2:746; Barbara M. Croner, ed., *A Sergeant's Story: Civil War Diary of Jacob J. Zorn, 1862-1865* (Apollo, PA, 1999), 66. Sergeant Zorn (Company F, 142nd Pennsylvania) said the regiment moved out at 7:00 a.m. That is probably when they sounded "Assembly." Other accounts state the column marched at 8:00 a.m.

8 *Pennsylvania at Gettysburg*, 2:652. The formation is based upon the "Bachelder Map," which shows the formation once it reached the field.

9 "In the Years '62 to '65; Personal Recollections of Edward R. Gearhart, A Veteran," *The Daily Times* (Stroudsburg, PA), Mar. 19-Aug. 6, 1900, Library, GNMP, typescript; *Pennsylvania at Gettysburg*, 2:651, 652; Survivors' Association, *History of the 121st Regiment* (Philadelphia, 1906), 51; Raus, Jr., *A Generation on the March*, 1. The 1906 regimental history cites information from the dedication of the monument at Gettysburg on September 11, 1889. Major Biddle claimed the brigade had sharpshooters to the front followed by the 121st Pennsylvania with skirmishers on both flanks. Evidence indicates the skirmishers belonged to the 142nd Pennsylvania.

few minutes to rest. Vail and Ovendorf of the 20th N.Y.S.M. hurriedly pulled their clothes from their bayonets and dressed. While there, the rest of the 121st Pennsylvania caught up with the column. The regiments had just gotten into proper marching order when the command to load and fix bayonets filtered down the formation. Major Alexander Biddle detached two companies from the 121st forward to reinforce the flankers.[10]

The brigade trudged northeast across Willoughby Run toward Pitzer's school house. Ovendorf, whose canteen was dry, told Vail he was thirsty. Without hesitating, Vail handed his nearly empty canteen to his brother in arms. The men in the 20th N.Y.S.M. marveled at the ripening orchards and massive German barns along the route, which were shockingly different from the war-ravaged wasteland of northern Virginia. Many of the Pennsylvania farm women greeted the passing soldiers with chunks of fresh buttered bread, which some of them only handed out to the Pennsylvanians. Captain John Cook (Company I) recalled a number of his disgruntled men returned to the ranks empty handed and vehemently swearing. The New Yorkers bypassed the obstacle by lying about the state from which they hailed. Unbeknownst to them, Cutler's brigade had already reached the hollow on the east side of McPherson's Ridge, and was marching north toward the Chambersburg Pike.[11]

Emmitsburg Road, Alexander Currens House

2.17 miles from Marsh Creek

Colonel Williams (19th Indiana) received word at 7:30 a.m. to recall his pickets. The division was marching at 8:00 a.m. He ordered his "boy" to pack up. Privates Bill Leavell and William Roby "Robe" Moore, tent mates in

10 Vail, *Reminiscences*, 117; *Pennsylvania at Gettysburg*, 2:651-652. Writing 52 years later made it difficult for Vail to add reliable specificity, including when he and Ovendorf put their uniforms back on. He did, however, note that the regiment marched an hour before loading and fixing bayonets. That would place them at Sachs Bridge. From then until he was wounded, Vail recalled no specific details about what he observed. Major Biddle did not record when the pickets caught up with the brigade, but it was probably at Sachs Bridge, from which point they could hear distant artillery fire. Sach's Bridge has been restored and preserved.

11 *Pennsylvania at Gettysburg*, 2:651-652; Cook, "Personal Reminiscences of Gettysburg," 322-323. The brigade reached the Fairfield Road, some three miles north of Sachs Bridge, about 10:30 a.m. after having covered six miles in two and a half hours, which puts the column's pace at 2.4 m.p.h. (common time).

Company K, began this day as they always had, with each rolling up their respective halves of the dog tent. One generally took care of the ground coffee, the sugar, and the hard crackers while the other toted the rest of the rations. That morning, hearing the crack of a rifled gun in the far distance, Moore believed they would not stay together and that Leavell would be killed or wounded. He stuffed both their haversacks with rations. "I, unconsciously, pass(ed) sentence upon my tentmate," he later penned. "I can say that it was not an uncommon thing for members of our Company to single-out certain ones, who in their opinion would get theirs in the next battle."

Williams assembled his Hoosiers and waited for their brigade to meet them. Cutler's brigade, with Hall's battery at the rear, tramped and rumbled past. Fifteen minutes later Generals Reynolds, Wadsworth, and their staffs cantered up the road behind Cutler.[12]

8:15 a.m. to 8:25 a.m.[13]
Joseph Sherfy's Peach Orchard
Intersection of the Emmitsburg Road and the Millerstown Road
1.75 miles south of Gettysburg

Colonel J. William Hofmann (56th Pennsylvania) watched Reynolds and Wadsworth dismount in front of Cutler's brigade to study what appeared to be a large county map while their staffs gathered on foot along the east side of the road. A couple miles to the northwest, white shell bursts pockmarked the sky. One of Reynolds's orderlies, Pvt. Bradford H. Tripp (Company F, 7th Wisconsin), with his veteran's acumen, listened intensely to the rate and sound of the fire and believed it came from a section of light guns.

An orderly from Buford reined in alongside the generals and confirmed his observation: the Confederates were driving in the cavalry on the Cashtown (Chambersburg) Road and had a section of light artillery in a "close place." The

12 Thompson, "In Their Own Words," 11; Report of Col. Samuel J. Williams, August 1, 1863, Vertical Files, VF-IN19, Library, GNMP; Ladd & Ladd, *Bachelder Papers*, 2:939, 940; R. K. Beecham, *Gettysburg: The Pivotal Battle of the Civil War* (Chicago, 1911), 61; Michele J. Mumaw, "A 'Bye' Goes Off to War," Honors thesis, Ball State University, Indianapolis, IN, 1997, 39-40. I believe Dudley erred in his report when he claimed Reynolds passed the regiment after it had joined the column. No other reports from the brigade verify that statement.

13 *OR* 27/1:927, 1030. At an average speed of 4.0 m.p.h., the general and his officers would have covered the 3.4 miles from Marsh Creek to the Peach Orchard in about an hour.

orderly passed along Buford's request that Reynolds bring up the I Corps as soon as possible. Other aides clattered past the column heading toward Marsh Creek, with one shouting something about the Rebels being "thicker than blackberries beyond the hill."[14]

The 76th New York, leading Cutler's brigade that morning, halted in the Emmitsburg Road with Sherfy's cherry trees lining the fence along its left flank. The veterans longingly eyed the overburdened trees. Major Andrew J. Grover, admonished the regiment as he passed: "Boys, the General charges you to be very particular to keep within the rules, and not meddle with those cherry trees! Be sure you don't break the trees down!" Wheeling his horse about, Grover trotted to the head of the regiment to screen the men from Reynolds and his officers. The line officers deliberately ignored what was transpiring as the rank and file descended on the trees like locusts on the fields of Egypt. "The trees," admitted the regimental historian, "did not remain quite uninjured."[15]

A herd of terrified but curious civilians from town thronged the road, blocking it completely. Wobbling old men, women dragging their young ones along, and children pulling other children along with them flowed around the column. Reynolds realized the danger posed by the growing crowd of townspeople and commanded Lt. Joseph Rosengarten, the I Corps' ordnance officer and his acting aide-de-camp, to post a guard from Company L, 1st Maine Cavalry, farther north on the road to turn the civilians back toward Gettysburg. He also told the lieutenant to find the mayor and tell him to keep his citizens inside their homes. The last thing he could afford was to have the I corps impeded by men, women, and children. Swinging into the saddle, Rosengarten

14 Hofmann, "Remarks on the Battle of Gettysburg," 3-4; Hofmann, "The Battle"; Ladd & Ladd, *Bachelder Papers*, 3:1566; *NYAG*, 3:990; Stephen Minot Weld, *War Diary and Letters of Stephen Minot Weld* (Boston, 1912), 229; Reynolds Memorial, *Addresses Delivered Before The Historical Society of Pennsylvania Upon the Presentation of a Portrait of Maj.-Gen. John F. Reynolds, March, 1880* (Philadelphia, 1880), 22, 62-63; "94-Year Old Letter From Orderly Tells How General Reynolds Was Killed," *Gettysburg Times*, January 23, 1958, 15; Charles H. Veil to David McConaughy, April 7, 1864, David McConaughy Papers, Civil War Era Collection, Special Collections, Gettysburg College; Bradford H. Tripp, "The Iron Brigade: They Open the Battle of Gettysburg," *NT*, June 18, 1891, 3. Tripp was wrong about the the time of the incident, but his description corroborates other accounts of the event.

15 Smith, *History of the Seventy-Sixth Regiment*, 236. According to Smith, a rumor stated that the home owner told the officers he was a secessionist. This does not make sense considering these were Federals.

galloped toward Gettysburg with a detachment of Company L close behind him.[16]

Reynolds and the rest of his staffers mounted and, with a small escort from Company L, headed for the town leaving Wadsworth's infantry standing in the road. Near the David Ziegler place, a frightened civilian reined in alongside the general, who halted momentarily to ask what concerned him. The man explained that the cavalry was fighting—something Reynolds already knew. The corps leader hurried toward the intersection of the Taneytown and Emmitsburg roads. He halted at a house on the southwest side of the crossroad where the Taneytown Road became Washington Street. From there, he got directions to the Chambersburg Pike. With his staffers in tow, Reynolds galloped northwest on Washington Street for the Eagle Hotel. Along the way, he shouted at the civilians lining the sidewalks to go to their cellars.[17]

Adams County Court House,
Middle and Baltimore Streets, Gettysburg

Lieutenant Rosengarten had already reined in at the courthouse on the southwest corner of Baltimore and Middle streets. Once there, he discovered that the provost-marshal and most of the city council, including council president Henry Rupp, had already left town. The lieutenant did manage to round up Burgess Robert Martin, at least one of the councilmen, and a couple of clergymen, and tell them to get the civilians off the streets, out of the army's way, and to a place of safety.[18]

16 Joseph Rosengarten to M. Jacobs, October 15, 1863, Reynolds Papers, Special Collections Dept., Franklin and Marshall College, Lancaster, PA. Rosengarten's letter did not say when he posted the guard or the regiment from which it came. The guard probably came from Company L, 1st Maine Cavalry (the general headquarters guard). Rosengarten likely posted them before Reynolds entered town because no one on the staff recalled running into civilians after that. It makes sense that Reynolds would have sent him ahead to see the mayor (president of the council) to keep the citizens off the streets.

17 "94-Year-Old Letter From Orderly Tells How General Reynolds Was Killed," 15; Veil to McConaughy; Murdoch, "Catherine Mary White Foster's Eyewitness Account," http://cupola.gettysburg.edu/ach/vol1/5, accessed Jan. 13, 2023.

18 Rosengarten to Jacobs; *History of Cumberland and Adams Counties, Pennsylvania* (Chicago, 1886), 193, in the *History of Adams County* section of the book. The courthouse would have been the most likely place for Rosengarten to have found any prominent person in town. According to the county history, Robert Martin served as the burgess in 1863.

8:35 a.m. to 9:00 a.m.[19]
Seminary Ridge
.45 miles west of Gettysburg

Once atop Seminary Ridge, Reynolds and several of his officers trotted south on the campus road to the seminary building. Looking up at the cupola, he spied General Buford and called out to him. When Buford poked his head over the railing, Reynolds shouted something along the lines of, "how are things going?" "Let's go and see," Buford replied. The cavalryman hurried down to the front door. The officers mounted and headed back for the rest of Reynolds's staff.[20]

The generals halted on the crest of McPherson's Ridge to the left of Calef's battery. The enemy, Buford informed Reynolds, were advancing in force from Cashtown. Orderly Charles H. Veil heard Reynolds tell Buford to "hold the enemy in check as long as possible, to keep them from getting into town."[21]

Calef trotted to Buford's side to receive further instructions. The general directed him to spread his guns to mislead the Confederates into believing the cavalry had more than one battery on the field. He also told Calef to leave one section north of the pike, deploy one section south of the road, and post the third farther to the left with the 8th New York Cavalry to cover the division's flank. Lieutenant John W. Roder stayed in the field north of the road. On the right of the line, Sgt. Joseph Newman rolled his guns into the hollow behind them and turned south. Passing through the destroyed sections of fence on both sides of the Chambersburg Pike, they turned west and rolled onto the slope adjacent to the McPherson barn. Dropping the trails of the two guns on the crest immediately opposite Roder's section, the limbers rolled down the hill and circled up again until they came on line along the north side of the barn.

19 The time is based upon the calculated rate of march.

20 Aaron Brainard Jerome, "Buford in the Battle of Oak Ridge," in John Watts DePeyster, *The Decisive Conflicts of the Late Civil War*, 152-153; Ladd & Ladd, *Bachelder Papers*, 1:201. Jerome's letter dated October 18, 1865, to Winfield Scott Hancock in *The Bachelder Papers* predates his account in DePeyster's work, which contains the more romanticized and dramatic dialogue including "The Devil's to Pay." His letter to Hancock is more straight forward and concise.

21 "94-Year-Old Letter From Orderly," 15; Veil to McConaughy; J. Willard Brown, *The Signal Corps, U. S. A. in the War of the Rebellion*, (Boston, 1896), 128; Signal Corps Association, *Signal Corps Reenactor's Service Manual*, www.civilwarsignals. org, accessed Jan. 16, 2023.

Sergeant Charles Pergel limbered his two-gun section and followed Calef to a new position in the open field south of the southeastern corner of Herbst Woods.[22]

While Calef redeployed, Col. Thomas Devin detached the 5th Squadron (Companies E and L) of the 17th Pennsylvania Cavalry from the left wing of the regiment to support Calef's two sections along the Chambersburg Pike. One company fell in mounted along the low ground east of Newman's guns at the McPherson barn, and the other in the hollow north of the road behind Roder's section.[23]

Herr's Ridge

At this point, James Archer's Confederate skirmishers were marking time. The thinly spread Rebel advance had halted on Herr's Ridge south of the tavern to await the deployment of their brigade. Joe Davis's skirmishers, facing minimal opposition, had started up the western side of the ridge north of the railroad bed. Simultaneously, Maj. Willie Pegram crested the hill ahead of Harry Heth's Division and began deploying his five artillery batteries. The guns dropped trail on both sides of the Chambersburg Pike, just east of the recently vacated ridge road.[24]

Meanwhile, north of the Giselman house the troopers belonging to Capt. William L. Heermance's squadron from the 6th New York Cavalry knew they were woefully outnumbered and decided it was best to hunker down under

22 Calef, "Gettysburg Notes," 48; *OR* 27/1:1030; Weld, *War Diary and Letters*, 229, 231, 234; Fleet, "In the Three Days' Battle," 240; Hayes, "The 2d U.S. Art."; http://wildcatbatterya2usarty.files.wordpress.com/2007/06/roster-officers-and-enlisted-men-light-company-a-second-artillery-1861-1865/, accessed Jan. 12, 2023. Battery A's roster shows that Pergel was a sergeant and Newman a First Sergeant at the time of the battle. Weld's two contemporary accounts agree as to finding Buford in the field and not at the seminary as often stated. I pieced together the events described above by blending those accounts with the 1912 recollection. The account of Reynolds and his officers riding forward to inspect the lines dovetails with Calef's account. I was unable to find any account that specifically mentions who destroyed the fence in the hollow. It is possible that it was done the evening before to allow the north-south passage of Buford's cavalry without being seen from the higher ridges to the west.

23 Moyer, *History of the Seventeenth Regiment*, 61, 381.

24 *OR* 27/1:677; Martin, *Confederate Monuments at Gettysburg*, 1:96, 99, 104-105, 110, 229.

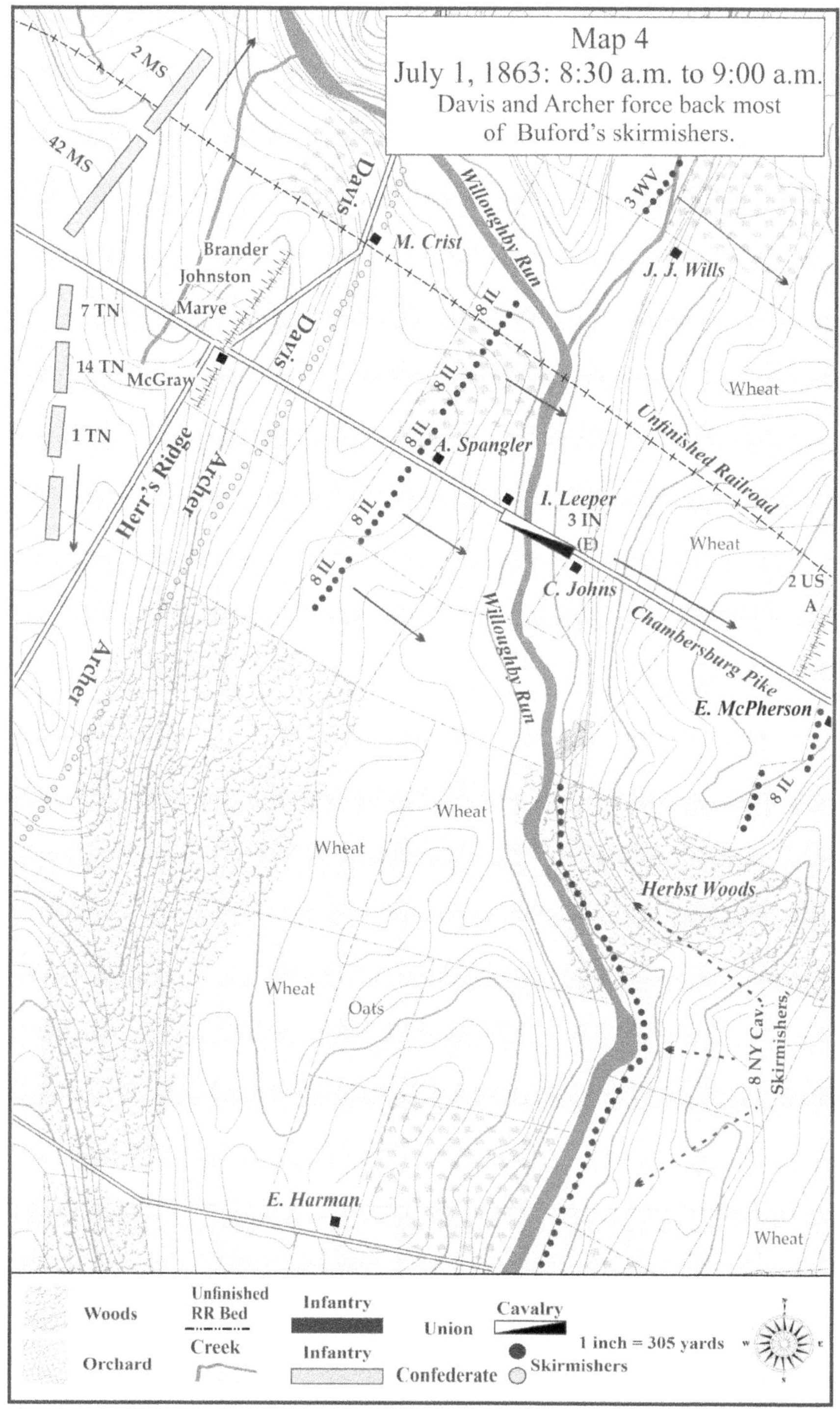
Map 4
July 1, 1863: 8:30 a.m. to 9:00 a.m.
Davis and Archer force back most of Buford's skirmishers.
2 MS
42 MS
Davis
Brander
Johnston
Marye
McGraw
7 TN
14 TN
1 TN
Herr's Ridge
Archer
M. Crist
Willoughby Run
3 WV
J. J. Wills
8 IL
A. Spangler
I. Leeper
3 IN (E)
C. Johns
Unfinished Railroad
Wheat
2 US A
Chambersburg Pike
E. McPherson
Herbst Woods
8 NY Cav. Skirmishers
Oats
E. Harman
Woods
Orchard
Unfinished RR Bed
Creek
Infantry
Union
Confederate
Cavalry
Skirmishers
1 inch = 305 yards

cover. They let the Rebels pass by their left flank rather than invite disaster by making their presence known.[25]

Seminary Ridge, Near the Chambersburg Pike

Captain Stephen M. Weld, Reynolds's youngest aide, watched 12 of the 17 Confederate guns wheel into position along Herr's Ridge on the west side of Willoughby Run. Major John L. Beveridge (8th Illinois Cavalry) also noticed them. A mile to the west he saw what appeared to be an infantry brigade in column crest a ridge and head northeast into a swale north of the Chambersburg Pike.[26]

Herr's Ridge on the Chambersburg Pike

Marye's two 12-pounder Napoleons and two 3-inch Ordnance Rifles unlimbered just northeast of Herr's Tavern, the right section on the south side of the road and the left in front of what Pvt. Charles R. Fleet described as "a beautiful oak grove." Captain Joseph McGraw's Purcell Battery, comprised of four 12-pounder Napoleons, went on line to his right just south of the road.[27]

McGraw planted his guns on the open ridge near the tavern about the time General Archer filed his brigade into the hollow along its western side near the Widow Hartzell's house. The 13th Alabama led the column. According to Pvt. William H. Bird (Company C), a "rather old lady" and her big yellow dog stood guard while the two lead companies passed her house. The angry canine lunged into the Rebs until they shot him down. The distraught widow gave them a tongue lashing and accused them of being terrible people. The soldiers retaliated by knocking over her ash bin.

With that skirmish behind them the Alabamians continued south with the 1st, 14th, and 7th Tennessee following. When the last regiment cleared the fence south of the Widow Hartzell's, Archer halted the brigade, faced it to the

25 Heermance Letters/Diary, 91. Heermance's July 4, 1863, letter to his fiancée indicates that the Confederates mistook his men for sharpshooters rather than dismounted cavalry. Apparently the New Yorkers were picking off North Carolinians from concealed positions.

26 Weld, *War Diary and Letters*, 231; Beveridge, "The First Gun at Gettysburg," 93. The infantry brigade belonged to Joe Davis.

27 Martin, *Confederate Monuments at Gettysburg*, 1:99, 110.

left into line, and waited for Davis to deploy. Archer filed his brigade south on the western side of Herr's Ridge, trying to keep the regimental colors and men below the line of sight from the high ground east of Willoughby Run. The 13th Alabama marched into the open woodlot on the knoll east of Frederick Herr's house, with its right wing extending into the open just south of the woods. From where he stood next to the color bearer, Pvt. William H. Moon (Company I) clearly saw the church spires of Gettysburg in the distance. The brigade anchored its left flank on the fence northwest of the house, about 2,000 feet south of the pike.[28]

Captain Ervin B. Brunson's Pee Dee Battery from South Carolina lost a gun when it broke an axle while trundling off the road. He rolled his remaining 3-inch Ordnance Rifles south on the Herr's Ridge Road and maneuvered into battery on the crest of a partially wooded knoll southwest of the Herr place. Lieutenant Andrew B. Johnston, having left his short-range 12-pounder howitzers below the ridge, swung into battery north of the road next to Marye. Captain Thomas A. Brander's Letcher Artillery finished out the formation with two 12-pounder Napoleons and two 20-pounder Parrott Rifles.[29]

From McPherson's Ridge, Major Beveridge observed Archer's skirmishers tramp over Herr's Ridge around Marye's and McGraw's batteries and fan down the eastern slope toward Willoughby Run. Captain Weld recollected the dismounted Federal troopers had "spread out like the fingers of the hand, falling back and firing." The severity of the situation was now more than clear. Reynolds, Buford, and a lone bugler, moved south along McPherson's Ridge.[30]

The 5th Alabama Battalion's skirmishers herded the 8th Illinois's dismounted troopers across Willoughby Run to the crest of McPherson's Ridge, south of Calef's center and right sections. Lieutenant William F. Fulton, Jr., the

28 Moon, "Beginning of the Battle of Gettysburg," 449. Moon places the regiment in a wood south of the Chambersburg Pike. The various maps of the field show a partially wooded knoll west to southwest of the Herr place. The elevation is high enough to see the town and Seminary Ridge over the woods on the eastern slope of the hill. He also said a three-gun battery went into position to the right-front of the regiment. Brunson's was the only three-gun battery on the field. Based on the size of the brigade, its left would have extended north of that fence and would have provided the brigade with something solid upon its flank to guide the line of march.

29 *OR* 27/1:677; Martin, *Confederate Monuments at Gettysburg*, 1:96, 99, 104-105, 110, 229; Moon, "Beginning of the Battle of Gettysburg," 449; http://www.wadehampton camp.org/pdla-sc-hist.html, accessed Jan. 16, 2023.

30 Weld, *War Diary and Letters*, 231; Beveridge, "The First Gun at Gettysburg," 2:93.

regiment's acting battalion commissary, casually rode in the road behind the left of the line, unconcerned about the sporadic small arms fire zipping in from the east.

The 8th New York's resistance stiffened as the Rebels got closer to the creek and woods. William H. Phipps (Company F) had just returned from a successful foray into to town for bread, his prize being a full cup of apple butter. Walking into the skirmish, he absentmindedly set the cup on a fence post and joined his men. Years later he recalled leaving the cup, which he had promised to return to its owner.[31]

Some of the Alabamians sheltered behind Isaac Leeper's house, out buildings, and blacksmith shop. Leeper kept a large watchdog, which bounded out of the house ready to fight. With his glasses pushed back on his head, Leeper clambered out of the basement wearing a leather apron and carrying what appeared to be a shoe knife in his hand. He was as excited as his dog. When he inquired about what was happening, one of the Alabamians told him that General Hill had sent them to drive back the cavalry and that there was going to be some hot fighting nearby. The news surprised him. "Tell General Hill to hold up a little, until I get my cow out of the pasture," he pleaded. Lieutenant Fulton shrugged off the absurd request as his "boys" took cover and went about their business.[32]

9:00 *a.m. to* 9:30 *a.m.*
Herr's Ridge, South of the Chambersburg Pike

Pegram's gunners opened against Calef's four exposed pieces as soon as Archer's skirmishers stepped below their muzzles. The pulling of lanyards initiated an artillery duel between the two ridges. Smoke engulfed the tops of the opposing hills and the drizzling atmosphere pushed the sulfuric clouds low to the ground, making it difficult for the opposing lines to see one another.

31 W. F. Fulton, "The Fifth Alabama Battalion at Gettysburg," *CV*, 31:379; Fulton, *Family and War Reminiscences*, 103; William H. Phipps, "Was at Gettysburg," *NT*, September 13, 1894, 3.

32 Fulton, "The Fifth Alabama Battalion at Gettysburg," 379; Fulton, *Family and War Reminiscences*, 103. The dialog from the two accounts was pieced together to make it more plausible. In the 1919 account, Fulton claimed Lee gave the order, as opposed to his 1923 account, which has Hill doing so. The shorter quote about the cow, given the circumstances in which the event occurred, is the more believable of the two.

One of Calef's rounds dropped short in the 5th Alabama. Burrowing itself in the soggy ground at Maj. Abram S. Van de Graaff's feet, it burst, blanketing him with dirt. The ground absorbed most of the blast. He wiped the soil from his eyes and continued after his men. Another shell screamed overhead and exploded well west of Herr's Ridge above the 26th North Carolina (Pettigrew's Brigade) as it marched east along the Chambersburg Pike. The column slightly wavered, prompting young Col. Henry K. Burgwyn to shout "Steady, men!"

Van de Graff's small Alabama regiment started taking casualties. A bullet killed the battalion's pet dog, which Lieutenant Fulton described as "an innocent bystander." Another round shattered Pvt. Columbus L. F. Worley's right ankle joint. The 21-year-old Tennessee-born draftee from Company A would refuse anesthesia when a surgeon told him he would lose the leg below the knee: "Doc, leave off the chloroform; if you can stand it, I can."[33]

The Emmanuel Harman House

.64 miles south of the Leeper Place

Sixteen-year-old Amelia E. Harman and her aunt, Rachel Harman, had been glued to a window on the east side of the house since about 9:00 a.m., when they heard the deep "boom" from Calef's first round at Herr's Ridge. Amelia remembered seeing what seemed like "hundreds" of Federal cavalrymen thundering west through the fields and down the Chambersburg Pike. Members of the 8th New York Cavalry splashed across Willoughby Run, galloping through their fields and around their house and outbuildings toward the wooded hillside to the west. A second shell burst brought more hollering troopers across their property.[34]

33 John T. McCall, "What the Tennesseans Did at Gettysburg," 2,Vertical Files, V-7 TN Inf., Library, GNMP; Moore, "Seventh Tennessee Infantry," 246; *OR* 27/2:646; A. S. Van de Graaff to his wife, July 8, 1863, Vertical Files, V7-Ala5Bn., Library, GNMP; Fulton, *Family and War Reminiscences*, 103; Busey & Busey, *Confederate Casualties at Gettysburg*, 1:57, 58, 61; "Southern Soldiers in Northern Prisons," *SHSP*, 23:159. The battalion lost nine wounded: Co. A: James Thomas Barnes, James D. Tureman, J. Wesley Cole, and Columbus Worley; Co. B: Capt. Archibald N. Porter, Lt. James R. Wilson, Duncan G. Bartlett; Co. C: George W. McKerley and Robert H. Yarborough.

34 www.findagrave.com/memorial/205139851/emanuel-harmon, accessed Jan. 13, 2023; "Burning of the McLean House on the First Day's Battle of Gettysburg," *Gettysburg Compiler*, July 3, 1915, 1. Emanuel Harman (Harmon) was an absentee landlord who did not live in the colonial-era house, which the locals called the McLean house after its builder,

Herr's Ridge, North of the Chambersburg Pike

Joseph Davis's column filed north of the road. The 55th North Carolina, led the brigade as it crossed Willoughby Run under the cover of Herr's Ridge to the west, followed by the 2nd and 42nd Mississippi regiments. Once clear of the creek, the North Carolinians and the 2nd Mississippi halted and faced east, their right flank resting on the creek bank.[35]

Heermance's stranded horsemen (6th New York Cavalry) north of the Giselman house on Herr's Ridge peppered the North Carolinians with sporadic but well aimed carbine fire. Colonel John K. Connally (55th North Carolina) detached Company B from the line to neutralize them.[36]

Colonel Hugh R. Miller's 42nd Mississippi formed between the southern side of the run and the railroad bed. Miller had his men clear their weapons. Private Andrew Park (Company I) remembered the colonel pacing the formation bellowing, "if there was a man there who could not stand the smell of gunpowder he had better step out, for we were going into a fight." To Park's astonishment, Pvt. Thomas C. Looney stepped forward and proclaimed, "Colonel, I just cannot go into a fight today, for if I do, I will get wounded or killed." Miller swore and yelled at him to get back into the ranks.

Colonel John M. Stone trooped the 2nd Mississippi's line, stopping in front of each company to give the men instructions preparatory to the advance they all knew was coming. Corporal Samuel W. Hankins recalled Stone's admonitions to his Company E. "Men, clean out your guns, load, and be ready. We are going to have it!" During the minutes it took to clear and load weapons, the colonel singled out Lt. Rodes R. Whitley. The lieutenant tagged along with his men despite being under arrest for a petty offense he had committed a couple of days

---

the Rev. Charles McLean. The New York-born Harman, who was something of an entrepreneur, built the Springs Hotel in 1869 near the allegedly medicinal Katysaline Spring along Willoughby Run near Herbst Woods and the Gettysburg Bottling Works. The troops on his property belonged to the 8th New York Cavalry.

35 Given the opportunity, formations tended to anchor at least one flank on a solid terrain feature like a road or fence to guide the line of march. Based upon the frontage of the brigade and Colonel Stone's description of the J. J. Wills farm lane, which split the 2nd Mississippi into wings, the brigade would have been north of the railroad bed. Travis W. Busey & John W. Busey, *Union Casualties at Gettysburg: A Comprehensive Record*, 3 vols. (Jefferson, NC, 2011), 2:772.

36 Hardee, *Light Infantry Tactics*, 1:5; Belo, "The Battle of Gettysburg," 165.

earlier. "Lieutenant Whitley, you can take command," Stone said. With the regiments ready to advance, General Davis ordered them forward.[37]

The infantry on both sides of the road stayed just below the crest of Herr's Ridge to let the gunners "soften up" the Federal cavalry across from them. Archer's Tennesseans and Alabamians stopped to the right rear of McGraw's guns, using the top of the ridge to shield themselves from Calef's artillerymen. Davis's regiments also halted below the Yankees' line of sight, north of Brander's battery.[38]

From his position with Company E, 2nd Mississippi, Cpl. Samuel W. Hankins could see the tall undulating wheatfields east of the James Wills place and Sheads Woods along Oak Ridge. He spied what he assumed were mounted officers riding to and fro. What he could not see was a line of prone enemy just in front of the officers. Lieutenant James B. Gambrell (Company I) went forward in charge of the skirmishers and quickly engaged the dismounted Yankee skirmishers in the wheat. The regiment had hardly come on line when one of Brander's guns hurled a shell toward the distant wood line. Almost immediately, a Federal gun responded. Hankins saw the smoke, heard the gun crack, and watched the shell burst harmlessly overhead.[39]

Meanwhile, Company B of the 55th North Carolina, having spread out as far north as the Mummasburg Road, flanked Captain Heermance's abandoned squadron and drove it toward the Hoffman place. The New Yorkers hooked up with the brigade skirmish line as it headed east toward the grain fields along Oak Ridge.[40]

37 Hankins, *Simple Story of a Soldier*, 43-44; A. Park, "Some of My Recollections of the Battle of Gettysburg," January 16, 1899, 1, Tom Elmore Collection.

38 Gottfried, *The Maps of Gettysburg*, 60-63; Hankins, *Simple Story of a Soldier*, 43-44. The infantry fighting got underway around 10:15 a.m. The Confederate artillery exchanged rounds with Calef from about 9:00 a.m. to 10:00 a.m. The infantry did not go into action during this time for fear of getting hit by its own guns. Hankins mistook Brander's guns for Bradford's Mississippi battery, which was not at Gettysburg.

39 Hankins, *Simple Story of a Soldier*, 43-44.

40 Cheney, *History of the Ninth Regiment*, 107-108; *NYAG*, 3:1134. Heermance said his men were flanked on the right. Company B, 55th North Carolina, was the only body of men across the squadron's front.

The Forney Farm, Near Oak Hill

With most of his regiments spread thinly across the northern end of the field to protect the approaches from Carlisle, Harrisburg, Hunterstown, and York, Colonel Devin decided to reinforce the picket line on the Mummasburg Road. The three squadrons of the 9th New York (Companies F/K, D/L, and I/G) were watering their mounts in the valley east of Oak Ridge when bugler Joseph Frappier (Company M) sounded "Boots and Saddles," "Double Quick," and "Prepare to Mount." The 1st Squadron (Companies F and K) got to horse and galloped up the road. Captain Timothy Hanley (Company F) sent Lt. Albert C. Robertson with 20 men over the ridge.

The troopers rode past the picket reserve at Forney's to the Hoffman place, where they encountered a large force of Rebs in the woods south of the Mummasburg Road. Wheeling about, they made for the fields east of Forney's, then occupied by the rest of the squadron and Companies B and C of the 6th New York. The Confederate skirmishers pursued them as far as Forney's, where they ducked into the outbuildings and put down a harassing fire. Several troopers from Company F of the 9th New York dismounted and dispersed them, losing Pvt. William A. Scranton to a wound. The Southerners counterattack made it too hot for the New Yorkers, who hastily mounted and under Captain Hanley's orders, raced back more than 350 yards to a dilapidated stone wall running along the crest of Oak Ridge.

The 1st Squadron dismounted behind the wall as the remaining two squadrons supported them on horseback. The two mounted squadrons of the 6th New York and the diminutive 3rd West Virginia (63 officers and men present), rather than risk getting gobbled up by the skirmishers on their right, also withdrew to the wall and dismounted.

Colonel William Sackett (9th New York) realized there was a gap on the left of the line between the troopers and the Chambersburg Pike, and that he had no idea where other enemy skirmishers might be. He sent out a 10-man mounted detachment under Sgt. Edward A. Holcomb to fill the void. They had orders to fire and retire to the main line if attacked. While riding into the wheatfield between the stone wall and McPherson's Ridge, Cpl. Cyrus "Ci" James turned to his best friend, Private Baker, and said, "John, if I am killed or wounded in this battle, you see than I am cared for or buried, and if you are killed or wounded, I will do the same for you." Baker agreed.

The pair halted on the first rise of ground west of the wall. James scanned the fields to the northwest. "There is a lot of Graybacks now," he announced.

Without warning, a squad of Rebels popped up behind a nearby fence and fired. One or more rounds killed him and his body fell off the right side of his horse. Reacting to the sudden tug of the reins, his mount whirled about and galloped southeast with James's right foot hooked in the stirrup. The horse dragged the lifeless body through the field toward the woods.

Baker followed the animal down a wood trail and across a low section of the railroad cut onto the Casper H. Dustman property, snagging the horse as it passed near the front door of the house about half a mile from where James had been killed. Hearing the commotion, Dustman, a 52-year-old German-born boat maker, rushed outside in time to help Baker free his friend's boot from the stirrup. Despite Dustman's objections that he was a poor man and did not want the badly broken body on his property, Baker pressured the frightened civilian into promising to bury the corpse. Dustman promised to inter James in the corner of his lot. With deep remorse, Baker left his friend behind. He would never learn whether the German kept his word.[41]

Roder's Section, Calef's Battery
North of the Chambersburg Pike

Lieutenant John Roder's left gun (Battery A, 2nd U.S.), the one closest to the pike, loosed a round at Brander's piece on Herr's Ridge. The sharp crack of the 3-inch rifle caught Lieutenant Calef's attention while Pergel's section trundled toward the 8th New York Cavalry's skirmish line. The projectile screamed through the air above the woods toward the right side of the Confederate battery line. Captain Marye's Fredericksburg Artillery responded with a single round, followed by shots from the remaining three guns.

One of the Virginia shells burst above Company C, 12th Illinois Cavalry, killing 18-year-old Pvt. Ferdinand Ushuer instantly. Another exploded over

41 Cheney, *History of the Ninth Regiment*, 107-108; John Baker, "The First Man Killed at Gettysburg," *NT*, September 12, 1901, 3; John Baker, "First Man Killed at Gettysburg," *NT*, December 24, 1903, 3; www.gdg.org/Research/People/safford.html, accessed March 6, 2023; www.segtours.com/files/gettysburg_census_1860.pdf, accessed Jan. 17, 2023. Baker believed that he had stopped at John Burns's house, but considering the distance from the field, that was too far away. The fact that he did not return to his company until after "exacting a promise" to have the civilian bury James suggests it was Casper H. Dustman. On the following day, Dustman, pleading personal poverty, reluctantly agreed to bury Lt. Winfield S. Safford (Company C, 24th Michigan). It is probably the same argument he gave to Baker.

Pvt. Gabriel Dunham of Company I, who, loaded down with canteens, was cutting through the field toward the rear to fetch water and carbine rounds. At the report, Pvt. Edwin DeReamer (Company I) rolled onto his back in time to see the shrapnel hurl Dunham forward, his arms flailing the air. DeReamer raced to his assistance and found Dunham laying in a bloodied heap, his left hip smashed and bleeding. DeReamer dragged him to the protection of a small stand of oaks.

Surgeon John Higgins arrived a few minutes later. He examined Dunham's wound and stanched the blood flow with a tourniquet, only to pronounce it mortal. (The dying 19-year-old would live until July 23, and pass away in his father's arms.) Seconds later, both Lieutenant Roder's and Sergeant Newman's guns engaged in counterbattery fire with Pegram's Battalion (17 guns) along Herr's Ridge. Calef ordered his four gun crews to fire slowly and accurately.[42]

Stone Wall on Oak Ridge at the Mummasburg Road

On the right of the line, the New Yorkers from the 9th Cavalry watched the tall wheat on the north side of the Mummasburg Road move on that windless sodden morning. The dismounted troopers hunkered down behind the northwest corner of the stone wall lining the road and waited for the oncoming Rebs, who were hunching or crawling through the field to get within effective range before cutting loose. At the right moment, the Yankees would pop up from their cover and pepper the Confederates, who ducked down or fled a short distance. At least one fellow flopped into the wheat, while another stopped behind a tree near the road. Nineteen-year-old Perry J. Nichols (Company F) bolted from cover and captured the Reb.[43]

42 www.daily-journal.com/news/local/gabriel-durham-the-first-to-fall-at-gettysburg/article_88f2fd56-53e0-5b9c-8add-d3f5f9cab834.html, accessed Jan. 17, 2023; *Illinois Monuments at Gettysburg*, 33; Beveridge, "The First Gun at Gettysburg," 93; Hankins, *Simple Story of a Soldier*, 44. According to the Monument Commission, Ushuer was killed about 7:00 a.m. The Southern artillery did not fire until the skirmishers had been pushed back to Seminary Ridge, which was much later. Marye claimed to have fired the first Confederate round, but it is possible that Brander provoked Calef's counterfire, to which Marye responded.

43 Calef, "Gettysburg Notes," 48; Cheney, *History of the Ninth Regiment*, 108. According to Lt. Newell Cheney, Company C, 9th New York, the Rebels opened fire a few minutes after 9:00 a.m.

McPherson's Ridge

Buford and Reynolds reined into the field in the shelter of the swale west of Seminary Ridge and halted. Artillery fire abruptly broke off their conversation. As Buford headed away, Reynolds gathered his staff, turned to Capt. Stephen Weld, and asked if Weld's horse was in good condition. Having pushed the animal 30 miles the day before, the aide frankly answered that the mare was not fit, but quickly added that he would take her anywhere the general wanted him to go. Reynolds told Weld and a nearby orderly who would accompany him how to find the Taneytown Road. "Ride at once at your utmost speed to General Meade," the general admonished, and "[t]ell him the enemy is advancing in strong force, and I fear he will get to the heights beyond the town before I can. I will fight him inch by inch, and if driven into the town I will barricade the streets and hold him back as long as possible."

Weld and the orderly took off at a dead run and disappeared into Gettysburg. Reynolds dispatched two more staffers—one to General Howard (XI Corps) and the other to Maj. Gen. Daniel Sickles (III Corps)—with instructions to bring their commands up as quickly as possible. The general and his officers rode into the Chambersburg Pike and headed south onto West Street to the western edge of town. At the intersection with High Street, the entourage turned east onto Washington Street and followed it south toward the George George house.[44]

Once there, they encountered Maj. Henry E. Tremain, General Sickles's aide-de-camp. When the major asked Reynolds if he had any instructions for the III Corps, Reynolds inquired as to the whereabouts of General Wadsworth and his division. Tremain fell in with Reynolds's staff, none of whom he knew, and rode with them south toward the Brien tenant house. Soon, the major spotted infantry marching up from the south. "There is General Wadsworth now."

44 Veil to McConaughy; Weld, *War Diary and Letters*, 229-232, 234-235; *Addresses Delivered Before the Historical Society of Pennsylvania*, 22; James Henry Stine, *History of the Army of the Potomac* (Philadelphia, 1892), 454. Weld's quote, cited in this work, predates his 1912 reminiscence, which he included in his published letters (p. 232) and very closely parallels his July 1, 1863, journal entry (p. 229-239) and his July 3, 1863, letter to his father (p. 234). Veil said the general took a "back Street" near John Burns's house on the corner of West and Chambersburg streets to the Emmitsburg Road. He probably took High Street to Washington Street and did not go cross-country with his staff and Company L of the 1st Maine.

Reynolds focused his attention east toward Cemetery Hill. "That would be a good place," he said quietly, apparently thinking out loud. "But I would like to save the town." Tremain listened without replying, unsure if Reynolds normally talked to himself. "If I form there it might destroy the town," he continued while visually sweeping the ground to the south, west, and northwest. The report of a distant gun did not interrupt his thoughts. "But I doubt if I shall have time to form on the other side of town."[45]

The Codori Farm

.7 miles southwest of Washington Street

The knot of officers made it as the rise of ground across from the Codori barn, from which they could clearly see the seminary on the ridge north of the Fairfield Road. Reynolds halted and directed Company L, 1st Maine, into the fields between the barn and the Fairfield Road with orders to tear down fences to open an unobstructed route for the infantry.

General Wadsworth rode up with his escort and saluted. Reynolds pointed to the open field west of the road. "You had better turn off here," he suggested, indicating the Codori farm, "and form your division as soon as you can." Tremain used the opportunity to edge alongside Reynolds. The III Corps staffer requested permission to return to Sickles unless the corps leader had other plans for him. Tremain also inquired whether the general had any instructions for him to relay to III Corps headquarters. "Tell General Sickles I think he should come up." The young major replied, "I shall report to him immediately." He rode away disappointed and somewhat sad that he achieved nothing while wasting too much time trying to reach Reynolds.[46]

45 Henry Edwin Tremain, *Two Days of War; A Gettysburg Narrative and Other Excursions* (New York, 1905), 10-12; "94-Year-Old Letter," 15; Veil to McConaughy; Samuel B. Holabird, comp., *Flags of the United States Army During the War of the Rebellion* (Philadelphia, 1887), unpaginated. Tremain describes meeting the general on the edge of town "where the highway [Emmitsburg Road] skirts a field at the base of the old cemetery [Cemetery Hill]." This places the meeting at or near the Emmitsburg-Taneytown roads intersection. It may have occurred on the rise in the road between the Ziegler and Brien houses, a position that would have given them a direct line of sight to the Codori barn. Wadsworth's division's standard was probably visible.

46 *Address Delivered Before the Historical Society of Pennsylvania*, 22; Tremain, *Two Days of War*, 12-14; "94-Year-Old Letter," 15; Veil to McConaughy. Private Charles H. Veil, one of Reynolds's orderlies, said the general ordered his escort to destroy the fences.

McPherson's Ridge, South of the Chambersburg Pike

With his two right sections cracking away at the Rebel artillery on both sides of Herr's Tavern, Lieutenant Calef turned south to check on Sergeant Pergel's two guns near Herbst's Woods. He found the unflappable General Buford and his lone bugler astride their horses, seemingly undisturbed by the intensifying chaos surrounding them. The lieutenant, keenly aware of the "demonic 'whir-r-r' of the rifled shot, the 'ping' of the bursting shell, and the wicked 'zip' of the bullet," noticed the general quietly smoking his pipe. "Our men are in a pretty hot pocket, my boy," Buford matter-of-factly observed. "We must hold this position until the infantry come up; then you withdraw your guns in each section by piece, fill up our limber chests from the caissons, and await my orders." Without warning, a shell exploded close by. Both horses reared without ditching either rider.

Calef continued on to the grass field on the ridge south of the eastern point of Herbst Woods to superintend the placement of Sergeant Pergel's section of guns. The right piece was about 1,000 feet south of the east-west fence line that continued along the southern edge of the tree line down to Willoughby Run. Dismounted troopers of the 8th New York covered both of Pergel's flanks along the crest.[47]

9:00 *a.m. to* 9:30 *a.m.*
Sherfy's Peach Orchard

Lieutenant Clayton Rogers cantered his mount past General Cutler with instructions for him to move out his infantry brigade. That was all Maj. Andrew J. Grover (76th New York) needed to bellow, "Forward—double-quick!" The New Yorkers trotted down the ridge toward Codori's, dragging the rest of the brigade behind them. The column obliqued slightly north by northwest,

---

That would have been Company L, 1st Maine Cavalry. The quote indicates that Wadsworth and Reynolds met at Codori's, where the infantrymen said they were turned off the road.

47 Calef, "Gettysburg Notes," 48; *NYAG*, 3:91; *OR* 27/1:1031; Weld, *War Diary and Letters*, 229-232, 234-235. To make Calef's fragmented 1907 recollection more intelligible, I had to weave it into his after-action report, Weld's reminiscences, and the *NYAG* account. I relied on the *OR* report to establish the framework and sequence of the events, and organized the remaining accounts to fit that schematic.

probably opposite the Codori house, parallel to and east of the nearly dry Stevens Run.[48]

The narrow breaches in the intervening fences, which the cavalrymen had left behind, temporarily halted the regiment. Realizing that the cavalry had not made the openings in the fences wide enough to allow the passage of a regiment moving by files (column of fours), Cutler yelled for pioneers from the 76th New York and 147th New York to come forward and remove the obstructions along the brigade's path. Hurrying to the front with their axes, the New Yorkers set about their work. While the two lead regiments slowly lurched northwest behind the pioneers, Lt. Col. Francis C. Miller bellowed at his 147th New York, "Forward, double-quick! Load at will!" Above the distant, rapid cracks of Calef's guns, Lt. J. Volney Pierce (Company G) distinctly heard what he described as "the wild rattle of jingling ramrods" from the men who had halted to charge and ram their cartridges.[49]

The Fairfield Road West of Middle Street

The route took the column northwest, east of the Bliss house and barn and across the "Long Lane." The 76th New York halted at Middle Street with the 56th Pennsylvania behind it, waiting for the pioneers to destroy the post and rail fences bordering both sides of the road. Behind this regiment, the 147th New York started crossing the dry creek bed of Steven's Run when the lead gun of Capt. James Hall's battery thundered past until the post and board fence along the Fairfield Road brought the horses pulling them to an inglorious halt. The

48 M. M. Whitney, "The 76th New York," *NT*, July 21, 1887, 5. This is my conclusion based up the lay of the land and the easiest access to Seminary Ridge.

49 Whitney, "The 76th New York"; Ladd & Ladd, *Bachelder Papers*, 2:910; Silas Casey, *Infantry Tactics*, 3 vols. (New York, 1863), 1:126, 203-205; Pierce, "Gettysburg"; *NYAG*, 3:991. It would have taken some time for the pioneers to widen the approach, which would necessarily have slowed the brigade's advance. Loading on a run was extremely difficult. Drill manuals provided for firing and loading while advancing and retreating, but at a slow pace, and admonished the men who were loading while moving to halt momentarily, like skirmishers, to "charge cartridges" and prime their weapons.To load on the run, a man had to halt, take a cartridge out of the cartridge box, tear it open, and put the powder down the bore. If loaded with a minié ball, he had to unwrap the greased round from another wrapper, insert it in the muzzle, then draw the rammer to drive the round home. Pierce's "wild rattle of the jingling ramrods" may imply that the men halted before executing the double quick, something the rest of the regiments also may have done.

pioneers tore into the fence along both sides of the road and widened the passage to allow the artillery to rumble through.

With the fences removed, Cutler's brigade tramped over the downed boards and threaded around the post stumps the pioneers had left in their wake. The general halted his men in the hollow east of the seminary where the east-west lane to the institution intersected the Chambersburg Pike. Part of the line ran through the southwest corner of the orchard between the pike and the Fairfield Road. The pioneers cut away the rails along the pike to ease the way for the ponderous artillery. Once done, the pioneers headed west onto Seminary Ridge south of the seminary building to remove portions of the rail fences bordering the west side of the main road through the campus. Colonel J. William Hofmann, meanwhile, ordered his Pennsylvanians to load their weapons. In the middle of the column, Adj. Henry H. Lyman of the 147th New York glanced at his watch. It was 9:30 a.m.[50]

8:55 a.m.
Alexander Currens Home on the Emmitsburg Road
2.17 miles from Marsh Creek

While the situation was becoming more threatening at McPherson's Ridge, Solomon Meredith's brigade intercepted the 19th Indiana near the Alexander

50 Hofmann, "The Battle"; *NYAG*, 3:990; Ladd & Ladd, *Bachelder Papers*, 1:385, 2:910, and 3:1001; Pierce, "Gettysburg"; "Private letter from an officer in the 147th About Gettysburg," *Oswego* [NY] *Commercial Times*, n.d., http://dmna.ny.gov/historic/reghist/civil/infantry/147thInf/147thInfCWN.htm, accessed Jan. 17, 2023; Markle, "The Story of Battle Told By Survivor." In 1882, Pierce recalled that the pioneers cleared the posts. By 1903 he was claiming the regiment climbed over the fences along the road, which the evidence does not support. Captain Hall wrote that his battery approached the field by the Chambersburg Pike from the eastern base of Seminary Ridge. The pioneers must have removed the post and rail fence to allow the guns through. According to Colonel Hofmann, the regiments halted at the eastern base of Seminary Ridge while the pioneers moved to the post and rail fence along the crest before the men headed west in column of fours. The seminary lane to the Chambersburg Pike would have forced the column due west and south of the seminary building. The intersection would have been the logical place to cut an opening for the artillery into the pike to allow passage west and parallel with the infantry. Private Markle (Co. B, 2nd Wisconsin) recalled that his regiment passed through an orchard. Gettysburg cartographer Steven Stanley's map of this area shows an orchard at the location described by Markle. It is also important to keep in mind that troops often advanced by anchoring one or both flanks on roads, creeks, fence rows, or other obstacles, and given the chance, approached under cover and by the line of least resistance.

Currens house. The regiments slowed their pace to allow the Hoosiers to slip into their assigned position between the 7th Wisconsin and the 24th Michigan. This action created a gap between the 19th and the two lead regiments. Colonel William W. Robinson halted his 7th Wisconsin to allow the regiments behind it to catch up. The 2nd Wisconsin kept marching, opening a lead of more than 100-yards ahead of the rest of the brigade.[51]

Shortly thereafter, Capt. James D. Wood, the brigade's assistant adjutant general, raced past Meredith's men yelling, "Boys, 'Little Mac' is in the command of the Army of the Potomac!" Cheering coursed along the road from one end of Meredith's column to the other. "McClellanites" to the core, the Westerners were overjoyed by the news. Farther ahead, the 2nd Wisconsin encountered a smattering of the locals, who pointed toward the blue mountain range some six miles to the northwest while shouting that Robert E. Lee's entire army had camped there the night before. The Badgers brushed aside their concerns by replying they would probably encounter the Rebs somewhere near there. "We rolled along quite merrily," recalled Pvt. Elisha Reed (Company H). "The boys felt well, and joke and song flowed freely."[52]

At the front of the 6th Wisconsin, Lt. Col. Rufus Dawes ordered Drum Major Robert N. Smith (Company I) to bring the regimental band to the head of the column, and ordered Sgt. Thomas A. Polleys to uncase the tattered Stars and Stripes. "The Campbells Are Coming" blared above the regiment as it approached Warfield Ridge. The "boys" closed up from their route step and slipped into the "common time."[53]

9:30 a.m.
Sherfy's Peach Orchard
1.23 Miles Northwest of A. Currens's House on the Emmitsburg Road

Artillery bursts in the distance reverberated above the 2nd Wisconsin as it reached the high ground at the Peach Orchard. From his position in the

51 Ladd & Ladd, *Bachelder Papers*, 1:140, 142; Thompson, "In Their Own Words," 11; Report of Col. Samuel J. Williams, August 1, 1863.

52 Beecham, *Gettysburg*, 61-62; Sullivan, "The Charge of the Iron Brigade"; Elisha R. Reed, "Gettysburg," *Wisconsin State Journal*, June 1887.

53 Rufus R. Dawes, *Service with the Sixth Wisconsin Volunteers* (Marietta, OH, 1890), 165; *Regimental General Order 23*, as cited in Herdegen & Beaudot, *In the Bloody Railroad Cut*, 165, fn 54.

regiment, Sgt. Cornelius Wheeler (Company I) heard what sounded like the sporadic cracks of carbines. Glancing northwest, he spotted what he thought were Union cavalrymen. Not too far away, carrying the colors in the center of the regiment, Private Reed (Company H) studied the ground to the west and saw no one at all. Corporal Robert K. Beecham (Company H) later reflected, "We had no idea that we were coming almost immediately into the presence of the enemy."[54]

Irish-born Cpl. Charles H. McConnell (Company B, 24th Michigan) heard the guns and hastily glanced at his watch. He later recollected it was around 9:30 a.m. Private James F. Clegg (Company H), marching alongside his chum Cpl. Charles E. Crary, Jr., saw a shell burst over the top of the Rev. Schmucker's house on distant Seminary Ridge. Sergeant Augustus F. Ziegler (Company A, 24th Michigan) observed white puffs of smoke to the northwest and matter-of-factly noted, "We knew right off what the order of the day was." He mistakenly believed Howard's XI Corps had arrived on the field ahead of them.[55]

Lieutenant Loyd G. Harris (Company C, 6th Wisconsin), commanding the brigade guard at the rear of the column, heard dull thumping off to the left front. He turned to his second in command, Lt. Levi Showalter (Company C, 2nd Wisconsin), and quipped, "The Pennsylvanians have made a mistake and are celebrating the 4th three days ahead of time." Colonel Dawes was of similar mind. He too described it as a "very dull" sound, and not at all indicative of an impending battle.[56]

For the most part, the Westerners listened to the distant bursts of shells over Seminary Ridge. Many brushed them aside as inconsequential.

54 Wheeler, "Reminiscences," 209; E. R. Reed, "What Our Veterans Have to Say About Their Old Campaigns," *NT*, March, 30, 1884, 7; Beecham, "The Second, or Fifty-Sixth, Which?" Reed apparently blended what he saw on the approach to the Codori farm with his recollection of the regiment's crossing the Fairfield Road onto the field near the seminary.

55 Earl Rogers, "The Second, or Fifty-Sixth, Which?"; Charles H. McConnell, "The First and Greatest Days Battle at Gettysburg," *NT*, July 20, 1916, 7; Augustus Ziegler, Letter, July 21, 1863, Vertical Files, VF-MI24, Library, GNMP; Hermann Bokum, *Wanderings North and South* (Philadelphia, 1864), 47.

56 *Milwaukee Sunday Telegraph*, February 15, 1885 and Rufus Dawes, *Milwaukee Sunday Telegraph*, April 27, 1890, as cited in Herdegen & Beaudot, *In the Bloody Railroad Cut*, 167, fn 57 and fn 58.

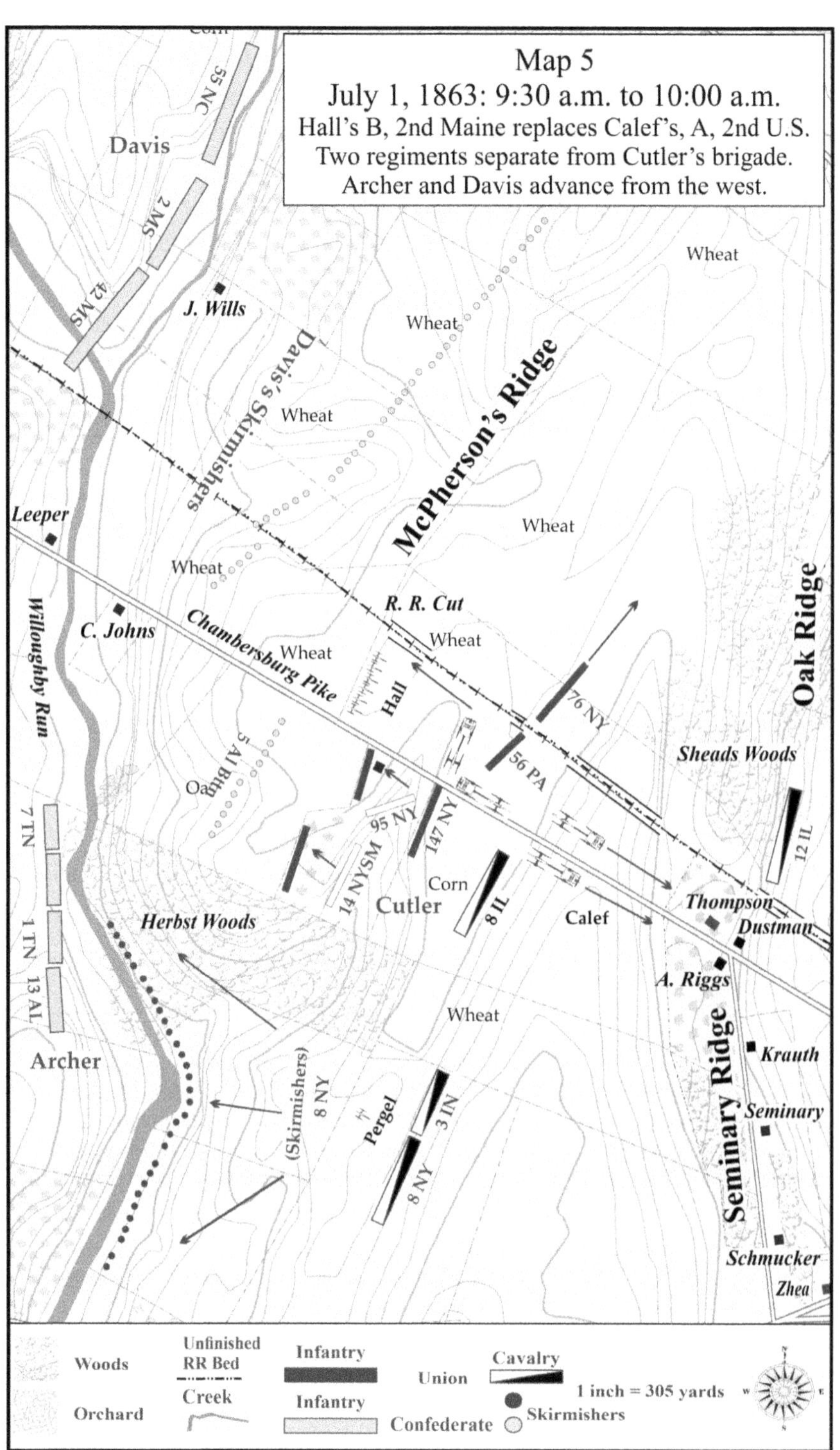

Map 5
July 1, 1863: 9:30 a.m. to 10:00 a.m.
Hall's B, 2nd Maine replaces Calef's, A, 2nd U.S.
Two regiments separate from Cutler's brigade.
Archer and Davis advance from the west.
55 NC
Davis
2 MS
42 MS
J. Wills
Davis's Skirmishers
Wheat
McPherson's Ridge
Leeper
Willoughby Run
C. Johns
Chambersburg Pike
R. R. Cut
Hall
76 NY
56 PA
Oak Ridge
Sheads Woods
5 AL Btn
95 NY
147 NY
14 NYSM
Corn
Cutler
8 IL
Calef
12 IL
Thompson
Dustman
A. Riggs
7 TN
1 TN
13 AL
Herbst Woods
Archer
(Skirmishers)
8 NY
Pergel
3 IN
Seminary Ridge
Krauth
Seminary
Schmucker
Zhea
Woods
Orchard
Unfinished RR Bed
Creek
Infantry
Union
Infantry
Confederate
Cavalry
Skirmishers
1 inch = 305 yards

Chapter Four

"Thar comes them old black-hats! It's the Army of the Potomac, sure!"

— Anonymous Confederate soldier, Archer's Brigade

The Death of a General

9:00 a.m. to 11:00 a.m.

9:00 a.m. to 11:00 a.m.
The Bridge over Marsh Creek on the Emmitsburg Road[1]

Colonel Charles S. Wainwright and temporary I Corps commander Maj. Gen. Abner Doubleday, together with their staffs, walked their horses past Colonel Stone's Pennsylvanians. The Keystone men stood in column facing the Emmitsburg Road, waiting for orders to advance. Major

1 William R. Ramsey, "The First Corps at Gettysburg," *NT*, April 30, 1908, 7. The article by Ramsey (Company F, 150th Pennsylvania) is the only source I have found that says Stone's brigade crossed Marsh Creek below Willoughby Run and came onto the Emmitsburg Road at the Sherfy Peach Orchard. The following sources say otherwise: Sanford N. Boyden (Company A, 149th Pennsylvania) to Capt. R. E. Gamble, March 15, 1906, Vertical Files, V6-PA149, Library, GNMP; Chamberlin, *History of the 150th Regiment*, 110; "Pennsylvania at Gettysburg, Address by Maj. J. F. Slagle," September 11, 1889, 2 and Address of 1st Lieutenant James A. Gardner, 2:878; OR 27/1:312. Boyden, Chamberlin, and Slagle all have Stone's brigade moving on the Emmitsburg Road. Slagle specifically said the 1st Brigade of the division (Biddle) marched by a parallel road. Gardner said Stone's brigade preceded Biddle's onto the field. Rowley noted that Biddle's brigade was detached and marched in front of Stone's brigade.

Thomas Chamberlin (150th Pennsylvania), at the rear of Stone's brigade, attributed the halt to allowing time for the skirmishers to come in and for Brig. Gen. John C. Robinson to join the column. Actually, Doubleday had instructed Wainwright's battalion to follow behind Rowley's Third Division. At 9:30 a.m., Stone's brigade took to the pike behind the general and his staff, apparently without realizing that Robinson's two brigades blocked Wainwright's batteries from getting to their assigned place in the line of march. The 143rd Pennsylvania led the column, followed by the 149th and the 150th regiments, respectively.

The officers did not realize the artillery was not in place until Stone's brigade reached the northern side of Marsh Creek. Doubleday immediately sent an orderly back to hurry the guns forward. The courier broke for the rear at a gallop, passed around the Pennsylvanians, and raced across the bridge shouting for Baxter's and Paul's muddied soldiers to make way for the batteries to pass. The infantrymen would have cleared the road for their own safety, though likely with much grumbling. Near the southern bank of Marsh Creek, Pvt. Rufus G. Northup (Company A, 90th Pennsylvania) recalled seeing at least two batteries —L, 1st New York and B, 4th U.S.—rattle across the small wooden bridge.

Once Stevens's 5th Maine Artillery got across, the infantry had to wait for the caissons, battery wagons, and traveling forges to pass at the "walk" before taking their assigned place back in the line of march. By then the sun had dissipated the mist, leaving the mud-spattered troops weltering in rising humidity and what would soon be stifling heat. Robinson's men finally shuffled their way across the rickety covered bridge, in no great hurry to get to the front. The ever-observant Private Northup took a quick glance at the sign posted on the south side of the bridge that warned travelers of a $5.00 fine for driving faster than a walk.[2]

2 *OR* 27/1:331; Peter Tomasak, ed., *The Avery Harris Civil War Journal* (Luzerne, PA, 2000), 59; John Shafer, "First In Gettysburg," *NT*, August 25, 1887, 3; Northup, "Going Into Gettysburg"; Nevins, *A Diary of Battle*, 232. Wainwright did not specify that the artillery was behind Stone when the advance began. According to Northup, an orderly raced past the column heading in the opposite direction, ordering the infantry to clear the road for the artillery, which came upon the column from behind. In 1906, the private incorrectly recalled that only two batteries—one iron and one bronze—crossed the creek. Wainwright clearly indicated that his battalion and all its caissons and wagons were in the column between the Third Division and the Second Division.

Stone's Brigade

The rains and heavy mist that had blanketed the area soaked the men and made the road slippery even though it was macadamized. Major Chamberlin noticed his Pennsylvanians struggling to bear up under the heat and humidity. They "perspired as they had rarely perspired before," he admitted. Officers allowed their men to occasionally stop and readjust their accoutrements, which disrupted the formations and staggered the march.

A little under half a mile north of the creek, Pvt. Avery Harris (Company B, 143rd Pennsylvania) noticed frightened old men, women, and children, many mounted on horses and mules, approaching the regiment from the left along the road running in front of the local post office. One individual, a young man of military age astride a mule, stood out among the group and was endlessly ribbed by the soldiers. "I would about as soon faced a battery of twelve pounder Napoleons as to have run the gauntlet of abuse that he got from our men," wrote Harris. The young man replied to the jeers and insults with a smile and kept heading south parallel to the Emmitsburg Road.[3]

Oppressive weather and approaching battle notwithstanding, Chamberlin remained enthralled by the ripening cornfields and vast stretches of untouched wheat—until the caravan reached him. Two children—a boy and a girl—astride a single horse clopped past. Their faces, red and swollen from incessant crying, left a doleful impression. "It was painfully apparent," he would recall years later, "that the miseries of war had penetrated this hitherto quiet pastoral region."[4]

Eastern Base of Seminary Ridge at the Chambersburg Pike

Battery B, 2nd Maine Artillery, passed slowly through the downed fence alongside Cutler's column, heading north under the cover of the ridge. By the time the lead gun entered the Chambersburg Pike at its intersection with the seminary lane, Cutler's regiments had started up the hill, in column, just south of the seminary. At the western end of the lane, the post and rail fence, which enclosed a small field to the left of the main building and bordered the eastern

3 James Fulton, "A Surgeon's Story of the Battle on Pennsylvania's Soil," *NT*, October 20, 1898, 1; Chamberlin, *History of the 150th Regiment*, 110; Tomasak, *Harris Journal*, 59.

4 Chamberlin, *History of the 150th Regiment*, 110.

side of the Rev. Schmucker's house, diverted the infantrymen to the south. When they struck the lane running west uphill from the Michael Zhea house to the Reverend Schmucker's place, the men turned west and crossed the campus road on top of the ridge and marched into the soggy field below the wood lot across from the campus.

As Cutler's brigade descended into the misty swale between Seminary and McPherson ridges, Lt. Col. James M. Sanderson, I Corps commissary officer, intercepted Capt. James Hall in the low ground northeast of the seminary. General Reynolds wished to see him "as soon as possible," announced Sanderson, and Hall was to bring his guns up at the trot.[5]

Hall spurred up the Chambersburg Pike with Sanderson and found Reynolds and Wadsworth riding west in the road north of McPherson's barn. The officers accompanied the generals to the ridgeline near Calef's guns. Reynolds was facing Wadsworth and within earshot of the captain. "General," he announced, "move a strong infantry support immediately to Hall's right for he is my defender until I can get the troops now coming on line." Wadsworth reined his horse about and dug spurs for the seminary.

Reynolds next turned toward the captain, and, indicating the 17 Confederate pieces along Herr's Ridge, exclaimed, "I desire you to damage the artillery to the greatest extent, and keep their fire from our infantry until they are deployed, when I will retire you somewhat as you are too far advanced for the general line." With that, Reynolds and his aides (Maj. William Riddle, Capts. Robert W. Mitchell, Craig W. Wadsworth, and Edward C. Baird), together with five orderlies, wheeled east to the low ground between McPherson's and Seminary ridges.[6]

5 Ladd and Ladd, *Bachelder Papers*, 1:385. For a full account of Cutler's brigade, see James L. McLean Jr., *"The Bullets Flew Like Hail": Cutler's Brigade at Gettysburg From McPherson's Ridge to Culp's Hill* (El Dorado Hills, CA, 2023). McLean's newly revised micro-history of the role played by the regiments comprising Cutler's command on all three days is a Gettysburg classic. The lane and fences at the seminary and Schmucker's show up in the Bachelder maps in *NYAG*. Soldiers follow the least line of resistance, and no one mentioned having to destroy a post and rail fence near the seminary.

6 Veil to McConaughy; Ladd and Ladd, *Bachelder Papers*, 1:385-386; Executive Committee, *Maine at Gettysburg* (Portland, ME, 1898), 16; James A. Hall to John B. Bachelder, February 27, 1868, Vertical Files, VF-ME2-Art., Library, GNMP; *Addresses Delivered Before The Historical Society of Pennsylvania*, n.p.; William Riddle to Lt. Bouvier, August 4, 1863, https://digital.fandm.edu/object/islandora5898, accessed Jan. 17, 2023; Harries, "The Iron Brigade in the First Day's Battle at Gettysburg," 4:341; Cheney,

Wadsworth, running the gauntlet of bursting shells, clattered up to Cutler riding at the head of his brigade and directed the general north across the Chambersburg Pike to protect the battery's right flank. Cutler and his staff led the way, followed closely by Sgt. Henry H. Hubbard and his 18-man headquarters guard from Company D, 147th New York. The 76th New York took off at the "double quick." The 56th Pennsylvania followed close behind. The two regiments passed over the pike through the destroyed portion of the fence in the hollow. In an effort to avoid the severe shelling, which had already inflicted numerous casualties in the 76th, the column veered northeast through the swale immediately east of McPherson's Ridge. Rather than follow them across the pike, Wadsworth and his staff stayed behind to attend to the disposition of the remaining three regiments in the brigade.[7]

John Buford, meanwhile, personally ordered Calef to quit the field. The 12th Illinois Cavalry, seeing the gun crews limber, retired east toward Oak Ridge. Lieutenant Roder's section trundled to the rear in good order by piece. Sergeant Newman's one gun also safely pulled away. An incoming solid shot, "whooshing" into the teams of the left limber, disemboweled the right horses of all three pairs and wounded a fourth animal. The three drivers, who miraculously survived the deadly round, sprang from their saddles and began cutting the dead and injured animals from their harnesses.

While Newman feverishly attempted to pair the two remaining horses to haul the gun away, Calef dispatched a man to the seminary to bring up a limber from one of the caissons. He next rode south to retire Sgt. Charles Pergel's section (Battery A, 2nd U.S.) south of Herbst Woods. Companies E and L, 17th

---

History of the Ninth Regiment, 111. Hall's account varies slightly between his 1868 and 1869 letters and the account in *Maine at Gettysburg*. The 1868 letter specifically recalled Reynolds being "extremely anxious, saying to Gen. Wadsworth in the exact following language . . . ", and predates his other descriptions of the conversation. In 1880, Hall wrote to Lt. Joseph Rosengarten that he met Reynolds on Seminary Ridge and rode forward with him to the place where he posted the guns. In fact, he met Sanderson on Seminary Ridge, not Reynolds. The five orderlies were Pvt. Bradford H. Tripp (Company G, 7th Wisconsin), Pvt. Charles Henry Veil (Company G, 9th Pennsylvania Reserves), Cpl. George D. Loop (Company B, 9th New York Cavalry), and Pvts. Morgan L. Bement and Henry Bentley (both Company C, 9th New York Cavalry).

7 Hofmann, "Remarks on the Battle of Gettysburg," 4; Hofmann, "The Battle"; *OR* 27/1:283; *NYAG*, 3:991; Edgar D. Haviland to Dear Mother, August 11, 1863, https://76nysv.us/76havilanded.html; Pierce, "Gettysburg"; Ladd and Ladd, *Bachelder Papers*, 3:1564; *NYAG*, 3: 991. The description of the 56th Pennsylvania's and 76th New York's route is from J. Volney Pierce in *NYAG*.

Pennsylvania Cavalry, returned to their regiment along the Mummasburg Road. With Cutler's two regiments passing behind them, the troopers of the 3rd Indiana cavalry mounted their animals. The troopers moved east and then south before forming with their left (Company E) behind Pergel. The 8th New York Cavalry continued the line to the south.[8]

Captain James Hall's limbers crested the ridge at the intersection of the campus lane and Chambersburg Pike while he was receiving his orders from Reynolds and Wadsworth. Trotting through the iron rain from the Rebel guns, which overshot Calef's former position, the lead team intercepted Hall at the breach in the fence in the hollow west of the seminary. Hall turned the battery to the northwest under the cover of McPherson's Ridge. In the process he cut off Cutler's three remaining regiments on the south side of the road. With no orders to proceed, Lt. Col. Francis C. Miller flanked the 147th New York to the left toward the shelter of the McPherson farm buildings and the hill.[9]

When the last team of Battery B, 2nd Maine, cleared the road Hall shouted, "To the left into battery!" The lead horseholders broke their limbers by pairs to the east in the hollow so the guns would face west. The artillerymen unhooked the pieces in the swale, while the drivers counter-marched the limbers so the teams faced the guns' trails. With the six 3-inch Ordnance Rifles at the regulation 14-yard intervals between hubs, Hall commanded his men to roll the pieces by hand to the top of the hill.[10]

Lieutenant Albert F. Thomas placed his section immediately north of the pike, followed on his right by Lt. Benjamin F. Carr's two guns. Lieutenant William N. Ulmer unlimbered his two pieces on Carr's right. Hall had not yet reconnoitered his front, so he did not know that the westernmost cut of the railroad bed ran perpendicular to his position a mere 60 yards from his right gun.

8 *OR*, 27/1:286, 1031; Calef, "Gettysburg Notes," 49; Hayes, "The 2d U.S. Art."; Moyer, *History of the Seventeenth Regiment*, 61, 381; Day, "Opening the Battle"; M. L. Trotter, "Opening the Ball at Gettysburg," *NT*, January 31, 1884, 3. In his postwar account, Calef has Pergel's encounter with Archer's Confederates occurring before he ordered the right sections to retire.

9 *NYAG*, 3:991; James Coey, "Cutler's Brigade: The 147th N. Y.'s Magnificent Fight on the First Day at Gettysburg," *NT*, July 15, 1915, 7. Coey, captain of Company E, said the 147th halted to let Hall's Battery pass, contradicting J. Volney Pierce's *NYAG* account, which claimed the battery passed the rear of the regiment before the regiment halted at McPherson's.

10 Ladd and Ladd, *Bachelder Papers*, 1:386 and 3:1566; *Maine at Gettysburg*, 15. Edward McPherson rented the farm to John A. Slentz.

Major General Henry Heth, who was new to both division command and service in the Army of Northern Virginia, made several tactical mistakes on the morning of July 1, 1863. LOC

No one in Lieutenant Ulmer's section knew it was there, either. Sergeant Charles E. Stubbs, the gunner of the right piece, noted a single apple tree in the tall grass about 50 yards to his right, but nothing more.[11]

Major General Henry Heth reached the front less than hour into the artillery fight. He did not like what he found there, and promptly sent a courier to get Davis's men moving. Riding south, he found Brig. Gen. James J. Archer with his command standing to arms under the cover of the woods west of Frederick Herr's house. Captain Jacob B. Turney (Company K, 1st Tennessee) heard Heth command Archer to determine "the strength and line of battle of the enemy." Archer protested: his skirmishers were meeting stronger resistance along Willoughby Run from the dismounted 8th New York Cavalry. An aggressive move would place his understrength regiments too far in advance to sustain the action. Heth reissued his order. Archer and all his regimental commanders except Lt. Col. Newton J. George (1st Tennessee) dismounted and sent their horses to the rear. The guns under McGraw and Brunson fell silent to allow the infantry to pass through their line.

As Company F of the 13th Alabama topped the ridge on the right of the formation, the sight of Gettysburg momentarily caught Pvt. Elijah T. Boland's attention. He quickly scanned southeast to the undulating low ground between the Fairfield and Emmitsburg roads, where his gaze latched onto what he described as "a long string of bluecoats" marching north. In the 7th Tennessee, on the extreme left of the brigade, Pvt. John T. McCall (Company B) surveyed

11 Ladd and Ladd, *Bachelder Papers*, 1:24 and 2:892.

Brigadier General James J. Archer was not pleased with Heth's orders. He and his men would pay a high price for the manner in which they were sent into battle. *LOC*

the ground ahead, which consisted of undulating grass and grain fields between the regiment and the overgrown banks along Willoughby Run.[12]

The regiments marched down the western slope of Herr's Ridge through the woods to its eastern side. They needed to get below the muzzles of their own artillery so they could neutralize the incoming artillery fire from Pergel's section, which continued lobbing shells at Brunson's guns on the crest behind them.

Brunson and McGraw cut loose as soon as Archer's men cleared the woods and entered the open fields in the basin along the creek. The air thundered with the reports of the projectiles "whooshing" and "screeching" just above the heads of the Alabamians. According to Pvt. William H. Moon (Company I, 13th Alabama), "it was the sweetest music I had ever heard."

To the northeast, Hall's Battery B, 2nd Maine Artillery, returned fire. Through the choking smoke, Private Moon witnessed a round dismount one of Pergel's guns on the ridge south of Herbst Woods. The "Rebel Yell" erupted from the ranks in response. Another shot killed five of the six horses on one of Pergel's limbers. The 13th Alabama's soused color-bearer, Tom Grant, wildly whooped and hollered while waving the flag from side to side. Moon, who was standing to Grant's left, knew these antics would draw fire. "Tom," he threatened, "if you don't stop that, I will use my bayonet on you." A sudden

12 Turney, "The First Tennessee at Gettysburg," 535; Boland, "Beginning of the Battle of Gettysburg," 308; Kimble, "Tennesseans at Gettysburg—The Retreat," 469; Moon, "Beginning of the Battle at Gettysburg," 449. Kimble claimed the advance started around 10:00 a.m.

spatter of carbine fire from the 8th New York along Willoughby Run snapped Grant into silence and halted the flag-waving.[13]

South of the Railroad Cut

From the top of the McPherson's Ridge, meanwhile, General Reynolds and his staff watched as the 5th Alabama Battalion, with the balance of Archer's Brigade tramping close behind, approached Willoughby Run. Wadsworth was visible deploying Cutler's brigade (the 95th New York, the 14th Brooklyn/84th New York, and the 147th New York) in the swale southeast of Edward McPherson's stone barn. The 147th was on the right, with the 95th and the 14th extending the line to the left. Air bursts rained scalding iron on their heads.

Reynolds rode back to Wadsworth and commanded him to take the center and left regiments forward to the crest. The two generals personally placed them on the ridge south of Hall's left flank before ordering them to lie down. Lieutenant Colonel Miller (147th New York) anxiously observed the entire maneuver from the picket fence surrounding a garden near the McPherson house.[14]

Major Beveridge of the 8th Illinois Cavalry also saw the infantry coming to his support. He ordered his troopers to horse and withdrew them into the hollow east of the ridge. The infantrymen of the 95th New York went prone west of the barn with their right flank on the Chambersburg Pike immediately across from Hall's Battery B, 2nd Maine. The 14th Brooklyn went to ground behind the stone wall along the ridge on the left of the 95th New York. Almost immediately, skirmishers from the 5th Alabama Battalion, moving through the tall field of wheat to their front, harassed the 14th with intermittent small arms

13 Moon, "Beginning of the Battle at Gettysburg," 449; Boland, "Beginning of the Battle of Gettysburg," 308; Day, "Opening the Battle"; Coey, "Cutler's Brigade"; http://nps gnmp.wordpress.com/2011/12/08, accessed Jan. 17, 2023; Flavius J. Bellamy to Parents, July 3, 1863, Rare Books and Manuscripts, Indiana State Library, Indianapolis, IN. Bellamy told his parents the battery was disabled, "one gun being dismounted and many of the horses killed." Private Day recalled that one horse remained alive at a nearby limber. The horse artillery, however, did not file returns registering lost guns or equipment for the battle. Moon, however, was taken to the rear as a prisoner and passed within a short distance of the gun. Calef lost 13 horses during the action.

14 *OR* 27/1:281; Ladd and Ladd, *Bachelder Papers*, 3:1564; *NYAG*, 3:991; Veil to McConaughy; Pierce, "Gettysburg." At the time, Cutler did not know that the rest of his brigade was not behind him.

fire. The Brooklyn men responded, initiating what was as yet a desultory firefight.[15]

Reynolds, Wadsworth, and their staffs moved south away from the pike toward Herbst Woods. Looking into the open woodlot, Reynolds spied some of the 5th Alabama's skirmishers working their way due north toward the 14th's exposed left flank. The rest of Archer's Brigade was visible marching down the slope in close support. The generals and their party reined toward the main campus road and halted on the west side, just south of the seminary.[16]

Archer's 13th Alabama marched through the right of the brigade skirmish line and slowed to a walk, firing and loading as it advanced—a methodical, disciplined skirmish tactic conducted by "comrades in battle" (four men in two ranks and two files). The first rank fired and loaded while the second passed through it, fired, and reloaded while the first pair walked through its ranks to repeat the procedure. The result was a rolling fusillade by ranks on a regimental front, a tactic that put a lot of ammunition and smoke downrange. It was intended to force the Yankee cavalry to hunker down in place—or skedaddle.

The advance through the sulfuric shroud impressed Pvt. William H. Bird (Company C), who thought the steady progress "was the prettiest line of battle I think I ever saw." As the 13th drew near the brush-covered ravine on the western side of the run, its leader, Col. Birkett D. Fry, saw mounted videttes from the 8th New York Cavalry to the south on the high ground west of the creek near the Harman farm. Fry sent Lt. Bailey A. Bowen (Company C) and a detail of about 20 men from the right of the line to protect the brigade's flank.[17]

15 Day, "Opening the Battle"; Trotter, "Opening the Ball"; *OR* 27/1:286.

16 Veil to McConaughy; R. K. Beecham, *Gettysburg*, 62; Hofmann, "The Battle, Twenty-Three Years Ago"; Charles Henry Veil, "An Old Boy's Personal Recollections and Reminiscences of the Civil War" (1908), Civil War Miscellaneous Collection, USAHEC, 41. Both of Veil's accounts said Reynolds saw Rebels in the woods moving north toward the Cashtown Road (Chambersburg Pike). Corporal Beecham erroneously recalled seeing Reynolds near the Emmitsburg Road, but Hofmann clearly said that Reynolds and his staff met him and his regiment in the field west of the seminary because they had ridden through town on a cleared road and had arrived there ahead of Cutler's brigade.

17 Hardee, *Light Infantry Tactics*, 1:191-196; Moon, "Beginning of the Battle at Gettysburg," 449; Bird, *Stories of the Civil War*, 7. Private Moon specifically noted the regiment walked slowly, loading and firing as it went. The maneuver, while written for skirmishers, could be implemented by a company, a battalion, or a regiment. Veterans, writing for other veterans, knew the intricacies of maneuvers need not be fully explained. Bird did not name who deployed Bowen, but the order came from Fry.

The Emanuel Harman House

Several rounds from the Alabamians sent the New Yorkers retreating about 500 feet downhill toward the opposite bank of Willoughby Run. The troopers used every bit of available cover—the barn, outbuildings, and the well pump—in an effort to slow the Rebs down. Amelia Harman watched several horses and a man or two fall. Fearful for their safety, she and her aunt scurried throughout the ground floor of the house locking the doors. Upstairs, they pushed open the shutters of a window on the west side to observe the skirmishing.

To them, it seemed as if all the Rebels in the world were moving about in the high timothy field between the house and the woods. The soldiers bobbed up and down to snap off potshots at Yankee troopers. A spent minié ball slapped into the shutter within a hair's width of Amelia's aunt's head. Simultaneously, a bullet dropped an officer's mount directly below them. The frightened women screamed, "Look, the field is full of rebels!"

"Leave the window or you'll be killed!" he yelled back.

The pair ran from the room and climbed into the cupola on the roof to witness the action from what they hoped was a safer spot.[18]

To the north, the men of the 1st Tennessee were lying along the west side of the creek. Farther north, the 14th Tennessee and the 7th Tennessee briefly hunkered down in the brush along the same bank before heading toward the northwest corner of Herbst Woods. Behind them, Capt. Jonathan S. Dowell (Company A, 7th Tennessee) lay in the field bleeding from a bullet wound in his right breast. Lieutenant Wilmouth Burgess assumed command of the rest of the company as it stepped into the knee-deep water.

The 14th and 7th Tennessee regiments went prone under the shelter of the bluff on the opposite bank. This mostly hid them from the small arms fire of the Yankee skirmishers, who had retired to the crest of McPherson's Ridge. "We halted to reform, reload, catch our breath, and cool off a little," was how Private Moon (Company I, 13th Alabama) recalled this part of the fight.[19]

A few minutes later, the two left Tennessee regiments cautiously worked their way east uphill through the open woods on the left, while the 1st Tennessee slipped through the band of trees and brush along the creek into the wheatfield

18 "Burning of the McLean House," 1.

19 Moon, "Beginning of the Battle at Gettysburg," 449; F. S. Harris, "From Gettysburg," *Lebanon* [TN] *Democrat*, Aug. 10. 1898.

farther south. Carbine rounds zipped through the trees. A conical ball found a billet with Company B, 7th Tennessee, when it shattered Pvt. Henry C. Rison's thigh. The intense resistance from the dismounted cavalrymen gave Pvt. "Bully Ike" Dawson (Company B) pause. If he was thinking about turning to run, he had no time to do so. Captain John D. Allen and Lt. "Jack" H. Moore flanked him and together the trio pushed forward.

The 1st Tennessee went to ground in the uncut wheat along McPherson Ridge. To its right rear, the 13th Alabama sheltered under the high rise of ground paralleling the creek. With the 5th Alabama Battalion and the Confederate artillery keeping the 14th Brooklyn pinned down, the 7th and 14th Tennessee passed virtually unmolested over the wooded plateau on the left front of the Brooklyn outfit. The Tennesseans went mostly prone once more along the top of the ridge west of a deep washout. From there through the open woodlot they could see the wheatfield running up the subtle incline to the top of McPherson's Ridge. The officers had a vantage point from which they could observe anything coming over the eastern horizon.[20]

9:50 *a.m. to* 10:05 *a.m.*
Emmitsburg Road

North of Sherfy's Peach Orchard, Lt. Clayton Rogers intercepted the head of Solomon Meredith's column at Codori's and directed the 2nd Wisconsin across the fields to the base of Seminary Ridge. Rogers wheeled about and spurred north along Cutler's route to inform Wadsworth that the rest of the division was just a mile from the front and coming fast.[21]

20 Moon, "Beginning of the Battle at Gettysburg," 449; Busey & Busey, *Confederate Casualties at Gettysburg*, 3:1398. The viewshed here is based on a personal familiarity with the terrain. The wounded Private Rison died a few weeks later.

21 "Synopsis of General Richardson's Speech," *The Cambridge City* [IN] *Tribune*, August 31, 1871, 2; Rogers, "The Second, or Fifty Sixth—Which." Hollon Richardson, in his speech at the first reunion of the Iron Brigade, claimed Wadsworth ordered the brigade through the fields from the Emmitsburg Road toward the seminary when the column was about a mile out of Gettysburg. Clayton Rogers, Earl Rogers's brother, stated that Meredith's brigade was about a mile from Gettysburg when he was sent to bring it forward. It is more likely that Clayton Rogers intercepted the column at Codori's, as opposed to Wadsworth doing it in person.

Brigadier General James S. Wadsworth's I Corps division bore the brunt of the Rebel attacks on the morning and afternoon of July 1, 1863. *LOC*

10:05 a.m. to 10:45 a.m.

With General Meredith in the lead, the 2nd Wisconsin reached the low ground east of the seminary around 10:05 a.m., more than 300 feet ahead of the the next regiment (7th Wisconsin). Occasional solid shots sizzled overhead from the west. Some crashed through the treetops in the grove along the crest south of the seminary, pelting the Wisconsinites with branches.[22]

At the terminus of the seminary lane with the Chambersburg Pike, the Wisconsin men turned west, parallel with the lane, and headed uphill toward the campus road. The front of the brigade veered south until it struck the lane at Zhea's, at which point it again turned west. Colonel Fairchild led the 2nd Wisconsin over the lane into the field across from Schmucker's.

Corporal Robert K. Beecham (Company H) noticed Generals Reynolds and Wadsworth with their aides and orderlies clustered in the road. To Beecham, Reynolds seemed both weary and sad as he sat astride his horse. "Forward, forward, men!" Reynolds anxiously exclaimed, probably motioning west. "Drive those fellows out of there. Forward, for God's sake, forward!"[23]

22 Ladd and Ladd, *Bachelder Papers*, 1:140.

23 Beecham, *Gettysburg*, 61-62; Harries, "The Iron Brigade in the First Day's Battle at Gettysburg," *Glimpses of the Nation's Struggle*, 4:340; Eleanor Reynolds to William Reynolds, July 5, 1863, Reynolds Family Papers: Eleanor Reynolds Scrapbook, Archives and Special Collection, Franklin and Marshall College Library, Lancaster, PA, quoted in https://digital.fandm.edu/object/islandora5858, accessed Jan. 17, 2023; Veil to McConaughy; Barnes to Dudley. Eleanor Reynolds, the general's sister, wrote "Forward, Forward Men, drive those fellows out of there, forward for God's sake, forward." Less than

General Meredith, who remained on the campus road, dispatched Capt. Hollon Richardson to order the other regiments to come forward into line and to load as they formed. To the front, through a sprinkling of rain, the men of the 2nd Wisconsin caught sight of sporadic puffs of carbine smoke hanging low along McPherson's Ridge. The cavalry's horseholders sheltered under the cover of the swale east of McPherson's Ridge.[24]

Lutheran Seminary

With the 2nd Wisconsin plowing west toward McPherson's Ridge, General Reynolds and his staff awaited the arrival of the remainder of Meredith's Westerners. The 7th Wisconsin crossed the campus road next. It rushed by the flank west along the same route taken by Fairchild's regiment past Reynolds. Lieutenant Benjamin T. Marten, one of Doubleday's aides, rode up to Reynolds to request orders for his general. Reynolds, who was still unsure of the strength and length of the Confederate line in front of him, bluntly replied, "Tell Doubleday I will hold on to this road [the Chambersburg Pike] and he must hold on to that one (pointing toward the Fairfield Road)." Marten saluted and spurred south.

Within quick order, Capt. Eminel P. Halstead, Doubleday's acting adjutant general, and Lt. Meredith L. Jones, an aide-de-camp, came alongside Reynolds and requested further instructions for Doubleday, who was still on the Emmitsburg Road ahead of the balance of the I Corps. The general emphatically told Halstead to bring up the corps' remaining two divisions as fast as possible,

---

a year later Veil penned, "Forward men forward and drive those fellows out of those woods." I used Eleanor's quote because she recalled it much closer to the incident. Beecham claimed the general urged them "forward with all possible speed to support Buford" from the west (north) side of the road, facing the regiment. Based on Tripp's and Beecher's accounts, the road Beecham referred to was almost certainly the main campus road connecting the Fairfield Road and the Chambersburg Pike. Beecham is the only witness from the Iron Brigade thus far discovered who recalled Reynolds saying anything to anyone in the regiment and ordering them forward. While Veil left the impression that these were the last words of the general and therefore occurred immediately before his death, this appears unlikely. Private Barnes (Co. H, 19th Indiana) saw Reynolds and his staff near the main seminary building.

24 *OR* 27/1:273; Huber, "At Gettysburg"; Ladd and Ladd, *Bachelder Papers*, 2:940; "Synopsis of General Richardson's Speech," 2. I described the weather and the condition of the field based upon other participants' accounts. It also makes sense that Meredith sent Richardson to tell the other regiments to load at this time.

and Jones was to hurry the corps artillery forward. While riding away, Halstead turned and saw the general and his staff riding toward Herbst Woods.[25]

The 19th Indiana struck west up the Fairfield Road simultaneous with the 7th Wisconsin's ascent of the hill toward the seminary. A staff officer approached the regimental color guard. "Do not unfurl the flag!" he instructed the color-bearers of the national and regimental banners. Rather than go over the crest, Col. Samuel J. Williams diverted the column into the narrow southern end of the grove on the crest and continued parallel to the campus road toward the seminary. From the rear of the column, on the left flank of the right wing, young Lt. Col. William W. Dudley would occasionally look toward the head of the regiment. He spotted newly promoted Sgt. Maj. Asa Blanchard coolly assisting the file closers to help maintain the formation's integrity as it maneuvered around the trees.[26]

The Hoosiers of the 19th regiment marched north behind Reverend Schmucker's house until the front of the regiment halted at the southeast corner of the seminary. Colonel Williams faced the regiment west by the rear rank, which placed the taller men in the front, thereby halving the regiment's fire effectiveness. Private William C. Barnes (Company H) caught a passing glance of Reynolds and his staff near the main campus building moments before the general headed toward Herbst Woods.

Rushing forward, the Indiana men stepped over the low stone fence on the east side of the road, crossed, climbed over the partially destroyed post and rail fence along its front, and hastily reassembled. The left of the regiment stood in a

25 *OR* 27/1:244, 278; Doubleday, *Chancellorsville and Gettysburg*, 130; Ladd & Ladd, *Bachelder Papers*, 1:140; Halstead, "The First Day of the Battle of Gettysburg," 1:4; Nevins, *A Diary of Battle*, 232. Doubleday implies that Reynolds was alive when he sent Halstead and Jones to get orders and that he was on the field at that time. Wainwright clearly stated in his diary that between 10:30 a.m. and 11:00 a.m. he was with Doubleday on the Emmitsburg Road when they got the order to hurry to the field. Doubleday wrote that Halstead gave him the instructions to hold the Fairfield Road, which contradicts his *OR* report in which he credits Lieutenant Marten with delivering that order. This occurred while Wainwright waited out a rain shower behind the brigade. Halstead and Jones delivered their directives around 10:35 a.m., by which time Wainwright had joined Doubleday on the road.

26 Ladd and Ladd, *Bachelder Papers*, 2:940; Thompson, "In Their Own Words," 3, 11; Barnes to Dudley; "Brief Sketch of Gallantry of Mr. B. Cunningham," *Bloomfield Monitor*, December 30, 1930, "Synopsis of General Richardson's Speech," 2; Lieutenant Colonel Dudley recorded that the regiment reached the Hagerstown Road; Colonel Williams described the grove and the regiment's route to the seminary, as did Capt. Hollon Richardson.

grass field and part of the right assembled in the oak wood lot. A stray round zipped into Company K and wounded Pvt. Bill Leavell as he stood next to "Robe" Moore. His premonition fulfilled, Moore recollected, "I never knew of a single failure of such a prediction or sentence, if you please, to come true."

A Virginia-born corporal named Burl Cunningham turned to his right and told 17-year-old Corporal Buckles, "It is time to show our colors; Abe, pull the shuck." The corporal removed the oil cloth cover and Cunningham unfurled the national colors. To his left, Cpl. David Phipps uncased the blue Indiana regimental banner. Colonel Williams directed the 19th almost due west toward the left of the 7th Wisconsin, which he could see in column to his right front heading toward the base of the ridge just south of Herbst Woods.[27]

The 24th Michigan left the Fairfield Road at the top of the hill and turned north onto the campus road. Colonel Henry A. Morrow halted it as soon as it cleared the road intersection and gave the order to load, but Capt. James D. Wood, Meredith's acting adjutant general, galloped up and peremptorily ordered him forward. "Boys, fall out, and give us 'Yankee Doodle'," Morrow instructed the regimental band. The Wolverine troops, with their weapons still unloaded, stepped over the destroyed fence, reformed, and started forward before the musicians had finished the first verse.[28]

Farther to the front, Companies B and F, 8th New York Cavalry, were mounted behind Pergel's guns under orders to advance. "It was certain death to us if we made that charge," Pvt. Frank E. Willett (Company F) recollected. From horseback they could clearly see Archer's Confederates heading toward them. Behind him, Willett could see Meredith's column doggedly tramping through the field from the seminary. A thought flashed through his head: "They might have hurried a little faster."[29]

27 Barnes to Dudley; Thompson, "In Their Own Words," 2; Mumaw, "A 'Bye' Goes Off to War," 40; "Brief Sketch of Gallantry of Mr. B. Cunningham." In his letter to George Blanchard, William Dudley noted the regiment crossed fences and fields en route to McPherson's Ridge.

28 *OR* 27/1:244, 245, 267, 940; Doubleday, *Chancellorsville and Gettysburg*, 130, 131; E. Cotton, "The Men Who Made the Music," *NT*, July 7, 1894, 2. Colonel Morrow (24th Michigan) claimed a staff officer from Wadsworth ordered his regiment to the front, not Doubleday. Private Edwin Cotton identified the officer as Capt. James D. Wood of Meredith's staff.

29 Willett, "Another Gettysburg."

The Hollow, East of McPherson's Ridge

The veterans in the 2nd Wisconsin did not wait for orders to dry out the bores of their unloaded rifles. Despite facing possible arrest for snapping caps while in the ranks, Pvt. Elisha R. Reed (Company H) capped his weapon and pulled the trigger, as did a considerable number of his comrades, in the hope of clearing any moisture from the bores. "Meeting no rebuke," explained Reed, "we felt sure the officers shared our suspicions as to what we were coming to." Reed, who had been wounded and captured at First Bull Run in July of 1861, recalled feeling the blood draining from his face. Wishing that he had never been born or had perished in his infancy, he lowered his head to conceal the fear coursing through him lest any of his comrades revile him for cowardice.[30]

Meanwhile, plunging fire from the Confederate guns on Herr's Ridge burst over the 2nd Wisconsin. Lieutenant Colonel John Kress, Wadsworth's aide-de-camp, materialized through the smoke along the top of McPherson's Ridge and galloped into the low ground on its eastern side. He reined in next to Colonel Fairchild at the front of his regiment as it approached the right flank of the 8th New York's mounted squadron. Kress yelled at Fairchild to put the 2nd Wisconsin into line and head into the woods to save the guns.[31]

Colonel Fairchild, Lt. Col. George H. Stevens, and Maj. John Mansfield dismounted. Throwing his reins to his hostler, Pvt. Henry W. Sanford (Company F), Fairchild shouted, "Non-combatants to the rear!" At the command "Load at will!" Private Reed planted his weapon in front of him while clawing at the flap on his cartridge box. He had just returned the rammer in the thimbles when he heard "Fix bayonets!" Most of the men had not yet finished loading their rifled muskets when the colonel called out, "Double Quick! "Forward, into line!" Acting Sgt. Frederick C. Waterman (Company A) recalled that a few of the dismounted cavalrymen, with permission, followed them into the action.[32]

30 Elisha R. Reed, "Gettysburg."

31 Incomplete Draft, Report of Lucius Fairchild, Fairchild Papers, Wisconsin Historical Society, Madison, WI, 1, hereafter cited as Fairchild Report; Ladd & Ladd, *Bachelder Papers*, 1:336.

32 *OR* 27/1:273; Beecham, *Gettysburg*, 62, 65-66; Fairchild Report, 1; Smith, *History of the Seventy-Sixth Regiment*, 368; E. Markle, "The Story of Battle Told By Survivor"; Wheeler, " Reminiscences of the Battle of Gettysburg," *War Papers*, 2:210; E. R. Reed, "Gettysburg"; Frederick A. Waterman, "At Gettysburg: Another Comrade Thinks the Iron

Reynolds spurred past Meredith and the 7th Wisconsin and headed north into the low ground east of Herbst Woods. "Long Sol" noticed the general riding toward the Chambersburg Pike. "But," he later wrote, "so hot was it about the time I had no disposition to be watchful of anything except the enemy and my brigade."[33]

Cresting the ridge, the 2nd Wisconsin passed through the dismounted cavalrymen and Pergel's guns before descending into the shallow swale along their front. Two hundred feet farther the ground rose again. The prone 1st Tennessee, directly opposite the Badgers, saw the colors bobbing above the wheat and waited until the 2nd maneuvered into line behind the worm fence on the opposite rise of ground before unleashing a devastating volley into the unsuspecting infantrymen. The rifle fire left gaps in the Yankee formation. Private Moon of the 13th Alabama watched the Tennesseans load by rolling over onto their backs in the trampled wheat, then "whirl" over onto their stomachs to shoot. "They were hotly engaged at close quarters, the Yanks charging them in column," was how Moon recalled the initial close-quarter infantry fighting.[34]

Within a short time the Confederates cut down about 90 officers and men in the 2nd Wisconsin. Lieutenant Colonel George H. Stevens collapsed, mortally wounded through the left side and the bowels. Sergeant Joseph O. Williams (Company I) perished in the initial volley, his death premonition fulfilled. A bullet plowed into Company H and struck Pvt. Virgil Helmes (Private Reed's file leader), in the chest. The lead bullet drilled through the top of Helmes's left lung, exited his back, and lodged in his knapsack. The critically wounded Badger turned about, pushed past Reed, and stumbled to the rear. Another bullet tore Reed's cap box away and ricocheted off his waist belt. The impact jarred him so hard that he was unsure if he was mortally wounded or just scared.

Reed stepped back from the line to check his wound and, finding no blood, painfully limped back into the ranks. He stopped momentarily alongside Lt.

Brigade Opened the Battle," *NT*, October 27, 1892, 4. According to Markle, the original command was "Forward, Double-quick, fix bayonets, load at will." Beecham contributed, "Forward into line." If some of the men loaded their weapons as the regiment advanced, the order to do so had to have been issued first, followed quickly by "fix bayonets" and then "advance." Reed accurately recorded the sequence of the order.

33 Huber, "At Gettysburg."

34 Moon, "Beginning of the Battle at Gettysburg," 449; Elisha R. Reed, "Gettysburg."

Alexander F. Lee (Company D) to get some percussion caps and had barely resumed his place when a spent minié ball hammered his left hip joint. When he realized again there was no blood and that he could walk on it, he once more rejoined his company, which was busy returning fire.[35]

The shock of the rounds zipping into Company E momentarily stunned Cpl. William H. Boyd. Before he could react, he and three comrades lay on the ground dead or grievously wounded. To his right, Pvt. Lawson C. Ward and the man behind him perished. The soldier covering him fell seriously wounded simultaneous with Boyd, who pitched face forward onto the ground. Six-foot-tall Sgt. John "Ben" Davids, Boyd's closest friend, dragged him away to the shade of an oak tree and propped him against its base. Once he was comfortable, he left Boyd with his canteen and returned to the line.

The injured corporal examined his wound and found that the minié ball had penetrated his right thigh about one inch below the hip joint and shattered his femur. Blood gushed from the wound, saturating his pants and making them heavier and warmer. The quick-thinking private cut away a length of his suspenders and, with a low-hanging dead branch he pulled from the tree, fashioned a tourniquet around his leg from the crotch to just above the wound. He slowly twisted it until the blood flow subsided. Once finished he sat and waited, hoping he was not about to die.[36]

Private William H. Phipps (Company F, 8th New York Cavalry), who had rejoiced at the sight of the infantry, found himself relieved from the line. Captain James Bliss, realizing that Phipps's mount could not withstand any more duty, shouted at him, "Your horse has given out; look out for yourself!" The private dismounted and, after helping a soldier from the 2nd Wisconsin

35 Wheeler, "Reminiscences of the Battle of Gettysburg," 208; Elisha R. Reed, "A Private's Story," *Milwaukee Sunday Telegraph*, June 12, 1887; Elisha R. Reed, "Gettysburg"; *OR* 27/1:273; E. B. Quiner, *The Military History of Wisconsin* (Chicago, 1866), 459-460; Otis diary, July 1, 1863; Fairchild Report, 1. For an account of Stevens's wounds see www.findagrave.com/cgi-bin/fg.cgi?page=gr&GRid=5903866, accessed Jan. 17, 2023. Reed mistakenly wrote that Lee was a sergeant. Quiner (1866), the *New York Times* (July 4, 1863). The Adjutant General's report noted that Capt. Ebenezer P. Perry, Lt. William A. Jamison, and Lt. Lee received their commissions on April 21, 1863.

36 "Suffers Since War: One of the Most Interesting Civil War Narratives is that of an Oshkosh Veteran," *Oshkosh* [WI] *Northwestern*, April 27, 1911; www.oshkosh museum.org/Virtual/exhibit3/e30036a.htm, last accessed Jan. 18, 2023; http://content. wisconsinhistory.org/cdm/ref/collection/quiner/id/27785, accessed Jan. 18, 2023. Boyd described the tree as a large "burro" tree, also known as a burl, burr, or burrow tree.

with a chin wound onto his animal, walked back toward the seminary. Phipps would not rejoin his regiment until after July 3.[37]

Bursting shells and over shots from the prone Tennesseans slammed into the 7th Wisconsin as the Badgers drew near Pergel's section, striking down several officers and men. Two stray buckshot slapped Lt. Col. John Callis's right hip and side. About the same time a bullet killed his horse and he went hard to the ground with it. Regaining his feet, Callis dismissed his wounds as slight and responded to the incoming rounds, which hammered his unsuspecting soldiers and disrupted their formation.

Major Mark Finnicum, who described the volley as "a shower of well-aimed balls," watched helplessly as the rounds knocked down an impressive number of enlisted men. Callis, unable to find Colonel Robinson, shoved the survivors into a battle line, trying his best to steady them before they went over the hill. The order to unsling knapsacks traveled along the regiment, and the encumbrances dropped to the soggy ground. Private Thomas G. Day (3rd Indiana Cavalry) watched the file closers stack them by companies and detach a man to guard each pile.[38]

A moment before, Reynolds and his staffers had reined to a halt in the low ground just east of Herbst Woods. The crash of rifle fire to the west, accompanied by the frequent air bursts from the Confederate artillery on Herr's Ridge, prompted the general to snap an order to Maj. William Riddle to have the artillery open "a very severe fire." The major had barely wheeled to leave when someone rushed up to Reynolds to announce that a Rebel line lay among the trees just over the top of the hill.[39]

37 Phipps, "Was at Gettysburg"; W. H. Phipps, "Saw Gettysburg Battle," *NT*, July 21, 1904, 3.

38 Ladd and Ladd, *Bachelder Papers*, 1:142; Day, "Opening the Battle"; Marc Storch & Beth Storch, "Unpublished Gettysburg Reports by the 2nd and 7th Wisconsin Infantry Regimental Officers," *GM*, #17, July 1, 1997, 21; Lance Herdegen & Sherry Murphy, eds., *Four Years With the Iron Brigade: The Civil War Journals of William Ray, Co. F, Seventh Wisconsin Infantry* (Cambridge, MA, 2002), 191; C. B. Bishop, "Starting the Gettysburg Fight," *NT*, June 2, 1910, 2; "Synopsis of General Richardson's Speech," 2. Ray claimed the men in the ranks fired as they advanced, as did Corydon Bishop. The regiment therefore loaded weapons as it came on line prior to the charge, as ordered by Captain Richardson.

39 "Synopsis of General Richardson's Speech," 2; *OR* 27/1:278. The 7th Wisconsin charged after the 2nd Wisconsin made initial contact with Archer's left. It seems reasonable to conclude that the Confederates belonged to Archer's Brigade and were on the eastern crest of the hill on which the brigade monuments stand today.

The general, who ignored protests by his staff that he had no right to risk his life, recklessly spurred his mount up the rise. Reynolds topped the ridge with Lt. John P. Carson (Company L, 1st Maine Cavalry) and the ever-present Capt. Craig Wadsworth by his side. A smattering of rifle fire caught him and his two officers near a small clump of trees just beyond the southeast corner of the woods. Reynolds instinctively swung his horse around at the same instant that the 1st Tennessee volleyed into the 2nd Wisconsin.

Lieutenant Carson's horse pitched forward dead and the officer flew feet first over the animal's head. Reynolds teetered in the saddle. The lieutenant reached him as the general started to topple and eased him to the ground. Assuming that Reynolds was either dying or dead, Carson laid him on his left side and vaulted onto the general's mount to go find Doubleday. Captain Wadsworth cut his horse south to halt Meredith's advance before it got trapped in the 1st Tennessee's fire.[40]

While the 7th Wisconsin struggled to regroup from the volley, Colonel Fairchild and his officers shoved the stunned men from the 2nd Wisconsin into a semblance of a line. The 1st Tennessee continued slamming the Westerners with small arms fire. The order to load rippled through the Badgers' line. Sergeant Cornelius Wheeler, still scanning the ground for casualties from Company I, caught a brief glimpse of Reynolds falling from his horse.[41]

Rather than face the likelihood of heavy losses, Fairchild ordered the Wisconsin troops to flank northwest into the eastern edge of Herbst Woods. The men knocked down the worm fence along their front and rushed into the woods. Not knowing the 7th and 14th Tennessee lay concealed along the ridge to his

40 Thomas B. Hopkins, "It Came From a Volley, Not From a Sharpshooter," *NT*, April 14, 1910, 6; Huber, "At Gettysburg"; Death of Reynolds—Gettysburg, http://loc.gov/resource /ppmsca.21792, accessed Jan. 18, 2023; Harries, "The Iron Brigade," 341. Solomon Meredith, in an 1867 letter to Huber, believed Reynolds was hit near "a small clump of trees standing out from the eastern edge and corner of the woods," but that he did not see the incident because he was too busy tending to his brigade. Huber noted that the monument stands at a spot far from the place described by Meredith, and is at a greater distance from the spot identified by Bachelder. Wartime artist Alfred Waud's contemporary map, based upon eyewitness accounts of the event, places Reynolds's death site at the southeast corner of the woods.

41 Fairchild Report, 1; Wheeler, "Reminiscences of the Battle of Gettysburg," *War Papers*, 210-211. In order for Wheeler to have seen Reynolds fall from his horse about 100 feet behind the right-rear of the regiment, the 2nd Wisconsin had to be in the open along the fence south of the woods.

Colonel Lucius Fairchild, commander of the 2nd Wisconsin, would lose his left arm in his attack into Herbst Woods. LOC

left, Fairchild halted his men just inside the tree line and commanded a change of front to the left. The Tennesseans opened fire through the open wood lot.

Most of the 7th Tennessee had remained prone except for two men. Private "Jack" K. Lane (Company K) stayed upright, calmly loading and firing as if at target practice. The other enlisted man stood a short distance behind and below the line, shooting over the men's heads, until Lt. William "Billy" Baber put an end to the fellow's nonsense. He grabbed the soldier by the hair and dragged him to the regiment.

The 2nd Wisconsin advanced slowly, the men halting in "comrades in battle" formation to load and return fire. A spent ball hit the twice-wounded Private Reed in the ankle, stopping him cold. Intense pain shot through his leg, forcing him to kneel and tear off his shoe. Rolling down his sock, Reed gingerly fingered the injury and discovered an ugly bruise but no apparent broken bones.[42]

Minie balls zipped through the color guard, one of them gouging a hole through Clr. Sgt. Philander B. Wright's high-crowned "Hardee hat." Barely missing the top of his skull, it was followed immediately by a second round near the same spot. Wright pushed ahead with the Stars and Stripes, while the color corporal carried the state flag close to his right. Some distance into the woods Wright spied through the smoke Sgt. William L. Oliver waving the flag of the

42 Fairchild Report, 1; *OR* 27/1:273; Harris, "From Gettysburg"; Reed, "Gettysburg." Reed said the regiment pushed down the fence along its front. Fairchild wrote, "We pushed forward slowly, loading and firing as we went." This may indicate that the men operated more as skirmishers than as a heavy battle line, much as Archer's men had done in their approach to Willoughby Run.

7th Tennessee. Nearby, Lt. Furgeson S. Harris (Company H, 7th Tennessee) spotted the 2nd Wisconsin's large U.S. flag and Wright with his big wide-brimmed black hat.[43]

A bullet shattered Wright's flagstaff and jarred his hands just as a second round smashed into his left leg. The simultaneous impacts sent him whirling through the air. Wright hit the ground so hard it nearly knocked him unconscious. Nearby lay the color corporal with the state flag, dead. Corporal Rasselas Davidson (Company H) pulled the state banner free while Cpl. Paul V. Brisbois (Company G) plucked the U.S. flag from the ground. Despite swearing he would never again go into another fight if he could "honorably" avoid it, Davidson pushed through the regiment and into the fray about 30 feet ahead of the line.[44]

To the left-rear of the 2nd Wisconsin, the boys in the 7th feverishly loaded their rifled muskets. The command "Fix bayonets!" reverberated overhead. Steel clanked against steel, followed by the rhythmic cold snaps of lock rings securing the 18-inch triangular bayonets in place. From his spot in the ranks, Pvt. William Ray (Company F) noticed the top of a Rebel battle flag jutting just above the ridge to his front. With the regiment steadied and armed, Lieutenant Colonel Callis shouted at his men to double-quick, only to have Captain Wadsworth gallop up behind him screaming "Halt! Halt!"

Callis repeated the order to stop, but no one heard his cry above the din. The men lurched forward into the bullets zipping through and about them. With their surviving officers herding them onward, the soldiers fired at any Confederate they saw, or at least in the general direction of the enemy. The moment the 7th Wisconsin stepped off, those watching the knapsacks burrowed into the piles to escape the incoming fire.[45]

43 Lance J. Herdegen, *The Iron Brigade in Civil War and Memory* (El Dorado Hills, CA, 2012), 370; William Thomas Venner, *The 7th Tennessee Infantry in the Civil War: A History and Roster* (Jefferson, NC, 2013), 190; Harris, "From Gettysburg." William L. Oliver, a 38-year-old overseer serving in Company G, carried the 7th Tennessee's flag. His regiment was directly opposite the 2nd Wisconsin. He is not listed in Busey & Busey, *Confederate Casualties at Gettysburg*, though he was shot in the leg on July 3. Venner, *The Weekly American* (Nashville, TN), July 6, 1887.

44 Herdegen, *The Iron Brigade*, 372; *OR* 27/1:275.

45 Ladd and Ladd, *Bachelder Papers*, 1:140; Day, "Opening the Battle"; Bishop, "Starting the Gettysburg Fight"; Herdegen & Murphy, *Four Years With the Iron Brigade*, 191. Callis's report, for the most part, disagrees with much of Robinson's account.

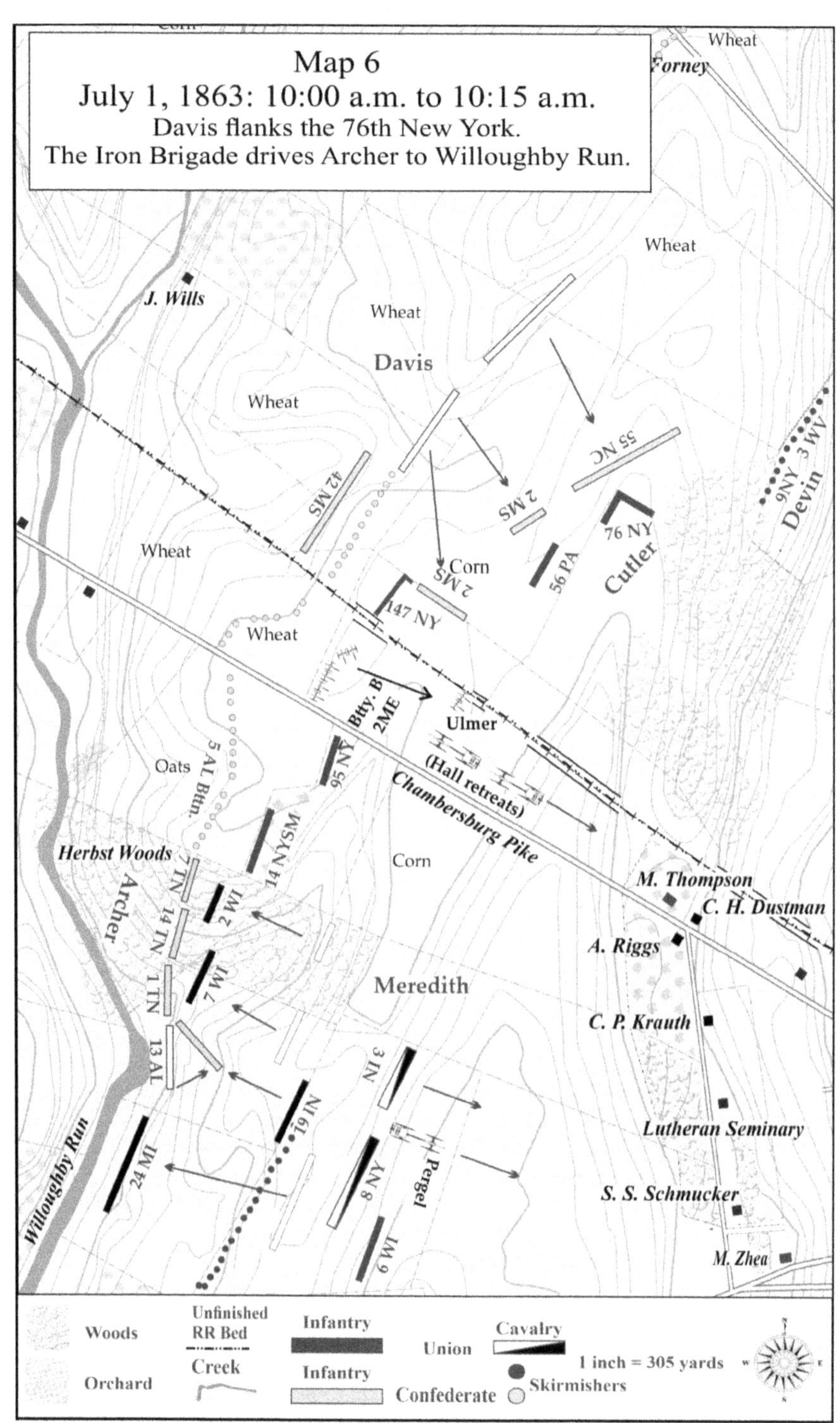
Map 6
July 1, 1863: 10:00 a.m. to 10:15 a.m.
Davis flanks the 76th New York.
The Iron Brigade drives Archer to Willoughby Run.
Wheat
Forney
Wheat
J. Wills
Wheat
Davis
Wheat
55 NC
42 MS
2 MS
9NY
3 WV
Devin
Wheat
76 NY
Corn
2 MS
56 PA
Cutler
147 NY
Wheat
Btty. B
2ME
Ulmer
Oats
5 AL Bttn.
95 NY
(Hall retreats)
Chambersburg Pike
14 NYSM
Herbst Woods
Corn
7 TN
2 WI
M. Thompson
C. H. Dustman
Archer
14 TN
A. Riggs
7 WI
1 TN
Meredith
C. P. Krauth
13 AL
3 IN
19 IN
Lutheran Seminary
24 MI
8 NY
Pergel
S. S. Schmucker
Willoughby Run
6 WI
M. Zhea
Woods
Orchard
Unfinished RR Bed
Creek
Infantry
Infantry
Union
Confederate
Cavalry
Skirmishers
1 inch = 305 yards

The charge triggered a chain reaction amongst the dismounted troopers of the 3rd Indiana. Cavalryman Matt Glaubner (Company E), whose horse had been killed earlier that morning, bolted into the fight on foot, carbine in hand. "Scharge! Scharge the bastards!" he shouted in his thick German accent. Glaubner intended to capture an unattended artillery horse on Pergel's one limber. Private William Rea (Company E), Col. George H. Chapman's orderly, also joined in the assault. He had his eyes locked on the saddle of a dead officer's mount and the revolvers sticking out of the saddle holsters.

While the infantry disappeared in the smoke along the ridge, the two troopers secured their war prizes and returned to their regiment. Sometime during the confusion, Lieutenant Calef showed up at Pergel's section and ordered him off the field. The corporal limbered his remaining rifled piece and headed back toward the seminary and the caissons. Calef never reported the loss of the dismounted piece.[46]

In the meantime, Lt. Col. Newton J. George (1st Tennessee), the only mounted officer in Archer's Brigade, watched the men of the 2nd Wisconsin recoil under the devastating volley loosed from his prone regiment. He rode south along the creek bottom looking for Archer and found the diminutive brigadier with Lt. Col. James Aiken (13th Alabama). Above the din of small arms fire, the 13th Alabama's Private Moon heard Aiken loudly request permission to left-wheel the Alabamians up the hill and catch the Yankees in a crossfire. Archer consented before trotting in the direction of his left flank.

Aiken called the men to their feet. Quarter-wheeling into line to face northeast, the colonel halted the right of the regiment about 130 yards west of the fence along McPherson Ridge. On the far right of the line, Private Bird (Company C) spied some skirmishers about 100 yards to the north. The Alabamians opened a desultory fire from the left as the companies came onto line, catching the 7th Wisconsin in the open ground between the fence and the 1st Tennessee.[47]

46 Day, "Opening the Battle." When Day quoted Glaubner, he inserted a long underscore in place of "bastards," but, having implied it, I filled it in. "S.O.B." usually appears as three underscores in the regimentals. More than likely the Confederates left the gun on the field when they retreated. The cavalry, for whatever reason, did not turn in reports of lost equipment. Nevertheless, Confederate and Federal accounts of an abandoned gun on the field appear credible.

47 Moon, "Beginning of the Battle at Gettysburg," 449; Bird, *Stories of the Civil War*, 7. The distance from the fence is approximate, based upon the brigade's estimated frontage.

Herbst Woods

A pall of thick smoke transformed Herbst Woods into a suffocating, sulfuric void, making it difficult to distinguish friend from foe. The 2nd Wisconsin continued its staggered yet determined advance. All the while Col. Lucius Fairchild endured the misery of watching Confederate rifle fire drop his officers and men with "terrible rapidity." Less than 50 yards into the woods, Pvt. Emanuel Markle (Company B) heard the colonel scream, "Charge, men. I mean charge."

Just after, a bullet killed Cpl. Oscar M. Bradfield on Markle's immediate right. A second later, a bullet passed under Markle's foot, ripped the sole off his brogan, and slammed into his heel. The impact knocked him flat. A short time later a round shattered Colonel Fairchild's left arm just above the elbow. He grasped his wounded arm with his right hand and staggered rearward while his regiment surged forward, some of them trampling over Markle.[48]

Meanwhile, at the southeast corner of the woods, orderly Charles H. Veil, together with Capts. Edward C. Baird and Robert W. Mitchell, dismounted and rushed to Reynolds's side. Veil rolled the general onto his back, but was unable to find a visible wound except for a bruise above his left eye. Believing he was severely stunned, Baird and Mitchell each grabbed a leg while Veil latched his hands under Reynolds's armpits. Together, they half-dragged and half-carried him over the rise into the low ground to get him out of the line of fire.

Baird hurried off to notify the officers in the vicinity that Reynolds was down. Mitchell remained nearby while Private Veil, Bradford Tripp (7th Wisconsin), and three orderlies from the 9th New York Cavalry placed him on a blanket and headed north toward the I Corps field hospital around the McPherson farmhouse. Mitchell was still there when the badly wounded Colonel Fairchild staggered from the woods. Mitchell surprised the officer by

---

Taken in conjunction with Callis's description of the volley disordering the regiment, it is conceivable that Bird thought he saw a skirmish line to the north. He did not fire his weapon until just before he was captured, which indicates the regiment did not deliver a traditional volley.

48 *OR* 27/1:273; Beecham, *Gettysburg*, 66; Charles Fairchild to Mother, July 6, 1863, Fairchild Papers, Wisconsin Historical Society, Madison, WI; Turney, "The First Tennessee at Gettysburg," 535; Markle, "The Story of Battle Told By Survivor." Beecham says Fairchild got hit 30 yards into the woods and the *OR* says 50 yards.

announcing that General Reynolds was dead, and then took off after the orderlies.[49]

Partway through the swale southeast of the farmhouse, the party stopped and gently lowered Reynolds to the ground. Orderly Veil thought he heard the general gasp. The private uncorked his canteen and carefully let a small amount of water fall onto Reynolds's mouth. The liquid trickled across his mouth onto the ground. There was no response. Captain Mitchell leaned over and asked Reynolds if he was suffering. The general responded with a faint smile, his chest heaved, and he expired.

The men transported the dead officer to Asst. Surg. John T. Stillman (147th New York), who was attending casualties along the Chambersburg Pike. Before examining the corpse, the doctor had them remove Reynolds's forage cap and sword belt, which they handed to Pvt. H. Sergent Jones (Company F, 14th Brooklyn). Stillman opened the general's tunic and felt his neck for a pulse; there was none. Major William Riddle recovered Reynolds's personal effects: the small gold ring he wore on his little finger, inscribed with the name "Kate," and the silk string around his neck with a 10-bead rosary ring and its attached crucifix. Riddle had the body placed on a stretcher and carried to the seminary.[50]

While Reynolds was being attended to, the 1st Tennessee and the 13th Alabama fired at the 7th Wisconsin from the front and left flank. The Yankees recoiled under the fire. John Callis, like Fairchild, decided it made more sense to get his men into the shelter of the woods. Once Capt. Jacob B. Turney (Company K, 1st Tennessee) realized the Yankees had ceased fire, he knelt to peer under the smoke and discerned legs dressed in blue shifting to the left

49 Veil to McConaughy; Ladd and Ladd, *Bachelder Papers*, 1:236; Tripp, "The Iron Brigade"; Cheney, *History of the Ninth Regiment*, 111; Eleanor Reynolds to brother. Tripp mistook the McPherson house for the toll house (Johns house), which was farther west on the Chambersburg Pike. The troopers were Cpl. George D. Loop (Company B) and Pvts. Morgan L. Bement and Henry Bentley (both of Company C).

50 Eleanor Reynolds to brother; Ladd and Ladd, *Bachelder Papers*, 1:332; Riddle to Bouvier; H. B. Rosengarten to Miss Reynolds, July 11, 1863, https://digital.fandm.edu/object/islandora5872, accessed Jan. 21, 2023. "Sergeant" Jones, mentioned in Rosengarten's letter, was H. Sergent Jones, the only Jones in Company F. The surgeon would have had the accoutrements removed to check the body. To check the pulse, he would have had to open the tunic, which exposed the ribbon. The beads and cross on a "short silken string"may have been an "Irish penal ring" worn under the clothing to conceal the wearer's faith in time of persecution. Reynolds was secretly engaged to Kate Hewitt, a Catholic. Lieutenant Bouvier was Lt. John Vernon Bouvier, Sr., Company K, 20th New York State Militia.

(north): The Yankees were flanking the brigade. Turney ran to the rear of the 14th Tennessee and found the visibly exhausted General Archer, who dismissed his admonition by saying that General Davis's Brigade was going to occupy the left of the line. In an attempt to save his men, the captain rushed back to his company to pull it out of the fight.[51]

When the 2nd Wisconsin closed to within 10 yards of their line, Cpl. Robert K. Beecham (Company H) heard someone to the front scream above the din, "Thar comes them old black-hats! It's the Army of the Potomac, sure!" The alarm sent a shockwave through the Tennesseans. Panic set in and they began breaking to the rear leaving, their few dead and badly wounded on the ground along the ridge. The Wisconsinites halted and loosed a wild volley into the Rebels' backs. Before the smoke dissipated, Maj. John Mansfield ordered a charge, and the Black Hats bolted through the woods in pursuit.[52]

Off to the south, the 19th Indiana appeared along the smoke- obscured ridge on the right flank of the 13th Alabama. "All of a sudden a heavy line of battle rose up out of the wheat," the startled Private Bird (Company C) remembered. The Indiana and U.S. flags rising above the powder smoke attracted fire from the 1st Tennessee. A bullet hit Cpl. Burl Cunningham in the left side and knocked him unconscious. He collapsed, seemingly lifeless, with the national colors still in his grasp. In the confusion, Cpl. Abram Buckles heard someone shout, "Abe, drop your gun and take the flag." Buckles lifted the banner from ground just as the Hoosiers shot back and surged forward.

51 Turney, "The First Tennessee at Gettysburg," 535; Moon, "Beginning of the Battle at Gettysburg," 449; Bishop, "Starting the Gettysburg Fight"; Ladd and Ladd, *Bachelder Papers*, 1:140; Herdegen & Murphy, *Four Years With the Iron Brigade*, 191; "Synopsis of General Richardson's Speech," 2; *OR* 27/2:647. The statements by Ray, Bishop, and Richardson corroborate that the regiment went into the fight with loaded rifles. Callis erred when he stated that the regiment joined the action with unloaded weapons. The firefight between Archer and part of the Iron Brigade was short, and may have only lasted a few minutes. Moon recalled the 13th Alabama firing a number of volleys into the Yankees at 75 yards. Lieutenant Colonel Samuel G. Shepard (7th Tennessee) reported, "he [Archer] appeared to be very much exhausted with fatigue."

52 Beecham, *Gettysburg*, 65; Dennis B. Dailey to Gen. Abner Doubleday, March 24, 1890, Bachelder Papers, Reel #1, Correspondence, Vertical Files, VF-W2, Library, GNMP; *OR* 27/1:274; Harries, "The Iron Brigade in the First Day's Battle at Gettysburg," 340; Cornelius Wheeler to Parents, July 11, 1863, Vertical Files, VF-WI2, Library, GNMP; Busey & Busey, *Confederate Casualties*, 3:1396-1414. According to this nominal list, the 7th Tennessee lost a confirmed one killed, two wounded, and 21 captured, while the 14th Tennessee had two killed, six wounded, and 44 captured, which indicates a short fight, the onset of panic, and then a rout.

Caught up in the frenzy, Buckles recklessly bolted ahead of the regiment. Colonel Henry Morrow's 24th Michigan, whose members loaded as they formed, crossed the fence in the 19th Indiana's left rear and enveloped the unsuspecting 13th Alabama. The order to fall back to the creek surprised Pvt. William H. Moon of Company I. The Alabamians were pouring it into the Yankees to the north while the Tennesseans slammed lead into the Wisconsin troops from the west. As far as Moon knew, only some bothersome skirmishers were pecking at the regiment's right flank.[53]

The Confederates peeled back from the right toward the creek, leaving behind more than a dozen dead, dying, disabled, or trapped men. The 1st Tennessee fell back with them. Among the abandoned lay Lt. William Jasper Muse (Company B, 1st Tennessee). He was hit in three places, including the right lung.

To the north, those Rebels who could do so ran over the sharp rise of ground east of Willoughby Run and dove for cover along its brush-covered banks. Private Major "Mage" H. Allen (Company H, 13th Alabama) was not one of them. A minié ball struck the right side of his head, hit his cheek bone below the eye, and passed through the auricle (cartilage or "burr") of his ear. The impact left him sprawled on the ground unconscious, his face bathed in blood. Unable to hear anything, and with his face paralyzed on the right side and his right eye locked open, Allen appeared dead.[54]

Private Bird (Company C, 13th Alabama) snapped off a wild shot before rushing into the marshy hollow behind him. The 19th Indiana halted on the rise of ground above the Alabamians while the 24th Michigan came into line to its left. The trapped Confederates struck the halted Wolverines with a hasty spattering of small arms fire. Color Sergeant Abel G. Peck (24th Michigan) was killed. Corporal Charles Bellore (Company E), the tallest man in the color guard, pulled the state flag from Peck's grasp and held it aloft. Lieutenant

53 "Brief Sketch of Gallantry of Mr. B. Cunningham"; Henry C. Marsh, "The Nineteenth Indiana at Gettysburg," Manuscript Department, USAHEC, 3; Moon, "Beginning of the Battle of Gettysburg," 449. Corporals Buckles and Cunningham with Private McKinney were all identified as members of the color guard. Phil Spaugy, researcher of the 19th Indiana, believes that McKinney was one of the three men wounded. See, "Flag of the Nineteenth," *Indianapolis Journal*, May 14, 1902.

54 Don Ernsberger, *Also For Glory Muster: The Story of the Pettigrew Trimble Charge at Gettysburg* (Bloomington, IN, 2008), 39. Ernsberger cited Allen's pension and family recollections. Allen, who survived his horrific wound, came to while being carried on the shoulder of a Union soldier.

William R. Dodsley (Company K) reeled under the impact of a rifle ball in his shoulder.[55]

The Western men rushed into the midst of the trapped Alabamians. Two officers and two enlisted men cornered Lt. Henry W. Pond of Company C, hollering, "Surrender! Surrender!" Startled by the suddenness of the attack, Pond turned to the equally frightened Private Bird. "Bird, what in the hell should I do?" "I don't see what you can do but surrender," came Bird's reply. Pond hurled his sword to the ground and, as fellow prisoner Pvt. William G. Martin sarcastically recalled, "got back in the Union."[56]

The 24th Michigan and 19th Indiana, with some mounted troopers from Company I, 8th New York Cavalry, flanked Archer's command from the south and pushed the 13th Alabama northward upon the rest of the brigade along Willoughby Run. Corporal. Abram Buckles (Company E) eagerly pushed too far in advance with the 19th Indiana's colors, prompting Lt. Col William W. Dudley to yell, "Come back with that flag!" He did.[57]

The collapse of the 13th forced the 1st Tennessee into the 14th Tennessee, creating a pocket from which almost half of them would not escape. A considerable number of Rebels, including some officers, crowded into a willow grove about 20 yards west of the run opposite the medicinal spring at the elbow in the creek. For a few seconds Lt. James W. Simpson (Company F, 13th Alabama) found himself alongside General Archer debating whether to stay or go. Simpson opted to make tracks.[58]

It was the 2nd Wisconsin that executed the *coup de grâce*. Companies B and G cornered the surviving Confederates in the willows. Newly promoted Capt. Charles Dow with his Company G, fighting on the left of Company B, crossed

55 Curtis, *History of the Twenty-Fourth Michigan*, 158, 164; Bird, *Stories of the Civil War*, 7-8; Busey & Busey, *Confederate Casualties at Gettysburg*, 3:1387; William J. Muse, "History of Captain Will J. Muse from his birth to the close of the Civil War," www.tennessee-scv.org/camp155/Dr%20Bradley,Civil%20War/cwrc/muse.html, last accessed Jan. 23, 2023.

56 Bird, *Stories of the Civil War*, 7-8; Busey & Busey, *Confederate Casualties at Gettysburg*, 1:132-150.

57 Marsh, "The Nineteenth Indiana at Gettysburg," 3; N. H. Decke, "Gettysburg," *NT*, May 1, 1902, 3.

58 Busey & Busey, *Confederate Casualties*, 1:132-150 and 3:1381-1414; James M. Simpson to Mother, July 8, 1873, Lt. James M. Simpson, 13th Ala. Inf. Regt., Allen-Simpson Papers, No. 29 Micro., Southern Historical Collection, University of North Carolina, Chapel Hill, NC; Dailey to Doubleday, March 24, 1890, Bachelder Papers, Reel #1.

west of the creek first. The Rebels, clustered around their officers, and cast aside their weapons. Many dropped on the ground to surrender. Private Patrick Maloney spied the handsomely uniformed General Archer in their midst. While the men near him rounded up prisoners, Maloney dashed into the thicket and literally collared the general. Archer struggled to keep his balance in the tussle until several other soldiers came to the Irishman's assistance and pulled him to the ground. With the general thus "subdued," Maloney and his boys rough-handled Archer back through the willows to Captain Dow.[59]

The dejected Archer—the first general in the Army of Northern Virginia captured in battle—offered the captain his sword. Dow refused to take it: "Keep your sword, General, and go to the rear; one sword is all I need on this line." Maloney guided Archer east toward the creek where Lt. William H. Harries (Company B) was busy disarming and organizing prisoners. The sight of Archer in a new gray uniform, complete with a magnificent blade in a steel scabbard hanging by his side, caught Harries' attention. He stopped what he was doing and studied the diminutive brigadier.[60]

Lieutenant Dennis B. Dailey (Company B), who served as an acting aide-de-camp on Meredith's staff, boldly approached Archer. The Confederate asked Dailey to protect him from Maloney, to which the Irish lieutenant impudently replied, "I'll relieve you of that sword." Archer protested that a captain had ordered him to keep it and that professional courtesy did not require him to surrender it again. Dailey would have none of it, and insisted on taking the sword. An outraged Archer unbuckled his belt and handed the blade to the lieutenant. The 2nd Wisconsin's Corporal Beecham witnessed the entire affair with a great deal of disgust. "It is not always that the man on the outmost line [Dow] receives the reward which he is due," the corporal lamented with justifiable bitterness.

Dailey ordered Harries, with Maloney and his comrades, to escort Archer and his men through Herbst Woods to General Meredith. The enlisted men prodded the general and the herd of prisoners to the western side of the creek. When Dailey noticed that the general's sword and scabbard were much lighter than his own, he unbuckled his and replaced them with Archer's. He handed the heavier weapon to a nearby soldier and told him to take it to brigade

59 Dailey to Doubleday; *OR* 27/1:274.

60 Harries, "The Iron Brigade in the First Day's Battle at Gettysburg," 340; Beecham, *Gettysburg*, 66-67.

headquarters for him. The man later turned the prizes over to Maj. John Mansfield, telling him they belonged to a Rebel general.[61]

By the time the 2nd Wisconsin bagged Archer and an impressive number of his men on the right of the line, the 7th Wisconsin had chased the 1st Tennessee into the open ground west of the creek. A confused Confederate officer with his sword unsheathed and extended toward the Yankee infantry, rushed Lt. Col. John B. Callis, shouting, "I surrender!" The Tennessean was so close that Callis could not use his sidearm to shoot him. Instead, the he responded with a counter-stroke that knocked the weapon from the Rebel's hand and barely missed the officer's throat. "Surrender?" Callis exclaimed. "That is no way to surrender! If you surrender, order your men to cease firing, pick up your sabre and order your men to go to the rear as prisoners." The officer complied. Callis mistakenly believed his regiment captured more men than remained in the 7th's ranks.[62]

Wood Line on the Eastern Side of Herr's Ridge

Colonel John M. Brockenbrough's Virginians, meanwhile, a brigade rife with discipline and morale problems, had reached the first fence east of the wood line on Herr's Ridge. When the colonel spotted the unfolding panic below him off his right-front, he ordered his regiments back to cover. With Rebels scrambling toward the woodlot, Colonel Morrow right about-faced the 24th Michigan by the rear rank and gave chase. He halted his line on the rise of ground about 800 feet west of the creek along the fence row running north from Emanuel Harman's farm lane. Rather than risk encountering bigger trouble in

61 Dailey to Doubleday; *OR* 27/1:274, 374; W. H. Harries, "The Sword of Gen. James J. Archer," *CV*, 19:420; Harries, "The Iron Brigade," 340; Beecham, *Gettysburg*, 67. In his after-action report, dated November 15, 1863, Maj. John Mansfield (2nd Wisconsin) wrote that Archer surrendered the sword to him, and that he passed it over to Lieutenant Dailey, a claim other eyewitnesses refute.

62 Busey & Busey, *Confederate Casualties*, 1:132-150 and 3:1396-1414; William W. Dudley, *The Iron Brigade at Gettysburg: Official Report Of the Part Borne by the 1st Brigade, 1st Division, 1st Army Corps, Army of the Potomac in Action at Gettysburg, Pennsylvania, July 1st, 2d, and 3d, 1863* (Cincinnati, 1879), 15; Ladd and Ladd, *Bachelder Papers*, 1:140. The exclamation marks do not appear in the original source. Callis probably captured one of the five officers bagged in 14th Tennessee, but it is impossible to determine his identity. That number included four junior second lieutenants and one captain, William S. Moore of Company H.

the woods 400 yards ahead, he decided to stay put and protect the brigade with skirmishers.

Company B spread west in an arc from the woods to Harman's house on Morrow's left flank and the colonel retired the remainder of the regiment to the west side of the creek. Lieutenant Colonel Callis's 7th Wisconsin came up on Morrow's right. Not too far to the west Callis spotted a line of Confederate infantry extending beyond his line of sight past his right flank. Gray-clad skirmishers across the regiment's front headed toward the line.[63]

With sporadic rifle fire reverberating across the ground to the west, the 2nd Wisconsin took a few minutes to regroup and take roll. The outfit had lost 116 of the 276 officers and men who had gone into the action. Lieutenant Colonel Stevens was dying and Colonel Fairchild had a shattered left arm that would require amputation. Captain Nathaniel Rollins, commanding Company H (the color company), started the day with 27 enlisted men and two officers, and finished with 11 enlisted men and himself. Lieutenant William S. Winegar perished along with three enlisted men. The Rebs wounded 13 more. The regiment counted an additional three captains and a lieutenant among the injured. Sergeant Cornelius Wheeler (Company I) tallied 150 Confederate prisoners.[64]

The brief affair cost Archer's command dearly. The four regiments engaged (1,058 officers and men) lost eight killed, 76 wounded, and 224 captured— or 29%. The 13th Alabama suffered 50% casualties, and the 1st and 14th Tennessee lost 27% and 25%, respectively. The 7th Tennessee managed to escape the tactical fiasco with about 90% of its original strength.

For the regiments of the Iron Brigade, losses suffered by the 19th Indiana and the 7th Wisconsin were not broken out from the total losses incurred throughout the three-day battle. The 24th Michigan lost about 10 men and the 2nd Wisconsin an estimated 116 in the area of Herbst Woods, for an average of 38%. Not counting the 6th Wisconsin, which fought farther north in the Chambersburg Pike area, these regiments entered the action with 1,470 soldiers.

63 Curtis, *History of the Twenty-Fourth Michigan*, 157, 188; Charles H. McConnell, "First and Greatest Days Battle at Gettysburg"; *OR* 27/1:267; Augustus F. Ziegler, Letter, July 21, 1863, Library, GNMP, hereafter cited as Ziegler Letter; Report of Col. Robert Mayo, 47th Virginia, August 13, 1863, Vertical Files, VF-VA47, Library, GNMP; Ladd & Ladd, *Bachelder Papers*, 1:141.

64 Otis diary, July 1, 1863; Wheeler to Parents; Rollins journal, July 1, 1863.

Overall, its estimated casualties amounted to about 10% of the total number present.[65]

10:30 a.m. to 10:45 a.m.[66]
Woodlot on Southern Herr's Ridge, North of the Fairfield Road

Colonel Biddle's Union column reached the intersection with the Fairfield Road around 10:30 a.m. A squadron of the 8th Illinois Cavalry was picketing the road and the open woodlot on its northern side near the David Finnefrock house. The colonel directed his men northwest into the shade of the trees. Captain John D. S. Cook (Company I, 20th N.Y.S.M.) noted the springy sod and how bucolic everything seemed—a verdant pasture lot heavily studded with mature hardwoods. The overheated infantrymen halted for a much-needed respite out of the direct sunlight. Battery B, 1st Pennsylvania Light Artillery, however, waited at the intersection.[67]

Around 10:45 a.m., Colonel Biddle cautiously walked his brigade north about 200 to 300 feet in column of regiments. Dismounted troopers from the 8th

65 Busey & Busey, *Confederate Casualties*, 1:132-150 and 3:1381-1414.

66 Cook, "Personal Reminiscences," 323; *OR* 27/1:315, 326. Captain Cook erred about the time by more than an hour. According to Colonel Biddle, the brigade arrived on the field around 11:00 a.m. and could hear heavy firing (i.e., The fight between Archer and the Iron Brigade); this places the time closer to 10:15 a.m. - 10:30 a.m. His men did not see the Iron Brigade at this time, which means it had passed into the valley along Willoughby Run before Biddle reached McPherson's Ridge. Lieutenant Colonel McFarland (151st Pennsylvania) places the arrival at the Fairfield Road at 10:30 a.m., which is the time the brigade would have taken at the "common time" without halting for a break.

67 Cook, "Personal Reminiscences," 323-324; *Pennsylvania at Gettysburg*, 2:877; the following three links were accessed Jan. 19, 2023: www.findagrave.com/memorial/32783303/elizabeth-keefauver; "Burning of the McLean House," 1; www.findagrave.com/memorial/32783314/william-keefauver; www.finda grave.com/memorial/205139851/emanuel-harmon; *The Gettysburg Compiler*, February 23, 1863, 3. At the postwar dedication of the monument, Lt. James A. Gardner noted the battery came up the Fairfield Road toward Seminary Ridge. The David Finnefrock house is also known by the landlord's name, Peter Stallsmith, and by another renter's name, William Keefauver. Keefauver rented the property before the war but lived on the Taneytown Road, four miles south of Gettysburg, and sold his farm on March 13, 1863. Apparently, Keefauver rented the Stallsmith house to David Finnefrock (pronounced "Finefrock"). Amelia E. Harman referred to Finnefrock as "our farmer," indicating that he was not married to Rachel Harman, her aunt, as some sources have cited. Emanuel Harman was not married and did not live on the property.

Illinois stationed about the Finnefrock buildings were skirmishing with Confederates on the wooded side of Herr's Ridge several hundred yards north of his regiments.[68]

10:15 a.m. to 10:45 a.m.[69]
Warfield Ridge

Lieutenant Benjamin T. Marten probably intercepted General Doubleday about a quarter mile or so southwest of Warfield Ridge. Doubleday, apparently sensing no real urgency in the directive to cover the Fairfield Road, continued at his casual pace. The intense humidity, punctuated with isolated and sometimes heavy showers, made the march more exhausting.[70]

Colonel Charles Wainwright had fallen out of the column about one and a quarter miles back with one of the battery forges to shod his horse "Billy." He waited there for a short while for a shower to blow past. Wainwright was traveling light. Since he anticipated a quiet day, he had tossed his saddle bags with his brush, comb, handkerchief, tobacco, and chocolate into the battalion wagon. Once the rain ended, he climbed into the saddle and trotted to the front of his artillery brigade, where he joined Doubleday and his staff about 400 yards beyond the Phillip Snyder place.[71]

The two officers discussed General Meade's promotion to command the Army of the Potomac. Doubleday commented that George Sykes, Meade's junior, "ought to be given a corps." Smoke from bursting shells at the front

68 Theodore B. Gates, *The "Ulster Guard" (20th N. Y. State Militia in the War of the Rebellion)* (New York, 1879), 432; Cook, "Personal Reminiscences," 324. Few of the officers and men expected a major engagement on July 1 and no one appeared in much of a hurry to get to the field.

69 The time is based on the rate of march at a walk for artillery. Bullfrog Road to the little bridge over the small stream north of Snyder's, at about four m.p.h., would take one hour and 15 minutes, putting Halstead's arrival time around 10:45 a.m.

70 Vail, *Reminiscences*, 117; Chamberlin, *History of the 150th Regiment*, 110; Nevins, *A Diary of Battle*, 232. Precisely where or when Marten contacted Doubleday is uncertain, but it is logical to assume he would have met the general before Doubleday got word to rush the corps forward. Wainwright makes it clear that the column was not in any hurry.

71 Nevins, *A Diary of Battle*, 232. The approximate locations of the column are based on progress at the "walk" (3.75 mph) from Marsh Creek. According to Wainwright, they were about two miles from Gettysburg. They were likely about 400 yards northeast of Snyder's on the Emmitsburg Road.

caught Wainwright's attention. Both officers listened intently for the "boom" of artillery fire, which thundered past them a few seconds later. Based on the time lapse between the shell burst and sound, the two agreed it was probably from Buford's position three or four miles off.[72]

Around 10:30 a.m., as the column drew near the Millerstown Road intersection at the Peach Orchard, Captain Halstead clattered up to the officers and shouted to hurry the corps forward because Reynolds was fighting west of the seminary. Without waiting for orders, Colonel Wainwright turned about and rode toward the rear to set his artillery in motion, unaware that General Doubleday and his staff were racing in the opposite direction toward Seminary Ridge.

Doubleday and his headquarters personnel took Wadsworth's route at Codori's, struck the Fairfield Road, and cut west uphill to the campus road. By 10:40 a.m. they reached the field in front of Reverend Schmucker's house, where Doubleday found himself in the middle of a chaotic situation. He turned to Lt. Jacob F. Slagle and ordered him to cut cross-country and send Rowley's division up in a hurry. He further admonished Slagle to be careful because they had no idea of the exact location of the Confederates.[73]

Meanwhile, Wainwright had gotten his artillery moving at the trot. Battery L, 1st New York, took the lead, followed by Battery B, 4th U.S. and Battery E, 5th Maine. At Codori's, he directed them to roll cross-country following the clearly marked route toward Stevens's Run. Halfway across the field they encountered Craig Wadsworth, who stopped to tell the colonel, "The General is killed; Reynolds is dead." The news shocked and saddened Wainwright, who continued on to the Fairfield Road. He turned west there, stopping momentarily to doff his hat as Reynolds's body was carried past. The artillery commander halted the batteries when he reached the opening in the Fairfield Road fence in the hollow southeast of the seminary.

72 When V Corps commander Meade was promoted to command the Army of the Potomac on June 28, 1863, Maj. Gen. George Sykes assumed command of the corps.

73 Doubleday, *Chancellorsville and Gettysburg*, 130; Slagle to Brother; OR 27/1:244. By pushing their horses, Doubleday and his staff could have reached the campus road within 5-10 minutes from the Peach Orchard if the staff had urged their horses into the equivalent of a modern canter/gallop (15-30 m.p.h.). Wainwright unjustly accused Doubleday of remaining behind. Slagle definitely places Doubleday on the field before the 6th Wisconsin went into action. He describes part of the First Division (6th Wisconsin) lying in the field to their front while the fighting was going on in the woods.

With regimental adjutant Lt. Angell Matthewson close at hand, Wainwright trotted up the road toward the campus. Unaware that Doubleday had preceded him onto the field, the colonel decided not to wait for orders but act on his own judgment. He erroneously assumed the general remained in the rear with the infantry. "I had no confidence in Doubleday," he later admitted, "and felt that he would be a weak reed to lean upon."[74]

The Field West of the Seminary

The Iron Brigade's 6th Wisconsin crested the Fairfield Road and right flanked onto the main campus road minutes before Doubleday's arrival. From there, it filed into the field through the opening in the fence south of the woodlot before heading southwest toward the Fairfield Road. Lieutenant Gilbert M. Woodward, another of Solomon Meredith's aides, intercepted the regiment at a gallop. "Colonel," he yelled to Rufus Dawes, "form your line, and prepare for action at once."

Dawes shouted the preparatory command above the din: "Battalion, by company into line, March!" By company, the men, their weapons at right shoulder shift, changed their intervals and faced to the right. "Load at will, load!" Rifle butts hit the soft ground. Men tore cartridges, charged their weapons, unwrapped their miniés, and inserted them into the bores. Ramrods clanged along the line as Dawes bellowed, "Forward into line, by companies, left half wheel. Double quick march."

The veterans executed the maneuver at the run, some with their weapons on their shoulders, others likely still ramming their cartridges while trying to keep up. Company G, at the front of the regiment, wheeled into line first to anchor the right, followed successively on the left by Companies C, K, B, and E (combined), the color guard, F, H, A and D (combined), and I. Dawes waited impatiently as the companies formed at a 45-degree angle to their original formation, facing northwest. Their left flank stood within 75 feet of the Fairfield

74 Nevins, *A Diary of Battle*, 233, 234; *OR* 27/1:355. Wainwright wrote, "All I could do then was to put my batteries in a position where they could be got at easily . . . and wait in a condition to start at a trot the instant orders came." Wainwright made no mention of Matthewson in his after-action report (July 17, 1863) or ordering the batteries to wait and be prepared to march. He makes it clear in his diary that he did send the lieutenant back to bring up two batteries to Seminary Ridge before reconnoitering the northern end of the Federal line.

Road. With the loading complete the colonel commanded, "Forward, right guide, March."[75]

Doubleday spied the 6th Wisconsin moving onto the crowded field and dispatched the diminutive Lt. Benjamin T. Marten at a gallop to direct it to stop where it was. Marten tore off across the soggy field and reined in alongside Dawes. "Colonel," the aide cried, "General Doubleday is now in command of the first corps, and he directs that you halt your regiment." Dawes did as directed and commanded his men to lie down.[76]

Moments later Lieutenant Harris arrived with the brigade guard under orders from General Meredith to join the 6th. Dawes split the guard, which consisted of 20 enlisted men from each regiment in the brigade, into two companies. Lieutenant Levi Showalter (2nd Wisconsin) went to the right of Company G on the northern end of the line. Lieutenant Harris took his "ad hoc" company to the left of Company I, with his left flank on the fence along the Fairfield Road. Lieutenant Remington (Company K) and his detachment from Company I took up a position behind Harris's men.[77]

75 Rufus R. Dawes, "Align on the Colors," *Milwaukee Sunday Telegraph*, April 27, 1890; Ladd and Ladd, *Bachelder Papers*, 1:323; Rufus R. Dawes, "With the Sixth Wisconsin at Gettysburg," *Sketches of War History, 1861-1865, Papers Prepared for the Ohio Commandery of the Military Order of the Loyal Legion of the United States, 1888-1890*, 9 vols. (Cincinnati), 3:365; Dawes, *Service with the Sixth Wisconsin*, 164; Sullivan, "The Charge of the Iron Brigade at Gettysburg"; Herdegen & Beaudot, *In the Bloody Railroad Cut*, 173 (diagram of the regimental line). There are variations in Dawes's post-battle accounts of the regiment coming onto the field. In order to have executed the maneuver from column into line as he described, the regiment would have had to have been in an unobstructed field and not in a road or on a hillside. In his *OR* report and in his 1890 newspaper article, he noted that he was ordered to halt and hold his men in reserve. In his 1868 letter to Bachelder and in *Service With the Sixth Wisconsin*, which he published the same year as the article in the *Milwaukee Sunday Telegraph* (1890), he identified the officer who ordered the halt as Lieutenant Marten of Doubleday's staff.

76 Dawes, *Service with the Sixth Wisconsin*, 165; Dawes, "With the Sixth Wisconsin," 365; Sullivan, "The Charge of The Iron Brigade at Gettysburg." "Mickey," the nickname of Sgt. James P. Sullivan, mentioned hearing Marten say something about Reynolds's demise, whereas Dawes did not. From this point on Sullivan merged the regiment's arrival on the field with the charge against the railroad cut, leaving the impression that they occurred nearly the same time. They did not.

77 *OR* 27/1:275; Dawes, "Align on the Colors"; Ladd & Ladd, *Bachelder Papers*, 1:323; Dawes, "With the Sixth Wisconsin," 365.

10:40 a.m. to 10:50 a.m.[78]

Lieutenant Slagle put spurs to his horse and took off at a gallop. Heading south across the Fairfield Road, he passed through Elizabeth Shultz's wood lot and veered southeast in a beeline for the Emmitsburg Road, which he reached near the Brien tenant cabin. Reining south in the road, he intercepted Col. Roy Stone's marching column about 600 yards north of the Philip Snyder farm lane. The lieutenant halted momentarily next to Brig. Gen. Thomas A. Rowley and Colonel Stone and shouted for the general to come forward at the double-quick. "Hurry up your columns," was how Sgt. Patrick DeLacy (Company A, 143rd Pennsylvania) recalled the order.[79]

A few minutes later, Sergeant DeLacy recalled seeing a boy of about 15 holding the reins of a fast-approaching horse, with four younger ones behind him, each clinging tightly to the child in front as they tried to stay on the animal's rocking back. Toward the front of the column, the sergeant heard one of the men exclaim, "My God, they are driving our people away from their homes!" The men sprang into a double-quick before the commands of their officers had carried through the ranks.[80]

Slagle rode alongside Stone's brigade and yelled at Colonel Wister of the 150th Pennsylvania, "Colonel, close up your men and move on as rapidly as possible." Drummer Henry "Harry" M. Keiffer (Company D) watched Slagle trot alongside the regiments behind the brigade, also urging them forward. After reaching the rear of the Third Division, Slagle wheeled his horse about and headed back toward Seminary Ridge.

Slagle reported back to Doubleday by 11:00 a.m., only to get sent out yet again. Since he had already contacted Rowley and Stone's brigade, the general directed the lieutenant to seek out Biddle's column of the Third Division.

78 This is based upon the approximate time Slagle left Doubleday until he encountered Rowley on the Emmitsburg Road.

79 Slagle to Brother; *Pennsylvania at Gettysburg*, 2:724; "Capt. DeLacy Describes Gettysburg Battle," *The Scranton* [PA] *Truth*, July 1, 1913; *OR* 27/1:331. According to Slagle, "I crossed through field and woods for about a mile, when I struck the road which they were upon and after following that for about two miles found Gen. Rowley, gave him his orders and went back." In 1889 at the dedication of the monument to the 149th Pennsylvania, Slagle clarified that Biddle's brigade took the side road and that Stone's brigade marched in the Emmitsburg Road from its morning bivouac.

80 "Capt. DeLacy Describes Gettysburg Battle."

Wheeling his mount south under the cover of McPherson's Ridge, Slagle rode to the Fairfield Road and then west into the valley south of the Harmon farm. He found the brigade in the Finnefrock woodlot and directed it uphill toward John Herbst's farm lane.

As the 20th N.Y.S.M. began its climb, a bullet from the woods knocked down one of the New Yorkers. Surgeon Robert Loughran slid off his horse and rushed to the man while the column continued on its way. Striking the Herbst lane, Slagle guided Biddle's brigade southeast into the Fairfield Road. No one had any real idea what was ahead of them.[81]

81 Henry M. Keiffer, "Recollections of a Drummer Boy," *NT*, December 31, 1881, 6; Slagle to Brother; Cook, "Personal Reminiscences," 324. Biddle did not specifically mention that Slagle led him onto the field, but the evidence implies that was the case. Biddle was isolated and had no knowledge of the developing battlefield, and he almost certainly would have remained in place until directed to move. In his letter, Slagle noted that Doubleday sent him to bring up Rowley, which was a mistake because he had already done that. The description of the terrain makes it clear that Slagle was sent to find Biddle, whose brigade was on the byroad to the field. The brigade's ascent up the western side of the creek bottom would have taken it to John Herbst's farm lane. To get into the Hagerstown Pike, from which the regiments finally deployed, they would have entered from the southern end of the lane.

Chapter Five

"We fight a little and run a little. There are no supports."

— *Brig. Gen. Lysander Cutler*

Davis Attacks Cutler

10:00 a.m. to 11:00 a.m.

10:00 a.m. to 10:15 a.m.
North of the Unfinished Railroad

Marching behind their mounted field and staff officers, the 76th New York and 56th Pennsylvania of Cutler's brigade continued north through the knee-high cornfield in the swale between the middle ridge and McPherson's Ridge. The misty atmosphere combined with the rising temperature and humidity to cast a ghostly veil over the low ground through which they marched. The New Yorkers were heading for the Mummasburg Road when their left flank came under sporadic small arms fire from the wheatfield on the western side of the corn. General Cutler responded by flanking the two regiments northeast into line on the middle ridge.[1]

1 *OR* 27/1:285; *NYAG*, 2:616, 3:991. The veterans wrote a great deal about the field contours on the northern side of the Chambersburg Pike. In volume 3, *NYAG*, J. Volney Pierce (Company G, 147th New York) mentioned three ridges. The westernmost, designated the "third ridge," refers to Captain Hall's artillery location on McPherson's Ridge. The "second ridge" is where Reynolds Avenue today crosses the middle railroad cut. The "first ridge" is Oak Ridge. From his description, Cutler, with the two lead regiments,

Preacher-turned-warrior Maj. Andrew Grover guided his 76th New York on line just north and to the rear of the Pennsylvanians. Unsure whether his New Yorkers had walked into hostile or friendly fire, he did not allow the regiment to respond. A 12-pounder ball plowed through Company B between Capt. Robert Story's legs without touching him. Another "whooshed" into Company E from the west and hurled a corporal into the arms of his file closer, Sgt. Edgar D. Haviland. "In such times," the sergeant coldly observed, "a man don't have much time to take care of the men so I threw him down." A bullet mortally wounded his messmate, Pvt. James B. Bush. Haviland, who described Bush as a "fine little fellow about my size," left him on the field. Major Grover cautioned the men to withhold their fire until he could determine the identity of the troops in front of the regiment.[2]

Colonel J. William Hofmann brought his 56th Pennsylvania to a halt slightly to the left front of the New Yorkers on a westerly bulge in the ridge, which placed them a little closer to the noisome skirmishers. From his saddle he could see through the mist and observe an infantry line moving through the tall wheat northwest of his position.

Mounted a few feet behind the colonel, Culter locked his field glasses upon the newcomers. "Is that the enemy?" inquired Hofmann. Cutler replied in the affirmative. The colonel turned toward his men. "Ready! Right oblique! Aim!" Cutler cautioned Hofmann to verify if they were close enough to fire effectively, but his warning came a second too late. "Fire!" The rounds zipped into the color guard of the 55th North Carolina of Joe Davis's Brigade, wounding one man and killing Pvt. William W. Gray (Company A). The North Carolinians responded with a lethal volley of their own. Pennsylvanians went down by the handful. Cutler and two of his staff officers hit the ground, their horses killed beneath them.

---

passed north between McPherson's and the "second ridge" and ascended the "second ridge" on the right flank to see what was going on off his left (west).

2 Haviland to Mother; *OR* 27/1:285; *NYAG*, 2:616; Ladd & Ladd, *Bachelder Papers*, 1:205. In his official report, Capt. John E. Cook noted Major Grover urged the men to hold their fire until the enemy presented a clear target. In *New York at Gettysburg*, John Bachelder wrote that he believed Grover withheld the regiment's fire until they could definitely identify who was shooting at them. The corn, which would not be harvested until September or October, was not very high and would not have provided any appreciable cover to a line of standing men. The rows were two feet apart and did not obstruct the passage of troops or horses.

When Major Grover realized the 55th North Carolina's left wing extended beyond his own right flank, he ordered the right wing of the 76th New York, with Company B (the color company) as its anchor, to about face and wheel to face south until it formed a right angle with the left half of the regiment. Once complete, the right companies faced north. The order had barely left the major's mouth when the Tar Heels hit them with a well-aimed volley. Corporal Chapin W. Merrick (Company G) collapsed with a bullet through his brain. In Company F, Pvt. Rulandus Pitts hit the ground hard, a minié ball having shattered his right kneecap. As he lay helpless, a second round slammed into his right shoulder.[3]

The Pennsylvanians could not see the 2nd Mississippi of Davis's command ascending the western side of the creek bottom west of the Wills house. The regiment straddled the east-west farm lane running from the Wills property to the crest of Herr's Ridge, a short distance north of the Christ house. The high post and rail fence bordering both sides of the lane made it impossible for the few companies on the north side to connect with the larger part of the regiment to the south.

Colonel John M. Stone, commanding the left wing, remained mounted between the two halves. Major John A. Blair, his second-in-command, had charge of the right wing of the regiment. The regiment crossed Willoughby Run and started uphill through the orchard around the Wills house. The angle of the slope slowed the northern end of the line, meaning the right side of the regiment moved ahead of it.[4]

3 Hofmann, "The Battle"; Hofmann, "Remarks on the Battle of Gettysburg," 4; https://76nysv.us/76merrickc.html; https://76nysv.us/76pittsr.html, accessed Jan. 20, 2023; Bates, *History of Pennsylvania Volunteers*, 2:220; Clark, *Histories of the Several Regiments*, 3:297; "The Battle of Gettysburg," *The Galveston Daily News*, June 21, 1896, 9; *NYAG*, 2:616; William J. Mantanye, "Camp Correspondence – 76th Regiment N. Y. S. V.," https://dmna.ny.gov/historic/reghist/civil/infantry/76thInf/76thInfCWN.htm, accessed on Jan. 20, 2023; Weymouth T. Jordan, Jr., ed., *North Carolina Troops, 1861-1865: A Roster*, 18 vols. (Raleigh, NC, 1998), 13:444; *OR* 27/1:282, 285. All of Cutler's aides and orderlies lost their horses during the early July 1 action. It is impossible to know which staffer was with Cutler when incoming fire killed his horse. Private Gray perished in the opening minutes of the fight, which makes it likely he was one of the two men shot at this time.

4 Ladd & Ladd, *Bachelder Papers*, 3:1699; J. M. Stone to H. H. Lyman, August 29, 1888, Lyman Papers, Oswego County Historical Society, Oswego, NY; Martin, *Confederate Monuments*, 1:104-105. The regiment had only two field officers, which meant each would control a wing. From his description, Stone apparently had command of the left of the line and Maj. John A. Blair the right side.

A shell burst above the 76th New York's color company and the color guard and cut down the two color-bearers. Corporals John Stephens and William Powers (both Company H) pulled the national and state flags from the ground and raised them above the smoke. Shrapnel whacked one of Sgt. William Cahill's hands; the impact numbed his entire arm. Rather than go to the rear, the sergeant, who still carried a pistol ball between his right eye and nose from Second Bull Run, stubbornly rubbed his arm until some feeling returned and remained at his post on the right of Company B. In Company C, a minié drilled through Lt. Lucius "Lute" Davis's gloved right palm. He tied and knotted his handkerchief around his upper arm and slipped a discarded ramrod through the handkerchief knot and twisted it to stop the blood flow. Holding the end of the ramrod taut with his injured hand, he unsheathed his sword with his left hand and returned to the fight.

Nearby, Major Grover's horse buckled beneath him and threw him to the ground. While trying to stand, a bullet tore through one of his feet. Painfully wounded, he obstinately hobbled along the line supervising the fighting. The New Yorkers had successfully folded back their line under a withering hail of bullets.[5]

The 55th North Carolina poured a devastating fusillade into the New Yorkers. Captain Robert D. Everett (Company E) died immediately. Lieutenant Phillip Keller took over the company, only to have a ball shatter his leg minutes later. With no commissioned officers left, Sgt. Edgar D. Haviland assumed command. A round cut down his second in command, Sgt. Walter B. Wood. Above the din, Haviland heard someone in Company A shout that Cpl. Benjamin F. Carpenter had "bought it."The sergeant trotted along the shrinking formation to check on his friend.[6]

Colonel John K. Connally, commander of the 55th North Carolina, saw the 76th New York pull back the right of its line. Knowing that he had the Yankees in a vulnerable position, Connally hollered for his Carolinians to fix bayonets. The sound of steel snapping into place rattled up and down the line as the officers repeated the order to their companies. The moment he yelled for the line

5 https://76nysv.us/davis-double.html, accessed Jan. 20, 2023; *OR* 27/1:285; Smith, *History of the Seventy-Sixth Regiment*, 375; "From the 76th Regiment," *Cherry Valley* [NY] *Gazette*, August 19, 1863; Mantanye, "Camp Correspondence – 76th Regiment N. Y. S. V."

6 Haviland to Mother.

to charge, Color Sgt. Marlin B. Galloway (Company E) hit the ground with a leg wound. Connally yanked the flag from his hands and rushed forward, pulling the rest of the guard and the regiment with him. The flag attracted the attention of the New Yorkers and several bullets stuck Connally in the arms and one hip. Major Alfred H. Belo rushed to his aid with a couple of hospital attendants in tow. When Belo asked the colonel if he was badly hurt, the injured officer replied, "Yes, but the litter bearers are here; go on and don't let the Mississippians get ahead of you."[7]

General Wadsworth, meanwhile, fully grasped the threat to Capt. James Hall's battery and Cutler's two lead regiments. Acting quickly, he dispatched an aide toward McPherson's to bring up the 147th New York. The officer found Lieutenant Colonel Francis Miller near the farmhouse. Captain Edward D. Parker (Company C) overheard the officer tell Miller that if he did not move immediately to the ridge north of Battery B, 2nd Maine, the guns would be lost in three minutes.

Lieutenant Colonel Miller ordered his men to their feet and hustled them northwest across the Chambersburg Pike. Passing behind Hall's limbers, the New York regiment continued north in the hollow and crossed the shallow part of the railroad bed immediately east of the cut and to the right-rear of the battery. Less than 100 yards north of the track bed, the head of the column crossed the remnants of the rail fence, which Lysander Cutler's men had destroyed, and entered a new cornfield.

Companies A and F filed into the corn, which allowed the rear of the regiment to clear the cut. Once the entire command was on the north side of the grade, Miller commanded, "By the left flank; guide center!" Mostly unheard amidst the battery thundering off their left and the incessant small arms fire to their right-rear, the New York infantrymen sidled left in a twisting line as each file successively followed the one to its immediate right. Adjutant Henry H.

7 A. H. Belo, "The Battle of Gettysburg," *CV*, 8:165; Clark, *Histories of the Several Regiments*, 3:297; "The Battle of Gettysburg," 9; *OR* 27/1:283. In his report, Cutler referenced "the good conduct of all the officers and men of the brigade, with but one or two exceptions." On November 5, 1863, he wrote a letter to Gov. Andrew Curtin specifically praising the conduct of the 56th and Colonel Hofmann and citing the regiment as having fired the opening shots of the engagement, saying, in part, "I have neglected a duty which I owe to one of your regiments, the Fifty-Sixth, and its brave commander." The effusive praise he heaped upon the regiment and the colonel imply that he had forgotten "to appropriately laud the regiment and the colonel for behavior upon the field." This is the first mention of the 56th having opened the battle.

Lyman observed the maneuver from his post behind the right of Company F and took note of the regiment's ragged alignment.[8]

The New York companies had advanced about 100 yards west to a point just below the crest of the ridge when Lt. J. Volney Pierce, commanding Company G on the left of the line, spotted Confederate skirmishers bobbing up and down to fire above the tall wheat on the top of the hill. The wheat stalks nodded and rippled as the bullets zipped through them. Men fell to the ground on both sides of the lieutenant. One of the minié balls killed Cpl. Fred Rife, who Pierce described as "one of the finest men I ever saw in personal appearance, gentlemanly conduct and as a soldier." The impact hurled Rife backward onto Pvt. Hiram Stowell's corpse. Celestin Birckley also perished in the wheat. Others staggered to the rear having been wounded without the chance of responding to the enemy fire.

Skirmishers from the 42nd Mississippi stood firing along the western side of McPherson's Ridge just 70 yards from the New Yorkers. Captain Delos Gary (Company G) collapsed to one knee behind Lieutenant Pierce, bleeding from a bullet in his head. Lieutenant Colonel Miller screamed, "Lie down! Fire through the wheat close to the ground!" The relatively untried men dropped like a row of dominoes on or just below the eastern lip of the ridgeline, 40 yards to the right-rear of Hall's battery.

Farther to the right in Company E, Capt. James Coey knelt in the ripened wheat watching the Rebs casually pop up, fire, and drop to cover to reload. The forestocks of their rifles poked above the crop as they thumped them on the ground to seat the powder from their cartridges.[9]

Coey wisely went prone behind his line. The first rounds went high, threshing the wheat above the Knickerbockers' heads and blanketing them with the severed stalks. The Yankees blindly fired at ground level through the field, which appeared to force the Mississippians to go prone. Despite the slow rate of fire (perhaps one shot per minute), Coey noted casualties rapidly escalating within the ranks. Most of the head and chest wounds proved fatal.

Lieutenant Pierce's Company G held the left of line at the top of the deep part of the cut opposite Hall's guns, with Companies D and K to its right. A minié ball zipped through Company D and gouged a track through Lt. William P. Schenck from his right shoulder into his chest cavity. The lead round

8 *NYAG*, 3:1003-1004.

9 Coey, "Cutler's Brigade."

shattered his shoulder, broke his collar bone, severed two ribs, and punctured an artery. Second Lieutenant, David G. Van Dusen lay dead. With his captain and Company D's two officers down, Lieutenant Pierce found himself commanding both companies. He lay behind his men and urged them to keep shooting. About five to eight minutes had elapsed since the 147th came under fire. The Yankees blindly slammed away through the sulfuric cloud enveloping their position. Above the din Pierce could distinctly hear "Give them hell!" He twisted his head to the right to see who was yelling. Close by, the wounded Capt. Nathaniel Albert "Than" Wright (Company K) was hammering his fist onto the ground, yelling out the order.[10]

In the cornfield on the 147th's right, Companies A and F saw the right wing of the 2nd Mississippi top the ridge southwest of Wills's orchard and opened on it. The Rebels halted and emptied a volley at the Northerners. Colonel John M. Stone, below the hill, heard the racket and urged his horse up the lane. Small arms fire from the cornfield in front peppered the 2nd Mississippi's left wing. Stone dismounted and was clambering up the post and rail fence along Wills's lane when a shot plucked him off the top rail. The Confederates north of the lane continued east against the beleaguered 56th Pennsylvania, while the right of the line executed a quarter wheel south against the 147th.[11]

10:15 a.m. to 10:30 a.m.

General Wadsworth realized Cutler's three regiments could not sustain their positions and dispatched aides to order them to retire in line of battle to the town and barricade the streets. Colonel J. William Hofmann (56th Pennsylvania), whose regiment was the closest to the general, received the directive before the other commanders. Hofmann shouted for his men to quit the

10 Burns E. Parkhurst, "At Gettysburg"; Coey, "Cutler's Brigade"; *NYAG*, 3:991; Ladd & Ladd, *Bachelder Papers*, 2:911, 3:1699; https://dmna.ny.gov/application/files/1515/5310/4190/147thInfCWN1.pdf, accessed Jan. 22, 2023. In his November 1, 1882, letter to Bachelder, Pierce said he commanded Companies G and D and, in 1900, he said Companies G and C were the left companies of the regiment. I think he erred in the *NYAG* account, or it was a transcription error. I opted to use the earlier Bachelder letter because of its proximity to the event.

11 Ladd & Ladd, *Bachelder Papers*, 3:1699. Colonel Stone recollected that the regiment moved southeast before swinging south. It seems logical that in moving southeast, the Mississippians would have hit the 56th Pennsylvania then turned south to take the 147th New York in the flank as the 56th Pennsylvania left the line.

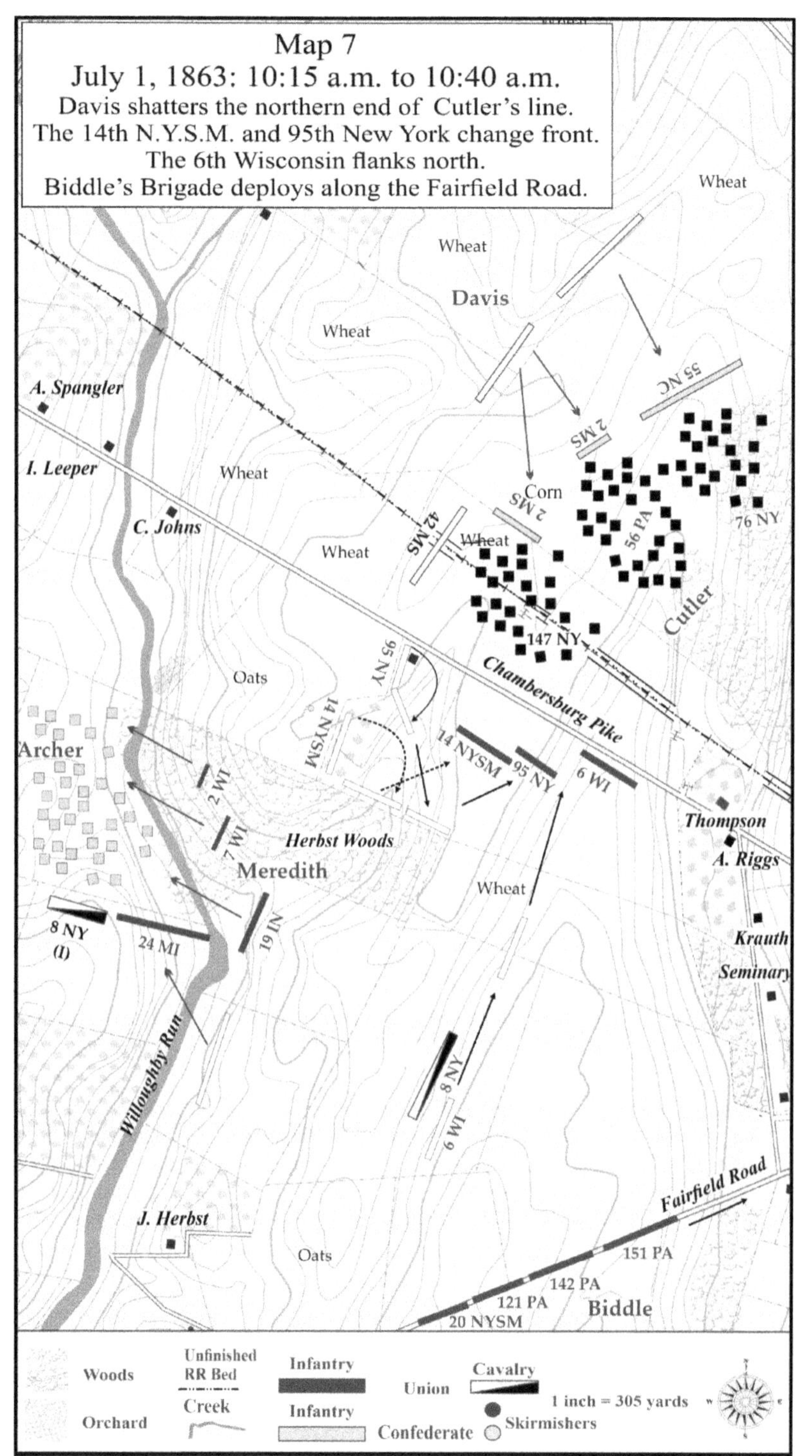
Map 7
July 1, 1863: 10:15 a.m. to 10:40 a.m.
Davis shatters the northern end of Cutler's line.
The 14th N.Y.S.M. and 95th New York change front.
The 6th Wisconsin flanks north.
Biddle's Brigade deploys along the Fairfield Road.
Wheat
Davis
55 NC
2 MS
Corn
42 MS
56 PA
76 NY
147 NY
Cutler
A. Spangler
I. Leeper
C. Johns
Oats
95 NY
14 NYSM
Chambersburg Pike
Archer
2 WI
7 WI
Herbst Woods
Meredith
19 IN
8 NY (I)
24 MI
6 WI
Thompson
A. Riggs
Krauth
Seminary
Willoughby Run
8 NY
J. Herbst
Fairfield Road
151 PA
142 PA
121 PA
20 NYSM
Biddle
Woods
Orchard
Unfinished RR Bed
Creek
Infantry
Union
Confederate
Cavalry
Skirmishers
1 inch = 305 yards

field. Mauled beyond recovery, the Pennsylvanians fled toward the woods on Oak Ridge some 50 yards behind them. Part of the 2nd Mississippi flowed into the gap and flanked the 76th New York from the south. As Maj. John A. Blair would vividly recall, "I could, I recollect, distinctly trace the line of the Union forces by the dead & wounded lying on the ground."[12]

In the 76th New York, Sgt. Edgar D. Haviland (Company E) found Cpl. Benjamin F. Carpenter (Company A) dead. He momentarily thought of rifling his friend's pockets for the $10.00 he owed him until he saw the 56th Pennsylvania heading toward the rear with the jumbled ranks of the 2nd Mississippi and 55th North Carolina close behind. The regiment was boxed in on three sides. Haviland rushed back to his company and reached it just as the order to retreat to the woods arrived. Major Andrew Grover hobbled over to Haviland and demanded he turn his weapon over to one of the enlisted men. Angered by the order, Haviland defiantly exclaimed that he wanted to fight alongside his "boys." "You must be a damned fool," the Methodist preacher hollered, "you have got your hands full now without a gun." Grover momentarily hesitated, then added, "You are a brave little devil."

The sergeant returned to his duties, not knowing he would never speak to the major again. Grover had just reached Company B when a case shot exploded overhead, indiscriminately knocking down soldiers in a leaden rain of .58-caliber balls and shards of hot jagged iron. Three of the balls slammed into the major. One struck his arm, another his leg, and the third penetrated his chest close to the heart. About the same time, a minié ball flew low into Company B and bored into Lt. A. Lyman Carter's ankle. He limped away from the line.[13]

12 Ladd & Ladd, *Bachelder Papers*, 1:205; Hofmann, "Remarks on the Battle of Gettysburg," 4; Bates, *History of Pennsylvania Volunteers*, 2:220; *Pennsylvania at Gettysburg*, 1:316; J. A. Blair to H. H. Lyman, September 6, 1888, Vertical Files, Library, GNMP; Haviland to Mother. Captain John A. Kellogg of Wadsworth's staff said the order was to barricade the streets.

13 Haviland to Mother; Richard F. Palmer, "A Newspaper Editor's View of Gettysburg," *The Crooked Lake Review*, March, 1996, www.crookedlakereview.com/articles/67_100/96march1996/96palmer.html, accessed Jan. 22, 2023; https://76nysv.us/76carteral.html, accessed Jan. 20, 2023. Carter carried the lead in his ankle until April 13, 1865, when Surgeon F. Hyde of Cortland, New York, amputated his infected leg below the knee. Palmer wrote that grapeshot hit Grover. Civil War infantry often called case shot "grape" because of the size of the .58-caliber slugs it contained. It appears all three of Grover's wounds occurred simultaneously. Captain John E. Cook (Company I) assumed command of the regiment, probably after the command rallied behind Oak Ridge.

Knowing that he was dying, Maj. Andrew Grover told the men to take his shoulder boards and pocket watch back to his wife and daughters. *New York Department of Military and Naval Affairs*

Captain Robert S. Story (Company B) crumbled under the impact of a minié ball that fragmented his thigh bone into three pieces. At the same time, a slower-moving musket ball drilled Sgt. William Cahill just below the hip. The lead hit the femur and ricocheted around it, lodging in the muscle on the opposite side. Someone pulled Cahill up from the ground and dragged him toward the relative safety of the woods on Oak Ridge. Sergeant Major Thomas Martin was not so lucky. He was left behind to slowly bleed to death from a minié ball that had passed through one arm and into his side.[14]

The mortally wounded Major Grover plaintively asked those examining him, "You will not go off and leave me, will you?"

Lieutenant Samuel E. Saunders (Company G) and three enlisted men picked up the major and lugged him toward Oak Ridge. The pain proved too much for the waning officer.

"Boys," he gasped, "it is no use carrying me farther, for I am dying."

They placed him on the ground. As Saunders knelt by his side, the major weakly told him to remove his shoulder boards and pocket watch and return them to his wife and three daughters. A burst of small arms fire buzzed through the field. One of them hit Saunders in the foot. Knowing they would be killed or captured if they remained in place, the lieutenant and enlisted men had no

14 Smith, *History of the Seventy-Sixth Regiment*, 353, 368, 372, 375; "Diary of Lieutenant Samuel E. Sanders," Cortland Historical Society, Cortland, NY, http://www.76nysv.us/76Saundersse.html, accessed Jan. 20, 2023; "From the 76th Regiment."

choice but to heed the major's instructions and race for the safety of the woods behind them.[15]

Back near the battle line, meanwhile, Company G was taking a beating. Sergeant Henry Cliff writhed on the ground with a shattered knee cap. Nearby lay Cpl. John L. Seeber, shot through the bowels. Corporal Franklin L. Gay also collapsed wounded. His messmate, Pvt. Charles W. Cook, immediately stooped to help him when a second round cracked into Gay's skull. Cook, realizing the regiment had already left the field, abandoned Gay and fled. With the young corn stalks snatching at his trouser legs and minié balls singing about his ears, he ignored enemy calls to "Halt, you Yank!"

Cook raced toward a cordwood stack on the top of the hill. He reached the ridge line and scurried around to the "safe" side of the woodpile, where he found Pvt. Charley Hills. When he asked Hills if he knew where the rest of the regiment was, the private pointed south along the ridge. "Yes. What is left of them are down there in the wood." The pair headed in that direction, where they found the wounded Lieutenant Saunders, unable to walk on his injured foot. The pair pulled him up and helped him down the east side of Oak Ridge toward the distant town.[16]

A few minutes after the 147th New York went prone, Wadsworth's aide reached Lt. Col. Francis C. Miller, shouted the order to withdraw, and galloped away. Simultaneously, Lt. J. Volney Pierce (Company G), who was lying behind the line between Sgts. Peter Shutts and Byron D. Parkhurst, glanced to the right and saw Miller catch a bullet in the skull. Knocked senseless, the colonel involuntarily tugged on the reins as he reeled in the saddle. His horse responded by careening to the rear with him still mounted. His second in

15 Smith, *History of the Seventy-Sixth Regiment*, 353, 368, 372, 375; "Diary of Lieutenant Samuel E. Sanders"; "From the 76th Regiment"; Palmer, "A Newspaper Editor's View of Gettysburg."

16 Cook, "A Day at Gettysburg"; C. W. Cook, "Who Opened Gettysburg"; Lt. and Acting Adjutant, C. A. Watkins, 76th New York to Editor of the *Herald*, July 21, 1863, http://museum.dmna.ny.gov/unit-history/infantry-1/76th-infantry-regiment/newspaper-clippings, accessed Jan. 22, 2023; *NYAG*, 2:616; *OR* 27/1:285. Cook indicated that the regiment broke under the Confederate attack. Bachelder claimed General Wadsworth had ordered the retreat, while Watkins wrote that Cutler did so. Captain John E. Cook, commanding the regiment after Grover's fall, also claimed the regiment held until Cutler commanded it to retreat. Private Cook's account sounds the most accurate given the smoke and confusion on the field. Cook spelled Seeber's name as "Scribner." The roster spelled it "Seaber."

command, Maj. George Harney, never heard the order to fall back and kept the regiment on the field.[17]

The fire slackened along the regiment's front. On his own initiative, Lieutenant Pierce ordered Companies G and D to their feet and advanced them cautiously the top of the ridge. He noted the twisted corpses of several Mississippians lying in the wheat on the hillside below them. Just west of the rail fence on the south side of the railroad bed, he spied a line of the 42nd Mississippi's skirmishers methodically inching uphill through the wheat toward Hall's guns.[18]

The grain field made it nearly impossible for Hall's artillerists (Battery B, 2nd Maine) to take out the attackers. A squad managed to ensconce itself near a fence corner to Hall's right front, directly opposite Pierce's two companies of the 147th New York. Simultaneously, around 40 more Mississippians disappeared into the railroad cut. Under its cover and masked by the thick smoke of Hall's guns, they flanked Lt. William N. Ulmer's right section. Climbing out of the 10-foot cut, they stood and, unnoticed, slipped in for the kill.

Ulmer spotted the threat through the smoke enveloping his guns. The Rebs were going to charge, he yelled. His men wheeled their pieces by hand to the right and loaded double canister. Sergeant Charles E. Stubbs was supervising his gun's placement when he heard the peculiar firecracker "snaps" of two exploding bullets bursting over his head. He instinctively faced toward the direction from which they came and spotted two Southerners wearing yellow slickers under the apple tree on his right flank. Passing themselves off as Yankees, they yelled at the artillerists to hold their fire.

In the meantime, Lt. Benjamin F. Carr, commanding the center section, raced over to Captain Hall and shouted that the Rebels had gotten within 20 yards of Ulmer's guns. Hall spurred to the right just as Ulmer turned his pieces and spotted a line of Mississippians leveling their weapons at his battery. He barked at Carr to change front by the oblique and load with double canister. The

17 "Private letter from an officer in the 147th About Gettysburg"; *Oswego Commercial Times*, not dated; http://dmna.ny.gov/historic/reghist/civil/infantry/147thInf/147thInf CWN1.pdf, accessed Jan. 22, 2023; *NYAG*, 3:991; Ladd & Ladd, *Bachelder Papers*, 3:1567.

18 "Private letter from an officer"; *NYAG*, 3:991; Ladd & Ladd, *Bachelder Papers*, 1:331 and 2:911. Pierce does not mention the fire slackening along the front of the regiment in his letter to the *Commercial Times* or his letter to Bachelder, November 1, 1882.

3-inch Ordnance Rifles cracked, their tubes rocking up and down on the trunnions as the pieces recoiled. The Mississippians scattered. Many leaped into the cut. From there, they methodically popped off rounds through the stifling smoke at the artillerists and their horses. Once again, Sergeant Stubbs heard exploding bullets "snap" around him.[19]

The 40 or so Confederates who slipped into the cut started pouring a fusillade into the Mainers. Lieutenant Pierce (147th New York) shouted at his "boys" to "Left oblique, fire!" into the Rebs on Hall's flank. The infantrymen stood up, rapidly loosed shots at the skirmishers, then hit the ground. The lieutenant remained on his feet to observe what was going on so he could direct his men's fire. With canister from the south pocking up the ground, the Rebs faced north and fired into Pierce's two companies, forcing them to retire to the main line.

Captain James Hall peered through the acrid sulfuric cloud engulfing his guns and spied Pierce and his two companies slipping back to the smoke-clogged regimental line. Hall erroneously believed the entire regiment was abandoning him. During the few seconds lost in deciding upon his next course of action, the noisome Mississippians, having forced Pierce to retire, fired once more at his artillerists and their horses as they sidled under the cover of the cut toward his right flank. Hall now had no choice but to abandon his position and save what men and guns he could.

He returned to the right of his battery and screamed at Lt. William N. Ulmer to retire his pieces by hand down to the section's limbers, move to the middle ridge (about 250 yards south), and enfilade the enemy in the narrow confines of the cut. "My idea," Hall later recalled, "was to get those two guns to safety . . . and perhaps by their aid save the other four." Ulmer responded immediately. From atop his horse, Hall observed the withdrawal and noted the lieutenant "went back handsomely."[20]

The prone Federals in the 147th New York, meanwhile, blindly cracked away at the fence along their front. Lieutenant Pierce snatched up a capped rifle from the several discarded weapons lying about. The cap snapped but the

19 *Maine at Gettysburg*, 17; Ladd & Ladd, *Bachelder Papers*, 1:24, 386, and 2:892. Despite postwar denials of using exploding bullets, Union soldiers at Antietam and Gettysburg reported being on their receiving end and recorded casualties.

20 Ladd & Ladd, *Bachelder Papers*, 1:386; *Maine at Gettysburg*, 18; *OR* 27/1:359. In his after-action report, Hall said he ordered Ulmer's section back 75 yards, which he amended in his letter to Bachelder.

weapon did not discharge. He took up a second rifle, drew a bead on a "strapping reb" as he jumped up and bolted away from the fence, and pulled the trigger—but nothing happened. "Jonny Reb got off with a whole skin," he lamented in a letter home.[21]

Time seemed to stand still for the hard-pressed Yankees. The dismounted Maj. George Harney stayed close to the 147th's line. With rounds zipping in from his right and right front, he recalled Companies A and F from the cornfield to the north. The companies scrambled over the fence running perpendicular to their line and took shelter behind it. From his post on the left of the line near the cut, Lieutenant Pierce watched the men form at right angles to the rest of the regiment. Captain James Coey (Company E), being closer to that part of the line, vividly recalled them shooting the 2nd Mississippi to a standstill. The Southerners along his front sporadically peeped above the wheat, cracked off shots, then took cover behind the crest. According to Coey, many of his dead or wounded lying along the crest of the ridge amidst the wheat had been been shot in the head or the upper body.[22]

Pierce and Adj. Henry H. Lyman watched in disbelief as Ulmer's guns rumbled along the south side of the railroad cut, heading east past the 147th's left flank. Meanwhile, Hall's remaining four pieces continued belching canister at the Rebels off their right flank. In the smoke and confusion, the two officers mistakenly assumed the entire battery had withdrawn.[23]

While his men of the 55th North Carolina surged ahead of him and over the 76th New York's casualties, Maj. Alfred H. Belo knelt alongside one of the wounded Yankees and asked him who commanded the men they had just repulsed. "We are Joe Hooker's men," the soldier winced, "and we have marched five miles this morning." Belo quickly informed one of his officers that their enemies were Army of the Potomac men, and not militia.

The North Carolinians lost some time gathering prisoners and reorganizing their ranks. Private John W. Cannon (Company E) impressively bagged 11 Yankees all by himself. The brief action had cost the New Yorkers and Pennsylvanians around 57% of their effective strength. Although they felled a considerable number of the Tar Heels, the Union troops had by far gotten the worst end of the bloody bargain. Nevertheless, the attack disorganized the

21 "Private letter from an officer."

22 Ladd & Ladd, *Bachelder Papers*, 2:911; Coey, "Cutler's Brigade."

23 Ladd & Ladd, *Bachelder Papers*, 1:332.

Mississippians and North Carolinians and forced them to halt, realign, and take stock of the field.[24]

The longer Major Harney kept the 147th New York in its untenable position, the more casualties it incurred. Turning southeast toward the railroad cut in the ridge behind them, Coey spied Rebel skirmishers swarming around one of Lieutenant Ulmer's guns. To the east was a mounted officer on the north bank of the cut behind the Rebs. It was Lt. Homer Chisman of Cutler's staff, spurring his horse in a tight circle while waving his cap to and fro, signaling the 147th to abandon its position. Coey knew what he was trying to communicate, and that it was suicidal for that officer to try and cross the field to deliver it in person.[25]

Middle Railroad Cut

Lieutenant Ulmer, having unlimbered both of his rifles on the south side of the deep railroad cut on the middle ridge, found himself caught in a metal maelstrom. Confederate skirmishers on his immediate right deliberately shot down the four horses remaining on the right limber. Rather than remain in place and be killed or wounded, the other crewmen limbered the left piece and made for the Thompson place. The artillerists on the disabled limber turned the gun about to face east, with one man holding up the trail while the other four rolled it off the field by hand. A spattering of small arms fire dropped all of them before they got too far.

Captain Hall witnessed the carnage and knew he would have to retire the rest of the battery unsupported—a difficult proposition at best. He instructed Lieutenants Carr and Thomas to fire their pieces as fast as they could to create an impenetrable cloud of smoke to mask their retreat. With the guns cracking behind him, Hall slipped down the reverse slope to the limbers and ordered the horseholders to reverse them to face east. When he returned to the crest, he instructed his embattled artillerists to roll the heavy guns, by piece, in

24 Busey & Martin, *Regimental Strengths and Losses*, 125; Jordan, *North Carolina Troops*, 13:477. Private Cannon received official recognition for his capturing prowess that day.

25 Coey, "Cutler's Brigade"; Ladd & Ladd, *Bachelder Papers*, 2:912; *NYAG*, 3:992. Lieutenant Pierce saw the officer but recollected that he rode toward them and waved his sword for the men to retreat.

succession, down the slope to their limbers and then evacuate the field as quickly as possible.[26]

While all this was transpiring, Lieutenant Pierce on the left of the 147th New York spotted an ominous sight through the veil of lingering smoke: the right wing of the 2nd Mississippi was climbing over a fence into the 147th's right rear. The precision with which it reformed under the direction of the officer in front of the colors momentarily mesmerized Pierce. The clatter of hooves snapped him back to the present. Captain Timothy E. Ellsworth, Wadsworth's adjutant-general, spurred across the bullet-swept low ground in the railroad cut, pulled up next to Major Harney, and shouted an order for the New Yorkers to retreat. Once his task was done, the captain reined his horse about and set spurs back toward Seminary Ridge.[27]

Harney had already seen two regiments to his right-rear retire. He hailed several of the officers within shouting distance for a quick conference. Captain James Coey distinctly heard the major offer them two choices: surrender or fall back like the 56th Pennsylvania and the 76th New York. To the man, they opted to withdraw rather than end up in Rebel prisons. Harney sent the order along the line for the men to cast aside everything but their rifles and cartridge boxes. When the order to retreat was announced, they were to stand, volley, and hit the

26 *OR* 27/1:359; Ladd & Ladd, *Bachelder Papers*, 1:386, 387; Calef, "Gettysburg Notes," 40:50; *Maine at Gettysburg*, 18. Later that morning, Lieutenant Calef recalled the dead and wounded gunners heaped around a gun. An account in *Maine at Gettysburg*, in a reference to Ulmer's abandoned piece, noted: "One gun was dragged off by hand, all the horses attached to it having been shot." In his December 29, 1869, letter to John Bachelder, Hall wrote, "I had but *three guns* [emphasis mine], the horses of one of Ulmer's all being dead, was moving [to] the rear hitched to a caisson, one was still upon the field [he is referring to the one with the dead horses on the fence along the Chambersburg Pike] and a third had been struck by a solid shot while returning [to the rear], and one wheel broken from [the] carriage, and it was going to the rear on one wheel." In his *OR* report, Calef merely wrote: "The men of the section dragged this gun off by hand," and that a caisson hauled the same piece away. It would have taken some time to get to the seminary to bring up the caisson, and this had to have happened after the 6th Wisconsin captured the railroad cut because no one noted a caisson in the road. The same applies to the gun with the broken wheel. Once Calef returned to the field, after the cut had been captured, he recalled, "Here was one gun of Hall's with all the horses dead in the harnesses [the one with the horses dead across the fence rails]. Another unlimbered and pointing toward our own line, left in that position by the cannoneers, who lay dead or dying beside it [Ulmer's abandoned piece]. Still another [the one with the broken wheel] with the cannoneers [volunteers of the 6th Wisconsin] making Herculean efforts to get it off the field, which was thickly strewn with the dead and dying infantrymen of Cutler's brigade."

27 *NYAG*, 3:992; Ladd & Ladd, *Bachelder Papers*, 1:331 and 3:1567.

ground to let the Rebel counterfire pass over their heads. While the Confederates reloaded, the New Yorkers were to stoop low and head to the rear at trail arms until they could independently turn and fire at will. The regiment was to close on center and rally around the colors at the tree line along Oak Ridge, which they could see through the haze on the field.[28]

Elements of the 42nd Mississippi crested the hill not 50 yards away from the prone New Yorkers. Private Andrew Park (Company I) was admiring the finest wheat field he had ever seen when "In retreat, March!" echoed along the front. Most of the Federals rose on one knee and let go a ragged volley. For the most part the shots went high. A few struck the Mississippians, who almost immediately returned fire. Captain Coey recalled the rushing sound the massive sheet of lead made in passing so close over his soldiers' heads. They could almost feel the wakes of the zipping bullets. According to plan, the infantrymen leaped to their feet. What they did not expect was that the Confederates had a second line loaded and waiting. The volley ripped into the surprised Federals. Their astonished officers behind the line helplessly watched the front "melt away," their men collapsing where they stood. Then the Rebels charged.[29]

The regiment broke and streamed toward the rear, leaving 42 dead and dying in the crushed bloodied wheat. Swedish-born Color Sgt. John Hinchcliff (Company K) about faced with the colors when a wave of lead struck him from behind. One of the bullets pierced his heart and he collapsed on top of the shattered flag staff and the shredded colors. Major Harney had turned about to observe the retreat when noticed the flag had gone down. He started moving toward it when Sgt. William A. Wybourn (Company I), who had not received the word to ditch his knapsack, volunteered to bring it off and raced back to Hinchcliff. Rolling his body off the flag, Wybourn ripped the riddled ensign from its staff, gathered it in his arms, and headed toward the railroad cut.[30]

On the left, Lieutenant Pierce turned to retreat with his men when he stumbled upon the mortally wounded Sgt. Edwin G. Aylsworth, whose pleas to

28 Coey, "Cutler's Brigade"; Ladd & Ladd, *Bachelder Papers*, 2:911; *NYAG*, 3:992. Lieutenant J. Volney Pierce, on the left of the line with Companies G and D, was not in that group of officers. He never heard the order.

29 Coey, "Cutler's Brigade"; *NYAG*, 3:992; A. Park, "Some of My Recollections of the Battle of Gettysburg," January 16, 1899, 1, Tom Elmore Collection.

30 Coey, "Cutler's Brigade"; *NYAG*, 3:991; Ladd & Ladd, *Bachelder Papers*, 3:1568. The next day Surgeon Algernon S. Coe, who was a prisoner at that point, walked the line and counted the bodies.

not be left on the field stopped Pierce in his tracks. He called over Sgt. Peter Shutts and the two struggled to get Aylsworth upright. When they tried to pick him up, Pierce could not lift him. They lowered the sergeant to the ground and headed toward the railroad cut, his gut-wrenching cries of "Don't leave me, boys!" rending the air around them. The memory still haunted Pierce 25 years later.[31]

To the north, disorganized squads of the147th New York halted, turned about, and loosed a sputtering fire in the direction of the 42nd Mississippi. The 55th North Carolina, with the 2nd Mississippi off the 147th's northern flank, quickly responded in kind. Yankee morale evaporated and they ran for the safety of the woods on Oak Ridge. The Tar Heels and Mississippians, now little more than a tangled mob, were close on their heels. Captain Coey swore that some of them hurled camp hatchets at he and his men. "In getting off the field," Adj. Henry Harrison Lyman recollected, "no order was observed." The New Yorkers left many of their comrades wounded or dying on the top of the ridge.[32]

James Hall and his four limbered pieces ran a hellish gauntlet of small arms and artillery fire. Near the low field immediately west of the Thompson orchard, a solid shot "whooshed" in on one of the pieces, breaking a wheel from the gun carriage. The piece dropped onto its lone axle, bringing the limber to a jarring halt. The artillerymen running alongside quickly manhandled the trail free of the pintle hook and rode on with their limber.[33]

Hall had led his remaining three guns into a tight spot. He noticed a section of fence down along the road in the southeast corner of the field, formed his teams into column, and made for the opening. Time seemed to stand still as the two lead pieces and the freed limber threaded their way through the opening into the Chambersburg Pike. Demoralized Union infantry thronged the area in a panic, followed closely by Davis's Confederate skirmishers, who halted to shoot the artillerists in the back. One shot hammered Hall's mount in the rump.

The Rebel skirmishers swarmed the lead pair of the fourth limber as it entered the passage into the pike. The horse holders leaped from their saddles and outran the frenzied Southerners, who mercilessly bayoneted the two front animals. The horses collapsed in place, their corpses lodged against the fence

31 *NYAG*, 3:992. Sgt. Edwin G. Aylsworth lingered for nine days before finally dying on July 10, 1863.

32 Coey, "Cutler's Brigade."

33 My interpretation of this event is based on accounts from the 6th Wisconsin.

posts. The skirmishers proceeded to slaughter the remaining four horses. "The enemy got so thick it was hard to tell which outnumbered, gray or blue," Hall recollected. Rather than face annihilation, he ordered his remaining pieces toward the safety of Seminary Ridge.[34]

The disorganized 2nd Mississippi and 55th North Carolina, which were not too far behind the skirmishers, topped the hill heading directly toward Sheads Woods. Color Corporal William B. Murphy, who was in advance of the line with the color guard, noticed what he thought was Yankee cavalry on the edge of the woods preparing to charge. Soon after he hollered back a warning to the regiment, a ragged volley drove the Yankees away.[35]

The Mississippians and Tar Heels crested the middle ridge in pursuit of Cutler's broken regiments about the same time that General Buford and his staff reached the western face of Sheads Woods to survey the situation. The small arms fire from the ridge spattered the trees around the mounted officers and sent them down the wagon track that cut east to west through the woods to the shelter on the opposite side. Buford immediately dispatched an aide to the seminary to fetch one of Calef's guns to stabilize the line, sweep the railroad cut, and drive out the skirmishers of the 42nd Mississippi harassing Hall's retreating battery. The staffer interrupted Calef's transfer of ammunition from the caissons to his remaining limbers. The embattled artillerist immediately dispatched Lt. John W. Roder and his right gun. The men swung into their saddles and took off to aid Buford.[36]

Farther to the west and unaware of anything beyond their immediate line of sight, Lt. J. Volney Pierce (Company G) and Sgt. William A. Wybourn (Company I), both of the 147th New York, jumped into the track bed and met a

34 Ladd & Ladd, *Bachelder Papers*, 1:386-387; *OR* 27/1:359; William B. Murphy to Dr. F. A. Dearborn, June 29, 1900, E. S. Bragg Papers, Box 1, #546, State Historical Society of Wisconsin, Madison, WI. Hall's letter to Bachelder letter mentions that the horses died by the bayonet. The after-action report does not specify how they perished.

35 Murphy to Dearborn; Smith, *History of the Seventy-Sixth Regiment*, 240. No one reported seeing cavalry in the area except William B. Murphy (2nd Mississippi).

36 Calef, "Gettysburg Notes," 40:49; *OR* 27/1:1031. Calef said Buford wanted to drive riflemen out of the cut by enfilading it. An artillery piece posted to fire down the length of the cut could have inflicted heavy casualties. Murphy said the piece was in front of the woods, which places it north of the cut. The trail through the woods would have provided the easiest access. According to Calef, the Rebs were blown away at the muzzle, and the 6th Wisconsin attacked the cut right after it fired. The gun forced the Confederates to change front and wheel into the cut and the 6th Wisconsin responded to that movement.

hail of small arms fire from the right flank: a Rebel squad had barricaded the cut. He and Wybourn clawed their way onto the southern bank and made tracks toward the Chambersburg Pike. They crossed the road with the sergeant in the lead and headed toward Alexander Riggs's peach orchard, immediately south of Mary Thompson's place. Wybourn had just reached the trees when a minié ball passed through his knapsack and knocked him face first to the ground. Supposing that Wybourn was dead, Pierce dropped by his side and tried to pull the riddled flag from his hands. The sergeant tugged back. "Hold on," Wybourn growled, "I will be up in a minute." The stunned lieutenant watched the stubborn Irishman roll over onto his side and painfully regain his feet. The two stumbled to the north side of the road, looking for their regiment.[37]

Seeing an opportunity to cut down as many Federals as possible, Col. Hugh R. Miller split the right wing of the 42nd Mississippi and ordered both parts to flank the cut and fire by the oblique from the north and south into the fleeing soldiers. According to Private Park (Company I), "I think there never was such slaughter as we made on this occasion." In some places the bodies of the dead and wounded lay three deep, and Park swore he could have walked three quarters of a mile down the track bed without touching the ground. The Mississippians took casualties, among them Pvt. Tom Looney (Company I), who had asked to be excused from duty when the regiment arrived on the field. A bullet snapped his left arm above the elbow.[38]

Meanwhile, Major Harney had rallied a company-size group of survivors from the 147th New York along the north side of the Chambersburg Pike. One of them, Sgt. Sidney G. Cooke (Company E), looked about and assumed the colors had not been carried off the field. General Cutler, who was feverishly attempting to rally the rest of his shattered brigade, also noted their absence and dashed up to Major Harney: "You have lost your colors, sir," he reprimanded.

The Irish major, who had seen Wybourn and Pierce approaching from the south, snapped back, "General, the 147th never loses its colors."

Cutler spotted toward the pair with the banner and immediately corrected himself. "Boys, I'll take it all back. It's just like cock-fighting to-day. We fight a little and run a little. There are no supports."[39]

37 *NYAG*, 3:992, 993.

38 Park, "Some Of My Recollections," 1.

39 Sidney G. Cooke, "The First Day at Gettysburg," *War Talks in Kansas*, 280.

Chapter Six

"Go like hell! It looks as though they are driving Cutler."

— Capt. James D. Wood, acting adjutant general to Doubleday

The Railroad Cut

10:15 a.m. to 11:00 a.m.

10:15 a.m. – 10:30 a.m.
The Chambersburg Pike on the Crest of Seminary Ridge

An artillerist with a crippled command and an embattled infantry division commander had an interesting encounter during the retreat toward the seminary.

It was during the move east that Captain Hall confronted Brig. Gen. James Wadsworth with an angry accusation: "It was cowardly to leave me as they [the infantry] did."

Wadsworth ignored the charge and instead replied, "Get your guns back to some point to cover the retiring of these troops."

Hall understood he was out of line and that there was still a lot of fighting left to do. "This, General, is that place right here in the road," he gestured.

"Oh, no," a discouraged Wadsworth retorted, "go beyond the town for we cannot hold this line." When Hall informed the general that his stranded gun (with the dead horses) was in danger of being captured and that he needed time to save it, the embattled Wadsworth lost his temper. "Lose no time in getting your guns in position to cover the retreat."

Convinced that he had lost the field, Wadsworth also directed General Cutler to salvage what he could of his brigade and fall back to Gettysburg and barricade the streets. He next trotted to the seminary, where he found Calef's artillerists transferring ammunition from the caissons to the limbers. The general personally directed him to take his remaining guns to the south side of the middle cut near where Ulmer's abandoned piece from Battery B, 2nd Maine, remained on the field.[1]

The Vicinity of Herbst Woods, South of the Chambersburg Pike

Looking north, Doubleday spied a strong Confederate force (Joe Davis's Brigade) tearing into Cutler's isolated regiments. Sensing that they were about to collapse, he snapped at his aide-de-camp, Lt. Meredith L. Jones, to bring up the 6th Wisconsin with the added directive to "move to the right." Doubleday dispatched another aide north to swing the 14th Brooklyn and the 95th New York to face parallel to the railroad cut. General Meredith also noticed the dilemma and dispatched acting adjutant general Captain James D. Wood with instructions for the Badgers of the 6th to "go like hell" because it looked like Cutler was being driven from the battlefield.[2]

Lieutenant Jones reined in alongside Rufus Dawes and tersely exclaimed, "General Doubleday directs that you move at once to the right." Dawes swung into the saddle. Jones wheeled about and headed toward Doubleday while

1 Ladd & Ladd, *Bachelder Papers*, 1:205, 387; *OR* 27/1:1031; Calef, "Gettysburg Notes," 49. I added the emphasis to Hall's statement and corrected Wadsworth's command from "Loose no time" to "lose no time." Captain John Kellogg of Cutler's staff claimed the brigade was ordered to fall back.

2 Ladd & Ladd, *Bachelder Papers*, 1:323; Dawes, "Align on the Colors"; Dawes, *Service with the Sixth Wisconsin*, 166; Halstead, "The First Day of the Battle of Gettysburg," *A Paper*, 1:5. Only in his regimental history did Dawes write that Lt. Meredith Jones delivered the order. In his previous writings, Dawes identified the officer as Benjamin Marten. Thus, *Sketches of War History* and *Service With the Sixth Wisconsin*, both published in 1890, contradict one another on this point. In "Align on the Colors," Dawes again cited the officer as Marten. Dawes and his wife, both meticulous researchers, would not have deliberately made such an error. Dawes's "With the Sixth Wisconsin" was published in *Sketches of War History* in January 1890. On November 10, 1890, Dawes penned the preface to his regimental history prior its publication before the end of that year. Apparently, it was during that time Dawes corrected the recollection , (which dates from March 18, 1868) so as to give the credit to Jones. Halstead noted that Dawes's attack occurred "very soon" after Doubleday met captured General James Archer.

Dawes shouted his men to their feet. They had hardly fallen in when Captain Wood unexpectedly skidded up to Dawes, yelling, "Go like hell! It looks as though they are driving Cutler!" The colonel faced the regiment by the right flank and set the column off at the double quick toward the Chambersburg Pike. Doubleday, seeing the Wisconsin men move out, probably spurred his horse toward the lane south of the seminary to watch for the rest of the I Corps to come up.

Immediately west of the seminary and some 80 rods south of the Chambersburg Pike, Dawes observed Cutler's brigade streaming southeast over the first ridge west of Sheads Woods and toward the low ground west of the Thompson place. Dawes simultaneously caught a glimpse of Hall's four guns in the distance on the northern side of the road, thundering east toward the same place. In all the mayhem, he never saw the Confederate skirmishers killing Hall's horses. Sergeant George Fairfield (Company C), however, clearly noticed the Rebs coming out of the low part of the cut into the field north of the road. They were, he recalled, "about to capture some of our artillery."[3]

Davis's Brigade distracted Dawes's attention as it emerged through the veil of low-hanging smoke on the middle ridge. He noted the enemy's advantage in numbers and sensed the threat they posed to the division. By then, Major Blair of the 2nd Mississippi, the only field officer in sight for the Rebels, found himself trying to control what was little more than a mob. He halted those men he could and asked them what to do next. As Blair would later put it, they decided to "capture Gettysburg."[4]

The Mississippians spotted John Roder's Union artillery piece rattle into position and unlimber. The Magnolia State soldiers cut loose with what one account claimed was a "deadly fire" and charged. The rifle fire slammed into Roder's gun just as the chief of piece, Cpl. Robert S. Watrous, pulled a double round of canister from the limber while the "Number two" man, Pvt. Thomas

3 Dawes, *Service With the Sixth Wisconsin*, 166; Ladd & Ladd, *Bachelder Papers*, 1:323; George Fairfield, "The Capture of the Railroad Cut," *NT*, September 1, 1910, 3; *Maine at Gettysburg*, 20. Dawes's exact words in his 1868 letter to Bachelder, as transcribed, read, "'go like hell' for it looked as though they were driving Cutler." It is difficult to ascertain where the right of Dawes's line would have been in relation to the deep end of the middle railroad cut. In line, his regiment would have taken up about 320 feet of frontage. Dawes wrote that the brigade guard detachment on his right hauled off Hall's gun. Captain Hall claimed that the piece was disabled while retiring beyond the second ridge, which places it in the low ground along the Chambersburg Pike.

4 Ladd & Ladd, *Bachelder Papers*, 1:323; Blair to Lyman.

Joseph Davis performed reasonably well during the early portion of the fighting on July 1 because he had capable regimental leadership. Unfortunately for President Davis's nephew, he lost control of his trio of regiments on the field, and the terrain sealed his fate. *LOC*

Slattery, shoved the powder bag down the bore. A minié ball shattered Watrous's leg and knocked him down. Slattery recovered the cans from Watrous and pushed them down the gun's muzzle. "Number one" rammed the cans home. The artillerists heard the Rebs scream, "There is a piece—let's take it!" as another Union gunner yanked the lanyard. The Ordnance Rifle bucked up and back in violent recoil.

The whizzing canister rounds flew high and inflicted minimal casualties on the Mississippians. The windy roar of the flying lead balls did, however, send them scrambling back as fast as they could move into the line reorganizing on the ridge behind them. Somehow amidst all the confusion Major Belo (55th North Carolina) spied the 6th Wisconsin rushing in column perpendicular to his line.[5]

Dawes placed himself at the head of the 6th Wisconsin, at the point where he wanted his command to turn. "Head of column to the right!" he yelled. An enlisted man acting as a guide rushed forward to direct the line of advance. Dawes latched his eyes on a group of officers along the south side of the Chambersburg Road carrying a dead general officer off the field on a stretcher.

5 Murphy to Dearborn; *OR* 27/1:1031; Calef, "Gettysburg Notes," 40:49; Belo, "The Battle of Gettysburg," 165. Calef's postwar account implies that Rebels were cut down close to the muzzle, but neither Confederate accounts nor casualty returns indicate any damage from artillery fire. More than likely the Mississippians fired at the gun crew and then maneuvered. In their haste, the gunners may have sighted the piece incorrectly and missed their target, or they fired high. Murphy's account has the 6th Wisconsin coming out of woods on his right, but there were no woods off his right. He likely mixed up the sequence of the action.

(He had no way of knowing it was General Reynolds.) When Dawes's mare reared and dropped her head, he instinctively pulled hard on the reins to bring her head up and also jabbed his spurs into her. She dropped onto her rump, hurling him to the ground. The officer struggled to his feet with the cheers of some of his men echoing in his ears. The horse regained her feet and limped away on three legs, badly wounded from a ball in the chest.[6]

While the column ran parallel to the Chambersburg Pike, Dawes belted out the command to face by the left flank into line and double-quick to the rail fence. The line peeled off by files to the left. The right wing (Companies B, E, K, C, G, and Lt. Levi Showalter's half of the brigade guard) quickly destroyed the rotten fence on their end of the formation and slammed into the new worm fence on the opposite side. Unable to climb it, they halted while the rest of the regiment, to their left rear, stalled along the sturdier section of the post and rail fence. Sergeant "Mickey" Sullivan of Company K vividly recalled waiting in the road for the rest of the line to assemble alongside. Dawes bellowed as loud as he could to fire by files from the right.[7]

Farther to the left, Lt. Loyd Grayson Harris, commanding the left half of the brigade guard, noticed the colors moving through the veil of black powder smoke hovering over the field. In bringing his company to the left of the line, he passed by the right flank of the immobile 95th New York. He momentarily slipped away from his men to run over in front of the 95th's right wing. "For

6 Dawes, "With the Sixth Wisconsin," 166-167. The minié ball had passed through the horse's chest, 17 inches into her left shoulder, and remained lodged just under the skin behind the shoulder blade. According to Dawes, the injury ruined her disposition: "[W]oe to the man who felt it, as her temper had been entirely spoiled."

7 Dawes, "With the Sixth Wisconsin," 166-167; Hardee, *Rifle and Light Infantry Tactics*, 55; Ladd & Ladd, *Bachelder Papers*, 1:323-324; Fairfield, "The Capture at the Railroad Cut"; William J. K. Beaudot and Lance J. Herdegen, *An Irishman In The Iron Brigade: The Civil War Memoirs Of James P. Sullivan, Sergt., Company K, 6th Wisconsin Volunteers* (New York, 1993), 94; Sullivan, "The Charge of the Iron Brigade at Gettysburg"; Dawes, "Align on the Colors"; Albert V. Young, *Milwaukee Sunday Telegraph*, April 22, 1888, as cited in Herdegen & Beaudot, *In The Bloody Railroad Cut*. Sullivan's two accounts are almost identical. Unless otherwise noted, I use the *Mauston Star* account. Dawes, in his *Service With The Sixth Wisconsin*, wrote: "The regiment halted at the fence along the Cashtown Turnpike and I gave the order to fire." According to Sgt. George Fairfield (Co. C), Cpl. S. Frank Gordon (Co. K), and Cpl. Albert V. Young (Co. E), from the colors to the left of Company G (the right company of the regiment), the fence on the south side of the road in front of the right wing was in disrepair. In "Align on the Colors," Dawes wrote that he did not remember that fence and that Cpl. Samuel F. "Frank" Gordon (Company K) told him later that his company tore it down.

God's sake," Harris accosted them, "why don't you move forward and join our left?" None of the New Yorkers responded to his plea. Frustrated, Harris hurried back to his part of the brigade guard and left the New Yorkers where they stood.[8]

Corporal William B. Murphy (Company A, 2nd Mississippi) watched Cutler's broken regiments reform inside Sheads's wood line. Simultaneously, Major Belo conferred with Major Blair (2nd Mississippi) to decide their course of action. Nearl\y four decades later, Belo explained his decision to charge the 6th Wisconsin. "I was so impressed with the fact that the side charging first would hold the field that I suggested to Major Blair that we should charge them before they had their formation completed." Blair yelled above the din for those who could hear to move "right into line."[9]

The change of front destroyed any remnants of organized regimental formations. "All the men were jumbled together without regard to Regt. or Company," Blair wrote in 1888. "The 2nd & 42nd & probably the 55th North Carolina were one mass of men." The right wing of the 55th North Carolina overlapped and intermingled with the left wing of the 2nd Mississippi, leaving the left of its line extended beyond the Mississippians' left. The west end of the line stumbled into the deep part of the cut. "It was therefore, a great surprise to us," Blair recalled with considerable understatement. The left ended up in the shallow eastern part of the excavation, which was only a few feet deep. Companies K and G (55th North Carolina) crossed onto the southern

8 Grayson (Loyd Harris's middle name and pseudonym), *Milwaukee Sunday Telegraph*, March 22, 1885, as cited in Herdegen & Beaudot, *In The Bloody Railroad Cut*, fn 35, 188; James P. Sullivan, "Gettysburg," *NT*, May 14, 1885, 3. Sullivan and Harris both insisted that the 95th New York did not participate in the charge, which contradicts Dawes's recollections. In his account, Harris said he encountered the 95th New York as the 6th Wisconsin was moving by files left into line along the Chambersburg Pike before Dawes ran back to the New Yorkers. Sullivan, on the right of the line and preoccupied with his malfunctioning rifle, did not notice the New Yorkers at all. Dawes was recovering from his horse throwing him and therefore had no way of knowing where the 95th New York was at that time. Jim McLean, the modern historian of Cutler's brigade and author of the recently published and outstanding *"The Bullets Flew Like Hail": Cutler's Brigade at Gettysburg, from McPherson's Ridge to Culp's Hill* (Savas Beatie, 2023), 106, concludes that the 95th New York did indeed participate in the attack.

9 Murphy to Dearborn; Blair to Lyman; Belo, "The Battle of Gettysburg." In Belo's quote I omitted the reference to Blair "commanding the Second Mississippi on my right" because it seemed superfluous. Blair made no mention of speaking to Belo; Belo's account, however, makes more sense. Blair said he went back and asked some men what they should do.

embankment, following the 2nd Mississippi's color guard and some of that regiment's left wing.[10]

Color Corporal Murphy, in advance of the line, headed toward Hall's two abandoned guns—one with a broken wheel and the other limbered behind its dead horses. Murphy dragged the color guard with him about 125 feet into Thompson's northwestern field, all the while screaming for the Mississippians and North Carolinians to follow him. The accurate, machine-like rifle fire emanating from along the Chambersburg Pike downed the entire color guard excepting Murphy, who somehow escaped unscathed. Bullets splintered the staff in two or more places and slapped through the flag in at least a dozen places. Murphy retreated to the line in the cut and sheltered as much as possible behind the shallow bank. As he fell back, so did the two left companies of the 55th North Carolina.[11]

The cut was not the defensive position the Confederates hoped it might be. In quick order, the 6th Wisconsin inflicted casualties in Company E, 2nd Mississippi. Private William King Weemes took a bullet in the left thigh, while Cpl. Charles L. Humphreys caught one through his right side and another in his liver. Sergeant William H. Keys was shot in the arm. All three managed to crawl north of the cut to a safer spot. The mortally wounded Cpl. George A. Wilson was dragged by comrades a few yards north of the ditch and placed with the other three.

About the same time, a minié ball shattered Cpl. Samuel W. Hankins's left foot and lodged against his heel. Willing hands hauled him out of the cut back to the other four injured men from his company. "Our place of 'safety' was very much exposed," lamented Hankins. Solid shot and shell fragments plowed up the ground around them. Rather than remain and face being wounded or killed,

10 John A. Blair to Rufus Dawes, October 31, 1893, Dawes Letters, Coll. M30, McCain Archives and Library, University of Southern Mississippi, Hattiesburg, MS; Clark, *Histories of the Several Regiments*, 3:298; Blair to Lyman; Belo, "The Battle of Gettysburg," 165. According to Lt. Charles M. Cooke of Company I, the adjutant of the 55th NC who wrote the history of the regiment in Clark, vol. 3: "About one-half of the Fifty-fifth Regiment being on the left extended beyond the cut on the embankment." Belo noted, "We were able to get out of the railroad cut after a severe struggle," which implies that he was in the cut when Sgt. Sullivan (Company K, 6th Wisconsin) entered it. It makes sense that the left wing advanced out of the cut then retired into it as the 6th Wisconsin advanced; this explains why Sullivan pursued him over the northern side of the embankment.

11 Murphy to Dearborn.

Keys struggled to his feet and made for the rear, leaving the unfortunate Wilson to bleed out.[12]

The frustrated Major Blair (2nd Mississippi) found himself trying to achieve the impossible: create a coherent fighting force from the inextricably mixed regiments. Except for the left wing of the 2nd regiment, most of the Mississippians could not see over the high side of the deep middle cut to fire at the more organized and better controlled Yankees, much less advance.[13]

The Badgers, meanwhile, had organized themselves on the southern side of the pike. The sudden disappearance of the Rebels surprised Lieutenant Harris, who was fighting on the far left of the line in Company G. It was as if the ground had opened and in the confusion and smoke and noise, the enemy had simply vanished. Harris was unaware of the cut's existence and had hoped for a stand-up fight in the open. Lieutenant Augustus Klein (Company A) bluntly denigrated the Mississippians as "kowardly sons of bitches" because they took cover. On the right end of the regiment, "Mickey" Sullivan of the 6th Wisconsin's Company K recalled that the ground swallowed up the Confederates. Any confusion about whether the Rebels were still there ended a short time later when a deadly fire from parts of the concealed position revealed that the enemy had not abandoned the fight.[14]

Sergeant Sullivan rested his prized silver-mounted 1861 Springfield on the top rail of the fence and pulled trigger. Nothing happened. Thinking he had not loaded the weapon, he charged it with a second round. Before he had time to pull the trigger a second time, Dawes shouted at the top of his voice, "Forward!" The infantrymen clambered over the rails under a slow but steady fire and reformed. Once organized they advanced, firing and loading by ranks as they inched forward. This wall of enemy infantry probably forced, or at least convinced, the

12 Hankins, *Simple Story of a Soldier*, 44; Busey & Busey, *Confederate Casualties*, 2:650, 651.

13 Ladd & Ladd, *Bachelder Papers*, 1:323-324; Dawes, "With the Sixth Wisconsin," 167; Blair to Lyman. Dawes's earliest account differs from "With the Sixth Wisconsin at Gettysburg." Murphy's somewhat confused recollection confirmed that the fence along the road impeded the Federal advance.

14 Sullivan, "The Charge of the Iron Brigade at Gettysburg"; Francis A. Wallar, "A Settled Question," *Milwaukee Sunday Telegraph*, July 29, 1883; Alan T. Nolan, *The Iron Brigade: A Military History* (Bloomington, IN, 1994), 239. The Augustus Klein letter resides in Nolan's personal collection, quoted on 239 and referenced in fn 21, 359. Klein was promoted to brevet first lieutenant on August 28, 1862.

men on the left side of the 55th North Carolina to retire into the muddy railroad bed.[15]

When Sullivan's weapon malfunctioned a second time, he drew the rammer and slammed it down the barrel only to discover he had accidentally double charged the piece. Quickly returning the rammer under the stock, he turned about and approached Adj. Edward Brooks, who had stationed himself behind Company K. "Brooks," he complained, "my gun won't go off." The adjutant handed a discarded weapon to Sullivan, saying, "Here take this."

Freshly armed, he passed his favorite but malfunctioning rifle to the officer and admonished him not to lose it. With that, Sullivan returned to his place in the ranks, loaded the new rifle, capped it, and squeezed the trigger. Nothing happened. The flummoxed veteran left the ranks once more, found Capt. John Ticknor, and excoriated his percussion caps as no good. The captain pointed to Cpl. John A. Crawford, who had just collapsed with a shattered knee. "Take Crawford's." Together, they rolled over the unconscious corporal. Sullivan unbuckled Crawford's accoutrement belt, which had the cap and cartridge boxes on it, and strapped them on.[16]

A short distance to the left in Company E, a minié ball broke Sgt. Michael Mangan's right ankle. Not realizing how badly he had been injured, Mangan attempted to stand only to fall hard onto his side. He forced himself to sit up and scan his surroundings. Several of his wounded soldiers sat around him, loading their rifles before struggling to their feet to return fire.[17]

That same fire coming from in and around the railroad cut hammered the color guard. Sergeant Thomas A. Polleys (Company H) was hit and dropped the flag. Two minié balls struck Cpl. Francis A. Deleglise (Company E) in the right leg; one of them drilled a hole through his calf and the other shattered his femur

15 Sullivan, "The Charge of the Iron Brigade at Gettysburg"; Dawes, "Align on the Colors"; Wallar, "A Settled Question."

16 Sullivan, "The Charge of the Iron Brigade"; Dawes, "Align on the Colors"; U.S. Surgeon-General's Office, *The Medical And Surgical History Of The War Of The Rebellion*, 3 vols., 6 books (Washington, D.C., 1883), 2/3:241; Sullivan, "Gettysburg." Crawford survived his injuries but lost his leg in the process. Dawes makes it clear in his article that he ordered the charge after the regiment had crossed the fence into the field south of the railroad cut. Sullivan's account substantiates this.

17 Hiram O. Brown and M. A. W. Brown, *Soldiers' and Citizens' Album of Biographical Record Containing Personal Sketches of Army Men And Citizens Prominent in Loyalty to the Union*, 2 vols. (Chicago, 1888), 1:170-171.

about four inches above the knee and lodged in the greater trochanter without destroying the head of the femur. The impact severely jarred Deleglise's entire right side, though for reasons unknown left him on his feet. The hearty Swiss, having previously recovered from a left thigh wound, a bullet through the right side of his frontal bone, and a broken tooth in the Cornfield at Antietam the previous year, turned about and staggered toward the Chambersburg Pike. In all the confusion, no one noticed which of the five remaining corporals in the color guard picked up the flag. Sergeant Mangan hailed Deleglise closer. The corporal hobbled to the man with the shattered ankle. He tried in vain to bind the sergeant's ankle only to discover that he could not use his right arm to do so: his wounded leg was too rigid to bend. He bluntly told Mangan he could not help him, and continued limping to the rear.[18]

"Mickey" Sullivan (Company K) was heading back toward the firing line when his captain, John Ticknor, staggered past, his arms and legs spread to resemble DaVinci's Vitruvian Man. A few steps beyond the sergeant, Ticknor pitched face forward onto the grass. Sullivan continued to his position behind the company when his tentmate, Sgt. Erastus Smith (Company K), brushed past. "Jerkey is shot," he explained in reference to the captain, "and I think he's killed, and I'm going to see about him."[19]

Within about 165 feet of the cut, Sgt. George Fairfield (Company C), on the right the line, noticed that the Confederates had stopped shooting. Only the 2nd Mississippi's battle flag stood out in the smoke-obscured field. Fairfield instinctively braced himself for the inevitable volley he knew would follow the silence.[20]

The Westerners had not traversed half of the distance to the cut when the Mississippians emptied a devastating volley into them. Colonel Dawes hastily surveyed the line. To his right was Capt. Joseph H. "Tall Sycamore" Marston (Company E) calmly herding his men forward with arms outstretched. Standing more than six feet tall, the captain—the second-tallest man in the regiment—

18 Brown & Brown, *Soldiers' and Citizens' Album*, 1:722-723.

19 Beaudot & Herdegen, *An Irishman In the Iron Brigade*, 95. The origins of Ticknor's nickname remain unclear.

20 Cornelius W. Okey, "Echoes of Gettysburg," *Milwaukee Sunday Telegraph*, April 29, 1883, as cited in Herdegen & Beaudot, *In the Bloody Railroad Cut*, fn 32, 184; George Fairfield to J. A. Watrous, no date, J. A. Watrous Papers, Box 2, "Civil War Materials," Wisconsin Historical Society, Madison, WI.

miraculously escaped injury. "How the rebels happened to miss Captain Marston I cannot comprehend," Dawes recollected. Lieutenant Orrin D. Chapman (Company C) fell mortally wounded in the volley, leaving the company under Sergeant Fairfield's command. [21]

No fewer than 15 men broke away from the flanks to outpace their comrades as they headed for the Confederate colors barely visible through the smoke. Private Cornelius Okey (Company C) made a dead run toward the center of the line. Simultaneously, drummer Lewis Eggleston and his "pards," Pvts. John O. Johnson, Barnard McGinty, and David "Rocky Mountain" Anderson (all of Company H) raced toward the colors. Privates Bodley Jones and William Pearson of Company A joined them. On the way they hooked up with Lt. William N. Remington (Company K), his six-man squad from Company I, and a stray member of the brigade guard, Pvt. Jasper Daniels (Company A, 2nd Wisconsin). Remington, who figured the regiment's firepower had forced the Confederates to shelter below the lip of the cut, thought he had a chance to capture the Mississippi flag. The disorganized platoon-sized mob burst through the hole in the center of their own line, stampeding toward Cpl. William B. Murphy and the waving colors of the 2nd Mississippi.

Murphy witnessed Pvt. Levi Stedman (Company I, 6th Wisconsin) die, struck by a bullet as he lurched for the colors. Stedman's comrade, Ed Lind, lay close by. Some 15 to 20 feet away, Lieutenant Remington—who had already been grazed on the left side of the neck—tried switching the sword in his right hand with the revolver in his left. The glimpse of a Rebel aiming at him from the cut caused him to throw his shoulder forward into the path of a minié ball that knocked him flat. (Murphy watched him go hard to the ground.) The injured Remington noticed Pvt. Jasper Daniels and a couple of other men rush at Murphy. The lieutenant crawled forward, regained his feet, and backed out of the fray toward his own regiment. "Flag-taking was pretty well knocked out of me," he later confessed.[22]

21 Ladd & Ladd, *Bachelder Papers*, 1:324; Dawes, "With the Sixth Wisconsin," 168.

22 Murphy to Dearborn; William N. Remington, *Milwaukee Sunday Telegraph*, April 29, 1883, as cited in Herdegen & Beaudot, *The Bloody Railroad Cut*, 194, fn 45, 195. It seems logical to place the attempt on the 2nd Mississippi's colors between the time the volley hit the 6th Wisconsin and the charge upon the cut itself because Remington's account indicates there was not much incoming small arms fire when he went for the flag. Sergeant Fairfield indicates that the regiment advanced under a steady fire that suddenly stopped, followed by a volley and a charge. The volley hit the regiment hard and temporarily stalled the advance.

Taken aback by the ferocity of the incoming rounds, Dawes realized that his small regiment had run into a formidable line. About 100 or so men were approaching his left flank from the south. "I did not then know or care where they came from but was rejoiced to see them," he later explained. Dawes rushed to the line and encountered Maj. Edward Pye and his small 95th New York. "We must charge. Are you with us?"

"Charge it is," Pye firmly responded.

Dawes raced back to the 6th Wisconsin's flag, screaming along the way, "Forward, charge!" Pye simultaneously bellowed at his men to do the same.[23]

The Wisconsinites surged ahead before the New Yorkers had completely come alongside. The 14th Brooklyn, trailing behind the right rear of the 95th, remained in the wake of the assault. The 6th's color guard bolted forward, forming the apex of a rough inverted "V," with the wings extended on either side. Companies disintegrated into squads with officers competing with their rank and file to reach the Confederates first.

"Align on the colors! Align on that color! Close up on that color!" Dawes repeatedly screamed above the din in an attempt to maintain a force sufficient to achieve his objective.

A bullet wounded the second color bearer and he dropped the flag. Dawes took a moment to hoist it when another member of the guard yanked the staff from him and started toward the railroad cut.[24]

Company I, on the left of the 6th Wisconsin, absorbed a number of the rounds. The impact of the minié balls slapping into his "boys" permanently burned an indelible image in Lt. Earl M. Rogers's mind. In the rear rank on the right of the company, Sgt. Andy Miller tumbled dead into the damp grass, just as Pvt. Gottfried Schoeber, the first man to Miller's left, fell wounded. Several

---

It also alerted Dawes to the presence of the Rebels in the railroad cut, which at this time he did not realize was to his front. Murphy's account in his letter to Dearborn confirms this impression. Corporal Murphy (2nd Mississippi) claimed more than a dozen Yankees tried to capture his colors.

23 Ladd & Ladd, *Bachelder Papers*, 1:324; Dawes "With the Sixth Wisconsin," 168. I quoted from *With the Sixth Wisconsin* because that source, based upon Dawes' meticulous postwar research about the charge, seemed the more accurate of the two.

24 Dawes, *Service With the Sixth Wisconsin*, 168; Ladd & Ladd, *Bachelder Papers*, 1:324; Dawes, "With the Sixth Wisconsin," 169; Letter, Earl M. Rogers to J. A. Watrous, not dated, J. A. Watrous Papers, Wisconsin Historical Society, Madison, WI. Rogers mentioned Dawes picking up the flag twice, while Beaudot and Herdegen, in *In The Bloody Railroad Cut*, claim it went down three times.

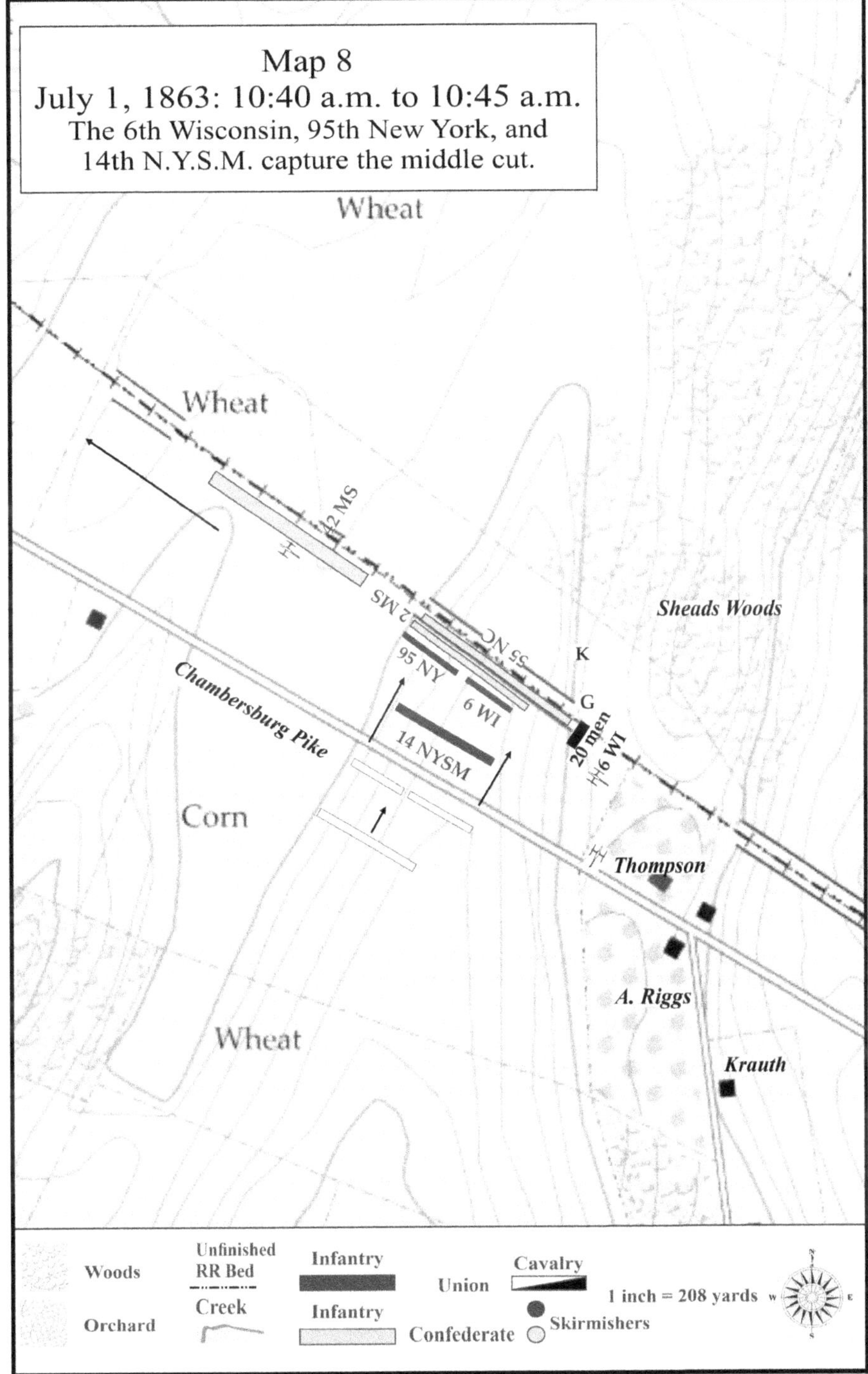
Map 8
July 1, 1863: 10:40 a.m. to 10:45 a.m.
The 6th Wisconsin, 95th New York, and
14th N.Y.S.M. capture the middle cut.
Wheat
Wheat
42 MS
2 MS
55 NC
Sheads Woods
K
G
95 NY
6 WI
14 NYSM
20 men
6 WI
Chambersburg Pike
Corn
Thompson
A. Riggs
Wheat
Krauth
Woods
Unfinished RR Bed
Infantry
Cavalry
Union
Creek
1 inch = 208 yards
Orchard
Infantry
Confederate
Skirmishers

steps farther, bullets killed Pvt. Lewis M. Boughton and felled Pvt. William Sweet. Corporals Jim McLane and Alf Thomas also went down wounded. Confederate rifle fire killed Pvt. George W. Sutton, removed Sgt. John M. Goodwin from the line, and knocked down Clr. Cpl. Charlie O. Jones. Color Corporal Clarence E. Bullard (Company B) left the field with a nasty flesh wound. Once again Dawes raised the colors from the ground, only to have Color Cpl. Charles W. Mead (Company G) pull them from him.[25]

One Rebel bullet hammered Sgt. George Fairfield (Company C) in the left hip. The sergeant instinctively felt the wound, found some blood, and discovered his water-filled canteen had slowed the round enough so that it only broke the skin. Sore but not disabled, he limped toward the cut. To his left, the Southern fusillade had swept away nearly half of the company. Farther to the left, Lieutenant Harris had just pushed his half of the brigade guard to the right when a piece of buckshot struck him in the neck. The bleeding lieutenant turned about and staggered off the field.[26]

To the east, Lieutenant Remington's fall pulled the cork out of the bottle. The now 14-man detachment went after the colors ahead of the line. Private Daniels fell back, thereby escaping the ensuing mêlée uninjured. Private Cornelius W. Okey (Company C), accompanied by drummer Lewis Eggleston and Pvts. John O. Johnson, Barnard McGinty, and "Rocky Mountain" Anderson, dashed past Lieutenant Remington. In the lead, Okey stooped low to pull the 2nd Mississippi's colors from the ground. Eggleston plowed into to him from the right rear and clasped the staff.

25 Rogers to Watrous; Herdegen & Beaudot, *In The Bloody Railroad Cut*, 165, fn 54. Herdegen identifies the following as members of the color guard: Sgt. Thomas Polleys (H) and Cpls. William Day (C), Francis A. Deleglise (E), Milo G. Sage (F), C. O. Jones (I), Charles Mead (G), Arland F. Winsor (K), and Clarence E. Bullard (B). Of the eight, Mead was killed and all the others but Sage wounded, which indicates Sage may not have been present that day. According to Rogers, Dawes repeated his command to "Align on the Colors!" Herdegen also notes that no one mentioned who carried the flag between Polleys and Mead.

26 Consul W. Butterfield, *History of Crawford And Richland Counties, Wisconsin* (Springfield, IL, 1894), 568; Fairfield to Watrous; Wallar, "A Settled Question"; Harris, *Milwaukee Sunday Telegraph*, March 22, 1885, as cited in Herdegen & Beaudot, *In The Bloody Railroad Cut*, 190, fn 44, 194; Lance J. Herdegen and William J. K. Beaudot, "With The Iron Brigade Guard At Gettysburg," *Gettysburg Magazine*, No. 1 (July 1, 1989), 30, 32. Herdegen and Beaudot did not document where they found the information on Harris's wounding, but it appears in the edited March 22, 1885 letter, to the *Milwaukee Sunday Telegraph* reproduced in *Gettysburg Magazine.*

Eggleston's weight on the flag made it impossible for Okey to jerk it from the ground. He stood up and found himself staring down the bayoneted muzzle of a musket in the hands of a Rebel corporal who was kneeling immediately in front of him. Okey instinctively threw his right shoulder forward to absorb the round when the weapon discharged. A .69-caliber round ball jerked through the skirt of his frock coat while the buckshot in the cartridge struck Okey in the left forearm and wrist, knocking him down.[27]

Private John O. Johnson, Eggleston's messmate, had gone into the action with the ramrod stuck in the bore of his rifle. He saw the Southerners around Color Cpl. William B. Murphy and the 2nd Mississippi's colors level their weapons at the drummer, whom he "loved as a brother." With no thought for his own safety, Johnson stepped over Okey with his rifle raised to protect Eggleston. Johnson was in the act of striking a Rebel with the butt of his rifle when a minié ball bored through his right arm and slammed through Eggleston's arms, sending both men to the ground.[28]

At the same time, a Confederate shot Pvt. Barnard McGinty through the leg. His messmate, Pvt. David Anderson, immediately crushed the Reb's skull with his rifle butt. Corporal William B. Murphy, who did not see the braining occur, tenaciously clenched the staff in one hand while trying to rip the flag from it with the other.[29]

Eggleston had barely hit the ground when Pvt. Bodley Jones, with William Pearson nearby, grabbed the flag. Jones, who Murphy described as a "large man," locked one hand on the staff and the other on the stubborn Mississippian.

27 Okey, "Echoes Of Gettysburg," as cited in Herdegen & Beaudot, *In The Bloody Railroad Cut*, fn 46, 195; Cullen B. Aubury, *Echoes From the Marches of the Famous Iron Brigade* (Milwaukee, 1900), 63. Okey republished his earlier account with a slight alteration. Despite misidentifying Lieutenant Remington as "Pennington," Okey, based upon other accounts, did get his hands on the flag staff—but he did not capture it. The bulk of his story is what he wanted it to be, rather than what had occurred.

28 John O. Johnson, "One Rebel Flag," *The Milwaukee Sunday Telegraph*, July 17, 1887, as cited in Herdegen & Beaudot, *In The Bloody Railroad Cut*, fn 47, 196. Tradition has it that David Anderson brained the Rebel who shot Eggleston, which Johnson's account debunks. Dawes repeatedly stated that David Anderson killed the man who shot Eggleston. William Murphy of the 2nd Mississippi, who was wrestling with Eggleston over the flag, would have almost certainly seen the braining had it transpired, but he did not. It apparently happened nearby, but not on the side where Eggleston was standing.

29 Murphy to Dearborn; Fairfield to Watrous. Fairfield identified David "Rocky Mountain" Anderson as the man who brained the Confederate after McGinty was shot.

The two Wisconsin soldiers died where they stood. Corporal F. Asbury Wallar and his brother, Sam, were rushing for the flag when they saw Bodley fall forward with it still in his hand. Asbury grabbed it before it hit the ground. Instead of following his initial thought to take it to the rear, he stepped back onto the southern bank of the cut, threw the flag on the ground, and stood on it to keep anyone else from taking the credit for it. He stayed put and calmly discharged his weapon into the desperate mass of rebels in front of him. By this time, Pvts. L. LeGrand Tongue and John Harland had come up with Company I, with the rest of the regiment behind them.[30]

"Surrender!" the Westerners yelled above the din. "Throw over your arms!" To their amazement a considerable number of the Confederates complied by grounding their weapons and waving their caps in the air. One Reb leveled his weapon at John Harland and fired, killing him instantly. As his body toppled into the muddy bottom of the cut, LeGrand Tongue brought his weapon to bear on the enemy. The man dropped his gun and pleaded for his life: "Don't shoot, don't kill me." Tongue's response shocked veteran Lt. Earl Rogers: "All hell can't save you now," snarled the private, who shot the unnamed Rebel from just a few feet away, his corpse falling across Harland's body.[31]

The 55th North Carolina's Major Belo, fighting on the left of the Confederate line, had received orders to cover the brigade's retreat by blocking the eastern end of the line so the other regiments could funnel west through the middle and western cuts to escape. They arrived seconds too late. Company K, on his exposed left flank, clambered out of the track bed and headed for safer ground. This action left Company G, under Lt. Mordecai Lee, isolated on the far end of the line.[32]

30 Philip Cheek and Mair Pointon, *History of the Sauk County Riflemen, Known as Company "A," Sixth Wisconsin Veteran Volunteer Infantry, 1861-1865* (Privately printed, 1900), 74; Rogers to Watrous.

31 Ladd & Ladd, *Bachelder Papers*, 1:324; Rogers to Watrous; George Fairfield, "The 6th Wis. At Gettysburg," *NT*, December 14, 1905, 3. Fairfield described how the mud had mixed with blood at the bottom of the railroad cut.

32 Belo, "The Battle of Gettysburg," 165; Clark, *Histories of the Several Regiments*, 3:297; Jordan, *North Carolina Troops*, 13:497. Belo later wrote: "just at that time we received orders to form a new alignment." Lieutenant Charles M. Cooke (Company I) described the change of formation as written in the text. Captain Walter A. Whitted (Company G) had escaped the trap with a bullet wound in his face or leg—the records are not clear. Company B had already been detached on skirmish duty near the Forney farm. This movement placed Company G on the left flank, followed respectively to the right by K,

Simultaneously, Adj. Edward P. Brooks flanked Lieutenant Lee's men with a mixed contingent of 20 soldiers from Companies C, G, and Lieutenant Showalter's brigade guard. The Yankees fired into the left of Company G, killing Lieutenant Lee and severely wounding five others. Nineteen Rebels surrendered.[33]

Trapped on the flank, those Confederates who were able to do so broke from the cut and headed back toward their own lines. Many dropped their weapons and surrendered. Forty-seven years later, Fairfield recalled that the 6th Wisconsin could have slaughtered the Southerners had they not capitulated.

Rufus Dawes pushed his way to the front of his men at the middle cut and stared down the four-foot embankment at the enemy crammed together below as his Badgers shouted, "Throw down your muskets! Down with your muskets!" "Where is the colonel of this regiment?" he shouted.

Major John Allen Blair of the 2nd Mississippi stepped forward. "Here I am," Blair defiantly responded; "Who are you?"

"I command this regiment. Surrender or I will fire," Dawes retorted.

Without uttering a word, the dejected major surrendered his sword and within short order six other Confederate officers handed their blades to Dawes. "Major," Dawes responded, "have your men fall in without arms." The infantrymen near Blair complied.[34]

Sergeant "Mickey" Sullivan watched as a number of Mississippians and North Carolinians stumbled over the northern side of the cut. Sullivan jumped into the railroad bed and was about to give chase when a Confederate officer

---

E, H, C, I, D, F, and A. Company K had no men captured, compared to the 59 taken prisoner among the other three companies in the left wing of the regiment. It is safe to conclude that that company escaped.

33 Fairfield to Watrous; Fairfield, "The Capture At The Railroad Cut"; *OR* 27/1:276. The 55th North Carolina apparently went into the action in the standard front as prescribed in Hardee's *Tactics*. The five right companies got trapped in the deep part of the cut and surrendered 89 officers and men.

34 Ladd & Ladd, *Bachelder Papers*, 1:325; Jordan, *North Carolina Troops*, 13:1993, 430, 452, 464, 506, 514; Busey & Busey, *Confederate Casualties*, 2:639, 648, 652, 651, 661; Dawes, Service *With the Sixth Wisconsin*, 169. I used Dawes's quotes from *Service With the Sixth Wisconsin*. Busey and Jordan identify the captured officers as follows: 2nd Mississippi: Maj. John Alan Blair, Company C: Capt. Romulus D. Sargent, Lt. David T. Walker; Company E: Lt. Peyton B. Bailey, Lt. Robert Whitley; Company I: Capt. Richard Leavell, Lt. John A. Stevens; 55th North Carolina: Lt./Adj. Henry T. Jordan; Company C: Lt. George J. Bethel; Company D: Lt. Silas Dixon Cabaniss; Company H: Lt. Benjamin J. Blount: Company I: Capt. Wilson High Williams.

abruptly handed him his sword. The surprised Badger took the blade in his right hand and brushed by the officer, intent upon stopping whomever he could from escaping.

The moment Sullivan stepped up on the northern bank, he saw Maj. Alfred Belo make a break toward safety. Sullivan shouted at the "big rebel" to halt. "Kill that officer," he shrieked, "and that will end it!" The infuriated sergeant twisted his body to throw the sword. In an instant, Belo yelled at the man nearest to him to shoot the Irishman down.

A minié ball drilled into Sullivan's left shoulder, slamming him to the ground just as he hurled the sword with his right hand. Lieutenant Charles M. Cooke (Company I), who was near Major Belo, saw the sword hit the man behind him. Numbed and badly jarred, Sullivan initially thought some Reb had struck him with the butt of his gun. As his head cleared, he realized he had been shot. Before he could get to his feet, Sgt. Albert Tarbox stooped to check on him. "They've got you down, Mickey have they," Tarbox asked in his thick brogue. As Tarbox stood, recalled a bitter Sullivan, "Some of the damned Rebs who had surrendered" shot him. "They did a good deal of that kind of work that day," he lamented.[35]

Sergeant Fairfield stepped into the blood-tainted mud of the track bed and started pushing through the armed mass of Confederates crowded in the deepest part of the cut. He quickly came upon Pvt. John Yates (Company E) sparring, at bayonet point, with a Rebel lieutenant armed with a sword. Fairfield yelled at the private to stand down and that the officer sheathe his blade (which he did, with a word of thanks). Not far away, Capt. John Marston (Company E) faintly heard someone among the Rebs shout "surrender." Private. Lyman White was preparing to lunge his bayonet into a Confederate captain. Marston, who did not think White had heard the command, leaped between the two and knocked the private's weapon aside, and immediately ordered the officer to surrender his sword to the enlisted man.[36]

35 Belo, "The Battle of Gettysburg," 165; Clark, *Histories of the Several Regiments*, 3:298; Beaudot & Herdegen, *An Irishman In The Iron Brigade*, 96; Sullivan, "The Charge of the Iron Brigade." Belo quoted Sullivan as shouting, "Kill that officer, and we will capture that command." The officer who surrendered his sword to Sullivan remains unidentified.

36 Fairfield to Watrous; Fairfield, "The Capture At The Railroad Cut"; Marston, *Milwaukee Sunday Telegraph*, April 24, 1881, as cited in Herdegen & Beaudot, *In the Bloody Railroad Cut*, 203.

The lieutenant whom Fairfield had saved sullenly marched his still-armed men toward the eastern end of the cut as prisoners. The sergeant continued to plow through the Southerners, ordering them to leave the cut as captives. Just as he reached the western flank of the 2nd Mississippi, Fairfield watched the rest of the brigade scrambling along the muddy track bed heading for the ridge and the safety of the creek bottom at its western base.[37]

Private David J. Hill (Company B, 2nd Mississippi) took advantage of the confusion to scurry under a muddy blood-soaked blanket alongside two wounded men. Once shrouded, he moaned as loudly as any desperately injured man could, hoping the Wisconsin troops would leave him to die. Lieutenant John C. Lauderdale, along with about 10 other Mississippians from his company, played dead among the casualties. The ruse worked; the Federals paid no heed to them.[38]

A short distance to the north, Cpl. Samuel W. Hankins (Company E) and his two surviving 2nd Mississippi comrades, Cpl. Charles L. Humphreys and Pvt. William K. Weemes, were evacuated to their own lines during the retreat from the cut. They left Cpl. George A. Wilson's corpse on the field.

Minutes after being left within his own lines, Hankins's leg started cramping. "Never have I felt such agony," he recalled. Hospital Steward James D. Shell (11th Mississippi) heard his friend's pleas and scrambled to his side while calling for more help. Shell and two other men massaged Hankins's leg and plied him with medicinal brandy, which was usually reserved for the surgeons. As soon as the muscle relaxed, Shell hailed a doctor.

The three sat on Hankins while the "doc" went to work with his scalpel. "It felt like he was using one that he had kept on hand for sharpening [a] slate pencil," was how Hankins later described the horrific procedure. The physician dug into the wound with what the corporal referred to as "tweezers." He extracted the ball, gave it to Hankins, and told him it was good for a furlough. Shell bandaged the wound and laid Hankins on an oil cloth with the mortally wounded Humphreys in the middle and Weemes on the other side.[39]

37 Ladd & Ladd, *Bachelder Papers*, 1:325; Fairfield to Watrous; Fairfield, "The Capture At The Railroad Cut." This lieutenant remains unidentified.

38 D. J. Hill to Rufus R. Dawes, September 12, 1893, Rufus R. Dawes Papers, Wisconsin Historical Society, Madison, WI.

39 Hankins, *Simple Story of a Soldier*, 44-45.

The 6th Wisconsin

According to Capt. John A. Kellogg of Lysander Cutler's staff, the fighting sputtered out within three minutes after the 6th Wisconsin reached the Confederate line at the railroad cut, about the same time reinforcements arrived. Corporal F. Asbury Wallar (Company I) had just loaded his rifle for the third time when the 95th New York and the red-legged infantry of the 14th Brooklyn came up behind the Badgers. One of the Brooklyn zouaves tugged at the flag under Wallar's feet in an attempt to steal it. The corporal warned the fellow to leave it be or he would shoot him dead. The would-be thief wisely backed away.[40]

The Wisconsinites scoured the eastern end of the middle cut looking for prisoners among the casualties. "They are getting away!" echoed overhead from the right flank. Corporal Isaiah F. Kelly looked down the grade. At least a dozen members of Company B, 2nd Mississippi, were running east through the cut. Despite a piece of buckshot in one leg and nick in his neck, Kelly tore after them with a few men from Company G. The Yankees caught up with 10 of the Mississippians.

A Confederate lieutenant, John Lauderdale, foolishly drew his revolver and cracked off a round into the Yankee squad. Private John Killmartin shot him dead. The Badgers left the lieutenant's body in the ditch and shoved and jostled the rest of the captives toward the rear to turn them over to the cavalry. Sergeant George Fairfield recalled that the 6th Wisconsin secured the cut around 11:00 a.m.[41]

The wounded Mickey Sullivan of Company K, who had been knocked briefly unconscious during the act of throwing his sword at Major Belo, said something to himself to verify that he could speak and breathe. Satisfied that he was still alive, Mickey picked up his rifle in his right hand and took to his feet. When he tried to shoulder the weapon, he discovered his left arm was next to useless. Lieutenant Colonel Dawes, meanwhile, handed his captured swords over to Lt. Edward P. Brooks. The adjutant later claimed one of the blades and turned the others over to an enlisted man with instructions to give them to Asst.

40 Wallar, "A Settled Question"; Ladd & Ladd, *Bachelder Papers*, 1:205. Wallar went by his middle name "Asbury," as indicated by an account from Sergeant Fairbanks.

41 Isaiah F. Kelly to Rufus Dawes, August 2, 1892, as cited in Herdegen & Beaudot, *In the Bloody Railroad Cut*, 208-209, fn 74; Fairfield, "The 6th Wisconsin at Gettysburg."

Surg. Abram W. Preston for safe keeping. That was the last anyone saw of them.[42]

Dawes ordered Maj. John F. Hauser to march the prisoners off by the left flank in column of twos. Sullivan spied Major Hauser's large number of lightly guarded Rebs and decided to join them. Exhausted from blood loss, he knew he could help no one. The bleeding, which had saturated the left side of Sullivan's tunic and his left leg and sloshed out of his left shoe, left a dark crimson trail with every step. At his request, one of the Rebels removed Sullivan's canteen from his neck and gently lifted it to the injured sergeant's mouth. Warm though it was, the "fresh" buttermilk, which a German farmer had given him that morning, helped to revive him a bit.

It was at this time that General Wadsworth rode forward with a cavalry detachment to take charge of the prisoners. The general recognized "Mickey's" critical condition. "My man, you are too badly hurt to be here." He commanded a sergeant to put Sullivan on his horse, escort him to the hospital, and stay with him until a surgeon had tended his wound. Hauser turned his charges over to the cavalrymen and returned to the regiment.[43]

While Wadsworth supervised the reorganization of Cutler's men, Rufus Dawes looked to consolidate his 6th Wisconsin. He called for a skirmish detail. Corporal Wallar, Rebel flag in hand, stepped forward. He passed the colors of the 2nd Mississippi to the unsuspecting lieutenant colonel before reporting for duty. Dawes had more to worry about than the Confederate flag. He hailed Sgt. William Evans (Company H) who, despite being severely wounded in both legs, was hobbling along using two muskets as crutches. Dawes gave the colors to Evans, who dropped the cumbersome weapons and painfully staggered off using the flag staff to support his weight.[44]

42 Dawes, *Service With the Sixth Wisconsin*, 169, 170.

43 Herdegen & Beaudot, *An Irishman in The Iron Brigade*, 96-97; Dawes, "Align on the Colors."

44 Wallar, "A Settled Question"; Dawes, "With the Sixth Wisconsin," 172; Grayson (Harris), "Adventures of a Rebel Flag," *Milwaukee Sunday Telegraph*, January 29, 1880, as quoted in Herdegen & Beaudot, "With the Iron Brigade at Gettysburg," 33. According to Dawes, he took the flag from the staff and wrapped it around Evans's body. Evans, while on furlough during the war, personally told Wallar that he tore the flag from the staff and broke the staff in two to keep it from capture by the Confederates during the retreat through town. Dawes's account does not sound fully accurate. Evans had no apparent reason to lie about what he told Wallar. It is also interesting to note that Miss Julia Hollinger, in whose house

North of the Middle Cut

Once the Wisconsin men vacated the track bed, Pvt. David J. Hill (Company B, 2nd Mississippi) crawled from beneath his bloodied blanket and lurched toward his own lines. He encountered an obviously wounded Yankee still wearing his knapsack aimlessly meandering about the body-strewn field. When Hill approached the man to assist him, the fellow turned his head to reveal a gory mess where his lower jaw had been, and a gaping hole in his throat. Hill led the man into some shade somewhere near the Wills place and eased him to the ground.

The Mississippian unhitched the Yankee's knapsack and rolled out the oilcloth, over which he spread the fellow's wool blanket, laid the injured man on top of the makeshift bed, and placed his knapsack under his shoulders to keep his head elevated. He also handed him a canteen and watched as the man plugged it into his open throat and try to drink. Unable to do much more for the Yankee, Hill left. He never learning his name or his regiment. "I suppose the poor fellow died," Hill would write years after the war.[45]

Nearby, a couple of Confederate prisoners came upon Cpl. Francis A. Deleglise painfully dragging himself by the left arm toward the Thompson place. They pulled him from the ground and turned him over to the cavalry provost guard. Two cavalrymen hauled him to Casper H. Dustman's cellar and placed him on the cold slab stone floor among the unattended casualties from both armies.[46]

Evans sheltered, wrote that her father made firewood out of the staff and hid the flag under her sheets.

45 Hill to Dawes.

46 Brown & Brown, *Soldiers' and Citizens' Album*, 1:723-724. Deleglise and his leg survived.

Chapter Seven

"If we can't hold them, where can you get men who can?"

— *Anonymous soldier, 143rd Pennsylvania, Stone's brigade*

I Corps on McPherson's Ridge

10:45 a.m. to 11:45 a.m.

10:45 a.m. to 11:00 a.m.
The Iron Brigade
Willoughby Run and Herbst Woods

Adjutant George E. Finney, Sgt. Maj. Asa W. Blanchard, and a detachment from the 19th Indiana began disarming and rounding up members of the 1st Tennessee. The 19-year-old Blanchard delivered the sidearms taken from three captured officers to 20-year-old Lt. Col. William W. Dudley and mistakenly told him one belonged to the Rebel lieutenant colonel. Without the slightest hesitation, Dudley graciously "invested" the sergeant major with the "lieutenant colonel's" sword and scabbard. Blanchard, who had not had a sergeant major's sword since his promotion, gladly buckled it on.[1]

1 Thompson, "In Their Own Words"; Busey & Busey, *Confederate Casualties*, 3:1381, 1383, 1391. The identity of the sword's owner is unclear. The 1st Tennessee reported two officers captured and two wounded and captured. The captured were Adj. William E. Watson, Jr. and Lt. James C. Grant (Company G). Lieutenants William Jasper Muse (Company B) and James M. Manley (Company G) were wounded and captured. Manley later died from his wounds. There is no way to ascertain whose sword Blanchard received.

While Blanchard and his squad busied themselves collecting small arms, Capt. Hollon Richardson of Brig. Gen. Solomon Meredith's staff rode out of Herbst Woods. Sergeant Augustus F. Ziegler (Company A, 24th Michigan) watched him trot to the skirmish line. The captain, wrote an admiring Ziegler, was "one of the bravest and noblest officers that ever drew a breath." Richardson apparently had seen the same Rebs spotted earlier by Lt. Col. John B. Callis of the 7th Wisconsin. He rode back to the woods and reported to Meredith, who sent orders to the 24th Michigan and the 7th Wisconsin to rejoin the brigade and return to the east side of Willoughby Run.[2]

Bullets from the Confederate skirmish line occasionally zipped through and above the ranks of the victorious Western men. Down at Willoughby Run, Pvt. Jonathan Bryan (Company H, 2nd Wisconsin) jubilantly waved his Hardee hat and cheered. Private Elisha Reed had just hobbled into the color company when a single shot from the distant woods hit the cheering Bryan in the heart, killing him instantly. Whatever joy the brief firefight and victory might have generated dissipated quickly. The fighting was far from resolved. The battered 2nd Wisconsin, together with the other regiments, sloshed across to the eastern bank.

Captain Richardson rode to the right of the Iron Brigade's line and directed the 7th and the 2nd Wisconsin to pull back to the top of next rise of ground 275 feet behind them and shift the line to the north. He placed the 2nd Wisconsin along the worm fence on the northern face of the woods. The 7th Wisconsin fell in along the western edge of the high bank above Willoughby Run at a right angle to the 2nd Wisconsin.[3]

2 Ziegler Letter; *OR* 27/1:245, 267; Ladd & Ladd, *Bachelder Papers*, 1:141. Callis implied that he ordered his regiment to retire on his own initiative, but Richardson's presence on the field seems to confirm otherwise. Doubleday would later write that he ordered the Iron Brigade to the eastern bank of Willoughby Run, but he had only recently arrived on the field and had no working knowledge of the tactical situation. Colonel Morrow claimed his 24th Michigan was ordered back to the creek.

3 Herdegen & Murphy, *Four Years With the Iron Brigade*, 191; *OR* 27/1:268; Curtis, *History of the Twenty-Fourth Michigan*, 157; Ladd & Ladd, *Bachelder Papers*, 1:141 and 2:941; Wheeler, "Reminiscences of the Battle of Gettysburg," 210; Reed, "Gettysburg"; Ziegler Letter; "Synopsis of General Richardson's Speech," 2; Barnes to Dudley. Barnes recollected that the 19th Indiana had re-crossed the creek and gone into line about halfway up the hill in the woods before it moved down to the creek and engaged in sharpshooting, which would explain why the left wing of the 24th Michigan was at an angle and downhill to the rest of the regiment. In Herdegen's and Murphy's book, Pvt. William Ray vividly described the right of the line's position on elevated ground.

The 2nd and 7th Wisconsin regiments went prone as Callis dispatched skirmishers to the front. The advance men spread out to the right to deal with the noisome Rebels to the northwest. They loped down to the east side of the run into a rather heavy but ineffective fire emanating from the north and west. Despite losing a few men, the Badgers nudged the Confederate skirmishers back to the fence along the hill to the west.[4]

Meanwhile, Colonel Morrow reformed the 24th Michigan in the sodden low ground about 100 yards south of Herbst Woods. He had barely halted the regiment when Captain Richardson pulled up and ordered him to "change front forward on the left battalion" and head into the woods. Morrow repeated the command and the regiment wheeled left into line to face north, its left flank near the creek and its right extending a short distance beyond the ridge to the east.

A couple of shots zipped through the air behind Richardson as he clattered back to the brigade. One of these rounds felled acting adjutant Capt. William H. Rexford with a groin wound. Another shattered Lt. Col. Mark Flanigan's left leg. Colonel Morrow, being afoot, quickly lowered Flanigan from his horse and climbed into his saddle. The men in the ranks shouted at him to dismount the big animal. Morrow refused, calling back that the regiment was too big for him to handle on foot.

Sergeant Ziegler watched his "boys" level their weapons at the horse. They hollered back that they would save Morrow by killing his mount under him if he did not heed them. The thought of losing the valuable officer to a Rebel sharpshooter was simply intolerable. Morrow reluctantly dismounted and started north on foot, leaving Flanigan to be cared for by the musicians, who eventually found him two hours later.[5]

Under directions from "Long Sol" Meredith, Richardson sent the 19th Indiana into the marshy southeast leg of the woodlot bordering Willoughby Run. A stretch of several hundred feet separated the left flank of the 7th from the right flank of the 19th Indiana. From where he stood, Col. Samuel J. Williams (19th Indiana) could see parts of the Confederate line extending south, well beyond the brigade's left flank. He sent a request to move his regiment out of its

4 Ladd & Ladd, *Bachelder Papers*, 1:141; Storch & Storch, "Unpublished Gettysburg Reports by the 2nd and 7th Wisconsin Infantry Regimental Commanders," *GM*, No. 17 (July 1, 1997), 22. Maj. Mark Finnicum's "Report to Governor Salomon of Wisconsin," July 24, 1863 is apparently describing the skirmishing to which Callis referred in his postwar writing.

5 Ziegler Letter; *OR* 27/1:268; Curtis, *History of the Twenty-Fourth Michigan*, 157.

A politically connected and controversial officer, Brig. Gen. Solomon "Long Sol" Meredith's questionable decision not to move his Iron Brigade to a more defensible position in Herbst Woods nearly destroyed the veteran command. *NA*

indefensible position only to hear, "It was expected that the Iron Brigade would hold the woods at all hazards." Lieutenant Isaac Wittemeyer (Company E) bitterly wrote home over a year later that the regiment was "left without orders."[6]

The Wolverines of the 24th, meanwhile, shifted into column by files and moved to fill the gap that existed between the 19th Indiana and the 7th Wisconsin. The 24th's right wing stood on the ridge parallel with the creek. The left wing filed into the ravine on a southwesterly line and connected with the right of the 19th, which had refused its line slightly uphill from the lower ledge.

Like Colonel Williams, Morrow did not like the formation. He immediately detailed Company B under Lt. Fred A. Buhl southwest to support the 19th Indiana's Company B under Lt. William B. Schlagle. By this time the field had quieted down to sporadic firing along the picket line. About the same time, John Callis sent Company B (under Lt. Amos D. Rood) and Company K (under Capt. George S. Hoyt) out on the skirmish line. When Rood pushed his men out too far forward, Captain Hoyt ordered him to pull them back to the fence between the creek and the woods. Just as quickly, Colonel Morrow dispatched an officer to find General Meredith and request permission to move his men to a more

6 Dudley, *The Iron Brigade*, 11; *OR* 27/1:268; Ladd & Ladd, *Bachelder Papers*, 2:941; Isaac Wittemeyer, "What a Soldier Says About Meredith," *Free Press* (Muncie, IN), March 24, 1864, 2; Harries, "The Iron Brigade in the First Day's Battle at Gettysburg," 344.

tenable defensive position from which to fight. According to the regimental historian, it was 11:00 a.m.[7]

While all this was transpiring, Confederate guns on Herr's Ridge continued their methodical pounding of the Shadowwoodlot. Augustus Ziegler, whose older brother William belonged to the 24th's color guard, found the pot shots particularly annoying. The case bursts, which he referred to as "rotten grape," showered the men on the ground with bark, splinters, and large branches. General Meredith had placed the 19th Indiana and the left wing of the 24th Michigan in an untenable position. The high ground along the west bank of the creek put both regiments in a defilade. Morrow impatiently waited for orders to retire to the main line.[8]

Three Miles South of the Seminary on the Emmitsburg Road[9]

Brigadier General John Robinson halted his brigades about one-third of a mile northeast of A. Currens's place and five miles from their bivouac. Stragglers needed to catch up, and his men needed a chance to get away from the stifling yellow dust churned up by the rumbling artillery ahead of them. The

7 *OR* 27/1:268; Curtis, *History of the Twenty-Fourth Michigan*, 157, 159; McConnell, "First and Greatest Days Battle at Gettysburg." Curtis and McConnell both cited the time of deployment as 11:00 a.m.

8 Amos D. Rood, "My Diary of the War," Wisconsin State Historical Society, Madison, WI, 60; Bokum, *Wanderings North and South*, 48; Roswell L. Root to Grand Father, August 23, 1863, Gregory A. Coco Collection, Harrisburg Civil War Round Table, Manuscript Department, USAHEC; Ziegler Letter; Curtis, *History of the Twenty-Fourth Michigan*, 157, 159; McConnell, "First and Greatest Days Battle at Gettysburg"; Ladd & Ladd, *Bachelder Papers*, 2:941. All times are approximate, of course, but help us chart the ebb and flow of battle. McConnell said he was on the skirmish line with Company B from 11:00 a.m. until 3:30 p.m. Augustus Ziegler (Company A) wrote on July 21, 1863, that the Rebs shelled the company for about an hour when Company A relieved Company B on the skirmish line and that half an hour later the Confederates attacked. Both erred on the time. Confederate Brig. Gen. Johnston Pettigrew started his advance at 2:00 p.m., which means Company A went on skirmish at 1:30 p.m.; Company B, which had deployed at 11:00 a.m., remained on the field until 1:30 p.m. Corporal Root (Company C, 24th Michigan) noted that the regiment lay in the woods about three hours (11:00 a.m. to 2:00 p.m.). Bokum, citing an account by Pvt. James F. Clegg (Company H) of the 24th, confirms that the brigade stayed in the woods for two to three hours. In his report to Bachelder, Lt. Col. William Dudley (19th Indiana) indicated that Schlagle's Company B remained on skirmish until the afternoon assault began.

9 Locke, *The Story of the Regiment*, 226.

thick powder coated their uniforms and packed their ears, eyes, nostrils, and mouths. Even breathing had become a chore. The men described the dirty nuisance as an "impalpable powder."

While 12th Massachusetts waited, listening to the sound of the distant fighting, Lt. Charles G. Russell (Company D) approached Adj. Charles C. Wehrum and Col. James L. Bates. Russell had never been in combat, and asked the two if they thought they would see any action. No doubt about it, one of the veterans replied, and probably in short order. The nervous lieutenant reassured himself and the others by responding, "I am right glad of an opportunity to show the men that I am no coward."[10]

The first reports of distant artillery fire reverberating over the hills to the northwest startled the men in the 11th Pennsylvania. Within a minute or two, Capt. Eminel P. Halstead reined in alongside Brig. Gen. Henry Baxter. "Close up, men, close up!" barked the officers. The brigade stepped off at the quick step. Someone in the regiment started belting out "Glory, Glory Hallelujah."[11]

Dr. Charles Wheeler, the 12th Massachusetts's assistant surgeon, rode with Capt. Erastus L. Clark. The soldiers referred to Wheeler, a short-legged man who sported a full black mustache and preferred wearing high boots, as the "Jack of Clubs." The tall Captain Clark took an inordinate amount of pride in his massive and meticulously groomed Nordic-blonde "shoe brush" mustache.

10 John D. Vautier, *History of the 88th Pennsylvania Volunteers in the War for the Union, 1861-1865* (Philadelphia, 1894), 105; Ladd & Ladd, *Bachelder Papers*, 2:989; Coburn diary, July 1, 1863; Hanna, "A Day at Gettysburg"; *Life in Southern Prisons*, 55; *Annual Report of the Adjutant-General*, 603. Vautier had been hospitalized in Washington sometime in November 1862, and did not rejoin the regiment until August 12, 1863. His accounts of Fredericksburg, Chancellorsville, and Gettysburg came from others in the regiment. The adjutant general reported hearing the artillery at 10:00 a.m.; it occurred sometime between 10:00 a.m. and 11:00 a.m. Coburn said the regiment marched eight miles to Gettysburg, which would have put five miles behind the regiment before it halted. Coburn added that they had covered a few miles before the three men heard artillery. Hanna said that they distinctly heard the guns and small arms fire around 11:00 a.m., before the column had reached Codori's. Corporal Smedley said the men halted because they needed a rest. He, like others, said the halt occurred at 9:00 a.m.

11 Locke, *The Story of the Regiment*, 227-228; George W. Grant, "The First Army Corps on the First Day at Gettysburg," in *Glimpses of the Nation's Struggle: Papers Read Before the Minnesota Commandery of the Loyal Legion of the United States, 1892*-1897, 6 vols. (Saint Paul, MN, 1902), 5:47; Vautier, *History of the 88th Pennsylvania*, 105; *NYAG*, 2:677. Chaplain Locke did not know the name of the aide-de-camp, but it was probably Halstead, who had just encountered Doubleday and Wainwright and who was hurrying the 2nd Division forward as instructed.

"Doctor," Clark began, "am I not a brave man? Do I not always do my duty?"

Taken aback, Dr. Wheeler replied, "Yes, captain. Why do you ask such questions?"

"Because I don't want you to think me afraid or superstitious," replied Clark. "I want to tell you that we are going to have a fight to-day. I shall be wounded. Look for me to-night, doctor, among the wounded. Remember!!"[12]

When they reached the high ground near the Sherfy farm, Lt. Samuel Boone (Company B, 88th Pennsylvania) distinctly heard the cracks of distant small arms fire and studied the shell bursts over the woodlot south of the seminary. Like Captain Clark, Boone was also troubled by a premonition of serious injury or worse. The lieutenant quick-stepped back to the hospital orderly, handed over his pocketbook, and instructed him to send it back to his family should "something bad" happen to him. Boone recalled hearing the cheers from both armies in the distance—the occasional "Hip! Hip! Huzzahs!" of the Federals, and the dog-like Confederate battle yelps.

Another aide-de-camp galloped to the front of Baxter's brigade. "Step out lively men," Chaplain William H. Locke heard the officer holler at the 11th Pennsylvania, "General Reynolds has been wounded, and every man is needed at the front." The brigade shifted into the double-quick in "orderly precision," recalled Lt. George W. Grant (Company B, 88th Pennsylvania).[13]

As the head of Brig. Gen. Gabriel Paul's brigade drew near the turnoff at Codori's, a throng of frightened civilians heading in the opposite direction appeared. The men, women, and children looked haggard, pale and frightened recalled Pvt. Bourne Spooner (Company K, 13th Massachusetts). Several soldiers asked them why they were running away. Others advised the passing throng, "Why don't you get into your cellars; if you leave your houses, you'll be likely to lose everything."[14]

12 Gaff & Gaff, *Corporal's Story*, 215-216.

13 Samuel G. Boone, "Personal Experiences," 21; Vautier, *History of the 88th Pennsylvania*, 106; Grant "The First Army Corps," 47.

14 Private Bourne Spooner's Memoir, "In the Ranks," http://13thmass.org/1863/gettysburg.htm, accessed Jan. 27, 2023.

11:00 a.m. to 11:30 a.m.[15]
Near the Seminary

Colonel Charles Wainwright and Lt. Angell Matthewson reined north along the seminary lane. As they approached the Chambersburg Pike intersection, Wainwright spied the 6th Wisconsin, 14th Brooklyn, and 95th New York securing the captured rail road cut. About that time, one of General Doubleday's staff intercepted Wainwright with a directive to post a battery along the pike on the crest of McPherson's Ridge.

Wainwright, a fine officer who had proved his mettle on previous fields and would do so again at Gettysburg, tasked Lieutenant Matthewson with specific instructions. The batteries were to send their caissons, battery wagons, and forges back to the Emmitsburg Road. Matthewson was to bring forward Capt. Reynolds's Battery L, 1st New York, and Lt. Stewart's Battery B, 4th U.S. and place them on the ridge in the woodlot about 200 yards south of the seminary building. They were to await further instructions and be ready to advance at the trot the moment they received his command.[16]

As he spurred west along the pike, Wainwright noted Captain Hall's abandoned limber with its six dead horses in the Thompson gateway. A little farther on he spied Ulmer's lone gun. Once he reached Hall's first artillery position, Wainright took note of the surrounding terrain. Deep ravines and

15 Biddle's brigade Marker, iron National Park Service tablet on Reynolds Avenue south of Herbst Woods on east side of the road. "July 1, Arrived and went into position about 11.30 a.m. left of Reynolds' (Herbst)Woods." This means the brigade was along the eastern base of McPherson Ridge by 11:30 a.m.

16 *OR* 27/1:356; Nevins, *A Diary of Battle*, 233-234; William Henry Shelton, "A Biography of a Period 1849-1890 by an Octogenarian," Mss., Vertical Files, V6-NY1AR, GNMP. In his report in the *OR*, Wainwright wrote that he placed Stewart's battery 200 yards south of the main building. He made no mention of having both batteries on the ridge until he revised his diary, apparently after the war. He would have placed the two batteries where he could easily find them after he reconnoitered the position. Both of his accounts make it clear that he ordered Reynolds's guns forward, but the diary confirms that he did not send him to McPherson's Ridge as he mistakenly noted in his report. In his diary, when Wainwright recorded that Wadsworth's division (implying infantry) secured the middle cut and held the southern side of the pike along McPherson's Ridge, he was likely referring to the 6th Wisconsin's assault along the railroad cut. He wrote, "I found that General Wadsworth had again occupied the ridge beyond from which he had fallen back"—something he would not have known since he had just arrived on the field. He had to have been referring to the middle cut because no Federal infantry remained north of the pike on McPherson's Ridge.

gullies abounded, and there was no infantry support on the northern flank. "I did not like this advanced position at all," he complained soon after the battle. He rushed back to the two batteries on the southern end of Seminary Ridge to supervise their placement. The approach of Lt. Jacob F. Slagle bringing Col. Chapman Biddle's brigade up the Fairfield Road from the west was a welcome sight.[17]

Herr's Ridge

With the field now relatively quiet, Confederate Maj. Gen. Henry Heth decided to advance his last two brigades commanded by Brig. Gen. James J. Pettigrew and Col. John M. Brockenbrough. Pettigrew kept his North Carolinians below the western side of the ridge about 300 yards south of the Chambersburg Pike. The regiments faced south in four parallel columns of fours. The large 26th (839 effectives) held the left, with the 11th, 47th, and 52nd extending the line westward.

"[M]ounted on a beautiful dappled grey," Pettigrew rode up in the front of the column and bellowed, "Echelon by battalion, the 26th Regiment by the left flank!" The regiment formed into battle line by files to the left and stepped off. Skirmishers fanned out from the line and disappeared over the top of the ridge and likely took up a position along the fence on the eastern side of the woods. The 11th marched south until it cleared the right flank of the 26th, at which point Col. Collett Leventhorpe, in his distinctive English accent, commanded, "By the left flank, march!" Once again the skirmishers loped forward, followed by their counterparts from the remaining two regiments. Cresting the ridge, the four regiments trod into the large woodlot doing their best to keep their staggered intervals as directed.[18]

17 Nevins, *Diary of Battle*, 234. Wainwright noted that he was "on the ridge" when the Third Division (Doubleday) passed into the field to his left front. He had to have been on Seminary Ridge to see that.

18 Busey & Martin, *Regimental Strengths and Losses*, 222; "Reminiscences of Thomas Perritt, 26th North Carolina, Company G," https://digital.ncdcr.gov/digital/collection/p15012coll8/id/12333, accessed Jan. 27, 2023; Bachelder Map, July 1, Map 10/14; Clark, *Histories of the Several Regiments*, 2:348; Albert Stacey Caison, "Southern Soldiers in Northern Prisons," 159; J. (John) C. T. Hood, "The 26th Regiment at Gettysburg, " *Lenoir* [NC] *Topic News*, April 8, 1896. The fence along the face of the woods would have provided the best protection for the skirmishers, with the Federal skirmishers along the next fence to the east between the Confederates and Willoughby Run.

From his post along the next fence east of the woods, Lt. Amos D. Rood (Company B, 7th Wisconsin) studied the cautious advance of Pettigrew's Brigade. Nearly all the men in the "Black Hat Brigade" could see the massive gray and brown formation approaching. Colonel Samuel J. Williams and his second in command, Lt. Col. William W. Dudley, dispatched a runner to find Solomon Meredith and inform him that the Rebels were outflanking them. Colonel Williams wanted to retire the regiment to the crest of the ridge in Herbst Woods and construct rail barricades. Likewise, Colonel Morrow (24th Michigan) recalled informing Meredith that the position they held at that time was untenable, and that his regiment needed to retire to higher, more defensible, ground.

Meredith passed the reports along with a request for support to Capt. Hollon Richardson, who quickly delivered it to General Wadsworth. The division leader ordered Meredith's brigade to fall back. Meredith disagreed. Retiring, he believed, would surrender the ridge to the enemy and make it possible for them to cut off the army and capture it. "Long Sol" turned to Richardson and declared that if Wadsworth would take care of the right, he would hold where he was until the army arrived or until "Hell freezes over."

The decision stunned Colonel Morrow, who appealed to Meredith three times and received the same response on each occasion: "The position must be held." The colonels along the creek would find out years later that their brigadier never forwarded their concerns to Wadsworth after Meredith told him the first time that the Iron Brigade would defend the position.[19]

Descending the eastern side of the hill, Col. Henry Burgwyn's 26th North Carolina went into line along a rail fence on the right of the 22nd Virginia Battalion (Brockenbrough's Brigade) about 300 yards east of the ridge road. Burgwyn placed the right flank of the 26th just north of the intersecting east-west fence running down the slope to the southwest corner of Herbst Woods. The line extended below the lane south of the Emanuel Harman farm. With the troops in their assigned locations, General Pettigrew ordered them to

19 Ladd & Ladd, *Bachelder Papers*, 2:94; Rood, "My Diary of the War"; Curtis, *History of the Twenty-Fourth Michigan*, 159, quoted from Morrow's July 30,1863 address in Detroit; "Synopsis of General Richardson's Speech," 2. At the 1871 Iron Brigade reunion, Richardson, without directly blaming Meredith for the damage done to the 19th Indiana, said they "appealed in vain." Dudley noted the 19th Indiana sent repeated requests to Meredith to fall back. Rood believed that General Doubleday sent the staffer who recalled them from the field. Richardson made it clear that Meredith was the person who decided to defend Herbst Woods.

unsling their knapsacks and lie down. Farther south, the remnants of General Archer's shattered brigade deployed in extended order to protect the exposed right flank from the 8th Illinois's dismounted skirmishers lurking around the Finnefrock buildings.[20]

Three of Col. John M. Brockenbrough's four Virginia regiments, meanwhile, had positioned themselves in the woods along a fence about 200 yards east of the ridge road. The 240 enlisted men of the 55th occupied the northern end of the line in the open field on the north side of the woods. The smaller 47th, with just 189 muskets, stood inside the woodlot, followed to the right by the 239-man 40th. The 22nd Battalion, 219-strong, completed the formation.[21]

In the Vicinity of the Seminary

In the meantime, Abner Doubleday, having ridden back toward the seminary, intercepted the prisoner escort from the 2nd Wisconsin under Lt. William H. Harries (Company B) somewhere along the campus road. Doubleday reined in alongside General Archer, whom he knew from his prewar Regular Army days.

"Good-morning, Archer, how are you?" he cordially asked. "I am glad to see you."

"Well, I am not glad to see you by a damn sight," shot back the disgruntled Confederate.

Taken aback by the unexpected rebuff, Doubleday simply announced, "Take him to the rear." With that, Doubleday abruptly rode south toward the Fairfield Road in search of the rest of Rowley's (Doubleday's) division. "The

20 Busey & Martin, *Regimental Strengths and Losses*, 222; "Reminiscences of Thomas Perritt"; Bachelder Map, July 1, Map 10/14; Clark, *Histories of the Several Regiments*, 2:348; "Southern Soldiers in Yankee Prisons," 159; Hood, "The 26th Regiment at Gettysburg."

21 Busey & Martin, *Regimental Strengths and Losses*, 225; Bachelder Map, July 1, Map 10/14; Report of Col. Robert Mayo, 47th Virginia, August 13, 1863, Vertical Files, Library, GNMP. Mayo confirmed that the brigade was in the woods on Herr's Ridge. The approximate frontage of the regiments offers a guide as to the location of these commands. The 26th North Carolina was separated from the 11th North Carolina by a fence on its right. That fence guided their line of advance to Herbst Woods. When Brockenbrough's regiments went into formation, the 55th Virginia extended into the open, with a fence separating it from the 47th Virginia.

meeting was far less pleasant to Archer than to Doubleday," observed Harries, who wrote about the exchange after the war.[22]

A squad from Company F, 8th New York Cavalry, took charge of the prisoners and with the infantry escort herded them east. Sergeant Frederick C. Waterman (Company A, 2nd Wisconsin) walked alongside the sullen Archer, chatting with him the entire way to Gettysburg. Corporal Nelson E. Evans, also with Company F, 8th New York Cavalry, surprised Pvt. Andrew Foulds, Jr. (Company K) when he hailed one of the captive Rebels by name. Evans, who recognized the man as someone he knew growing up with in Seneca Falls, New York, inquired how he had come to wear "those clothes." According to the unnamed prisoner, he had moved to Mobile, Alabama, before the war. He was exposed there to pro-secessionist sentiments and decided to join the Confederate Army because they seemed as right as anybody up North. Before he was hauled off to headquarters, he admonished his fellow New Yorkers, "Now, you boys, if you know when you are well off, you will get out of here as soon as you know how. Our forces are marching on Gettysburg and they will gobble you up as though you were nothing."[23]

The Low Ground East of the Seminary

After sending Archer away, General Doubleday headed down the east side of Seminary Ridge. While doing so he spotted the vanguard of Col. Roy Stone's brigade column and made a beeline toward it. He rode alongside the 143rd Pennsylvania as it double-quicked across the nearly dry Stevens Run.

"It's General Doubleday," declared one of the enlisted men.

"What command is this?" Doubleday shouted.

"The Pennsylvania Brigade," someone yelled back.

22 Harries, "The Iron Brigade," 340-341; Willett, "A Comrade"; Waterman, "At Gettysburg."

23 Harries, "The Iron Brigade," 4:340-341; Andrew Foulds, Jr., to Rev. R. S. McArthur September 7, 1890, Library, GNMP; Busey & Busey, *Confederate Casualties*, 1:57. Only one New York-born Confederate appears in the records from Archer's two Alabama regiments: Lt. Charles E. Denison (Company A, 5th Alabama Battalion), from Oswego County, born around 1838. Denison moved to Chicago in early 1857 and relocated later that same year to Gainesville (Sumter County), AL. He enlisted in 1861 and was present with the battalion on July 1, 1863. According to the records, he was shot between the scapulae near the 4th dorsal vertebrae (between the shoulder blades) and captured on July 3, 1863. I corrected the punctuation and spelling in the quote.

"Pennsylvania!" Doubleday exclaimed, "Go in for Pennsylvania!"

A cheer reverberated along the column. "We have come to stay," shouted an unnamed voice.

"Hold them, boys, when you get there," Doubleday demanded as the regiment trotted past him.

A Pennsylvanian hollered back, "If we can't hold them, where can you get men who can?"[24]

Rowley and Colonel Stone trotted up alongside about this time, and the three officers spurred toward the top of the ridge. The heat and exhaustion left a considerable number of men sweltering and heaving along the route from the Emmitsburg Road to the eastern base of Seminary Ridge. Sergeant DeLacy watched several fellows in the 143rd stumble and scramble to their feet in an effort to keep up.

Company I's scrounger, a sergeant, had marched the entire route with three "found" beef ribs skewered on his bayonet. With a battle looming, he threw them on the ground and quickened his pace. The obese and profusely sweating Lt. William P. Dougal (Company D, 150th Pennsylvania) asked Maj. Thomas Chamberlin if he could fall behind. The major consented, provided the exhausted lieutenant rounded up stragglers and herded them to the front. Within the hour Dougal had collected about 50 soldiers.[25]

Near the Seminary

Surgeon John H. Beech (24th Michigan) commandeered the regimental musicians. "The stretcher corps is six miles in the rear," he explained, "and you will have to go in and help carry the wounded." Bugler Arthur S. Congdon (Company E) and his friend Edwin Cotton (Company H) fashioned a makeshift stretcher out of fence boards and a blanket and hurried forward. The first man

24 "Capt. DeLacy Describes Gettysburg Battle," *The Scranton* [PA] *Truth*, July 1, 1913. In *Chancellorsville and Gettysburg*, 130, and *OR* 27/1:244, Doubleday almost certainly mistakenly attributed the quote to the 24th Michigan in *Chancellorsville and Gettysburg*, and to the Iron Brigade in the *Official Records* report. The fighting had ended by the time Doubleday received the order to hurry to the front. It is highly probable that his exchange was with Stone's command.

25 "Capt. DeLacy Describes Gettysburg Battle"; *Pennsylvania at Gettysburg*, 2:731; Chamberlin, *History of the 150th Regiment*, 111, 112. Doubleday likely picked up Stone and Rowley after his encounter with the 143rd Pennsylvania. From there, they rode up the ridge and found Biddle's brigade either in the road or just north of it.

they encountered was a heavy fellow shot through both legs who had collapsed face first in the marshy field. The two musicians worked the unnamed soldier onto the "stretcher" and made for the rear.[26]

11:30 a.m. to 11:45 a.m.[27] *The Gatekeeper's House on Cemetery Hill*

Captain James Hall (Battery B, 2nd Maine) had just rolled his three remaining guns into battery front, facing west, when Lt. Col. John A. Kress of Wadsworth's staff rode up with orders for him to return to the front; Wadsworth had decided to hold the line. Kress told Hall to follow him and abruptly left the battery when it reached the eastern end of the railroad bank descending from the cut through Seminary Ridge. Hall studied the elevated track bed in front of him and observed artillery fire raking the top of the hill. Based on the rate of fire, he believed a section of Rebel artillery was responsible, and the enemy guns were making the passage too dangerous to use.

Hall opted to take his three guns up the north side of the embankment to give his men some shelter from the incoming fire. He parked the pieces on the east side of Sheads Woods and rode ahead to get orders. Kress intercepted him at the woodline. "Move your battery up through this clump of woods (Sheads) and into position on the right of them on a knoll (Oak Hill)," the colonel instructed.

Hall led his guns along the eastern face of the woods until they encountered a Federal cavalryman riding in from the north who warned Hall that Confederates were coming directly toward them from the north. Hall halted the battery while he and a sergeant spurred to the northern side of the tree line, where they immediately came under fire from Rebel skirmishers. Hall

26 Edwin Cotton, "The Men Who Made the Music," *NT*, July 7, 1894, 2; Curtis, *History of the Twenty-Fourth Michigan*, 177, 178. As stretcher bearers, the musicians would probably have taken care of the wounded of their own regiment. According to the regimental history Pvts. Samuel T. Lautenslager (Company G), John Renton (Company D), and Thomas Brennan (Company E) were all shot through both legs.

27 Edmund L. Dana, Diary, July 1, 1863, Edmund L. Dana Papers, Wyoming Historical and Geological Society, Wilkes-Barre, PA, as cited in James J. Dougherty, "We Have Come to Stay!': The 143rd Regiment Pennsylvania Volunteer Infantry and the Fight for McPherson's Ridge," *GM*, No. 24 (Jan. 1, 2000), 43, fn 21. Dana put the time of arrival at McPherson's as 11:45 a.m. It probably took the regiment about five minutes or so to cross the field from Seminary Ridge.

countermarched his pieces back to the sheltered spot they had left but a few minutes earlier.[28]

Fairfield Road-Campus Road Intersection

The 151st Pennsylvania, marching at the front of Biddle's brigade, stopped just below the intersection of the Fairfield Road with the seminary lane and faced north. The rest of the regiments followed suit. The order to scale the post and board fence and reassemble on the other side traveled down the formation. Private Edwin R. Gearhart (Company G, 142nd Pennsylvania), who would have seen the trampled valley to the north as well as McPherson's Ridge started climbing the fence. An officer who knew Gearhart was ill ordered him to stay behind with the musicians. Gearhart reluctantly complied. Ambling west about 50 yards along the road, he came upon a sick enlisted man propped against the fence. Without hesitating, he asked the man for his weapon and accoutrements. Once he strapped on the cartridge and cap boxes about his waist, Gearhart shouldered the rifle and jogged slowly up the hill to rejoin the regiment. The "boys" cheered when he fell in amongst them. "I felt real happy because I was in Pennsylvania," recalled Gearhart.[29]

The sporadic sound of small arms crackled through the air while artillery rounds swooshed from the north through the sky. Captain John D. S. Cook (Company I, 20th N.Y.S.M.) gazed west across the valley while waiting for orders to deploy. Cook remembered seeing the tops of Gettysburg's church spires poking above the valley on his right before the brigade went into regimental front.

From his vantage point on horseback through his field glasses, Maj. Alexander Biddle (121st Pennsylvania) could see Confederate skirmishers from

28 Ladd & Ladd, *Bachelder Papers*, 1:388; *OR* 27/1:360; *Maine at Gettysburg*, 20. While colorful, the account from *Maine at Gettysburg* varies too much from both the letter to Bachelder of December 29, 1869 and Hall's after-action report written on July 16, 1863. In the Bachelder account, Hall wrote that Col. Clement Best (XII Corps artillerist) led him back to the cut. As noted by the editors, that man was probably John A. Kress of the I Corps.

29 "In the Years '62 to '65," 34; *OR* 27/1:317, 320, 323, 327; R. D. Sayre, "A Day at Gettysburg," *NT*, April 13, 1893, 3. Sayre [Sayn] mistook the Fairfield (Hagerstown) Road for the Emmitsburg Pike. Both Lt. Col. George McFarland (151st Pennsylvania) and Col. Theodore B. Gates (20th N.Y.S.M.) said they occupied the left of the brigade line. I chose Gates's report based upon the Bachelder Maps. Whoever transcribed Sayre's letter for the *Tribune* misread it. Sayre was in fact Randle D. Sayn.

Pettigrew's Brigade lying on the hillside along the eastern face of the woods on Herr's Ridge.[30]

Once Doubleday reached the summit at the point where the Fairfield Road crossed Seminary Ridge, he instructed Colonel Stone where to deploy his brigade. He next turned his attention to Colonel Biddle's regiments, which had just halted on the northern side of the Fairfield Road. Rowley ordered Biddle to front his brigade facing west and oblique the line northwest and align it along the eastern side of McPherson's Ridge with its right flank immediately south of Herbst Woods.

That move would place Biddle's command parallel with Seminary and McPherson's ridges. As the 142nd Pennsylvania wheeled by company to the left, Sgt. Jacob J. Zorn (Company F) overheard Doubleday, whom he admired, advise Rowley, "General, take care of my men." With much pride, Zorn later recorded in his diary, "Let it be Said for Gen Doubleday that very few Generals in the Army at Just Such a time as this would ever think of the men of their Division as this genl after taking the Responsible position of Commanding a Corps."[31]

Rowley established his headquarters on the south side of the seminary and placed his headquarters guard (Company D, 149th Pennsylvania) across the Fairfield Road/seminary lane intersection to support Stewart's and Reynolds's batteries. A mounted squad of about 10 men from Company L, 1st Maine Cavalry, stood ready in front of Elizabeth Shultz's house.[32]

30 Croner, *A Sergeant's Story*, 67; *OR* 27/1:315, 317, 320, 323, 326; Gates, *Ulster Guard*, 432; Cook, "Personal Reminiscences," 324; *Pennsylvania at Gettysburg*, 2:652, 653, 746. Colonel Chapman Biddle was elevated from the 121st Pennsylvania to command the brigade, and his 1st cousin, Maj. Alexander Biddle, given command of the 121st. (Neither man was related to Col. George H. Biddle of the 95th New York.) Major Biddle claimed the brigade formed facing west on the edge of an open woods (Seminary Ridge) prior to advancing northwest and forming in the left-rear of the First Division (Meredith's Iron Brigade). To have seen the Confederates that far off, Biddle would have needed binoculars or a spyglass. He also claimed the men saw Reynolds on the field or while being carried off.

31 *OR* 27/1:315, 317, 320, 323, 326; Croner, *A Sergeant's Story*, 67.

32 John W. Nesbit, comp., *General History of Company D, 149th Pennsylvania Volunteers* (Oakdale, PA, 1908), 14. The squad could consist of one sergeant, one or two corporals, and eight privates, depending on the size of the company from which it originated. It may have come from Company L, 1st Maine Cavalry, because that unit performed guard and courier duty for the I Corps. It makes sense they would have provided details for the division commanders.

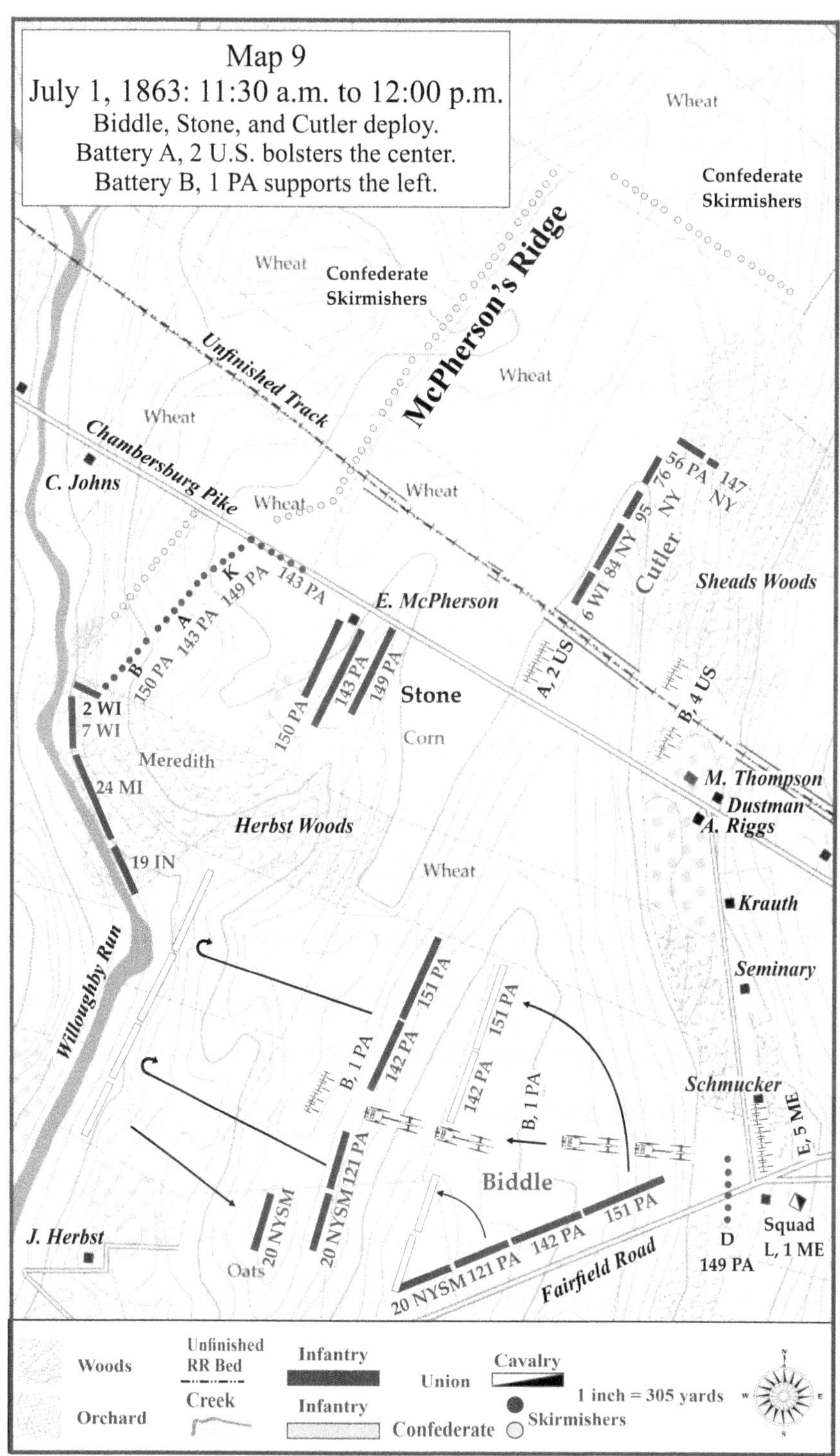
Map 9
July 1, 1863: 11:30 a.m. to 12:00 p.m.
Biddle, Stone, and Cutler deploy.
Battery A, 2 U.S. bolsters the center.
Battery B, 1 PA supports the left.
Wheat
Confederate Skirmishers
Confederate Skirmishers
McPherson's Ridge
Unfinished Track
Chambersburg Pike
C. Johns
E. McPherson
56 PA
147 NY
76 NY
95 NY
84 NY
6 WI
Cutler
Sheads Woods
143 PA
149 PA
150 PA
143 PA
149 PA
150 PA
Stone
Corn
A, 2 US
B, 4 US
2 WI
7 WI
Meredith
24 MI
19 IN
Herbst Woods
M. Thompson
Dustman
A. Riggs
Krauth
Seminary
Willoughby Run
151 PA
142 PA
B, 1 PA
151 PA
142 PA
B, 1 PA
Schmucker
E, 5 ME
Biddle
20 NYSM
121 PA
20 NYSM
20 NYSM 121 PA 142 PA 151 PA
Fairfield Road
J. Herbst
Oats
D
149 PA
Squad L, 1 ME
Woods
Orchard
Unfinished RR Bed
Creek
Infantry
Union
Infantry
Confederate
Cavalry
Skirmishers
1 inch = 305 yards

With Biddle's brigade out of the road, Capt. James H. Cooper rolled his battery up to the intersection. There, he encountered Col. Charles Wainwright, who ordered him make for McPherson's Ridge. Wainwright told Cooper to go into battery on the crest south of Herbst Woods and "to await events." While Cooper's rifles rattled and creaked toward Sergeant Pergel's former position, Wainwright rode north toward the railroad cut. The minute Cooper came into sight, Confederate riflemen and artillery directed their attention at his pieces. Once on front, the four 3-inch rifles unlimbered and responded.[33]

Vicinity of the Seminary (North of Biddle's Brigade)

Roy Stone's 143rd and 149th Pennsylvania regiments tramped up the Fairfield Road from the east to the seminary lane and turned right. Private Avery "Orr" Harris (Company B, 143rd) heard what he described as "the crack of the carbine" and "the plunk, plunk of light caliber artillery" intensify as his regiment neared the crest. Generals Doubleday and Rowley sat astride their horses in the lane. The brigade veered downhill, northwest through an open white oak woodlot on the western slope of Seminary Ridge and halted in the sprouting cornfield immediately beyond the destroyed worm fence west of Alexander Riggs's place. While they stood there, a dismounted cavalryman armed with a carbine approached Company B grousing about how he wanted to avenge the death of his horse at the hands of the Rebels earlier that morning. Private Harris thought he heard him say he was from the 8th Michigan. Colonel Edmund L. Dana apparently told the trooper to go somewhere else.[34]

With the 150th Pennsylvania marching at the tail of his marching column, Colonel Stone ordered the soldiers to pile their knapsacks and blanket rolls. The word traveled by companies through the ranks of his first two Pennsylvania regiments. Private Harris recalled instinctively feeling that he and the boys

33 Nevins, *Diary of Battle*, 234; *OR* 27/1:355, 364; *Pennsylvania at Gettysburg*, 2:877. Lieutenant James A. Gardner wrote that the battery went in position at noon. In the after-action report, Cooper also claimed it was around noon.

34 Fulton, "A Surgeon's Story of the Battle"; Isaac B. Noecker to Editor, *Lebanon* [PA] *Courier*, July 9, 1863; *OR* 27/1:334; Tomasak, *Harris Journal*, 59. The trooper, Dennis Buckley, Company H, 8th Michigan Cavalry, had been "left behind" when the Michigan Brigade passed through the town several days earlier. He is not in the Adjutant General's report, however, and there is only one piece of paperwork on him in Army files. No other cavalrymen mention seeing or knowing him. Doubleday lauded him by name in his report. It is more likely than not that Buckley had, for whatever reason, gone AWOL.

Colonel Roy Stone's brigade was composed of mostly green soldiers, but they held the McPherson farm area against numerous attacks until being driven off late in the afternoon. LOC

would never see their belongings again. Doubleday and Rowley trotted along the formation. Sergeant Patrick DeLacy (Company A) recalled a fragment of what Doubleday said as he quickly briefed the men on what had preceded them. The general specifically mentioned that Capt. Michael Flynn (Co. C, 56th Pennsylvania) had ordered the first fire on the field, thereby emphasizing what those in the ranks already knew: Doubleday entrusted the Pennsylvanians with securing a victory in defense of their home state. With that, the two regiments started across the soggy fields toward McPherson's farm. Sporadic bursts of artillery projectiles launched from Herr's Ridge peppered the field.[35]

Colonel Edmund L. Dana's 143rd Pennsylvania led the advance with Lt. Col. Walton Dwight's 149th behind it. An artillery round killed "Charley," Lt. Col. John D. Musser's favorite mount. "I had to double quick some distance with the regt.," Musser explained in his after-action report. The 143rd reached the vicinity of the McPherson barn. Dana anchored his right (Company I) near the barn and extended his left south into an orchard. Artillery projectiles "whooshed" or screamed low over the ridge. Corporal Simon Hubler (Company I) recalled that small arms rounds buzzed overhead with "uncomfortable frequency." A loud crack startled Hubler and Pvt. Jacob Yale, who was standing

35 Tomasak, *Harris Journal*, 59; Ladd & Ladd, *Bachelder Papers*, 2:953; William S. Downing to Dear Wife, July 6, 1863, Vertical Files, VF 143PA, Library, GNMP; Diary, July 1, 1863, Pvt. Charles D. W. Hoover, Vertical Files, VF143PA, Library, GNMP; *Pennsylvania at Gettysburg*, 2:731; Fulton, "A Surgeon's Story of the Battle"; *OR* 27/1:331, 332, 334, 346; "Capt. DeLacy Describes Gettysburg Battle." DeLacy did not say who briefed the line or told them about Flynn. Doubleday addressed the brigade before it advanced, and was probably the source for DeLacy's recollection.

alongside him, fell against his leg and landed across his feet. The blood pouring onto his face from the hole above one of Yale's eyes told Hubler all he needed to know.[36]

On the left of the line, Capt. M. Lewis Blain (Company E) helped a wounded man over the fence along the farm lane to Surgeon James Fulton, who helped the man into the McPherson farmhouse east of the line. The floor was already blanketed with wounded artillerymen. The surgeon hunted for his mounted orderly, only to discover that he and his medical field kit were nowhere to be seen. Unable to assist anyone, Fulton mounted and headed toward the seminary to fetch his much-needed equipment.[37]

Colonel Dana, meanwhile, ordered his 143rd Pennsylvanians to lie down. All save a few complied until their company officers coerced them to go prone. The almost comical scene of some of the men bobbing their heads up and down between air bursts amused the now-dismounted Lieutenant Colonel Musser. Confederate artillerymen along Herr Ridge managed to get in a few good shots, one of which wounded Pvt. Charles C. Davis (Company C). The distinct "Bang! Flup! Thud!" of a ricochet close to Company B attracted Pvt. Avery Harris's attention. The round skipped through Company I on his right and ripped away Lt. Oren E. Vaughen's haversack—all without touching him. "Well, boys, they have cut off my supplies," joked the startled file closer. The same sergeant from Company I who had tossed aside his beef ribs showed up with a crock of thick milk, which he had miraculously "found" on the premises. He did not hesitate to share it with some of the boys and Colonel Dana.[38]

While the 143rd regiment was in place, the 149th Pennsylvania came up on its right in the farm lane and faced west. On the extreme left of the line in the dirt road, Capt. Francis Bacon Jones (Company G) watched what he mistook for 6-pounder rounds ricochet off the ground behind the regiment and bound

36 Hoover diary, July 1, 1863; Lt. Col. John D. Musser, unpublished report, September 15, 1863, John D. Musser Papers, Ronald D. Boyer Collection, USAHEC, 1; Shafer, "First in at Gettysburg"; Tomasak, *Harris Journal*, 59; Simon Hubler, "Just the Plain, Untarnished Story of a Soldier in the Ranks," *New York Times*, USAHEC; Fulton, "A Surgeon's Story of the Battle." Participants referred to the trees as either an apple or a peach orchard.

37 Fulton, "A Surgeon's Story of the Battle."

38 Musser Report; Hoover diary, July 1, 1863; Shafer, "First in at Gettysburg"; Tomasak, *Harris Journal*, 60. Company I had two sergeants, Jesse Harrison and Edward P. McCreary, with one of them probably being the scrounger. Shafer identified the officer who lost his haversack as Lieutenant Vaughen; Harris did not specify the fellow's rank.

toward the seminary, shattering whatever blocked their paths—stray horses, hapless soldiers, and rail fences. Small arms fire passed over the line from the west but failed to strike anyone in the 149th's left wing.[39]

The Seminary Woodlot

Colonel Stone, meanwhile, rode up to Col. Langhorne Wister's 150th Pennsylvania, which had just lurched to a halt in column of fours, and told Wister where to deploy his men. With shells bursting above McPherson's Ridge and over the valley along the 150th's front, Wister formed the companies on battalion front. When the command "Forward!" rang out, a shout went up from the ranks, "Colonel, we are not loaded yet!" Major Thomas Chamberlin and Lt. Col. Henry Huidekoper spat out nervous laughs, despite having just learned of Reynolds's death. The embarrassed Wister commanded his men to load. As soon as they came to "order arms," he instructed them to unsling their knapsacks. With his regiment finally prepared, the colonel ordered it forward at the double-quick.[40]

It took about five minutes for the 150th Pennsylvania to join the other two regiments of the brigade. Company B was on the left of the line, followed on the right respectively by Companies H, I, G, and C, then the color guard. Companies E, D, F, and A finished out the formation to the right. With the brigade complete, Colonel Stone instructed his regimental commanders to detach one company west as skirmishers. Colonel Wister chose Capt. George W. Jones and his Company B. He specifically instructed Jones to advance until he met the enemy, and to engage him. Colonel Edmund Dana of the 143rd

39 John H. Bassler, "The Color Episode of the One Hundred and Forty-Ninth Regiment Pennsylvania Volunteers in the First Day's Fight at Gettysburg, July 1st, 1863," *Paper Read Before the Lebanon County Historical Society, October 18th, 1907*, 5; "Excerpt from Chronicles of Francis Bacon Jones," Robert Brake Collection, USAHEC, 4-5; Chamberlin, *History of the 150th Regiment*, 114. Bassler said about 1/3 of the regiment faced north along the Chambersburg Pike. The regiment did face west and north, but not at this stage of the action.

40 *Pennsylvania at Gettysburg*, 2:731; Chamberlin, *History of the 150th Regiment*, 112; *OR* 27/1:334. At the 1889 dedication of the monument at Gettysburg, Chamberlin said he ordered an advance then had the men discard their knapsacks. Six years later in the regimental history, he changed the order: the men piled up their knapsacks then he said, "Forward!" Of the two, I chose the latter account because other primary documents support that assertion.

Pennsylvania detached Capt. Charles M. Conyngham's Company A to cover the front of his regiment. Dana also directed Company F's Capt. Robert Crockett to take his sharpshooters along the Chambersburg Pike on the right of Company A. Captain John C. Johnson (Company K, 149th Pennsylvania) was singled out to join the other three companies.[41]

Sergeant Patrick DeLacy recalled decades later that the boys in Company A, 143rd Pennsylvania, cheered as they headed over the ridge. The skirmishers from the three companies fanned out, firing in pairs as they advanced. Captain Crockett and his 30 sharpshooters kept to the road, using the post and rail fence as cover. Fire from Confederate skirmishers behind the fence along the quarry lane inflicted casualties. Private Abraham N. Ide took a bullet in the side and collapsed. Sergeant William H. Bennett went down next. Sergeant Herbert N. Nogle ran back to DeLacy shouting, "Billy is dead. Billy is done for!" before wheeling about and returning to his friend. Nogle threw Bennett over one shoulder and ran a gauntlet of small arms fire and shell bursts all the way to the field hospital at the barn, saving his comrade's life.[42]

Despite their losses the Pennsylvanians drove the Rebs away from the fence, across the creek, and finally occupied the abandoned fence row. The walking wounded stumbled back through the ranks of the 143rd to the aide station at the barn and house. Lieutenant Colonel John D. Musser noted with a certain amount of understatement that they made the men nervous and uneasy. Most of the artillery rounds harmlessly passed over the prone regiment on the eastern side of the ridge. One, however, burst in Company C, killing one enlisted man and injuring two others, one of whom, Pvt. Alonzo Platt, lost his leg and later his life.[43]

Colonel Wister moved the 150th past the barn and uphill to the low worm fence along the crest. The color guard came under long-range fire the moment the center formed along the southern side of a duck pond between the fence and

41 Chamberlin, *History of the 150th Regiment*, 112; *OR* 27/1:329, 335; "Captain DeLacy Describes the Battle of Gettysburg"; John F. Krumwiede, "A July Afternoon on McPherson's Ridge," *GM*, No. 21 (July 1, 1999), 29. Krumwiede did not cite the source from which he obtained the details on the organization of the regimental line. I placed Company B on the far left of the line, next to H, because Wister would have detached a flank company for skirmish duty.

42 "Capt. DeLacy Describes the Battle."

43 Musser Report; Wheeler, "Reminiscences," 210; William L. Perry to Dear Friends, July 2, 1863, William R. Brown, Private Collection.

the barn. A one-ounce ball (probably from a case shot) slammed into Cpl. James Monroe "Roe" Reisinger's right foot. The iron ball shattered his instep, passed along the base of his second toe, and lodged in the ball of his foot. Color Sergeant Samuel Peiffer (Company I) and the other members urged him to go to the hospital. Reisinger, who discovered that he could walk if he put his weight on the right heel, adamantly refused to leave the line.[44]

Biddle's Brigade

Earlier, on the way across the field to support Cooper's guns, Maj. Alexander Biddle (121st Pennsylvania) noticed Colonel Stone's brigade, in column of regiments, rushing across the northern end of the valley toward the north side of Herbst Woods. Colonel Chapman Biddle's brigade went prone as soon as it reached the eastern side of McPherson's Ridge southeast of Stone's position. The 151st Pennsylvania anchored its right flank perpendicular to the southern face of the woods. The 142nd Pennsylvania formed on its left with Cooper's guns to its left front. About 65 yards south, to the left-rear of the battery, the 121st Pennsylvania extended the line, with the 20th N.Y.S.M. holding the far left. Since Cooper's battery divided the brigade in half, Colonel Biddle decided to place both the 20th N.Y.S.M. and the 121st Pennsylvania under the former regiment's commander,. Col. Theodore B. Gates, while Biddle controlled the two remaining Pennsylvania regiments on the right.

General Rowley's command to unsling knapsacks, followed immediately by "fix bayonets," squelched most of the joking in the ranks of the 121st Pennsylvania. Color Sergeant Edward "Ned" Beckit, Sr. (Company F) ordered the color guard of the 20th N. Y. S. M. to move five paces forward to the top of the ridge. The moment the guard advanced, a notorious slacker and troublemaker nicknamed "Jersey" dropped his rifle and bolted from the regimental line behind the guard toward Cooper's guns. An astonished Cpl. Enos Vail of the color guard stared in amazement as "Jersey" assumed the "Number one" man's post at the right front of one of Cooper's pieces.

The 20th's flags diverted some of the pressure from the battery. Minié balls buzzed around the color guard like angry yellow jackets. The armed members of the guard calmly and deliberately replied. Nineteen-year-old Corporal Vail

44 "Three Bullets at Gettysburg: Medal of Honor Recipients," *Military Images*, vol. 35, no. 3 (2017), 13, http://www.jstor.org/stable/26112024, accessed Jan. 27, 2023.

managed to get four shots off and was ramming his next cartridge when something clubbed him forcefully enough to hurl him to the ground. Ignoring his aching back, Vail forced himself to stand upright to finish loading his weapon. His legs went out from under him. Struggling to his feet a second time, he turned about and, fueled by fear verging on panic, raced toward the seminary and the low stone wall in front of it.[45]

Pursuant to orders, Colonel Biddle's had his men stand to march them over the crest into the bottomland east of Willoughby Run to get them out of the line of fire. Intermittent small arms rounds cracked through the marshy low ground from the fenced-in grain field on the top of the hill west of the Emanuel Harman buildings. Projectiles occasionally screamed overhead from the artillery on Herr's Ridge. Colonel Gates and his veterans of the "Ulster Guards" knew the timothy field was rife with enemy sharpshooters, and they could not understand why Rowley had placed them in a defilade from which they could not return fire. After several annoying minutes Biddle retired the brigade, except the 20th N.Y.S.M., and moved the regiments back to their prior position on the eastern side of the ridge. Biddle kept the Ulster Guards in plain sight of the enemy on the brow of the hill.[46]

By this time, one of Cooper's Ordnance Rifles had broken an axle during its recoil. The artillerist dispatched an orderly to alert General Wadsworth of the situation and had the piece dragged by the limber to the rear. "Old Waddy" personally rode up to Colonel Gates and demanded he deploy a company across Willoughby Run to flush the sharpshooters. Gates assigned the job to Capt. Ambrose N. Baldwin and his sharpshooters of Company K.[47]

45 *OR* 27/1:317, 320, 323, 326; *History of the 121st Regiment*, 51; Gates, *Ulster Guard*, 432, 440; Cook, "Personal Reminiscences," 324; Vail, *Reminiscences*, 117, 118, 127; "Colonel McFarland's Diary Reveals War-School Career," *Gettysburg Times*, June 27, 1941.

46 *OR* 27/1:317; Cook, "Personal Reminiscences," 324; Gates, *Ulster Guard*, 432-433; *OR* 27/1:317. Colonel Gates said the brigade was moving west into the Willoughby Run valley 10 minutes after arriving at McPherson's Ridge, which places the line on the move by 11:40 a.m. If they stayed there a few minutes longer it is conceivable that the regiment would have returned to the top of the ridge around 11:45 a.m.

47 *OR* 27/1:315, 317, 320, 364-365; Gates, *Ulster Guard*, 433; Vail, *Reminiscences*, 66. In his official report, written in 1864, Gates said the regiment was in the open "about" 20 minutes before Wadsworth told him to silence the skirmishers. In the 1879 regimental history, he asserted that the incident occurred "ten minutes later." Cooper did not say how he got the piece off the field; since it was not captured, the crew likely hauled it away.

As they dashed southwest across the field toward the Harman place, Pvt. Alexander Tice (Company E), volunteered to go along. Private Tice, who had drawn noncombatant duty in all of the regiment's previous engagements, had confessed earlier that morning to his close friend Vail, "You know I have never been in battle, and I have a presentiment that am going to be killed." At the time, Vail laughed it off by telling Tice that he had been in every engagement and was still alive and well. But Private Tice was right. Enemy metal soon found and killed him.[48]

Rachel and Amelia Harman observed much of the morning's fight from the cupola of their home. From that vantage point, they witnessed General Cutler coming onto the field and watched as the Iron Brigade overpowered Archer's command. What they did not see was Baldwin and his sharpshooters of Company K rush onto their property. The New Yorkers created such a racket at the kitchen door at the rear of the house that it sent the two women hurrying down to the first floor, which was shaking from the infantrymen trying to destroy the heavy door.

"Open, or we'll break down the doors!" Baldwin bellowed.

One of the ladies began pulling open the door, which slammed all the way open as "maddened, powder blackened bluecoats" stormed into the kitchen. The horseshoe-clad heels of the soldiers' brogans thudded across the wood floors and then up the stairway. Baldwin, meanwhile, sent the women into the cellar while his men dispersed into the rooms on the western side of the house and opened fire. Huddled in the dank blackness of the basement, Amelia recalled how she and Rachel could hear their racing hearts pounding above the racket overhead.[49]

The New Yorkers were peppering the right side of Colonel Burgwyn's 26th North Carolina. "We still await orders with the enemie's sharp shooters occasionally reminding us that we had better [lie down]," Private Thomas Perritt (Company G) wryly noted. Burgwyn ordered an enlisted man to roust the pesky Union sharpshooters out of the structure, but Perritt's lieutenant, John Anderson Lowe, volunteered to go instead. Crawling south along the fence row, he finally spied the sharpshooters on the roof of the Harman house, lurking behind the chimney. A couple of well-placed rounds neutralized any more

48 Vail, *Reminiscences*, 127.

49 "Burning of the McLean House on the First Day's Battle of Gettysburg," https://genealogytrails.com/penn/adams/burning_McLeanHouse.html, accessed Feb. 4, 2023.

threats from that quarter. In the interim, the Carolinians sent canteen details to the rear to fetch water and alleviated the tension by nervously joking and "braving up" one another.[50]

50 Clark, *Histories of the Several Regiments*, 2:350; John R. Lane, "Anniversary of Gettysburg Forty Years After the Battle," *Charlotte Daily Observer*, July 4, 1903; John R. Lane, "Address at Gettysburg," *News and Observer* (Raleigh, NC), July 5, 1903; "Reminiscences of Thomas Perritt," https://digital.ncdcr.gov/digital/collection/p15012coll8/id/12333, accessed Feb. 4, 2023. Underwood, who wrote the history of the 26th North Carolina for Clark, *Histories of the Several Regiments*, 2:350, plagiarized Perritt's "A Trip That Didn't Pay," which recounted his experiences at Gettysburg. Colonel Lane, in his renditions of the battle, admitted that he quoted Underwood verbatim. Lifting large sections of the work of a previous writer was not uncommon for veterans of both armies.

Chapter Eight

"Can I fight in your regiment?"

— *John Burns, civilian*

The I Corps Reorganizes

11:30 a.m. to 1:00 p.m.

11:30 a.m. to 11:45 a.m.
Seminary Ridge

General Wadsworth was deeply concerned about the state of his bloodied division. It was still early in the fighting, but it had been seriously mauled and was in danger of being routed. To bolster his position, he detached Battery A, 2nd U.S. forward toward the ridge south of the middle cut. Lieutenant Calef led his four remaining pieces across the Chambersburg Pike into the casualty-strewn ground west of Mary Thompson's place.

An ominous quiet had settled over the field. According to Calef, "It seemed as though both sides had retired to their corners, awaiting the call of 'time.'" The wounded pleaded with the drivers not to roll over them. Calef cautioned his men to be mindful of them as the battery, in column of piece, slowly maneuvered its way through the bodies.

The 21-year-old Calef studied everything within his line of sight. Hall's piece was stuck in the Thompson's gate, all its horses dead. Just to the east, infantrymen strained to get the gun with the broken wheel to the pike. Wending farther toward the cut, he spied Lt. Frederick Ulmer's abandoned gun facing his approach, its crew dead or dying about it.

Calef's pieces rolled into battery front by piece under what he described as "a heavy musket fire" from Confederate skirmishers. The crews unlimbered the guns from left to the right and the drivers wheeled the limbers into place behind their respective pieces. The carnage wrought by the morning's combat deeply troubled the young lieutenant: "The field presented a true battle picture, seen in all the horrors of its reality, can never be effaced from my memory."

There was not much time to dwell on the sea of wounded, dying, and dead. Rebel skirmishers were already targeting his cannoneers. Turning in the saddle, Calef looked back at the eastern railroad cut. Union infantry was still reforming there, and he concluded Wadsworth was having trouble getting the men to move out. With his battery ready to get down to business, the lieutenant told his gunners to fire by piece. The first 3-inch Ordnance Rifle cracked and recoiled, the tube violently rocking on its trunnions as it sent a round screaming toward Herr's Ridge. Battery A, 2nd U.S. Artillery had just reopened the battle.[1]

Colonel Pegram's 14 Confederate field pieces responded immediately from Herr's Ridge and the Wills farm. Calef saw the white puffs of smoke before he heard the reports. His veteran artillerists took the shelling in stride, returning fire slowly and deliberately against both targets. The drivers, deeply attached to their animals, scooped up the oats that Hall's Mainers had jettisoned during their retreat and fed them to the horses. The harnessed teams were indifferent to the shell bursts. Calef marveled at how calmly they munched the grain and grass. A horse occasionally reacted to an exploding shell by lazily raising its head. Several would perish in their harnesses.[2]

After recalling Cutler's brigade from the eastern side of Oak Ridge, General Wadsworth observed increased small arms fire near the middle cut. The 147th New York, numbering only about 75 enlisted men, held the right of the line, with the 56th Pennsylvania, 76th New York, 95th New York, and 14th Brooklyn finishing the formation to the south. The battered regiments passed west through Sheads Woods and picked up the 6th Wisconsin on the way to the top of the ridge on Calef's right.

1 *OR* 27/1:1031; Calef, "Gettysburg Notes," 50, 51.

2 Calef, "Gettysburg Notes," 50-51; *OR* 27/1:1032. In his after-action report, Calef wrote that 12 guns opened on him. In his 1907 account he increased it to 36 guns between McIntosh's and Pegram's battalions. McIntosh's guns did not go into action until a few hours later. Pegram had 17 pieces in action during the day, but at this time only 14 opened on Calef's battery.

Lieutenant Joseph F. Slagle, who had rejoined Doubleday in the grove west of the seminary, watched the ragged line dash for the ridge north of the cut. Six of Pegram's guns south of the Chambersburg Pike shelled the formation as it advanced, taking out several members of the 6th Wisconsin. Upon reaching the eastern base of the ridge, Colonel Dawes ordered his men prone below the crest to protect them from the air bursts. The rest of the line went to ground while skirmishers fired over the ridge.[3]

Once again, Captain Hall ventured out to find a superior officer to tell him where to deploy his three Ordnance Rifles. He found Col. Charles Wainwright in the Chambersburg Pike. The colonel took note of the battery's depleted condition and instead of placing it somewhere to fight, ordered Hall to take his guns to the rear. He also bluntly castigated Hall that one of his guns remained on the field and that he had refused to place the battery where Wadsworth had wanted it posted. While what was left of his battery rolled toward Cemetery Hill, Hall commandeered one of his sergeants, a private, and a limber with four horses. The small group headed into the turnpike and turned west back toward the battlefield.[4]

11:45 a.m. to 12:00 p.m.[5]

Following the same track as the brigades that had preceded them, Brig. Gen. Henry Baxter's regiments (Robinson's Second Division) cut northwest off the Emmitsburg Road across the fields at the Codori farm. The 11th Pennsylvania led the brigade, followed by the 97th New York, 90th Pennsylvania, 88th Pennsylvania, 9th New York State Militia (83rd New York), and 13th Massachusetts. Private Thomas L. Hanna (Company F, 9th N.Y.S.M.) was

3 *Pennsylvania at Gettysburg*, 2:725; Ladd & Ladd, *Bachelder Papers*, 1:204, 205, 331 and 3:1170; *OR*, 27/1:276; Dawes, *Service with the Sixth Wisconsin*, 174. For a different interpretation of Cutler's position on the field, particularly during Alfred Iverson's attack, see McLean, *"The Bullets Flew Like Hail,"* 127-139.

4 Ladd & Ladd, *Bachelder Papers*, 1:388; *OR* 27/1:360; *Maine at Gettysburg*, 21. In Bachelder, Hall wrote that he took two men and four horses back with him. In his earlier report in the *OR*, he claimed that he had a limber and a sergeant with him. The road he referred to in the letter to Bachelder is probably the Chambersburg Pike. In *Maine at Gettysburg*, Hall asserted that he, not Wainwright, broached the suggestion to recover the field piece.

5 Dana diary, July 1, 1863, 43, fn 21.

struggling to get over the discarded rails of the stone and rider fence along the road when an orderly galloped by and yelled at the men that General Reynolds had been killed. Hanna recalled glancing up at the sky overhead and remembering how bright blue it seemed at that moment.[6]

Baxter's brigade was approaching Middle Street when an aide from General Doubleday arrived to inform General Robinson of the unfolding situation and that Robinson needed to secure the seminary. The division commander directed Col. Richard Coulter (11th Pennsylvania) to take his regiment and the 97th New York and follow the aide. As acting commander, Coulter passed the word on to Col. Charles Wheelock of the 97th New York, who in turn told Lt. Col. John P. Spofford to get the two regiments moving. Reining in his mount in front of both regiments Spofford joked, "You are detailed to-day for a support. They don't want to let you meet the enemy as they are afraid you will run." The soldiers laughed at the jest as they assembled to step off.[7]

General Robinson detached Brig. Gen. Gabriel R. Paul's brigade and sent it northwest across Middle Street and the Fairfield Road toward the seminary. Lieutenant Slagle intercepted Robinson on the ridge and directed him to put the brigade in the woodlot west of the seminary building. As soon as the regiments halted, Robinson ordered them to construct a semicircular rail breastwork in the

6 *Pennsylvania at Gettysburg*, 1:166; Boone, "Personal Experiences," 21, 22; George W. Grant "The First Army Corps," 47; Ladd & Ladd, *Bachelder Papers*, 2:677; Hanna, "A Day at Gettysburg"; Jaques, *Three Years' Campaign of the Ninth N.Y.S.M.*, 154; Todd, *History of the Ninth Regiment*, 268; Isaac Hall, *History of the Ninety-Seventh Regiment New York Volunteers* (Utica, NY, 1890), 134, 136; Frank Jennings, "Reminiscence," 3, CWTI Collection, USAHEC. Corporal Frank Jennings (Company A, 90th Pennsylvania) wrote that the regiment formed the right of the line, which meant that it would march at the front of the column. Since the 11th Pennsylvania and 97th New York were detached from the head of the brigade and the 11th reached its position ahead of the 97th, it would have to have led the column, which would have placed the 90th immediately behind the 97th.

7 *OR* 27/1:289, 307; Vautier, *History of the 88th Pennsylvania*, 105; *NYAG*, 2:677; *Pennsylvania at Gettysburg*, 1:166; Locke, *The Story of the Regiment*, 229; Todd, *History of the Ninth Regiment*, 269; Hall, *History of the Ninety-Seventh Regiment*, 140; https://cwl.dhinitiative.org/islandora/object/HamiltonCivilWar%3A1044, accessed Feb. 1, 2023; Sgt. Michael Kirby [Company K] to Mr. Daniel (Cady), September 7, 1863. Although there is no specific mention of an aide leading the two regiments onto the field, the troops would not have known where to go unless they followed someone who knew the ground. According to Vautier's sources, the regiments arrived on the field with unloaded weapons. I added punctuation and proper capitalization.

grove close to the seminary lane. Any wood, anywhere to be found, would do the job.[8]

In Paul's brigade, Pvt. Bourne Spooner (Company D, 13th Massachusetts) remembered how the tree canopy darkened the woods. He noticed a large group of saddled cavalry horses with their holders under the cover of the eastern slope of Seminary Ridge. Several projectiles screamed into the treetops and burst, throwing the horses and men into a panic. The brigade moved into the rocky hillside west of the seminary unmolested by the guns. "I have no recollections as to the length of time we were in reserve, for this is a thing impossible to determine amid the great strain and excitement of actual battle," he penned in 1871. The 13th, being the lead regiment, loaded its weapons.[9]

12:00 p.m. to 12:15 p.m.

In the low ground east of the seminary, Baxter's small column encountered scores of bleeding and wounded men limping away from the battle. The "manly" Yankee "Huzzahs" and the shrill Rebel "Yi-yis" reverberated across the ridge, mingling with the crashes of artillery airbursts. A couple of rounds ricocheted off the top of the hill in the vicinity of the seminary and flew harmlessly overhead.[10]

The three regiments halted in the orchard south of the Chambersburg Pike. Word traveled through the ranks that they were being held in reserve. The men in the 88th Pennsylvania unhitched their traps and started scrounging the area for kindling to start coffee fires. Before they got their cups heated, Lt. George W. Grant (Company B, 88th Pennsylvania) saw an aide "riding like mad" toward the brigade. He clattered to a halt alongside General Baxter and shouted an unintelligible order, which the general quickly repeated for all to hear: "Fall in!"[11]

8 Slagle to brother; *Maine at Gettysburg*, 45.

9 Spooner, "In the Ranks."

10 John D. Vautier, "At Gettysburg, The Eighty-Eighth Pennsylvania Infantry in the Battle," *Philadelphia Weekly Press*, November 10, 1886; Hall, *History of the Ninety-Seventh Regiment*, 135.

11 Vautier, *History of the 88th Pennsylvania*, 105; Grant "The First Army Corps," 47-48; James Beale, *The Statements of Time on July 1 at Gettysburg PA* (Philadelphia, 1897), 22-23. Beale, a private in Company I, 13th Massachusetts, said the regiment (the right of the

Major Benezet F. Foust called the 88th Pennsylvania to its feet and gave the order to load. By the time the troops moved out, Cpl. Charles Smedley (Company G, 90th Pennsylvania) believed that about half an hour had elapsed. A glance skyward told him it was around noon. The column cut north, crossed the railroad embankment, and halted momentarily along the eastern side of Sheads Woods, apparently awaiting orders. From where he stood, Smedley could clearly see the fighting in the fields to the west, which he described as 'pretty sharp." Skirmish fire echoed from the north. He knew now without a doubt the regiment would "see the elephant" very soon.[12]

Seminary Ridge

Colonel Wainwright, who watched Baxter's approach into Sheads Woods from the vicinity of the Thompson place, returned to the Chambersburg Pike. Once there, learned that Wadsworth had placed Calef's battery on the middle ridge. He continued south on the seminary lane to where he had parked both Lt. James Stewart's Battery B, 4th U.S. and Capt. Gilbert H. Reynolds's Battery L, 1st New York. Wainwright ordered Reynolds to the middle ridge to support Calef's four guns and dispatched Stewart's six 12-pounders to report to Robinson north of the pike.[13]

Stewart left Lt. James Davison in charge of the guns while he and the battery bugler rode ahead to survey the ground. Passing into Sheads Woods, they scouted north toward the Mummasburg Road. Hall encountered both Col. Thomas C. Devin, commanding Buford's Second Brigade, and General Robinson, who was bringing his Second Division of the I Corps onto the field. Robinson, preoccupied with his own men and having no idea where to post a battery, told the Stewart to report to Wadsworth.

Devin informed Stewart (neither of whom knew John Reynolds was dead) that his cavalry was working to keep the Rebels at bay long enough for

line) was west of the seminary in what was then a narrow lane and that artillery was in the grove in front of the seminary. The lane was the campus road. The guns were in the grove south of the building.

12 *Life in Southern Prisons*, 55; Vautier, *History of the 88th Pennsylvania*, 105; Cyrus S. Detre, "The 88th Penna Regt at Gettysburg," NARA, G 94, War Records Office, Union Battle Reports, Vol. 27, Boxes 48-52; Coburn diary, July 1, 1863. Private Robert S. Coburn (Company H, 9th N.Y.S.M.) noted in his diary that his unit "arrived around noon."

13 *OR* 27/1:356.

Reynolds to bring up the rest of the I Corps. Stewart scanned the area to the north and west with the battery's field glasses. The size of the Confederate forces coming over the high ground beyond Willoughby Run astonished him.

The artillerist wheeled about and rode to the top of the middle ridge, from which he could clearly observe every deployment of Harry Heth's Confederate division along Herr's Ridge. Having a better grasp of the situation, he galloped to the seminary to study the action along McPherson's Ridge, where he learned that Reynolds had perished early that morning. Stewart reined north again and raced to the Thompson place, where he found General Wadsworth and his staff.[14]

Stewart sent the bugler to Lieutenant Davison to bring up the battery. He also warned Wadsworth of the enemy massing along his front. He advised that he would put half his battery on the north side of the cut and half to the south of it. According to Stewart, "The general said he would be much obliged if I would do so." Stewart ordered Capt. Greenlief T. Stevens (5th Maine Battery) to bring his six Napoleons forward from the valley to the east to unlimber on Stewart's vacated position. Stevens's gunners had just finished clearing the gun carriages for action when the order arrived.[15]

McPherson's Ridge, Southeast of Herbst Woods

Colonel Gates and his 20th N.Y.S.M. remained on the top of the trampled crest in clear view of the Confederate gunners and skirmishers. Although well within artillery range, the men felt relatively secure from sharpshooters despite the bullets buzzing their line. The rank and file grumbled about being stranded in such an exposed position. Someone generated a rumor that Wadsworth, their old brigade commander, had deliberately placed them there because, as Captain Cook (Company I) later explained, "He knew our regiment would go where it was sent and stay where it was put."[16]

14 Stewart, "Battery B at Gettysburg," 183-184, 186; *OR* 27/1:356. In his 1896 rendition of his role in the battle, Stewart explained that he had ridden ahead of the battery to join Craig Wadsworth on the firing line. Had he done that, he would have known of Reynolds's death and of the fighting of the Iron Brigade in Herbst Woods.

15 Stewart, "Battery B at Gettysburg," 184; *Maine at Gettysburg*, 83.

16 Cooke, "The First Day at Gettysburg," 324, 325; Gates, *Ulster Guard*, 433; *OR* 27/1:320, 323, 326; *History of the 121st Regiment*, 52; "Colonel McFarland's Diary"; *Pennsylvania at Gettysburg*, 2:653, 746. It is clear from Maj. Alexander Biddle's after-

McPherson's Ridge, North of Herbst Woods

The noonday sun beat down on Col. Langhorne Wister's 150th Pennsylvania. Wister remained behind the center of the line, with Lt. Col. Henry S. Huidekoper overseeing the right wing of the regiment and Maj. Thomas Chamberlin on post behind the left wing. While pacing the line, Major Chamberlin noticed a boney old man striding with purpose toward him with a weapon at trail arms in his right hand. Chamberlin took particular note of the bluish tint in the old man's clean-shaven face and his quaint attire.

Once he was close to the major, John Burns asked, "Can I fight with your regiment?"

Chamberlin replied that he could, but the unexpected approach of Colonel Wister forced him to change tack. "Here is our colonel; speak to him."

"Well, old man, what do you want?" Wister asked.

"I want a chance to fight with your regiment," Burns replied.

"You do?" The colonel was obviously surprised by the request. "Can you shoot?"

"Oh, yes," Burns answered.

"I see you have a gun, but where is your ammunition?" continued Wister.

Burns used his left hand to brush back his coat and slap his pants pocket. Both officers saw it was bulging with cartridges.

Wister grinned. "Certainly you can fight with us and I wish there were many more like you." The colonel advised him to go into the woods with the Black Hats to keep himself in the shade and under the protection of the trees.[17]

The old man strode into the woods, where he turned west for several hundred yards, until he came across Lieutenant Colonel Callis of the 7th

---

action report that the entire brigade was facing north supporting a battery when it changed front to the west and moved south to the left of the 20th N.Y.S.M so as to not block the battery (Battery L, 1st New York). The brigade would have initially been to the left of Cooper's battery before noon, as shown on the Bachelder Map. The reports indicate that the regiments changed face at least three times to escape artillery fire. By 11:45 a.m., the brigade supported Cooper, facing west. At noon, it shifted north to face Confederate Lt. Col. Thomas H. Carter's Second Corps guns on Oak Hill. By 12:15 p.m. Cooper withdrew and was replaced by Reynolds's New York battery. Within about 15 minutes, and without the 151st Pennsylvania, the balance of the brigade shifted west, with the 121st Pennsylvania moving to the far left of the brigade.

17 Chamberlin, *History of the 150th Regiment*, 120-121.

The cantankerous John Burns posed for this photograph after recovering from his Gettysburg wounds. *LOC*

Wisconsin. The bell crowned hat, waistcoat, and old-fashioned swallow-tailed coat caught the colonel's attention as Burns halted and came to "present arms."

"Colonel, is this your regiment?" he rasped.

"Yes."

Burns immediately went to "order arms" and responded with, "Can I fight in your regiment?"

Unlike Wister, Callis did not think much of the idea. "Old man," he scoffed, "you had better go to the rear or you'll get hurt. The rebels are very careless about how they shoot, and you are liable to get killed any moment; see the bullets are flying pretty thick now."

Burns dismissed the idea. "I've heard the whistle of bullets before." When the perturbed colonel told him to go to the rear, Burns shot back. "No sir. If you won't let me fight in your regiment I will fight alone."

The old shoemaker started toward the skirmish line on his own when Sgt. George Eustice and some of the fellows from Company F started teasing him about his stove-pipe hat and shouting that he should be allowed to fight. Callis relented.

"Fix him up, boys," Eustis insisted, "He'll soon get tired of it and go home."

The sergeant handed him a newly captured silver mounted rifle, which they had taken from one of Archer's sharpshooters, and exchanged it with his standard army rifle. Commenting that it would make him look more like a soldier, Eustice also tried to hang a cartridge box over Burns's shoulder, but he shrugged it off. "I can get my hands in here," Burns replied while slapping his pants pocket, "quicker than in that box; I am not used to those new-fangled things." When the sergeant asked him why he had come to the front, the civilian muttered something about the Rebs driving off his cows and that he wanted to get even.

Burns stepped over the prone Badgers, saying, "I want to get a sight at one of them." Callis was right behind him. Burns earned the admiration of the surprised veterans when he planted himself behind a tree and began plinking away, despite the shell bursts in the branches overhead and incoming small arms fire.

"Are you a good shot?" The old man obviously intrigued Callis.

"Tolerable good," came the reply.

Callis pointed and asked, "Do you see that Rebel riding yonder?"

"I do."

"Can you fetch him?"

"I can try," Burns coolly responded.

He took aim and squeezed the trigger. In the smoky woods, he could not be certain if he knocked the Rebel off, but the cheer from the line behind him, which could see under the sulfuric veil, told him he probably did bag the fellow. When Burns spied the riderless horse in the distance, he felt quite sure that he had gotten his man. Soon after, a Wisconsinite stepped up to the tree nearest him and, according to Burns, the two "picked off every Rebel that showed his head."[18]

Oak Hill

After a grueling nine-mile march from Heidlersburg that left a trail of unconscious or exhausted stragglers along its route, the large Confederate infantry division under Maj. Gen. Robert E. Rodes reached the Samuel Cobean farm just north of Gettysburg. The command, part of Lt. Gen. Richard Ewell's

18 Thaddeus S. Kenderdine, *A California Tramp and Later Footprints* (Newtown, PA, 1888), 342-344; "The Field of Gettysburg," *The Atlantic Monthly*, vol. 16, no. 97 (November 1865), 621-622; Ladd & Ladd, *Bachelder Papers*, 1:141; "John Burns at Gettysburg," *NT*, August 19, 1886, 4; Aubery, *Echoes From the Marches of the Iron Brigade*, 1900, 59-60. Kenderdine and Aubery based their renditions, with slight variations, upon Callis's April 14, 1885, letter to Aubery. A similar undated letter from Callis to Bachelder appears in *The Bachelder Papers*. Callis is the only person who claimed Burns carried bullets in his pocket and a powder horn. Kenderdine, in quoting Sergeant Eustis, makes it clear that the sergeant gave him the better rifle and that Burns already had cartridges in his pockets, not just the lead balls for a small-caliber squirrel gun. Callis takes credit for giving Burns the rifle, but the contemporary accounts, and Burns's in particular, do not substantiate that assertion.

Second Corps, was composed of five brigades, and had arrived on the exposed right flank of the Union I Corps. With Brig. Gen. Stephen D. Ramseur's Brigade bringing up the rear of the long column, behind the wagon train, Rodes could initially only position four of his brigades to flank the Federal position on Oak Ridge.[19]

Brigadier General Alfred Iverson's four-regiment North Carolina brigade stood to arms along a fence row about 500 yards north of the N. Hoffman house. Iverson's largest regiment, the 5th North Carolina, held the left of the line in the woods, followed to the right by the 23rd, the 20th, and his smallest regiment, the 12th.

About 200 yards behind Iverson, Brig. Gen. Junius Daniel aligned the left of his five Tar Heel regiments on Iverson's left, bringing the force to around 3,500 officers and men. With Daniel's front measuring about 1,900 feet, his right extended over 700 feet beyond Iverson's.

Colonel Edward A. O'Neal commanded the Alabama brigade to Daniel's immediate left. O'Neal's front extended from the wooded eastern crest of Oak Ridge into the valley across the fence south of the Cobean farm buildings. The 3rd anchored the right of the formation, followed respectively to the east by the 13th, 26th, 6th, and 5th Alabama regiments. Brigadier General George P. Doles's four Georgia regiments secured the division's left flank.[20]

Using the road running south from the northeast corner of the woods, Rodes ordered his chief of artillery, Lt. Col. Thomas H. Carter, to roll his two lead batteries, Capt. William P. Carter's King William Artillery and Capt. Charles

19 G. Ward Hubbs, ed., *Voices from Company D: Diaries by the Greensboro Guards, Fifth Alabama Infantry Regiment, Army of Northern Virginia* (Athens, GA, 2003), 182; *OR* 27/2:566. Junius Daniel would report that at this time he was 200 yards behind Iverson's Brigade, which would have placed Iverson command along the fence row in the woods to the south.

20 Busey & Martin, *Regimental Strengths and Losses*, 194, 210, 212; *OR* 27/2:566, 592; Clark, *Histories of the Several Regiments*, 1:634-635 and 2:236. I based the frontage upon Martin and Busey, but there are some facts that give pause to the positions of the 20th and the 23rd regiments. Bachelder placed the 20th on the left of the 23rd, as described in Clark's first volume. A study of the field and the alignment of the regiments on both sides according to estimated frontage, however, puts the 20th facing the front of the 88th Pennsylvania and the 23rd the 97th New York. However, in order for the 88th to capture the 23rd's colors, and the 97th to capture the 20th's colors (as they both did), the two Union regiments would have had to cross each other's paths during the charge in the afternoon. None of the members in either regiment ever mentioned doing so. It is thus likely that the 20th was next to the 12th, and the 23rd next to the 5th.

Major General Robert E. Rodes was widely considered one of the rising stars in the Army of Northern Virginia. He fumbled his advantageous tactical situation on the afternoon of July 1 by attacking piecemeal off Oak Hill, and in doing so lost control of his division. *LOC*

W. Fry's Orange Artillery, into battery on the south end of the ridge. Captain R. Channing Page's Morris Artillery and Capt. William J. Reese's Jeff Davis Artillery remained behind as a reserve. Carter had barely positioned his eight guns (two 12-pounder Napoleons, two 3-inch rifles, and four 10-pounder Parrott rifles) when Rodes sent an aide to him asking for a battery. Carter offered him Page's four Napoleons.[21]

Rodes ordered his brigades forward to support the artillery on the southern face of Oak Hill. When he realized the advance would create a significant gap between O'Neal's left and Doles's right, the general personally assumed command of the 5th Alabama but neglected to tell O'Neal why he detached the regiment. Instead, Rodes kept it back at Cobean's as a reserve, forcing O'Neal to continue without it.

The brigade got as far as the second fence line south of its original position, where it went to ground while Colonel O'Neal awaited further orders. On the right front of Rodes's Division, Iverson marched to the Hoffman farm lane. Daniel advanced with him, trying to maintain the 200-yard interval between the

21 Thomas H. Carter to D. H. Hill, July 1, 1885, B21, Box 3, Virginia Historical Society, Richmond, VA; *OR* 27/2:553. Carter referred to Page by his middle name, Channing. I concluded that since Rodes wanted the woods to mask his advance, he used the sheltered road along the western side of the ridge. Interestingly enough, O'Neal asserted that the brigade moved out after the artillery had withdrawn. He probably saw Carter take his two batteries to the south and did not know where the other two had halted.

two brigades. None of the brigades in the division had direct contact with the other.[22]

Leaving Reese's Jeff Davis Artillery parked northwest of the Cobean house, Rodes led Page along the farm lane paralleling the lower east side of the ridge that connected Cobean's farm with McLean's. About 290 yards south of the buildings, the general placed Page's guns on the sloping spur along the east side of the first band of woods. This space was insufficient for the battery to go into front, so Page placed one section toward the base of the slope and the other up-hill behind it, with all the guns facing southeast. In so doing, he put the lower gunners in jeopardy from the wooden sabots and the metal bands that fastened the spherical rounds to the powder bags.[23]

From his position, Page spotted two manned bronze guns on an isolated hill in the valley about 1,400 yards to the southeast. The two Napoleons were under Lt. Clark Scripture (Battery I, 1st Ohio Light); Capt. Hubert Dilger was in charge of the remaining four. A line of skirmishers from the 45th New York (Howard's XI Corps) protected Scripture's flank, with the main body of the 45th behind it supporting the rest of the guns.[24]

The Middle Cut

At 12:10 p.m., General Wadsworth scratched a hurried note to Doubleday or Howard, whichever could be found first: "I think the enemy are retiring, and that we should advance promptly upon them. I am not sure that they are not moving round on our right flank, though I do not see any indication of it."[25]

22 *OR* 27/2: 523; Hubbs, *Voices from Company D*, 182. Private Pickens clearly noted the 5th Alabama advanced to the McLean barn to catch up with the rest of the brigade, which was behind a fence. That advance had to have occurred during the afternoon advance around 1:00 p.m. Based upon the alignments of the brigades, it is likely that O'Neal, once the artillery was silenced, moved forward to the second fence north of the McLean barn, which would have put him on an obtuse line to Daniel.

23 Bachelder Maps; Hubbs, *Voices from Company D*, 182; Carter to Hill. Carter expressed his disgust over the battery's deployment. Private Samuel Pickens (Company D, 5th Alabama) wrote that a battery was 150 yards to the regiment's front, which is the distance from the southern fence on Cobean's property to the spur. The best approach to the spur was along the eastern side of the ridge.

24 *OR* 27/1:734, 754.

25 *OR* 27/1:345 and 27/3:462; Beale, *Statements on Time*, 21; Dana diary, July 1, 1863, 43, fn 21. In his after-action -report, Dana cited the arrival time on the McPherson farm at 11:45

A few minutes later, Thomas Carter's two batteries opened fire from Oak Hill, confirming what Wadsworth had suspected. The rounds caught Calef's unsuspecting artillerists on the flank. The lieutenant watched the incoming shot skip between the gun trails and the teams, slaughtering several of his horses. That same fire dropped rounds on top of Cutler's battered brigade and the bloodied 6th Wisconsin.[26]

Wainwright Deploys Captain Reynolds

During those tense minutes, Capt. Gilbert H. Reynolds hurried Battery L, 1st New York to Calef's support. The guns ran a veritable gauntlet of case shot and iron to Calef's right flank. Lieutenant George Breck, who recalled that the Regular battery "had been blown almost to pieces," unlimbered his section fronting north, the muzzles pointing over a crumbled stone wall, only to find the position completely exposed to fire from the west as well.

The first burst gashed Cpl. John P. Conn's scalp and grievously injured Captain Reynolds. A ricocheting fragment hit the ground and threw dirt and stone into the captain's face. Something, whether an iron fragment or a rock, struck the point of his left cheekbone and cut him right below the left eye. Simultaneously, a second missile—this one an iron shard—hammered him in the right side. Badly stunned and bleeding, Reynolds clapped his hand over the injured eye and turned to announce to his second in command, Lieutenant Breck, that he had just been wounded. The sight of the captain's bloody face momentarily startled the lieutenant, who turned and rode toward his hard-pressed section.

Reynolds reined away from the battery, found Sgt. Charles DeMott, and asked him to stay by his side. The two encountered Colonel Wainwright near the seminary. The captain insisted on returning to the battery, but Wainwright countermanded him and had DeMott take him to the hospital at the seminary.

---

a.m. Captain Irvin reported that the regiment remained on the farm for fifteen to twenty minutes, which would place the time somewhere between 12:00 p.m. and 12:05 p.m. before the regiment went into action. According to the battlefield plaque, Carter's guns arrived on the battlefield "soon after noon." Wadsworth's note of it being quiet at 12:10 p.m. is accurate.

26 *OR* 27/1:1032; Calef, "Gettysburg Notes," 51; Dawes, *Service With the Sixth Wisconsin*, 174.

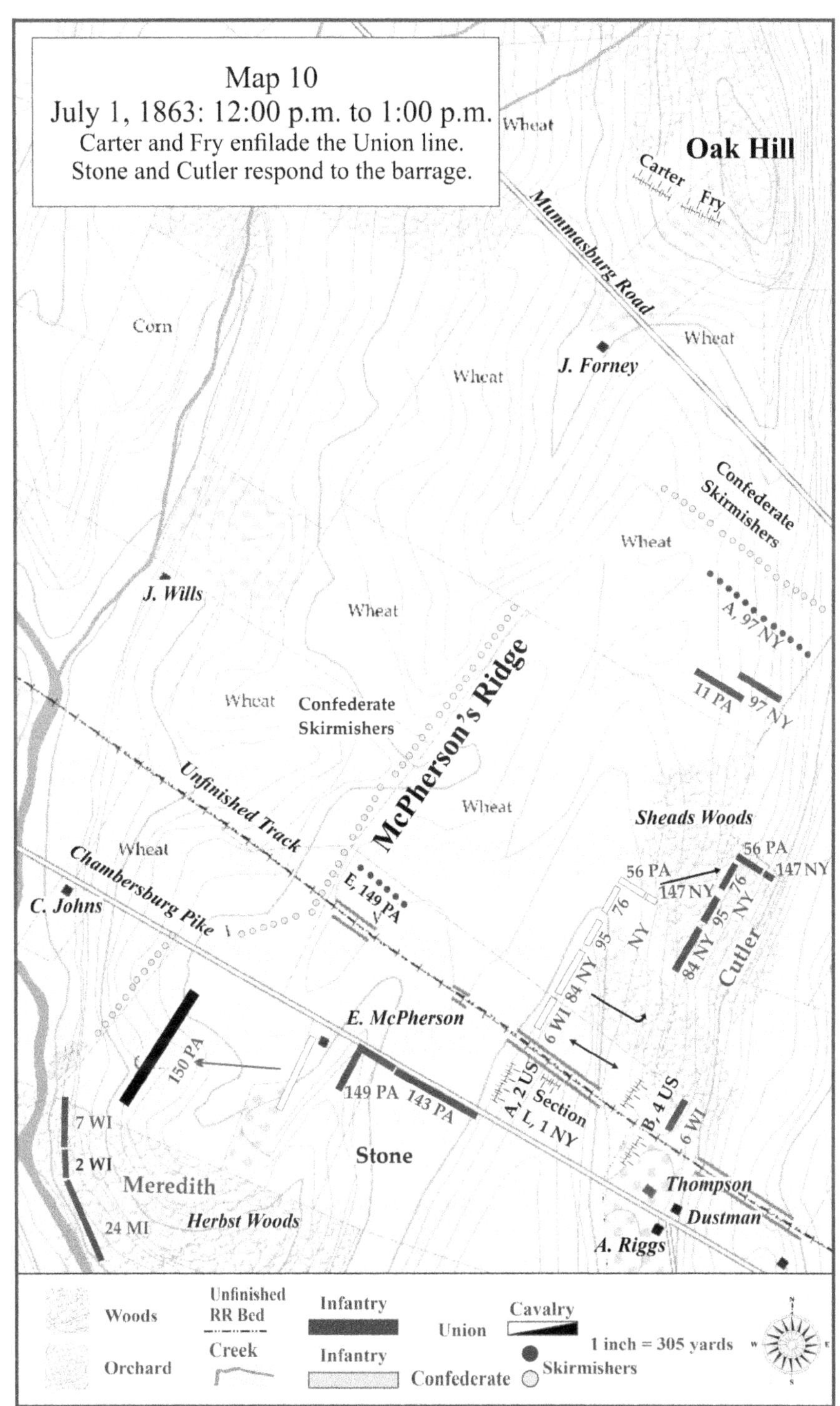
Map 10
July 1, 1863: 12:00 p.m. to 1:00 p.m.
Carter and Fry enfilade the Union line.
Stone and Cutler respond to the barrage.
Oak Hill
Carter
Fry
Mummasburg Road
Wheat
Corn
J. Forney
Confederate Skirmishers
J. Wills
A, 97 NY
11 PA
97 NY
Confederate Skirmishers
McPherson's Ridge
Unfinished Track
Sheads Woods
56 PA
147 NY
76
95
NY
84 NY
Cutler
C. Johns
Chambersburg Pike
E, 149 PA
E. McPherson
6 WI
150 PA
149 PA
143 PA
A, 2 US
Section L, 1 NY
B, 4 US
7 WI
2 WI
Meredith
Stone
24 MI
Herbst Woods
Thompson
Dustman
A. Riggs
Woods
Orchard
Unfinished RR Bed
Creek
Infantry
Union
Confederate
Cavalry
Skirmishers
1 inch = 305 yards

The sergeant left Reynolds there under the care of the diminutive Pvt. Isaac "Ikey" Weinberg.[27]

Sergeant William H. Shelton dismounted and threw the reins over the handle on the limber seat. The officers and men knew they would have to clear out or get as badly mauled as Calef's artillerists to their left. Shelton untethered his mount while the drivers pulled the limbers about, hooked up the guns, and took off at a trot to the south. The cannoneers ran alongside the teams, implements in hand.

Shelton had just slipped his foot in the stirrup when he heard, "For God's sake, Sergeant, save me." Turning toward the plea, he spotted Cpl. John Conn stumbling toward him, arms flailing. When Conn fell, Shelton noticed the corporal's profusely bleeding scalp. The injured corporal staggered to his feet as Shelton dropped the reins to grab the wounded man's extended arm. As he did so, Shelton's well-trained chestnut ran after the limbers; the men struggled to work their way through the muddy stubble field.

Forced to move at what must have felt like a snail's pace, Shelton captured everything in front of him with his artist's eye, and wrote about it. The wheels sank into the soft field, and the horses churned up more muck until they got mired down. The implements, which some of the men had returned to the hooks on the gun carriages, rattled. The water and grease buckets swayed back and forth under the limbers. The two buglers rode immediately behind Lieutenant Breck. A riderless gray horse, with the guidon anchored in the stirrup, assumed its position on the right of the lead team.

27 https://museum.dmna.ny.gov/unit-history/artillery/1st-artillery-regiment-light, accessed Feb. 1, 2023; *OR* 27/1:356, 362; *NYAG*, 3:1256; Blake McKelvey, ed., "Rochester in the Civil War," *The Rochester Historical Society*, XXII (1924), 131, 132; https://museum.dmna.ny.gov/unit-history/artillery/1st-artillery-regiment-light/newspaper-clippings, last accessed Feb. 1, 2023; Shelton, "A Biography of a Period," 75, 76. Breck considered Weinberg, whom he referred to as the "little Jew," an excellent soldier. In his after-action report, Breck said the battery took fire from the left flank, and therefore was pointed north, whereas in his postwar writing he reversed the flank fire to the right, which meant the guns would have to have been facing west. Shelton did not record his experiences until 1920, when he was 80. Like Breck, he admitted the battery moved several times and that he could not remember all of its positions. He claimed that at the time Breck's section unlimbered, the guns were pointed over a "crumbled stone wall." There was not a wall in front of Calef's guns, which means it was likely along the railroad cut, and probably stone from the excavation that had not been cleared away. He was mistaken when he wrote that the fire from the right and forced the guns to leave. Those shots had to have come in from the west (left). I used the official report to establish the position of the guns.

Unexploded shells and solid shot burrowed into the ground on every hand, showering the retreating gunners with what one eyewitness described as "fountains" of black topsoil. The experience left indelible impressions on Shelton and Breck. The battery trotted about 500 yards south into the swale directly west of the seminary and unlimbered, facing north on the right of Capt. James H. Cooper's Battery B, 1st Pennsylvania Light Artillery, which Wainwright had redeployed from McPherson's Ridge to counter the Rebel guns. With their nine guns in battery, they opened fire on Fry's and Carter's pieces on Oak Hill.[28]

The Thompson Place on the Chambersburg Pike

Amid all the chaos, Captain Hall and his two enlisted men parked their limber just under the cover of the eastern crest of Seminary Ridge. Leaving the extra man with the limber, the captain and the sergeant, using the road banks for some shelter, ran up to the gate and started feverishly cutting the dead horses free of their harnesses. Plunging small arms fire and shell bursts drove them to the road berm several times.

Tying the traces together, they ran over to the rear of the limber, unhitched the trail of the gun, and fastened their "rope" through the iron eye of the lintel. By then the man with the limber had turned the carriage about. The sergeant and the captain tied the other end of their trace rope to the lintel hook on the back of the limber, and the limber pulled the gun into the road. Once the driver backed the limber up and the other two attached the gun to the carriage, they all headed for Cemetery Hill.[29]

28 Shelton, "A Biography of a Period," 76; *NYAG*, 3:1257; *OR* 27/1:362; *Pennsylvania at Gettysburg*, 2:878. Neither officer mentioned the presence of the other's battery, but they definitely occupied the field at the same time.

29 Ladd & Ladd, *Bachelder Papers*, 1:388; *OR* 27/1:360; *Maine at Gettysburg*, 21. As so often happens when veterans penned their experiences, they assumed their audience, being veterans themselves, knew the minute details of how Hall would have extracted the piece and what "road" and "road bank" to which he referred. I reconstructed this based upon my knowledge of how they would have approached the problem. The railroad cut was rocky and too narrow to turn about a limber with four horses. Hall would have needed one man to "hold the horses" of the team. The Chambersburg Pike was wide enough to wheel a limber around. The drainage ditch and the resulting road berm would have provided at least minimal cover.

12:15 p.m.
Stone's Brigade, McPherson's Farm

Artillery fire from the right flank cut through the air behind the 143rd Pennsylvania and caught the Keystone soldiers unaware. Colonel Dana, having seen the Confederate artillery cut loose, mistook them for Federal guns and dispatched a man to tell them to cease fire. Simultaneously, to his dismay, he watched Cutler's brigade evacuate the eastern side of the middle cut. The infantrymen had not waited for the New York artillerymen to go into battery. The Rebels bracketed the ground between them and Sheads Woods, negating any direct escape to the east.

Lieutenant Colonel Rufus Dawes directed his men of the 6th Wisconsin to follow him single file south into the middle cut in an effort to keep them from being slaughtered by the incoming artillery rounds. The fire at this time, according to Dawes, threw a "cart load" of dirt over their heads as they ran. The 14th Brooklyn (84th New York) and 95th New York followed close behind. The 76th New York and the 56th Pennsylvania, with the 147th New York in the lead, faced by the right flank and stampeded to the relative security of Sheads Woods.

Once the latter three regiments reached the rail fence running north from the railroad bed, they halted and began constructing a low barricade out of fence rails and debris. When they finished, they wheeled north to the rail fence along the northern edge of the woods and started skirmishing with their Confederate counterparts along the new high fence 200 yards to the north.[30]

While Baxter's brigade formed to move out from the vicinity of the seminary, an aide led the detached 97th New York and 11th Pennsylvania in column north across the southern end of the railroad cut before turning west until the Pennsylvanians cleared the far side of the wood lot. The aide directed the New Yorkers to advance to the east-west fence bordering the northern side of Sheads Woods, where they halted to load their weapons. Before they stepped off, Colonel Wheelock detached Company A of the 97th New York under Capt. Isaac Hall forward along the eastern side of Oak Ridge to a small strip of trees south of the Mummasburg Road. The skirmishers cautiously approached the

30 *Pennsylvania at Gettysburg*, 2:725; *OR* 27/1:335; Ladd & Ladd, *Bachelder Papers*, 1:331 and 3:1570; "Three Bullets at Gettysburg: Medal of Honor Recipients," *MI*, vol. 35, no. 3 (2017): 13, http://www.jstor.org/stable/26112024, accessed Feb. 2, 2023. The anonymous author in the *Bachelder Papers* wrote that the men used hay bales in the works.

small woodlot but veered off when they came under a less-than-intimidating fire from a couple of Confederate riflemen. Captain Hall counted two shots with their accompanying puffs of smoke. Sensing no serious problem in that direction, Hall headed back toward the regiment.[31]

By that time, the New Yorkers of the 97th had reached the southernmost fence running east from the Forney property. In so doing they timely relieved Cutler's three regiments, which had expended all of their ammunition. Isaac Hall's skirmishers rejoined the 97th New York there and assumed their post on the right of the regiment. Colonel Coulter dispatched Companies A and B from the 11th Pennsylvania's flanks. Once they cleared the fence, he sent the rest of the regiment over it into the high timothy grass on the opposite side. The Pennsylvanians marched several yards north and went prone.

From where he stood, Colonel Wheelock could see the Confederates deploying into the second field to the north. He ordered his men of the 97th to unhitch their knapsacks and leave them in piles behind the line because he did not want to send his men into combat loaded down with gear. He also ordered Isaac Hall to take Companies A and F forward as skirmishers. Hall spread his men out in the regulation "comrades in battle" (groups of four men in two ranks) to cover the front of the 97th New York and the right rear of the 11th Pennsylvania. The skirmishers on the left passed over the 11th Pennsylvania line, trampling paths through the grass toward the high rail fence some 200 yards farther north.[32]

The Confederates sporadically popped up to fire while crawling through the tall grass. They wounded several of the Federals and killed one man in Company F before being driven back to the Mummasburg Road. Captain Hall peered toward the wooded crest of Oak Hill, around 600 yards to the north, and

31 Hall, *History of the Ninety-Seventh Regiment*, 135, 136, 140. In a letter to Hall dated April 29, 1890, Ebenezer B. Harrington (Company C, 97th New York) mistakenly wrote that the entire brigade, not just the two regiments, had crossed the railroad embankment before the skirmishers went forth.

32 Hall, *History of the Ninety-Seventh Regiment*, 135, 136; Eldred, "Gettysburg"; Ladd & Ladd, *Bachelder Papers*, 1:331, 3:1570; M. Kirby to Mr. Daniel (Cady), September 7, 1863, https://cwl.dhinitiative.org/islandora/object/HamiltonCivilWar%3A1044, accessed Feb. 1, 2023. Traditional interpretations have both the 97th New York and 11th Pennsylvania moving upon the sparse woodlot on the eastern slope of Oak Ridge along the Mummasburg Road, which is probably a misinterpretation of Hall's map in his regimental history. No record has been found showing that the 11th Pennsylvania deployed skirmishers on the eastern side of the ridge.

thought he caught sight of a Confederate battle flag and what appeared to be a line of infantry.[33]

McPherson's Farm

With artillery rounds screaming overhead from the west, the sound of one crashing farther north attracted the attention of Col. Roy Stone. The adept colonel shifted the brigade to meet the new threat. The 150th Pennsylvania immediately threw down the worm fence along its front and came under skirmish and artillery fire as it rushed down the hill toward the quarry. The regiment halted about 180 yards down the slope to the right rear of the 2nd Wisconsin.[34]

With Stone's brigade securing his right flank, Solomon Meredith finally decided to correct his brigade line. With so many companies on skirmish, he strengthened it by closing the 2nd Wisconsin to the left and shifting the 7th Wisconsin to the right, thereby placing the 2nd between the 24th Michigan and the 7th Wisconsin.

The painfully wounded Pvt. Emanuel Markle (Company B, 2nd Wisconsin), perhaps using his rifle as a crutch, hobbled toward laughter

33 Hall, *History of the Ninety-Seventh Regiment*, 135; Smith, *History of the Seventy-Sixth Regiment*, 240-241. According to Smith, the brigade participated in the assault on Iverson's Brigade, but he also claimed the 76th New York was not relieved until 2:00 p.m., which was not the case. There are no reliable accounts that state the 76th or 147th New York engaged Iverson's line. The accounts from the 147th New York assert two different things. One reports the regiment retired after half an hour (approximately 1:10 p.m.) and were pursued by the Rebels, Surgeon Coe of the 147th noted the line retired because they used up all their ammunition. He implied the brigade took part in Iverson's repulse, but that makes no sense. Had the brigade right wheeled, as commonly shown, it would have outflanked the 12th North Carolina, which it did not. Since the regiment was under fire from Carter's battery for about 15 to 20 minutes (roughly noon to 12:20 p.m.) before falling back to the woods, it probably encountered the same skirmishers the 97th New York and 11th Pennsylvania met and ran out of ammunition as those two units came onto the field. This explains why Bachelder's map shows Cutler's mauled brigade mistakenly flanking Iverson.

34 "Three Bullets at Gettysburg"; Chamberlin, *History of the 150th Regiment*, 117; Tomasak, *Harris Journal*, 60, 62; Wheeler, "Reminiscences," 110. Traditional accounts do not have the 150th Pennsylvania so far advanced on the ridge; Wheeler, however, wrote that a new Pennsylvania regiment formed on his right and perpendicular to it. Roe Reisinger (150th Pennsylvania) and Avery Harris wrote about the regiment advancing over the ridge. Harris mistakenly recalled Dana sending a man to identify the guns. By the afternoon, he definitely would have known that the Confederates had artillery on Oak Hill.

emanating through the woods. A short time later he stumbled across Cpl. Charles C. Bushee, also from Company B, disabled by a severe hip wound. A few feet farther on he found another friend, Mike Brennan, gut shot and sitting against a tree.

"Markle," he winced, while shakily handing him a sheet of paper, "here is a letter and if things don't [turn] out right with me . . . write that address and tell them what happened."

Markle took the letter, limped on, and shortly encountered his captain, Robert Hughes. He told the officer he would find Brennan sitting against a tree and that he should see what he could do for him. Hughes walked over and returned in less than a minute.

"The man is dead," he said matter-of-factly. Markle eventually mailed the letter to the corporal's friends.[35]

Most of the artillery projectiles lobbed from Herr's Ridge passed harmlessly over the 150th Pennsylvania and either burrowed into the ground or bounced away. One, however, struck Sgt. Maj. Thomas M. Lyon across the chest and hurled the soldier to the ground. The projectile ripped away the front of his uniform. Although Sergeant Lyon was in horrific pain, he was a miraculously fortunate man. The iron shot had only bruised his chest without breaking the skin.[36]

Colonel Walton Dwight (149th Pennsylvania) moved his regiment partially to the right. The three right companies (left to right: I, F, and A) went to cover behind the road berm and in the drainage ditch running along the Chambersburg Pike, facing north. The remaining five companies of the regiment went prone in the farm lane. Company C, the color company, held the right where the lane intersected the pike, with Companies H, E, B, and G completing the formation to its left.

Captain John Irvin (Company B) estimated they had been on the farm about 15 to 20 minutes. The men watched artillery shells fly harmlessly overhead from the west into the fields behind the line. The 143rd Pennsylvania remained

35 Meredith statement to Bachelder, Ladd & Ladd, *Bachelder's History of the Battle of Gettysburg* (El Dorado Hills, CA, 2021), 229-230; www.secondwi.com/second wisnews/jim%20kennedy/2dwiswoulded%20gg.htm, accessed Feb. 2, 2023; Markle, "The Story of Battle Told By Survivor."

36 Chamberlin, *History of the 150th Regiment*, 117.

on the eastern side of the ridge between the barn and the orchard. They were ordered to hold their fire because their own men were in front of them.[37]

A round hurtling in from the north smashed through the cherry trees along the farm lane, forcing the left wing of the 149th Pennsylvania to change its front. Colonel Dwight ordered it into line on the left of Company C; this movement concealed them from the Rebs, who would have to cross the open wheatfield to the north.

Corporal James Logan, the tallest man in Company G, lay next to Capt. Francis B. Jones. Logan raised himself onto his elbows to peer over the road berm when an incoming 12-pounder shot struck him full in the head. The corporal's blood sprayed all over Jones and the impact hurled Logan's decapitated corpse onto the captain. The shot burrowed into the ground at the captain's feet. Jones rolled the body off. Almost immediately a shell exploded in the middle of Company B to Jones's right. The round killed Pvt. William Fleming and seven others outright and wounded eight more, two of whom would die from their wounds.[38]

The enfilade from the north forced Colonel Stone to file the 143rd Pennsylvania by the right into the drainage ditch on the right of the 149th. The line went to ground behind the road bank, which Pvt. Avery Harris (Company B) noted protected "some" of the men. An incoming solid shot from Herr's Ridge bounced through the ranks, killing one soldier and inflicting several other casualties.

37 *Pennsylvania at Gettysburg*, 2:725; Bassler, "The Color Episode," 5; Hubler, "Plain, Untarnished Story"; *OR* 27/1:345; Captain Ralph Gamble to Capt. John H. Bassler, May 8, 1907, Ramsey-Bassler Collection, USAHEC; "Excerpt from Chronicles of Francis Bacon Jones," 5. Based on Captain Jones's account, Company G of the 149th Pennsylvania was on the left of Company B. Company C was in the center as the color company. Logically, Company A was on the right of the line. Bassler and Gamble both said that three companies faced north along the Chambersburg Pike. I estimated that those three companies covered about 126 feet of front. Adding the remaining four companies (approximately 168 feet) would place the left flank somewhere near the current flank marker, around the Chambersburg Pike and Meredith Avenue. The regiment had to have been lying in two ranks to fit in that area.

38 Musser, Unpublished Report; James L. Clark to Maria Funk, July 9, 1863, Vertical Files, VF 6 -PA 149, Library, GNMP; "Excerpt from Chronicles of Francis Bacon Jones," 5; Bates, *History of Pennsylvania Volunteers*, 4:635, 636. Only four men in Company G died outright on July 1: Cpl. James Logan and Pvts. Charles Brewer, John Davis, and Ross M. Hood.

Soon thereafter, Capt. Charles M. Conyngham, despite having been wounded, brought Company A back from skirmishing along Willoughby Run intent upon returning to its assigned place on the right of the regiment. Colonel Dana intercepted him and ushered the company into the space between the 149th and Company B of the 143rd.

Captain John H. Bassler (Company C, 149th Pennsylvania) assumed the Confederate batteries on Herr's Ridge had detected movement and were firing by guess at the regiment's location. He quickly realized that the incoming projectiles from the north, while annoying, posed no real danger to the men along the road. The guns to the west, however, would slaughter the line in the ditch once they found the range of the pike. Roy Stone reached the same conclusion.[39]

Within about 20 minutes, one of those "annoying" shells from Oak Hill crashed into the file closers of Company A of the 143rd. It struck Sgt. Patrick DeLacy, shredding his sack coat to ribbons. Private James Kelly, seeing the sergeant hit the ground, ran to his side. "Jim," the winded and frightened DeLacy sputtered while fingering the damaged breastplate on his cross belt, "the cartridge box and the Lord saved me this time." Bruised and shaken, DeLacy returned to his position behind the line.[40]

Colonel Stone set upon a clever plan to draw the fire away from the brigade by sending out a decoy to distract the Confederate gunners. He directed Col. Walton Dwight to dispatch the 149th's color guard northwest to the high ground, with orders to stay there until ordered to return. One of the colonel's orderlies approached Clr. Sgt. Henry G. Brehm and told him to march the guard about 200 to 300 feet northwest away from the regiment. Sergeant Brehm and Cpl. Franklin W. Lehman stepped out as ordered, carrying the national and state flags, respectively. The rest of the guard, Cpls. John H. Hammell, Henry H. Spayd, John Friddell, and Frederick Hoffman, followed close behind, armed with rifles.

They settled on a low rail lunette that Federal cavalrymen had cobbled together sometime before daylight. Their position, about 50 yards north of the Chambersburg Pike and about 115 yards south of the western railroad cut,

39 *OR* 27/1:3289, 339, 345; Tomasak, *Harris Journal*, 60; Bassler, "The Color Episode," 6. Bassler erred about the time the shift occurred: it was noon, not 1:00 p.m.

40 "Capt. DeLacy Describes Gettysburg Battle."

allowed enough room for the regiment to maneuver freely through the low ground to the east.

The color bearers planted the two banners in the makeshift barricade and hunkered down. With the outpost masked by the tall wheat along the western side of the crest, only the two flags presented themselves as targets to the Confederate artillerists on Herr's Ridge. For all the Rebels knew, the colors represented a concealed Yankee regiment. The ruse succeeded: Pegram's batteries shifted their fire from the Chambersburg Pike to the crest of McPherson's Ridge, and a shell that failed to explode punched a hole through the blue state flag.[41]

At the same time, Colonel Dwight sent Company E of the 149th Pennsylvania forward to handle Confederate skirmishers deploying south from Oak Hill in advance of a regiment that had just moved out of the southern edge of the woods west of Carter's Virginia battery. The Pennsylvanians literally stumbled into the deep part of the western cut. Climbing up to the northern side, they propped themselves on the ledge and opened fire. In conjunction with Baxter's skirmishers to the north and northeast, the New Yorkers triggered sniping and sporadic small arms fire along the entire northern end of the field. Colonel Richard Coulter (11th Pennsylvania) noted the time. It was 12:30 p.m.[42]

When someone in Company A of the 143rd Pennsylvania shouted that the 149th's colors were in the open and that the Rebs were closing in on them, Sgts. Charles H. Riley and the indefatigable Patrick DeLacy bolted into the field. Captain Charles M. Conyngham yelled at them, "Back to the line. You must stay with your company!" The two noncommissioned officers returned and lay down behind their men.[43]

41 Noecker to Editor; Bassler, "The Color Episode," 6; Ladd & Ladd, *Bachelder Papers*, 2:761, 766. Captain Bassler listed all five corporals. Spayd identified them by seniority, 1st through 4th, but did not mention Hoffman, who would have been the 5th corporal.

42 *OR* 27/1:345; Sanford N. Boyden to Capt. R. E. Gamble, March 15, 1906, Library, GNMP.

43 "Capt. DeLacy Describes Gettysburg Battle."

12:30 p.m. to 1:00 p.m.
Oak Ridge Near the Cobean Farm

Captain Page's four Confederate guns rumbled partway down the hillside, where the gunners unlimbered and opened fire on Lt. Clark Scripture's pair of Napoleons. The pulling of their lanyards immediately stirred up a hornet's nest. Under instructions from Capt. Hubert Dilger, the Ohioans fired slow and deliberately, each shot well-aimed. Dilger hurried the other four guns into battery to Scripture's left; they, too, delivered a deliberate and accurate fire into the Confederates. Private Pickens (5th Alabama) watched the Yankees methodically destroy two caissons, dismount one gun, and butcher a half dozen horses. Page took such a drubbing that Rodes called Reese to put his four 3-inch Ordnance Rifles on line with him.[44]

The Union guns did not escape unscathed. The incoming rounds inflicted several casualties. Dilger sent someone to fetch Lt. William Wheeler's 13th New York rifled battery from Cemetery Hill to bolster his position. Handkerchief-waving ladies lined the streets as Wheeler's men rumbled through town on the way to the field. Their speed over the rough road jarred the wheels apart on two of his caissons; two of the ammunition chests survived the crash. The other carriage completely shattered on impact, destroying its pair of ammunition chests.[45]

Despite being short four ammunition boxes, Wheeler left his dismounted artillerymen to jog behind the guns while he hurried the pieces to the front. He wheeled into battery on Dilger's right and halted to wait for his panting men to catch up. Several minutes later, Wheeler's rifles opened fire on Page's and Reese's guns. The rifled percussion shells tore Carter's battery apart, forcing him to redeploy one section. The pieces limbered and trotted south to the open plateau northwest of the McLean barn, about 800 yards west of the Federal pieces, where the guns again unlimbered. Dilger, having assumed command of

44 *OR* 27/1:754 and 2:602; Hubbs, *Voices from Company D*, 182; Carter to Hill. Dilger and Thomas Carter also refer to Page's heavy losses in horses and personnel. In his letter to Hill, Carter wrote that he sent six guns to Rodes. Dilger reported seeing eight, two of which moved closer to him. The additional four guns had to have been Reese's battery. Thus it is reasonable to assume that the maps showing Page having four guns on the southern end of Oak Hill should be two guns.

45 Guy Breshears, ed., *Loyal Till Death: A Diary of the 13th New York Artillery* (Bowie, MD, 2003),185; *OR* 27/1:752.

both batteries, turned the attention of his smoothbores on those two guns, eviscerating the Virginia artillery position.

Within 15 minutes Page lost 10 more horses and about four men killed or dying and another 26 injured. The Yankees destroyed at least one other limber, dismounted another gun, probably shattered the mouth of an additional piece with a round in its muzzle, and drove back every Rebel attempt to remove the pieces from the field with fresh horses.[46]

The heavy damage suffered by his battery angered Channing Page. He sent an aide galloping through the woods to find his battalion commander, Lt. Col. Thomas Carter, and inform him of the situation. Carter, in turn, rode down the hillside through the trees and found General Rodes and his staff in Cobean's field behind the 5th Alabama.

Glancing or gesturing up at the six guns on the slope, Carter shouted, "General, what fool put that Battery yonder?"

An abrupt silence fell over the group of officers. As Carter later put it, "queer" expressions spread across all of their faces.

The general softly replied, "You had better take it away, Carter."

As Carter was turning to withdraw what was left of the battery, an aide whispered to him, "The General put it there himself."[47]

46 Louis Fischer, "At Gettysburg," *NT*, December 12, 1889, 3; A. R. Barlow, "A Defense of the Eleventh Corps," *NT*, January 15, 1885, 1; A. R. Barlow, "Another Shot at Comrade, Beale," *NT*, April 23, 1885, 3; *OR* 27/1:752, 754; *NYAG*, 1:375; James S. Pula, *Under the Crescent Moon with the XI Corps in the Civil War, Volume 2: From Gettysburg to Victory, 1863-1865* (El Dorado Hills, CA, 2018), 19; Edward Marcus, ed., *A New Canaan Private in the Civil War: Letters of Justus M. Silliman, Seventeenth Connecticut Volunteers* (New Canaan, CT, 1984), 42; Barlow (1/15/1915) identified the Rebel battery as being under the hill, or at or near its base. Three months later he clarified his statement by writing, "When Capt. Dilger drove out the Rebel battery (Page's) on our left front (northwest) it took position (what remained of it) on the bluff still further to the left (south)." Dilger stated that the Rebels added four more guns to the other pieces and advanced two of the guns to within 800 yards of his battery, which by moving the guns south from Cobean's would place them on the eastern side of Oak Hill overlooking the McLean barn. At the dedication of the 45th New York's monument on October 10, 1888, Christ Boehm, in an address delivered in German, identified the Rebel battery (Page's) as being bronze and that Dilger destroyed it as well as the other four guns (Reese's) that joined it. Pula quoted Col. Philip P. Brown, Jr. (157th New York), who stood by Dilger when the captain fired the round that hit the Rebel gun in the muzzle. He also cited contemporary sources from Jacob Hoke and Pvt. Justus M. Silliman (17th Connecticut) to substantiate the accuracy of the colonel's observation.

47 *OR* 27/2:603; Carter to Hill, July 1, 1885. The emotions and expressions as set forth in the text are found in the Carter letter.

Chapter Nine

"The line gradually disappeared on the same spot where it stood."

— *Adj. Augustus Horstmann, 45th New York*

Rodes Attacks

12:30 p.m. to 2:00 p.m.

12:30 p.m. to 1:15 p.m.
Shead's Woods

Henry Baxter's brigade formed in column of fours. The 90th Pennsylvania took the advance, followed respectively by the 88th Pennsylvania, the 9th New York State Militia (83rd New York), and the 12th Massachusetts. Together, they headed west along the north bank of the railroad grade as far as the Thompson place, then turned north behind Cutler's reformed brigade.

Lieutenant George W. Grant (Company B) heard his men in the 88th reassuring themselves. "Boys, do your duty today for the old Keystone," "Home and fireside now." "The man who runs should be shot in his tracks." From the right of the line the lyrics "John Brown's body lies a moldering in the grave" reverberated above their heads.[1]

1 Grant "The First Army Corps," 48; *OR* 27/1:307. Baxter wrote that his regiments fell in line on the right (97th New York), which Hall confirmed in the regimental history. The regiments would have taken the least restricted approach into Sheads Woods.

On the Confederate side that morning, Maj. David G. McIntosh had reinforced the southern end of Willie Pegram's artillery line on Herr's Ridge. Captain William B. Hurt's section of breech-loading Whitworth Rifles and Capt. Robert S. Rice's four 12-pounder Napoleons rolled to the right of McGraw's Battery. The smoothbores [not visible on the map] directed their attention toward McPherson's Ridge while Hurt's Alabamians focused their guns on Sheads Woods. The section chief spotted movement of some sort and sent a solid shot hurtling at the suspected target. Private Thomas L. Hanna (Company F, 9th N. Y. S. M.) heard the bolt shrieking through the air overhead "like a frightened bird."[2]

Colonel Coulter's 11th Pennsylvania and 97th New York, meanwhile, still faced north toward Oak Hill. Coulter dispatched General Robinson's mounted orderly to scout the Moses McLean buildings. Sergeant Ebenezer S. Johnson (Company L, 1st Maine Cavalry) spurred his horse across the Mummasburg Road and headed toward the farm's conspicuous red barn in the low ground on the eastern side of Oak Hill.

Baxter arrived along the stone wall running perpendicular to the 11th Pennsylvania and the 97th New York and halted as soon as the left of his 12th Massachusetts aligned on the right end of the 97th. He faced the regiments west just as Sergeant Johnson returned from McLean's with a report of Confederates (Edward O'Neal's Brigade) heading south toward the farm. "Indications being that we should be attacked on our right flank," explained Baxter, "I at once changed front."[3]

Baxter's regiments reformed into column with the 90th Pennsylvania in front. They filed right, forward on the first battalion, down the steep eastern hillside under the cover of the thin belt of trees paralleling their route. The 90th Pennsylvania and the 88th Pennsylvania crossed the lane running toward the Mummasburg Road and went to ground in the open field with the 88th's left on

2 Hanna, "A Day at Gettysburg"; Martin, *Confederate Monuments*, 1:63, 96, 228; Ladd & Ladd, *Bachelder's History*, 216.

3 Hall, *History of the Ninety-Seventh Regiment*, 135, 136, 140; Isaac Hall, "Iverson's Brigade, and the Part the 97th New York Played in Its Capture," *NT*, June 26, 1884, 7; *OR* 27/1:291, 293 307; Beale, *Statements of Time*, 23. The evidence indicates that Johnson was with Coulter. Johnson probably conducted his reconnaissance prior to Baxter's arrival. Private James Beale (Company I, 12th Massachusetts) recalled seeing a cavalryman, whom he later concluded was Johnson, ride around the red barn and return. Someone told Baxter of a threat from the north. It makes sense that the news was delivered by Sergeant Johnson.

the lane. The 9th N.Y.S.M. and the 12th Massachusetts went prone along the rail fence bordering the north side of the tree line. Coulter filled the void left by the rest of the brigade by placing the 97th New York and the 11th Pennsylvania behind the wall, perpendicular to the rest of his command. They stayed along the eastern side of the wall on the slope, with their heads just below the top. The New Yorkers leaned their rifles against the large boulders at its base and waited.[4]

By this time the brigade's ammunition train guard under Capt. Edward P. Reed (Company G, 12th Massachusetts) had been relieved and came to a halt nearby under the shade of a few trees. The men were restless and wanted to join their respective regiments, but Captain Reed believed General Baxter wanted to use them as the provost guard.

"We want to join our regiments!" shouted the veterans.

The ruckus attracted the general's attention. He galloped over to the disgruntled soldiers. "What is the matter here?" he demanded.

"We want to go to our regiments!"

"You do?" replied Baxter. "Well, if that is the case, you are just the men I want there. Go to your regiments!"

The small band scattered at full speed to their respective commands. Corporal George Kimball (Company A, 12th Massachusetts) fondly recollected how his comrades rolled over on their sides and cheered their arrival.[5]

In Company G, 90th Pennsylvania, Pvt. Charles Smedley threw away his personal letters lest they be found upon his corpse after the battle, but secreted away a couple envelopes and some writing paper in his notebook.

Sporadic fire from the stone wall along the Mummasburg Road began peppering the line. Colonel Peter Lyle (90th Pennsylvania) ordered Company A forward from the right of the regiment on skirmish.

At the same time, Col. James L. Bates (12th Massachusetts) ordered Capt. Edwin Hazel's Company K to drive the Confederates out at the points of their bayonets. The vigorous dash from both companies took Cpl. Frank Jennings (Company A, 90th Pennsylvania) aback. "I never saw the men more willing to fight than they were at Gettysburg," he would later reminisce. Within minutes

4 *OR* 27/1:307 Hall, *History of the Ninety-Seventh Regiment*, 136 (map). Baxter said he formed his regiments on the right of Coulter's before moving down the hill. He likely halted along the stone wall before changing front.

5 Gaff & Gaff, *A Corporal's Story*, 217.

the two companies flushed the Rebel skirmishers from the road and pursued them into the fields to the north.[6]

Colonel Charles Wheelock (97th New York) returned Companies A and F to the right of the regiment. Their withdrawal pulled the Confederate skirmishers out of the woods on Oak Hill, who pecked away at the Federal line behind the stone wall with annoying accuracy. Despite ordering his men to maintain proper intervals and minimize casualties, Captain Hall lost another man killed and several more wounded. The rundown wall provided minimal protection.

General Baxter advanced the 12th Massachusetts to the narrow band of trees skirting the berm along the southern side of the Mummasburg Road. Private James Beale (Company I, 12th Massachusetts) looked to the brow of the ridge and saw a Rebel skirmisher drop to one knee, take deliberate aim at Company I, and fire. The bullet slammed into Pvt. George Bates's arm, knocking him out of the ranks. The regiment took cover in the belt of trees bordering the post and rail fence on south side of the Mummasburg Road. The left flank remained "in the air" close to the top of the ridge. The Confederates had forced the 97th New York and the 12th Massachusetts to hunker down.

Captain Hall's men attempted to gain fire superiority over the Southerners by jumping up in groups to fire in unison at individual puffs of smoke rising from the tall grass. When Pvt. Lloyd Reese was killed, Pvt. John Manchester immediately rifled Reese's cartridge box for more ammunition. The flank fire from the north continued to wreak havoc on the company.[7]

To the right, Capt. George L. Schell and his Company I, 88th Pennsylvania fanned out in "comrades in battle" to the north and systematically picked away at O'Neal's Alabamians. Colonel Peter Lyle (90th Pennsylvania) dispatched Company A (17 officers and men) north onto the David Heagy farm. Shortly after they arrived, Companies A, B, D, and E of the 45th New York (Brig. Gen. Alexander Schimmelfennig's brigade), advanced under D Company's Capt. Friedrich Irsch to relieve them. Minutes later, Lt. Col. Adolphus Dobke hurried

6 *OR* 27/1:307; Jennings, "Reminiscence," 3; *Life in Southern Prisons*, 55; *Annual Report of the Adjutant General*, 603.

7 Hall, *History of the Ninety-Seventh Regiment*, 137; Hall, "Iverson's Brigade"; *OR* 27/1:309; Beale, *The Statements of Time*, 23. The map in the 97th's regimental history shows the 12th veering northwest toward the Mummasburg Road. Dobke said he arrived on the field at 11:30 a.m. He apparently kept his skirmishers back, supporting Dilger until he drove the Rebel artillery off.

the rest of his New Yorkers forward to the right of those men to cover the northwestern flank of the XI Corps. With their arrival, six of the Pennsylvanians, among them Cpl. Frank Jennings, returned to their regiment.[8]

12:30 p.m. to 1:15 p.m.
Oak Ridge

For at least an hour the North Carolinians in the brigades of Junius Daniel and Alfred Iverson (Rodes's Division) waited under the counterbattery barrage from Cooper's and Breck's guns, taking casualties throughout. In Iverson's Brigade, Sgt. Henry C. Wall (Company D, 23rd North Carolina) vividly recalled that case shot (which he mistakenly called "grape shot") inflicted "some loss." Behind Iverson, Lt. Col. Wharton J. Green and General Daniel had dismounted in front of the prone 2nd Battalion. They were holding the reins and quietly observing the artillery at work when a shell burst just in front of the left of the regiment, killing and wounding nine men.[9]

With Carter's and Reese's guns withdrawn to safer ground, Dilger concentrated his 12 guns on O'Neal's and Doles's regiments. Exploding shells splintered the trees above the right of O'Neal's Alabamians and also struck the regiments lying in the open field behind the worm fence south of the 5th Alabama. Lieutenant Thomas S. Taylor (Company G, 6th Alabama) recalled the Yankee shells "[k]illing some & wounding many." Company B absorbed four of those hits: Capt. Thomas R. Lightfoot and three privates, the latter of which each suffered leg, hip, or thigh wounds. One slew Capt. James T. Davis (Company D, 12th Alabama), splattering his brains all over Capt. Robert E. Park (Company F) next to him. Shortly thereafter another shell exploded in Company F, wounding Cpl. James H. Eason and Pvt. Lucius Williams.[10]

8 *OR* 27/1:734; Cook, *History of the 12th Massachusetts*, 100; Detre, "88th Penna Regt. at Gettysburg"; Jennings, "Reminiscence," 3. Lieutenant Levan's capture of the colors of the 26th Alabama implies Company I was among the skirmishers Detre noted went out. "Heagy" appears on other maps, including Bachelder's, as "Hagy."

9 Clark, *Histories of the Several Regiments*, 2:235 and 4:255; *OR* 27/2:553, 601; Thomas H. Carter to D. H. Hill, July 1, 1885. Colonel Samuel B. Pickens (6th Alabama) reported that the artillery fire lasted about an hour.

10 Thomas S. Taylor to Dear Wife, July 17, 1863, Alabama Department of Archives and History, Montgomery, AL; "Casualties in the 12th Alabama Regiment," *Montgomery Weekly Advertiser*, July 27th, 1863; Robert E. Park, *Sketch of the Twelfth Alabama Infantry*

The skirmishers of the 45th New York, particularly the four left companies under Capt. Friedrich Irsch (Company D), lost men to the incoming artillery bursts and to Rodes's sharpshooters. Before the day ended, Irsch's boys accounted for seven of the 11 combat fatalities in the entire regiment.[11]

1:15 p.m. to 2:00 p.m.

With the guns silenced on the eastern side of Oak Hill, Rodes commanded O'Neal's men to advance; Iverson had orders to march at the same time O'Neal moved out. Iverson, however, had no direct line of sight over Oak Ridge to the Alabamians in the valley to the east. Rodes also failed to give Daniel instructions on the direction of his march, other than that he should cover Iverson's right.

O'Neal's four regiments had not yet started their rush toward the fence south of McLean's barn when Rodes personally directed Colonel O'Neal to flank south onto the farm lane that connected with the McLean farm. Colonel Cullen A. Battle's 3rd Alabama was maneuvering into column of twos when Rodes—without consulting O'Neal—ordered Battle to march his regiment west into the woods and connect with the left of Daniel's Brigade.

Captain Irsch observed the remaining three regiments stealing along the lane heading toward the Mummasburg Road west of the Heagy place. He ordered his 45th New Yorkers to hit the ground and sent a runner to Captain Dilger to direct canister or explosive rounds against the enemy infantry. Dilger

---

(Richmond, 1906), 58; "War Diary of Capt. Robert Emory Park," *SHSP*, 26:12-13; Busey & Busey, *Confederate Casualties*, 1:55. Of the five enlisted men wounded in Company B, 6th Alabama, Wade Armstrong, William Jones, and Snowden S. Kirkland had gunshot wounds in the lower extremities consistent with being prone and being hit from above by case shot.

11 *NYAG*, 1:378; *OR*, 27:1, 734-736; Busey & Martin, *Regimental Strengths and Losses*, 140; Regimental monument inscription from the field. According to the *OR*, all of the casualties occurred on July 1. The regimental roster shows the four companies lost five killed, two mortally wounded, eight wounded, two missing in action, one deserter, and 13 captured during the first day's battle, with the latter occurring during the retreat through town. The regiment reported 11 killed, 35 wounded, and 164 captured on July 1. The four companies accounted for 64% of the regiment's fatalities, 23% of the wounded, and 10% of the missing and captured. By the end of the day, 165 of the 375 officers and men in the regiment remained fit for duty.

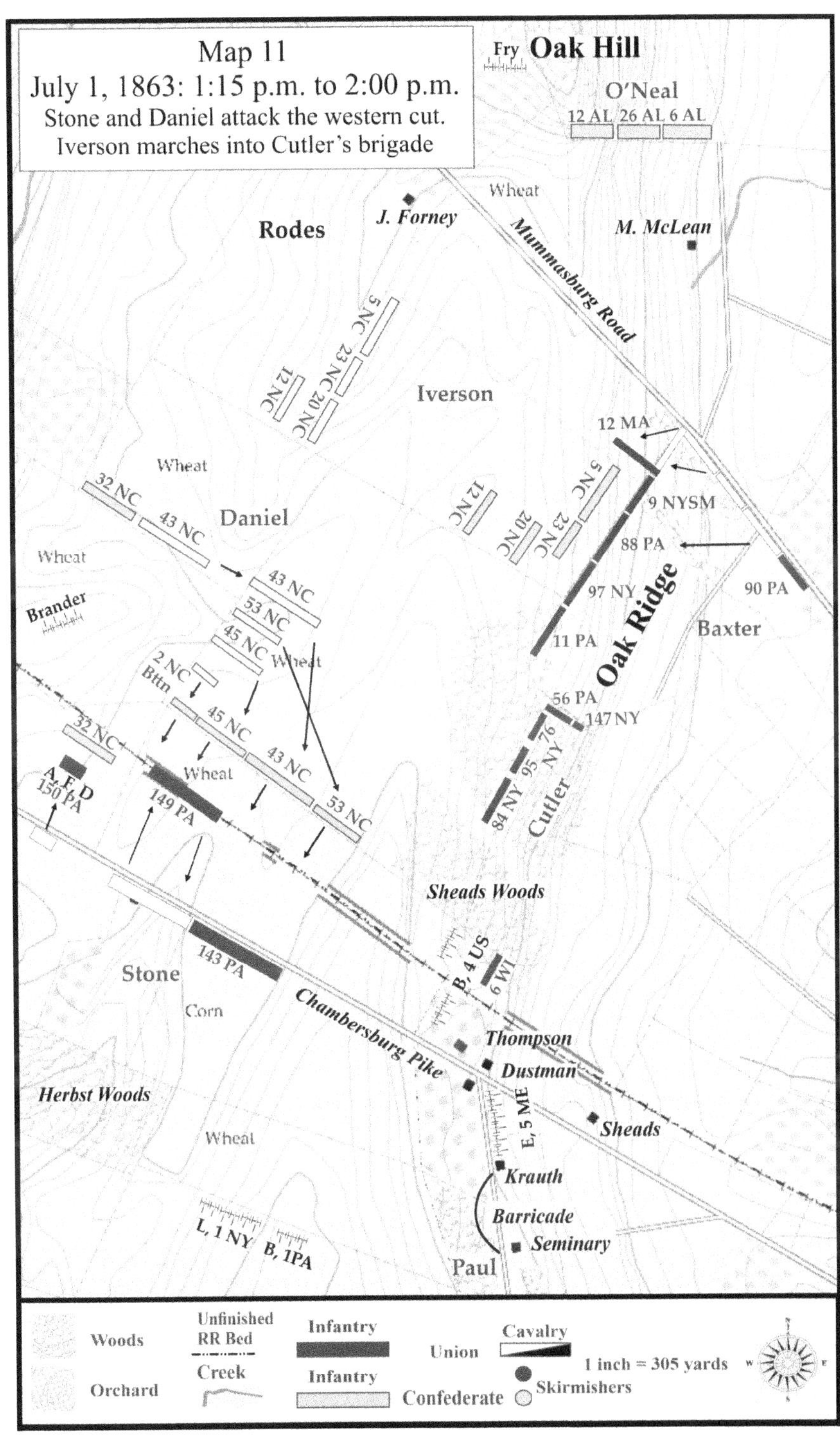
Map 11
July 1, 1863: 1:15 p.m. to 2:00 p.m.
Stone and Daniel attack the western cut.
Iverson marches into Cutler's brigade
Fry
Oak Hill
O'Neal
12 AL
26 AL
6 AL
Wheat
J. Forney
Rodes
Mummasburg Road
M. McLean
5 NC
23 NC
20 NC
12 NC
Iverson
12 MA
Wheat
32 NC
43 NC
Daniel
12 NC
5 NC
9 NYSM
20 NC
23 NC
88 PA
Wheat
43 NC
53 NC
45 NC
97 NY
90 PA
Brander
Oak Ridge
Baxter
11 PA
Wheat
2 NC Bttn
56 PA
147 NY
45 NC
32 NC
76 NY
95
43 NC
A, F, D
150 PA
Wheat
149 PA
53 NC
84 NY
Cutler
Sheads Woods
143 PA
B, 4 US
6 WI
Stone
Chambersburg Pike
Corn
Thompson
Dustman
Herbst Woods
E, 5 ME
Sheads
Wheat
Krauth
Barricade
L, 1 NY
B, 1PA
Seminary
Paul
Woods
Unfinished RR Bed
Infantry
Union
Cavalry
Orchard
Creek
Infantry
Confederate
Skirmishers
1 inch = 305 yards

knew the distance was too far for canister to be effective, and instead cut loose with spherical case and shell.[12]

Without orders and under an intense shelling, O'Neal changed front by files to the right and left into the field north of the barn. Heedless of the sporadic shots from the Federal skirmishers to the south and east, the men threw down the worm fences lining the road and deployed into line of battle. The 12th and the 26th regiments went to the right and the 6th to the left. The 12th formed in column of battalions, with the right wing in the lead, which gave it room to clear the west side of the barn and keep the right flank out of the orchard on the steep hillside of Oak Hill. The farm buildings shattered the 26th Alabama's formation and turned it into a confused mob for a time, while the 6th Alabama remained intact east of the lane.[13]

Air bursts of case crashed into the Alabamians' left flank. The skirmishers from the 88th Pennsylvania dropped on their stomachs along with the half-dozen from the 90th Pennsylvania to their right while Baxter's right wing hammered the Alabamians with a volley followed by firing at will. Company F,

12 *OR*, 27/2:523-553, 566, 592; *NYAG*, 1:378, 379; Brandon H. Beck, *Third Alabama! The Civil War Memoir of Brigadier General Cullen Andrews Battle, CSA* (Tuscaloosa, AL, 2000), 82. Colonel O'Neal specifically stated that Rodes detached the 3rd Alabama and the 5th Alabama without telling him why. In his report, Rodes explained that he had to include the "temporary" and "unimportant" dispositions of O'Neal preceding the attack "because they are necessary to a full understanding of Colonel O'Neal's report," which implies Rodes did not agree with the colonel's observations regarding how the general split up his brigade. Rodes asserted that O'Neal detached the 3rd Alabama without consulting him, and that O'Neal remained behind with the 5th Alabama as the Alabamians advanced, which contradicts the general's own admission that he personally commanded the 5th Alabama. It is interesting to note that Colonel Battle wrote in his memoirs that Rodes told him to "Keep well up on Daniel's left." According to the historian of the 45th New York, the skirmishers saw the Alabamians moving south along the farm lane east of the McLean farm, which confirms Rodes's assertion that the brigade "moved with alacrity (but not in accordance with my orders as to direction)."

13 "Casualties in the 12th Alabama Regiment"; Busey & Busey, *Confederate Casualties*, 1:129-133. The lane was too narrow to accommodate the normal column of fours. Deployment is based upon contemporary tactics. Neither side specifically noted how the brigade left the confines of the farm lane. No Confederates mentioned being in the lane, but Captain Irsch placed them there. According to Lt. Robert E. Parks (Company F, 12th Alabama), "Every officer on the right wing of the regiment was either killed or wounded." He named the eight officers, including himself, and an inspection of the casualty returns shows they came from Companies B, D, F, G, and H, which accounted for 39 of the 64 casualties in the regiment. The right wing accounted for eight of the nine officers listed as casualties on July 1.

12th Alabama, lost their Baptist preacher, Pvt. Edmond J. Rogers, when a gunshot shattered his left thigh. In Company I, a spent ball broke the skin on Pvt. Oscar C. Whitaker's left arm leaving a bruise, while another one grazed his head, leaving a burn mark and a lump. The 12th Alabama held its ground for a few minutes, but incurred 50 casualties doing so.

A bullet thudded into the chest of Lt. William "Bill" L. Branyon (Company K, 26th Alabama). Sergeant J. E. Tomlin heard Branyon gasp "O Lordy!" as he collapsed onto his back. A shell fragment killed a man in front of Capt. David Ballenger (Company D) and a projectile nearly ripped an arm off the man standing next to the captain. In quick order no less than seven bullets struck Ballenger: three nicked one of his wrists, and four went through his coat but only bruised him. He later attested that God had surrounded him and stood there with him.[14]

On their own initiative, Captain Irsch's four left companies stood and fired directly into the 6th Alabama's left flank and rear as the line passed them, cutting down a large number of the Confederates. The regiment broke and ran back to the fence north of the house. Another fusillade hit the 26th Alabama from the front and flank at it cleared the buildings. Fire superiority and advantage of position reduced the Rebels' ability to respond effectively.

In the span of some 10 minutes, the Germans of the 45th New York took out around 40 of the disorganized Rebs. Seeing the devastating impact of the .58-caliber minié balls on human beings just 50 or so yards away imbedded itself in Adj. Augustus Horstmann's memory: "The breaches in their ranks widened rapidly under our incessant & well-directed fire from our Springfields."

The heavy lead slugs traveling about 800 feet per second lifted some of the enemy a few feet in the air and threw them on their faces or backs. Others collapsed where they stood, while some of the wounded tried to crawl to cover. Above the din the New Yorkers repeatedly shouted, some in English and others in their native German, "Remember Chancellorsville!" It was, recalled Horstmann, "a terrible sight to see this splendid line annihilated in such [an] incredibly short time. The line gradually disappeared on the same spot where it stood."

14 J. E. Tomlin to William L. White, February 1922, Vertical Files, Library, GNMP; David Ballenger to Dear Nancy, July 8, 1863, Vertical Files, Library, GNMP; "O. to Dear Ma," *Mobile* [AL] *Evening News*, July 24, 1863; Park, *Sketch of the Twelfth Alabama Infantry*, 58.

From the eastern side of the McLean barn, Col. Samuel B. Pickens of the 6th Alabama watched the 26th Alabama get flanked west of the McLean barn. Most of its members retired to the fence north of the barn, where they joined the rest of the brigade. About 40 uninjured men surrendered to the Yankees, something that infuriated their commander, Lt. Col. John C. Goodgame: "It is my opinion that every man could have escaped being captured had they done their duty," he complained in his after-action report.[15]

Before the smoke cleared, the skirmishers from the 88th and 90th Pennsylvania (Baxter's brigade), in conjunction with Companies A and B of the 45th New York (Schimmelfennig's brigade), charged the barn and the house. The New Yorkers quickly captured 72 uninjured Rebs in the barn and a nearby drainage ditch. They turned the captives over to Adjutant Horstmann, who hurriedly sent them to the rear under guard. The Pennsylvanians also mopped up 35 wounded men. In the process, Lt. Eldridge Levan stumbled over the abandoned flag of the 26th Alabama lying in the grass, picked it up, and walked it back across the Mummasburg Road. He handed the banner over to the newly arrived General Robinson and returned to his company.[16]

15 *OR* 27/1:734 and 2:600, 602; Augustus Horstmann, "Battle of Gettysburg Pa. July 1st 1863, Day 1," 13, Vertical Files, Library, GNMP; Busey & Busey, *Confederate Casualties*, 1:63-73, 129-133, 173-179; *NYAG*, 1:379.

16 Ladd & Ladd, *Bachelder Papers*, 2:1062; *OR* 27/1:307, 310; Vautier, *History of the 88thPennsylvania*, 107; *Pennsylvania at Gettysburg*, 1:477; *NYAG*, 1:375, 380; Horstmann, "Battle of Gettysburg," 13; Busey & Busey, *Confederate Casualties*, 1:63-73, 129-133, 173-179; Richard Rollins, "*The Damned Red Flags of the Rebellion." The Confederate Battle Flag at Gettysburg*, (Redondo Beach, A, 1997), 102, Appendix A, n.p; Hall, *History of the Ninety-Seventh Regiment*, 136. The issue of who captured what flag from Iverson's and O'Neal's brigades is a confusing mess. In his comprehensive list of the flags captured at Gettysburg, Rollins identifies the following flags and the men who captured them: (1) O'Neal: 26th AL by 88th PA, unknown captor; (2) Iverson: 5th NC by Capt. Erastus Clark (12th MA); 12th NC by unknown captor (76th NY); 20th NC by Sgt. Sylvester Riley (97th NY); 23rd NC, by Sgt. Edward Gilligan (88th PA). Rollins credited both Capt. Hershel Pierce (76th NY) and Lt. Edlridge Leven [Levan] (88th PA) with the possible capture of the 26th's flag. However, Lieutenant Wagner (*Pennsylvania at Gettysburg*) cites Bates (*History of the Pennsylvania Volunteers, 1861-1865*), who credits the 88th PA with the capture of the flags of 23rd NC and 26th AL (which was misnamed in the after-action report as the 16th Alabama, which did not serve in the Army of Northern Virginia). Given where the 26th AL saw action and from other information from the various sources too complex to discuss here, I concluded it was probably Levan who picked up the 26th's flag from the grass during the regiment's mop up operation.

Edward A. O'Neal had a fairly distinguished career as a regimental leader, but lost control of his brigade and quarreled with General Rodes at Gettysburg, which doomed his expected promotion to brigadier general. *Wiki*

Near the Hoffman Farm

During the artillery fire, Iverson sent an aide to Rodes to find out when he was to advance his brigade. The aide returned with the directive to remain in place until his skirmishers became "hotly" engaged. Shortly thereafter, Rodes sent word to meet the enemy, who were advancing upon the batteries. He also ordered Iverson to ask Daniel to support him, and informed Iverson that O'Neal's Brigade would go forward on his left after the batteries stopped shooting. Iverson hurried a messenger to Daniel to tell him he was getting ready to march, and sent a man to alert each of his regiments of his intentions. He further advised his left regiment, the 5th North Carolina, to watch for O'Neal's advance. Minutes later the artillery ceased fire and Iverson received word the Alabamians had stepped off. Colonel Daniel H. Christie detailed Company G, 23rd North Carolina, to screen the brigade as skirmishers.[17]

McPherson's Farm

From the McPherson place, Col. Roy Stone took notice of the increased skirmish activity along the railroad cut. When the Confederate batteries ceased

17 *OR*, 27/2:579; Cpl. John Fuller Coghill to Dear Sister, Folder 1, John Fuller Coghill Papers, 1724-z, Southern Historical Collection, Wilson Library, University of North Carolina, Chapel Hill, NC. According to Coghill, he was sent out to the front and opened the battle before the brigade came up to support them, which is what a skirmisher would have experienced in that situation.

firing, he saw an enemy line of battle (Iverson) off to the north marching out of the woods on Oak Ridge heading south across the Mummasburg Road toward Sheads Woods. The colonel estimated the time as 1:30 p.m. About 520 yards south of the Hoffman lane, Iverson left quarter-wheeled his brigade to the fence immediately east of the Forney farmhouse.[18]

The sudden change of front surprised General Daniel. Having just passed through Hoffman's wood lot, he wheeled his regiments to face due south to cover Iverson's right flank. The maneuver placed the right of the 32nd North Carolina along the bank of a small tributary that fed into Willoughby Run south of the Wills place. A fence 420 yards to the left separated the 53rd regiment from the 45th to its left. As the brigade continued its march, the ground began dropping more sharply to the west, which forced Daniel to flank east. Being crowded against the fence separating it from the 45th and the 2nd Battalion, the 53rd halted and stepped backward to allow the 43rd to maneuver in front it. By the time the 32nd regiment reached the northern side of Wills's orchard, the regiment had its left upon that fence, with the 43rd on the opposite side and the 45th and the 2nd Battalion to its left.

Daniel once more flanked left and fronted before the brigade reached the Wills farm lane on the southern side of the orchard. This forced the 2nd Battalion across the fence on its right, immediately north of the western railroad cut. Once there, he aligned his brigade for an assault. The 2nd Battalion walked forward about 20 feet into the field before halting. The 45th knocked down a section or two of the fence and filed left until it covered the 2nd and faced front. Daniel ordered the regiments to lie down. At that point, Carter's and Fry's

18 Clark, *Histories of Several Regiments*, 1:137, 139, 635; Hall, *History of the Ninety-Seventh Regiment*, 137, 139; Ladd & Ladd, *Bachelder Papers*, 2:1061; Charles C. Wehrum, "The Adjutant of the 12th Mass. Replies to the Captain of the 97th N.Y.," *NT*, December 10, 1885, 3; Cook, *History of the Twelfth Massachusetts*, 100; *OR* 27/1:329. Bachelder, on "Map 10: 2:30 p.m.," shows Iverson's left on the Mummasburg Road, whereas in a letter to Bachelder, Hall said no Confederate casualties occurred north of the high rail fence. Wehrum (12th Massachusetts) confirmed this by noting the regiment did not get attacked along its front during the charge but rather took casualties from skirmishers on the right in the woods along Oak Hill. Both Hall and Captain Egleston (Company D, 97th New York) wrote that the 12th Massachusetts got a flank fire on the Confederate line, and that the high fence prevented many of the New Englanders from charging. Bachelder's time is likely off by an hour. Like the historians who cited him, he apparently believed the charge against Iverson occurred immediately after the volley that sent the brigade to cover in the drainage, when evidence suggests it did not.

Despite this being his first serious combat as a brigade commander, Junius Daniel performed well as he executed his original mission—to protect Iverson's right-rear. He would be killed at Spotsylvania in May of 1864. *Wiki*

artillerists on Oak Hill resumed shelling the Pennsylvanians along the Chambersburg Pike.[19]

Iverson's skirmishers fanned out to the brigade's flanks to protect the advance from any surprises. Clearing the fence east of the Forney house, the 23rd and the 20th regiments had enough room to fit on the right of the 5th, which aligned its left on the high worm fence along the northern side of the timothy field. The fence bordering the southern edge of the field, however, cut off the 12th, forcing it to fall back and realign about 50 yards behind the 20th. The distance between the fences narrowed quickly as the brigade plowed east through the thick grass. Less than 200 yards into the advance, the 20th found itself crowded into line close behind the 23rd.[20]

19 *OR* 27/1:342 2:566, 573, 576; Clark, *Histories of Several Regiments*, 3:256 and 4:255. Colonel James T. Morehead (53rd North Carolina) wrote that the regiment was pulled from the line because of crowding between the brigade on the left and the one on the right. This is based on the estimated frontage of the brigade and Daniel saying he had to flank to the left "some distance." Lieutenant Colonel William A. Owens (53rd North Carolina) reported his regiment moved "forward some 200 yards," and then "by the left flank some 300 yards" before moving forward "some 50 or 100 yards." Lieutenant Colonel William G. Lewis (43rd North Carolina) noted they advanced about one mile before engaging the Federals, and that his regiment was between the 32nd and the 45th, but did not mention the 53rd, which may indicate that it was not in the brigade line at that time. Lewis added that the 43rd halted in a farm lane. The only lane south of the Mummasburg Road was the one on the south side of the Wills orchard. Putting the left of the 45th on the fence south east of the orchard would place the 43rd and the 32nd in the Wills's lane and the 2nd Battalion in front of the western cut.

20 Coghill to Sister; Clark, *Histories of the Several Regiments*, 1:137, 139, 635; Hall, *History of the Ninety-Seventh Regiment*, 137, 139; Ladd & Ladd, *Bachelder Papers*,

Farther south, Roy Stone patiently waited for Daniel's men to step within rifle range. By the time Iverson's right presented itself to the Pennsylvanians, the gap between it and the Keystone troops had narrowed to under 700 yards. The marching abilities of the North Carolinians impressed some of the Union men. Private Lysander S. Jordan (Company B, 143rd Pennsylvania) exclaimed, "See yonder, boys, that line of Rebels coming from our right front. Don't they do that fine? But, if they don't change direction, we will take them in the flank. All eyes to the front, now!" continued the talkative private. "They are swinging their right now and that means us. Don't fire, men, until they get to that fence."

Lieutenant Colonel Walton Dwight ordered the 149th Pennsylvania to aim over the heads of their skirmishers. The men adjusted the ramp sights on their model 1853 Enfields and cut loose. To the right, the 143rd Pennsylvania also joined in the shooting. Corporal Simon Hubler (Company I) recalled pouring an additional charge of powder down the muzzle of his Enfield before charging the bullet. He adjusted the sight to 900 yards and pulled trigger.[21]

For reasons unknown, once the brigade headed east, Iverson did not advance with his command. Rather than strike Sheads Woods, the veterans steadily marched through the chest-high timothy field, ignoring the bothersome long-range rounds zipping about from the Pennsylvanians along the Chambersburg Pike. With the undulating ground and grass shielding their approach, they had turned away from their skirmishers, heading toward what seemed to be an unoccupied part of the Union line.

2:1061; Wehrum, "The Adjutant Replies"; Cook, *History of the Twelfth Massachusetts*, 100; *OR* 27/1:292. Bachelder shows Iverson's Brigade in a perfectly straight line. Colonel Coulter and the historian of the 12th Massachusetts claim the Confederates attacked in three lines. Sergeant Walter Montgomery (12th North Carolina) wrote that much of the brigade had pushed ahead before the 12th could come "well up," meaning it was behind the advance. The fence on the brigade's right flank constricted the front of the brigade the farther east it progressed. It probably constricted the front of the 23rd North Carolina, forcing it to fall in behind the right rear of the 20th North Carolina.

21 *OR* 27/1:329-330, 341, 345 and 2:566; Beale, *Statements of Time*, 15; Noecker to Editor; Hubler, "Just the Plain, Untarnished Story"; Tomasak, *Harris Journal*, 60. Colonel Stone said the Confederates advanced about 1:30 p.m. Daniel said his brigade reached the field around noon within 2.5 miles of the town, which puts it about due west of the Cobean farm, and that they did not advance until around 1:30 p.m. The colonel of the 32nd North Carolina placed the time of advance at 2:30 p.m. While the 45th North Carolina's report made no mention of the time it became engaged, the remaining three after-action reports all noted the time of advance as around or by 1:00 p.m. Stone probably observed the Confederate advance between 1:00 p.m. and 1:30 p.m.

General Robinson halted his mount atop Oak Ridge and watched as the heavy force of Rebels tramped toward his him. The division commander rode below the crest of the ridge and hastily prepared to fill the gap in the line to the right of the 97th New York. He ordered General Baxter to change front to the west with his brigade, and sent an aide to the seminary to bring up Brig. Gen. Gabriel R. Paul's regiments.

Baxter kept the 90th Pennsylvania along the Mummasburg Road to contend with the potshots coming from the McLean farm, then relayed the orders to his individual regimental commanders to right about and head uphill to the crest. He admonished them to keep their flags and heads below the top of the wall. The 88th Pennsylvania went to the right of the 97th New York. The officers kept the men down on one knee out of sight on the steep eastern slope of the ridge. "Await command. Aim low," they ordered.[22]

Thirty-eight years later, former Pvt. Thomas L. Hanna (Company F, 9th N.Y.S.M.) distinctly remembered how, as the regiment struggled up the hillside, the faces of his comrades lost their color and he tightly gripped his rifle until his muscles ached. From behind, Baxter's voice thundered overhead, "The ridge, men! Forward! Quick! Double-quick!" The New Yorkers lay down to the right of the 88th Pennsylvania, along the base of the boulders of the deteriorated wall. A thin fringe of scrub oak lined their side of the ridge. Baxter calmly trooped the line. "Keep cool, men and fire low," Thomas Hanna (Company F) heard the general advise them.

To the immediate north, the 12th Massachusetts's adjutant, Charles W. Wehrum, suggested to Col. James L. Bates that he throw the right wing, which in facing about became the left wing, forward. Bates consented, and the adjutant yelled for the right and left general guides to go forward to indicate the flanks as instructed in the manual. Laughing because he knew the situation did not require "by the book tactics," Bates countered, "Adjutant, we will dispense with them on this occasion." The right wing, followed by all but the two right companies that remained along the south side of the Mummasburg Road, sheltered behind the rocks on the crest, unseen by the Rebels. While maneuvering into line, a bullet struck Lt. Charles G. Russell (Company D) in the

22 Todd, *History of the Ninth Regiment N.Y.S.M.*, 270; *OR* 27/1:306, 310; Grant "The First Army Corps," 49; Vautier, "At Gettysburg"; Vautier, *History of the 88thPennsylvania*, 106.

head and killed him. The 90th Pennsylvania shifted to the left to fill the space just vacated.[23]

Within moments, the 5th and 23rd North Carolina, followed closely by the 20th to its right rear, descended into the drainage bottom about 150 yards west of Baxter's line. As they ascended the shallow slope, the 11th Pennsylvania spotted them moving forward in nearly parade-ground alignment, with flags flying and weapons at right shoulder shift. The Southerners marched with the rhythmic step of veterans. The "Keystaters" immediately poured it into the right wing of the 20th and 23rd regiments. In the 23rd, two bullets struck Maj. Christopher C. Blacknall, one through the jaw and the other in the neck. Corporal William J. O'Daniel (Company H) went to the rear with a lead buckshot imbedded in his left cheek.[24]

Iverson's three regiments responded with a determined "Rebel Yell" as they shifted the advance slightly northeast to escape the incoming Pennsylvania rounds. When they got within perhaps 50 yards of the Federal line, Baxter's regiments volleyed. Tar Heels dropped by squads. Others turned in a panic and fled toward the security of the demolished fence row west of the Forney place. The 12th North Carolina walked into the maelstrom as it reached the western lip of the depression about 80 yards behind the 20th, its two left companies absorbing Yankee fire. Lieutenant Colonel William S. Davis flanked his small regiment south under the helpful cover of the stream bottom to his right front. Davis kept his men moving until he lost sight of the rest of the brigade and found himself in front of Sheads Woods facing the rocky western slope of southern Oak Ridge.

The 9th N.Y.S.M. and Company A on the left of the 12th Massachusetts caught the 5th North Carolina from the front while the right of the 12th left-wheeled parallel with the high rail fence on the left of the North Carolinians' and mercilessly cut down about 200 officers and men. Some of the shocked

23 Ladd & Ladd, *Bachelder Papers*, 2:989; Cook, *History of the Twelfth Massachusetts*, 100; *NYAG*, 2:678; Coburn diary, July 1, 1863; Hanna, "A Day at Gettysburg"; *Pennsylvania at Gettysburg*, 1:487.

24 Hall, *History of the Ninety-Seventh Regiment*, 137; Vautier, *History of the 88th Pennsylvania*, 106; Hanna, "A Day at Gettysburg"; James L. McLean, *Cutler's Brigade at Gettysburg* (Baltimore, 1995), 222; Clark, *Histories of Several Regiments*, 2:236; Busey & Busey, *Confederate Casualties*, 2:983; Monroe Haskell, ed., "The Road to Gettysburg': The Diary and Letters of Leonidas Torrence of the Gaston Guards," *The North Carolina Historical Review*, vol. 36, no. 4 (October 1959), 515.

Rebels replied with a quick burst of small arms fire before rapidly falling back to the creek bottom. "See them run!" someone in the 9th N.Y.S.M screamed. Once under the shelter of its shallow banks, and despite their horrendous casualties, the Tar Heels partially reassembled the three mauled regiments into a single formation. An attempt was made to launch a charge, but the heavy musketry made short work of the effort and Iverson's men scrambled back for cover once again.[25]

The men of the 88th Pennsylvania coolly and methodically rested their rifles on the rocks in front of them and plinked away at the Rebels. Swiss-born Lt. Col. Joseph A. Moesch paced his horse back and forth behind his small 9th N.Y.S.M. urging the soldiers to do their duty. The New Yorkers' fighting blood was up. Cursing and shouts of "Give them Hell!" mingled with the screams and pleas of the wounded. The entire affair settled into a prolonged heavy exchange of fire.[26]

The Pennsylvanians eviscerated the 23rd North Carolina. Colonel Daniel H. Christie received a mortal wound in his back. Lieutenant Colonel Robert D. Johnston was wounded in his jaw, neck, and collarbone, near to the injuries to his face and neck he had suffered at Seven Pines on May 31, 1862. Adjutant Julius B. French collapsed in the ditch, mortally wounded. Corporal Leonidas Torrence (Company H), who had recovered from a serious wound at Sharpsburg on September 17, 1862, suffered two hits. One minié lodged deep in the muscle of his thigh but did not strike the bone. The other wound, also from a large-caliber minié, struck his hairline between the ear and eye and may have

25 Busey & Busey, *Confederate Casualties*, 2:895-902; Clark, *Histories of the Several Regiments*, 1:635-636; Hanna, "A Day at Gettysburg"; *Annual Report of the Adjutant-General*, 104; Grant, "The First Army Corps," 49; Jaques, *Three Years' Campaign of the Ninth N.Y.S.M.*, 156. McLean, *"The Bullets Flew Like Hail,"* 189. Grant claimed the regiment opened on the Confederates at 50 yards and the Rebs fell back to the dry creek bottom "about" 150 yards from the line. Sergeant Montgomery (12th North Carolina) wrote that the stone 80 yards west of the 88th Pennsylvania monument marks the spot where the Yankees captured the North Carolina flags. This means that the Pennsylvanians were about 70 yards east of their monument along the steep bank of Oak Ridge. Captain Hershel W. Pierce (Company A, 76th New York) claimed he shot down the color bearer of the 26th Alabama with his carbine, but the 76th New York never engaged O'Neal's Brigade. Busey and Busey positively confirmed three killed and 13 wounded in the 12th North Carolina. The other casualties are listed as having occurred sometime during the remainder of the battle. If that is the case, the 12th did not get as heavily involved as the account in Clark suggests.

26 Hanna, "A Day at Gettysburg."

Colonel Daniel H. Christie was mortally wounded during Alfred Iverson's bungled attack, lingered for more than two weeks, and died on July 17, 1863, at the age of 30. *Histories of the Several Regiments and Battalions from North Carolina*

penetrated his brain. The company's butcher bill continued. A private named Samuel L. McClure was shot five times—thrice through the body and twice in his left arm, which the surgeon later removed just above the elbow. The bullet that shattered Pvt. Hugh M. Wallace's right wrist resulted in the loss of his right arm. The trio of gunshot wounds in Pvt. Samuel Eller's left thigh cost him his leg, and, like Private Wallace, his life. Unlike his mortally wounded comrades, the more fortunate Pvt. E. S. Freeman survived a serious right elbow wound.[27]

2:00 p.m.
Along the Chambersburg Pike

Colonel Stone watched the northern end of Oak Ridge burst into smoke and flashes as Baxter's men rose and blasted Iverson's regiments at point-blank range. A considerable number of the ambulatory wounded and uninjured Rebs raced helter-skelter for the downed fence west of the Forney buildings.

Back at the fence, Capt. Don Peters Halsey, Iverson's assistant adjutant general, rallied the mob into something resembling a demi-brigade. The mixed-up regiments fell in and took cover behind the downed rails. The rest, along with

27 Haskell, "The Road to Gettysburg," 515; Busey & Busey, *Confederate Casualties*, 2:996-997; Clark, *Histories of the Several Regiments*, 2:236.

most of the brigade's surviving officers, took cover in the drainage ditch under the cover of Oak Ridge. Colonel Stone watched as two more Confederate lines marched en masse toward the western railroad cut and the 149th Pennsylvania's skirmishers.[28]

Stone ordered Lt. Col. Walton Dwight (149th Pennsylvania) to move forward to secure the cut. Colonel William A. Owen's 53rd North Carolina of Daniel's Brigade, meanwhile, tramped unseen 300 yards southeast and fronted a considerable distance behind the 45th North Carolina. The 53rd closed the interval between the two regiments to just a handful of yards.

The 149th's unexpected advance surprised the 143rd Pennsylvania on its right. When the men grumbled about why it was moving, the loquacious Private Jordan (Company B) announced his conclusion: "I'll tell you, boys, what they mean. Old Roy Stone is after a big chunk of glory for his tails and don't intend the 143rd Pa. should have any of it. But see, the fools have planted their colors beyond the railroad cut!"

The undulating ground and tall hayfield screened the advances of the opposing sides from one another. The Pennsylvanians of the 149th, leaning forward under the heavy canopy of projectiles and shell bursts from Oak Hill, reached the embankment before Daniel's Rebels. The ground unexpectedly fell out from under the feet of many on the left of the line. Unable to see the southern lip of the cut, men in Companies G, B, H, C, and I plummeted, in some cases, more than 10 feet, into the muddy track bed. Those who could do so picked themselves up from the jarring fall, scaled the steep northern bank, and crawled into the high grass. Captain Jones (Company G) remembered peering over the top of the grass to scan the terrain to the north. To the right, Companies F and A knelt along its much shallower eastern end.[29]

28 *OR* 27/1:330, 342, 345 and 2:554; Krick, *Staff Officers in Gray*, 146. Halsey led an interesting life. He was a scholar from the University of Virginia (Charlottesville) and Emory and Henry (Emory, VA) and had studied abroad at three German colleges. He left his professorship in languages at Roanoke College (Salem, VA) and joined Company G, 2nd Virginia Cavalry as a lieutenant. He transferred to serve as an aide-de-camp and assistant adjutant general in the North Carolina brigade. Halsey was wounded three times during the war (Seven Pines, Sharpsburg, which cost him the sight in his right eye, and Spotsylvania), and captured twice (Sharpsburg and Waynesboro). He died in 1883 at the age of 46.

29 *OR* 27/1:330, 342, 345 and 2:576; "Excerpt from Chronicles of Francis Bacon Jones," 6; Ladd & Ladd, *Bachelder Papers*, 2:830; William H. Wright to Mary E. Wright, July 7, 1863, Vertical Files, Library, GNMP; Noecker to Editor; Sanford N. Boyden to Capt. R. E. Gamble, March 15, 1906; Tomasak, *Harris Journal*, 60. Captains Jones (Company G),

From where he stood, Lieutenant Colonel Dwight could see three regimental flags rhythmically swaying in step with the Confederates. He arranged his men in a single rank along the precipitous northern side of the western cut and admonished them to withhold their fire until the Rebs got close enough to cut down all three lines in one volley. The very ill Capt. John Bassler privately disagreed with the decision. "Col. Dwight had orders to take his regt. across to the cut," he groused after the war, "but unfortunately he took us across the cut." Dwight had inadvertently put his men in a position difficult for the enemy to reach, but one from which his men could not easily leave.[30]

From the south side of the cut, Dwight observed Daniel's skirmishers press back Capt. Zara B. McCullough's Company E. He recalled the captain and his troops to the right of the line next to Company A. Dwight paced from one end of the position to the other waiting for the North Carolinians to attack, all the while instructing his men to aim below the knees and fire by battalions upon his command.[31]

While Dwight paced, the 2nd North Carolina Battalion crossed the rails of the worm fence about 100 yards from the cut and the hidden Yankees. It was not until they were within about 50 feet of the Pennsylvanians that men from the 2nd Battalion spied the state and national colors of the Keystone regiment jutting above the tall grass on the ridge to the southwest. The Tar Heels halted, leveled their weapons, and pulled their triggers. The minié balls zipped harmlessly above the out-of-sight infantry.

Dwight belted out the command to fire by battalions. In quick succession, the right wing cut loose, followed almost immediately by the left. The result, or so it seemed at the time, was a devastating volley. A wall of lead struck down a swath of Daniel's exposed troops. With their formation destroyed, the remnants of the three regiments scrambled toward the rail fence 100 yards behind them. Many officers had been hit, among them Lt. Col. Hezekiah L. Andrews, who refused to leave his men despite a painful hip wound. As Dwight's men

---

Irvin (Company B), and Bassler (Company C), Sergeant Noecker (Company C), and Private Wright (Company I) all mention being in a deep cut. Corporal Boyden (Company A) did not mention its depth, which concurs with Bassler's assertion that the right companies (A and F) occupied the lower part of the railroad bed.

30 *OR* 27/1:342; Ladd & Ladd, *Bachelder Papers*, 2:830; "Excerpt from Chronicles of Francis Bacon Jones," 6.

31 *OR* 27/1:342.

reloaded, he calmly directed them to hold their fire until the Rebels had reached the muzzles of their guns.[32]

The North Carolinians rallied and surged forward. Ninety feet from the 149th Pennsylvania they ran into another sheet of lead. They retreated to the fence a second time and started shooting through the tall grass heedless of their hundreds of dead and wounded blanketing the field. Several rounds struck home. Three Pennsylvanians were wounded in the left hand. A bullet glanced off the skull of Capt. John Irvin (Company B), who was acting major. As he staggered away from the line, he noticed Colonel Dwight recoil under the impact of a bullet in the thigh. Dwight refused to leave his post and kept his men at their work.[33]

Herr's Ridge

Unbeknownst to the Pennsylvanians, Maj. David G. McIntosh's artillery battalion had arrived on the field. Captain Robert S. Rice's four Napoleons (the Danville Battery) rolled into front straddling the railroad bed west of the western cut. Case shot unexpectedly hit the 149th from the left. The wounded Dwight saw the smoke billowing from near the orchard on the high ground west of the Christ place.[34]

Junius Daniel, meanwhile, reorganized his brigade line. The 32nd North Carolina slipped across the track bed downhill and west of the Pennsylvanians, heading toward the Chambersburg Pike and McPherson's barn. The 43rd North

32 *OR* 27/1:330, 342 and 2:576, 578; Busey & Martin, *Regimental Strengths and Losses*, 290; Busey & Busey, *Confederate Casualties*, 2:791-803; "Excerpt from Chronicles of Francis Bacon Jones," 5. The report filed by the 53rd North Carolina did not mention the attack on the cut or its casualties. The 53rd's nominal casualties amounted to 102 casualties (25%). The 2nd Battalion also lost 102 officers and men (42%). The impact of the volley probably left the impression of much heavier losses. Colonel Stone claimed the Confederates were shot within pistol range, staggered, then climbed over a fence and were hit again at ninety feet.

33 *OR* 2:578; Martin, *Confederate Monuments*, 1:96.

34 *OR* 27/1:342, 343, 345; 2:578; "Excerpt from Chronicles of Francis Bacon Jones," 6; *Pennsylvania at Gettysburg*, 2:725; William Wright to Wright; Oliver W. Phillips to Rosaltha Gertrude Phillips, July 7, 1863, Vertical Files, Library, GNMP; Privates Oliver W. Phillips, Miles Swope, and Jacob Kiphart, Jr., of Company A, 149th Pennsylvania had left hand wounds. According to the battlefield marker, the battery enfiladed the Union line at the cut, which meant it had to have deployed on the left of Pegram's Battalion.

Carolina, followed by the 53rd, fell in on the left of the 45th. Once all the regiments had assumed their positions in the brigade line, he ordered a charge. Colonel Dwight, who realized it "would have been certain surrender or destruction" if he did not act quickly, yelled for his men to retreat. In so doing, he abandoned the color guard with the flags on McPherson's Ridge. His men raced pell-mell toward the pike, something Pvt. Avery Harris (Company B, 143rd Pennsylvania) duly noted.[35]

The North Carolinians, with their line disrupted by the tall grass, randomly halted to fire as they advanced, hitting the Pennsylvanians in their backs as they climbed their way out of the deep end of the cut. Several dropped killed or wounded to the bottom. Others lost their grip and plummeted into the roadbed. Company B lost at four men: Pvts. Jacob D. Birsch, Jacob T. Lions, and William Lewis went missing, and Cpl. Ellis Lewis perished on the south side of the cut. Private Reuben D. Spangler (Company C), despite breaking his arm in a fall, regained his feet and miraculously pulled himself over the southern wall to safety. The confused affair lasted about 10 minutes.[36]

The 45th North Carolina, rushing ahead of the 2nd Battalion, discovered the cut the hard way when about a quarter of its men cascaded into it. To the east, the 42nd and the 53rd rushed across the low end and opened fire at the Union troops rallying along the Chambersburg Pike. The stunned Carolinians to their right rounded up around 30 startled Pennsylvanians and herded them to the rear. Daniel, having witnessed the disappearance of part of the line, realized the 2nd Battalion and the 45th could not advance beyond the cut. The brigadier yelled for the two regiments to retire about 100 feet to the protection of the west-to-east spur of McPherson's Ridge, which paralleled the cut. The 43rd and the 53rd, unaware of what had happened with the right wing, raced after the retreating Pennsylvanians. Daniel was on the verge of losing control of his brigade.[37]

Colonel Stone, meanwhile, rode out into the smoky field to observe the situation at the cut while Col. Edmund Dana (143rd Pennsylvania) walked his

35 *OR* 27/1:342 and 2:566, 573; Noecker to Editor; Tomasak, *Harris Journal*, 60. The scenario in the main text is reconstructed from the reports of Daniel and the 32nd and 43rd regiments.

36 Ladd & Ladd, *Bachelder Papers*, 2:830; James L. Clark to Maria Funk, July 9, 1863; Noecker to Editor; Sanford N. Boyden to Capt. R. E. Gamble, March 15, 1906. Birsh (Berk), and Lewis apparently deserted.

37 *OR* 27/1:330, 342 and 2:567, 573, 574; "Excerpt from Chronicles of Francis Bacon Jones," 6; Chamberlin, *History of the 150th Regiment*, 117.

line. "Steady now, my men," he instructed them. "Every one of you pick your man." The sound of hammers metallically clicking to full cock traveled through the ranks. "Ready," Dana barked. "Now Fire!" A billowing white sulfuric cloud spouting tongues of flame engulfed the regiment. The North Carolinians in the track bed between the western and the middle cuts took cover and shot back. The 43rd and the 53rd were caught between the opposing lines of fire.

In quick order, two minié balls thudded into Stone; one nicked his arm and the other bored into his right hip bone. He rode back to the turnpike, where volunteers helped him from his mount and carried him to the McPherson barn. Sergeant John C. Kensill (Company F, 150th Pennsylvania) vaguely recalled someone saying to his superior, Col. Langhorne Wister, "Roy Stone is badly wounded and you have to take command of the brigade." Immediately thereafter, an officer Kensill assumed was an aide, rode up to Wister shouting something about a large body of Rebs, possibly as many as 2,000, advancing toward them.[38]

Wister spurred his horse down to Lt. Col. Henry S. Huidekoper, commanding the right wing of the 150th, and ordered him to lead Companies A, F, and D to the top of the ridge to counter the unseen threat. While Huidekoper double-quicked his men by the right flank toward his assigned position, Wister placed Maj. Thomas Chamberlin in charge of the rest of the regiment.[39]

Halfway between the cut and the road, a minié ball hammered Capt. Francis B. Jones (Company G, 149th) in the left leg at the same instant that a shell exploded directly over his head. A fragment snapped his leg and sent him to the

38 Ladd & Ladd, *Bachelder Papers*, 2:833; Tomasak, *Harris Journal*, 60; *OR* 27/1:330, 335, 345; Chamberlin, *History of the 150th Regiment*, 117; Mark Reinsberg, "General Stone's Elevated Railroad: Portrait of an Inventor, Part III," *The Western Pennsylvania Historical Magazine*, vol. 50, no. 1 (January 1967), 8. Federal accounts clearly state that the Confederates attacked the road south of the track bed. Doctor John Dickson operated on Stone's hip on August 1, 1863, and removed a minié ball from the bone and separated the muscle (*iliacus internus*) from the bone (*Iliac Fossae*). This procedure allowed the colonel return to active duty much faster. The arm wound did not need serious medical attention. Stone said he was shot while the 149th retreated.

39 Bassler, "The Color Episode," 24; Ladd & Ladd, *Bachelder Papers*, 2:833. In a letter to John H. Bassler dated March 9, 1906, Huidekoper placed the 150th on the western side of the hill east of the lane running down to the quarry. Sergeant Kensill said Wister ordered the right wing under Huidekoper to right wheel and the left wing to "right turn" (face right), neither of which makes sense. The right wing would have faced right (north) in column of fours and approached the road that way. The left wing would have stayed in place facing the enemy.

Following Col. Roy Stone's wounding, Col. Langhorne Wister (150th Pennsylvania) took over brigade command, only to fall wounded himself a short time later with a shot to the mouth. *History of the One Hundred And Fiftieth Regiment, Pennsylvania Volunteers*

ground in a heap. While lying there, he watched small arms fire and artillery projectiles cut the hay as low as a scythe. The yelling Confederates passed around him.[40]

The routed Pennsylvanians reached the pike in absolute disorder, where Colonel Dwight vehemently berated them as cowards. The sick and feverish Capt. John H. Bassler (Company C) barely made it back to the reforming regiment. Despite the overwhelming chaos, he noticed Companies A, F, and D from the 150th Pennsylvania move to the post and rail fence on the left of his own regiment and commence shooting northeast toward the Rebels.

Meanwhile, across the pike, Colonel Wister noticed what appeared to be a battalion moving through the tall wheat on the lower western slope of McPherson's Ridge, heading toward the isolated colors of the 149th Pennsylvania. He yelled at Adj. Richard L. Ashurst to order Lt. Col. Huidekoper to charge the Rebs. Rather than return to the right rear of Company A, Ashurst stayed with Capt. William P. Dougal to participate in the attack.[41]

Huidekoper and his men scaled the fence under musket fire from the 32nd North Carolina. They left behind Sgt. John Kensill (Company F), unconscious from a bullet wound to the skull. A portion of the three companies stepped over the demolished worm fence on the northern side of the road and executed a partial left wheel to the northwest. They reached the western crest of the ridge

40 "Excerpt from Chronicles of Francis Bacon Jones," 6.

41 Chamberlin, *History of the 150th Regiment*, 118; John C. Kensill, "A Gettysburg Coincidence," *NT*, January 21, 1882, 8; Bassler, "The Color Episode," 29, 30; Tomasak, *Harris Journal*, 60.

and unexpectedly stumbled upon the North Carolinians not 20 yards in front and below them. A costly firefight erupted. The rotund Lt. William P. Dougal (Company D) was shot as he cleared his revolver from the holster and had to leave the field. In Company F, the Southerners killed Lt. Charles P. Keyser and Pvt. Frank E. Northrup, and mortally wounded Pvts. Charles F. Gibson and John Boyer. Company D lost two corporals and two more privates wounded. Rather than risk another ambush, the North Carolinians backed out of the fight; Huidekoper ordered the companies to return to the road.[42]

After dispatching the orders for Huidekoper to move out, Wister took his horse into the road, drew his sword, and yelled for Dwight to advance his reorganizing regiment. Dwight complied, much to the displeasure of Captain Bassler, who never forgave him for what followed. Bassler erroneously believed the colonel was drunk.

Dwight's exhausted Pennsylvanians staggered into the field again just as Huidekoper's three companies of the 150th crossed to the north side of the road. Glancing northwest toward the ridge, Colonel Dana spied one of the 149th's isolated flags above the smoke. "143rd," he yelled, "defend that flag!" The Pennsylvanians scrambled over the fence into the road and entered the field to the north. To their left, Huidekoper's and Dwight's men continued shooting into the North Carolinians. Private Avery Harris (Company B, 143rd Pennsylvania) saw dead Rebels hanging on the fence along the top of the ridge. He watched them fall in a heap close to the 149th's colors and attributed their fanatical attempts to "Dutch Whiskey."[43]

The demoralized North Carolinians stampeded over and around the hapless Captain Jones (Company G, 149th Pennsylvania). Seconds later, Jones heard familiar voices announce, "Here he is," and recognized two enlisted men from his company. While lying there, Jones spied Col. Walton Dwight limping after his men using his sheathed sword as a cane. Two more of Jones's soldiers joined the rescue party and worked the injured officer onto a blanket. With one on each

42 Bassler, "The Color Episode," 31; Chamberlin, *History of the 150th Regiment*, 118-119.

43 *OR* 27/1:335; Bassler, "The Color Episode," 8; Chamberlin, *History of the 150th Regiment*, 118, 119; Tomasak, *Harris Journal*, 60. While Chamberlin wrote a very good regimental history, he was downhill from Huidekoper's charge and did not see it. Contrary to current descriptions of the fight, a careful reading of the accounts suggest the right wing stood along the Chambersburg Pike on the left of the 149th. The left wing remained on the right of the Iron Brigade near the quarry on the western slope of McPherson's Ridge.

corner, the four men struggled south under a canopy of incoming rifle and artillery rounds. It did not take long for a bullet to hit one of the stretcher bearers. Nevertheless, they got Jones as far as the south side of the pike, where he asked them to lay him in the drainage ditch.[44]

Rallied Confederates stopped what was left of the 149th short of the railroad cut. The Pennsylvanians fell back under a hail of small arms fire and intermittent shelling. One of the shells tore Capt. Albert Sofield (Company A) in half. His second lieutenant, Lewis Bodine, was also wounded. Private Oliver W. Phillips referred to them as "two of the best men that ever lived."

The long-suffering Captain Bassler collapsed with a leg wound. Lieutenant John G. Batdorff pulled the captain to his feet, but when he discovered Bassler could not stand, hoisted him onto his back and staggered for the safety of the McPherson house. Batdorff lowered the captain to the ground near the northwest corner of the house and left him to rejoin the company.[45]

The right wing of the 150th Pennsylvania and what remained of the 149th Pennsylvania regrouped along the south side of the Chambersburg Pike while the 143rd Pennsylvania, on the right of the line, covered their retreat. In the 149th, Sgt. Isaac Noecker (Company C) estimated that only some 80 officers and men remained in the regiment from the original 450 engaged that day.[46]

With the Federals driven back to the Chambersburg Pike, General Daniel shifted his line about 300 yards north of the western cut and faced it east behind the fence about 450 yards west of Sheads Woods. Captain John A. Hopkins (Company E, 45th North Carolina) reported that the "regiment suffered more than it ever did in the same length of time." The 45th anchored the right, followed to the left (north) by the 2nd Battalion, 43rd, and the 53rd regiments, respectively.

The afternoon fight had cost Daniel's North Carolinians dearly. About one-third of the total number engaged were killed, wounded, or captured/

44 Bassler, "The Color Episode," 8, 21, and manuscript copy of statement from Asst. Surgeon Jonas H. Kauffmann (151st Pennsylvania) attached to that article, January 4, 1914; Ladd & Ladd, *Bachelder Papers*, 2:830; Captain Ralph Gamble to Capt. John H. Bassler, May 8, 1907, Ramsey-Bassler Collection, USAHEC; Noecker to Editor; *OR* 27/1:345; "Excerpt from Chronicles of Francis Bacon Jones," 6, 7. Surgeon Kauffmann attested that Dwight was not intoxicated.

45 Noecker to Editor; Oliver Phillips to Rosaltha Phillips.

46 Sanford N. Boyden to Capt. R. E. Gamble, March 15, 1906, Vertical Files, Library, GNMP; Busey & Martin, *Regimental Strengths and Losses*, 28; Noecker to Editor.

missing. One of the dead was Lt. Col. Hezekiah L. Andrews (2nd Battalion). Wounded officers included Maj. John Hancock, Col. Samuel Hill Boyd, and Adj. Jedethan H. Lindsay, Jr., of the 45th, and Lt. Col. James T. Morehead of the 53rd. Although his losses were among the highest in the entire corps, Daniel—in his first real fight as a brigade commander—had excelled. He led his men with courage and resolution, and he protected Iverson's right-rear as originally directed.[47]

East Side of McPherson's Ridge, South of Herbst Woods

In Chapman Biddle's brigade, Lt. John M. "Jack" Young (Company K) scampered into the 20th N.Y.S.M. giddy with excitement. Standing in the open, silhouetted against the sky and exposed to artillery shells and skirmishers, he ripped into his favorite verse from a bawdy ballad he normally blurted out when intoxicated. Waving his forage cap above his head, he croaked, "Colonel, it's damned hot out there!" He spat out something about there being too many Rebs for the company to handle at the Harman place and that they could not hold the ground. Colonel Theodore B. Gates shouted back that they had to hold as long as possible and sent the lieutenant on his way, only to dispatch Company G under Capt. William H. Cunningham to support them.[48]

Under orders from Brig. Gen. Abner Doubleday, Lt. Jacob F. Slagle directed Colonel Biddle to file his regiments south across the Fairfield Road onto the hillside east of Willoughby Run. In so doing, he left Companies K and G (20th N.Y.S.M.) stranded at the Harman farm. The regiments remained there for perhaps 10 minutes, subject to increasingly accurate fire from Confederate guns on Oak Hill.

47 Gottfried, *The Maps of Gettysburg*, 117; *OR* 27/2:567, 574, 576. I based the order of the brigade upon Gottfried's book and Lieutenant Colonel Owens's report for the 53rd North Carolina. The brigade apparently incurred most of its casualties in the cut and while reforming north of it rather than during the last attack against Sheads Woods.

48 Cook, "Personal Reminiscences," 325-326; Gates, *Ulster Guard*, 433. Cook's statement that the two left companies were sent on skirmish when the regiment reached McPherson's Ridge contradicts the colonel's assertion in the regimental history: "Sometime subsequently, Captain Baldwin sent word that he was severely pressed and that the enemy were multiplying around him and asked for reinforcements." At that point, the colonel sent out Company G. The fact that Young was under artillery fire indicates the incident occurred during the Confederate advance.

Biddle marched his four regiments into the road and moved them east up the hill until the 20th N. Y. S. M. came within a short distance of the seminary lane. Its right flank stood directly opposite the southwest corner of the woodlot fronting the seminary. He sheltered them there, facing north under the protection of the board fence and the road bank. Thus far, only the members of the color guard of the 20th had discharged their weapons at the Confederates.[49]

The Valley Between Herbst Woods and the Seminary

Pursuant to General Wadsworth's orders, Colonel Wainwright retired Cooper's trio of Ordnance Rifles (Battery B, 1st Pennsylvania Light) to the low stone wall in front of the seminary. He attached himself to the center and left sections of Breck's Battery L, 1st New York Light, commanded by the one-armed subordinate Lt. William H. Bower, and directed them to occupy Pergel's and Cooper's former position on McPherson's Ridge southeast of Herbst Woods. At the same time, Wainwright detached Breck with Lt. Benjamin W. Wilber's right section to the orchard on the McPherson farm, with instructions to keep the barn on his right flank.[50]

Seminary Ridge

Battery E, 5th Maine (Capt. Greenlief T. Stevens) went into battery behind the stone fence fronting the Reverend Krauth's house north of the seminary, adding six more Napoleons to Wadsworth's artillery line between Sheads Woods and the northern terminus of Seminary Ridge. That brought the total number of guns to 12 smoothbores and two 3-inch Ordnance Rifles.

Shortly thereafter, Capt. James H. Cooper (Battery B, 1st Pennsylvania) rolled his guns into position as ordered. He placed his left piece at the northwest corner of the seminary. The remaining two guns formed in battery farther north along the wall at the prescribed 14-yard interval between carriage wheels. No

49 *OR* 27/2:320; Slagle to brother. Because of their extreme range and accuracy, Colonel Gates mistook the Parrotts on Oak Hill for Rodman siege guns.

50 *Pennsylvania at Gettysburg*, 2:878; *OR* 27/1:362, 364. In his report, Captain Cooper said Wainwright commanded him to assemble the battery in front of the seminary. In 1889, Lt. James A. Gardner informed Bachelder that the battery deployed in front of the professor's house (Krauth). Gardner apparently erred; he did not have enough guns to fill that spot, which Stevens would occupy at 2:00 p.m.

sooner had Cooper done so than the pieces came under fire from a Rebel battery to the northwest.

During Daniel's assault against the railroad cut from the north, Maj. William Pegram had detached Capt. Thomas Brander's four guns across Willoughby Run to provide backup for the struggling infantry. The guns arrived by way of the Wills' farm lane and turned southeast and went into position on the hill immediately north of the western cut. The men from Pennsylvania and Maine responded with spherical case and shell.[51]

General Doubleday, having heard from Wadsworth of Solomon Meredith's decision to hold Herbst Woods, dispatched his ever-present aide Jacob Slagle to ride to General Rowley and send Biddle's brigade to the front.[52]

51 *OR* 27/1:360, 364 and 3:678; *Pennsylvania at Gettysburg*, 2:878; *Maine at Gettysburg*, 84.

52 Slagle to brother.

Chapter Ten

"Here are those damned black-hat fellows again! This is no militia."

— *Anonymous Confederates in Herbst Woods, Archer's Brigade*

The Collapse of McPherson's Ridge

2:00 p.m. to 3:00 p.m.

2:00 *p.m.* – 2:30 *p.m.*
The Harman Farm

For Amelia and Rachel Harman, it must have seemed like time stood still and that the raging battle being fought just outside would never end. The crashes of artillery fire and sheets of small arms rifle fire were becoming nearly unbearable.

The pair huddled in their basement while Companies G and K of the 20th N.Y.S.M. sniped at Johnston Pettigrew's Rebels in the woods west of their farm. "The suspense and agony of uncertainty were awful! We could hear the beating of our own hearts above all the wild confusion," Amelia recollected half a century later. Suddenly, hard-soled shoes clattered about the upper floors followed by the loud slamming of what seemed like every door in the house. Then, silence. Sick to their stomachs, the two women listened apprehensively to the rhythmic swishing of the grass in the front yard. The minimal light from the narrow basement windows turned darker. They ran to one of the high openings and peered through the horizontal slats into the front yard; legs clad in gray tramped past. Their "boys in blue" had abandoned them.

The women raced up the steps into the kitchen as Rebels flooded the house. A reddish glare illuminated a nearby window. Staring through it into the barnyard, Amelia gasped at the sight of their large barn engulfed in flames. To her horror, the Rebs had piled a stack of old newspapers on the floor, dumped books and rugs on top, and used a match to ignite them. The women tried to stomp it out and pleaded for help, but the soldiers stopped them. Colonel James K. Marshall had ordered the buildings burned. Some of the Carolinians deliberately misidentified themselves as "Louisiana Tigers" and told the women to get out or burn up with the house.[1]

Amelia and Rachel watched the 47th North Carolina press into the low ground below the first rise of east of Willoughby's Run. The 52nd North Carolina passed by the barn while air bursts painted the sky above them. As the women pushed through the regiment, men gathered around them. "Go on, go on out of the reach of grape and canister," shouted the soldiers.[2]

The Situation Along Willoughby Run

At 2:00 p.m., division commander Harry Heth ordered his final two brigades under Pettigrew and Brockenbrough to advance under the cover of the batteries along Herr's Ridge. Colonel Henry K. Burgwyn, Jr., increasingly restless about the seemingly endless delays, mounted his horse behind the center of the 26th North Carolina and called the regiment to attention. Lieutenant Colonel John R. Lane positioned himself on the right wing and Maj. John T. Jones covered the center of the left wing. Color Sergeant Jefferson B. "Jeff" Mansfield stepped forward with the color guard 10 feet in front of the line and awaited the command to march.[3]

On Pettigrew's left, Colonel John Brockenbrough filed his Virginians north toward the Chambersburg Pike until the 40th cleared the woodlot, when it faced to the right. The 22nd Battalion remained in the woods with its left flank on the fence, which left enough room for the 26th North Carolina to get to the creek

1 "Burning of McLean Home," 1; "Account of Captain Benjamin F. Little." The Tar Heels probably capitalized on the notoriety of the "Tigers." Much like John Mosby's guerillas, the Louisianans were accused of more crimes than they perpetrated.

2 "Burning of McLean Home," 1.

3 *OR* 27/2:643; "Reminiscences of Thomas Perritt"; Martin, *Confederate Monuments*, 1:230; Busey & Busey, *Confederate Casualties*, 2:1003; John R. Lane, "Anniversary of Gettysburg."

without the Virginians crowding its formation. Brockenbrough's men marched steadily down the slope at the quickstep toward Willoughby Run with no intimation that the terrain along the creek was about to fragment a textbook line of battle.[4]

The left side of Brockenbrough's front, under fire from the left wing of the 150th Pennsylvania, forded the creek south of the Catherine Johns house. The 55th and the 47th Virginia regiments broke into a trot up the steep hill to the lane north of the quarry, where they went prone and initiated a firefight with the Pennsylvanians. The 40th Virginia occupied a rock quarry and opened on the 7th Wisconsin with an oblique fire, while the 22nd Battalion took cover along the overgrown western bank of the creek to engage the Westerners from the front. The intense pressure forced Capt. George W. Jones and his Company B, 150th Pennsylvania, off the skirmish line and back into Herbst Woods, where they fell in with the 7th Wisconsin.[5]

4 Only maps have straight battle lines. At best, Confederate and Federal accounts remain sketchy on this part of the field. The estimated Confederate frontages and the tactical deployments they would have used to advance in this area suggest they engaged in a heavy shootout with the Federal regiments mentioned in this paragraph. The large 26th North Carolina spanned almost the entire front of Herbst Woods, which would have left room for only the small 22nd Virginia Battalion on its left flank, as shown in Gottfried, *The Maps of Gettysburg* (Map 8.3) but not in Bachelder's Map, July 1, 11/14. Bachelder shows the 22nd Battalion and the 40th Virginia extending halfway across the eastern face of the woods. Gottfried's map is the more accurate of the two. If the fence row on the 26th North Carolina's right is used to guide the line of march, the description of the frontage stated in Clark, volume 2, makes sense.

5 Martin, *Confederate Monuments*, 1:230; Clark, *History of the Several Regiments*, 2:849; *OR* 27/2:643; Gottfried, *Maps of Gettysburg*, 97, 99, 101; Bachelder Map no. 11/14 (July 1); Christian to Daniel; William J. Hatchett to Dear Parents, July 7, 1863, Hatchett Family Papers, *Civil War Times Illustrated* Collection, USAHEC; Wayland Fuller Dunaway, *Reminiscences of a Rebel* (New York, 1913), 85-86; Report of Col. Robert M. Mayo; Chamberlin, *History of the 150th Regiment*, 120. The 55th and the 47th did attack, but did not sweep the Federal position as is often presumed. Mayo (47th Virginia) noted the Federals put up "an obstinate resistance." Dunaway (40th Virginia) wrote: "On a field of battle the dead and mortally wounded are usually scattered promiscuously on the ground, but here I counted more than fifty fallen heroes lying in a straight line . . . the wounded must have numbered as many as two hundred and fifty." Private Hatchett (22nd Battalion) wrote his parents, "I am in hope I will never see as hard a time again." Christian (55th Virginia) noted that the regiment pressed "the enemy back foot by foot." Martin said the fighting lasted from 2:00 p.m. to 3:00 p.m. These accounts allude to a prolonged fight, and not a charge and quick retreat. Brockenbrough's two left regiments probably sheltered along the quarry lane because the ground and the fence provided them with good cover.

2:00 p.m. to 2:30 p.m.[6]
Western Side of Seminary Ridge, Near Fairfield Road

Colonel Chapman Biddle and his soldiers watched the situation to the north rapidly deteriorate, as had General Rowley, who directed the colonel to move his regiments north out of the Fairfield Road for a second time and form them in two lines of two regiments each. The 121st Pennsylvania, with the 142nd Pennsylvania on its right, comprised the front line, with the 20th N.Y.S.M. covering the 121st. The 151st Pennsylvania flanked north in the road then crossed the fence, going into line on the right of the New Yorkers. When they stepped out, Rowley unexpectedly held the 151st back and placed it along the southern face of the oak grove on Seminary Ridge. Lieutenant Slagle intercepted the three regiments and marched them northwest to support Bower's two sections of artillery on McPherson's Ridge. General Rowley personally shifted the 151st Pennsylvania into the grove west of the seminary and positioned it behind the makeshift barricade of tree stumps and fence rails there.[7]

Slagle directed the 20th N.Y.S.M along the reverse side of McPherson's Ridge on the immediate left of two sections of Battery L, 1st New York. The 121st Pennsylvania came up on the right of the four guns before Colonel Biddle realized that they blocked the position normally assigned to the 142nd Pennsylvania. Therefore, he moved the Pennsylvanians in column south, directly across the fronts of Bower's guns to allow room for the 142nd to come on line on the east side of the ridge between the right piece and the woods.

Major Alexander Biddle was leading his men across the front of the silent pieces onto a seemingly insignificant rise of ground south of the guns when he looked west toward Willoughby Run and spotted the 47th North Carolina (Pettigrew's Brigade) steadily marching over undulating ground. Farther to the left, flames and billowing smoke from the Harman property darkened the horizon. Not over 150 yards to the southwest, the 52nd North Carolina

6 These are the times cited by the officers and men of Biddle's Brigade.

7 *OR* 27/1:320, 321, 327, 356, 362; Ladd & Ladd, *Bachelder Papers*, 1:27; Slagle to brother. Wilber had recently received the promotion and had not yet been assigned to Battery C of the regiment. In the *OR*, Colonel Gates said the brigade was on the ridge at 2:30 p.m.

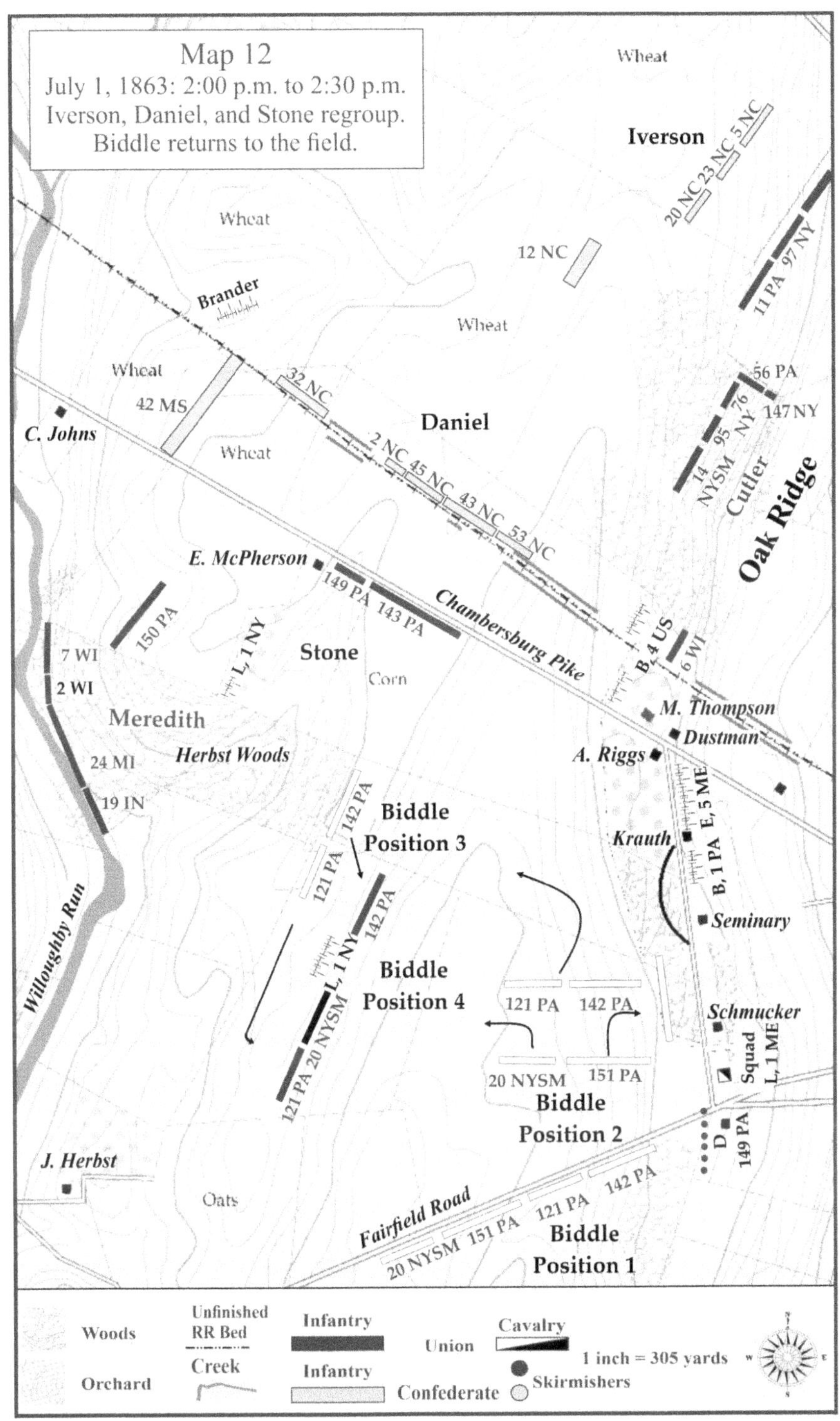
Map 12
July 1, 1863: 2:00 p.m. to 2:30 p.m.
Iverson, Daniel, and Stone regroup.
Biddle returns to the field.
Wheat
Iverson
20 NC
23 NC
5 NC
12 NC
97 NY
11 PA
Brander
Wheat
42 MS
32 NC
56 PA
147 NY
76 NY
95 NY
14 NYSM
Cutler
Oak Ridge
Daniel
C. Johns
2 NC
45 NC
43 NC
53 NC
E. McPherson
149 PA
143 PA
Chambersburg Pike
150 PA
L, 1 NY
Stone
Corn
B, 4 US
6 WI
7 WI
2 WI
Meredith
M. Thompson
Dustman
24 MI
Herbst Woods
A. Riggs
19 IN
142 PA
Biddle
Position 3
E, 5 ME
Krauth
B, 1 PA
121 PA
142 PA
Seminary
Willoughby Run
L, 1 NY
Biddle
Position 4
20 NYSM
121 PA
121 PA
142 PA
Schmucker
Squad
L, 1 ME
20 NYSM
151 PA
Biddle
Position 2
D
149 PA
J. Herbst
Oats
Fairfield Road
142 PA
121 PA
151 PA
20 NYSM
Biddle
Position 1
Woods
Unfinished RR Bed
Infantry
Union
Cavalry
1 inch = 305 yards
Orchard
Creek
Infantry
Confederate
Skirmishers

(Pettigrew's Brigade) moved by the right oblique, trying to flank Biddle's unsuspecting regiment.[8]

Infuriated by the Pennsylvanians blocking his front, Col. Charles Wainwright ordered Bower to take the four guns to their previous position on Seminary Ridge, about 100 yards south of the seminary near the Reverend Schmucker's house. According to Wainwright, "There was no shadow of a chance of our holding this ridge even had our Third Division commanders had any idea of what to do with the men, which they had not." In the meantime, the 121st Pennsylvania cleared the left of the 20th N.Y.S.M. and went prone along the east side of the ridge facing west, which left a large gap between the 20th N.Y.S.M. and the 142nd Pennsylvania. Biddle closed them to the left, creating a hole between his right flank and the southeast corner of Herbst Woods.[9]

2:00 p.m. to 2:45 p.m.[10]
The Situation on Oak Ridge

In Company B, 88th Pennsylvania, Lt. Samuel G. Boone watched with grim satisfaction as his men and others from Baxter's brigade remained steadfastly at their work. The men took deliberate aim before firing. Although pinned in an untenable position, Iverson's Tar Heels still managed to pick off some Yankees foolish enough to overly expose themselves.

8 *Pennsylvania at Gettysburg*, 2:653; *History of the 121st Regiment*, 58, 169; *OR* 27/1:323, 356; Lt. Slagle to brother. In his July 2, 1863 report, Biddle said the 121st had to move to the left of the brigade because its "proper position" placed it in front of the battery, which confirms Wainwright's complaint that Bower's four guns could not fire because their "own infantry" moved in front of the guns. Biddle further stated that they fired at the enemy when their faces showed over the top of the ridge, which implies the 121st stood below the ridge and the enemy walked into them.

9 *Pennsylvania at Gettysburg*, 2:653; *History of the 121st Regiment*, 58, 169; *OR* 27/1:323, 356; Slagle to brother; Nevins, *A Diary of Battle*, 235.

10 *OR*, 27, pt.1, 292; Detre, "88th Penna Regt at Gettysburg"; Boone, "Personal Experiences," 22; Todd, *History of the Ninth Regiment N.Y.S.M.*, 270; *Annual Report of the Adjutant General*, 2:604; *Life in Southern Prisons*, 55. Colonel Coulter (11th Pennsylvania) said the regiment mainained a "brisk fire" until 3:00 p.m. Adjutant Detre placed the retreat from the charge just before the regiment left the field. Boone said the men kept the Rebs "pinned for hours." Todd placed the movement back to the wall at the time of Stephen Ramseur's attack off Oak Hill around 3:00 p.m. The adjutant general said the regiment kept the enemy at bay for about an hour. Smedley wrote that the fighting lasted about an hour.

When Sgt. Henry "Harry" Evans spotted a Confederate color bearer to his front, he saw what he thought was a good opportunity. "John," he informed Sergeant Whitmoyer (Company H), "I will take a whack at those colors." Evans stood to take his shot. Whitmoyer heard a bullet thud into Evans, whose rifle clattered to the ground. He asked Evans if he was hit. "No," he slowly replied as he stooped to pick up his weapon. Instead, he fell flat on his back, dead from a round through his heart.

Boone left Capt. Edmund A. Mass and Lt. George W. Grant in charge of the line while he relieved a wounded man of his weapon and scrounged cartridges from the fallen. Stepping up to the firing line, he plugged away. "I done some wicked firing into the mass of confederate soldiers lying down within the field within short musket range," he would later proudly boast.[11]

2:30 p.m. to 2:45 p.m.
Herbst Woods

Colonel Burgwyn's 26th North Carolina slugged it out with the 24th Michigan and 19th Indiana as it advanced toward the brush and briars along the western bank of the creek. A bullet hit Sgt. Hiram Johnson (Company G), bringing him and the colors to the ground. Private John Stamper (Company A) lifted the flag and took a step toward the overgrown creek bank. A minié ball struck his right shoulder and dropped him.

Colonel Collett Leventhorpe, meanwhile, using the dense smoke to screen its advance, wheeled the left wing of the 11th North Carolina (Companies B, G, K, E, and H) uphill to flank the 19th Indiana from the south. Leventhorpe's men poured a devastating fire into the surprised Hoosiers.[12]

Major Egbert Ross urged the right half of the 11th North Carolina (Companies C, I, D, F, and A) east against what he probably thought was an

11 Boone, "Personal Experiences," 22; Grant "The First Army Corps," 50-51; Vautier, "At Gettysburg"; Vautier, *History of the 88th Pennsylvania*, 106-107.

12 Busey & Busey, *Confederate Casualties*, 2:1006, 1034; Mrs. B. A. C. Emerson, "The Most Famous Regiment," *CV*, 25:353; Edmund Jones, letter, May 11, 1865, Collett Leventhorpe Papers, as cited in William Thomas Venner, *The 11th North Carolina Infantry in the Civil War: A History and Roster* (Jefferson, NC, 2015), Kindle Edition, Ch. 7, fn 4, not paginated. The company alignment is based upon Hardee's *Tactics*. Thomas Venner identified the companies in each wing and I arranged them in their appropriate positions from left to right.

English-born Col. Collett Leventhorpe, leading one wing of his 11th North Carolina, flanked the Iron Brigade's 19th Indiana. He was severely wounded soon thereafter and captured during the retreat. He would eventually be promoted to brigadier general of state troops—the only English-born officer to hold that rank. *Histories of the Several Regiments and Battalions from North Carolina*

unoccupied ridge. The moment the regiment topped the first rise east of Willoughby Run, it walked into the line of fire of Lieutenant Bower's four guns waiting at the intersection of the Fairfield Road and the seminary lane near Elizabeth Shultz's house.[13]

A round plowed down the six members of the 11th North Carolina's color guard. A canister ball brushed Lt. William B. Taylor without injuring him while another one bored a hole the size of an egg through Major Ross's right side, mortally wounding him. Nineteen-year-old Adj. Henderson C. Lucas picked up the standard. The five companies threw themselves to the ground under cover below the line of sight.[14]

About the same time, a minié ball shattered Colonel Leventhorpe's left arm and a second one struck his hip, knocking him from the saddle. Leventhorpe had

13 Nesbit, *General History of Company D*, 14; *OR* 27/1:1032. Nesbit served with Company D, headquarters guard. Bower placed the guns in the Fairfield Road.

14 Lemuel J. Hoyle to My Dear Mother, July 12, 1863, Lemuel J. Hoyle Papers, #4746, Southern Historical Collection, Wilson Library, UNC; William B. Taylor to Dear Mother, July 29, 1863, Vertical Files, VF-7-11NC IN, Library, GNMP; *OR*, 27, pt.1, 323; *Fayetteville Observer*, September 17, 1863. Taylor (Company A, 11th North Carolina) described Ross's wound. Based upon the frontage of the 26th North Carolina, Leventhorpe, with the 11th North Carolina's left wing, probably wheeled against the 19th Indiana and the right wing sheltered below the ridgeline after getting hit by Bower's canister. The 11th's color guard was slaughtered about this time. Alexander Biddle wrote that the Confederates to their front advanced slowly.

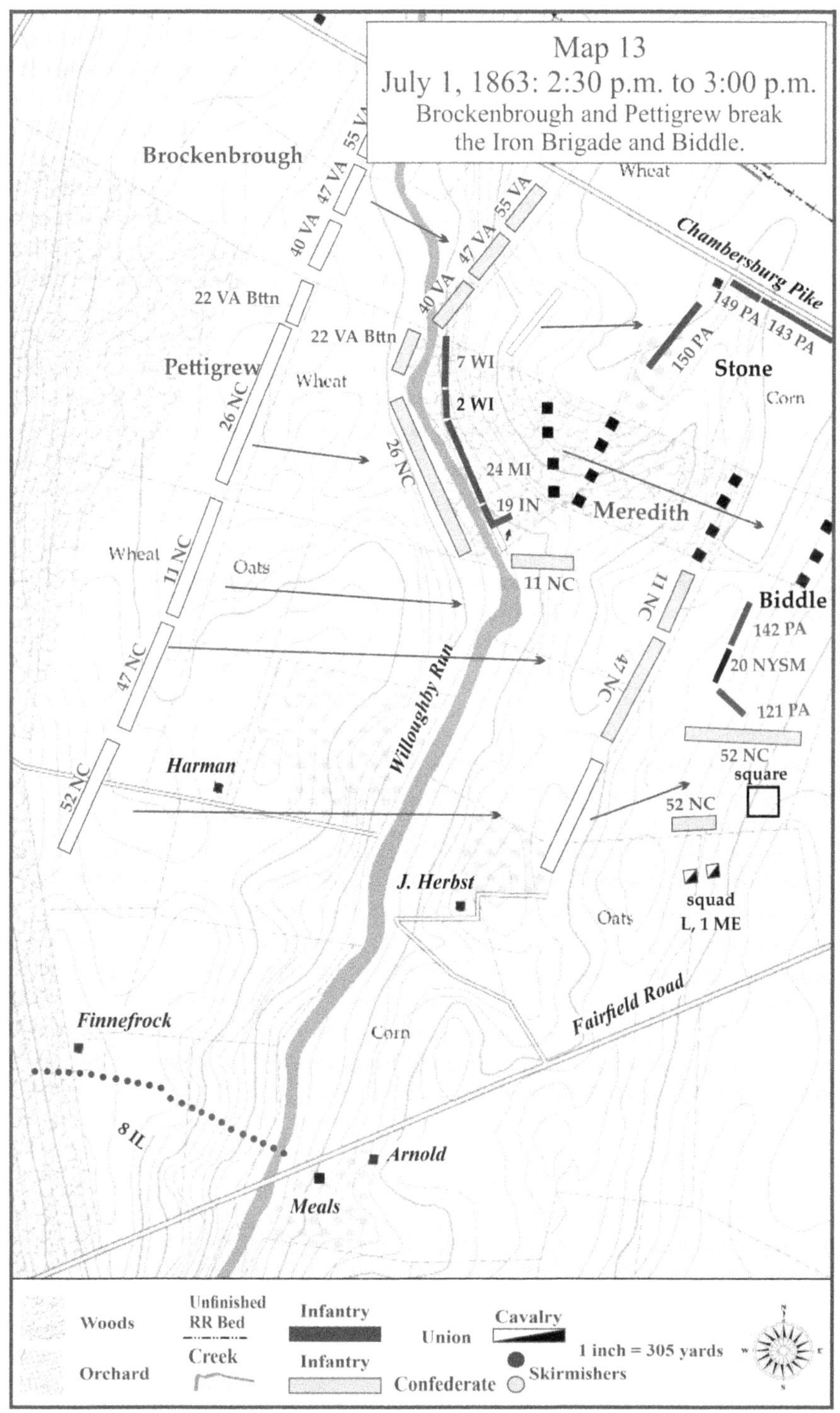
Map 13
July 1, 1863: 2:30 p.m. to 3:00 p.m.
Brockenbrough and Pettigrew break the Iron Brigade and Biddle.
Brockenbrough
55 VA
47 VA
40 VA
22 VA Bttn
Pettigrew
26 NC
11 NC
47 NC
52 NC
Wheat
Oats
Corn
Chambersburg Pike
149 PA
143 PA
150 PA
Stone
7 WI
2 WI
24 MI
19 IN
Meredith
Biddle
142 PA
20 NYSM
121 PA
52 NC
square
squad
L, 1 ME
Harman
Willoughby Run
J. Herbst
Fairfield Road
Finnefrock
8 IL
Arnold
Meals
Woods
Orchard
Unfinished RR Bed
Creek
Infantry
Union
Infantry
Confederate
Cavalry
Skirmishers
1 inch = 305 yards

to be carried from the field, and the wing's command devolved to 55-year-old Capt. Mark D. Armfield (Company B). Within a minute's time the regiment had lost its command staff.[15]

The Indianans were enduring their own hell. The last 20 minutes had cost them 20 killed and another 120 wounded, including Lt. Col. William Dudley with a shattered right knee. What remained of the regiment fragmented and retired uphill toward the next ridge on the hillside, about 100 yards behind them. "We did not cut and run," insisted Pvt. Roby Moore of the color guard. The veterans lined up behind the large trees four to five deep and sniped in succession at the Confederates below them, while the man in front peeled toward the rear to the next tree. There was little or no attempt to maintain a line.

Private William "Wes" Payton (Company K) leaped into the air grasping his middle, his eyes bulging in terror. "Robe," gasped the 23-year-old, "I'm shot." The unflappable Moore pried his friend's hands away from his gut. A sardonic smile rippled across his face. Barely able to withhold his laughter, he told Wes that a button on his coat had deflected the round. The injury may have been painful, but it was not mortal.[16]

In backing out of its untenable position, the 19th Indiana shifted its front to deal with the left wing of the 11th North Carolina on the high ground to the south. Corporal Charles H. McConnell (Company B, 24th Michigan) watched the Hoosiers realign at what was nearly a right angle to his company's left rear, which in turn exposed the Wolverines to a horrific enfilade. Captain William J. Speed (Company D), then acting major, was frantically trying to change the front of the two left companies (B and G) to face south and align on the Indianans when he died instantly from a bullet through the heart. The failed

15 Collett Leventhorpe, Letter, undated, Vertical Files, VF7-NC11, Library, GNMP; George Phifer Erwin to Dear Father, July 3, 1863, George Phifer Erwin Papers, #246, Southern Historical Collection, Manuscripts Department, Wilson Library, UNC; Lt. Hoyle to Dear Mother. Hoyle and Leventhorpe both described Leventhorpe's wounds.

16 Mumaw, "A 'Bye' Goes Off to War," 40, 41; William R. Moore to Sister Lizzie, July 4, 1863, Vertical Files, Library, GNMP; William Roby Moore, *Autobiography*, William Moore Family Collection, William Henry Smith Memorial Library, Indiana State Library, Indianapolis, IN, n.p.; Curtis, *History of the Twenty-Fourth Michigan*, 188; William W. Dudley to George R. Blanchard, August 9, 1887, Vertical Files, VF6-IN19, Library, GNMP; Barnes to Dudley; Report of Col. Samuel J. Williams; Jesse N. Potts, "Army Correspondence," *Winchester* [IN] *Journal*, July 17, 1863, 2; Busey & Martin, *Regimental Strengths and Losses*, 23. Williams counted 288 engaged to Busey & Martin's 308 of all ranks.

attempt left Company B on its own, its survivors stubbornly retiring from tree to tree, yielding ground foot by foot. Colonel Henry A. Morrow watched helplessly as the Carolinians mowed down his men "like grass before the scythe."

The tallest man in the regiment, Clr. Cpl. Charles E. Bellore (Company E) was shot in the head and perished immediately. Private Thomas B. Ballou (Company C) plucked up the national flag only to go down mortally wounded. Private August Earnest (Company K) grabbed the staff and started rearward with the left of the line toward the next ledge, some 50 yards behind them. The regiment left 50 of its officers and men behind, among them Lt. Gilbert A. Dickey (Company G) and probably half of Company B's 54 officers and men.[17]

The Rebels in the broad center of the damaged 26th North Carolina line, unable to plow through the brambles, started crowding the middle in an effort to find the low spots in the brush. Many were attempting to cross to the eastern bank of the creek under the cover of their own artillery barrage, subjected to a continuous fire. Private George W. Kelly (Company D), having relieved the wounded Private Stamper of the regimental battle flag, leaped across the run with Pvt. Larkin A. Thomas (Company F) by his side. Kelly lost his footing and went face first into the muddy bank.

Thomas stopped abruptly. "Get up, George," he shouted, "and come on!"

"Can't, Larkin," Kelly groaned, as he worked himself into a sitting position. "I'm hit. I believe my leg is broken."

"What hit you?"

Kelly grimaced, "Piece of shell. There it lies," he pointed. "Give it to me. I'm going to take it home for a souvenir. Take the flag, Larkin." Thomas took up the staff.

The fire of the Westerners gouged holes in the ranks of the Carolinians, but the Rebels managed to cross the creek and form some semblance of a battle line. On the left of the 26th, the mounted Capt. Louis G. Young (Pettigrew's aide-de-

17 www.findagrave.com/memorial/10954534/charles-henry-mcconnell, accessed Feb. 6, 2023; Curtis, *History of the Twenty-Fourth Michigan*, 160, 165, 175-179, 188; Ziegler Letter; Mary A. Livermore, *My Story of the War: A Woman's Narrative of Four Years Personal Experience* (Hartford, CT, 1889), 35; McConnell, "First and Greatest Days Battle at Gettysburg." Speed was serving as acting major because Maj. Edwin B. Wright was acting lieutenant colonel. McConnell's *Tribune* article was published four months after his death. Corporal McConnell reported eight uninjured of 54 present. The regimental history nominally listed nine of the 54. Based upon McConnell's testimony, Companies B and G likely accounted for the greater portion of the casualties during the flanking incident.

camp) happened upon a large group of men huddled in a mud pit along the creek bank. Once again a bullet plucked Young's kepi from his head. He caught it in the air and put it back on before rousting the skulkers into line on the bank. Farther to the right the Yankees shot Capt. William W. McCreery's horse out from under him, so he chased after the 26th North Carolina on foot. "Bullets rained around like hail in a storm," Pvt. Thomas Perritt (Company G) recollected.

The left and right companies of the 26th crossed the creek ahead of the center because of the lower vegetation in their fronts. Lieutenant Colonel John R. Lane reformed the right wing and ran to Colonel Burgwyn to assess the situation in that part of the regiment.

"It is all right in the center and on the left; we have broken the first line of the enemy," yelled back the colonel.

"We are in line on the right, Colonel!" Lane shouted back.[18]

The "Rebel Yell" echoed upward from the creek bottom through the impenetrable smoke hovering in the woods. According to Colonel Morrow, the Confederates "came on yelling like demons." From the ledge about halfway up the hill, the equally frenzied Yankees shot into the Stygian pall. A large number of the Yankee wounded, recalled Captain Young, foamed at the mouth "as if mad, and evidently unconscious of the sound of their voices. This was the only occurrence of the kind which came under my observation during the war, and I attribute it to the effect upon the nerves of the quick, frightful conflict following several hours of suspense."[19]

The 26th North Carolina closed ranks. The wounded and dead blanketed the ground. The lines had thinned considerably; gaps appeared along the formation as individual soldiers wove in and around the trees. Captain Young, miraculously still in the saddle atop his mount, Coosy, trotted up behind Lt. Thomas J. Cureton and his Company B, calling to him to close to the right on the colors. Looking to the right, the startled lieutenant saw only four men from

18 "Reminiscences of Thomas Perritt"; John R. Lane, "Anniversary of Gettysburg."

19 Busey & Busey, *Confederate Casualties*, 2:1020, 1030; Emerson, "Most Famous Regiment," 353; Curtis, *History of the Twenty-Fourth Michigan*, 160; *OR* 27/2:643; Rod Gragg, *Covered With Glory: The 26th North Carolina at the Battle of Gettysburg* (New York, 2000), 123; Krick, *Staff Officers in Gray*, 207; Clark, *Histories of the Several Regiments*, 5:119. Emerson put a "please" in Kelly's request for the shrapnel and mistakenly called Larkin "Lewis." Young's foaming at mouth reference is in Clark (fn on 119).

Company F on the field. One of them, Sgt. John T. C. Hood (Company F), raised his rifle on a squad of Yankees with a flag 75 to 100 feet to his right front. He pulled the trigger the instant Pvt. Larkin Thomas (Company F) stepped between him and the Westerners. The hammer snapped but did not ignite the round.

Hood examined the nipple and discovered he had put two caps on it by mistake. He recapped the piece and discharged his weapon while simultaneously getting hit in the foot. His left leg went completely numb. Weak from his earlier hip wound and his profusely bleeding foot, Hood inverted his rifle and used it as a crutch to hobble downhill away from the fighting. Only three of the 86 enlisted men in Company F remained on the field: Sgt. Henry C. Coffey and Pvts. Larkin Thomas and James Daniel "Jimmie" Moore.[20]

In the heat of the mêleé, a minié ball struck Thomas in the left arm. Private John Vinson (Company G) snatched the furled colors from him as he fell. A second later Vinson himself was wounded. Private John R. Marley (Company G) grabbed the flag staff, unwrapped the colors, and collapsed dead. Of the two remaining members of the color guard, Pvt. William Ingraham (Company K) shook it open.[21]

On the other side of the firing line, part of what remained of the 19th Indiana weakly anchored the left of the 24th Michigan. The companies had broken into groups of individual soldiers firing from behind trees to the south and west. Part of the Hoosiers' left wing had refused its line to shoot at the left half of 11th North Carolina on the higher ground across the ravine. The 24th Michigan covered the center of the line. On the extreme right, the two isolated Wisconsin regiments, the 2nd and the 7th, assumed a rough "V" formation in their original position along the first rise of ground east of Willoughby Run.

The national flag of the 19th Indiana fell again. Private Roby Moore (Company K), standing not eight feet from it, had just finished reloading his rifle when he saw it drop. "The flag is down!" he shouted.

20 Thomas J. Cureton to J. R. Lane, June 15, 1890, John R. Lane Papers, #411-z, Southern Historical Collection, Louis Round Wilson Special Collections Library, UNC; J. T. C. Hood, "The 26th Regiment at Gettysburg"; William H. S. Burgwyn, "Unparalleled Loss of Company F, 26th North Carolina Regiment, Pettigrew's Brigade, at Gettysburg," *SHSP*, 28:201. According to an account from the 24th Michigan, Coosy might have been a mule.

21 "Reminiscences of Thomas Perritt"; Emerson, "The Most Famous Regiment," 354; Clark, *Histories of the Several Regiments*, 2:374; Busey & Busey, *Confederate Casualties*, 2:1030, 1033, 1035. The unidentified color bearer about whom Emerson wrote appears to have been William Ingraham, who is listed in Clark. Busey also reported two more of the guard wounded: Clr. Cpls. John Bowman (right leg and thigh) and John Parsons.

Lieutenant William Macy (Company C) hollered back, "Go and get it!"

The justifiably frightened Moore spat out an oath. "I won't do it!" When he came to the realization that he had no other option, Moore threw down his weapon and darted to the dead man's side and raised the flag, all the while doubting his chances of surviving. "I got the impression that I would be a goner," he later wrote with considerable understatement.[22]

Within a minute, a minié ball zipped in from the left and carried away the bone and tip of Moore's left index finger. By this time some of the regiment had backed about 75 feet farther up the hill and northeast from where he stood. From that elevation they could shoot over the heads of the men below them. Through the smoke to the north Moore spotted Sgt. Maj. Asa Blanchard with Old Glory in his hand. He yelled at Blanchard that he had better get up the hill to the regiment but the sergeant major, whom Moore considered somewhat pompous, ignored him.[23]

Blood spurted from Moore's fingertip but there was little pain. He slung the flag staff over his shoulder and walked toward the new line, leaving Blanchard to his fate. Colonel Williams stopped Moore as he passed through the left wing. "Robe, are you wounded?" he asked. When Roby told him it was nothing more than a scratch, the ordered him to "give up that flag and go back to the rear."

Moore found Cpl. "Old Joe" Carder (Company K) lying behind some fence rails plinking away. When he asked the loyal Virginian to relieve him of the flag, Carder, having long served as one of the regimental color bearers, refused. "I don't want it," the corporal drawled, "I can do more a shooting." A big sergeant named Israel Blair (Company I) approached Moore and announced he would carry "Old Glory." Free of his burden, Moore left the regiment and headed for Gettysburg. He carried with him a premonition about getting wounded a second time: "I knew though that going back to the rear was a

22 Mumaw, "A 'Bye' Goes Off to War," 41; Henry C. Marsh, "The Flag of the Nineteenth," *Indianapolis Journal*, May 14, 1902, 6, provides the "I won't do it" quote. Marsh's version has Macy going down and removing a body off the flag in response to the denial to retrieve it; Moore's response, however, dovetails perfectly with the account and makes sense. Macy's accounts of the fight, as told to others by Macy rather than in his own published personal account, tends to focus on his individual heroism and appear self-serving. Phil Spaugy, one of the most knowledgeable individuals about the 19th Indiana, agrees that Moore refused to grab the flag, and then complied.

23 Mumaw, "A 'Bye' Goes Off to War," 41.

ticklish undertaking, for the minnie balls would be zipping all around me as they came down."[24]

Sergeant Blair, one of the five remaining color guards, only had the flag in his hands for a few seconds when a "bullet found its billet" and knocked him to the ground seriously injured. Corporal David Phipps (Company I), to whom Blanchard had given the regimental banner, had just escaped the slaughter along the creek when he saw Pvt. Joel B. Curtis (Company B) fall with a dangerous hip wound. Phipps had no way of knowing that only four of the original men in the guard remained upright and among the living.

After Blair fell, Phipps took the national flag in his free hand. By then the regiment's survivors had backed up several more yards, leaving him between the lines. He waved the "Stars and Stripes" about three times before enemy fire took him out of action. He fell face-first on top of both flags.[25]

Four men darted downhill from the line to retrieve them. Lieutenant William W. Macy and Lt. Jesse N. Potts (both Company C) got there first. Corporal Burr Clifford (Company F) and Company K's acting Lt. Crockett T. East arrived seconds later. Macy rolled the unconscious Phipps off the standards and furled the regimental banner. East tried to shuck it when a round killed him. Macy hurried back to the regiment with Potts right behind him. Clifford, who had thrown down his weapon and stripped off all his accoutrements, took the U.S. flag and headed back up the hill.[26]

Clifford quickly reached the conclusion that he would not survive carrying an unfurled U.S. flag. He stopped and, with the staff in his left hand and his side turned toward the enemy to make himself a smaller target, furled the colors and began slipping the shuck over it. A bullet hit the staff below his left hand, and another went through the top of his Hardee hat. A third cut his left pants leg just below the knee, and two others ripped through the tail of his frock coat.[27]

24 http://www.19thindianaironbrigade.com/Company_K.html, accessed Feb. 6, 2023; Mumaw, "A 'Bye' Goes Off to War," 41-42; Moore to Sister Lizzie.

25 "'Boys' of the Nineteenth And Some of Their Deeds of Valor on Bloody Fields of Battle," *Muncie* [IN] *Evening Press*, October 8, 1908, 5.

26 "'Boys' of the Nineteenth," 5; William W. Dudley to George R. Blanchard, August 9, 1887; Marsh, "Flag of the Nineteenth," 6; Burr Clifford to H. C. Marsh, February 20, 1911, Marsh Family Collection, Manuscripts Division, Indiana State Library. Macy and Potts alleged that Macy took the regimental colors from Blanchard and carried them all the way to Seminary Ridge.

27 Clifford to Marsh.

Clifford soon realized "our line had been swept away." With no officers in sight, he shouldered the flag and proceeded uphill about 125 feet when Blanchard rushed up and accosted him. "Here, what are you running away with that flag for?" The sergeant major yanked the staff from Clifford, jerked the shuck free, and tucked it under his sword belt. Captain Hollon Richardson (of Meredith's staff) had just ridden up to the line when he saw Blanchard waving the regimental banner screaming, "Rally, 19th, Rally!"

Behind Richardson, the much sterner voice of his brigadier "Long Sol" Meredith bellowed, "Steady, men! Steady!" Richardson heard the distinct thud of a bullet strike someone beside him. The flag quivered as Blanchard collapsed against a tree. "Don't stop for me," he gasped. "Don't let them have the flag. Tell mother I never faltered." Burr Clifford stepped aside to avoid the blood spurting from the sergeant's severed femoral artery, and it splattered Cpl. William N. Jackson (Company E) instead.

Sergeant William H. Murray (Company K) pulled the shuck from Blanchard's waist and was considering taking the standard when Clifford picked it up and walked toward the right wing of the regiment on the higher ground behind them. Looking back over his shoulder, he saw a sergeant he did not recognize with the regimental banner; Lieutenant Macy had handed it off. Instead of staying to learn the banner's fate, he headed to the rear with the "crowd" that had been the 19th Indiana.[28]

Simultaneous with Blanchard's demise, Richardson heard a loud groan echoing behind him. A case shot had burst in front of Meredith. A fragment fractured his skull and four case balls slammed into his mount. The dying horse plummeted to the ground, crushing the hapless general's leg and side. Before anyone could pull him free, the horse's thrashing head detached several of the general's ribs from his breastbone. Once freed from the animal, Meredith dispatched Richardson with a hastily scribbled note to the isolated 2nd and 7th Wisconsin with orders to withdraw.[29]

28 Marsh, "Flag of the Nineteenth," 6; Clifford to Marsh; Charles Carleton Coffin, *Four Years of Fighting* (Boston, 1866), 273; "Synopsis of General Richardson's Speech," 2. Blanchard's alleged last words are from Coffin. Marsh never cited who heard the sergeant major utter those words. By the mid-1880s onward, perhaps in an attempt to romanticize the war, heroic quotes abounded in memoirs and regimental histories.

29 "General Meredith," *Indianapolis Journal*, August 20, 1863; *Elkhart* [IN] *Review*, July 18, 1863, 1; Ladd & Ladd, *Bachelder Papers*, 1:142.

The 24th Michigan, meanwhile, held its own. The men hammered the Carolinians for several long minutes. Private August Earnest (Company K) died in the first fire and collapsed across the feet of Sgt. Everard B. Welton (Company H), who took the colors from him. Two of the color guard also got hit. Corporal William Ziegler (Company A) expired instantly and Cpl. Thomas Suggett (Company G) lay dying on the forest floor.

A bullet struck Maj. Edwin B. Wight in the right eye. Sergeant Augustus Ziegler (Company A) saw the round throw the major down. Two soldiers had dragged Wight back a short distance behind the line when he abruptly told them to return to the ranks because they might be needed. The partially blinded major struggled to his feet and stumbled toward the seminary. Lieutenant Winfield S. Safford (Company C) staggered away after a bullet passed through his stomach and lodged in his spine. Lieutenant Walter H. Wallace (Company K) perished. Colonel Morrow took the flag from Sergeant Welton and handed it to Clr. Cpl. Andrew Wagner (Company F). Wounded men between the opposing lines heard Rebels yelling, "Here are those damned black-hat fellows again! This is no militia."[30]

Farther to the right, Pvt. Emanuel Markle (Company B, 2nd Wisconsin) was hit four times defending his tree. A spent minié ball went through his left pants pocket and lodged in his wallet. A second spent ball bored through the handkerchief in his left breast pocket and bruised his chest. The third drilled a hole through his tunic and shirt. The final hit his right hand and tore the rifle from his grasp. He lay on the ground expecting the inevitable when a Reb dropped to his knee alongside him.

"We've got you Yank," he drawled. "Well, you haven't got very much," Markle retorted. The Reb snapped back that "[h]e'd just as soon kill me as look at me." Not to be outdone, the stubborn Badger told him that if he was anxious to kill someone there were thousands out yonder for him to try his hand on. The Southerner asked him to what command he belonged and how many Yanks were in front of them. The whole army was up, Markle quipped, "dressed and ready to do business." At that, the Rebel walked off. Skulkers soon picked up

30 Curtis, *History of the Twenty-Fourth Michigan*, 160, 162, 165, 176, 181. On July 30, 1863, Morrow wrote that the entire color guard went down at the second position in the woods. His account, being the most contemporary, implies that those two died in the woods. He also noted that is where Earnest died (and not at the third position as stated by Curtis, who did not participate in the battle).

Markle, Cpl. Robert Burns, Pvt. Edward Weeks, and others from Company B and herded them rearward toward captivity.[31]

2:30 p.m. to 2:45 p.m.

Farther to the west, in Roy Stone's brigade, Lt. Col. Henry S. Huidekoper (150th Pennsylvania) had watched Pettigrew's and Brockenbrough's regiments come down Herr's Ridge toward Willoughby Run. Huidekoper took his three companies and executed a reverse left wheel to connect with Maj. Thomas Chamberlin's left half of the regiment. Stray rounds knocked several men from the ranks but did not stop the realignment. After several minutes of exchanging rounds with the Virginians, Huidekoper started backing his regiment uphill and east toward their former position in front of the McPherson barn.[32]

By the time the 150th reached the duck pond on the ridge, Lt.Benjamin N. Wilber (Battery L, 1st New York) had unlimbered his two pieces on the rise between the barn and Herbst Woods. Huidekoper, who was preoccupied with both redeploying his regiment and a bullet lodged against the bone in one of his legs, can be excused for failing to notice the artillery.

A brief lull fell over the field in front of the Pennsylvanians: the Confederate artillery stopped shelling the brigade. Unbeknownst to the Keystone men, the 26th North Carolina—reinforced by the two right regiments of Brockenbrough's Brigade—had started pushing the 24th Michigan east through Herbst Woods. Huidekoper realized that Major Chamberlin had disappeared during the withdrawal. He presumed him dead and shouted for volunteers to find and bring in his body. Sergeant William R. Ramsey (Company F) and four others stepped forward for the grim and dangerous task of returning to "no man's land" to find a corpse. The soldiers found Chamberlin lying on the ground between the lines. A minié ball had drilled through his back just under his right shoulder blade and exited through his left breast. Somehow the officer was still alive.

On their way back to the line, the Confederate artillery on Herr's Ridge renewed its shelling. One of the rounds exploded just above and behind the rescuers. An iron fragment sizzled past Sergeant Ramsey, slightly grazed the

31 Markle, "The Story of Battle By Survivor."

32 Chamberlin, *History of the 150th Regiment*, 119-120; Ladd & Ladd, *Bachelder Papers*, 2:948-959 and 3:1592; *OR*, 27/1, 345.

Major Thomas Chamberlin of the 150th Pennsylvania was severely wounded while commanding the left half of the regiment, and lay between the opposing lines until discovered by his own men. *History of the One Hundred And Fiftieth Regiment, Pennsylvania Volunteers*

man across from him, passed above Chamberlin's head, and slapped into the dirt just in front of them. They struggled past the regiment and hauled the major to the McPherson house. As they placed him on the floor in the front room, he calmly rasped, "Now, boys, raise my head up, give me a drink of water, and go out to your work."[33]

By this time Lieutenant Colonel Huidekoper had withdrawn the 150th Pennsylvania into the hollow south and west of the McPherson house and established a new firing line. The banged-up soldiers had discharged several rounds from that new position when he decided to push up to the fence again. According to regulations, the color guard, including the hobbled Corporal Reisinger, followed the stalwart and conspicuously courageous Clr. Sgt. Samuel Peiffer with the regimental flag toward the top of the ridge.[34]

While his men ascended the hill toward the fence just west of the McPherson barn, Huidekoper observed General Pettigrew herding the Iron Brigade beyond the right flank of the 151st Pennsylvania and Lieutenant Wilber's guns on the ridge top in the orchard south of the barn. Believing that the section had just arrived on the field, Lieutenant Colonel Huidekoper sent a runner to advise Wilber to retire. The lieutenant, having fired a few shots, lost no time getting his pieces limbered and heading to the rear. He dropped trails

33 Wilber letter, July 2, 1863; Ladd & Ladd, *Bachelder Papers*, 2:949; Chamberlin, *History of the 150th Regiment*, 122.

34 "Three Bullets at Gettysburg"; Chamberlin, *History of the 150th Regiment*, 121.

around 165 yards east of McPherson's Ridge and waited for the infantry to catch up with him.[35]

The Pennsylvanians occupied their original position and again the Confederates counterattacked with heavier numbers from the front and the left flank. The Federals dropped with increasing frequency. Private William L. Perry (Company H) had no less than six men cut down alongside him. The color guard also lost heavily. Corporal Joseph J. Gutelius (Company D) went down, mortally wounded. Corporal Rodney Conner (Company C) buckled under the impact of a minié ball in his side, but somehow recovered himself sufficiently to hobble off the field. Sergeant Samuel Pieffer was shot in the right arm and a second later, a bullet shattered the bones in Huidekoper's right arm. He relinquished command to his senior captain, Cornelius C. Widdis (Company A).[36]

Grasping his mangled arm, Colonel Huidekoper walked back to the field hospital at the barn. In the chaos he never saw Sergeant Ramsey (Company F), who had just left Major Chamberlin in the McPherson house, stop by the pump to fill his canteen. When he tried to return to the regiment, Ramsey discovered it had moved and disappeared in the dense smoke. He had no idea where it had gone.

During Ramsey's absence, Adj. Richard L. Ashurst was hit three separate times: once in the shoulder, again almost immediately by a spent ball that lodged painfully in his heavy boot against his shin, and a third ball that broke his scabbard. Disabled but not fully lame, Ashurst managed to remain upright and with his regiment. While standing behind his Company C cheering the men on, Lt. Gilbert B. Perkins went down with a thigh wound. Captain John W. Sigler

35 https://museum.dmna.ny.gov/unit-history/1st-artillery-regiment-light, accessed Feb. 9, 2023; Ladd & Ladd, *Bachelder Papers*, 2:953-954; *OR* 27/1:346, 356, 362.

36 For more on Huidekoper's postwar account of his wounding, see https://civilwartalk.com/threads/a-wounded-mans-walk-through-st-francis-xavier-gettysburg.159196/#post-2077624, accessed Feb. 9, 2023; Ladd & Ladd, *Bachelder Papers*, 2:954; Perry to Dear Friends; Chamberlin, *History of the 150th Regiment*, 121. Chamberlin identified Sgt. Samuel Peiffer (Company I) and Cpls. Joseph J. Gutelius (Company D), Samuel Barnes (Company A), Roe Reisinger (Company H), and Rodney Conner (Company C) as the color guard. The regiment likely had a sixth man, who may have been Sgt. Duffy B. Torbett (Company C) because Huidekoper cited Torbett for gallantry in the after-action report. The regiment had only one flag, meaning the guard would have had six men, including the color sergeant.

(Company I) and Lt. Chalkey W. Sears (Company F) refused to leave their men despite both having suffered leg wounds.[37]

What remained of the 150th Pennsylvania fragmented. The right wing under Adjutant Ashurst headed to the right toward the 149th Pennsylvania along the Chambersburg Road. At Captain Widdis's direction, the left wing surged toward the rear to the fence row east of the farm lane. Only two of the six-man color guard remained uninjured. One died, and three others remained with the colors in spite of their wounds. A .69 caliber minié ball slammed into the back of Cpl. "Roe" Reisinger's right leg above the knee. The bullet flattened against the femur and prostrated him. Corporal Samuel Barnes (Company A) pulled Reisinger upright and assisted him in staying in the ranks.[38]

While searching for the 150th along the farm lane in front of the barn, Sergeant Ramsey stumbled upon Sgt. Elias B. Weidensaul (Company D).

"Where is the regiment?" he asked.

"To hell with the regiment," Weidensaul spat," let us go over there." He nodded at a gap between the left of the 149th Pennsylvania and the barn.

Joined by a few others, they ran to the Chambersburg Pike, took cover in the drainage ditch, and opened fire into the field north of the road. They soon discovered that their regiment had already attached itself to the company-sized 149th Pennsylvania.[39]

The badly wounded Capt. Francis Bacon Jones (Company G, 149th Pennsylvania) lay nearby. Glancing skyward, he spied Col. Langhorne Wister with blood rolling down his chin onto his tunic from a bullet wound through his mouth. Choking on his own blood and unable to speak clearly, Wister motioned for Col. Edmund L. Dana (143rd Pennsylvania) to take over the brigade, though he remained on the field.[40]

37 Ladd & Ladd, *Bachelder Papers*, 2:949, 954; Chamberlin, *History of the 150th Regiment*, 122; Perry to Dear Friends. Perry mistakenly wrote that Lieutenant Perkins belonged to Company B.

38 "Three Bullets at Gettysburg." The adjutant would have had charge of the right wing and the senior captain (Widdis) the left of the line. A .69 caliber musket ball weighed .9 ounces (394.6 grains). A .58 minié weighed 1 ounce (437.5 grains). The .69 minié, at 750 grains, weighed 1.7 ounces. A .58 minié inflicted the first wound and a .69 minié the second.

39 Ladd & Ladd, *Bachelder Papers*, 2:949.

40 "Excerpt from Chronicles of Francis Bacon Jones," 7.

2:30 p.m. to 2:45 p.m.
Seminary Ridge

Lieutenant Jacob Slagle galloped up to Doubleday; the general immediately sent him to find Colonel Wainwright, who was supposed to be with a battery somewhere in an open field. Slagle located the colonel on Seminary Ridge with the center and left sections of Battery L, 1st New York Artillery. He spurred back to Doubleday, who almost immediately dispatched him to Wadsworth at the center of the line. Wadsworth informed Slagle of the gap between the left of the XI Corps and the right of the I Corps.Turning about, Slagle galloped to I Corps headquarters and delivered his report. Doubleday sent an aide into the woodlot immediately west of the seminary and ordered Brig. Gen. Gabriel Paul to advance his brigade north to fill the gap in the line.[41]

Since their arrival on the field around noon, Paul's five regiments had been constructing a knee-high semicircular barricade of downed trees, fence rails, rotten tree stumps, and other debris across the western slope of the woodlot west of the seminary. Starting opposite the southwest corner of the building, the rough line arced its way northwest to a point along Alexander Riggs's southern fence about 180 feet from the northwest corner of the woodlot. From there, it turned northeast to a point about 280 feet south of the seminary lane–Chambersburg Pike intersection. While not particularly formidable, it afforded some protection along an estimated 740-foot front.[42]

Within a few minutes General Paul shifted his regiments to the right front into the James Thompson orchard, where he formed them into three lines. The first was comprised of the 13th Massachusetts on the right and the 104th New York on its left. The 107th Pennsylvania fell in behind the 13th, with the 16th Maine on its left. The 94th New York centered itself behind the second line. Despite being prone, the movement apparently attracted the attention of Carter's guns on Oak Hill, and the men soon found themselves the target of incoming artillery rounds.[43]

41 1st Brigade, 2nd Division, I Corps marker at Doubleday and Robinson avenues, GNMP; Slagle to brother. The shooting started at 2:30 p.m., which places his departure for Howard around that time. Paul's brigade advanced around 2:30 p.m.

42 *Maine at Gettysburg*, map on 45; *NYAG*, 2:756. I based my calculations on the diagram in this map and converted it to the scale I use with this manuscript.

43 Spooner, "In the Ranks."

Captain Stephen C. Whitehouse (Company K, 16th Maine) approached Adj. Abner R. Small. "Adjutant," he quietly began. "I wish I felt as brave and cool as the colonel [Charles W. Tilden] appears."

Small waved off the statement. "Why, captain, he is as scared as any of us. Cheer up, 'twil soon be over."

"Well, the colonel may be scared, but he looks as happy as though we were to have an old-fashioned State of Maine muster," countered Whitehouse.

"I know that, Captain," replied the adjutant. "No man ever saw him appear differently in a fight. Notice, the men just idolize him. They would be perfectly happy if Colonel Farnham were here too."[44]

Within a few minutes, a staffer from General Robinson clattered into the brigade asking for a regiment to go on skirmish. The news drained the courage from nearsighted jeweler Pvt. Bourne Spooner (Company D, 13th Massachusetts). The regiment often drew skirmish duty, which he found extremely trying on his nerves. He breathed easier when Colonel Tilden yelled for the 16th Maine to take its feet. A sullen Captain Whitehouse turned to Abner Small to announce, "Good bye, Adjutant, this is my last fight." The regiment double-quicked north to plug a hole in Robinson's formation.[45]

44 Abner Small, *The Sixteenth Maine Regiment in the War of the Rebellion, 1861-1865* (Portland, ME, 1886), 117, 138. Lieutenant Colonel Augustus B. Farnham was home on sick leave and did not return until July 25, 1863.

45 Spooner, "In the Ranks"; *Maine at Gettysburg*, 46; Small, *Sixteenth Maine*, 117; *OR* 27/1:297; Annual Report of the Adjutant General, 615. See the 16th's regimental history for the exchange quoted here. The adjutant general's report paraphrases the after-action report of the 13th Massachusetts, which supports Spooner's recollection that the brigade deployed piecemeal by regiment.

2:45 p.m. to 3:00 p.m.[46]
The Color Detachment of the 149th Pennsylvania
McPherson's Ridge, South of the Western Railroad Cut

Color Sergeant Henry G. Brehm, with the national flag, was on the left of the prone Corporal Lehman, who carried the state banner. A small interval separated the two men. Corporals John H. Hammell, Henry H. Spayd, John Friddell, and Frederick Hoffman were on their stomachs in the trampled wheat behind as close support. Both color bearers had jammed their flag staffs into the soft ground and crouched below the rails. So far only one Rebel shell from the north had passed through the folds of the Pennsylvania banner. Wherever it ended up, it did so without bursting.

Peering over the rails and the top of the virtually undisturbed wheat on the western slope of the ridge, Brehm and Lehman spotted dismounted officers they mistakenly thought were cavalry videttes. Hearing them shout at infantry to advance changed their minds. The corporals wanted to return to the regiment, but Brehm refused, saying they did not have orders to do so.

"There was a hot discussion among us," Hoffman recalled. Brehm finally ordered Hoffman to find Col. Walton Dwight (their regimental commander) or Colonel Stone and tell them the colors were in danger. The corporal took off at a dead run in the direction of where he thought the officers would be. The guard reasoned that their superiors would not abandon them in such "an exposed position."[47]

That feeling changed about 2:45 p.m. When one of the two color bearers looked west into the tall wheat and saw nothing. He slid down behind the rails, unaware that a number of Mississippians from Brig. Gen. Joseph Davis's Brigade, including the 2nd Mississippi's wounded Col. John M. Stone, had noticed the two flags sticking up above the grain.

Stone called for volunteers to take the banners. Twenty-year-old Lt. Atlas K. Roberts and Pvt. Henry "Tobe" McPherson (both Company H, 2nd

46 See Ladd & Ladd, *Bachelder Papers*, 2:759-766, 830-831 (entries with have affidavits and statements from the survivors of the color guard); Bassler, "The Color Episode," 6-12, 14-18; J. H. Strain, "Heroic Henry McPherson," CV, 31:205. This interpretation describes a very brief action of maybe three minutes' duration, and emphasizes how seconds often seemed like minutes, and minutes hours, during the stress and confusion of combat.

47 Bassler, "The Color Episode," 6, 12; Ladd & Ladd, *Bachelder Papers*, 2:761-762, 763, 766; Burgwyn, "Unparalleled Loss of Company F," 199.

Mississippi) offered their services, as did two other unnamed men. In the 42nd Mississippi, Sgt. Franklin D. Price (Company A) told a few of his boys that he wanted the big blue state flag (149th Pennsylvania). Privates Andrew Park (Company I) and 14-year-old William "Willie" P. Clarke (Company H) decided to go with him.[48]

Led by Roberts, the six men scrambled through the wheat to within striking range of the Yankees. A "Rebel Yell" cut through the air. The startled five Pennsylvanians jumped to their feet, three of them with their weapons loaded. Brehm and Lehman collided with each other. The former, being the bigger of the two, sent Lehman to his knees and he dropped the state flag as he went down. The staff fell at an angle against the barricade. Henry Spayd, standing behind Lehman, saw him topple and assumed he was wounded.[49]

According to one account, Lieutenant Roberts (2nd Mississippi) sprinted ahead of the men and gripped the staff of the national flag.

"This is mine!" he shouted.

"No, by God it isn't!" Brehm yelled back, who reached out and clenched his hands around Roberts's throat.

Friddell, Hammell, and Spayd leveled their rifles and pulled their triggers. Only Friddell's and Hammell's fired; Spayd had forgotten to cock his piece. One of the rounds killed an enlisted Rebel. The other knocked Lieutenant Roberts onto his back with the flag staff still in his hands, killing him. The momentum pulled Sergeant Brehm over the barricade on top of the dead Confederate officer.

Frank Price, meanwhile, tugged on the state flag to jerk it across to the Confederate side, but Corporal Lehman grabbed the staff with his right hand

48 Strain, "Heroic Henry McPherson," 205; Ladd & Ladd, *Bachelder Papers*, 2:763, 765; *Richmond Enquirer*, July 24, 1863, 1; Bassler, "The Color Episode," 14; John W. Moore, *Roster of North Carolina Troops in the War Between the States*, 4 vols. (Raleigh, NC, 1882), 3:190; Park, "Some Of My Recollections," 1. It is hard to reconcile Strain's account with Lt. William R. Bond's and identify most of the men in the attack. Park mistakenly recalled that Clarke belonged to Company F, whereas Moore cites him in Company H. Strain names McPherson and Roberts with three other unnamed volunteers (five total). Bond and the *Richmond Enquirer* confirmed Price's role in the affair, with Bond mentioning that Price and six others (seven total) participated with him. The Pennsylvanians counted five plus a number of others in the vicinity. Roberts was one of the dead; the other two remain anonymous.

49 Strain, "Heroic Henry McPherson," 205; Bassler, "The Color Episode," 16; Ladd & Ladd, *Bachelder Papers*, 2:763, 765.

and held on. A Rebel popped up across from him and put the muzzle of his weapon against Lehman's chest. The corporal shoved the rifle barrel aside with his left hand just as Spayd, having finally cocked his weapon, shot the Southerner through the abdomen before he could get the round off.[50]

Sergeant Price yanked the flag from Lehman's right hand. Empty-handed, Lehman noticed Mississippians swarming past both flanks. He also saw Brehm on the ground throttling the lifeless Roberts, and Rebel "Tobe" McPherson, whose rifle had misfired, raising his weapon to strike Brehm. McPherson lost his balance and toppled over the top rail onto the Yankee side of the "fence." Brehm rolled off the dead lieutenant onto his back and propped himself on his left elbow as Friddell and Hammell hurried to pick him up.

Before they got to him, Lehman watched the sergeant "flip" McPherson a defiant gesture with his fist. Lehman started running toward the road while Spayd hurled his empty weapon at Price, striking him in the back) before snatching the flag and skedaddling for the McPherson farm. On the way he threw off his canteen and haversack to lighten his load. Brehm defiantly slung the national colors over his shoulder at the right shoulder shift and quick-stepped ahead of Friddell and Hammell. Confederates Sergeant Price and Privates Park, Clarke, and McPherson—the latter of whom had recapped his piece the moment he got to his feet—gave chase.[51]

Along the Chambersburg Pike

During the flag incident, Lt. Dudley A. Fish (Company A, 149th Pennsylvania), the only remaining officer with the company, ordered his men into the upper level of the barn and loft to shoot at the Rebs through the ventilation slits. Corporal Sanford N. Boyden conferred with his brother, Cpl.

50 Bassler, "The Color Episode," 12, 16; Ladd & Ladd, *Bachelder Papers*, 2: 763, ("The Colors of the 149th Pa. at Gettysburg," Statement by H. H. Spayd). A wounded Pennsylvanian who witnessed the entire incident told Bassler that he saw three Confederates on the ground.

51 Ladd & Ladd, *Bachelder Papers*, 2:761; Bassler, "The Color Episode," 10, 11, 12; J. H. Strain, "Heroic Henry McPherson," 205; *Richmond Enquirer*, July 24, 1863, 1; Park, "Some Of My Recollections," 2. Lehman probably saw the sergeant give the Confederate his middle finger, but could not bring himself to write that in a letter to Bachelder. In his 1907 affidavit, as opposed to his 1881 letter to Bachelder, he did not claim that he saw Brehm get clubbed or shake his fist. He did explain how he got knocked down and how he escaped. This scenario is reconstructed from Confederate witnesses.

Alfred Boyden, and decided that being cooped up in a building did not seem advisable. Along with several others from their company, they asked Captain Widdis if they could join his men. Widdis agreed.[52]

2:45 p.m.-3:00 p.m.
The Ledge on the Northwest Corner of Herbst Woods

For the better part of half an hour (roughly 2:10 p.m. – 2:40 p.m.), Lt. Col. John B. Callis had held the right side of the Iron Brigade with his two-regiment demi-brigade against the 22nd Virginia Battalion and harassing fire from stray members of the 26th North Carolina. A hurried inspection along the refused line of the 2nd Wisconsin confirmed what he had suspected: the Confederates were double-quicking through the woods past his left flank. His regiments were on their own hook.

Callis ran to the 7th Wisconsin, which still fronted the 22nd Battalion, and Capt. Henry F. Young (Company F), who apparently commanded the regiment in his absence.

"Captain," Callis yelled above the din, "they are going to flank us on both flanks!"

"Let them flank us and be damned!" Young spat back. "We are giving them hell in front." The words had hardly dissipated in the noise when Richardson rode up to Callis, handed him the note from Solomon Meredith, and spurred back to the rest of the brigade. The note read: "I am hurt and cannot get to you, take command of the brigade and get out of that little end of the 'v' as best you can."

"By right of companies to the rear, march!" screamed Callis. Incoming rifle fire slammed into the column from more than one side. Callis belted out an impossible order to execute under the circumstances: "Halt! Right face, right into line wheel, double quick march, march!"

His veterans did the best they could and executed the command in less than perfect alignment. As soon as they created some semblance of a formation, they delivered a volley.

Before the smoke cleared, Callis yelled, "By right of company to the rear, load while marching!"

52 Chamberlin, *History of the 150th Regiment*, 119-120; Ladd & Ladd, *Bachelder Papers*, 2:948, 949 and 3:1592; *OR* 27/1:345.

The two small regiments, together with Company B, 150th Pennsylvania, grew smaller with each yard they covered. The regiments pulled out of the fight as they made their way toward the right of the 24th Michigan.[53]

The 26th North Carolina reacted to the dwindling resistance by surging through the smoke. The men stumbled into a deadly fusillade delivered at close range by the Westerners on the crest of the ridge. By then, Captain McCreery from Pettigrew's staff had reached Colonel Burgwyn behind the center of the 26th regiment. McCreery rasped out a message from the general that the regiment "had covered itself with glory today." The colonel hailed over Lt. Col. John R. Lane, repeated the message, and told him to spread it along his wing.

The flag once more hit the ground. Without thinking, McCreery snatched it up, waved it, and stepped forward, only to die from a single gunshot wound to the heart. He collapsed on the flag, saturating it with his blood. Lieutenant George Willcox (Company H) dragged the flag from under McCreery's corpse. He took but a few steps forward when two bullets struck him simultaneously—the first in the right side and the second in the left foot, which completely numbed his leg. Unable to walk, Willcox dropped to one knee behind the line to examine his wounds.

The Yankees pummeled the remnants of the Tar Heel regiment to a standstill. The companies shrank so quickly that officers barely had time to tighten their ranks and close on the colors. During this heavy exchange of fire Colonel Burgwyn noticed that the flag was no longer on the line, turned around, and saw Lieutenant Willcox with it. He snatched the flag staff, rushed over to Lt. Thomas J. Cureton (Company B), and asked if he had anyone from the color company who could take it. Cureton ordered Pvt. Franklin "Frank" Honeycutt to step up. Burgwyn commanded him to advance. Two steps toward the front, a minié ball hit Honeycutt in the head and killed him.

53 Ladd & Ladd, *Bachelder Papers*, 1:141-142; Norman N. Shapiro, "John Benton Callis: Madison County's Republican Congressman," *The Huntsville Historical Review*, vol. 29, no. 2 (Spring-Summer, 2004), 10. The low-hanging smoke and uneven terrain made it difficult to maintain any genuine parade round alignment. Callis may have issued those commands, but with the incoming rounds and the shell bursts overhead, the men did not execute the maneuvers "by the book." No other available information suggests that Meredith passed the brigade command to Callis. It is interesting to note that in a letter dated September 3, 1893, to Col. Thomas S. Kenan (43rd North Carolina), Callis mentioned the "little end of a 'v'" and withdrawing by right of companies to the rear, but did not mention that he had assumed command of the brigade.

Cureton and his second lieutenant, Milton Blair, rushed forward to raise the flag just as a burst of small arms fire struck the center of the regiment, killing Capt. William Wilson (Company B). Colonel Burgwyn had stepped in front of the men and was turning back toward them when a minié ball penetrated his left side and knocked him flat on his back. Lieutenant Willcox, who by this time had rubbed some feeling back into his foot, limped over to the young colonel, knelt by his side, and asked Burgwyn where he had been hit.

The colonel moved his hand toward his left side and tried to speak, but Willcox could not understand what he muttered because of the thunderous racket of the battle. Convinced his colonel lay dying, Willcox remained by his side as the regiment continued forward. A short time later, Willcox spotted two of the regimental stretcher bearers, Pvt. Neill B. Staton (Company B) and the wounded Pvt. William P. Ellington (Company E) wandering among the casualties with a blanket. The lieutenant called them over and pleaded with them to do everything they could for Burgwyn. With that, the wounded officer set out to find what was left of his company.

Lieutenant Blair reached Honeycutt's body ahead of Cureton. He yanked the blood-saturated St. Andrew's Cross from under the dead private and carried it forward a short distance. Lieutenant Colonel John H. Lane shouted at him to hand over the flag. As he passed it off, the lieutenant quipped, "You will get tyred of [it]."[54]

By this time, a stretcher party had evacuated General Meredith to the rear. Captain Hollon Richardson unofficially assumed command of the shattered Iron Brigade. As each regiment, in succession from the right of the line, emptied a parting volley into the shadowy woods, the captain retired it by right of

54 "Reminiscences of Thomas Perritt"; Emerson, "The Most Famous Regiment," 354; Clark, *Histories of the Several Regiments*, 2:375; "Brave Carolinian Fell at Gettysburg," *SHSP*, 35:321; Busey & Busey, *Confederate Casualties*, 2:1041; George Willcox to W. H. S. Burgwyn, June 21, 1900, William Hyslop Sumner Burgwyn Papers, PC 4, Vol. 2, 200; Curtis, *History of the Twenty-Fourth Michigan*, 188; Thomas J. Cureton to J. R. Lane, June 15, 1890, John R. Lane Papers, #411-z, Southern Historical Collection, Louis Round Wilson Special Collections Library, UNC. Cureton's and Willcox's accounts lacked the Victorian sentimentality of traditional renditions and seem more credible. Willcox noted that he alone stayed with the dying colonel. The bullet may have passed through the lower lobes of both lungs, which would have made it difficult for Burgwyn to have spoken because breathing would have been difficult with his lungs slowly filling with blood. Cureton definitely asserted that Honeycutt had the flag before Burgwyn, and that Burgwyn did not have the flag in his hand when he was shot, as is so often asserted. There does not appear to be any primary evidence that Blair said, "No man can take those colors and live."

company to the rear. According to Colonel Morrow, "No General seems to have been giving orders to them [the 24th Michigan] or to the brigade." The four battered regiments retreated over the top of the ridge as far as the partially destroyed fence line along the original position of Archer's Brigade some 100 yards behind them. The fence ran downhill from a barely perceptible runoff on its north end along the crest of a chest-high ravine. The Yankees reformed along that same line, using the creek bottom at its westerly end as a natural earthwork.[55]

2:45 p.m.-3:00 p.m.[56]
Eastern Side of Herbst Woods

A bullet zipped into the 24th Michigan and struck Clr. Cpl. Andrew Wagner in the breast. He collapsed next to Colonel Morrow. The colonel went to one knee beside him to retrieve the flag. He assured Wagner (mistakenly) that the wound would not kill him. Private William Kelly (Company E) pulled the standard from Morrow's grasp, yelling, "The Colonel of the Twenty-Fourth Michigan shall not carry the colors while I am alive!" The next instant a round dropped Kelly lifeless across Morrow's feet. When Pvt. Lilburn A. Spaulding (Company K) picked up the flag, Morrow yanked it from him.

The Rebels shot down the Michiganders with unnerving frequency. Lieutenant Reuben H. Humphreyville (Company K) was yet another Wolverine who died where he stood. The regiment lost an estimated 100 men in mere

55 Report of Colonel Williams; Curtis, *History of the Twenty-Fourth Michigan*, 162; "Synopsis of General Richardson's Speech," 2; Brown & Brown, *Soldiers' and Citizens' Album*, 1:580. Williams described the location of the fence. In a communiqué dated July 14, 1863, to Governor Randall of Wisconsin, General Wadsworth wrote: "In the battle of Gettysburg, as the senior staff officer of the Brigade, a large and unusual amount of responsibility devolved upon him [Richardson]. Amounting at times to the command of the brigade." This preceded General Cutler's letter to the governor on August 13, 1863, which stated: "At Gettysburg, he [Richardson] virtually commanded the brigade for a portion of the day. It cannot be known how many lives he saved by the manner in which brought off the troops from the field on the 1st of July. There seemed to be no one else to give orders, most of field officers having been killed or wounded."

56 *OR* 27/1:333; Chamberlin, *History of the 150th Regiment*, 121. Chamberlin noted the heavy Confederate attack started at 2:45 p.m., which was the approximate time of Pettigrew's uphill assault in Herbst Woods. In his after-action report, Wister said he was hit five minutes after Huidekoper, and five minutes after that the brigade was forced from the field. The entire action took only about 10 minutes.

Caught up in the frenzy of the charge, Lt. Colonel John R. Lane of the 26th North Carolina held the flag and shouted orders to the regiment. He was later shot through the neck, a wound many thought mortal. *Histories of the Several Regiments and Battalions from North Carolina*

minutes. Morrow gave the order to retreat, and the remnants of the Iron Brigade fled through the woods toward the open field on its eastern side.[57]

The battered 26th North Carolina walked into a lead buzzsaw during its approach to the Westerners. The Tar Heels halted and returned fire. Lieutenant Colonel Lane, still clenching the flag, darted through the woods to Company K on the right of the line. He shouted to Capt. John C. McLaughlin, "Close your men to the left. I am going to give them the bayonet." Lane next ran to the far left of the regiment to order those men to close to the right. As he passed Company G, Pvt. Thomas Perritt heard him exclaim, "Close on the center, I am going to give the enemy the bayonet!"

Perritt had just brought his rifle to front to load his fifteenth round when two bullets thudded into his body. Private G. Preston Kirkman saw him reel under the impact and asked him if he was wounded. "Yes," Perritt gasped. Kirkman asked him for his rifle; Perritt gave it to him. The 18-year-old grasped the weapon, took a step or two, and crumpled mortally wounded. Captain McLaughlin was also hit, a minié ball shattering his thumb and forcing him to quit the field.[58]

57 Curtis, *History of the Twenty-Fourth Michigan*, 162, 163, 165, 188.

58 "Reminiscences of Thomas Perritt"; Lane, "Address at Gettysburg," July 5 1903; Busey & Busey, *Confederate Casualties*, 2:1047; James Adams's "Reminiscences: 26th Regiment North Carolina Inf.," 1911, in the state archives of North Carolina, is identical to Lane's newspaper article. Lane's article is so self-serving that he places himself next to the dying Burgwyn's instead of Willcox, whose letter to the deceased colonel's father predates Lane's story by three years. Perritt distinctly recalled being wounded after hearing the

Lieutenant Colonel Lane returned to the front center of the regiment and impetuously rushed toward the Federal line, calling over his shoulder, "26th, follow me!"[59]

The North Carolinians from the 26th regiment howled like banshees as they crashed through the woods, stumbling over the undulating ground littered with human debris from the morning fight. When within 75 feet of the retreating Wolverines, Lane turned about to urge his men forward. A minié ball fired from a lower angle bored through the back of his neck near the base of his skull. Spinning upward, the slug fractured his lower jaw, clipped off a chunk of his tongue, and broke off his upper front teeth as it exited his mouth.

Acccording to Lt. Thomas J. Cureton, Lane "fell limp as a rag." Given the nature of the gruesome wound, Cureton believed his superior was dead and hurried forward with his men. Captain Stephen W. Brewer (Company A) pried the flag from the unconscious Lane's hands and followed what remained of the shattered 24th Michigan.[60]

The 26th North Carolina's charge against the 24th Michigan freed up the survivors from the 11th North Carolina's left wing, which entered the open ground east of the gully and realigned itself with the battered right half of the regiment. At the same time, the 47th North Carolina came up to the right of the 11th and halted to realign its disorganized ranks.

With their blood up and no incoming rounds harassing their front, the Tar Heel troops of the 47th stood in the chest-high wheat and charged, the "Rebel Yell" echoing over their heads and trailing behind them. To the left, Company A

---

command to close on center. Cureton clearly stated that Blair handed the flag to Lane, who did not pick it up from the ground. Lane almost surely concocted the quote, "No man can take those colors and live." He had to have had the flag with him before he ordered the charge and not after, because he took it from Blair almost immediately after the lieutenant had picked it up.

59 Lane, "Address at Gettysburg."

60 www.findagrave.com/memorial/10954534/charles-henry-mcconnell, accessed Feb. 6, 2023; Lane, "Address at Gettysburg"; Cureton to Lane; Busey & Busey, *Confederate Casualties*, 2:1002. Busey provided a detailed explanation of Lane's wound. On Find A Grave, the author infers Cpl. Charles H. McConnell (Company B, 24th Michigan) claimed the colonel "fell like a rag." Nowhere in his postwar account of Gettysburg does McConnell credit himself with shooting down Lane as later asserted by both parties. He clearly noted that he did not remember falling back to several positions, and that he was probably caught up with the 19th Indiana throughout the retreat. Lane generated the myth that McConnell shot him, and McConnell apparently went along with it, even though his own account does not acknowledge any part of it.

of the 11th North Carolina and parts of Companies D, F, and I followed young Adjutant Lucas who bolted ahead with the flag. Those companies and part of the left wing tried to keep up with the bloodied 26th in its final attack. They caught the Wolverines attempting to rally, for the third time in less than half an hour, in the open field immediately east of the woods.[61]

Sergeant August Ziegler (Company A, 24th Michigan) recalled seeing the remains of the bloodied 19th Indiana retreating in a panic, accompanied by Company B of the 24th. Not 30 feet away, toward the center of the line, Col. Henry A. Morrow stood alone with the national colors, frantically waving them to and fro while screaming, "Will you desert your Colors, boys, rally to your flag!"

"I thought on the instant you cant see your Col. shot," Ziegler later recalled, and started to take the colors. Unable to stem the butternut and gray tide, Morrow simply said, "Never mind," and handed the flag over to the color corporal from Company D. The Carolinians continued firing into the stampeding Yankees.

In the 24th's Company H, Pvt. John Malcho pulled the wounded Edward B. Harrison to his feet and started walking away with him. Harrison's best friend, John G. Welsh, quickly took hold of Harrison from the opposite side. Two bullets quickly killed Harrison and Welsh, while a third tore the sole off one of Malcho's shoes. Malcho left his dead comrades side by side in the wheat and made tracks east for Seminary Ridge.[62]

West Side of the Seminary Oak Grove

Brigadier General Thomas Rowley watched the 19th Indiana and the left company of the 24th Michigan stream through the hole in Col. Chapman Biddle's line. Rowley ordered the 151st Pennsylvania forward, but by that time it was too little, too late.[63]

61 Taylor to Dear Mother; *Fayetteville Observer*, September 17, 1863; Curtis, *History of the Twenty-Fourth Michigan*, 188.

62 Ziegler Letter; Curtis, *History of the Twenty-Fourth Michigan*, 181. The color corporal remains unidentified.

63 *OR* 27/1:327.

2:45 p.m. to 3:00 p.m.
Sheads Woods

By the time the 16th Maine reached the fence along the northern edge of Sheads Woods, Henry Baxter's regiments still had Alfred Iverson's men pinned in the drainage along their front. For the better part of an hour they had stubbornly exchanged rounds with the Rebs across the smoke-obscured field.

The New Englanders lined up along the fence and put down a hot fire into the flank of the 23rd North Carolinian. The Confederates replied immediately. Corporal William N. Yeaton (Company C) of the color guard died first, followed by Captain Whitehouse (Company K) when a fragment or small arms fire ripped a gory wound in his throat. Corporal Frank Devereaux (Company K) perished shortly afterward.

Lieutenant Isaac H. Thompson (Company G) became acutely aware of a round zipping just past him from the rear. Twisting about, he spied a soldier he did not know loading his rifle about 15 paces behind the line. Thompson rushed the man and they exchanged words, at which point the lieutenant decked the fellow with a single punch. Thompson grabbed the soldier by his collar, pulled him upright, spun him about, and kicked him in the rear away from the regiment. The few men who witnessed the incident hooted and howled.

The shooting had escalated to such a point that Lt. George A. Deering (Company F) picked up a discarded weapon and stepped into the ranks. In his excitement, he forgot to remove the ramrod from the bore and, much to his men's amusement, sent it swishing through the trees into the field beyond. Canister and case shot from Oak Hill, coming in too high, showered the New Englanders with branches and leaves. In Company I, Lt. Lewis Bisbee stepped behind a tree to protect himself from the miniés singing about. Captain William H. Waldron crouched on one knee under the cover of another oak to Bisbee's right.

Colonel Tilden trooped the embattled line on horseback. Blood flowed freely from the animal's wounded flank and the beast soon foundered, forcing Tilden to dismount. Lieutenant Bisbee saw blood spurting from Captain Waldron's neck. Fearing the bullet had severed his jugular, the lieutenant leaped to his side and lowered Waldron onto his back. Soaking his handkerchief with water from his canteen, Bisbee bound Waldron's wound and managed to stop the flow. He had no idea that the minié ball had passed just behind the jugular and then traveled down into the captain's lung. "We were hotly engaged for some time, suffering severely in officers and men," recalled Pvt. Samuel Peabody (Company I). [64]

Several minutes into the action, the 94th New York (Paul's brigade) came up on the left of the 16th Maine and was immediately subjected a deadly fusillade. An anonymous infantryman caught a round through his haversack that struck the man behind him in the elbow. A shell fragment knocked down the man by his side and several other comrades were hit. "I have abundant reason to be thankful to my Heavenly Father for protecting me from the bullets which flew in all directions and thick as hailstones in a hail storm," the unnamed man later wrote a friend.

In an effort to avoid further slaughter, the regiment went prone behind the rail fence.[65]

64 Francis Wiggin, "Sixteenth Maine at Gettysburg," *War Papers*, 4:157; Samuel Peabody, "The 16th ME. At Gettysburg," *NT*, April 18, 1901, 3; Account of Lt. Lewis Bisbee, Company I, 16th ME, Lewis Bisbee Papers, Minnesota Historical Society, St. Paul, MN; Small, *Sixteenth Maine*, 119.

65 *OR* 27/1:299; Letter to Friend John, July 12, 1863, Vertical Files, V6-NY94, Library, GNMP; "From the 94th," Chaplain Philos G. Cook, to *Editors Journal*, July 15, 1863 and "Letter from Colonel Root, July 14, 1863," https://museum.dmna.ny.gov/application/files/4215/5308/9201/94thInfCWN2.pdf, accessed Feb. 10, 2023.

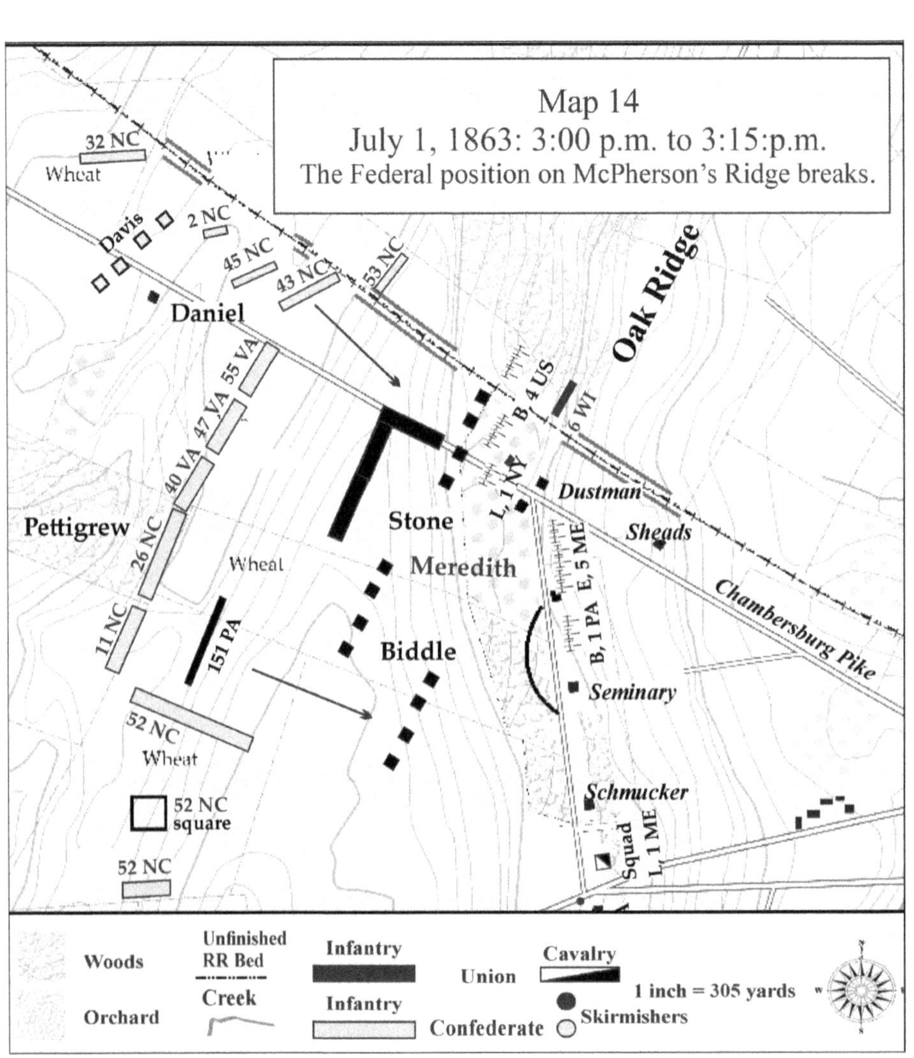
Map 14
July 1, 1863: 3:00 p.m. to 3:15:p.m.
The Federal position on McPherson's Ridge breaks.
32 NC
Wheat
Davis
2 NC
45 NC
43 NC
53 NC
Daniel
Oak Ridge
55 VA
47 VA
40 VA
26 NC
11 NC
Pettigrew
Wheat
151 PA
52 NC
Wheat
52 NC square
52 NC
B, 4 US
6 WI
L, 1 NY
Stone
Meredith
Biddle
Dustman
Sheads
E, 5 ME
B, 1 PA
Seminary
Chambersburg Pike
Schmucker
Squad
L, 1 ME
Woods
Orchard
Unfinished RR Bed
Creek
Infantry
Union
Infantry
Confederate
Cavalry
Skirmishers
1 inch = 305 yards

Chapter Eleven

"Life never seems so sweet, or so near the end."

— *Sgt. Patrick DeLacy, 143rd Pennsylvania*

Retreat to Seminary Ridge

3:00 p.m. to 3:30 p.m.

3:00 p.m. to 3:15 p.m.
Herbst Woods

The 151st Pennsylvania (Biddle's brigade) had reached the rise of ground 60 yards east of Herbst Woods by the time a remnant of the 24th Michigan attempted to rally in the soggy basin about the same distance behind the 151st's right wing. Lieutenant Colonel George F. McFarland, the commander of the Pennsylvania regiment, watched the Black Hats try to rally behind him. "I saw this attempt to reform distinctly and clearly," he later told Col. John B. Bachelder, "and remember the officers moving up and down the line acting with great coolness and bravery. I cannot say, however, that the whole brigade thus formed. It may have been a portion." The Rebels shot down several of the Pennsylvanians before they could completely dress their line.[1]

Biddle's other men in the remaining regiments stood with their heads barely showing above the tall wheat along their front. To their surprise, the 11th and

1 Ladd & Ladd, *Bachelder Papers*, 1:300; *OR* 27/1:327; Sayre (Sayn), "A Day at Gettysburg."

the 47th North Carolina (Pettigrew's Brigade) had reached the rail fence on the ridge about 60 to 75 yards away. From his position in the ranks of Company G, 142nd Pennsylvania, Pvt. Edwin R Gerhardt saw the 11th's officers leading the regiment in the front of the line, waving their swords as they cheered their men forward.[2]

From the other side of the field, the Carolinians watched as the Yankees leveled their rifles all along the line to fire. During those few brief seconds, the Rebels got the drop on them and started shooting by files as they reached the fence. Union Private Gearhart saw the smoke, heard the miniés zip by, and noticed several men on his right collapse. "Fire! Fire! Fire!" the officers screamed. Biddle's line exploded in flame and smoke. The 151st Pennsylvania also fired, despite Lieutenant Colonel McFarland's specific admonishment not to do so.

Unable to see any troops on his left through the low-hanging smoke, Capt. Lafayette Westbrook (Company B), without any permission to do so, dispersed the company as skirmishers by "comrades in battle." Private Randle D. Sayn (Company B), who during the short interval before the firing caught his first glimpse of the St. Andrew's Cross, recalled how the men separated quickly on Westbrook's order.[3]

Adjutant Henderson C. Lucas carried the colors of the 11th North Carolina to within 50 yards of the rail fence, where a bullet through the left hip dropped him. Undaunted and with the flag still in his grasp, he forced himself upright just in time for a minié ball to knock his right leg out from under him. He lay there helpless but managed to keep the banner aloft until a third ball disabled his left arm. The colors fluttered to the ground. Eighteen-year-old Rebel private D. Cameron Waddell (Company G) and Cpl. William G. Ivey rushed to his side. Waddell picked up the standard and, with Ivey by his side, knelt next to Lucas to ask if there was anything they could do for him. "Boys, I have played out," the young officer gasped, "go on to victory."

Waddell rushed forward, leaving Ivey—who had just been shot and was the mortally wounded—lying beside the adjutant. Waddell got as far as the fence,

2 "In the Years '62 to '65," 34-35. Edwin's name was sometimes spelled as "Edward."

3 *OR* 27/1:323, 327; Clark, *Histories of the Several Regiments*, 3:89; "In the Years '62 to '65," 35; *Pennsylvania at Gettysburg*, 2:747; Sayre, "A Day at Gettysburg." Sayn (his name was transcribed as Sayre) reported that the regiment volleyed first before being ordered to fire at will.

jabbed the staff into the ground, and looked rearward only to find himself alone. Captain Armfield had judiciously ordered the men back to the shelter of their jump-off point. The now lightly wounded Waddell, standard in hand, wheeled about and made tracks to catch up with them.[4]

The Pennsylvanians and New Yorkers had shot the stubborn Carolinians to a standstill. The Tar Heels held their ground while returning an accurate fire at close range. The pungent smoke hovered low to the ground, held down by the high humidity. Captain John H. Thorp (Company A, 47th North Carolina) noticed that his rank and file, their hands wet with sweat, were having a tough time gripping their ramrods to shove the bullets home. Some resorted to pounding the inserted rammers on the ground or against field rocks to finish charging their weapons.[5]

After the first volley, Lieutenant Colonel McFarland (151st Pennsylvania) once again ordered his men to pick their targets in Herbst Woods. This time the men heeded his command. He repeatedly heard soldiers yell, "There he goes!" or "I brought my man [down]!" McFarland became so focused on what was transpiring around him that he lost all perception of time. "In battle," he later admitted, "all our senses are quickened, and moments seem to contain many times sixty seconds. It is hard therefore to estimate time."[6]

For the next five minutes the opposing forces slaughtered each other. While trying to load, Pvt. Alexander Collins (Company H) reeled under the glancing impact of a minié ball to the left side of his head. The ball hit him just above the left eye and burned across his temple and his ear, leaving him deaf on that side and unable to open his eye. He would have fallen had he let go of his weapon. Nauseated and partially blind, he stood there until his stomach settled and his vision cleared well enough to see the Rebels, who were now uncomfortably close. Collins finished loading his rifle and resumed fighting.

4 *Fayetteville Observer*, September 7 and 17, 1863, 3; Busey & Busey, *Confederate Casualties*, 2:866, 887, 888. Waddell is listed as Duncan C. Waddell. The September 7 and 17th editions described the incidents set forth. The September 7th paper, whch did not identify Wadell or Ivey, claimed the first man was shot down instantly and the man who stooped by the adjutant's side also perished. The September 17 edition identified both men by name but stated that Waddell was not wounded, and that Ivey was hit and no one seemed to know his fate. Busey & Busey listed Waddell as wounded and captured and Ivey as mortally wounded and captured.

5 Clark, *Histories of the Several Regiments*, 3:89.

6 *OR*, 27/1:327; *Pennsylvania at Gettysburg*, 2:747.

A bible inside the tunic breast pocket of Company A's Lt. Frank M. Powell stopped a bullet and saved his life. Acting Adj. Andrew G. Tucker, Gov. Andrew Curtin's nephew, took two hits but refused to leave his post. In Company I, Pvt. James Bower stepped forward from the line and coolly shot down a Confederate color bearer, only to get hit in the left lung as he returned to his place in line.

English-born acting Maj. James Ashworth (121st Pennsylvania) fell with 11 wounds. Sergeant Frank H. Evans (Company E) had just risen to his feet to fire when a minié ball drilled into his neck. "When the bullet struck me, it jarred my body as a blow on the neck with a fist. I felt it enter my neck but did not feel it go out," he recollected. Evans staggered about 75 yards to the rear and crumpled into the grass, completely exhausted and waiting to bleed out. He heard groans and looked up to see his former tent mate, Pvt. Harry Gouldy, walking past him grasping a wounded arm. A step or two later, Gouldy staggered back to his sergeant and despite the bullets whizzing about, begged Evans to get up. The latter, who could hardly breathe, shook his head, "No." He blacked out at that point.

The Rebels also dropped Capt. J. Frank Sterling (Company C), acting Capt. James Ruth (Company I), and Lt. West Funk (Company G). Corporal John M. Bingham (Company A), a tough 19-year-old who took a minié ball through his side (his first of four wounds that day), refused to leave the line or to tend to his wound. His tenacity would later earn him a first lieutenancy. Color Sergeant William Hardy held onto the national flag even though its staff had been shot into three pieces; somehow Hardy himself emerged from the maelstrom unscathed. Sergeant William G. Graham (Company D), with the blue state banner, also miraculously escaped injury.[7]

The 52nd North Carolina, Pettigrew's command, had flanked northeast under the cover of the ridge behind which Biddle's brigade lay. Without warning, the Tar Heel regiment appeared through the smoke on the Yankees'

7 Collins Pension File; *OR* 27/1:323; *Pennsylvania at Gettysburg*, 2:653; *History of the 121st Regiment*, 141-142, 171-173, 189-190, 191, 276, 277; Horatio N. Warren, *Two Reunions of the 142d Regiment, Pa. Vols* (Buffalo, NY, 1890), 23, 59; Robert McCalmont, ed., *Extracts From Letters Written by Alfred B. McCalmont, From the Front During the War of the Rebellion* (Stroudsburg, PA, 1901), 58; L. Ward Smith to Mrs. Bower, July 20, 1863, Vertical Files, VF6-PA 142, Library, GNMP. Ashworth and Ruth, both from Company I, were commissioned major and captain, respectively, on April 20,1863, but apparently had not mustered in at those ranks as of July 1. In the *OR* they are referred to by their original ranks in Company I.

flank. A deadly shower of lead that Maj. Alexander Biddle described as a "crushing fire" hammered the left of the 121st Pennsylvania. Despite Major Biddle's efforts to refuse the line, the regiment buckled and streamed into the flank of the 20th N.Y.S.M., which, in turn, acted to herd the two regiments into the left of the 142nd Pennsylvania.[8]

Near the Shultz House

An intrepid sergeant commanding the cavalry squad protecting General Rowley's headquarters on Seminary Ridge watched as the 52nd North Carolina wheeled north. He apparently decided to lead his detachment in a "forlorn hope" attack to "put the skeer" into the Rebs. With weapons drawn, the troopers charged in column down the hill through the downed fence into the small field between the seminary's oak woods and the Fairfield Road. When he realized he was being threatened from behind, Col. James K. Marshall (52nd North Carolina) dispatched Lt. William E. Kyle and his Company B to disperse the noisome cavalry. He also ordered two companies to form a square to discourage further cavalry forays.[9]

Farther north and east, Private Gearhart (Company G, 142nd Pennsylvania) caught sight of the small band of cavalrymen as they scattered. Gearhart, who had just expended his fifth round, lost heart at what was unfolding within his vision: the seven companies of the 52nd North Carolina was forcing the fractured 121st Pennsylvania into the smaller 20th N.Y.S.M. and rolling them into his 142nd. Someone screamed, "Retreat!" Parts of the regiment began trying to back out of the fight. A heavy volley poured out of Marshall's 47th North Carolina at close range, killing or wounding many including the entire color guard of the 142nd.

Someone picked up the flag and handed it to Colonel Biddle, who was spurring his horse back and forth behind the line in an unsuccessful effort to get his men to hold their position. He finally planted the flag next to Col. Robert P. Cummins and told him to make a stand around it.

8 *Pennsylvania at Gettysburg*, 2:652; *OR* 27/1:321, 323.

9 "In the Years '62 to '65," 35; Nesbit, *General History of Company D*, 15; Clark, *Histories of the Several Regiments*, 3:106, 236; "The Battle of Gettysburg: Illinois' Share in That Struggle," *Chicago Tribune*, November 24, 1863, 2. The infantry square, an ancient tactical design against cavalry charges, was only used a few times during the Civil War.

Colonel Robert P. Cummins, commander of the 142nd Pennsylvania, fought in several battles before falling next to the flag. He died the next day. His body was sent back home for burial to his birthplace in Somerset County, Pennsylvania. *USAHEC, Carlisle, PA*

Colonel Cummins was standing by the colors waving his sword hollering, "Rally round the flag!" when Private Gearhart and a handful of other soldiers clustered around him. Gearhart managed to snap off one round before the squad dissolved. Cummins collapsed mortally wounded and the colors fell to the ground next to him.

Captain Horatio N. Warren (Company A, 142nd Pennsylvania) recalled seeing four men working to carry the dying colonel from the field. The Rebs shot three of them down. The fourth, though bleeding from the mouth, unbuckled Cummins's sword belt and made for Seminary Ridge, swearing revenge while waving it triumphantly overhead. Sergeant James R. Balsey (Company H) stooped to retrieve the flag but was hit by two bullets. The wounded Pvt. Alexander Collins (Company H) attempted to leave when ordered to do so, but a bullet knocked him unconscious.[10]

The Chambersburg Pike

The situation along the turnpike deteriorated rapidly for the hopelessly entangled 149th and 150th Pennsylvania (Roy Stone's brigade). Corporal Sanford N. Boyden was standing next to Capt. Widdis (Company A, 149th Pennsylvania) when he thought he saw an enemy column trying to outflank the

10 "In the Years '62 to '65," 35; Clark, *Histories of the Several Regiments*, 3:90; James Robinson Balsey, "On the Field Among the Enemy, and in the Hospitals Cared for by Patriotic Women," *NT*, May 19, 1898, 3; Warren, *Two Reunions*, 9-10; *OR* 27/1:323; Collins Pension File.

regiment off to his left from the rise of ground east of Herbst Woods. Captain Widdis nodded to the U. S. flag they seemed to be carrying and instructed that no one shoot at them because they were friendly troops. Boyden, who studied the approaching soldiers through the smoke and could clearly make out Confederate battle flags behind the leading regiment, disagreed, and told the captain they had no time to lose and had best skedaddle.[11]

Lieutenant Colonel Henry S. Huidekoper of the 150th Pennsylvania, his right arm tied off above the elbow with his saddlebag cord and hobbled with a leg wound, made his way back to his regiment near the barn. Huidekoper realized the futility of trying to main their position and told Captain Widdis to slowly take the regiment to the rear. Widdis began moving the survivors away from the road. Huidekoper headed for the rear.[12]

By this time Col. Edmund Dana (commanding Stone's brigade) knew the 149th and 150th Pennsylvania could no longer hold their position around the McPherson barn. Dana sent the brigade's acting assistant adjutant general, Lt. William M. Dalgliesh to order their withdrawal. The 150th's adjutant, Richard L. Ashurst, was present when Dalgliesh rode into the vortex and announced the order to pull out. With no other officer of higher rank than himself present, Ashurst yelled for his three remaining officers—Lt. Chalkey W. Sears (Company F), acting Lt. George Bell (Company H), and acting Lt. Elias B. Weidensaul (Company D)—to gather around him and announced the order. "Adjutant," Bell protested, "it is all damned cowardice; we have beaten them and will keep on beating them back!"

A quick survey of the field to the south undermined Bell's defiance. What was left of the 2nd and 7th Wisconsin were coming out of Herbst Woods en echelon, by battalions. During the retreat, Sgt. William S. McGinley and a handful of men from his Company E bolted south into the first piece of low ground east of Herbst Woods and formed with the 150th's Company B on the right flank of the 7th Wisconsin.[13]

11 Boyden to Gamble.

12 Ladd & Ladd, *Bachelder Papers*, 2:954. Huidekoper's memorandum to Bachelder notes that he turned the regiment over to Colonel Wister, but this could not have been the case because Wister had already been severely wounded. In a 1906 interview, Huidekoper also claimed that his men rescued the flag of the 149th Pennsylvania, that men wearing bucktails on their caps brought the flag to him, and that he turned it over to Colonel Dwight of the 149th. These were also events that did not occur.

13 Chamberlin, *History of the One Hundred and Fiftieth Regiment*, 134, 135.

On the far right of the line, the 143rd Pennsylvania (Stone) found itself facing what must have seemed like an insurmountable Confederate force coming from the north and the west, respectively. A bullet cut down the state color bearer. With no thought for his own safety, Cpl. William S. Downing (Company I) took it up and somehow managed to keep it for the rest of the day.[14]

A minié ball in the shoulder incapacitated Capt. George N. Reichard (Company C) and another killed Pvt. Charles S. Bertells. Lieutenant Charles C. Plotze (Company A) absorbed a round but stayed with the line. Lieutenant Charles W. Betzenberger (Company I) suffered a hand wound but refused to leave the line.

In Company I, Pvt. Josiah M. Wolf hollered at Simon Hubler: "Corporal, I have two charges in my gun, and I'm afraid to shoot them out!" Hubler took the piece, raised the rifle to his shoulder, aimed, and pulled the trigger. The recoil kicked as hard as a mule. He handed the weapon back to Wolf, and told him that if he double loaded his rifle again, he would have to fire it himself. Hubler would later note that the recoil was so severe that the weapon probably had five or six rounds jammed into it.

Sergeant Patrick DeLacy (Company A) noticed the Rebs trying to cross the road on the right of the regiment. When Lt. Col. John D. Musser discovered the enemy had turned the 149th's left, he ordered the bugler to sound the retreat.[15]

McPherson's Ridge, North of the Chambersburg Pike

Corporal Frank Lehman led the color guard of the 149th Pennsylvania (Stone) in retreat. Henry Spayd carried the state banner right behind him. With "Old Glory" over his right shoulder, Color Sergeant Brehm marched east in a deliberate quickstep, with John Friddell and John Hammell following him toward the Chambersburg Pike. Instead of running into their own men in the dust- and smoke-clogged area, they found themselves behind a thin disordered Rebel line of battle.

14 The Confederates between the Chambersburg Pike and the railroad cut were probably Daniel's 32nd North Carolina and Davis's 42nd Mississippi.

15 Hubler, "Just the Plain, Untarnished Story"; Hoover diary, July 1, 1863; Downing to Wife; *OR* 27/1:338, 339; "Capt. DeLacy Describes Gettysburg Battle"; Chamberlin, *History of the One Hundred and Fiftieth Regiment*, 132-133; Ladd & Ladd, *Bachelder Papers*, 2:95.

Brehm, Lehman, Hammell, and Fridell had no choice but to thread their way through the enemy. Lehman was shot on the north side of the road. Spayd, who had stripped off his haversack and canteen, made it about 100 yards with "Surrender you, Yankee!" echoing in his ears when Pvt. "Tobe" McPherson (Company H, 2nd Mississippi) shot him. The bullet penetrated Spayd's right thigh. He made another few strides in a zigzag pattern before throwing himself on top of the flag in an unsuccessful effort to keep it from being captured.

Sergeant Price (Company A, 42nd Mississippi), still set upon claiming the Yankee "blue flag," jerked the banner from beneath Spayd's seemingly lifeless body and was on the way back to his own lines when a minié ball clipped his hand. Spayd, meanwhile, remained motionless in an effort to play dead. Hammell was killed in the McPherson farm lane. Despite a chest wound, Friddell managed to reach the barnyard, where he hunkered down until the fighting shifted farther east. Brehm got as far as the corner of the field northeast of the house, some 100 yards beyond where Spayd fell.

Captain John Bassler (149th Pennsylvania), meanwhile, ill and suffering from a leg wound, had been resting between the southeast corner of the barn and the house. He could hear the Rebs on the western side of the barn yelling at the Pennsylvanians to surrender. He watched as Brehm, about 50 yards distant with the flag at "right shoulder shift," ran through the meadow along the pike. "My heart," he later wrote, "beat heavily as I thought of the tremendous odds against the gallant sergeant as he quickly disappeared from [my] line of sight."[16]

From where he stood with the rallying 149th and 150th Pennsylvania about 100 yards east of the barn, Lt. John G. Batdorff (Company C) also spotted Brehm rushing toward the gathering line. He was nearly to his company when a shell burst above and to his left, prostrating him. Batdorff rushed over to pull the big sergeant behind the line, leaving the broken flag staff and torn flag in the field.

16 Ladd & Ladd, *Bachelder Papers*, 2:760, 762, 763; Strain, "Heroic Henry McPherson," 205; Bassler, "The Color Episode," 12, 16, 18; *Richmond Enquirer*, July 14, 1863, 1. I interpreted the sequence of events as follows: Bassler, on September 5, 1881, said he saw "immediately after" a red-headed Rebel (Price) heading west with the state flag. By June 4, 1907, he had changed it to "our flag" (U.S.) with the dying Brehm trailing stubbornly "immediately after" the Reb. In that same affidavit, he initially stated that he saw "sometime after" a Confederate soldier (with no one following him) going by with the flag. While it sounds good, it is highly unlikely the second memory is accurate.

Color Sergeant Samuel Peiffer of the 150th Pennsylvania was already wounded when a bullet to the head mortally wounded him while holding the regimental colors. *History of the One Hundred And Fiftieth Regiment*

The command to fix bayonets ran along the ragged regimental line, which was now barely a company strong. Sergeant William Ramsey (Company F) had just fastened the "pig sticker" on his rifle when Sgt. Henry B. Evans nudged him with his elbow and showed him his weapon. A bullet had hit the barrel mid-forestock and bent it a little to the left. Grinning, Evans secured his bayonet on the wayward muzzle and quipped, "Bill, look at my bayonet, won't it be bully to reach around the corner for them."

Seconds later the bugler sounded the retreat. The survivors of the 150th turned and ran. In the midst of the chaos, Cpl. Samuel P. Gilmore (Company C) watched as Color Sgt. Samuel Peiffer (Company I, 150th Pennsylvania) fell . Gilmore ran over, noticed a fatal head wound, and grabbed the flag before continuing to distance himself from the fighting.[17]

Corporal "Roe" Reisinger (Company H, 150th) lay on the field with a .69-caliber musket ball in his right hip. The lead slug had passed at a downward trajectory through the hip into his thigh, where it stopped just beneath the surface of the skin opposite his scrotum. This was his third wound. Too weak to move, he remained motionless where he fell.[18]

17 Bassler, "The Color Episode," 12, 18; Ladd & Ladd, *Bachelder Papers*, 2:760, 766, 957; Chamberlin, *History of the One Hundred and Fiftieth Regiment*, 138; Noecker to Editor. Both Noecker and Boyden (149th Pennsylvania) noted the regiment retreated directly to the seminary. In his December 17, 1881, letter to Bachelder, Bassler said Lieutenant Batdorff saw the shell hit Brehm.

18 "Three Bullets at Gettysburg," 13. Reisinger received the Medal of Honor for his conspicuous gallantry at Gettysburg.

Captain Bassler, from his spot at the southeast corner of the McPherson barn, watched as the red-headed Sgt. Franklin Price (Company A, 42nd Mississippi) limped west with the 149th's blue state flag. Bassler recalled the time as between 3:10 pm and 3:15 p.m. Private Willie Clarke (Company H, 42nd Mississippi) rushed forward, snatched up the national flag and the broken staff of the 149th from the ground, and raced toward his regiment, which had fallen back to the crest of McPherson's Ridge. On the way he passed the wounded Price (Company A), who turned his prize over to the boy to take to Colonel Miller.[19]

The Iron Brigade Leaves Herbst Woods

Captain Hollon Richardson, now unofficially in command of the Iron Brigade, had successfully pulled what was left of the 2nd and 7th Wisconsin from Herbst Woods. The two regiments, along with Company B of the 150th Pennsylvania, retired by companies to the right. The men loaded as they withdrew, and repeatedly reformed and faced the slowly pursuing Rebs. Their steadiness left an indelible impression on Sgt. William Ramsey (Company F, 150th Pennsylvania), who observed the retiring Yankees from a point between the McPherson house and barn. "I have often since spoken of the cool, orderly manner in which Meredith's brigade fell back," recalled Ramsey, "their movement seemed to be almost as deliberate as though they were on dress parade."

The 2nd and 7th Wisconsin withdrew toward the creek bottom to join what was left of the brigade. Richardson galloped to the left in an unsuccessful attempt to rally Biddle's demoralized regiments. When he came upon the downed colors of the 142nd Pennsylvania, the staff officer grabbed them and spurred back to his rallying fragments of the Iron Brigade. From the southern side of Sheads Woods north of the railroad bed at the Thompson place, Col. Rufus Dawes (6th Wisconsin) spotted Richardson trooping the line on his

19 Ladd & Ladd, *Bachelder Papers*, 2:760; Park, "Some Of My Recollections"; *Richmond Enquirer*, July 24, 1863, 1; Bassler, "The Color Episode," 9.The *Enquirer* described in detail how Price got his "blue flag," and that another man (McPherson) shot the color bearer (Spayd) in the thigh. McPherson's colonel offered McPherson a lieutenancy, He declined the promotion. Neither Price nor Clarke received any formal recognition for the flags they captured.

mount with the flag in hand, which he mistakenly thought belonged to the 7th Wisconsin.[20]

Colonel Henry Morrow (24th Michigan), still carrying the bullet riddled U.S. flag, halted in the creek bottom some 350 yards east of the woods on the left of the 2nd and 7th Wisconsin. Civilian John Burns, who had gotten caught up in the retreat of the 142nd Pennsylvania, fell in with the Wolverines and was wounded. A stray round from the northwest killed Capt. Malachi O'Donnell (Company K) as he waved his sword above his head to rally his men. Lieutenant Newell Grace (Company H) collapsed with three wounds, all mortal.[21]

With the 7th Wisconsin as its anchor, the dwindling 143rd Pennsylvania made a stand along its right flank. The command to fix bayonets carried down the line. "Life never seems so sweet, or so near the end," thought Sgt. Patrick DeLacy Company A). The sight of Confederates surging down the hill toward them prompted one of the Pennsylvanians to scream, "Get you Rebels!" Others took up the cry. With a "manly cheer," recalled one eyewitness, the regiment charged and drove the Southerners back to the ridge.

During the sudden but brief lull that followed, the right wing of the 143rd executed the movement, "On the right of company, in reverse order, left half wheel to the rear." The men right about faced and, stepping over their own casualties, established a line at a 45-degree angle to the rest of the regiment. Once that was completed, they right about faced. They anchored their left on 18-year-old Clr. Sgt. Benjamin Crippen, who marked the point of the angle in the road southwest of the left half of the 143rd. The Rebels soon opened fire from the northwest across the pike, catching the Pennsylvanians from the left rear while they were changing the line. Private Avery Harris (Company B) remembered the screams of the injured men writhing around him. Ben Crippen stood in the road, defiantly shaking his fist at the Rebs.[22]

20 *OR* 27/1:280; Ladd & Ladd, *Bachelder Papers*, 1:142 and 301, and 2:956; "Synopsis of General Richardson's Speech," 2; Dawes, *Service With the Sixth Wisconsin*, 174. In the newspaper article, Richardson claimed he ordered the brigade to retire by the right of companies to the rear, as did Lieutenant Colonel Callis (7th Wisconsin). Both wrote their accounts in the early 1870s. In his 1867 letter to Bachelder, Lt. Col. George McFarland (151st Pennsylvania) identified the officer with the flag as probably being Richardson. In the after-action report for the 7th Wisconsin, Colonel Robinson claimed Clr. Sgt. Daniel McDermott (Company K) carried the flag throughout the battle.

21 Curtis, *History of the Twenty-Fourth Michigan*, 165, 175, 181, 183.

22 "Capt. DeLacy Describes Gettysburg Battle"; Tomasak, *Harris Journal*, 60, 62.

With rounds coming in from the front and both flanks, a squad from Company B, on the left of the regiment, impetuously rushed forward from the line and halted to shoot from a more advantageous position. With Stephen E. Miller to his right, Avery Harris managed to get off three rounds before they decided they had better return to the ranks.

No sooner had they wheeled about in place when Miller dropped his rifle, grasped his upper right arm, and gasped, "God, Orr, 'un shot." A bullet also hit Harris, forcing him down on one knee. Struggling for air, Harris tried to reply, "So am I, Steve," but could only mouth the words. When Miller took off in a panic, Harris stood, his rifle clenched in his left hand and his right forearm pressed against his right side to help him breathe. Hunched over, he stumbled toward Gettysburg.[23]

Whatever stand these Federals made did not last more than a couple minutes, which was time enough for the 143rd to loose a "salute" or two, as Col. John D. Musser reported. When the bugler once more sounded "Retreat," the musical order triggered a stampede. The regiment fragmented into clusters, with some begrudgingly falling back and others running for the rear.[24]

The heavy Confederate counterattack successfully smashed the entire Federal line along McPherson's Ridge and generated a chaotic withdrawal east toward Seminary Ridge. The Union line peeled away from south to north. According to one of the survivors, the 121st Pennsylvania, on the left, broke: "[T]he time made by the 121st getting to the cover of the wood beyond [at the seminary] was remarkable, probably set a record,"

The Tar Heels shot down or captured a large number of the Keystone soldiers, but stopped cold on the ridge rather than risk crossing open ground into waiting Federal troops. Colonel Theodore B. Gates, finding his 20th N.Y.S.M. in an untenable position, gave the order to retreat. The regiment scattered east toward Seminary Ridge. To Gates's amazement, the Rebels did not chase after them on that end of the field. "The enemy's pursuit," he recalled, "was cautious and tardy."

23 Tomasak, *Harris Journal*, 68-69.

24 Musser, Unpublished Report; *OR* 27/1:338; Hubler, "Just the Plain, Untarnished Story"; "Capt. DeLacy Describes Gettysburg Battle." In the *OR* and his report dated September 19, 1863, Musser wrote that the regiment moved rearward in "good order." DeLacy and Hubler, however, indicated that the regiment skedaddled. All three were likely correct given their point of view.

To the left, the seriously wounded acting Maj. James Ashworth (121st Pennsylvania) recalled that very few Rebs ran over him as he lay immobilized on the ground. Rather than pursue, the 52nd North Carolina left behind a detachment to keep an eye on their rear and continued north to roll up the rest of Biddle's brigade. Refusing to show panic, Maj. Alexander Biddle of the 121st and Lt. Henry H. Herbst (Company A) walked back toward the seminary.[25]

On the right of the brigade, the 142nd Pennsylvania also put up a minimal defense. Several men halted at the dilapidated worm fence about 150 yards east of the regiment's former position and shot a few rounds at the 47th and 11th North Carolina as they topped the ridge to their front. Private Edwin R. Gearhart (Company G) knew from the rifle reports on his side of the regiment that most of his comrades had not stopped running from the fight. Someone foolishly ordered a charge, but the sight of the North Carolinians loping down the hill toward them sent the remnants of the 142nd racing without order into the valley west of the seminary.

During his skedaddle, Gearhart caught a glimpse of Union men moving along the woodlot with rails in their hands. He breathed easier, thinking he would never get bagged by the Rebels. An unexpected burst of canister, followed immediately by explosions from long-range Confederate artillery, dismissed that thought. Gearhart threw himself face first into the tall timothy grass.[26]

Sergeant James R. Balsey (Company H) did not fare as well. While lying on the ground between the fence and the Rebs, a bullet from his own men struck him. Before long, small arms fire cut away his haversack and his cartridge box. Like so many of the wounded who could not remove themselves from the line of fire, Balsey lay trapped between the two hostile forces. Lieutenant Colonel Alfred B. McCalmont (in command of the 142nd Pennsylvania after Cummins was mortally wounded) and an enlisted man trailed behind the regiment. Unwilling to leave Balsey to die in the hands of the Confederates, they pulled him upright and dragged him toward the seminary hospital.[27]

25 *History of the 121st Regiment*, 55, 169; *OR* 27/1:321; *Pennsylvania at Gettysburg*, 2:653.

26 "In the Years '62 to '65," 35; Warren, *Two Reunions*, 22.

27 Balsey, "On the Field Among the Enemy"; McCalmont, *Extracts From McCalmont Letters*, 58.

While the flanking fire from the 47th North Carolina ripped into the left of Lieutenant Colonel McFarland's 151st Pennsylvania, one of John Brockenbrough's Virginia regiments burst from the woods to its right front. In the few minutes since they had joined the fighting, McFarland's Pennsylvanians had lost more than 150 officers and men. Still seated on his horse, McFarland surveyed the smoky field on his flanks and spotted the Rebels try to cut him off from the rear. Intent on forming on the left of the Black Hats, he decided to extricate his men from the collapsing front and gave the command to retreat while firing.[28]

Private Randle D. Sayn (Company B) had just started to pull out when someone yelled from behind, "For God's sake, don't let them devils in town to-night and we will give you all you can eat and drink!" The statement was unusual enough to turn around and see who had yelled it. "Old man," he spat back at John Burns, "we have to obey orders."

By the time the Pennsylvania's reached the bottomland, however, the Iron Brigade had left. The Rebels, who had expended their ammunition and energy in the enervating heat and were now under fire from Union guns posted along Seminary Ridge, did not pursue. The Pennsylvanians reached the hurriedly erected barricade at the seminary.[29]

Seminary Ridge North of the Seminary

Stevens's Battery E, 5th Maine, unlimbered in Krauth's yard, and Cooper's Battery B, 1st Pennsylvania, did so on elevated ground from the seminary to Stevens's flank. Together, they hurled case and shrapnel through the battered woodlot the moment Confederates came into view along McPherson's Ridge. The billowing smoke from the smoothbores combined with the bluish haze from the rifle fire in the stream bottom about 300 yards to their front to make positive target identification nearly impossible. The artillerists switched to canister.[30]

During the sprint toward Riggs's peach orchard, Clr. Sgt. Benjamin Crippen (143rd Pennsylvania) turned to defiantly shake his fist at the oncoming Rebs when a bullet toppled him face first into the road with the national flag beneath him. His blood splattered over Sgt. Patrick DeLacy (Company A). The

28 *Pennsylvania at Gettysburg*, 2:747; Ladd & Ladd, *Bachelder Papers*, 1:300, 301.

29 Ladd & Ladd, *Bachelder Papers*, 1:301; Sayre, "A Day at Gettysburg."

30 *Maine at Gettysburg*, 84; *OR*, 27/1:360-361, 364.

bleeding Capt. Charles M. Conyngham (Company A) saw Crippen collapse and yelled, "One hundred and forty-third, rally on your colors!" Before anyone could respond, DeLacy rolled Crippen onto his back and made off with the flag, something Pvt. Avery Harris (Company B) did not realize. He believed Daniel's Rebels had gotten it.[31]

Colonel Wainwright was in the orchard with Lt. Benjamin Wilber's section of 3-inch rifles. The infantry along his front was getting too close for his guns to fire without slaughtering their own men, so Wilber's pair of the iron guns remained silent while some of the 143rd Pennsylvania swarmed around them. Confederates popped over the middle ridge and their skirmishers approached to within 50 yards of the guns before anyone noticed because the smoke was so heavy. When Wilber realized what was happening, he yelled at the infantry crowding his two pieces, "My God, boys, save my guns!" Lieutenant Colonel Musser rallied a portion of the regiment to protect the artillery.

Lieutenant Colonel Walton Dwight (149th Pennsylvania) and Adj. Richard L. Ashurst (150th Pennsylvania), commanding the mixed contingents of both regiments, also heard or learned of Wilbur's plea for help. Ashurst hesitated, believing the Rebs would overrun the section. Dwight, however, still bleeding from his leg wound, urged him to make a stand. Ashurst acquiesced. Together, they merged their men into a company-sized line. Almost immediately Lt. Elias B. Weidensaul bent over, tightly clasping his chest.

"Are you wounded?" Ashurst asked.

"No," Weidensaul blurted out, "killed!" With that, he twisted to one side and dropped stone dead at the adjutant's feet.[32]

One particularly reckless soldier in Company F, 150th Pennsylvania, stood and watched as the shell burst like a fireworks display overhead. Sergeant William Ramsey heard the young man holler, "Come, boys, don't you hear the

31 "Capt. DeLacy Describes Gettysburg Battle"; *Pennsylvania at Gettysburg*, 2:685, 686; Hubler, "Just the Plain, Untarnished Story"; Tomasak, *Harris Journal*, 60, 64; *OR* 27/1:338.

32 Chamberlin, *History of the One Hundred and Fiftieth Regiment*, 134-135; *OR* 27/1:356, 362, 363; Musser, Unpublished Report; Hubler, "Just the Plain, Untarnished Story." Based on Breck's report, it appears likely that Breck placed Wilber's gun in the orchard while Wainwright took charge of Bower's four pieces. Prior to Pettigrew's attack, with no immediate threat to that end of the line, Wainwright returned to Wilber's section and ordered Breck to the two sections below the seminary. In his report, Wainwright has Stevens to Cooper's left and not to his right, as the captain reported.

music? The ball is going to open. Why don't you get up and choose your partners?"[33]

The heavily thinned 24th Michigan managed to get as far as the makeshift barricade near the Krauth house. There, Col. Henry Morrow, who still carried "Old Glory," hailed Capt. Albert M. Edwards (Company F), handed him the flag staff, and began climbing over the rails. A minié ball glanced off the top of Morrow's skull, staggering him. Somehow the stunned officer crossed to the other side. By this time his face was covered in blood, but Morrow refused to have his wound dressed or to leave the regiment. Some of his men ignored his protests and led him away to get his injury tended. Captain Edwards, who was now the senior officer of the regiment on the field, kept the flag and assumed his duties. Sergeant Augustus F. Ziegler (Company A), who witnessed the entire incident, wrote admiringly of Morrow: "He wasn't going to leave the boys until the Cotillion was over."

Corporal Charles H. McConnell was one of the eight uninjured soldiers left in what had been the 54-man Company B. He refused to turn and run. Instead, he walked backward, his face to the enemy, to Seminary Ridge, his loud and colorful swearing trailing behind him in a streak so blue it "would have done credit to the mate of a Mississippi steamboat."[34]

The Michiganders anchored themselves on the right of the 151st Pennsylvania. The rest of Biddle's fragmented brigade was to its left in the following order: 142nd Pennsylvania, 20th N.S.Y.M, and 121st Pennsylvania. In all, maybe 400 survivors between the five regiments—Maj. Alexander Biddle described them as "broken"— hunkered behind the low rail fence in an effort to remain below the muzzle blasts of the Cooper's battery. The Rebs, meanwhile, continued to "peg" at them from McPherson's Ridge.[35]

33 Ladd & Ladd, *Bachelder Papers*, 2:958.

34 Livermore, *My Story of the War*, 35; McConnell, "First and Greatest Days Battle"; Ziegler Letter; Curtis, *History of the Twenty-Fourth Michigan*, 163, 188. Curtis offered two different versions in the regimental history. On p.163, he wrote that Morrow gave the flag to an anonymous private and that Edwards took it from that man's corpse. On p.188, Curtis quotes Morrow's July 30, 1863, speech in Detroit in which Morrow claimed that he was hit in the head and handed the flag to Edwards. The July 30 speech was only weeks after the event and there is no reason to doubt it.

35 *OR* 27/1:316, 320, 323; *History of the 121st Regiment*, 55; Busey & Martin, *Regimental Strengths and Losses*, 125, 126. Of the 1,287 engaged, the brigade lost 440 killed/wounded and 457 missing which left 390 officers and men between four regiments. The 24th

The men sheltered behind the rails just below the ledge under the west side of the campus road. Major Biddle and Lt. Henry Herbst (Company A) joined his cousin, Col. Chapman Biddle, Lt. Col. Alfred McCalmont (142nd Pennsylvania), and Lt. Col. George F. McFarland (151st Pennsylvania) in front of the seminary to determine what to do next.

Lieutenant James Stewart, who had left his three guns under cover on the western edge of Sheads Woods, joined Lt. James Davison in the field west of Mary Thompson's orchard. He spotted Junius Daniel's Confederates when they topped the middle cut and ordered the lieutenant to open with double canister at 300 yards into the advancing Confederates. The Yankee canister and small arms fire swept some of the North Carolinians away, but also killed a few of their own. Part of the 2nd Wisconsin had gone to ground in what appeared to be a safe place when one of the canister rounds from Davison's section decapitated Cpl. David Gudger (Company C).[36]

Case shot with a short fuse and canister hurtling from 12-pounder smoothbores cut down whatever was in it their path, pulverized fences, shredded trees, tore up the ground, and wreaked panic with flesh and bone. While crossing to the north side of the Chambersburg Pike, the few remaining men of the 7th Wisconsin under Lt. Col. John Callis accidentally walked into the wall of iron being thrown from Davison's three guns. Callis unsheathed his sword and faced the guns. Through the smoke, he screamed at the lieutenant to cease fire.

A minié ball hammered Callis in the right chest and glanced downward into his lung's lower lobe. The impact knocked him unconscious. While his survivors and the remnant of the 19th Indiana scrambled to get behind the artillery, Capt. Martin C. Hobart (Company B) detailed several men to haul Callis to the north side of the seminary. When the smoke eventually settled, the

---

Michigan numbered around 140 men of all ranks. There is no way to determine an exact number of men present because there is no way to ascertain how many men did not stop at the barricade. The force behind the barricade likely was much smaller.

36 Stewart, "Battery B," 185; Aubery, *Echoes From the Marches of the Iron Brigade*, 49. Company C, 2nd Wisconsin only had one corporal killed that day. The other, William Y. Cunningham, was missing in action. There does not seem to be enough information to place the regiments in their precise order. The Iron Brigade apparently closed to the north, with the road on the right, and at least the survivors of the 19th Indiana, 2nd Wisconsin, and 7th Wisconsin ended up in Thompson's orchard with Davison's three guns; the 24th Michigan ended up there as well.

four regiments of the Iron Brigade occupied a front typically covered by a 400-man regiment.[37]

Just before 3:00 p.m., Lieutenant Slagle informed Abner Doubleday of Wadsworth's discouraging report, which confirmed Doubleday's assessment of the deteriorating situation at the front. Doubleday scratched a hasty note in his order book and took note of the time: 3:00 p.m. He tore the page out and passed it to his dependable aide to get it to Maj. Gen. Oliver O. Howard, the commander of the XI Corps, as fast as he could. He admonished Slagle to inform Howard that the entire army was in danger of being flanked, and that he needed a brigade to reinforce the line. Lieutenant Slagle galloped into Gettysburg, but was unable to locate either Howard or anyone who knew the general's whereabouts. Slagle finally happened upon a major en route to Howard and followed him. He found the general at the Evergreen Cemetery gatehouse along the Baltimore Pike.

Howard listened to the lieutenant's request for reinforcements as he read the message that Doubleday could not hold out any longer. Howard told Slagle he did not have a man to spare. The aide, who did not believe the corps commander, wheeled his horse about and set his spurs to gallop back to Doubleday. In a letter to his brother pened two months later, Slagle explained his doubt thusly: "I satisfied myself afterwards he [Howard] did not have a man engaged at the time." Slagle, of course, was wrong. Most of the XI Corps was in the process of being wrecked and routed just above the town by Richard Ewell's Second Corps. The lieutenant reported the unwelcome news to Doubleday, who sent him to Wadsworth once again to find another infantry regiment. Doubleday also ordered Capt. Eminel P. Halstead, his acting adjutant general, to race to the cemetery and repeat the request to General Howard for immediate reinforcements.[38]

37 Williams Report; Ladd & Ladd, *Bachelder Papers*, 1:142; Shapiro, "John Benton Callis: Madison County's Republican Congressman," *The Huntsville Historical Review*, 29:10. Callis's earliest account of his wounding is in *The Bachelder Papers*.

38 Slagle to brother; Halstead, "The First Day of the Battle"; Charles H. Howard, "The First Day at Gettysburg," 15. Oliver Otis Howard's brother Charles, who served on his staff, later wrote that the note from Doubleday was written at 3:00 p.m. Halstead cited his departure time around 4:00 p.m., but it had to have been be closer to the first quarter of the hour because Halstead reached Cemetery Hill shortly before Maj. Gen. Winfield Scott Hancock (II Corps) arrived there at 3:30 p.m. Slagle, who did not know the name of the cemetery, recorded that he was sent to Wadsworth a second time, and then to division commander Robinson, for reinforcements.

Captain Hollon Richardson, the indefatigable staff officer who for some time unofficially commanded the battered Iron Brigade, retrieved the fallen colors of the 142nd Pennsylvania. *Wisconsin Historical Society*

3:15 p.m. to 3:30 p.m.[39]

Chapman Biddle's regimental officers at the front of the seminary dispersed when a flurry of small arm shots cut down some of the men in the 151st Pennsylvania. As Lieutenant Colonel McFarland returned to the rear of his line, Capt. Hollon Richardson rode up with the flag he had picked up during the retreat.

"Colonel, is this your flag?" asked Richardson, who was unaware which regiment McFarland commanded.

The question momentarily took the colonel aback. He had lost track of his banner in the confusion of the attack. A breeze rustled the folds showing the colonel its designation.

"No," McFarland answered, "it is the flag of the 142nd Pennsylvania. And it belongs on my left. Give it to that man there and let them rally round it."

A nearby soldier, who the colonel knew belonged to the 142nd, stepped up and declared, "I'll take it." McFarland watched the man rally a few comrades around him before returning to his duties.[40]

Sporadic rifle fire and artillery discharges peppered the tenuous Federal line thrown together along Seminary Ridge. Captain Cooper used the brief lull to refill his limbers from the caissons before sending them to the rear. Over in Mary Thompson's orchard, the artillerymen in Lieutenant Davison's left half of

39 *History of the 121st Regiment*, 56. In a letter to Capt. John M. Clapp (Company F, 121st Pennsylvania) dated January 27, 1892, Col. Newton Brown (14th South Carolina) wrote, "There was some considerable interval, however, between Pettigrew's advance than ours [Perrin's Brigade]."

40 Ladd & Ladd, *Bachelder Papers*, 1:301-302.

Battery B, 4th U.S., took a much-needed breather while Davison and Lt. James Stewart complimented themselves on the battery's excellent performance. Thus far, they had sustained few casualties.[41]

41 *Maine at Gettysburg*, 85; *Pennsylvania at Gettysburg*, 2:879; Nevins, *A Diary of Battle*, 236; Stewart, "Battery B," 185.

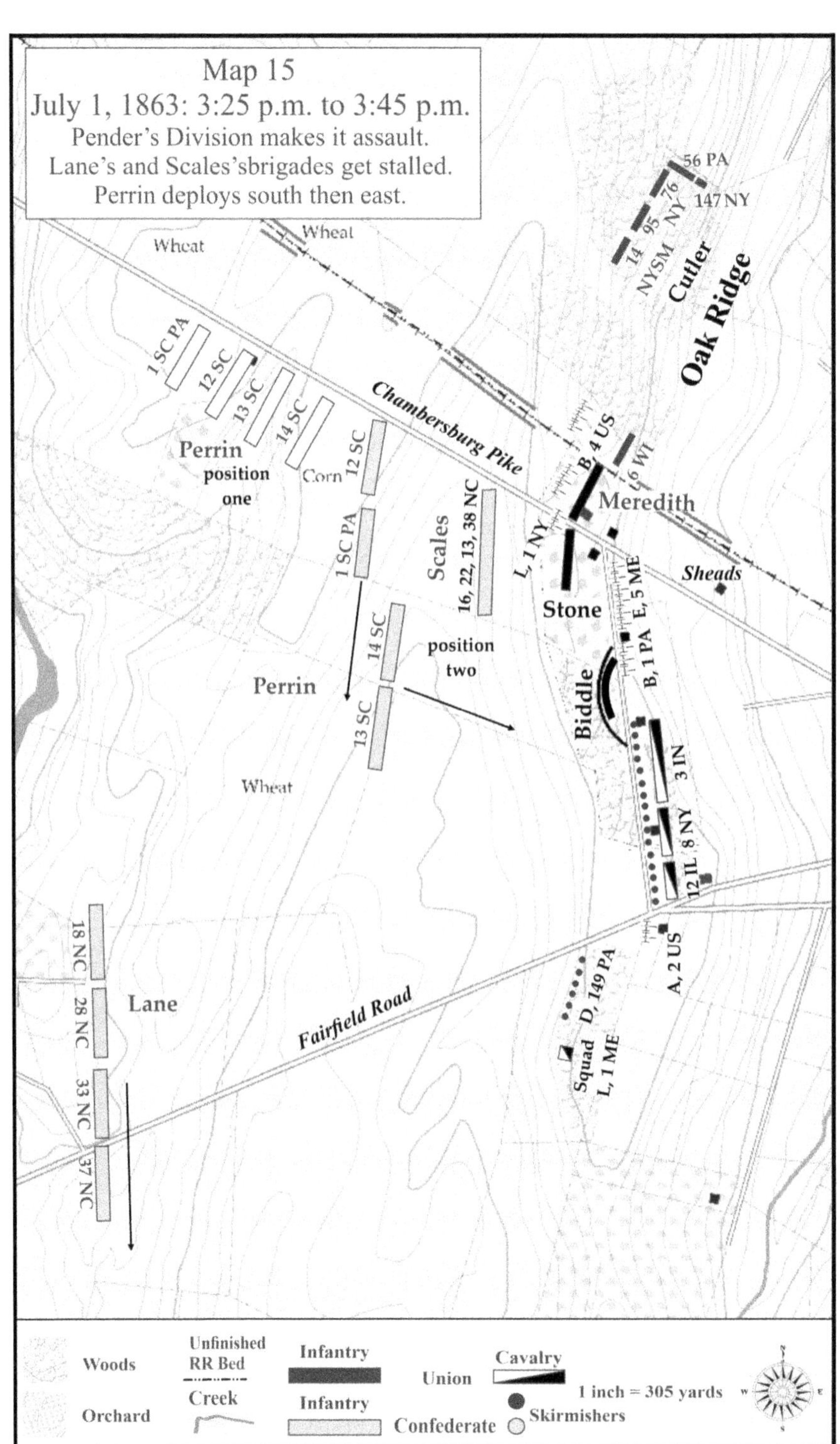
Map 15
July 1, 1863: 3:25 p.m. to 3:45 p.m.
Pender's Division makes it assault.
Lane's and Scales'sbrigades get stalled.
Perrin deploys south then east.
56 PA
147 NY
14
95
76
NY
NYSM
Cutler
Oak Ridge
Wheat
Wheat
1 SC PA
12 SC
13 SC
14 SC
Perrin
position
one
Corn
12 SC
Chambersburg Pike
B, 4 US
6 WI
Meredith
L, 1 NY
Scales
16, 22, 13, 38 NC
1 SC PA
Stone
E, 5 ME
Sheads
14 SC
position
two
B, 1 PA
Biddle
Perrin
13 SC
Wheat
3 IN
8 NY
12 IL
A, 2 US
D, 149 PA
18 NC
28 NC
33 NC
37 NC
Lane
Fairfield Road
Squad
L, 1 ME
Woods
Orchard
Unfinished
RR Bed
Creek
Infantry
Infantry
Union
Confederate
Cavalry
1 inch = 305 yards
Skirmishers

Chapter Twelve

"It seems miraculous how I escaped injury."

— *Pvt. George O. Dibble, Company A, 8th New York Cavalry*

Final Defense of Seminary Ridge

3:30 p.m. to 4:00 p.m.

3:30 p.m. to 3:45 p.m.
Cemetery Hill

Capt. Eminel P. Halstead arrived at Cemetery Hill with a message from Abner Doubleday shortly before 3:15 p.m. According to Halstead, a despondent-looking General Howard was standing in the field immediately west of the Evergreen Cemetery gatehouse. When asked about reinforcements, Howard replied, "Tell General Doubleday I have no reinforcements to send him. I have only one regiment in reserve." After reflecting a moment he added, "Go to General Buford, give him my compliments, and tell him to go to General Doubleday's support."

Halstead asked about the whereabouts of the cavalry, and the general pointed the way.[1] Captain Halstead rode off and found Col. William Gamble's

1 Halstead, "The First Day," 6; Ladd & Ladd, *Bachelder Papers*, 1:3. Halstead's self-serving account exhibits a deep dislike for Howard and his XI Corps. To put it bluntly, he worshiped Winfield Hancock (II Corps) at Howard's expense. According to chief of staff Maj. Charles H. Morgan, he and Hancock arrived at Cemetery Hill at 3:30 p.m. and found a

mounted brigade (without the 8th Illinois) in the low ground west of the Emmitsburg Road.[2]

About 15 minutes before Halstead reached Buford, the cavalry commander fired off a dispatch to the chief of cavalry, Brig. Gen. Alfred Pleasanton:

> I am satisfied that Longstreet and Hill have made a junction. A tremendous battle has been raging since 9:30 a.m., with varying success. At the present moment the battle is raging on the road to Cashtown, and within short cannon range of this town. The enemy's line is a semicircle on the height, from north to west. General Reynolds was killed early this morning. In my opinion, there seems to be no directing person. . . . P.S.—We need help now.[3]

The order to support Doubleday riled the cavalryman. According to Halstead, Buford rose in the stirrups and loudly protested, "What in hell and damnation does he think I can do against those long lines of the enemy out there!"

"I don't know anything about that, General," the captain responded. "Those are General Howard's orders."

"Very well. I will see what I can do."

Halstead returned to Doubleday.[4]

---

depressed General Howard and his brother, aide-de-camp Maj. Charles H. Howard, standing west of the gatehouse. (Halstead's account has General Howard alone.)

2 Halstead, "The First Day of the Battle," 6; W. S. Hancock, "Gettysburg: Reply to General Howard," *The Galaxy: Magazine of Entertaining Reading*, vol. 22 (June 1876 – January 1877), 22:823, 829. Compare Ladd & Ladd, *Bachelder Papers*, 3:1350-1351 with Howard's report in the *OR*, 27/1:704. (Note that Howard's times are probably inaccurate.) In his account, Halstead claimed Howard sent him east, he could not locate Buford, returned to Cemetery Hill, and found Howard and Hancock talking. Halstead claimed he was close enough to hear Howard refuse to cede command of the army's left wing to Hancock, and after that he rode west on his own initiative to find Buford. Howard (and Halstead) could have seen Gamble's brigade along the western side of the Emmitsburg Road and Howard would not have sent the lieutenant in the wrong direction.

3 *OR* 27/1:924-925.

4 Halstead, "The First Day," 8. Following this incident, Halstead wrote that the cavalry formed to charge, forcing Confederates to form a square. He was evidently referring to the oft-told (but still questionable) story that credited the maneuver to the 8th Illinois Cavalry south of the Fairfield Road against Lane's Rebels. Buford accompanied the rest of the brigade, not the 8th Illinois.

One mile west of Willoughby Run

Before 3:00 p.m., a Confederate officer recently promoted to major general used the relative quiet on the field to align two of his brigades on Herr's Ridge to support Harry Heth's embattled division. William Dorsey Pender's Division was about to enter the fight. Colonel Abner Perrin's South Carolina brigade had marched along the Chambersburg Pike toward Gettysburg at the head of Pender's column, with Brig. Gen. Alfred Scales's North Carolinians behind it, followed by Brig. Gen. Edward L. Thomas's Georgians and Brig. Gen. James H. Lane's North Carolinians.

Pender detached Lane when his brigade reached the back road intersecting the Chambersburg Pike near Ephraim Wisler's place. At that time, word arrived that Yankee cavalry (the 8th Illinois) was harassing James Archer's exhausted brigade; Lane would cover the division's southern flank along the Fairfield Road.

The route took Lane south along Marsh Creek to Black Horse Tavern on the western base of Bream's Hill. The 7th North Carolina held the right of the line on the north side of the Fairfield Road with the 37th, 28th, 18th, and 33rd regiments finishing out the formation to the north. For all practical purposes, from that point onward the North Carolinians operated as an independent command.[5]

By the time Lane deployed near the tavern, Colonel Perrin's command had reached Herr Ridge Road. Pender ordered Perrin to file his brigade of South Carolinians to the right along the road. The 13th South Carolina, the point regiment, halted in the road about 3,500 feet south of the pike fronting east along a destroyed rail fence. The 14th, 12th, and 1st regiments followed suit. By then Scales's North Carolinians had come up. Pender had them repeat the

5 Clark, *Histories of the Several Regiments*, 1:379 and 2:477; *OR* 27/2:665; Busey & Busey, *Confederate Casualties*, 2:854-865, 733-941, 1050-1068, 1089-1099, 1109-1124. In Clark, volume 2, Lane explained: "Lane's Brigade was ordered from the centre of A. P. Hill's line to 'the post of honor' on the right to protect that flank of the army from the enemy's cavalry while we fought his infantry in front." In his after-action report in the *OR*, he wrote that the brigade marched in line almost a mile before moving to the southern side of the road. This means the brigade deployed on or near of the first ridge east of Black Horse Tavern. (Many maps mistakenly show Lane's deployment a good distance east of Willoughby Run.) Busey & Busey record the following :nominal losses for the brigade as follows: 7th NC: 0; 18th NC: 10; 28th NC: 8; 33rd NC: 9; 37th NC: 3, for a total of 30 casualties.

maneuver. The 16th, 22nd, 34th, 13th, and 38th North Carolina left faced. With the left of the line aligned on the northern face of the woods, the two brigades stepped over the fence and started down the eastern slope of Herr's Ridge. The 13th South Carolina's surgeon, Spencer G. Welch, riding on the left of the regiment admired the military bearing of the Carolinians.[6]

While Lane was moving along the Fairfield Road, Pender was busy sheltering the nine regiments under Scales and Perrin inside the western edge of Herr's Woods for a much-needed rest. Sweltering in his sweat-soaked uniform, Lt. James F. J. Caldwell (Company B, 1st South Carolina) welcomed the relative relief from exposure to the heat and humidity. Sporadic shelling and overshot miniés zipped overhead and slapped into the trees.

Farther left, artillery projectiles inflicted casualties in the 16th North Carolina. Lieutenant George H. Mills (Company G) witnessed a shell fragment strike Lt. George Woodie, a file closer in Company A (34th North Carolina) in the head. Mills, who was behind his company, watched as the panicked officer bound toward the rear yelling, "I'm dead! I'm dead!" Mills, who mistook Woodie for a captain, spotted nothing but a couple minor scalp wounds. Woodie's colonel, William Lee Lowrance, who also believed the injury was minor, mockingly called out for stretcher bearers to "Go and take that man off — if you can catch him." One Yankee shell almost eliminated General Scales, who was calmly seated on his horse. The projectile screamed behind his back just above his horse's rump and burrowed into the forest floor, leaving a hole he thought large enough to hold a man.[7]

6 Spencer Glasgow Welch, *A Confederate Surgeon's Letters to His Wife* (New York, 1911), 64; Joseph Brown, "McGowan's South Carolina Brigade at Gettysburg," *The* [Charleston] *News and Courier*, July 12, 1882, n.p.; *The Charleston Weekly News*, n.d.; *The Anderson* [SC] *Intelligencer*, July 27, 1882, 1; *The Newberry* [SC] *Herald*, August 3, 1882, 1; J. F. J. Caldwell, *The History of a Brigade of South Carolinians, Known First As "Gregg's," And Subsequently As "McGowan's Brigade"* (Philadelphia, 1866), 96; Bachelder, Map 13 of 27.

7 *OR* 27/2:655; J. F. J. Caldwell, *The History of a Brigade*, 97; Busey & Martin, *Regimental Strengths and Losses*, 231; Ladd & Ladd, *Bachelder Papers*, 2:904, 906 (map), and 3:1696-1697; George H. Mills, *History of the Sixteenth North Carolina Regiment* (privately printed, 1901), 36; Varina Davis Brown, *A Colonel at Gettysburg and Spotsylvania* (Columbia, SC, 1931), 83; Busey & Busey, *Confederate Casualties*, 2:1099. In his February 2, 1890, letter to Bachelder, Scales noted that his brigade, while under sporadic artillery fire, rested about half an hour in a grove of trees. Lieutenant Mills (Company G) confirmed the break before his regiment advanced. In *The Bachelder Papers*, volume 2, Pvt. John A. Leach (Company E, 1st South Carolina), in a missive dated

Alfred Scales enlisted as a private and rose quickly through the ranks. He was promoted to brigadier general a few weeks before Gettysburg. His storied career with the Army of Northern Virginia was nearly cut short on the first day at Gettysburg, first by a shell that barely missed him, and then with a severe leg wound. *LOC*

Thompson's Orchard

An aide reined in alongside Union Lts. James Davison and James Stewart to announce that the Confederates were making another advance. Stewart told Davison to handle the situation along the Chambersburg Pike, as he had in the last attack, while he used his three guns on the Rebel left flank from Sheads Woods. With that, the Scot swung into his saddle and galloped back to his sheltered position inside the western face of the woods. Using the left piece as the pivot, he had his remaining two guns rolled by hand forward at a 45-degree angle to the original line until they faced southwest toward the high ground at the middle cut. With the middle ridge protecting his right flank and the rise of ground on the southern side of the middle cut blocking the line of sight, it would be nearly impossible for the Southerners to realize they would be advancing into a sweeping fire. He ordered his Napoleons charged with double canister and, with nothing more to do, waited for the action to start anew.[8]

September 12, 1882, mentioned the brigade being in a woods and advancing to the top of a hill into an open field. Of all the officers injured in the five regiments, only Lieutenant Woodie suffered a head wound (fractured cranium). He survived, only to be disabled by a foot wound at the Battle of the Wilderness on May 5, 1864.

8 Stewart, "Battery B," 185.

3:25 p.m. to 3:45 p.m.

"Attention!"

The order traveled through the regiments of Pender's Division. It was about 3:25 p.m. The men got to their feet and went to "right shoulder shift." At the command "Guide left, march!" Scales's North Carolinians marched left in column of twos into the meadow north of the woods. The brigade broke into two separate battle lines facing east as the men entered the open hillside. They were aligned, from north to south as follows: 38th (186 muskets), 13th (200 men), and 34th (278 rank and file) in the front line, and the 22nd (238 men) and 16th (301 muskets) in the second line.

Without changing their order of battle, Perrin's South Carolinians sidled to the north edge of the woods. The men fixed bayonets as their officers paced the regiments, repeating orders from General Pender. They were to keep their alignments and not break the momentum of the attack by stopping to fire until specifically commanded to do so. Scales's Brigade stepped off at the quick time (110 steps per minute). With its left flank between 125-150 feet south of the Chambersburg Pike, the brigade quickly descended into the Willoughby Run Valley and crossed the creek under occasional bursts of shell and case shot.

With their right flank north of the burning Harman house, Perrin's South Carolinians crossed over the same marshy ground Pettigrew's men had traversed an hour or so earlier. Forty yards from the creek, an errant round of case hammered Capt. John A. Hinnant (Company C, 12th South Carolina) in the upper left leg, spun him around, and threw him to the ground. Lieutenant J. R. Boyles marched past him. The veterans stepped gingerly over the ashen dead and the non-ambulatory wounded while swarms of injured men passed around the flanks of the formation.[9]

The line abruptly halted along the western bank of Willoughby Run. The right side faced the casualty-strewn marshy hollow south of the woods. The 1st South Carolina ended up in front of a steep bluff at the northwest corner of Herbst Woods near the stone quarry. Unable to keep pace with Scales, whose men had already started marching up the hill north of the quarry, Perrin hastily reformed his regiments at the double-quick to the north. The 14th South Carolina, with the 13th behind it, peeled north in column of twos. When the 13th cleared its rear, the 12th fell in behind it, followed by the 1st.

9 J. R. Boyles, *Reminiscences of the Civil War* (Columbia, SC, 1901), 41.

Once the 14th South Carolina passed beyond the northern edge of Herbst Woods and the quarry, it flanked right into line and halted. The 13th fell into line at full interval immediately behind it; the 12th and the 1st Palmetto regiments did likewise. With his regiments aligned in column, Perrin hurried his command forward to support Scales.[10]

Halfway up the slope Scales's North Carolinians came upon Brockenbrough's prone Virginians. Their officers had pulled them back from the front line because they had run out of ammunition. Shortly thereafter Perrin's South Carolinians followed suit. Lieutenant Caldwell (1st South Carolina) heard the Virginians cheering them on.[11]

Shells and case shot burst behind and in front of Scales's men the moment they topped the ridge. The regiments changed their pace to double-quick (280 feet per minute) to lessen their exposure to the enemy fire. Their professionalism impressed the general. The soldiers, he wrote, marched "in as good [a] line as I ever saw."

Colonel Wainwright, astride his horse near Wilber's guns south of the Chambersburg Pike, watched Scales's advance and thought the same thing. "Never have I seen such a charge," he wrote in his journal. "Not a man seemed to falter. Lee may well be proud of his infantry." From Lt. James Stewart's position at Sheads Woods, Rufus Dawes (6th Wisconsin) marveled at the Rebel discipline. "Their bearing was magnificent," he recollected. "They maintained their alignment with great precision. In many cases, the colors of [the] regiments were advanced several paces in front of the line." The southwesterly course of the pike narrowed the left flank's distance from it to less than 50 yards.[12]

The Carolinians negotiated the dilapidated worm fence at the bottom of the swale and pressed onward despite shelling from Seminary Ridge. About 75

10 Joseph Brown, "McGowan's South Carolina Brigade at Gettysburg," *The Newberry Herald*, August 3, 1882, 1; Ladd & Ladd, *Bachelder Papers*, 1:90; Nevins, *A Diary of Battle*, 236; Ziegler Letter; Calef, "Gettysburg Notes," 51; Day, "Opening the Battle." There is some confusion as to the number of lines Perrin carried into battle. Some Union witnesses saw three lines, and others four. Based on the sources, it is likely Perrin attacked in four separate lines.

11 Ladd & Ladd, *Bachelder Papers*, 3:697; Caldwell, *The History of a Brigade*, 97; *OR*, 27, pt. 2, 670; Daniel A. Tompkins and A. S. Tompkins, *Company K, Fourteenth South Carolina Volunteers* (Charlotte, NC, 1897), 19-20. Caldwell described it as "a general cheer."

12 Ladd & Ladd, *Bachelder Papers*, 3:1697; Nevins, *A Diary of Battle*, 236; *OR* 27/2:670.

yards into the hollow before reaching the middle ridge, a shell fragment slammed into Alfred Scales's leg, forcing him to turn the brigade over to Col. William L. Lowrance of the 34th. When the front regiments crested the middle ridge between Herbst Woods and the Chambersburg Pike, Stewart's masked half of Battery B, 4th U.S., unloaded its canister into the unsuspecting Rebels. Simultaneously, Lt. James Davison's three pieces cut loose with solid shot from Thompson's orchard. To his left, Lt. Benjamin Wilber's two 3-inch Ordnance Rifles slammed the Confederates head on with canister. Dense whitish-gray clouds punctuated with tongues of flame enveloped the Federal position.

Augustus Ziegler of the 24th Michigan witnessed the iron and lead assault against Scales's formation from his place on the right side of the line at the seminary barricade. "It was a splendid sight to see how the canister mowed them down," admitted. "You could see avenues cut right through the rebel column." Command control disintegrated as artillery rounds punched through the ranks from front to rear as each line appeared along the horizon.[13]

Under the shelter of the western side of the middle ridge, Pvt. John H. Bradley (Company G, 16th North Carolina) stopped to charge his weapon but the rammer got stuck. Lieutenant George H. Mills, his file closer, stopped to help him pull it out then followed the company with Bradley to his left and Lt. John B. Ford on his right.

The men ran into a sheet of iron and lead—canister from the Federal gunners to their front, and the blue-clad infantry behind the makeshift barricade in front of the seminary. A shot through both legs above the knees brought down Private Bradley. Lieutenant Ford also collapsed with a severe wound. Lieutenant Mills rushed to Ford's side and realized he would bleed out if he did not get immediate help. He spied Surgeon F. T. Fry riding nearby and begged him to come to Ford's assistance, but the doctor ignored his pleas. It was only then that Mills noticed that Fry had suffered a head wound. The bitter lieutenant would later refer to the doctor as "doughty," meaning he thought Fry was more than foolish for being on the line and not attending to his duties.[14]

In all the smoke and chaos, it looked for a time as if the entire brigade had shattered. It was not so. The Confederates were pressing forward with

13 Ziegler Letter; Nevins, *A Diary of Battle*, 235.

14 Mills, *History of the 16th North Carolina*, 36; Busey & Busey, *Confederate Casualties*, 2:902-916, 922-933, 970-982, 1099-1109, 1124-1136. Fry survived his wound but was no longer on the rolls as of December 1863.

astonishing determination, closing the gaps in the front line. From Riggs's orchard, Colonel Wainwright admired how the second line slipped into the gaping holes punctuating the front regiments. Nearby, Col. Samuel J. Williams (19th Indiana) watched the Confederate line maneuvering beyond his flank and knew the "game was up." He began trying to pull his "boys" back along the railroad cut. "I found it impossible to form my command," he honestly reported.

By the time Scales's troops reached the drainage ditch about 120 yards west of Riggs's orchard it was one long single front rank of varying depth stretching from the turnpike south for 700 to 800 feet. The regiments went to cover there and opened fire. Of the 180 enlisted men in the ranks of the 13th North Carolina at the start of the fighting, 30 remained. Some of the Rebels, including Lt. George H. Mills (Company G, 16th), attempted to move beyond the ditch. A shell fragment gouged Mills's right thigh, leaving in its wake a deep raw cut and mangled muscle. Still conscious, he flattened himself where he fell, trying not to get hit again. Something broke the left elbow of Clr. Sgt. William Franklin Faucet of the 13th before snapping his upper arm in two. Color Sergeant Richard T. Blackwell (Company G, 22nd) felt a severe blow on his left side, which miraculously only burned his skin and knocked him off his feet.[15]

Perrin's South Carolinians topped the middle ridge about the same time Scales stalled at in the drainage area—and ran into an unnerving barrage of case and canister. In the 1st South Carolina, Lt. James F. J. Caldwell (Company B) watched as the Yankee artillery fire tore a chunk out of the left of the front line. An empty tin canister can barely missed Pvt. John A. Leach (Company E). A case round in front of Company C of the 12th South Carolina took out three men. Private James Williamson caught one of the round's .58-caliber musket balls in the left leg. A private named John A. Robertson collapsed about four feet away with a shattered right foot. Lieutenant Boyles, the 12th's file closer, fell when one of the lead balls shattered his right leg into splinters below the knee. In the single second it took for him to hit the ground, he distinctly

15 Clark, *Histories of the Several Regiments*, 1:698; Mills, *History of the 16th North Carolina*, 37; *OR* 27/2:670; Ziegler Letter; Nevins, *A Diary of Battle*, 235-236; Busey & Busey, *Confederate Casualties*, 2:922-933, 970-982, 1124-1136; Busey & Martin, *Regimental Strengths and Losses*, 231; Williams Report. The brigade took into action 1,250 (National Park Service) or 1,351 (Busey & Martin) and lost 470 from all causes in the first day's action. This translates into 35% (Martin & Busey) or 38% (NPS). According to Bachelder's Map 13, the regiment, including officers and file closers but excluding men who left the field uninjured, probably had around 950 armed troops along the drainage area.

remembered seeing his right shoe sailing through the air and landing out of sight.[16]

From Battery B, 4th U.S., Rufus Dawes watched Scales's front line deliver a ragged fire and saw a number of the Rebels scramble back to the safety of the reverse side of the middle ridge. Some of them rallied with Perrin's 13th and the 14th South Carolina, reformed, and moved off at the quick step toward Scales's pinned line. The 1st and 12th South Carolina regiments followed at the prescribed "full distance" (about 100 yards). This time, recalled Dawes, the Southerners seemed more cautious than before. When his faster-moving brigade stepped within several yards of the North Carolinians, Perrin moved his regiments by the right flank to extend the division's front. Veterans of the assault did not recall being under direct small arms fire up to that point.[17]

3:35 p.m. to 3:45 p.m.[18]

In Riggs's orchard, meanwhile, Lt. Col. John Musser (143rd Pennsylvania) watched solid shot gouge and plow through the ground around him and his men. Incoming miniés hissed through the air and shell bursts slapped the ground with scalding iron shards. Captain William A. Tubbs (Company F) received a minor

16 Ladd & Ladd, *Bachelder Papers*, 2:1046; Boyles, *Reminiscences of the Civil War*, 41; Busey & Busey, *Confederate Casualties*, 3:1328.

17 *OR* 27/1:363; Dawes, *Service With the 6th Wisconsin*, 175; Boyles, *Reminiscences*, 41; Caldwell, *The History of a Brigade*, 97; Tompkins & Tompkins, *Company K*, 19-20; Ladd & Ladd, *Bachelder Papers*, 2:1046. In a second letter to Bachelder (June 2, 1884) Private Leach (Company E, 1st South Carolina) recalled that part of the brigade (14th and 13th South Carolina) went prone "well down in [the] valley" in front of the seminary before his line continued the advance at the "double-quick," which would have been done with weapons at "right shoulder shift." Federal witnesses generally agree that they saw the Confederates extending their line along Seminary Ridge by flanking south almost in parade ground formation, as opposed to getting hit head on. To do that the Confederates would have to have come on line from behind the North Carolinians.

18 *Pennsylvania at Gettysburg*, 2:747, 749; Boyden to Gamble; Brown, *A Colonel at Gettysburg*, 84; Bachelder's Map 13 has Scales and Perrin crossing Willoughby Run in battle lines at 3:30 p.m. Federal testimony states the brigades crossed in column of three or two regimental fronts, and did not pass through Herbst Woods but perpendicular to it. McFarland (151st Pennsylvania) noted the action near the seminary lasted about 10 minutes (3:35 p.m. to 3:45 p.m.) In his notes in the same work, Bachelder posited 10 to 15 minutes. (3:35 p.m. to 3:50 p.m.) Boyden noted about 20 minutes (3:35 p.m. to 3:55 p.m.), and Brown said it lasted, at most, 15-20 minutes (3:35 to 3:55 p.m.). Bachelder reasonably concluded that the Confederates overran Seminary Ridge at 4:00 p.m.

head wound, while Lt. Henry M. Gordon lay helpless on the ground with a crippled leg. Captain Asher Gaylord (Company D) was shot through both legs. Lieutenant Lyman R. Nicholson (Company G) incurred a fatal shoulder wound but refused evacuation from the field.[19]

The Seminary

The 400 or so officers and men comprising the 24th Michigan and Biddle's survivors crouching behind the hasty barricade cut loose at long range as soon as the North Carolinians crossed the middle ridge. Colonel Theodore B. Gates (20th N.Y.S.M.) believed his brigade sent the Rebs skedaddling. For the next 10 minutes they put down a scathing fire that helped pin the Carolinians in the drainage area; being prone, the Rebels replied at a much slower rate. Still, many of their bullets found their marks.[20]

Colonel Chapman Biddle trotted his horse behind the regiment-sized brigade, encouraging the men to hold fast. A bullet smacked into his mount and another grazed the colonel's skull. When he yanked on the reins, the horse reared and the stunned Biddle plummeted to the ground. He staggered to his feet, apparently uninjured except for the spot where the minié ball had skinned his scalp. Turning the brigade over to Colonel Gates, he wobbled to the seminary to get his wound bandaged.

Despite suffering from a wound in his side, Cpl. John M. Bingham (Company A, 121st Pennsylvania) refused to leave the ranks. Acting Adjutant Andrew G. Tucker (142nd Pennsylvania) got hit for the third and last time. Lieutenant Alfred McCalmont and an enlisted man carried him to the seminary, where he would die two days later. In Company A, Capt. Horatio N. Warren recalled that the men shot so fast they burned their hands on their rifle barrels. Many tossed their fouled weapons aside and picked up others to fire.[21]

19 Musser, Unpublished Report; *OR* 27/1:339, 343.

20 *OR* 27/1:321; *Pennsylvania at Gettysburg*, 2:747, 749. Colonel McFarland said the 151st Pennsylvania was behind the barricade for 10 minutes. Two pages later, Bachelder noted the regiment was in the woodlot for about 10-15 minutes.

21 *History of the 121st Regiment*, 53, 55, 59; Warren, *Two Reunions*, 22, 23, 25; McCalmont, *Extracts From McCalmont Letters*, 58.

Low Ground, West of the Emmitsburg Road

General Howard's orders to John Buford to support the embattled infantry, relayed via Captain Halstead, could not have sat well with the cavalryman. Misgivings aside, he was a soldier's soldier and orders were orders. "Come on, boys," he ordered.

With the 3rd Indiana in the lead, Buford spurred his white horse ahead of the brigade column. Lieutenant Calef followed with two depleted limbers and two 3-inch rifles. The ground was too uneven to charge over, so the cavalry trotted northwest to the Fairfield Road and then turned north into the woodlot south of the seminary. Three companies of the 3rd Indiana (150 enlisted men) dismounted behind the low stone wall closest to the seminary and formed the first line. The right wing, under Maj. Charles Lemon, remained mounted behind them as the second line. The horseholders for the front line fell in behind Lemon's troopers. Two squadrons (180 men) from the 8th New York took cover on the 3rd's left, and one squadron from the 12th Illinois (110 men) completed the line to the Fairfield Road.[22]

Fairfield Road

22 Flavius Josephus Bellamy to Dear Parents, July 3, 1863, Indiana State Library; Day, "Opening the Battle"; Calef, "Gettysburg Notes," 51; *OR* 27/1:934; Busey & Martin, *Regimental Strengths and Losses*, 106; Ladd & Ladd, *Bachelder Papers*, 1:130; George Oliver Dibble to Dear Brother Albert, July 7, 1863, Vertical Files, V6-NY8-CA, Library, GNMP, typescript; Nesbit, *General History of Company D*, 15. Colonel Gamble stated that half of each regiment dismounted behind the stone wall, which should have consisted of: 3rd Indiana (three companies, 115 men/230-foot front); 8th New York (three companies, 135 men/270 foot-front), and 12th Illinois (two companies, 110 men/220 foot-front). Six days later, however, Pvt. George O. Dibble (Company A, 8th New York) informed his brother Albert that the regiment deployed two squadrons (four companies/180 men/360 feet) along the wall, which added about 100 more men to the line and extended the front another 200 feet. If that was the case, the cavalry brigade front would have taken the line from the south side of the seminary to the Fairfield Road. Private Thomas G. Day (Company E, 3rd Indiana) wrote that the line stretched to the south side of the Fairfield Road near the Shultz house and remained mounted behind the stone wall. If that regiment deployed in two lines, the others likely did also, with the horseholders behind the second line to protect the men and mounts from incoming fire. Nesbit, *General History*, noted two guns supporting the provost company. The only place from which their fire could have covered the field to the northwest was from north of the Fairfield Road. The cavalry placements from north to south are according to Bachelder, Map 13, though I disagree with his placement.

VMI graduate James "Little Jim" Lane assumed command of a brigade when its commander was killed at Sharpsburg. On July 1, his men were still living with the stigma of having shot Thomas "Stonewall" Jackson at Chancellorsville. His command was fortunate to avoid heavy losses on the first day at Gettysburg, but was selected to participate in "Pickett's Charge" on July 3. *LOC*

Earlier, operating without oversight from commander Dorsey Pender, Brig. James H. Lane's Brigade reached Willoughby Run. There, he ordered the 7th North Carolina (on the south side of the Fairfield Road) to move east and to the right about 450 yards. This allowed the brigade to cross the road through the downed fence at the Finnefrock woodlot. The 7th maneuvered into skirmish formation and easily drove back their counterparts from the 8th Illinois Cavalry, who wanted to annoy but not fully engage an infantry regiment. With his right flank covered, Lane began his advance west with his North Carolinians.

Lane's movement attracted the attention of the main body of the 8th Illinois on the Rebel brigade's right rear. The Hoosiers made several annoying dashes upon the 7th, which made it nearly impossible for the regiment to keep up with the rest of the brigade extending out on its right. This, in turn, forced Col. William M. Barbour of the 37th to detach Capt. Daniel L. Hudson with his 40-man Company G to extend the skirmish line to the left of the 7th.[23]

23 *OR* 27/2:665; "The Battle of Gettysburg," *Chicago Tribune*, November 24, 1863, 2. A July 4, 1863, letter from Maj. William Medill (8th Illinois) noted that the regiment pestered the Confederates from the right-rear, and not from behind a stone wall south of the Fairfield Road.

Elizabeth Shultz House

Artillerist Lt. John Calef unlimbered his two rifled pieces in front of the Elizabeth Shultz place, which provided his artillerists with a good view of the northern end of the middle ridge. Thus began a slow and deliberate fire against Lane's regiments, which had finally come into range to the southwest. The artillery fire attracted Lane's attention. He spotted infantry and mounted cavalry inside the woodline between his position and the Shultz house.

Private John W. Nesbit (Company D, 149th Pennsylvania) kept an eye on the Federal troopers. "The cavalry squad kept up appearances in good style, and it was thought they would charge, but they didn't," he later wrote. "They charged to the rear and left us in a hurry." The abandoned provost guard joined in the shooting from behind the rail fence bordering the western face of Shultz's wood lot. Combined with pressure from dismounted troopers (8th Illinois) on the right flank, and unsure what was off his right flank, Lane's attack stalled.[24]

The Railroad Cut to the Seminary

Most of the Northerners along the Seminary Ridge line knew they could not hold out much longer. By the time Pender's two brigades (Scales and Perrin) reached the middle ridge, Brig. Gen. John Robinson's division front to the north (Paul and Baxter) was starting to collapse. Mixed regiments from his command were gathering along the northern side of the railroad grade behind Seminary Ridge. The wounded and discouraged men of his division were already filling the track bed or heading for town. The loss of so many regimental and company-level officers had destroyed command control. With their brigades reduced to regiments, and regiments to companies, many surviving officers

24 *OR* 27/2:665; Nesbit, *General History of Company D*, 15. Lane reported that he ran into enemy cavalry and some infantry, but he did not mention that they were behind a stone wall. His men, he continued, gave a Rebel Yell and charged. No other contemporary accounts support his claim. By the end of the fighting on July 1, Lane's entire brigade had suffered 30 confirmed casualties, which indicates his men did not engage in serious fighting. (Compare those numbers to losses incurred by Scales and Perrin farther north.) The stone wall that today runs along the tour road opposite the Shultz house may not have existed in 1863. Some veterans wrote that the lower stone wall was replaced with a taller one.

decided on their own that the time had leave. Robinson's men had reached their breaking point, and his division was unraveling.[25]

In no particular order, officers took it upon themselves to pull their men out of the fighting along Seminary Ridge. Lieutenant Colonel John D. Musser (143rd Pennsylvania, Stone's brigade) reluctantly gave the order to fall back, leaving his dead and wounded behind. Sergeant Patrick DeLacy (Company A) carried the bloodied national flag while Cpl. William S. Downing (Company I) brought off the state banner. Nursing his wounded hand, Lt. Charles W. Betzenberger (Company I) found himself moving to the rear, as did the injured Capt. Charles M. Conyngham (Company A) and Lt. Orin E. Vaughan (Company K). Captain Asher Gaylord (Company D) lay in the orchard shot through both legs and unable to move. Close by, Lt. Henry M. Gordon (Company F), disabled by a leg wound, attempted to crawl after the command but could not catch up.[26]

The 143rd dragged along some of the survivors of the Lt. Col. Walton Dwight's 149th Pennsylvania. Private William Wright (Company I) chucked his knapsack and cumbersome haversack in the road and left the field armed only with his canteen. A few men stayed behind with Lieutenant Wilber's section to assist the gunners.[27]

Colonel Wainwright rode over to Stevens's battery to find out why his guns had fallen silent. To his ire, he found the battery limbering up. Wainwright (who still believed he was defending what he thought was Cemetery Ridge) loudly demanded they stop. Lieutenant Edward N. Whittier retorted that General Wadsworth had advised them to leave. Wainwright countermanded the general and galloped to each of his batteries to the north (except Stewart's) and told them to stay at their posts and fight. It was then that an aide informed him that the Rebels had flanked him on the right.

Looking northeast, Wainwright initially thought the lines of men coming in from that area belonged to Oliver Howard's XI Corps. A volley in the wrong direction indicated otherwise. Union infantry was moving to escape along the elevated railroad bed. There was no position left to defend. Wainwright spurred

25 *OR* 27/1:321. According to Col. Theodore Gates, most of the infantry had left before his end of the line departed.

26 Musser, Unpublished Report; Downing to Wife, July 6, 1863; *OR* 27/1:339.

27 Tomasak, *Harris Journal*, 64-65; William Wright to Mary Wright, July 7, 1863.

back along his line yelling at his officers to limber and retire at a walk to avoid generating a panic.[28]

Unfortunately, the word arrived too late for some of the gunners in the Thompson orchard. A private named Benjamin H. Stillman (detached from Company B, 7th Wisconsin) served as "Number 5" on the piece in the road. He was back at the limber handing off a 12-pounder canister round to Charley Sprague, the "Number 4." Sprague, who was going to run it to the piece, turned his head to look toward the front and a minié ball struck him in the forehead and killed him.

Stillman stepped over his friend at a run, intent on placing the three rounds he cradled in his arms close to the gun to make them more accessible to "Number 2," the man who loaded the piece. On the way, Stillman saw the diminutive Lieutenant Davison begin to buckle under the impact of a bullet that broke his leg. Seeing that the gun had plenty of ammunition stacked nearby, the private dropped his rounds in the road and caught the lieutenant as he was falling. He supported Davison as the injured lieutenant ordered the men to load with canister and wait for the command to fire.

At that point, Stillman hoisted Davison over his shoulder, ran back perhaps 50 feet, and lowered him behind a slight rise of ground to protect him from incoming rounds. What he did not realize was that by that time the guns had retired to the ridge crest behind him.

With the artillery falling quiet, another temporary, unnerving silence fell over the Chambersburg Pike. Except for a few rifle and musket potshots, both sides—having expended most of their ammunition and now partially shielded from one another by the low-lying smoke—used the abatement to catch their collective breath and figure out what to do next.[29]

At the left center of the barricade, Maj. Alexander Biddle (121st Pennsylvania) stared through the thick pall of smoke in the woods and caught sight of infantry moving by the right flank across the front "as if on parade" not more than 150 yards from the works. Trooper Thomas G. Day (Company E, 3rd Indiana) spotted them, too. Day, atop his horse immediately south of the seminary, watched the mystery soldiers marching by platoons by fours toward

28 Nevins, *A Diary of Battle*, 236.

29 B. H. Stillman, "B. H. Stillman and His Civil War Record," *Eugene* [OR] *Guard*, February 18, 1912.

the southern end of the barricade. He took note that many of them wore blue uniforms, or parts of them, and carried what looked to be U.S. colors.

Without orders, the Union infantry at the barricade shot at them, deliberately trying to provoke a response. In the haze their officers mistook the targets for their own men and immediately ordered a cease firing. Major Biddle stooped to look under the smoke and recognized them as Confederates. What he did not know was that they were the 13th and 14th South Carolina, part of Abner Perrin's Brigade. It looked as though they possibly overlapped the unoccupied southern part of the works. Biddle rushed back to the seminary to warn Brig. Gen. Thomas A. Rowley of the threat. Rowley ordered Biddle back to the line.[30]

Colonel Chapman Biddle returned to his brigade with his head bandaged. The dismounted Colonel Gates (20th N.Y.S.M.) hurriedly briefed him on the situation. Biddle and Gates noticed the two South Carolina regiments had not completely cleared Scales's right flank and ordered the brigade to retreat to the low stone wall running north from the front of the seminary along the lane. Though Gates later claimed the "troops moved off in tolerable order," men in the 121st Pennsylvania referred to it as a "skedaddle." Just like others would on different part of the line, eyewitnesses saw the same event and reported it in starkly different terms.[31]

A short distance to the north, Capt. Albert A. Edwards realized the "cotillion" had ended. He ordered the 24th Michigan to join the remnant of the Iron Brigade in the retreat. Colonel Wainwright rode up to order Captain Cooper's battery about the same time Lt. Col. Alfred B. McCalmont (142nd

30 *OR* 27/1:321, 323-324; Day, "Opening the Battle"; *History of the 121st Regiment*, 55. Popular knowledge claims Rowley was drunk at Gettysburg, and even fell from his horse. Not so, claims John F. Krumwiede, *Disgrace at Gettysburg: The Arrest and Court- Martial of Brigadier General Thomas A. Rowley, USA* (Jefferson, NC: McFarland & Co., 2006), 59-102, 108-132. A wide number of primary sources convincingly argue that Rowley was not drunk, but was suffering from large painful boils, could barely ride a horse, and his doctor advised that he not go into battle.

31 Caldwell, *The History of a Brigade*, 98; Ladd & Ladd, *Bachelder Papers*, 2:904; Boyles, *Reminiscences*, 41; Brown, *A Colonel at Gettysburg*, 81; *OR* 27/1:315, 321, 323; *History of the 121st Regiment*, 55; *Pennsylvania at Gettysburg*, 2:652, 653. Neither Gates nor the Survivors Association mention the stone wall. Major Biddle wrote that around 4:00 p.m. the brigade retreated to the front of the seminary, as did the account in *Pennsylvania at Gettysburg*. His cousin Col. Alexander Biddle (121st Pennsylvania), claimed the regiment defended the "fence" on the hospital grounds. Four Rebel accounts reference the stone wall.

Pennsylvania) trotted up to inform him of the obvious: the infantry to his left had gone and he had better leave also.[32]

While Stevens's and Cooper's artillerists hastily hooked the trails of their pieces to the limbers, the 14th and 13th South Carolina moved into line to the right of the 16th North Carolina. "Charge, bayonets!" reverberated above them. The men in the front rank leveled their weapons, those in the rear rank kept their rifles shouldered. and all advanced at the quick step. Despite the horrendous racket, some of the men distinctly recalled hearing Yankee officers along the wall loudly admonishing their soldiers not to fire until ordered to do so.[33]

3:45 p.m. to 4:00 p.m.[34]

Charles Wainwright looked toward the western side of the woodlot and saw Sgt. T. Rutledge Owens (Company F, 14th South Carolina) with the regimental battle flag climbing the barricade. Private James A. Gardner (Cooper's battery) noticed him, too. On command, the men in Biddle's brigade stood and fired by files from the right, cutting down the Rebels like a farmer wielding a scythe. By the time the shooting had traveled to the left of the line, the Northerners had reloaded on the right flank and initiated a second round of killing.[35]

Their initial volley hit the 14th South Carolina hard. Private W. Scott Allen (Company K) watched as 34 of the 39 men in his line fell, four of them dead. Four of the five men with the family name Ouzts in the company were among them. George Ouzts died from a head wound, Franklin took a bullet in the leg, Martin caught one in the thigh, and a minié grazed Cpl. William H. in the head. Marion Ouzts passed through unscathed, but the carnage may have prompted him to desert on July 3. Of the regiment's officers, only Allen's brother, Lt. James Allen, escaped injury. Lieutenant Brantley Bryan and Lt. Simon Cogburn lay among the wounded. With the exception of one man, the members of the regimental color guard died at their posts, including Sgt. Rutledge Owens, who

32 Nevins, *A Diary of Battle*, 236; *Pennsylvania at Gettysburg*, 2:879.

33 Tompkins & Tompkins, *Company K*, 19-20.

34 *OR*, 27/1:266. Wadsworth reported the time of the retreat as 3:45 p.m.

35 Ladd & Ladd, *Bachelder Papers*, 3:1621; Nevins, *A Diary of Battle*, 236; Tompkins & Tompkins, Company K, 20; *History of the 121st Regiment*, 52; *Pennsylvania at Gettysburg*, 2:653.

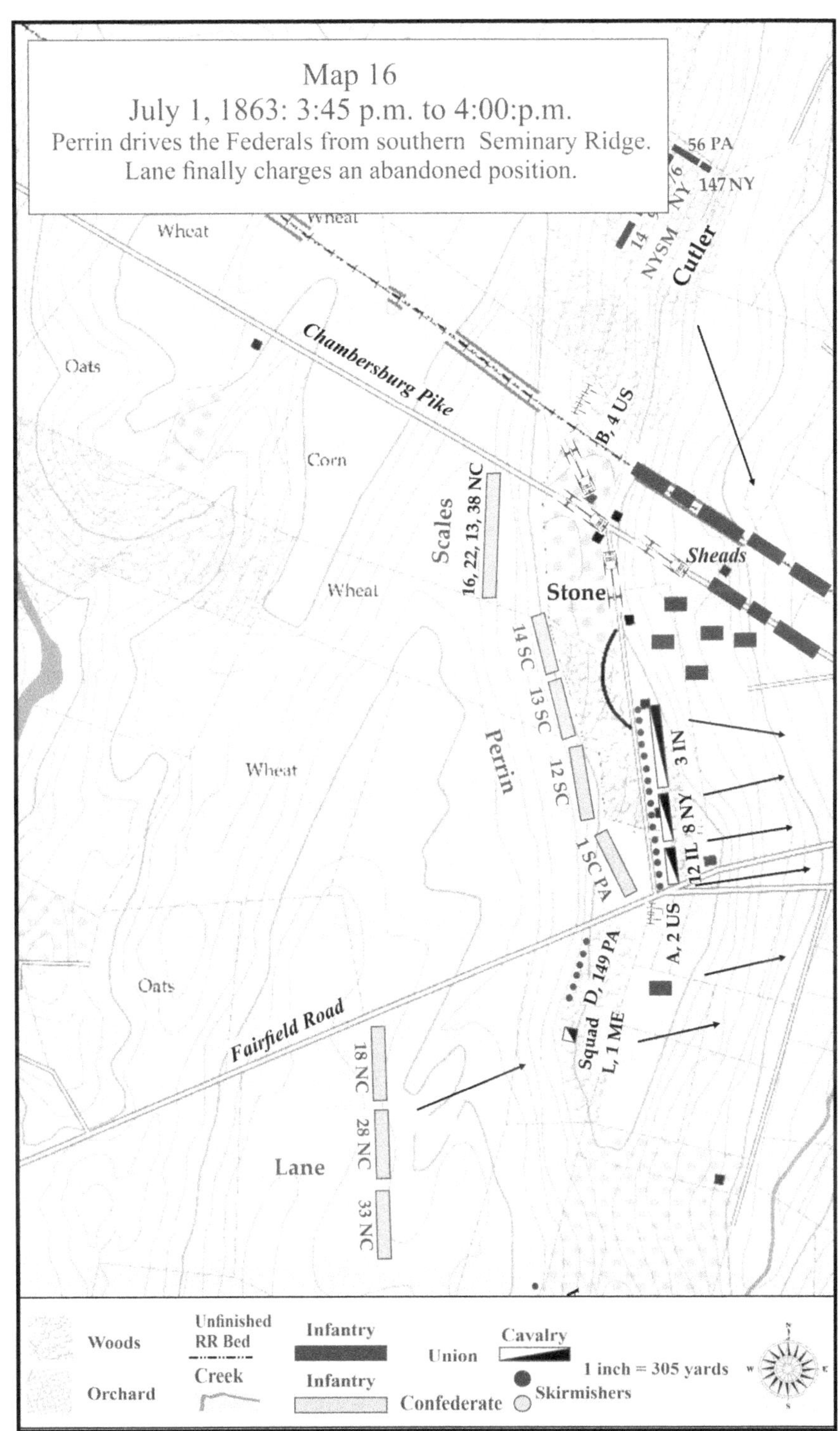
Map 16
July 1, 1863: 3:45 p.m. to 4:00:p.m.
Perrin drives the Federals from southern Seminary Ridge.
Lane finally charges an abandoned position.
56 PA
147 NY
76 NY
14 NYSM
Cutler
Wheat
Oats
Chambersburg Pike
B, 4 US
Corn
Scales
16, 22, 13, 38 NC
Sheads
Stone
Wheat
14 SC
13 SC
12 SC
1 SC PA
Perrin
3 IN
8 NY
12 IL
A, 2 US
D, 149 PA
Squad L, 1 ME
Wheat
Oats
Fairfield Road
18 NC
28 NC
33 NC
Lane
Woods
Orchard
Unfinished RR Bed
Creek
Infantry
Union
Infantry
Confederate
Cavalry
Skirmishers
1 inch = 305 yards

took five rounds and bled out. The South Carolinians closed ranks, returned the volley, and went to ground, pinned in place by gunfire.[36]

From the left side of the Seminary Ridge line, several of Gamble's cavalrymen snapped off rounds at the 13th South Carolina when it reached the edge of the woodlot. Major Charles Lemon (3rd Indiana) shouted, "Don't shoot, they are our men!" Moments later, the color bearer of the 13th dropped the Federal flag and held aloft the Saint Andrew's Cross. The Rebels opened fire. As Pvt. George O. Dibble (Company A, 8th New York) put it in a letter to his brother, "The rebels deceived us making us think they were our soldiers until quite near us."[37]

Many of their rounds went high and struck the horses in the second and third lines. Company E, 3rd Indiana lost 10 mounts in a matter of minutes. Major Lemon was struck twice, once in the forehead and again in the chest. Private Day (Company E, 3rd Indiana) watched him tumble from the saddle, fatally wounded. In response, troopers mounted and dismounted unleashed a devastating wall of lead at the Confederates with their breechloading carbines.

One of the injured troopers lived to vividly describe the action. "We went popping at them. They fell like rain," wrote Pvt. Daniel W. Pulis (Company D, 8th New York) in a letter home to his parents. "The ground soon got covered with them." As much of the seminary lane crackled with riflery from both sides, Lieutenant Calef decided it was time to limber his pair of rifles and make for the rear.[38]

Back near the Shultz house, the ill General Rowley told Capt. James Glenn (Company D, 149th Pennsylvania) to quit the field with the provost guard. It was too little, too late: the men in the provost guard decided to act on their own.

36 John A. Chapman, *History of Edgefield County From the Earliest Settlements to 1897* (Newberry, SC, 1897), 124; *Pennsylvania at Gettysburg*, 2:747, 748; Ladd & Ladd, *Bachelder Papers*, 1:90, 147; Busey & Busey, *Confederate Casualties*, 3:1360-1362; Brown, *A Colonel at Gettysburg*, 85. At one time as many as 14 men with the name Ouzts served in Company K. All were from Edgefield County, South Carolina.

37 Day, "Opening the Battle"; Dibble to Brother. For a different perspective of Perrin's attack and the cavalry involved in the action, see Wittenberg, *"The Devil's to Pay,"* 139-145.

38 Daniel Pulis to Parents, July 6, 1863, in "Regimental Histories, 8th New York Cavalry," http://www.beach-mcgee.com/Beach/Military%20Records/8th%20New%20York%20Cavalry%20Regimental%20History.pdf, accessed Feb. 17, 2023; Bellamy to Parents; Dibble to Brother; "First Shot at Gettysburg," 5; "List of Casualties in the Eighth New York Cavalry," https://museum.dmna.ny.gov/index.php/?cID=2551, accessed Feb. 12, 2023.

Mexican War veteran Abner Perrin led a brigade as a colonel at Gettysburg because its commander, Samuel McGowan, was wounded that May at Chancellorsville. His gallant conduct earned him brigadier's stars that September. The ambitious officer would die leading a counterattack at Spotsylvania on May 12, 1864, shot seven times. *Generals in Gray*

Corporal Henry B. Callahan hollered something about getting off the ridge to avoid capture. He snatched up a loose cavalry horse, climbed into the saddle, dug in his heels, and galloped down the Fairfield Road toward town. Private David H. Morton grabbed another unclaimed horse and followed him.

Captain Glenn, with Sgt. John Snodgrass and Pvts. John W. Nesbit, Joseph C. Bell, and several others took off on the road down the east side of the ridge. They left behind the dead Pvt. Joseph Baldwin, the dying Sgt. Alexander M. Stewart, and the lamed Pvt. Andrew Crooks. Private James Roach and a couple of others on the south side of the road never heard the order to leave.[39]

Rowley soon passed the word to retreat to the men north of the seminary. As the regiments peeled away from the left, discipline evaporated and a mob of Union men surged toward the closest avenue of escape: the Chambersburg Pike. Lieutenant Colonel George McFarland (151st Pennsylvania), whose horse had just been shot out from under him, realized he had no one on his left flank. He was about to retreat when the cavalrymen fired into the 13th South Carolina. When he saw the Rebels waver, McFarland yelled at his stalwarts, "Give them another volley, boys!" A "manly" cheer coupled with gunfire erupted from the

39 Nesbit, *General History of Company D*, 15. If Captain Glenn assumed temporary command of Biddle's brigade, as noted in *Pennsylvania at Gettysburg*, it likely occurred after what remained of the brigade reached Cemetery Hill.

Pennsylvanians. The 13th South Carolina began retreating toward the 1st and 12th regiments.[40]

Surprised at the repulse of one of his regiments, Col. Abner Perrin reacted by unsheathing his sword, flashing it above his head, and charging through the 1st and 12th regiments into the retreating 13th. His prompt action and obvious gallantry helped stem the tide, herd the troops back to the edge of the woods, and regain control. Once he was satisfied the regiment was reorganizing, Perrin spurred his horse back and forth behind the 1st and 12th South Carolina, shouting and pointing his sword toward the stone wall. He knew momentum was everything, and that the attack must be pressed ahead. In a few minutes, the two regiments flanked south and went into line on the right of the 13th and 14th South Carolina. The Fairfield Road constricted the brigade's frontage and squeezed the right wing of the 1st South Carolina into a disorganized mass along the southern face of the woodlot. The Yankee troopers there hammered the Palmetto troops with rapid carbine and pistol fire. Tactical confusion notwithstanding, the South Carolinians responded by pushing forward, firing from tree to tree.[41]

"Retreat, men! Fall back in good order!" shouted Colonel McFarland.

With his exhausted Pennsylvanians scattering from the wall, the colonel stopped to look under the smoke to ascertain what the Rebs were doing.As he did so, a bullet fired from the southwest shattered both of his legs. He fell heavily on his left side with his head toward the woods. Private Randle D. Sayn (Company B), standing just a few feet away, knelt by by his side. The wounded officer waved him off. "Never mind me, but run." Sayn took the advice to heart and ran as fast as he could to catch up with what remained of the regiment.

Company F's Pvt. Lyman D. Wilson, however, would not abandon his colonel. He pulled McFarland's arm around his neck, hauled the officer to his feet, and dragged him toward the seminary. A bullet clipped off the middle button on the colonel's coat sleeve before Wilson lowered him against the north wall.[42]

The firefight between the cavalry and the 1st South Carolina on the southern end of the line lasted for several minutes. Federal casualties escalated. "It seems

40 Ladd & Ladd, *Bachelder Papers*, 1:302. None of Bachelder's maps regarding Perrin's assault are consistent with firsthand accounts.

41 Ladd & Ladd, *Bachelder Papers*, 1:302.

42 Sayre, "A Day at Gettysburg," 3; Ladd & Ladd, *Bachelder Papers*, 1:90.

miraculous how I escaped injury," wrote Private Dibble (Company A, 8th New York) to his brother. "I was in the front rank. The dead and wounded lay on all sides of me while I received not a scratch." Companies B and K, which were mounted, suffered the most. Each lost seven men wounded, one of whom—Cpl. Edward Marriott (Company K)—was mistakenly reported as killed. Before the fighting ended, the 8th New York lost 36 men killed, wounded, and captured, which were heavy losses by cavalry standards. Together, the 3rd Indiana and the 12th Illinois lost more than 60 men.[43]

Artillerist Wainwright sat astride his horse anxiously studying the infantry funneling into the railroad cut and the Chambersburg Pike. He despaired of getting his guns away in time and counted it as good fortune that the batteries, except those of B, 4th U.S., had sent their caissons to the rear. Lieutenant Benjamin Wilber remained at his two rifles in Riggs's orchard, providing covering fire to keep the Rebels in front at bay.

While the cavalry slowed down Perrin's 1st and 12th South Carolina regiments, Stevens's 5th Maine battery and Cooper's Pennsylvanians entered the road three limbers abreast and started toward town at the "walk" as ordered. Davison's three caissons followed. By the time Private Stillman left the wounded Lieutenant Davison under cover, his limbered piece had halted in the road on top of the ridge, waiting for its turn to leave the field. Stillman ran over to his gun where the chief of the piece, Sgt. Andrew McBride, told him they were out of canister. The private recalled leaving three rounds in the road and offered to go back and get them. He raced to within 50 feet of the stalled Rebel line, picked up the discarded rounds, and ran back to the battery only to find that it was already halfway to town. He chased after it.[44]

43 Ladd & Ladd, *Bachelder Papers*, 2:1046; Dibble to Brother; "List of Casualties in the Eighth New York Cavalry"; *OR* 27/1:185; Bellamy to Parents; George W. Shears, "The 12th Illinois Cav., Its Part in the Gettysburg Campaign," *NT*, February 5, 1891, 3. Company A, 8th New York, lost one killed and one wounded. Companies B and K suffered the heaviest losses and the recorded wounds in K indicate they remained mounted behind the wall. The company reported the following wounds: one leg, two knee, one shin, one arm, one head, and one unknown. The leg and lower extremity injuries indicate the injured were higher than the wall. Bellamy and Shearer report, respectively, one major, one captain, and two lieutenants killed (3rd Indiana) and one lieutenant (12th Illinois) killed. The *OR* states that the 3rd Indiana lost one officer killed (Lemon) and one wounded. The 12th Illinois had no officers killed and three wounded, for a total of five officers between the two units.

44 Wilber Letter; Stillman, "B. H. Stillman and His Civil War Record"; Nevins, *A Diary of Battle*, 236. Wilber fired until the infantry reached him, when he was ordered to retreat.

To the south, the 14th South Carolina charged the seminary and the 1st South Carolina advanced on the stone wall. Buford ordered his men to skedaddle. The mounted troopers escaped, leaving the dismounted and those who had not heard the order to scramble after their horses. The 8th New York's Private Dibble found himself alone at the wall. His horse had disappeared, so he ran for his life. The less fortunate Capt. Charles D. Follett (Company D) lay behind the line, mortally wounded. The morning skirmishing and the stand at the wall drained Gamble's three regiments of 80, and perhaps more, in killed, wounded, and missing.[45]

45 "List of Casualties in the Eighth New York Cavalry"; *OR*, 27/1:185.

Chapter Thirteen

"The order to retreat was given, or understood, for few orders were given on that field."

— Lt. Walter T. Chester, Company D, 94th New York

Collapse

3:00 p.m. to 4:30 p.m.

3:00 p.m. to 3:15 p.m.
The Situation on Oak Ridge

For a considerable amount of time, Colonel Baxter's Pennsylvanians, Bay Staters, and New Yorkers kept up a steady skirmish fire against Alfred Iverson's survivors in the drainage area paralleling Oak Ridge. Despite being pinned down, the Rebels showed no obvious intention of breaking off the engagement.

On the left of the Union line, the 11th Pennsylvania's mascot, a male mutt named "Sallie," entertained the men by snapping at the dust kicked up by low-flying bullets. A shell burst over Company A and barely missed crippling Pvt. George Cramer, who informed his wife that had a rock not deflected the fragment, which bruised his right arm just above the elbow, no knife would have been needed to remove the limb.[1]

1 Eldred, "Gettysburg," 4; William Edward Foster to My own dear Mother, July 6, 1863, https://sparedcreative21.art.blog/2020/03/26/1863-william-edward-foster-to-martha-willi

Lieutenant Rush Cady (Company K, 97th New York) won the admiration of Sgt. Michael Kirley for calmly encouraging the men heedless of the whistling minié balls that flew past them. Cady went from man to man, taking cartridges from their boxes and methodically tearing them open and placing them back in their tins to save reloading time. "I must say," Kirley recollected, "it is the only battle I have been in where I could see the Rebs. Every time I fired I took good aim."[2]

In front of the 88th Pennsylvania, Lieutenant Boone spotted white flags on bayonets poking up from the drainage. Lieutenant Colonel John P. Spofford (97th New York), sitting atop his mount, also noticed them. General Baxter thought more Rebels might be in the area and feared a trap. He loudly discussed the matter with the 88th's officers. Without warning, however, Spofford yelled as loud as he could, "Boys of the 97th, let us go for them and capture them!" Sergeant Kirley had just fired his first prepared cartridge when he heard the order to charge. Steel clanking on steel rippled up and down the line as the New Yorkers fixed bayonets. Company C, the color company, bolted over the low wall, dragging the regiment and part of the 11th Pennsylvania into the action. "We were scattered all over the field," Kirley recollected. The 97th's charge

ams-foster/, accessed Feb. 12, 2023; Cook, *History of the Twelfth Massachusetts Volunteers*, 101; *OR* 27/1:130; Detre, "88th Penna Regt at Gettysburg"; Vautier, *History of the 88th Pennsylvania*, 310. Traditional interpretations have Baxter charging Iverson's men within a very short time after repulsing and pinning them down. The four sources listed above, however, uniformly confirm that the brigade was essentially out of ammunition when it charged. This can only mean Baxter's troops fired heavier and longer than we may have realized.

2 M. Kirby to Mr. Daniel [Cady], September 7, 1863, https://cwl.dhinitiative.org/islandora/object/HamiltonCivilWar%3A1044, accessed Feb. 15, 2023; "From the Memoirs of Capt. Lewis T. Hicks. of Co. E, 20th Regiment," *The State Journal* (Raleigh, NC), April 27, 1917, 11, 14. I added correct punctuation to Kirley's quote to make his run-on sentences more understandable. Hicks's memoirs should be used with caution. For example: he claimed artillery fire singed off half his beard, but the 20th North Carolina was not close to any artillery; that his men waved boots and hats on their bayonets to indicate surrender, but no other accounts (and there are many) mention that unusual method); that his men killed a Federal general as well as many of his 30-man mounted escort (no other accounts support this openly preposterous claim); that the smoke was so thick no one could see more than 10 feet (no other accounts support this and some, like Sgt. Kirley's refute it). Finally, he claimed his lieutenant was shot in the head by an Alabama regiment from behind, but according to Busey & Busey, *Confederate Casualties*, 2:951-952, Hicks and his two lieutenants were captured, and his company only had one man killed outright—a corporal.

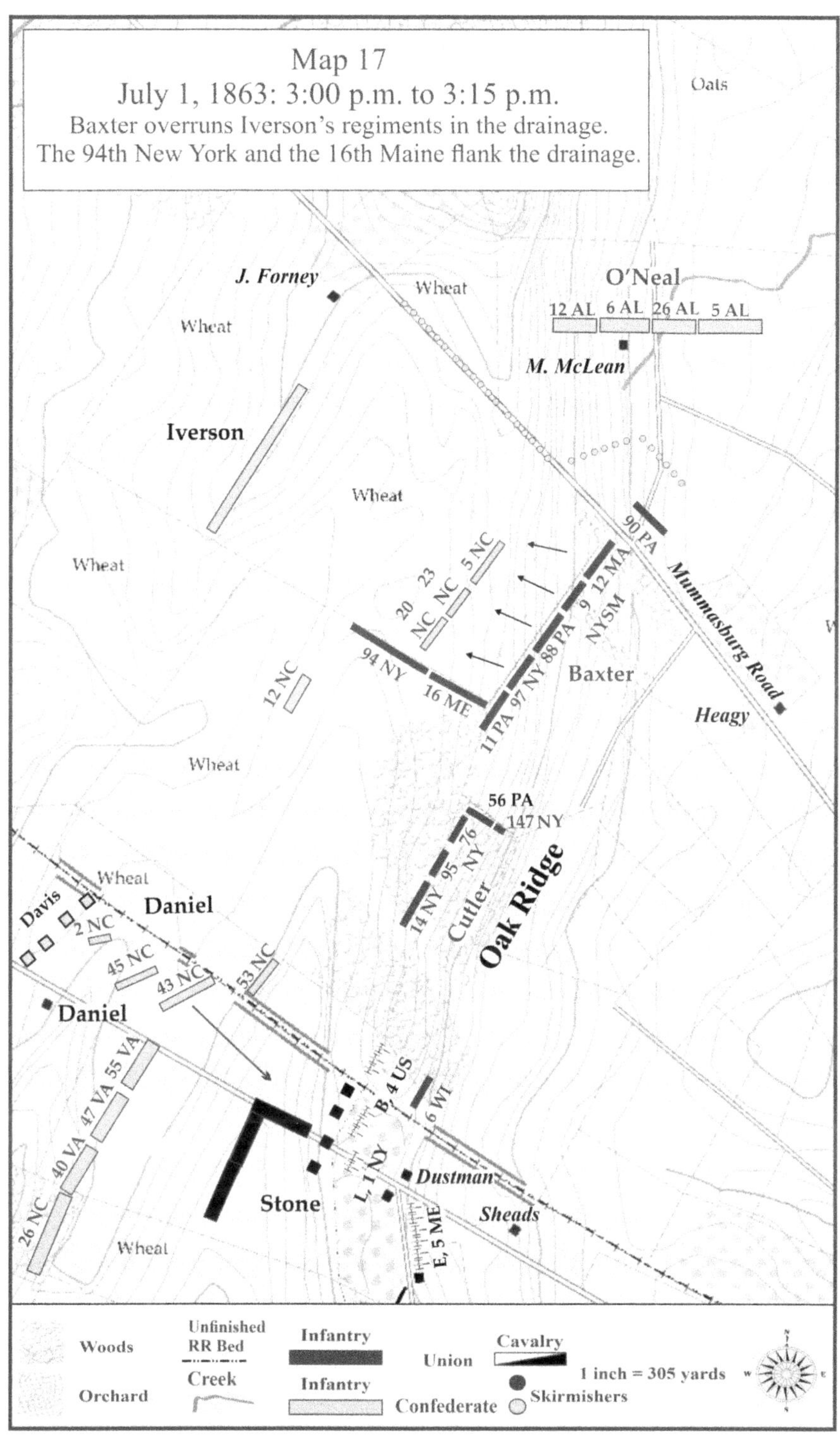
Map 17
July 1, 1863: 3:00 p.m. to 3:15 p.m.
Baxter overruns Iverson's regiments in the drainage.
The 94th New York and the 16th Maine flank the drainage.
Oats
J. Forney
Wheat
O'Neal
12 AL
6 AL
26 AL
5 AL
M. McLean
Iverson
90 PA
12 MA
9 NYSM
88 PA
97 NY
11 PA
Baxter
5 NC
23 NC
20 NC
94 NY
16 ME
12 NC
Mummasburg Road
Heagy
56 PA
147 NY
76 NY
95 NY
14 NY
Cutler
Oak Ridge
Davis
Daniel
2 NC
45 NC
43 NC
53 NC
55 VA
47 VA
40 VA
26 NC
B, 4 US
6 WI
L, 1 NY
Dustman
Stone
Sheads
E, 5 ME
Woods
Orchard
Unfinished RR Bed
Creek
Infantry
Union
Confederate
Cavalry
Skirmishers
1 inch = 305 yards

caught Col. Charles Wheelock unawares, but he followed his men into the fight. The surprised Baxter joining in screaming, "Up, boys, and give them steel!"

The sudden blue rush startled the pinned Tar Heels. A majority of the still ambulatory North Carolinians stood frantically waving white handkerchiefs in attempts to avoid getting skewered or shot. Some ran toward and even through the knots of approaching Union men. Judging from the scores of Rebel casualties lying about, Kirley concluded. "The 97th did not fire for nothing."[3]

Privates Joseph Trainer and George Penair led part of Company D, 88th Pennsylvania, into the scrap as the momentum and wild cheering traveled north through the ranks. Color Corporal Lewis W. Bonnin stayed with the color company despite being badly wounded. The 9th N.Y.S.M. joined them. When the four regiments off to the south sprang over the wall, the men on the left end of the 12th Massachusetts started hollering and screaming, "Forward!" "Charge!" to which the officers bellowed in reply, "Charge bayonets!" "Fire away!" "Cease Fire!"[4]

Colonel Bates and Adj. Charles C. Wehrum, behind the right flank of the regiment with Companies H and G, heard the confusion. Bates dispatched Wehrum to find out what was happening and gave him the authority to charge if the situation warranted it. Wehrum approached Company A and spotted the injured Cpl. William L. Kimball stubbornly attempt to rest his weapon in the crotch of a short tree so he could get one more shot at the Rebs. His younger brother, Cpl. George Kimball together with Captain Erastus Clark, were insisting William go to the rear when they heard Wehrum call out, "What is the order?"

Corporal Kimball pointed toward the left and exclaimed, "They are going forward!" "Forward!" "Forward!" "Forward!" the soldiers in the line chanted.

Unsheathing his sword, the adjutant leaped over the wall and cried, "Forward, Twelfth!"

About 50 officers and men from the regiment heard the call above the din and responded. Captain Clark bolted ahead of all but one man in the dash for the

3 Kirby to Daniel [Cady]; Vautier, "At Gettysburg"; Boone, "Personal Experiences," 22; Grant, "The First Army Corps," 50; Hall, *History of the Ninety-Seventh Regiment*, 138, 141; Hall, "Iverson's Brigade"; *OR* 27/1:310. In his report, Colonel Wheelock claimed credit for ordering the charge, but he also mistakenly claimed none of his men were killed and only a few wounded in the assault.

4 *Pennsylvania at Gettysburg*, 1:477; Vautier, "At Gettysburg"; Vautier, *History of the 88th Pennsylvania*, 108.

colors of the 5th North Carolina; Corporal William H. Miller (Company C, 9th N.Y.S.M.) had a lead on him.[5]

The 11th Pennsylvania and 97th New York bolted toward the 20th North Carolina under a sporadic rain of small arms rounds. The bulk of it struck the New Yorkers. A bullet struck the detached sword scabbard carried by Capt. Isaac Hall in his right hand. The impact jarred him but the scabbard stopped the round from hitting his right thigh. A shot to the head killed Color Cpl. James Brown (Company B). Sergeant James B. McGurren (Company G) snatched the colors and continued with the attack. Company C of the 97th reached the Carolinians first. Sergeant Sylvester Riley wrested the flag from the Confederate color bearer and immediately turned it over to his second lieutenant, Ebenezer B. Harrington. Captain Dennis J. Downing (Company H) broke his leg when he leaped into the ditch among the Rebels. At least 125 officers and enlisted Rebels readily surrendered, 99 of whom were uninjured. Dropping their weapons, they headed back toward the stone wall.[6]

To the right, the 88th Pennsylvania encountered little resistance. As the regiment approached the 23rd North Carolina, around 115 officers and men, including more than 30 wounded, stood with hands raised and rushed through the regiment. One of them, still carrying his rifle, stooped and headed for Lt. Samuel Boone, who screamed, "Drop your arms, get back quick!" Boone slapped him hard across the back with the flat of his sword. At that moment, he noticed blood trickling from beneath the man's accouterment belt. Had he known the Rebel was injured, he later admitted, he would not have struck him.[7]

Company E's Capt. Joseph H. Richards (88th Pennsylvania) rushed the defiant color bearer of the 23rd North Carolina, Cpl. Edward S. Hart (Company D). Richards put both hands on the staff and tried to jerk it out of Hart's grasp. "Sip" Hart, however, had vowed that he would never let go of the flag as long as he remained "on his pegs." Pennsylvania sergeant Edward L. Gilligan settled the matter by slamming his rifle butt against the Tar Heel's skull and knocking

5 Ladd & Ladd, *Bachelder Papers*, 2:989; Gaff & Gaff, *A Corporal's Story*, 221; Kimball, "Iverson's Brigade."

6 Hall, *History of the Ninety-Seventh Regiment*, 141-142; Hall, "Iverson's Brigade," 7; Busey & Busey, *Confederate Casualties*, 2:941-961.

7 Boone, "Personal Experiences," 2; Busey & Busey, *Confederate Casualties*, 2:983-1001.

him unconscious. Richards kept the flag and carried it triumphantly back to the stone wall.[8]

Squads from the 9th N.Y.S.M. and 12th Massachusetts headed for the 5th North Carolina while the New Englanders who did not participate in the charge formed along the high rail fence perpendicular to the stone wall and enfiladed the Carolinians. New Yorker Thomas Hanna (Company F) distinctly recalled Pvt. Patrick Burns (Company H) bumping him as he sped past, hollering in his brogue, "Follow me, bays; follow me!" Just then Hanna heard the all-too-familiar "thud" of a bullet striking something solid. Burns collapsed with blood gushing from his chest. Almost simultaneously, Hanna felt something burn his scalp and knock him half silly. He staggered to the rear with his hand clapped to his head.[9]

Adjutant Charles C. Wehrum (12th Massachusetts) looked to the south and estimated that no more than 200 of Baxter's brigade reached the Confederate line. As with the 88th Pennsylvania, unarmed Rebels—over 60 of them—rushed into the ranks of the New Englanders and New Yorkers. Company C's Corporal Miller (9th N.Y.S.M.) reached for the Rebel flag just as Captain Clark of the 12th Massachusetts got a grip on it. Rather than get in a dispute with an officer, the corporal let him have the colors while he attended to the prisoners, who had readily surrendered. "The prisoners were simply ordered to the rear, and I can tell you they needed no second order, but 'got up and got,'" Miller recollected after the war.

8 "Gallantry under fire: Sip Hart survived on general's likker, cat stew," The next three links were accessed Feb. 15, 2023: http://rchs-nc.net/2015/11/12/gallantry-under- fire-sip-hart-survived-on-generals-likker-cat-stew/; www.findagrave.com/memorial/95 96871/joseph-h-richards; www.findagrave.com/memorial/ 10385451/Edward-Scipio- Hart; 23rd North Carolina Infantry; Clark, ed., *Histories of the Several Regiments*, 2:244; Walter. F. Beyer and Oscar. F. Keydel, eds., *Deeds of Valor*, 2 vols. (Detroit, 1901), 1:223; Vautier, *History of the 88th Pennsylvania*, 107; Boone, "Personal Experiences," 23. There is confusion surrounding Hart's refusal to let go of the flag. In Clark, Sergeant Well refers to it while describing the action at Spotsylvania on May 12. Hart's service record in his Find A Grave entry, however, notes that he was wounded in the right arm (not the head) on May 12, 1864, was captured the next day, and remained a prisoner until June 16, 1865, when he took the oath of allegiance. The record shows no evidence of him being wounded at Gettysburg. Wells said he let go of the flag only once, when he was knocked unconscious. Sergeant Gilligan received the Medal of Honor in 1892 for hitting the color bearer with the butt of his weapon, which allowed Richards to secure the flag. I concluded that Hart was the man with the flag.

9 Hanna, "A Day at Gettysburg."

The spectacle of a company of armed Rebels limping and running unescorted over the wall left of the 90th Pennsylvania frightened Sgt. Richard W. Morris (Company C), who thought they had broken the line and flanked his regiment. For a moment he envisioned himself "going South" to a prison pen. Meanwhile, Lt. Col. Joseph A. Moesch (9th N.Y.S.M.), having heard the men cheering Corporal Miller for his courage, took a moment to shake Corporal Miller's hand and to promise him a promotion.[10]

A minute or two after the charge began, Col. Peter Lyle ordered the 90th Pennsylvania to wheel northwest to support the two right companies of the 12th Massachusetts. Brigadier General Stephen Dodson Ramseur's brigade of North Carolinians, General Rodes's final brigade in his division, was now on the front line, and hit them with a volley from the north. The right wing of the regiment waivered. Major Alfred Sellers unsheathed his sword and bolted through the line to steady his troops. As they fell in at right angles to Companies H and G of the 12th Massachusetts, the Pennsylvania men of the small regiment screamed while emptying their buck and ball into the Confederates.[11]

Meanwhile, the small contingent of Federals who had broken through as far as the small rise of ground on the western side of the drainage ditch ran into rifle fire from Junius Daniel's mostly prone Confederates stacked along the fence row to the southeast, and from the survivors of Iverson's Brigade who were arranged behind the fence east of the Forney place.

Carter's Rebel artillery on Oak Hill opened on them, as did infantry on the north side of the Mummasburg Road. General Baxter and the contingent from the 88th Pennsylvania got caught in this crossfire. Despite his continual exhortations to "give them cold steel," Baxter's veterans decided otherwise. The bullets slicing through the grass at their feet struck down friend and foe alike. Without any attention to order or protocol, the Pennsylvanians about-faced and headed helter-skelter back toward Oak Ridge.[12]

10 Charles C. Wehrum, "Iverson's Brigade," *NT*, August 21, 1884, 3; Miller, "They All Helped To Do It"; J. Madison Drake, "Captured Flag on Gettysburg Field," *Newark Sunday Call*, January 16, 1910, 14; *OR*, 27/1:307; Hall, *History of the Ninety-Seventh Regiment*, 138; Morris, "The First Corps," 3; Busey & Busey, *Confederate Casualties*, 2:823-840. The five-minute affair netted Baxter's brigade 119 enlisted men and nine officers (all uninjured), and 101 wounded (four officers, 97 rank and file), for a total of 220 captives.

11 Sellers Letter, July 9, 1863.

12 *OR* 27/2: 554; Grant "The First Army Corps," 50; Vautier, "At Gettysburg"; Vautier, *History of the 88th Pennsylvania*, 107.

Sergeant Kirley of the 97th New York watched as the Confederate brigade north of the Mummasburg Road opened fire about the same time the regiment reached the ditch. A bullet from that volley nicked his right leg. The 11th Pennsylvania and the 50 or so men from the 97th responded by turning about and racing to catch up with their compliant prisoners. During the 97th's retreat, Lt. Rush Cady (Company K) tried to reform his men. He turned to face the North Carolinians, who had rallied along the fence bordering the western end of the field, when he flopped onto his back uttering "Oh, I am hit." Privates Richard Deane (Company B) and Stephen Nailor (Company G) saw Cady collapse and ran to his assistance. The bullet had passed through his right and arm into his chest, lodging in his lung. He asked his comrades to get him off the field.[13]

Farther north, the officers and men of the 9th N.Y.S.M. and 12th Massachusetts decided to fall back as quickly as possible. They, too, came under flank fire from the Mummasburg Road area. Corporal Miller (Company C, 9th N.Y.S.M.), who had just come within a whisker of capturing the flag of the 5th North Carolina, quaked under the impact of two rounds to his left arm. One penetrated his chest and lodged dangerously close to his heart; the other destroyed the arm.

On the far right of the 12th Massachusetts, Company G, the color company, came under fire from the Rebels to the north. The company responded by surging alone into a tiny corn patch, but just as quickly righted about and returned to its former position. The color bearer, Pvt. Patrick Cullen (Company K), miraculously came away from the foray unscathed. Sergeant Charles L. Emmons (Company G) ran out of luck and went down critically wounded. Corporal Henry Damon and two other men from Company G placed him onto a blanket, and, with Lt. Jonathan B. Whitman (Company I) on the fourth corner, picked him up and started off the field. When they encountered the color guard, Whitman, whom Colonel Bates had ordered to stay with the regiment, volunteered Pvt. James Coullahan of the color guard to take his place. While the lieutenant returned to his duties, the four men struggled with the dying Emmons down the eastern side of Oak Ridge toward Gettysburg.[14]

13 Hall, *History of the Ninety-Seventh Regiment*, 138; Kirby to Daniel (Cady).

14 Drake, "Captured Flag on Gettysburg Field," 14; Miller, "They All Helped Do It"; James Coullahan, "The Story of the Colors," Vertical Files, VF6-MA12, Library, GNMP.

Corporal George Kimball (Company A) did not return with the rest of the 12th Massachusetts. Instead, he engaged in a conversation with a dozen or so captured Tar Heels. When they started laughing and suggested that he stay with them for a trip down south to a "durned sight better" country than the prisons up north, Kimball realized that he had not retreated with his comrades. He continued talking with the Rebs while slowly backing up toward his own lines. When he reached a point from which he could sprint to safety, he whirled about and began running.

"Halt!"

"Go to Hell!" he shouted over one shoulder. Several of his former prisoners snapped off a few ineffectual shots after him.

The corporal now found himself coming under fire from the enemy on his left and his own men to the front. Artillery shells burst uncomfortably overhead, which too him appeared as though they were aimed at him alone. He yanked his handkerchief from his pocket and stuck it on the end of his bayonet to keep from dying by "friendly fire." About 50 yards from the stone wall a bullet struck him in his left groin and dropped him like a rock. He tried to get up, but could not.

Kimball raised his head and recognized red-bearded Sgt. Uriah Macoy (Company F) motioning for him to lie low. Kimball worked his knapsack off his back and placed it upright in front of his head with the cast iron skillet he had strapped onto it facing the gunfire. He lay between the lines, never expecting to survive the ordeal. For the next hour he listened to the bullets hit the skillet at a rate of one per minute.

Charles F. Weakley, the boy they had unofficially recruited into Company A on June 30, lay nearby, too injured to move. Despite a hip wound received early in the fight, Weakley hobbled into the charge until shot through the right arm. Exhaustion, pain, and blood loss prostrated him.[15]

3:15 p.m.

Lieutenant Jacob Slagle rejoined General Doubleday just as the Federal line started to disintegrate. The general ordered Slagle to ride hard to General Robinson and bring back a regiment. Slagle clattered off through a seemingly

---

Coullahan mistakenly identified the color bearer as Patrick A. Mullen, who entered the regiment as a draftee on July 14, 1863.

15 Gaff & Gaff, eds., *A Corporal's Story*, 213-214, 221-223.

unrelenting "shower of musket balls." As he approached Robinson's division, he encountered a staffer on his way to Doubleday to get reinforcements because the Rebels had flanked Robinson. The frustrated Slagle reined his horse about and galloped back.[16]

After being apprised of the situation, Doubleday dispatched Slagle to send Gabriel Paul's three remaining regiments north. Private George E. Jepson (Company A, 13th Massachusetts) watched the aide gallop up to Paul. "

Fall in!" rippled along the three regimental lines.

Relieved that what he described as "a long and an anxious" halt was over, Jepson took his place in the formation.

"Forward, double quick!"

The 13th Massachusetts led the column. Company D was at the head of the regiment and Company K had the back. The 104th New York, accompanied by General Paul, came next with the 107th Pennsylvania at the rear. The Bay Staters tramped over the Chambersburg Pike past the badly wounded Capt. J. Otis Williams (Company D, 12th Massachusetts), who lay along the side of the road. Shells burst overhead as they drew near the railroad bed. A hot fragment mortally wounded Pvt. John Flye (Company K) before the regiment cleared the bed to veer northwest into Sheads Woods.[17]

16 Slagle to brother.

17 Arthur A. Kent, ed., *Three Years With Company K* (Madison, NJ, 1976), 179; "William Warner's Account of the Battle," http://13thmass.org/1863/gettysburg.htm#mozTocld956094, accessed Feb. 16, 2023; Davis, *Three Years in the Army*, 226; *NYAG*, 2:752, 756; George E. Jepson, "Reflections of a Private," 13th Regiment Association Circular #15, December 1902, 14. Like many veterans, Jepson preferred to discuss grand tactics rather than his own role in the battle. The only long halt that occurred with his brigade was near the seminary. This is my explanation of making sense of Paul's disjointed deployment. Either Doubleday or Robinson deliberately held back the three regiments to feed into the line where needed. Robinson, who knew Paul's regiments were the last reserve of the I Corps, probably had a hand in creating that last reserve. The order of the column is based on the sequence of events described by the participants. The 13th Massachusetts deployed before the 104th reached the field. The 104th New York was heading for the right of the 13th under orders from Paul when Robinson ordered it to the left of the 13th. I believe Paul intended to put the 107th Pennsylvania on the left of the 13th, but Robinson placed it along the stone wall where the 97th New York had been.

3:15 p.m. to 3:30 p.m.
The Stone Wall on Oak Ridge

While under fire from both the west and north, Baxter's regiments tried to reform and fight despite not having enough ammunition for a sustained action of any sort. Adjutant Wehrum (12th Massachusetts) discovered that the 90th Pennsylvania had formed at right angles to his Bay Staters, facing north to withstand pressure from Ramseur's disjointed assault.

Wehrum also found his colonel, James L. Bates, hemorrhaging from a bullet wound in his neck. Wehrum tied his own handkerchief around the wound to stem the bleeding. When he told Bates he needed to leave the field, the colonel stubbornly refused. "We need every available officer at his post," he insisted.

Captain Erastus L. Clark, the 12th's towheaded captain of Company A with the impressive shoe brush mustache, was not among them. Shortly after returning to the wall, Clark removed the colors of the 5th North Carolina from the staff and shoved them inside his tunic. Just after doing so, a shell fragment struck him full in the face. The jagged iron destroyed the roof of his mouth, carried away most of his teeth, and broke part of his nasal passage and a number of upper facial bones. A couple of men helped him from the field. "I would much rather have lost my life than my mustache," he is recorded as having uttered. His premonition of being wounded had been fulfilled.

The nearly 300 Rebel prisoners had rather suddenly become a burden by clogging the position and making it difficult to maneuver. General Robinson intervened and ordered Capt. Benjamin F. Cook (12th Massachusetts) forward with the provost guard, which he had posted on the eastern base of the slope, to remove the prisoners. While he complied with the command, Baxter's brigade prepared for a counterattack.[18]

Colonel Charles Wheelock (97th New York) was rather conspicuously waving the captured flag of the 20th North Carolina about and in doing so, attracted the attention of Maj. Eugene Blackford's sharpshooter battalion on Oak Hill. The sight of the distant officer deliberately taunting the Confederates

18 Gaff & Gaff, eds., *A Corporal's Story*, 215-216, 226; Ladd & Ladd, *Bachelder Papers*, 2:550; Wehrum, "Iverson's Brigade"; Cook, *History of the Twelfth Massachusetts*, 101; Sellers Letter; Drake, "Captured Flag on Gettysburg Field," 14.

irritated Baxter, who demanded the colors be taken to the rear. Wheelock blatantly refused: "My regiment captured these colors and will keep them."

Baxter immediately put Wheelock under arrest, but before this could be carried out, Wheelock called over Lt. William J. Morrin (Company A), handed him the flag, unsheathed his sword, and cut about half of it from the staff. Together, the officers continued taunting the Confederates with the large swaths of flag until a bullet in Morrin's forehead terminated their foolishness.[19]

General John C. Robinson (Second Division) did not wait for General Paul to reach the field. He intercepted the 13th Massachusetts and sent it north to the small woodlot and the destroyed worm fence paralleling the Mummasburg Road. Skirmishers sprinted ahead of the line toward the right of the 90th Pennsylvania, at which point Baxter retired the brigade, with the exception of the 97th New York, southeast through Sheads Woods into the low ground between the town and Oak Ridge. The 97th found itself, temporarily at least, operating with Paul's brigade.[20]

The 12th Massachusetts and 90th Pennsylvania had no sooner vacated the stone wall and its intersection with the Mummasburg Road than skirmishers from the 26th Alabama, undetected by the Yankees, occupied the apex on the crest. At the same time the 13th Massachusetts planted its right flank on Heagy's lane about 33 feet south of the small woodlot. Sergeant Austin C. Stearns (Company K) spied a long line of infantry north of the McLean barn and initially thought they were Federal troops. Within a short time that formation advanced close enough for him to discern the Confederate battle flag and dirty uniforms. Federal skirmishers in the Mummasburg Road, unaware they had been flanked, snapped off shots at the Rebs to the north. The 26th Alabama and 5th Alabama quickly drove them off and dropped into the shelter of the road.

Sergeant Stearns took note of the large gap between his regiment and the 104th New York on the ridge to his left and rear. The New Englanders pushed a

19 Grant "The First Army Corps," 51. Grant later claimed that the officer killed next to Wheelock was a captain. He was incorrect. Company A (97th New York) on the right side was under Capt. Isaac Hall, who was not killed at Gettysburg. Hall's second in command, however, was Lieutenant Morrin, who was killed while standing alongside Wheelock.

20 *OR* 27/1:292; Locke, *The Story of the Regiment*, 230; Detre, "88th Penna Regt at Gettysburg"; Boone, "Personal Experiences," 23; Grant, "The First Army Corps," 49; *NYAG*, 2:756. Colonel Prey (104th New York) wrote that the 97th New York was on his left along the stone wall. Coulter's report for the 11th Pennsylvania reported his men were relieved by a part of Paul's brigade.

short distance into the open field between them and the road. Without any advance warning, they encountered enfilade fire from the left and "brisk" accurate shooting from the front, some of which seriously wounded Pvt. George Atkinson (Company F).

On the far right of the line in Company D, Pvt. Bourne Spooner watched the incoming rounds pock marking the field and drilling into the pile of fence rails between him and the northern side of the woodlot. Calmed by the fact that the Rebels had concentrated the bulk of their fire on the center of the 13th, his nervousness vanished. "I rather like this," he mused.[21]

Newly commissioned to Company G from Company K, Lt. William R. Warner, who had turned in his rifle and accoutrements that morning, still wore his sergeant's chevrons into action. Picking up a discarded rifle, he scrounged some percussion caps and cartridges from nearby casualties. He saw Sgt. Willard Wheeler (Company K) fall onto his back. Austin Stearns also noticed Wheeler lying in the grass, but in the smoke and deafening noise he could not tell if he was alive. He rushed to Wheeler's side but received no response to his queries. Blood and brains were running out a bullet hole in the sergeant's left temple. Gurgling through his partially open mouth, Wheeler raised his left arm to wipe his forehead. As Stearns later put it, "There was no time now to be wasted on dead men," and returned back into the ranks. During his brief absence the Rebels had cut down eight of the tallest men on the right side of the company. Three had died instantly, four suffered serious injuries, and Sgt. Melvin H. Walker had caught a slug in his right foot. Fortunately for him, two friends in the 12th Massachusetts came upon him as their regiment retired from the field and helped him hobble to safety.[22]

With the national flag held aloft, Color Corporal Roland B. Morris (Company C, 13th Massachusetts) was knocked backward and up into the air before thudding onto his back, the prey of a Southern sharpshooter in the McLean barn. Company A's commander, Lt. Jacob A. Howe, watched Morris writhe about, screaming uncontrollably with a bullet through his intestines.

21 Kent, *Three Years in Company K*, 179-180; William A. Newhall to Dear Sister, July 8, 1863, http://13thmass.org/1863/aftermathprisoners.html, accessed Feb. 16, 2023; *Boston Traveler*, July 10, 1863; Spooner, "In the Ranks."

22 "Warner's Account"; Kent, ed., *Three Years With Company K*, 180; Melvin H. Walker, "A Personal Experience," https://13thmass.org/1863/Gettysburg.html#mozTocId960759, accessed Feb. 16, 2023.

Howe ordered two men to carry Morris away. Within a few minutes, five other members on the color guard had fallen.

An anonymous corporal raised the national flag. Sergeant David Sloss (Company B) kept the regimental banner aloft. Private George H. Lehman (Company E), fighting on the left of the colors, found himself being pushed uncomfortably close to the guard. A bullet grazed his left leg, but he calmly remained in the ranks. Not long afterward a second ball broke his right leg and knocked him off his feet. Lehman found a discarded towel and bound his wound to stop the bleeding. He regained his feet and limped painfully toward Gettysburg.

Five minutes into the firefight, a bullet struck Pvt. Charles F. Adams (Company A). He had leaned forward on his left leg and raised his weapon to his shoulder when a minié ball drilled through his leg behind the knee and ripped the flesh off his right leg upon exiting. The shock hurled him to the ground, where he lay unable to move.[23]

Fry's Rebel battery on Oak Hill also opened on the 13th Massachusetts. Shrapnel struck Pvt. Thomas J. Downey (Company E) as he loaded his rifle. The large shard hit his knapsack, ripped his blanket off, and threw him about 10 feet behind the line. Downey picked himself up and limped back into the formation. He was plugging away when a second minié struck his right knee. He stubbornly remained with the regiment.

Corporal Stearns felt the sudden tug and sting of a minié ball cutting across his left shoulder. His arm dangled lifelessly against his side. Handing his weapon to a comrade whose own gun had malfunctioned, Stearns walked a short distance behind the line and sat down to massage his arm. Nearby, he found Pvt. James Ryan (Company I) shot through both wrists, frantically struggling to get his knapsack unhitched so he could get to the rear and get medical help. Stearns helped Ryan out of his pack and resumed massaging his paralyzed arm.[24]

"Close to the left. Close to the left!" Pvt. Bourne Spooner heard officers yell.

23 Jepson, "Reflections of a Private," 17; "Found a Friend Among His Captors," *Boston Sunday Globe*, July 29, 1913; "His Wound, a Surgeon's Marvel," *Boston Sunday Globe*, July 29, 1913.

24 Kent, *Three Years in Company K*, 180; Boston Traveler, July 10, 1863.

With each passing minute the regimental front diminished in size. The men of Company D sidled to the west and encountered a Dantean landscape of corpses on their backs with gashed heads, wounded men pleading hideously for help, and one man Spooner was never able to forget. A soldier was laying on his side wounded in the leg or hip. Mute and with an anxious expression on his face, he lay staring at the smoldering cartridge box on his waist belt, awaiting the inevitable ignition of the live ammunition still inside.

Unable to assist the man, Spooner kept his place in the ranks. As the formation continued shrinking, he came across one of the two Blanchard brothers of Company B, Brainard P. and William F. Both ignored the pleas from injured men to be carried off the field. When a soldier said something about the sad plight of the injured and that they needed help, one of the Blanchard brothers refused: "No, no, I can't attend to the wounded now." Neither could Spooner. General orders prohibited anyone other than the ambulance department personnel from assisting the casualties. "The regulation,"concluded Spooner, "though harsh and rigorous, was necessary."[25]

Another Massachusetts man, Cpl. Herschel A. Sanborn (Company C) was back with the regiment after a long convalesce from a wound he suffered at Antietam. Sanborn stepped to the rear of the line and stood motionless for a second before collapsing dead. Former company teamster, 33-year-old Pvt. Sylvester A. Hayes (Company H), screeched, "Who will take care of my children now?" as he lay dying with a bullet in his left lung. Next to him, a swarthy private named John M. Brock died quickly with a round through the heart. Lieutenant William Warner (Company G) recalled how fast the tall young man's face paled, his flesh sharply contrasting with his raven hair.[26]

While the 13th Massachusetts slugged it out in the Mummasburg Road with O'Neal's Alabamians, General Paul with the 104th New York came onto the ridge behind 97th New York. Paul directed Col. Gilbert G. Prey to move his New Yorkers east (downhill) to the right of the 13th Massachusetts. Prey had hardly reached the gap between the crest of the ridge and the New Englanders when Robinson bellowed from the top of the ridge, "Colonel Prey, God damn you, where are you going? Form on the left!"

25 Spooner, "In the Ranks." Both Blanchard brothers were reported as missing on July 1, but both managed to escape and eventually return to the Union lines.

26 "Warner's Account."

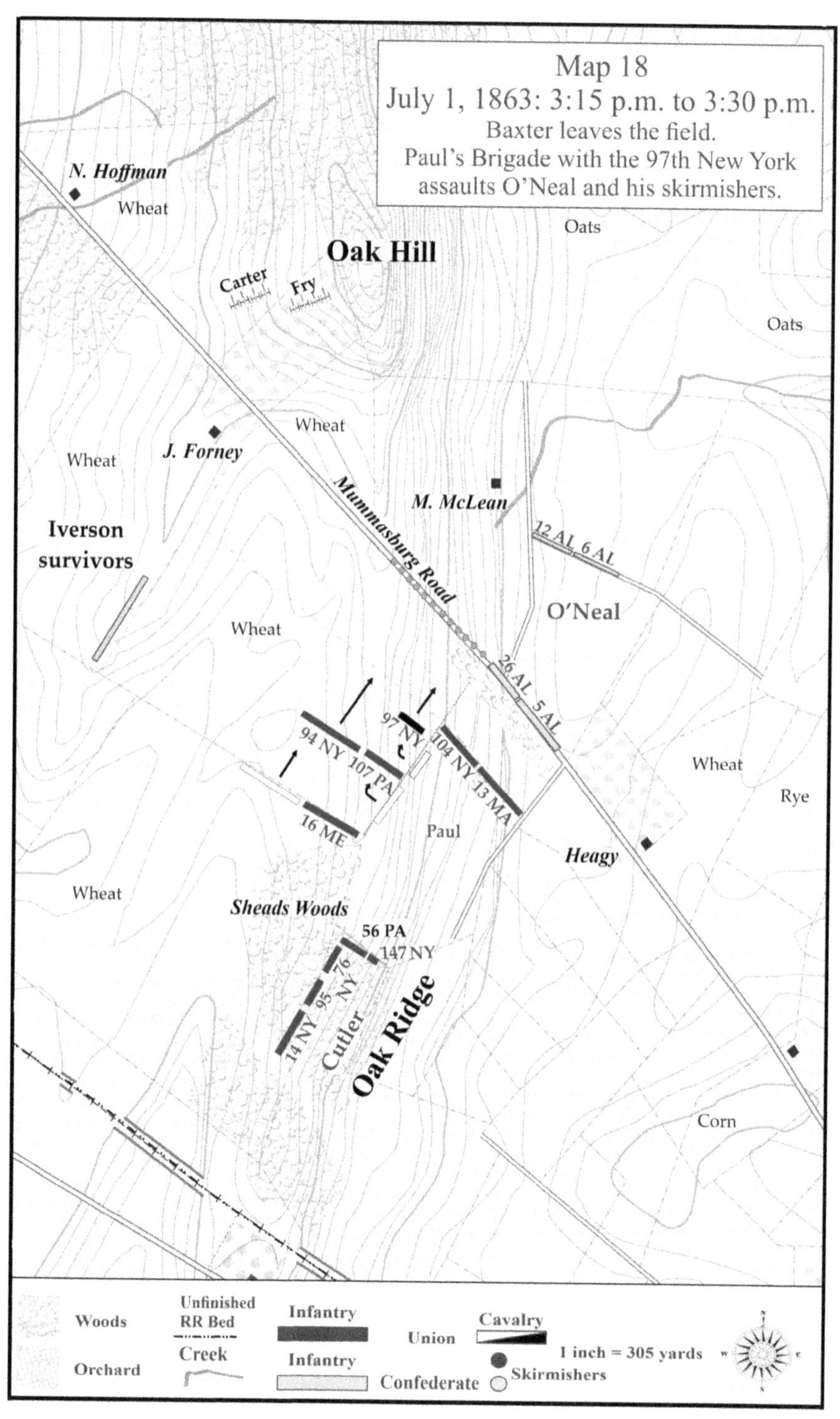
Map 18
July 1, 1863: 3:15 p.m. to 3:30 p.m.
Baxter leaves the field.
Paul's Brigade with the 97th New York assaults O'Neal and his skirmishers.
N. Hoffman
Wheat
Oats
Oak Hill
Carter
Fry
Oats
Wheat
J. Forney
Wheat
Mummasburg Road
M. McLean
Iverson survivors
12 AL
6 AL
O'Neal
Wheat
26 AL
5 AL
97 NY
94 NY
107 PA
104 NY
13 MA
Wheat
Rye
16 ME
Paul
Heagy
Wheat
Sheads Woods
56 PA
147 NY
76 NY
95
14 NY
Cutler
Oak Ridge
Corn
Woods
Orchard
Unfinished RR Bed
Creek
Infantry
Infantry
Union
Confederate
Cavalry
Skirmishers
1 inch = 305 yards

Prey did as ordered. "March!" he shouted, "March! Load at will!"[27]

The regiment incurred casualties almost immediately while forming into line. O'Neal's two Alabama regiments in the Mummasburg Road had them in their sights. Colonel Prey's horse was hit, forcing him to dismount in spite of Robinson's directive for all regimental commanders to stay mounted. General Paul was riding behind the colors of the 13th Massachusetts when he suffered one of the most hideous wounds on the field and lived to tell the tale. A minie ball struck him in the right side of the head one and a half inches behind his eye and exited out his left eye. The impact knocked him unconscious and he was lifted down from the saddle. Sergeant Charles A. Drew (Company A) helped carry the semi-conscious and now fully blind Paul away from the front. Brigade command passed to Col. Samuel Leonard (13th Massachusetts) until an arm wound knocked him out of the fight. He left the field, apparently without informing any of his staff.

Major Jacob Parker Gould strode from one end of the left wing to the other, exhorting loudly, "Do your duty, you noble sons of Massachusetts, do your duty! Remember your state!"

Robinson and Colonel Wheelock noticed the 13th's unsteadiness and dispatched the exhausted 97th New York down the slope to shore up the line. The New Yorkers quickly help restore order. When Wheelock recalled the men, Capt. Isaac Hall and a handful of his soldiers from Company A did not hear the command.[28]

When Colonel Prey spotted Robinson just below the top of the ridge, he approached on foot: "Who is in command of the brigade?"

"Where is Colonel Root?" asked Robinson.

"Don't know; not here," Prey replied.

"Where is Colonel Leonard?" inquired Robinson.

27 NYAG, 2:756; OR 27/1:301. Prey wrote this in his afteraction report: "I was ordered to form line by Brigadier General Paul on the right of the Thirteenth Massachusetts Regiment, and while doing so, was ordered by Brigadier General Robinson, commanding division, to form to the left..." In *NYAG*, he made no mention of Paul and simply noted that Robinson deployed him. In that same piece, he left the expletives blank. I filled them in.

28 *NYAG*, 2:756; Warren H. Freeman and Eugene H. Freeman, *Letters From Two Brothers Serving in the War For the Union to Their Family at Home* (Cambridge, MA, 1871), 77; Hall, *History of the Ninety-Seventh Regiment*, 138-139; "Warner's Account." Hall described the regiment as "a new regiment along the Mummasburg Road, facing north." That had to have been the "newly arrived" 13th Massachusetts, which means that the 97th New York did not leave the field with the rest of the brigade.

"Not with his regiment," shot back Prey.

"You are next in rank, take command of the brigade!" directed Robinson.

Robinson turned to an aide and directed him to find Colonel Root (94th New York) and tell him he needed to take over the brigade.[29]

The 107th Pennsylvania (Paul's brigade) arrived on the eastern slope of Oak Ridge shortly after the 97th New York returned to the wall and faced west with its right flank perpendicular to the narrow woodlot running down to the farm lane. The Pennsylvanians ascended the hillside to the stone wall with their right wing behind the reforming 97th. The left wing covered the rest of the stone wall to the south to the point where the right end of the 16th Maine anchored its intersection with the westerly running fence.[30]

Robinson's aide finally found Colonel Root and the 94th New York at the moment the colonel determined to put his regiment behind the high rail fence just south of the Mummasburg Road, and from that position open fire on Carter's Virginia guns firing from Oak Hill. The order to charge shocked Lt. Walter T. Chester, the commander of Company D, who later complained to the *Buffalo Courier* that the New York regiment obeyed "a diabolically reckless order, which could proceed from the mouth of drunkenness, to charge, in the face of a brigade of rebels, across an open field." With a cheer, the veterans stepped over the low rail fence into the corpse-strewn and trampled grass field in front of them.[31]

The attack spread to the east. Colonel Charles W. Tilden, whose horse had just been shot from under him, commanded the 16th Maine to stand and attack. Color Sergeant Wilbur F. Mower (national flag) and Cpl. Sampson A. Thomas (state banner) scrambled over the fence first. The order caught Lt. Lewis Bisbee (Company I) off guard as he tended to the seriously injured Captain Waldron.

29 *NYAG*, 2:756.

30 Mary Warner Thomas and Richard A. Sauers, eds., *The Civil War Letters of First Lieutenant James B. Thomas* (Baltimore, 1995), 173-174; *Pennsylvania at Gettysburg*, 2:558-559. Adjutant Thomas wrote his father on July 13, 1863, that the color bearer died before the charge and that an anonymous 3rd corporal took the colors.

31 Letter from Colonel Root to Editors, *Commercial Advertiser* (Buffalo, NY), July 14, 1863, https://museum.dmna.ny.gov/unit-history/infantry-1/94th-infantry-regiment/news paper-clippings, accessed Feb. 17, 2023; "Interesting Letter from the 94th—The Buffalo Company and Its Losses," https://museum.dmna.ny.gov/application/files/9415/5308/9201/94thInf CWN1.pdf, accessed Feb. 17, 2023.

Bisbee told the captain he had to leave him, gave Waldron his revolver, and followed his men over the fence and into the field.[32]

Colonel Wheelock (97th New York), however, got the jump on Paul's two regiments. The New Yorkers of Baxter's brigade leaped over the wall for the second time and into a small arms fusillade. A number of bullets passed through the ranks of the New Yorkers and into the 107th Pennsylvania behind them. One killed Col. Cpl. Thomas Breash (Company C), who carried the national flag. Corporal George A. McConnelly (Company H) grabbed it only to die along with another member of the color guard. The third corporal in the guard grabbed the flag before the Pennsylvanians crossed over. Colonel Thomas McCoy bitterly recalled, "Some excited fellows on our right pushed over the wall, and a charge was made, our regiment joining." The New Yorkers immediately swung north with the Pennsylvanians scrambling into line behind them. They connected with the right of the 94th New York, and in doing so blocked the 16th Maine's advance.[33]

Rebel fire from behind the stone wall along the Mummasburg Road northwest of the 104th New York sliced through the regiment. Color Sergeant Maurice Buckingham with the U.S. flag died, and Sgt. William H. Shea with the state flag collapsed with a broken leg that would eventually kill him. Despite a slight wound, Pvt. David E. Curtis secured the state banner. A second member of color guard went down a moment or two after raising the Stars and Stripes. Sergeant Thomas J. Curtis picked up the flag and just as quickly got hit. When ordered to the rear, he loudly refused. A bullet in the head knocked him down, but in death he grasped the staff so tightly that the next man in the guard had to pry it from his frozen hands.

Both that man and the next color corporal who took it up were shot. Sergeant Moses Wallis, the last of the color guard, pulled the flag from that fellow's hands. Colonel Prey shouted at Maj. John R. Strang to take the left wing and attack the wall or they would all be dead men. Strang yelled the order,

32 Small, *Sixteenth Maine*, 117; *Maine at Gettysburg*, 51; George D. Bisbee, "Three Years a Volunteer Soldier in the Civil War: Antietam to Appomattox," *War Papers Read Before the Commandery of the State of Maine, Military Order of the Loyal Legion of the United States*, 4 vols. (Portland, ME, 1915) 4:121-122; "Bisbee Account"; *Pennsylvania at Gettysburg*, 2:557. Small identified Mower as the first man across the fence; it makes sense that Thomas was with him. *Maine at Gettysburg* identifies both men.

33 *Pennsylvania at Gettysburg*, 2:558; Hall, *History of the Ninety-Seventh Regiment*, 139, 140-141; Thomas & Sauers, *Thomas Letters*, 173-174; "Bisbee Account"; Root to Editors.

but the men hesitated. Prey pushed his way in front screaming, "I will lead you, boys!" They bolted after him.[34]

"Forward! Forward!" echoed through the 13th Massachusetts. After the men repeated it a couple of times, the regiment advanced in a disorganized rush. Bourne Spooner (Company D) had not had time to ram his cartridge home when the attack started. He ran a few steps with his weapon in his left hand and the ramrod in his right. Realizing his predicament, he halted to finish loading. His file closer, Lt. Henry Washburn, asked him why he had stopped. A hasty glance apprised Washburn of the situation, and he went forward to attend to genuine stragglers.

The color bearer and several other members of the 5th Alabama, meanwhile, moved out of the lane heading away from the fighting. When Maj. Jacob Gould (13th Massachusetts) spotted them, he ordered the men closest to him to cut them down. Someone yelled, "Give it to 'em for Fredericksburg!" The Confederate flag disappeared in the tall grass. Spooner and others reached the road a handful of seconds later. White towels and handkerchiefs bobbed over the top of the road bank; the Rebs were surrendering. Wounded and injured alike, men of the 5th Alabama cast their weapons aside and scrambled over the rail fence along the road. For the most part they greeted the victorious New Englanders with handshakes and congratulations on their "well done" charge. With the two sides so closely intermingled, the Confederate artillery on Oak Hill appears to have shifted its fired against the New Yorkers on the western side of the stone wall rather than risk hitting their own men on the Mummasburg Road.

The 13th Massachusetts hauled in 80 Alabamians of all ranks, and a detachment that reached the McLean barn brought in another 11; they had captured a force nearly the size of their own small regiment. Lieutenant Jacob A. Howe (Company A) watched as his second in command, Lt. David Whiston, approached with a pair of officer's swords in each hand. A perplexed Howe asked Whiston what he expected him to do with them.

Spooner used the lull to walk among the Confederate casualties. He stumbled across a young soldier lying on his side. The sight of the Rebel opening and closing his mouth reminded him of a beached fish, gasping for air.

34 *NYAG*, 2:751, 757; Bell to State Historian. The color guard consisted of the following: Clr. Sgt. Maurice Buckingham (C), Clr. Sgt. William H. Shea (I), Sgt. Thomas J. Curtis (A), Clr. Cpls. Andrew McMullen (F), Andrew J. Pierce (E), and Moses Wallis (E), and Pvts. David E. Curtis (D) and Edgar J. Fancher (A).

Spooner knelt and offered the boy some water, but he shook his head "no." He walked away, the memory of that moment seared in his mind.[35]

The 104th New York was also on the receiving end of a large surrender. The New Yorkers took in 38 enlisted men and three officers from the 26th Alabama. Colonel Prey did not have enough personnel to handle the Rebs so he turned them over to Pvt. Frank N. Bell (Company C), who had just armed himself with a discarded, though nonoperational, weapon. Bell, in turn, handed them off to the prisoner detachment of the 13th Massachusetts. The consequence of all this was that the 13th's lieutenant colonel, N. Walter Batchelder, would later claim that his regiment captured seven commissioned officers and 125 enlisted men.[36]

To the west of the wall, Col. Adrian Root, now commanding less than half of Paul's brigade, watched the 94th New York alongside the 97th New York, with the 107th Pennsylvania and the 16th Maine trailing behind, charge the strong high worm fence south of the Mummasburg Road. He rode east and reported to General Robinson for further instructions while informing him of the left wing's advance. Root paraphrased the general's reaction thusly: Robinson "thought it hardly desirable to attempt to carry the enemy's position and directed me to recall my men to their original position."

Racing over the crest, Root rode up between his two front lines and bellowed for the regiments to turn back. A shell that burst close overhead as he wheeled his horse around to lead the withdrawal severely concussed him. One of the shards ripped his cap from his head and jerked him from the saddle. He hit the ground hard. "My share in the battle had ended," he later explained.[37]

Root's veterans also realized that their "share of the battle had ended." It did not matter whether they heard their colonel's command to withdraw or not; they were savvy enough to know the time had come to leave. "The order to retreat was given, or understood," Lt. Walter T. Chester (Company D, 94th New York) informed the *Buffalo Courier*, "for few orders were given on that field." With all

35 Spooner, "In the Ranks"; Jepson, "Reflections of a Private," 17; George Henry Hill to Dear Father, August 4, 1863, accessed Feb. 17, 2023.

36 *OR* 27/1:298, 301; *Annual Report of the Adjutant-General*, 615; Bell to State Historian. According to Prey, he turned his captives over to the 13th Massachusetts. Batchelder took charge of the prisoners then claimed his regiment. the 13th Massachusetts, captured them rather than the New Yorkers.

37 Root to Editors.

unit cohesion lost, the three regiments morphed into clots of frightened soldiers following the closest flag.

Adjutant James B. Thomas (107th Pennsylvania) realized that the color corporal had not joined the herd. He wheeled around and noticed the man still standing at the fence, defiantly waving the colors at the Rebels along the woodline on Oak Hill. Thomas hollered at him to retreat, to no avail. The exhausted lieutenant bounded up to the corporal and dragged him away. The fleeing soldiers raced through a devastating plunging fire from Carter's Virginia battery on Oak Hill. Two enlisted men stumbled across the semiconscious Colonel Root and dragged him into Sheads Woods, where they emptied two canteens of water on his face in an effort to bring him around. Failing to do so, they abandoned him.[38]

With the front regiments rapidly disintegrating, Colonel Tilden commanded the 16th Maine to pull out of the fight. The attack had taken just a few minutes. By the time Lt. Lewis Bisbee caught up with his company, its men had turned about and were heading back to their original position, where they went prone. On the east side of Oak Ridge, General Robinson with his staff and orderlies frantically scrounged cartridges from the wounded and the dead to disperse them to the demoralized survivors of the 107th Pennsylvania along the wall. Corporal John C. Delaney, a 15-year-old Irish immigrant, never forgot his division commander pressing three rounds into his hand at that critical moment.[39]

Eastern Slope of Oak Ridge

Colonel Gilbert Prey untangled some of the 104th New York from the 13th Massachusetts and withdrew the New Yorkers to the ridgeline, where they fell in on the right flank of some survivors from the 97th New York. Prey informed General Robinson that enemy troops were maneuvering into the woods on Oak Hill, on their northern flank. The disorganized 13th Massachusetts formed a makeshift line at right angles to the 104th. The sounds of heavy fighting off to

38 "Interesting Letter from the 94th-The Buffalo Company and Its Losses"; Root to Editors; Warner and Sauers, *Civil War Letters of James Thomas*, 174.

39 "Bisbee Account"; https://www.findagrave.com/memorial/6172366/john-carroll-delaney, accessed Feb. 17, 2023; J. C. Delaney, "Robinson's Division," *NT*, September 17, 1908, 7; *Pennsylvania at Gettysburg*, 2:559; *NYAG*, 2:757.

the south was gradually drawing closer. All the signs, recalled Sgt. George H. Hill (Company B, 13th Massachusetts), indicated the left wing of the I Corps was being driven back—or worse. "We had no orders to fall back, and we would not be driven," he insisted.[40]

One of Robinson's aides trotted up to Tilden with orders for him to move the 16th Maine by the right to the east side of the ridge south of the Mummasburg Road. The Mainers executed the maneuver "in considerable disorder," recalled Lt. Lewis Bisbee, who together with Clr. Sgt. Wilbur F. Mower (with the national flag) reached the thin belt of maples behind the 13th Massachusetts. "You take position here and let the regiment form on you," Robinson's aide directed Mower. The men in the 13th cheered the Mainers when they arrived on the line.

A staff officer clattered up to Lt. Jacob A. Howe (Company A) and asked who commanded the 13th Massachusetts. Given the woefully depleted line, Howe had a feeling that he had just received a temporary field promotion. The officer told him to withdraw and rode away. The exhausted soldiers could see large chunks of Howard's XI Corps to the northeast disintegrating in the face of heavy Confederate lines moving against them. The rest of the brigade retired south, leaving the 16th Maine on its own.[41]

Sergeant Frank Wiggin (Company H, 16th Maine) recalled an aide riding up and speaking to General Robinson, who in turn rode to Colonel Tilden with orders to move the regiment by the right along the ridge to the Mummasburg Road and go into position there. Tilden argued that the Rebels had superior numbers there, and the ground was completely untenable. "Take that position and hold it at any cost," Wiggin heard Robinson yell back. "Boys, you know what that means!" Tilden is said to have exclaimed as he executed the order.[42]

40 Charles H. Richmond, "The 104th N.Y. Vols. At the Battle of Gettysburg," Charles H. Richmond Account, GAR Surveys B1706-00, New York State Archives, Albany, NY; "Bisbee Account"; Hill to father; John Boudwin, Diary, July 1, 1863, https://civilwartalk. Com /conversations/need-information-on-these-individuals.59885 (link inactive when last checked on Feb. 17, 2023). Lewis Bisbee claimed the Confederates only attacked from the front (north), and not against either flank.

41 "Bisbee Account"; Spooner, "In the Ranks"; Jepson, "Reflections," 41.

42 "Bisbee Account"; Spooner, "In the Ranks"; Wiggin, "Sixteenth Maine at Gettysburg," 158, *Maine at Gettysburg*, 41-42, 46. There are several sources on this exchange, each slightly different. Considering the tense and confusing situation on the field, there is little doubt it was animated and blunt.

Tilden advanced what remained of his 16th regiment northwest into the road. At least two companies faced west behind the stone wall, while the rest of the line hunkered down in the sunken road facing north. Even when standing, the men could not see through or over the dense brush covering the bank facing the McLean buildings. The irrepressible Lieutenant Bisbee strolled to the crest of the ridge at the apex in the line and discovered what he believed to be two Rebel brigades emerging from the woods on Oak Hill in parade ground formation. He reported the news to Tilden. It was around 3:30 p.m.[43]

3:30 p.m. to 4:00 p.m.
Forney Farm

The minutes ticked away as Junius Daniel watched for supports to arrive on his right flank. As soon as Alfred Scales's North Carolinians topped McPherson's Ridge below the Chambersburg Pike, Daniel ordered his North Carolinians forward. With the 32nd North Carolina on the northern side of the western cut, the 2nd Battalion, 45th, 43rd, and 53rd regiments (south to north) stepped over the fence along their front and obliqued southeast toward the Federal center along the pike. Iverson's three mauled regiments also moved ahead through the very fields over which they had marched not two hours before. The 14th and the 30th North Carolina, under Brig. Gen. Stephen D. Ramseur's personal command, left-wheeled into the field to the north and rear of Iverson, at which point Col. Cullen A. Battle and his 3rd Alabama came up on the right-rear of the 30th. Battle, who had been told by Daniel that he was on his own, rode up to Ramseur and asked if his orphan unit could join his pair of regiments. Ramseur agreed. Ramseur's 2nd and 4th North Carolina, meanwhile, attached themselves to O'Neal's left flank on the McLean farm. Rodes's Division was not acting as a cohesive unit.[44]

Colonel Tilden saw what was happening and gave the order for his 16th Maine to retire. The two left companies along the stone wall flanked south and ran for the cover of Sheads Woods. The right companies in the road about-faced

43 "Bisbee Account." Bisbee probably saw the 14th and the 30th North Carolina of Brig. Gen. Stephen Dodson Ramseur's Brigade moving toward the Forney farm.

44 Gottfried, *Maps of Gettysburg*, 117; *OR* 27/2:525, 567, 573. Daniel's report mentions the cut as the object of his assault. The report of the 43rd North Carolina clearly indicates Daniel's troops went after Stewart's guns south of the cut.

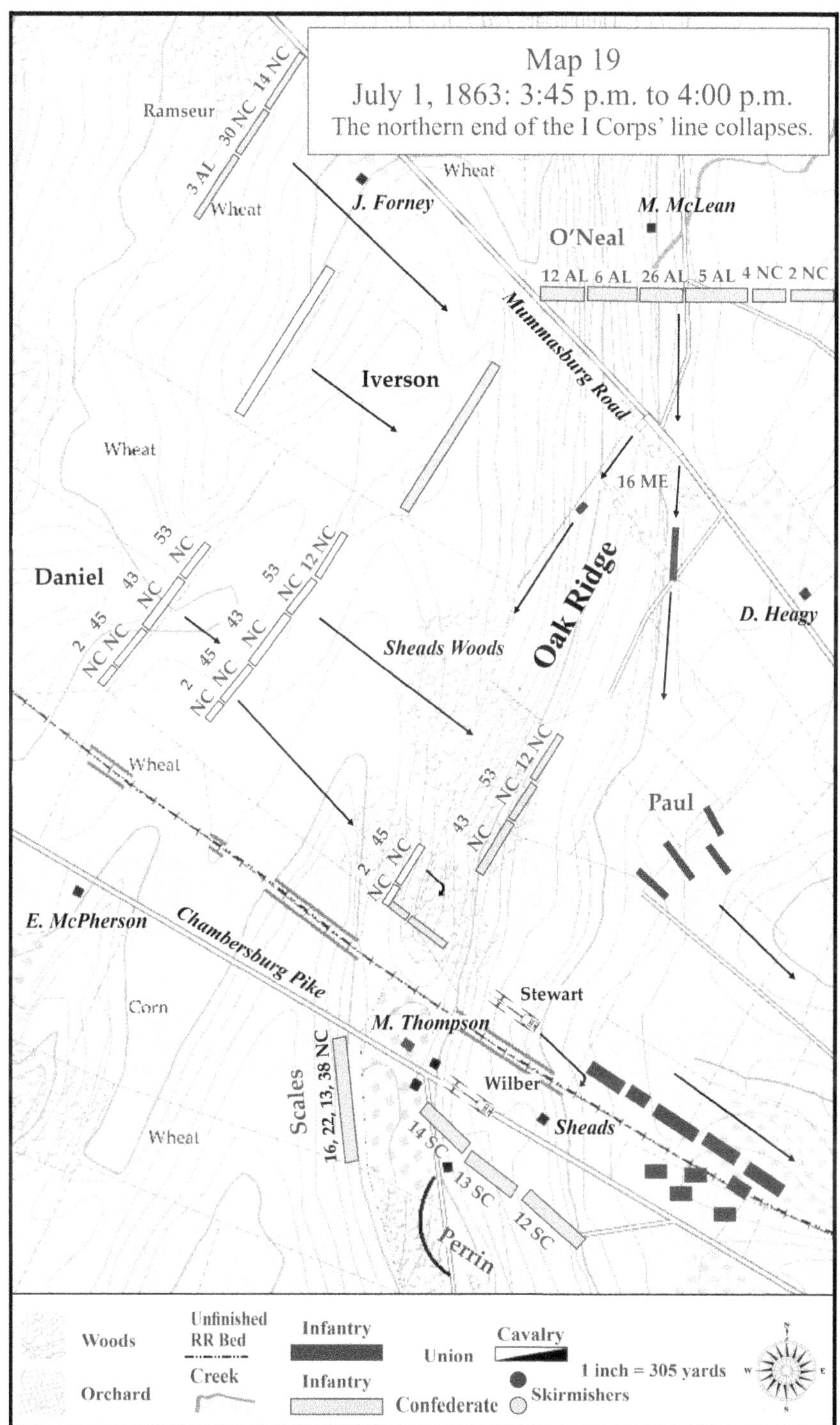
Map 19
July 1, 1863: 3:45 p.m. to 4:00 p.m.
The northern end of the I Corps' line collapses.
Ramseur
14 NC
30 NC
3 AL
Wheat
J. Forney
M. McLean
O'Neal
12 AL
6 AL
26 AL
5 AL
4 NC
2 NC
Mummasburg Road
Iverson
Wheat
16 ME
Oak Ridge
Daniel
53 NC
43 NC
45 NC
2 NC
12 NC
D. Heagy
Sheads Woods
Paul
E. McPherson
Chambersburg Pike
Corn
Stewart
M. Thompson
Wilber
Sheads
Scales
16, 22, 13, 38 NC
14 SC
13 SC
12 SC
Perrin
Woods
Orchard
Unfinished RR Bed
Creek
Infantry
Union
Cavalry
Confederate
Skirmishers
1 inch = 305 yards

Brigadier General Cullen Battle would attach his 3rd Alabama regiment to Stephen Ramseur's command and fight with it on the last two days of the battle. He would replace O'Neal as brigade commander and lead it until a wound knocked him out of the war in the fall of 1864. *Generals in Gray*

and clambered over the southern bank into the low ground formerly held by the 13th Massachusetts and reformed along the fence line inside the strip of woods from which they had initially deployed. The Rebel gunners on Oak Hill zeroed in on them and quickly made that position untenable.[45]

Private James M. Lyford (Company E), recalled the regiment withdrew in "fairly good order," with the men hunched over as they tried to get out of the artillery's range. Lyford lagged behind to help his lamed cousin Pvt. William T. Bates get away from the fighting. Artillery rounds lopped off treetops and shattered their trunks and branches, forcing Lyford to concentrate on both his cousin and the debris raining down from above. A short distance into the woods, Sheads Woods, the concussion from an air burst threw Lyford to the ground unconscious. Lyford was the lucky one. A large chunk from a tree fell and snapped Bates's neck. The 24-year-old hospital steward fell a few feet behind his cousin.

45 *Maine at Gettysburg*, 43; "Bisbee Account"; Peabody, "The 16th ME. At Gettysburg"; James M. Lyford, "How One May Be Mistaken," *NT*, January 6, 1898, 2. The 20 minutes of relatively light engagement by the 16th Maine probably occurred while Daniel waited for Scales to come up on his right. *Maine at Gettysburg* also alludes to the regiment doing some long-range firing, but that it retired south through the woods when the Rebels got within close range. Withdrawing troops tend to escape in the opposite direction of the attack. Therefore, it seems more likely that the right side of the line would have fallen back to the maple tree lot perpendicular to the stone wall, and the men along the wall would have flanked south into Sheads Woods.

When Pvt. Samuel Peabody (Company I) spotted what he believed was a Rebel battle line across their front to the south, he dodged west into the woods. Once through the woodlot, he ran into another line of Southerners just 100 yards away. Some shouted "Halt!" and then fired. Bullets zipped around him as the New Englander dove for cover behind an oak tree.[46]

As Daniel's Brigade drew closer to Sheads Woods with each step, one of General Robinson's aides clattered up to Lt. James Stewart. He apologized to the artillerist for the general forgetting about the guns, and informed him that Robinson wanted him "to fall back to the town as rapidly as possible."

"How far is the division from here?" inquired Stewart.

"Probably half a mile," the aide replied. "Colonel Dawes's regiment, the Sixth Wisconsin, has been moved to another part of the field."

"Then for the first time that day did I realize what the horrors of war meant. As I gave the command to limber to the rear, I could not bring my wounded with me," Stewart recalled decades later, "and the beseeching looks that these men gave me quite unnerved me, I was sorry indeed to leave them to their fate." The upset Scot led his three pieces east through the woods toward the railroad cut.

Robinson had no sooner rallied the 11th and 88th Pennsylvania to cover the battery's withdrawal than Stewart's three teams trampled through and over the center of the 88th. The shock destroyed the formation, and many of the enlisted men and a few of the officers stampeded toward town. Captain Joseph H. Richards (Company E, 88th Pennsylvania) was still clutching the captured flag of the 23rd North Carolina. Richards cut the flag from the staff to keep it for himself. Lieutenant Samuel Boone (Company B) received the brass hilt below the spear point on the top of the pole. Another officer took the spear point and a fourth claimed the staff. The four decided to assist the withdrawing gunners who were stalled at the road grade.[47]

Daniel's command, meanwhile, split as it crested the middle ridge. The 2nd North Carolina Battalion and the 45th North Carolina wheeled right against the middle cut. A stray round seriously wounded Lt. Col. Wharton J. Green in the head, forcing Daniel's aide-de-camp to leave the front. With the 53rd to its left, the 43rd continued tramping east. It halted about 100 yards short of Sheads

46 Peabody, "The 16th ME. At Gettysburg." "Fairly good order" implies some confusion and a less-than-orderly exit from the field.

47 Stewart, "Battery B," 186-187; Grant, "The First Army Corps," 52; Locke, *The Story of the Regiment*, 230; Boone, "Personal Experiences," 23, 24.

Woods, where the men connected with the right of Iverson's isolated 12th North Carolina.

The 12th's 23-year-old Lt. Col. William Smith Davis had seen Private Peabody (16th Maine) dart into the open along the rock ledge in front of him and run for cover when the 53rd sent him packing. Incoming fire began picking up when Pvt. Thomas Gould from Peabody's Company I arrived. After a few minutes of annoying the Rebs, the two bolted for the rear and plummeted down a steep embankment. Peabody kept running, but the fall stunned Gould and he stayed behind.

"The men in our front are listening to the firing on both their flanks, and if we could get up into the woods and surprise them with a charge and a yell they would run," recalled Lieutenant Colonel Davis. The 12th's North Carolina's commander discussed the plan with his company officers, who agreed. The assignment fell to Lt. William N. Sneed (Company B) and 15 hand-picked skirmishers, who advanced to within 40 yards of the retreating Yankees. The moment the skirmishers disappeared into the trees, the remaining 160 or so officers and men in the 12th rent the air with the "Rebel Yell" and charged. The 53rd and 43rd North Carolina regiments of Daniel's command off to the right picked up the war cry and attacked with them. The Yankees who were still in the woods ran—most without firing a shot.[48]

South of the Chambersburg Pike

Scattered groups from the mauled 13th and 14th South Carolina regiments (Perrin's Brigade) swarmed both sides of the seminary, overrunning the hospital and all its occupants. Private Lyman D. Wilson (Company F, 151st Pennsylvania) had just dragged Lt. Col. George McFarland inside the main hall when Rebels entered the building. With his right leg shattered beyond repair and his left one permanently disabled, McFarland already knew his days of field service had ended. Now he was a prisoner of war. The South Carolinians bagged around 50 officers and men from the 121st Pennsylvania in the same vicinity.[49]

The Confederates trapped Lt. Benjamin Wilber's rear piece (Battery L, 1st New York) near the intersection of the seminary lane and the Chambersburg

48 *OR* 27/2:573, 576, 578; Clark, *Histories of the Several Regiments*, 1:638, 3:6, and 4:258; Krick, *Staff Officers in Gray*, 142; Peabody, "The 16th ME at Gettysburg."

49 Ladd & Ladd, *Bachelder Papers*, 1:90; *Pennsylvania at Gettysburg*, 2:653.

Pike. When a minié ball coming from the south killed the wheel horse, Wilber dismounted and cut the dead animal from its harness. By time he got the limber rolling, South Carolinians broadsided him with a volley that killed the wheel driver in his saddle and slaughtered the remaining horses in their traces. A bullet tugged through the lieutenant's beard and another passed through his coat. His mount collapsed beneath him but he slipped from the saddle before the animal hit the ground. Yelling at the remaining drivers to save themselves, Wilber rushed after the lead gun and managed to get it safely off the field.[50]

The rail bed east of the Seminary Ridge cut began rising from two feet to as high as 12 feet as it crossed the valley to the town. To support the elevated track bed, the construction company had piled large rocks along its exterior sides, creating what the men referred to it as a "quarry dump." Though it was only a couple of feet high, the lowest section north of the Sheads house created a treacherous obstacle to the teams pulling the limbers. The first two of Stewart's three guns managed the difficult passage, but the pintle hook that fastened the gun to the third limber broke in the ascent. The gun's trail clanged on the rocks and the 2,600-pound gun free-wheeled into the field below. The crew instantly struggled to uncoil the prolonge from the trail at the same time some of Daniel's North Carolinians emerged from the tree line about 100 yards to the northwest.

"Halt that piece!" one of the Southerners hollered.

A quick-thinking artilleryman defiantly called back, "Don't you see that the piece is halted?"

Fearing the Rebs would capture the gun, Stewart spurred after the two limbers that had gotten away and hurried them back to the southern side of the cut. They rolled into battery with their muzzles over the road bank, loaded canister, and fired. The North Carolinians scrambled back into the woods.

The crew hauled the limber over the low bank to the far side of the cut. After clearing it they had to physically manhandle the gun up over the bank onto the road and then drag it over the opposite side into the field below—all the while underfire and trying not to let the cannon roll over them. Once on better ground, they tied it by the prolonge to the limber. The moment the piece rolled over the bank, the Carolinians charged to within 60 yards of the battery and volleyed, killing the swing driver and wounding the wheel driver and his two horses. The two other pieces fired and temporarily halted the Rebel advance. Stewart used the resultant smoke to limber his guns and get them to the Chambersburg Pike.

50 Wilber Letter; Nevins, *A Diary of Battle*, 237.

The four officers from the 88th Pennsylvania carrying the dismembered remains of the flag and staff of the 23rd North Carolina arrived seconds after the guns departed. Lieutenant Boone (Company B) darted to the northern side of the grade into Confederate skirmishers. He wheeled about, bolted to the opposite side of the bed, and fled toward Gettysburg. Although they were less than 60 yards away, South Carolinians closing in from the south never tried to drop him. They had settled on a larger, more target rich, environment than a single man.[51]

The Palmetto State soldiers halted and volleyed into the right flank of the 143rd Pennsylvania. Their fire forced Lt. Col. John D. Musser and his contingent to the north side of the 10-foot-high railroad grade. The men clawed their way to the top and exposed themselves to more rifle fire from the south. A bullet wounded Pvt. Charles Hoover (Company C) in the leg above the knee; the exhausted soldiers stretched out along the berm to await capture. Lieutenant Charles Plotze (Company A) received his second wound of the day, but survived. Already wounded in the hand, Lt. Charles W. Betzenberger (Company I) did not survive the second bullet that hit him.

A minié grazed Lieutenant Colonel Musser above the knee. He dropped down the opposite side of the cut from the "frying pan into the fire," as shells and small arms volume seemed greater there than on the other side. To the west, North Carolinians streamed from Sheads Woods in extended order. Musser directed whoever was left within ear shot to run along the bank toward the town. On the way, a bullet scratched Cpl. William S. Downey's arm above the elbow. He hung onto the state flag and made a successful getaway.[52]

Abner Perrin's Rebels struck the pike as Stewart's caissons entered it. Wainwright observed the mass exodus from the road and saw an chance to prevent the slaughter of his teams. The infantry cleared the right of way for his guns. "Trot! Gallop!" he screamed. The drivers whipped their horses and the battalion made a dash for safety before the graybacks had time to reload.[53]

Lieutenant Stewart turned his limbers over to Sergeant McBride and spurred west toward the Thompson place to check on Lieutenant Davison's guns. "I could not believe he would have left without informing me of the fact," fumed Stewart, who found nothing but Confederates in the vicinity. The enemy shouted at him to surrender. Instead, he wheeled his horse about and galloped

51 Stewart, "Battery B," 188; Boone, "Personal Experiences," 24.

52 Hoover diary, July 1, 1863; Musser Report; *OR* 27/1:339.

53 Nevins, *A Diary of Battle*, 236.

east to catch up with his battery—and ran into more Rebels between him and his limbers. Determined the avoid capture, Stweart reined to the southeast and galloped cross-country toward a high fence obstructing his path. His horse leaped over without difficulty, but a shell fragment hit Stewart's right thigh in mid-air. The impact nearly knocked him from his horse. He landed on the other side of the fence, felt the leg and determined it was not broken, and pressed on toward West Street. All in all, his was a rather miraculous escape.[54]

Part of the 45th North Carolina (Daniel) swept into the shallow roadbed west of the deep eastern cut while part of it, along with the 43rd, 53rd, and 12th regiments, swung south into the valley north of the elevated track bed. By then the 16th Maine had backed into the rocky side of the track grade alongside part of the 97th New York. The situation quickly devolved into a fight, flee, or surrender moment. Lieutenant Colonel John Spofford of the 97th called together his six remaining officers to discuss their options. Lieutenants James A. Stiles and William B. Judd decided to make a run for it. The others, including Spofford, raced back to the relative shelter of the deep cut.

Stiles, Judd, and others bolted east. "I beg leave to state that it was running the gauntlet in the strict sense of the word," he recalled. "The bullets were flying from each side a perfect shower. The air seemed so filled that it seemed almost impossible to breathe without inhaling them. Someone fell beside me almost every step. It was here that Serg. Fred. Munson fell mortally wounded, and Lieut. James Stiles was killed." Judd reached the outskirts of town unscathed.[55]

The others did not fare as well. The 45th North Carolina trapped the 97th's officers and 73 men in the cut. The 45th's Capt. Alexander H. Gallaway (Company F) searched Lieutenant Colonel Spofford and reclaimed his half of the 20th North Carolina's flag, which he had wrapped beneath his tunic.

The North Carolinians stepped to within 100 feet of Colonel Tilden and his stalwarts of the 16th Maine. Looking rearward, the colonel saw more Rebels (Perrin's South Carolinians) closing in from behind. When he turned back around to face north, he found himself staring at a rifle leveled at him from just

54 Stewart, "Battery B," 188.

55 Letter, R. S. Eggleston, July 7, 1863, and Letter, Lt. Wm. B. Judd, n.d, both found at https://museum.dmna.ny.gov/index.php/?cID=2602, accessed Feb. 20, 2023; Hall, *History of the Ninety-Seventh Regiment*, 142. The officers were Capt. Rouse S. Eggleston and Lts. James A. Stiles (Company D), Henry B. Chamberlain (Company I), Francis Murphy (Company G), Justus O. Rockwell (Company E), and William B. Judd (Company F). The mortally wounded sergeant was Fred Munson (Company D, 97th New York).

30 feet away. "Throw down that sword or I will blow your brains out," the man blustered. Resigned to his fate but unwilling to surrender his sword, Tilden plunged the blade into the ground as far as he could and snapped it off at the hilt.

With Tilden's permission, acting Maj. Samuel Clifford Belcher had the color bearers strip the flags from their staffs and rip them into small pieces. They distributed as many of the fragments as they could before laying down their arms. After completely disarming them, the North Carolinians captured the staff of the national flag with its tassels intact. Pieces of the U.S. flag lay all about the place. As the Rebels led him away, Lt. Lewis Bisbee glanced back at Gettysburg and grinned. The last of the men on the grade had made it into the town.[56]

As he approached town, Colonel Wainwright believed he had safe. He was wrong: "The Rebs pulled off the skirt of my coat," he quipped.

The record offers few specifics, but guns from Lt. Col. John J. Garnett's battalion (Donaldsonville Battery) were called to the front and may have taken up a position on the ridge, perhaps on the open hill north of the seminary. According to Brig. Gen. William Nelson Pendleton, General Lee's chief of artillery, "Garnett's battalion moved to the front, slightly participating in the fight, and then, under cover of a hill near the brick seminary, awaited orders." Whether these rounds struck home is unknown, but there were few if any other Southern guns firing into this area. What we do know is that about this time a solid shot decapitated Lt. Francis Thomas of General Baxter's staff right in front of Lieutenant Judd just as he reached the town. Three other projectiles destroyed three of Lieutenant Stewart's limbers as they entered Gettysburg.[57]

56 *OR* 27/2:575; Eggleston Letter; Judd Letter; *Maine at Gettysburg*, 43, 44; Wiggin, "Sixteenth Maine at Gettysburg," 4:159; "Brisbee Account." Judd claimed the colonel had the colors of the 23rd (20th) North Carolina wrapped around his body. Captain James A. Hopkins (Company E, 45th North Carolina) described the 16th Maine's flag staff as "very fine" with tassels. According to *Maine at Gettysburg*, the 16th surrendered 12 officers and 92 men at the grade. The 97th surrendered five officers and 73 rank and file, for a total of 184. The 45th North Carolina captured 188 men plus "smaller squad[s] in other places."

57 Nevins, *A Diary of Battle*, 237; William N. Pendleton, "A Review of the First Two Days' Operations at Gettysburg," *SHSP*, 5/4:196; OR 27/2:346-354. Bachelder does not show Garnett's Battalion on the field at this time. Garnett's report (*OR* 27/2:652), which contradicts Pendleton's description of the duration of the firing, states that Capt. V. Maurin, with six rifled pieces, "opened upon the enemy, and with apparent effect. These pieces kept up a slow and steady fire *for about an hour* . . . [emphasis added]."

Postscript

Aftermath

4:00 p.m. to 5:00 p.m.

By 4:30 p.m., the battle for Seminary Ridge and Oak Ridge had shifted to street fighting and complete chaos in the streets of Gettysburg, the rounding up of Union stragglers, and general mopping-up operations.

Those Federals who managed to reach the security offered by Cemetery Hill and beyond were left to deal with the horrific losses of their friends and the sanguinary memories of what had just transpired. Sergeant Patrick DeLacy (Company A, 143rd Pennsylvania, Stone's brigade) stopped at a footbridge at the base of the Chambersburg Pike on the edge of town. The indelible image of a corpse on the creek bank, just touching the surface of the stream with its head barely attached to the torso, lingered until the day he died more than half a century later.

Lieutenant Amos D. Rood (Company B, 7th Wisconsin, Iron Brigade) never forgot the ricocheting canister ball that miraculously bounced off his left shoulder blade as he raced down a Gettysburg street in a mad dash to save himself, or the suffocating heat he and his comrades had endured. It was, he recalled simply, "[h]ot as hell."[1]

Lieutenant Colonel John D. Musser (143rd Pennsylvania, Stone's brigade) remembered how he and the few exhausted soldiers left under his command tried to rest when they finally regrouped at the cemetery. They found it impossible to do so. Musser and his fellow Keystone soldiers were overpowered by fatigue but coursing with adrenaline; they could not stay still. Officers and enlisted men anxiously walked about, shaking hands and weeping over the ones who were not there. "We were almost afraid to ask each other where the rest of our regiment was, we knew most of them were either killed or wounded," Musser recalled.

Sergeant Augustus Ziegler (Company A, 24th Michigan, Iron Brigade) was escaping through the town when he noticed the cellars and houses crammed with men from Oliver Howard's routed XI Corps. Some, insisted Ziegler, were so insistent on finding shelter that they had pushed wounded men from the I Corps onto the pavement to clear the way. "I wished at the time," he wrote in a letter after the battle, still upset by what he had witnessed, "that we had the time to commence at one end of the City and shoot everyone that could be found in the town that wasnt wounded. I tell you it would have been a terrible slaughter." The sergeant finished by claiming outright that some of the shirkers had been summarily punished: "I can tell you as a fact that there was as many or more killed by our own officers than by the rebs."[2]

While trying to escape capture, Capt. John D. S. Cook (Company I, 20th N.Y.S.M, Biddle's brigade) cut down a side street toward Baltimore Street. He clambered over the first of a series of fences that ran across his front only to find himself deep in hog manure. Cook had no choice but to slog his way through the offensive muck, angered all the while about the poor sanitation in the town.

The manure-coated New York captain finally staggered into Baltimore Street with artillery rounds crashing into the houses around him. One of the first things he saw was another Federal shrieking as a bullet slammed into him and whirled him in a circle, a hand flailing helplessly in the air as he collapsed face first into the ground. Rifle fire swept the street as Cook bolted into a crowd of

1 "Capt. DeLacy Describes Gettysburg Battle"; Rood, "My Diary of the War," 63, 64.

2 Ziegler, Letter.

frightened soldiers. By some miracle the officer managed to reach Cemetery Hill.[3]

Pursuant to orders, Pvt. Henry Hunterson (Company B, 88th Pennsylvania) and his wounded prisoner arrived at the division hospital located in the Christ Lutheran Church on Chambersburg Street. Hunterson brushed past Assistant Surgeon William F. Osborn (11th Pennsylvania) and Chaplain Horatio Howell of the 90th Pennsylvania, both of whom were ascending the steps into the hospital. Despite being a non-combatant, Howell wore the prescribed straight sword at his side as well as his shoulder boards.

Simultaneously, Dr. Edgar Parker (13th Massachusetts), with the bandaged Sgt. Archibald Snow (Company I, 97th New York) on his heels, stepped onto the landing from the church. Private Hunterson reached the door at the same instant. At that same moment Osborn and Howell stopped on the first step below the porch. Something distracted the chaplain, who turned toward the street in response to the commotion. Hunterson did the same.

A Rebel soldier was rushing toward the base of the steps from the opposite side of the street, lifting his rifle as if to shoot. Hunterson instinctively pulled his prisoner in front of him as a shield and backed through the door. The skirmisher braced one foot on the first step and yelled for Chaplain Howell to surrender. Howell was about to say something when the Rebel pulled his trigger. The minie ball entered the chaplain's forehead and exited the back of his head before glancing off Dr. Parker's skull. Before the chaplain's corpse hit the porch, Surgeon Osborn had bolted inside the church, as had the wounded Sergeant Snow.

The quick-thinking Snow abandoned his prisoner, tied a white rag around his arm, and got a nearby doctor to certify him as a nurse—and escaped capture by doing so. By this time a Confederate lieutenant had arrived with a squad of men to secure the church. When the surgeons complained that one of them had murdered a chaplain, the lieutenant waved off the accusation by explaining that the deceased was armed.[4]

Howell was the only chaplain killed during the battle.

3 Cook, "Personal Reminiscences of Gettysburg," 329.

4 Henry Hunterson, "Escaped Capture," *National Tribune*, March 23, 1911, 7; "The Shooting of Chaplain Howell," www.13thmass.org/1863/gettysburg_4.html#mozToc Id288058; William F. Osborn, "Letter of a Union Chaplain," Vertical Files, Library, GNMP. According to Mary McAllister, Parker was hit with the same bullet that killed Howell. Snow claimed he was right behind Howell, when in all probably it was Parker.

* * *

Major General John Reynolds's I Corps was thoroughly wrecked on July 1, 1863. In addition to the loss of Reynolds, four brigade commanders were wounded: Brig. Gens. Solomon Meredith and Gabriel R. Paul, and Cols. Chapman Biddle and Roy Stone. The corps committed 28 infantry regiments to the battle. Fourteen of the 28 regimental commanders became casualties: 76th New York (killed); 142nd Pennsylvania (mortally wounded); 12th and 13th Massachusetts (wounded); 24th Michigan, 94th, 95th, and 147th New York, 107th, 149th, 150th, and 151st Pennsylvania, and 2nd Wisconsin (wounded); 16th Maine and 97th New York (captured).[5]

Seven of the 28 regiments lost approximately 47% of their original numbers engaged (killed, wounded, missing/captured). Five incurred 54% casualties. Ten left 65% on the field. The remaining six accrued losses totaling 75%. The corps recorded an astounding 2,361 men captured or missing. Put another way, about 40% of the casualties suffered that day were missing or captured.[6]

Just four days later, a grieving Lt. Walter T. Chester (Company D, 94th New York, Paul's brigade) wrote a letter to the *Buffalo Courier*: "Many brave, strong men of the regiment sobbed like children thinking of the seemingly utter wreck of our noble corps."[7]

5 Raus, *A Generation on the March*, 25, 34,44,75, 75, 83, 88,130, 135, 138,139, and 179.

6 Some of the I Corp units, such as Cutler's brigade. were engaged on all three days of the battle. They did not separate and tabulate casualties for each day. The overwhelming majority of the losses, however, were sustained on July 1.

7 Musser Report; "Interesting Letter," July 5, 1863.

Appendix

Order of Battle / Casualties, July 1, 1863

Army of the Potomac: Maj. Gen. George G. Meade

Cavalry Corps (11,846): Maj. Gen. Alfred Pleasanton

First Division (2,752[1]): Brig. Gen. John Buford

1st Brigade (1,600): 8th IL, 12th IL, 3rd IN, 8th NY. Casualties: 99 (6%)

2nd Brigade (1,148): 6th NY, 9th NY, 17th PA, 3rd WV. Casualties: 28 (2%)
Artillery (75): A: 2nd U.S. Casualties: 12 (16%)

Left Wing Commander: Maj. Gen. John F. Reynolds

I Corps (9,836[2])

Maj. Gen. John F. Reynolds / Maj. Gen. Abner Doubleday

General Headquarters 1st Maine Cavalry, Co. L; 121st Pennsylvania, Co. B

1 Division strength does not include the Reserve Brigade of 1,321 officers and men.

2 Martin & Busey, *Regimental Strengths and Losses*, 125-127, 143-144, 146. The numbers for I Corps do not include Stannard's Vermont brigade and the 7th Indiana because neither participated in the July 1 battle. Most of these Federal casualties occurred on July 1. Federal regimental strengths and casualties are from Martin & Busey.

First Division (3,423[3]): Brig. Gen. James F. Wadsworth

1st Brigade (1,829): 19th IN, 24th MI, 2nd WI, 6th WI, 7th WI. Casualties: 1,153 (63%)

2nd Brigade (1,583[4]): 76th NY, 84th NY,[5] 95th NY, 147th NY, 56th PA. Casualties: 992 (62%)

Second Division (2,995): Brig. Gen. John C. Robinson

1st Brigade (1,536): 16th ME, 13th MA, 94th NY, 104th NY, 107th PA, Casualties: 1,021 (67%)

2nd Brigade (1,451): 12th MA, 83rd NY[6], 97th NY, 11th PA, 88th PA, 90th PA. Casualties: 663 (46%)

Third Division (2,751[7]): Brig. Gen. Thomas A. Rowley

1st Brigade (1,361): 80th NY[8], 121st PA, 142nd PA, 151st PA. Casualties: 898 (66%)

2nd Brigade (1,317): 143rd PA, 149th PA, 150th PA. Casualties: 853 (65%)

I Corps Artillery (596): Col. Charles S. Wainwright

B: 2nd ME, E: 5th ME, L: 1st NY, B: 1st PA, B: 4th US. Casualties: 106 (18%)

XI Corps (9242): Maj. Gen. Oliver O. Howard

45th NY (375). Casualties: 224 (60%)

Artillery (127), I, 1st OH. Casualties: 13 (10%)

* * *

3 Each corps, division, and brigade had supernumeraries (staff) added into the number engaged. Brigade numbers included regimental returns, plus brigade staff. Division added its staff to the brigade counts, and corps added its staff to all of the division returns.

4 The 7th Indiana (434) did not participate in the first day's battle; therefore their number is not included in the Order of Battle.

5 Also known as the 14th Brooklyn.

6 Also known as the 9th New York State Militia.

7 The number engaged does not include the 1,950 officers and men of Brig. Gen. George Stannard's 3rd Brigade, which was not involved in the July 1 action.

8 Also known as the 20 New York State Militia.

Army of Northern Virginia: Gen. Robert E. Lee

Second Corps (13,461[9]): Lt. Gen. Richard S. Ewell

Rodes's Division (6,659[10]): Maj. Gen. Robert E. Rodes

Iverson's Brigade (1,384): 5th NC, 12th NC, 20th NV, 23rd NC. Casualties: 751 (54%).

Daniel's Brigade (2,161): 2nd NC Bttn., 32nd NC, 43rd NC, 45th NC, 53rd NC. Casualties: 683 (32%)

O'Neal's Brigade (1,688): 3rd AL, 5th AL, 6th AL, 12th AL, 26th AL. Casualties: 380 (23%)

Ramseur's Brigade (1,027): 2nd NC, 4th NC. 14th NC, 30th NC. Casualties: 117 (11%)

Division Artillery (385): Lt. Col. Thomas H. Carter

Batteries: Reese (AL), W. Carter (VA), Page (VA), Fry (VA). Casualties: 39 (10%)

Third Corps (19,706[11]) : Lt. Gen. Ambrose P. Hill

Heth's Division (6,470): Maj. Gen. Henry Heth

Brockenbrough's Brigade (972): 22nd VA Bttn., 40th VA., 47th VA, 55th VA. Casualties: 116 (12%)

Pettigrew's Brigade (2,580): 11th NC, 26th NC, 47th NC, 52nd NC. Casualties: 978 (38%)

Davis's Brigade (1,713): 2nd MS, 42nd MS, 55th NC. Casualties: 831 (49%)

Archer's Brigade (1,197): 5th AL Bttn., 13th AL, 1st TN PA, 7th TN, 14th TN. Casualties: 336 (28%)

Pender's Division: (4,989): Maj. Gen. William Dorsey Pender

Perrin's Brigade (1,516): 1st SC PA, 12th SC, 13th SC, 14th SC. Casualties: 460 (30%)

9 Confederate troops strengths are drawn from Martin & Busey, *Regimental Strengths and Losses*, 289-305, 313-314. Confederate casualty returns are based on the compilation of numbers drawn from Busey and Busey, *Confederate Casualties at Gettysburg*. Richard H. Anderson's Division (7,136) of Hill's Second Corps was not engaged on July 1.

10 This number does not include Brig. Gen. Doles's Brigade (1,322), which did not engage the I Corps.

11 This total does not include the 11th Mississippi (592), 1st South Carolina Rifles (366), and Brig. Gen. George Thomas's Brigade (1,248), which were absent on other duty or not engaged on July 1.

Lane's Brigade (1,734): 7th NC, 18th NC, 28th NC, 33rd NC, 37th NC. Casualties: 30 (2%)

Scales's Brigade (1,351): 13th NC, 16th NC, 22nd NC, 34th NC, 38th NC. Casualties: 466 (35%)

Third Corps Reserve Artillery (736): Col. R. Lindsay Walker

McIntosh's Artillery Battalion (357): Hurt (AL), Rice (VA), Johnson (VA), Wallace (VA). Casualties: 3 (1%)

Pegram's Artillery Battalion (375): Zimmerman (SC), Johnston (VA), Marye (VA), Brander (VA), McGraw (VA). Casualties: 5 (1%).

Numbers Engaged / Casualties / Percentage of Losses

Army of the Potomac

I Corps: Infantry/Artillery: 9,765 / 5,686 / 58%

Buford's Cavalry Division / Artillery: 2,827 / 139 / 5%

45th NY / 1st OH Btty: 502 / 237 / 47%

Total: 13,094 / 6,062 / 46%

Army of Northern Virginia

Second Corps: Infantry / Artillery: 7,044 / 1,970 / 28%

Third Corps: Infantry / Artillery: 12,195 / 3,225 / 27%

Total: 19,239 / 5,195 / 27%

Bibliography

Primary Sources

Manuscript Collections

Alabama Department of Archives and History, Montgomery, AL

Taylor, Thomas S. to Dear Wife, July 17, 1863

Archives of the Grand Army of the Republic Museum and Library, Philadelphia, PA

Davis, Jacob M. "History of the 19th/90th Pennsylvania Volunteers" (copy)

Ball State University, Indianapolis, IN

Mumaw, Michelle J. "A Boy Goes Off to War: An Honors Thesis," April and May, 1997.

Bowdoin College Library, George J. Mitchell Department of Special Collections & Archives, Brunswick, ME

Howard, Charles Henry. Collection

William R. Brown, Private Collection, Youngstown, OH

Perry, William L. to Dear Friends, July 2, 1863

Clarke Historical Library, Central Michigan University, Mount Pleasant, MI

Hampton Family Papers, 1816-1992

Hampton, Charles George. Diary

William R. Perkins Library, Manuscripts Department, Duke University, Durham, NC

Luttrell, Thomas J. Confederate Diary

Special Collections Department, Franklin and Marshall College, Lancaster, PA

Reynolds, Eleanor. Scrapbook, Reynolds Family Papers

Reynolds, Eleanor. Letter to brother, July 5, 1863: https://digital.fandm.edu/object/islandora5858

Riddle, William. Letter to Lt. Bouvier, August 4, 1863: https://tinyurl.com/48n8h62a

Rosengarten, H. B. Letter to Miss Reynolds, July 11, 1863: https://tinyurl.com/2cd6ysmh

Vertical Files, Library, Fredericksburg and Spotsylvania National Military Park, Fredericksburg, VA

Heermance, William L. Letter to Susie Leeds, July 4, 1863

Special Collections Department, Gettysburg College, Gettysburg, PA

McConaughy, David. Papers

Vertical Files, Library, Gettysburg National Military Park, Gettysburg, PA

Account of Captain Benjamin F. Little, Co. F, 52nd North Carolina

Anonymous Veteran, 8th Illinois Cavalry, *New York Times*, July 1, 1913

Ballenger, David. Letter to Dear Wife, July 8, 1863

Barnes, William C. Letter to W. W. Dudley, March 28, 1883

Bentley, Wilber G. Letter to the Illinois Commandery of the State of Illinois

Blair, J. (John) A. Letter to H. (Henry) H. Lyman September 6, 1888

Blanchard, Elisha A. Letter to Parents, July 5, 1863

Boyden, Sanford N. Letter to Capt. R. [Ralph] E. Gamble, March 15, 1906

Clark, James L. to Maria Funk, July 9, 1863

Christian, W. S. Letter to John W. Daniel, October 24, 1903

Collins, Alexander. Pension File, Certificate No. 68.644, April 17, 1905

Coullahan, James. "The Story of the Colors"

Cramer, George. Letter to Dear Wife, July 11, 1863

Dibble, George Oliver. Letter to Dear Brother Albert, July 7, 1863

Dodge, T. [Theodore] A. Diary

Downing, William S. Letter to Dear Wife, July 6, 1863

Dudley, William W. Letter to George R. Blanchard, August 9, 1887

Fischer, Louis. Memoirs

Foulds, Andrew. Letter to Rev. R. S. Mc Arthur, September 7, 1896

Gamble, William. Letter to W. S. Church, March 10, 1864

Hall, James A. Letter to John B. Bachelder, February 27, 1868

Hoffman, John E. Diary

Hoover, Charles D. W. Diary

Horstmann, Augustus. "Battle of Gettysburg Pa. July 1st 1863, Day 1."

"In the Years '62 to '65, Personal Recollections of Edward R. Gearhart, A Veteran," *The Daily Times*, Stroudsburg, PA, March 19, 1900-August 6, 1900, typescript, paginated

Jones, Marcellus E. Journal, Monday, June 29, 1863, Perrin-Wheaton Chapter, National Society of the Daughters of the American Revolution, Wheaton IL

Hofmann, J. William. "The Battle, Twenty-Three Years Ago," *Gettysburg Compiler*, June 29, 1886.

Krolick, Marshall. Chicago Civil War Round Table, F. Tilberg Copy

Letter to Friend John, July 12, 1863

McCall, John T. "What the Tennesseans Did at Gettysburg"

Markle, Emanuel. "The Story of Battle By Survivor," *Lacrosse Chronicle*, n.d.

May, Robert M. Report of the 47th Virginia, August 13, 1863

Moore, William R. Letter to Sister Lizzie, July 4, 1863

Osborne, William F. "Letter of Union Surgeon"

Phillips, Oliver W. Letter to Rosaltha Gertrude Phillips, July 7, 1863

Sellers, Alfred. Letter, July 9, 1863

Shattuck, Mrs. M. D. Letter to Mother (Mrs. Ira Donelson), July 26, 1863

Slagle, Jacob. Letter to Brother, September 13, 1863

Smith, L. Ward. Letter to Mrs. Bower, July 20, 1863

Thompson, Michael. "In Their Own Words: 19th Indiana at Gettysburg, PA, 1863"

Tomlin, J. E. Letter to William L. White, February 1922

Wheeler, Cornelius. Letter to Parents, July 11, 1863

Williams, Col. Samuel J. Report, August 1, 1863

Wright, William H. Letter to Mary E. Wright, July 7, 1863

Van de Graaff, A. S. Letter to wife, July 8, 1863

Ziegler, Augustus. Letter, July 21, 1863

Huntington Library, San Marino, CA

Webster, Samuel. Diary

William Moore Family Collection, William Henry Smith Memorial Library, Indiana Historical Society, Indianapolis, IN

Moore, William. Autobiography

Indiana State Library, Indianapolis, IN

Bellamy, Flavius Josephus. Letter to Parents, July 3, 1863

Lebanon-Wilson County Library, Lebanon, TN

Fite, John A. Memoirs

Minnesota Historical Society, St. Paul, MN

Account of 1Lt. Lewis Bisbee, Co. I, 16th ME

Bisbee, Lewis Papers

National Archives and Records Administration, Washington, D.C.

Detre, Cyrus S. "The 88th Penna Regt at Gettysburg" (G 94, War Records Office, Union Battle Reports, Vol. 27, Boxes 48-52)

New York State Archives, Albany, NY

GAR Surveys B1706-00

Bell, F. N. Letter to State Historian (Hugh Hastings), February 22, 1898

Richmond, Charles H. "The 104th N.Y. Vols. At the Battle of Gettysburg"

North Carolina State Archives, Raleigh, NC

Willcox, George. Letter to W. H. S. Burgwyn, June 21, 1900, William H. Sumner Burgwyn Papers

North Carolina State Library/Archives, Raleigh, NC

"Reminiscences of Thomas Perritt, 26th North Carolina, Company G"

Oswego County Historical Society, Oswego, NY

Lyman Papers

Pennsylvania State Archives, Harrisburg, PA. Diaries and Journals Collection

Wallace, Stephan A. Diary, September 18, 1862-July 12, 1863

Tom Elmore Private Collection

A. Park, "Some of my Recollections of the Battle of Gettysburg."

United States Army Heritage and Education Center (USAHEC), Carlisle, PA

Boone, Samuel G. "Personal Experiences" (Michael Winey Collection)

Calder, William. Letter (Robert L. Brake Collection)

Coburn, Robert S. Diary (Civil War Times Illustrated Collection)

Chapman, George Henry. Diary

Frank, Abner. Diary

Gamble, Ralph. Letter to John H. Bassler, May 8, 1907 (Ramsey-Bassler Collection)

Hatchett, William J. Letter to My Dear Parents, July 7, 1863 (Civil War Times Illustrated Collection)

Hoffman, John E. Diary (Robert L. Brake Collection)

Heller, Calvin S. Diary (Civil War Miscellaneous Collection)

Hubler, Simon. "Just a Plain, Untarnished Story of a Soldier in the Ranks," *New York Times*

Jennings, Frank. "Reminiscence" (*Civil War Times Illustrated* Collection)

"Excerpt from Chronicles of Francis Bacon Jones" (Robert L. Brake Collection)

Marsh, Henry C. "The Nineteenth Indiana at Gettysburg"

Mesnard, Luther B. "Recollections," May 6, 1901 (Civil War Miscellaneous Collection)

Musser, John D. Unpublished Report, September 15, 1863, John D. Musser Papers (Ronald D. Boyer Collection)

Root, Roswell L. Letter to Grand Father, August 23, 1863 (Gregory A. Coco Collection)

Veil, Charles Henry. "An Old Boy's Recollections and Reminiscences of the Civil War" (Civil War Miscellaneous Collection)

Southern Historical Collection, University of North Carolina, Chapel Hill, NC

Allen-Simpson Papers

Coghill, John Fuller. Papers

Erwin, George Phifer. Papers

Hoyle, Lemuel J. Papers

Lane, John R. Papers

Lineback, Julius A. Papers

McCain Archives and Library, University of Southern Mississippi, Hattiesburg, MS

Dawes (Rufus R.) Letters

Virginia Historical Society, Richmond, VA

Carter, Thomas H. Letter to D. H. Hill, July 1, 1885

Wisconsin Historical Society, Madison, WI

Dawes, Rufus. Papers

Hill, D. J. Letter to Rufus Dawes, September 12, 1893

Dillion, Henry Papers
Winkler, Frederick C. "The 26th Wisconsin at Gettysburg," Box 2, Folder 17
Fairchild, Charles Papers
Fairchild, Lucius. Incomplete Draft of Report
Rollins, Nathaniel. Journal: https://tinyurl.com/4zmah66u
Rood, Amos D. "My Diary of the War"
Watrous, J. A. Watrous Papers
Fairfield, George. Letter to J. A. Watrous, undated, Box 2, Civil War Materials
Rogers, Earl M. Letter to J. A. Watrous, undated, Box 2, Civil War Materials

Websites and Online Sources

"23rd North Carolina Infantry": www.23rdnorthcarolinainfantry.weebly.com/about.html
"26th North Carolina Infantry Regiment": https://tinyurl.com/mfz6w2xt
"The 94th in the Battle at Gettysburg": https://tinyurl.com/3thnhwry
"1860 U.S. Federal Census, Borough of Gettysburg, Adams County, Pennsylvania": https://tinyurl.com/mr44yhwh
"1868 Map of Washington Township, PA": https://tinyurl.com/4rfxjuf4
"Army Correspondence," C. A. Watkins, July 21, 1863: https://tinyurl.com/2f9jue7h
"The Burning of the McLean House on the First Day's Battle of Gettysburg": https://tinyurl.com/bd5ycrc6
"Camp Correspondence—76 Regiment N. Y. S. V.": https://tinyurl.com/39ruapj9
"The Cannoneer Redux": https://tinyurl.com/3nhhudpm
"Charles Henry McConnell": https://tinyurl.com/3tk6bwuu
"Confederate Couriers at Gettysburg": https://tinyurl.com/2tzxvey2
"Corporal Chapin W. Merrick, Co. G": https://www.76nysv.us/76merrickc.html
"David Schriver": www.findagrave.com/memorial/39383726/david-schriver
"David S. Finefrock": www.wikitree.com/wiki/Finefrock-93
"Death of Reynolds—Gettysburg": http://loc.gov/resource/ppmsca.21792
"Diary of Lt. Samuel E. Sanders": https://76.nysv.us/76saundersse.html
"Diary of Sergeant John Boudwin": http://13thmass.org/1863/gettysburg.html#mozTocld346526
"Edward Scipio 'Sip' Hart": www.findagrave.com/memorial/10385451/edward-scipio-hart
"Elizabeth Keefauver": www.findagrave.com/memorial/32783303/elizabeth-keefauver
"Emanuel Harmon": www.findagrave.com/memorial/205139851/emanuel-harmon
Extracts from Letters of William B. Judd, 97th New York: https://tinyurl.com/3etmwavb
"Frances Amanda Morrill Hazelton": https://tinyurl.com/ahcsw932
"From Reynolds' Battery": https://tinyurl.com/yc48bkna
"From the 94th": https://museum.dmna.ny.gov/index.php/?cID=2557
"From the 147th Regiment (officer letter, 147th New York)": https://tinyurl.com/yck5vjpx

"From the Gallant Old Twentieth": https://museum.dmna.ny.gov/index.php/?cID=2461

"Gabriel Durham, the First to Fall at Gettysburg": https://tinyurl.com/yve54hft

"George H. Stevens": www.findagrave.com/memorial/5903866/george-h-stevens

Hannah Catherine Schriver Spangler: www.findagrave.com/memorial/18347356

Edgar Haviland to "Dear Mother": https://www.75nysv.us/76havilanded.html

Hartwig, Scott. "From the Library: 'Consolidated Return of the Loss and Expenditure of Artillery and Artillery Materiel in the Battle of Gettysburg'": https://tinyurl.com/yckpcmju

Interesting Letter from the 94th—The Buffalo Company and Its Loss: https://tinyurl.com/27ensbar

John Carroll Delaney: www.findagrave.com/memorial/6172366/john-carroll-delaney

Joseph H. Richards: www.findagrave.com/memorial/95968710/joseph-h-richards

Letter from Capt. R. S. Eggleston: https://tinyurl.com/3etmwavb

Letter from Colonel Root: https://museum.dmna.ny.gov/index-php/?cID=2557

Letters of Sergeant George Henry Hill, Aug. 4, 1863: https://tinyurl.com/mrye7bdt

Letter on Death of Winfield Scott Safford: gdg.org/research/people/safford.html

Letters of Rush Palmer Cady (97th NY Infantry): elib.hamilton.edu/cady

Letters of Warren Freeman & William Newhall; Parole Camp, West Chester, PA: https://tinyurl.com/4kx868pz

Levi Spangler: www.findagrave.com/memorial/18347348/levi-spangler

Lieutenant A. Lyman Carter: https://76nysv.us/76carteral.html

List of Casualties in the Eighth New York Cavalry: https://tinyurl.com/2yfux8z2

Map #22, Adams County, Pennsylvania, 1858: https://tinyurl.com/ye2y42rz

Map of Franklin County, PA: http://usgwarchives.net/maps/pa/county/frankl/frankln2.jpg

Map of Washington Township, Franklin County, PA: https://tinyurl.com/35kb5kjf

Memoirs of Private Bourne Spooner, Company D, "In the Ranks": https://tinyurl.com/yz4hcf84

Miller, John A. War Returns to South Mountain: https://southmountaincw.wordpress.com

Murdock, David A. "Catherine Mary White Foster's Eyewitness Account of the Battle of Gettysburg, with Background on the Foster Family Union Soldiers": https://tinyurl.com/mryeukdc

Paddy's Wedding sung by Peter Dawson: https://www.youtube.com/watch?v=bk7AsG0ZxnI

Palmer, Richard F. "Lucius Davis Meets General Doubleday": https://76nysv.us/davis-double.html

———. "A Newspaper Editor's View of Gettysburg": https://76nysv.us/ed-getty.html

Pee Dee Artillery: http://www.wadehamptoncamp.org/pdla-sc-hist.html

Pulis, Daniel. Letter to Parents, July 6, 1863, in "Regimental Histories, 8th New York Cavalry": https://tinyurl.com/ycenncjt

Reed, Elisha Rice. "General Lee at Gettysburg, Pa.": https://tinyurl.com/5n7psd6v

Riggleman, Michael. "Poinsett's Cavalry Tactics for Reenactors": https://tinyurl.com/yeyub4nk

Rosalie the Prairie Flower: https://www.youtube.com/watch?v=OfNZUX4VMZ4

Roster of Officers & Men, Co. A, Second Artillery, 1861-1865: https://tinyurl.com/42c6ymbm

Rulandus Pitts: https://76nysy.us/76pittsr.html

Sergeant Melvin H. Walker's Reminiscence: https://tinyurl.com/2p8c8ape

Signal Corps Reenactor's Service Manual: https://tinyurl.com/mncr9wpe

Suffers Since War: One of the Most Interesting Civil War Narratives is that of an Oshkosh Veteran: http://content.wisconsinhistory.org/cdm/ref/collection/quiner/id/27588/rec/3

Thompson, D. G. Brinton. "From Chancellorsville to Gettysburg, A Doctor's Diary": https://www.jstor.org/stable/20089816

William Cline Diary: https://rarebooks.nd.edu/digital/civil_war/diaries_journals/cline/

William Cross Hazelton: https://tinyurl.com/ykxa8dwu

"William Edward Foster to Martha (Williams) Foster": https://tinyurl.com/ycyp93w2

"William H. Boyd": www.oshkoshmuseum.org/Virtual/exhibit3/e30036a.htm

"William Keefauver": www.findagrave.com/memorial/32783314/william-keefauver

"William R. Warner's Account of the Battle": https://tinyurl.com/ppuzad6v

"A Wounded Man's Walk-Through St. Francis Xavier, Gettysburg": https://tinyurl.com/2u938xd4

Newspapers

The Adams Sentinel (Gettysburg, PA)

The Anderson Intelligencer (Anderson Court House, SC)

Baraboo Republic (Baraboo, WI)

Bloomfield Monitor (Bloomfield, NE)

The Boston Journal (Boston, MA)

The Boston Sunday Globe (Boston, MA)

Boston Traveler (Boston, MA)

Cambridge City Tribune (Cambridge City, IN)

The Charleston Weekly News (Charleston, SC)

Charlotte Daily Observer (Charlotte, NC)

Cherry Valley Gazette (Cherry Valley, NY)

Daily Times (Stroudsburg, PA)

Elkhart Review (Elkhart, IN)

Eugene Register Guard (Eugene, OR)

The Evening Star (Washington, D.C.)

Free Press (Muncie, IN)

The Galveston Daily News (Galveston, TX)

Gettysburg Compiler (Gettysburg, PA)

Gettysburg Times (Gettysburg, PA)

Indianapolis Journal (Indianapolis, IN)

Lebanon Democrat (Lebanon, TN)

Lebanon Courier (Lebanon, PA)

Lenoir Topic News (Lenoir, NC)

The Mauston Star (Mauston, WI)

Milwaukee Sunday Telegraph (Milwaukee, WI)

Mobile Evening News (Mobile, AL)

Montgomery Weekly Advertiser (Montgomery, AL)

Newberry Herald (Newberry, SC)

The News and Courier (Charleston, SC)

The News and Observer (Raleigh, NC)

Newark Sunday Call (Newark, NJ)

New York Times (New York, NY)

Richmond Enquirer (Richmond, VA)

Richmond Palladium (Richmond, IN)

Rochester Daily Union and Advertiser (Rochester, NY)

Philadelphia Weekly Press (Philadelphia, PA)

The Scranton Truth (Scranton, PA)

The Star Press (Muncie, IN)

The State Journal (Raleigh, NC)

Winchester Journal (Winchester, IN)

Wisconsin State Journal (Madison, WI)

Published Primary Sources

Articles and Pamphlets

"A Company Officer." "Reminiscences of the Battle of Gettysburg," *Lippincott's Magazine*, New Series, (Philadelphia, PA, 1883), 23:54-60.

Anonymous. "Buford's Cavalry at Gettysburg," *National Tribune*, August 27, 1891, 3.

Baker, John. "The First Man Killed at Gettysburg," *National Tribune*, September 12, 1901, 3.

———. "First Man Killed at Gettysburg," *National Tribune*, December 24, 1903, 3.

Balsey, J. R. "On the Field Among the Enemy, and in the Hospitals Cared for by Patriotic Women," *National Tribune*, May 19, 1898, 3.

Barlow, A. R. "A Defense of the Eleventh Corps," *National Tribune*, January 15, 1885, 1.

———. "Another Shot at Comrade Beale," *National Tribune*, April 23, 1885, 3.

Bassler, John H. "The Color Episode, of the One Hundred and Forty-Ninth Regiment Pennsylvania Volunteers in the First Day's Fight at Gettysburg, July 1st, 1863," *Paper Read Before the Lebanon County Historical Society, October 18th, 1907*, 1-34.

Beecham, Robert K. "Adventures of an Iron Brigade Man," *National Tribune*, October 30, 1902, 3.

Belo, A. H. "The Battle of Gettysburg," in *Confederate Veteran*, 40 vols. (1893-1932), vol. 8 (1900), 165-168.

Beveridge, John L. "The First Gun at Gettysburg," in *Military Essays and Recollections; Papers Read Before the Commandery of the State of Illinois, Military Order of the Loyal Legion of the United States*, 8 vols., 2:79-98.

Bisbee, George D., "Three Years a Volunteer Soldier in the Civil War, Antietam to Appomattox," in *War Papers Read Before the Commandery of the State of Maine, Military Order of the Loyal Legion of the United States*, 4 vols., 4:114-149.

Bishop, C. D. "Starting the Gettysburg Fight," *National Tribune*, June 2, 1910, 2.

Blodget, William D., to "Dear Wife" [Esther Spencer Blodget], July 2, 1863, "Stepping Stones," Warren County Historical Society, No. 1 (March 1956), 2:36-37.

Boland, E. T. "Beginning of the Battle of Gettysburg," *Confederate Veteran*, vol. 14 (1906), 308.

Bradshaw, E. [Elmer] M. "That March to Gettysburg," *National Tribune*, September 30, 1909, 7.

"Brave Carolinian Fell at Gettysburg," in *Southern Historical Society Papers*, 52 vols. (1876-1959), vol. 35 (1907), 320-322.

Burgwyn, William H. S. "Unparalleled Loss of Company F, 26th North Carolina Regiment, Pettigrew's Brigade, at Gettysburg," *Southern Historical Society Papers*, vol. 28 (1900), 199-203.

Burrell, A. B. *No! Never Surrender: Last Words of the Rev. H. S. Howell, Chaplain of the 90th P.V., Who Fell In Front of College Church Hospital on the First Day of the Battle of Gettysburg,"* Handbill, Delaware Water Gap, PA, 1863.

Caison, Stacey Albert. "Southern Soldiers in Northern Prisons," *Southern Historical Society Papers*, vol. 23 (1895), 158-164.

Calef, John H. "Gettysburg Notes: The Opening Gun," in *Journal of the Military Service Institution of the United States*, vol. 40 (1907), 40-58.

Coey, James. "Cutler's Brigade: The 147th N. Y.'s Magnificent Fight on the First Day at Gettysburg," *National Tribune*, July 15, 1915, 7.

Cook, C. W. "A Day at Gettysburg," *National Tribune*, April 7, 1898, 2.

———. "Who Opened Gettysburg?" *National Tribune*, November 14, 1892, 4.

Cook, John D. S. "Personal Reminiscences of Gettysburg," in *War Talks in Kansa;, A Series of Papers Read Before the Kansas Commandery of the Military Order of the Loyal Legion of the United States*, 1906, 321-341.

Cooke, Sidney G. "The First Day at Gettysburg," in *War Talks in Kansas; A Series of Papers Read Before the Kansas Commandery of the Military Order of the Loyal Legion of the United States*, 1906, 276-286.

Cotton, E. (Edwin). "The Men Who Made the Music: How the 24th Michigan Band Went Through the War," *National Tribune*, July 7, 1894, 2.

Dawes, Rufus R. "With the Sixth Wisconsin at Gettysburg," in *Sketches of War History, 1861-1865. Papers Prepared for the Ohio Commandery of the Military Order of the Loyal Legion of the United States, 1888-1890*, 3:364-384.

Day, Thomas G. "Opening the Battle. A Cavalryman's Recollections of the First Day's Fight at Gettysburg," *National Tribune*, July 30, 1903, 3.

Decke, N. (William H.) "Gettysburg," *National Tribune*, May 1, 1902, 3.

De Peyster, John Watts. "The Death of Reynolds," *Army and Navy Journal*, vol. 4, no. 43 (June 22, 1867), 694-695.

Dodge, Horace O. "Opening the Battle: Lieut. Jones, the 8th Ill. Cavalryman, Fired the First Shot at Gettysburg," *National Tribune*, September 24, 1891, 3.

Ebersole, Jacob. "Incidents of Field Hospital Life With the Army of the Potomac," in *Sketches of War History 1861-1865, Papers Prepared for the Ohio Commandery of the Military Order of the Loyal Legion of the United States, 1890-1896*, 4:327-333.

Eldred, William D. "Gettysburg," *The National Tribune*, February 25, 1892, 4.

Fairfield, George. "The 6th Wis. At Gettysburg," *National Tribune*, December 14, 1905, 3.

———. "The Capture of the Railroad Cut," *National Tribune*, September 1, 1910, 3.

"The Field of Gettysburg," *The Atlantic Monthly*, vol. 16, no. 97 (November 1865), 616-624.

"First Shot at Gettysburg," *National Tribune*, October 30, 1902, 5.

Fischer, Louis. "At Gettysburg," *National Tribune,* December 12, 1889, 3.

Fleet, C. B. "In the Three Days' Battle at Fredericksburg, 1863," *Southern Historical Society Papers*, 52 vols (1876-1905), 32:240-242.

Fulton, James. "A Surgeon's Story of the Battle on Pennsylvania's Soil," *National Tribune*, October 20, 1898, 1.

Fulton, W. F. "The Fifth Alabama Battalion at Gettysburg," *Confederate Veteran*, vol. 31 (1923), 379.

Gardner, James M. "Union vs. Rebel Cavalry," *National Tribune*, May 24, 1888, 4.

Grant, George W. "The First Army Corps on the First Day at Gettysburg," in *Glimpses of the Nation's Struggle; Papers Read Before the Minnesota Commandery of the Loyal Legion of the United States, 1892-1897*, 5:45-57.

Hall, Isaac. "Iverson's Brigade, and the Part the 97th New York Played in Its Capture," *The National Tribune*, June 26, 1884, 7.

Halstead, Eminel Potter. "The First Day of the Battle of Gettysburg," *A Paper Read Before the District of Columbia Commandery of the Military Order of the Loyal Legion of the United States*, 1:3-10.

Hancock, Winfield Scott. "Gettysburg: Reply to General Howard, 'The war's over, but the fighting has just begun.'" *The Galaxy: Magazine of Entertaining Reading*, vol. 22 (June 1876-January 1877), 821-831.

Hand, J. W. "Gettysburg," *National Tribune*, July 24, 1890, 3.

Hankins, Samuel W. "Simple Story of a Soldier," *Confederate Veteran*, vol. 20 (1912), 442, 457, 571.

Hanna, Thomas L. "A Day at Gettysburg," *National Tribune*, May 23, 1901, 6.

Harries, William H. "The Iron Brigade in the First Days' Battle at Gettysburg," in *Glimpses of the Nation's Struggle; Papers Read Before the Minnesota Commandery of the Loyal Legion of the United States, 1892-1897*, 4:37-350.

———. "The Sword of Gen. James J. Archer," in *Confederate Veteran*, vol. 19 (1911), 420.

Hawkins, Norma Fuller. "Sergeant Major Blanchard at Gettysburg," *Indiana Magazine of History*, vol. 34, no. 2 (June 1938), 212-216.

Hayes, Michael. "The 2d U.S. Arty," *National Tribune*, December 29, 1892, 4.

Hazelton, William C. "People of Gettysburg," *National Tribune*, March 24, 1892, 4.

Hofmann, J. William. "Gettysburg," *National Tribune*, June 19, 1884, 7.

———. "Remarks on the Battle of Gettysburg," *Paper Read Before the Historical Society of Pennsylvania, March 8th 1880*. Philadelphia: A. W. Aunes, Printer, 1880, 3-8.

"Hon. William W. Dudley, Commissioner of Pensions," *National Tribune*, August 20, 1881, 5.

Hopkins, Thomas B. "It Came From a Volley, Not From a Sharpshooter," *National Tribune*, April 4, 1910, 6.

Huber, A. H. "At Gettysburg," *National Tribune*, December 8, 1892, 1.

Hughes, Morgan. "Buford's Cavalry at Gettysburg," *National Tribune*, August 27, 1891, 3.

Ivy, William T. "At Gettysburg," *National Tribune*, July 11, 1901, 3.

———. "The Battle of Gettysburg," *National Tribune,* March 21, 1901, 3.

Jepson, George E. "Reflections of a Private," 13th Regiment Association Circular #15 (December 1902), 13-23.

"John Burns of Gettysburg," *National Tribune*, August 19, 1886, 4.

Keiffer, Harry M. "Recollections of a Drummer Boy," *National Tribune,* December 31, 1881, 6.

Kelley, T. Benton. "An Account of Who Opened the Battle By One Who Was There," *National Tribune*, December 31, 1891, 4.

Kelley, Thomas B. "First Shot at Gettysburg, It Was fired by Lieut. E. M. Jones, 8th Ill. Cav.," *National Tribune*, October 15, 1908, 7.

Kensill, John C. "A Gettysburg Coincidence." *National Tribune*, January 21, 1882.

Kimball, George. "A Young Hero of Gettysburg," *Century Magazine* (November 1886- April 1887), 133-134.

Kimble, June. "Tennesseans at Gettysburg—The Retreat," *Confederate Veteran*, vol. 18 (1910), 460-463.

Lyford, James M. "How One May Be Mistaken," *National Tribune*, January 6, 1898, 2.

Lyman, H. H. "General Howard Criticized," *National Tribune*, March 12, 1885, 8.

Marye, John L. "The First Gun at Gettysburg, With the Confederate Advance Guard," in Charles H. Browning, ed., *The American Historical Register* (March 1895-August 1895), 1225-1232.

McCall, W. M., "I was much gratified…," *Confederate Veteran*, vol. 3 (1895), 19.

McConnell, Charles H. "The First and Greatest Days Battle at Gettysburg," *National Tribune*, July 13, 1916, 7.

Miller, William H. "They All Helped To Do It," *National Tribune*, October 15, 1885, 5.

Monroe, Haskell, ed. "The Road to Gettysburg"—The Diary and Letters of Leonidas Torrence of the Gaston Guards," *The North Carolina Historical Review*, vol. 36, no. 4 (October 1959, 476-517.

Moon, W. H. "Beginning of the Battle of Gettysburg," *Confederate Veteran*, vol. 33 (1925), 449-450.

Moore, J. H. "Seventh Tennessee Infantry," in John Berrien Lindsley, ed., *The Military Annals of Tennessee, Confederate, First Series* (1886), 227-259.

Morris, R. W. "The First Corps at Gettysburg," *National Tribune*, May 19, 1887, 3.

Northrup, Rufus P. [G.] "Booze Made Tigers Reckless," *National Tribune*, December 30, 1909, 7.

———. "Going Into Gettysburg," *National Tribune*, October 11, 1906, 6.

Norton, Walter B. "The Last Word About the First Shot," *National Tribune*, April 24, 1884, 7.

Parkhurst, Burns E. "At Gettysburg: Heroism of the 147th N. Y.," *National Tribune*, November 1, 1888, 3.

Peabody, Samuel. "The 16th ME. At Gettysburg," *National Tribune*, April 18, 1901, 3.

Pendleton, William N. "A Review of the First Two Days' Operations at Gettysburg," *Southern Historical Society Papers*, vol. 5 (January-June, 1878), 194-201.

Phipps, William H. "Was at Gettysburg," *National Tribune*, September 13, 1894, 3.

———. "Saw Gettysburg Battle," *National Tribune,* July 21, 1904, 3.

Pierce, J. V. "Gettysburg," *National Tribune*, April 3, 1884, 7.

Reed, E. R. "What Our Veterans Have to Say About Their Old Campaigns," *National Tribune*, March 30, 1884, 7.

Robertson, John P. "Opening the Battle. How I Saw the First Shot Fired at Gettysburg," *National Tribune*, April 2, 1903, 3.

Sayre [Sayn], R. [Randle] D. "A Day at Gettysburg," *National Tribune*, April 13, 1893, 3.

Shafer, John. "First In at Gettysburg," *National Tribune*, August 25, 1887, 3.

Shapiro, Norman M. "John Benton Callis: Madison County's Republican Congressman," *The Huntsville Historical Review*, vol. 29, no. 2 (Spring-Summer, 2004), 7-56.

Shearer, Robert A. "The Cannoneer," *National Tribune*, April 17, 1890, 5.

Shears, George W. "The 12th Illinois Cav., Its Part in the Gettysburg Campaign," *National Tribune*, February 5, 1891, 3.

Smith, Lucien A. "Recollections of Gettysburg," in *War Papers Read Before the Michigan Commandery of the Military Order of the Loyal Legion of the United States*, 3 vols., 2:297-308.

Stewart, James. "Battery B Fourth United States Artillery at Gettysburg," in *Sketches of War History, 1861-1865, Papers Prepared for the Ohio Commandery of the Military Order of the Loyal Legion of the United States 1890- 1896*, 8 vols., 4:180-193.

Storch, Marc and Beth Storch, eds. "Unpublished Gettysburg Reports by the 2nd and 7th Wisconsin Infantry Regimental Officers," *Gettysburg Magazine* (July 1, 1997), 20-25.

Sweetland, A. F. "The 55th Ohio at Gettysburg," *National Tribune*, September 9, 1909, 7.

Tripp Bradford H. "The Iron Brigade: They Opened the Battle of Gettysburg," *National Tribune*, June 18, 1891, 3.

Tripp, Bradford H. "At Gettysburg: Substantiating the Claim That the Iron Brigade Opened the Battle," *National Tribune*, September 24, 1892, 4.

Trotter, M. L. "Opening the Ball at Gettysburg," *National Tribune*, January 31, 1884, 7.

Turney, J. B. "The First Tennessee at Gettysburg," *Confederate Veteran*, vol. 8 (1900), 535-537.

"War Diary of Capt. Robert Emory Park," *Southern Historical Society* Papers, vol. 26 (1898), 1-31.

Waterman, Frederick C. "At Gettysburg: Another Comrade Thinks the Iron Brigade Opened the Battle," *National Tribune*, October 27, 1892, 4.

Wehrum, Charles C. "Iverson's Brigade," *The National Tribune*, August 21, 1884, 3.

———. "What Our Veterans Have to Say About Their Old Campaigns," *National Tribune*, August 21,1884, 3.

Wehrum, Charles C., "The Adjutant of the 12th Mass. Replies to the Captain of the 97th N.Y.," *The National Tribune*, December 10, 1885, 3.

Wells, Edmund. "A Personal Reminiscence of July 1st to July 4th, at Gettysburg, Penna.," *Montgomery County Historical Society Publication*, vol. 6 (1929), 63-67.

Wheeler, Cornelius. "Reminiscences of the Battle of Gettysburg," in *War Papers. Read Before the Commandery of the State of Wisconsin, Military Order of the Loyal Legion of the United States*, 4 vols., 2:207-220.

Whitney, M. M. "The 76th New York," *National Tribune*, July 21, 1887, 5.

Wiggin, Francis. "Sixteenth Maine at Gettysburg," in *War Papers Read Before the Commandery of Maine, Military Order of the Loyal Legion of the United States*, 4 vols. (1910), 150-170.

Willett, Frank E. "A Comrade Who Says the 8th N. Y. Cav. Opened the Great Battle," *National Tribune*, December 1, 1892, 4.

Books

Alleman, Tillie Pierce. *At Gettysburg, or What a Girl Saw and Heard of the Battle*. New York: W. Lake Borland, 1889.

Annual Report of the Adjutant-General of the Commonwealth of Massachusetts, December 31, 1863. Boston: Wright & Potter, State Printers, 1864.

Atkinson, William B., ed., *The Physicians and Surgeons of the United States*. Philadelphia: Charles Robson, 1878.

Aubery, Cullen B. *Echoes From the Marches of the Famous Iron Brigade*. Milwaukee: privately published, 1900.

Baker, Levi. *History of the Ninth Massachusetts Battery*. Lancaster, OH: Vanberg Publishing, 1996.

Barlow, A. R. *Company G: A Record of the Services of One Company of the 157th N. Y. Vols. in the War of the Rebellion*. Syracuse, NY: A. W. Hall, 1899.

Bates, Samuel P. *History of Pennsylvania Volunteers, 1861-5*, 5 vols. Harrisburg, PA: B. Singerly, 1869 71.

Beck, Brandon H. *Third Alabama! The Civil War Memoir of Brigadier General Cullen Andrews Battle, CSA*. Tuscaloosa, AL: University of Alabama Press, 2000.

Beale, James. *The Statements of Time on July 1, 1863, at Gettysburg PA*. Philadelphia: James Beale Printer, 1897.

Beaudot, William J. K. and Lance J. Herdegen. *An Irishman In The Iron Brigade: The Civil War Memoirs of James P. Sullivan, Sergt., Company K, 6th Wisconsin Volunteers*. New York: Fordham University Press, 1993.

Beecham, Robert K. *Gettysburg: The Pivotal Battle of the Civil War*. Chicago: McClurg & Co., 1911.

Beyer, Walter F. and Oscar F. Keydel, eds. *Deeds of Valor*, 2 vols. Detroit: Perrien-Keydel Co., 1901.

Bird, William H. *Stories of the Civil War*. Columbiana, AL: Advocate Print, n.d.

Boies, Andrew J. *Record of the Thirty-Third Massachusetts Volunteer Infantry From Aug. 1862 to Aug. 1865*. Fitchburg, MA: Sentinel Printing Co., 1880.

Bokum, Hermann. *Wanderings North and South,* Philadelphia: King and Baird, Printers, 1864.

Boyles, J. R. *Reminiscences of the Civil War*. Columbia, SC: The Bryan Printing Co., 1892.

Breshears, Guy, ed. *Loyal Till Death: A Diary of the 13th New York Artillery*. Bowie, MD: Heritage Books, Inc., 2003.

Brown, Hiram O. and M. A. W. Brown. *Soldiers' and Citizens' Album of Biographical Record Containing Personal Sketches of Army Men And Citizens Prominent in Loyalty to the Union*. Chicago, IL: Grand Army Publishing Co., 1888.

Brown, J. Willard. *The Signal Corps, U. S. A. in the War of the Rebellion*. Boston: U.S. Veteran Signal Corps Association, 1896.

Brown, Varina Davis. *A Colonel at Gettysburg and Spotsylvania*. Columbia: State Company, 1931.

Butterfield, Consul W. *History of Crawford and Richland Counties, Wisconsin*. Springfield, IL: Union Publishing Co., 1894.

Butts, Joseph Tyler, ed. *A Gallant Captain of the Civil War; Being the Record of the Extraordinary Adventures of Frederick Otto Baron von Fritsch*. New York: F. Tennyson Neely, 1902.

Caldwell, J. F. J. *The History of a Brigade of South Carolinians Known First as "Gregg's," and Subsequently as "McGowan's Brigade."* Philadelphia: King & Baird, Printers, 1866.

Chamberlin, Thomas. *History of the One Hundred And Fiftieth Regiment, Pennsylvania Volunteers, Second Regiment, Bucktail Brigade*. Philadelphia: J. B. Lippincott Co., 1895.

Chapman, John A. *History of Edgefield County From the Earliest Settlements to 1897*, Newberry, SC: Elbert A. Aull, Printer and Publisher, 1897.

Cheek, Philip and Pointon, Mair. *History of the Sauk County Riflemen Known as Company "A," Sixth Wisconsin Veteran Volunteer Infantry 1861-1865*. Madison, WI: Democrat Printing Company, 1900.

Cheney, Newel. *History of the Ninth Regiment, New York Volunteer Cavalry*. Poland Center, NY: Martin Merz & Son, 1901.

Clark, Walter, ed. *Histories of the Several Regiments and Battalions from North Carolina in the Great War*, 5 vols. Goldsboro, NC: Nash Brothers, 1901.

Committee on Regimental History. *History of the Sixth New York Cavalry (Second Ira Harris Guard), Second Brigade-First Division-Cavalry Corps, Army of the Potomac, 1861-1865*. Worchester, MA: Blanchard Press, 1908.

Cook, Benjamin F. *History of the Twelfth Massachusetts Volunteers, (Webster Regiment)*. Boston: Twelfth (Webster) Regiment Association, 1882.

Croner, Barbara M., ed. *A Sergeant's Story: Civil War Diary of Jacob J. Zorn, 1862-1865*. Apollo, PA: Closson Press, 1999.

Cross, Andrew. *The War, The Battle of Gettysburg and the Christian Commission*. Baltimore: 1865.

Curtis, O. B. *History of the Twenty-Fourth Michigan of the Iron Brigade*. Detroit: Winn and Hammond, 1891.

Davis, Jr., Charles E. *Three Years in the Army: The Story of the Thirteenth Massachusetts Volunteers*. Boston: Estes and Lauriat, 1894.

Dawes, Rufus R. *Service with the Sixth Wisconsin Volunteers*. Marietta: E. R. Alderman & Sons, 1890.

De Peyster, John Watts. *The Decisive Conflicts of the Late Civil War, or Slaveholders Rebellion, No. 3*. New York: Macdonald & Co., 1867.

Doubleday, Abner. *Chancellorsville and Gettysburg*. New York: Charles Scribner's Sons, 1882.

Dudley, William W. *The Iron Brigade at Gettysburg. Official Report of the Part Borne By The 1st Brigade, 1st Division, 1st Army Corps, Army of the Potomac, in Action at Gettysburg, Pennsylvania, July 1st, 2d, and 3rd 1863*. Cincinnati: Privately printed, 1879.

Dunaway, Wayland Fuller. *Reminiscence of a Rebel*. New York: Neale Publishing Co., 1913.

Executive Committee. *Maine at Gettysburg*. Portland, ME: Lakeside Press, 1898.

Freeman, Warren H. and Eugene H. Freeman. *Letters From Two Brothers Serving in the War For the Union to Their Family at Home*. Cambridge, MA: H. O. Houghton and Co., 1871.

Fulton, William Frierson, Jr. *Family and War Reminiscences of William Frierson Fulton, Jr.*, Livingston, AL: Privately Printed, 1919.

Gaff, Alan D. and Donald H. Gaff, eds. *A Corporal's Story: Civil War Recollections of the Twelfth Massachusetts*. Norman OK: University of Oklahoma Press, 2014.

Gates, Theodore B. *The "Ulster Guard" (20th N. Y. State Militia) and the War of the Rebellion*. New York: Benjamin H. Tyrrel, 1879.

Girvan, Jeffrey M. *"Deliver Us from This Cruel War": The Civil War Letters of Joseph J. Hoyle, 55th North Carolina Infantry*. Jefferson, NC: McFarland & Co., 2010.

Hall, Isaac. *History, of the Ninety-Seventh regiment New York Volunteers ("Conkling Rifles") in the War for the Union*. Utica, NY: L. C. Childs & Son, 1890.

Hard, Abner. *History of the Eighth Cavalry Regiment Illinois Volunteers During the Great Rebellion*. Aurora, IL, 1868.

Hauer, Earl W. *A Record of the Descendants of Levi Nelson Tongue and Adeline Sutton Morse*. Privately printed, 1949.

Heitman, Francis B. *Historical Register and Dictionary of the United States Army*. Washington, D.C.: U.S. Government Printing Office, 1903.

Helm, Thomas B. *History of Delaware County*. Chicago: Kingman Brothers, 1881.

Herdegen, Lance and Sherry Murphy, eds. *Four Years With the Iron Brigade: The Civil War Journals of William R. Ray, Co. F, Seventh Wisconsin Infantry*. Cambridge, MA: Da Capo, 2002.

History of Cumberland and Adams Counties, Pennsylvania. Chicago: Warner Beerst & Co., 1886.

Holabird, S. B. *Flags of the Army of the United States During the War of the Rebellion*. Philadelphia: Burk and McFetridge, 1887.

Howard, Oliver Otis. *Autobiography of Oliver Otis Howard, Major General United States Army*, 2 vols. New York: Baker & Taylor, Co., 1907.

Hubbs, G. Ward, ed. *Voices from Company D: Diaries by the Greensboro Guards, Fifth Alabama Infantry Regiment, Army of Northern Virginia*. Athens, GA: University of Georgia Press, 2003.

Hurst, Samuel. *Journal History of the Seventy-Third Ohio Volunteer Infantry*. Chillacothe, OH, 1866.

Index to the Reports of Committees of the House of Representatives for the First Session of the Forty-Ninth Congress, 1885-'86, 12 vols., vol. 7, Report 2060. Washington, D.C.: U.S. Government Printing Office, 1886.

Jacobs, M. *Notes on the Rebel Invasion of Maryland and Pennsylvania and the Battle of Gettysburg, Jul 1st, 2d and 3d, 1863*, Philadelphia: J. B. Lippincott & Co., 1864.

Jaques, John W. *Three Years' Campaign of the Ninth, N.Y.S.M., During the Southern Rebellion*. New York: Hilton and Co., Publishers, 1865.

Jerome, Aaron Brainard. "Buford in the Battle of Oak Ridge," in John Watts DePeyster, *The Decisive Conflicts of the Late Civil War Or Slaveholders' Rebellion, No. 3*. New York: McDonals and Co., 1867.

Kenderdine, Thaddeus S. *A California Tramp and Later Footprints*. Newtown, PA, 1888.

Kent, Arthur A., ed. *Three Years With Company K*. Madison, NJ: Fairleigh Dickinson U. Press, 1976.

Kiefer, W. R. *History of the One Hundred Fifty-third Regiment Pennsylvania Volunteer Infantry Which Was Recruited in Northampton County, PA, 1862-1863*. Easton, PA: The Chemical Publishing Co., 1909.

Ladd, David L., and Audrey J. Ladd, eds. *John Bachelder's History of the Battle of Gettysburg*. El Dorado Hills, CA: Savas Beatie, 2021.

Ladd, David L. and Audrey J. Ladd, eds. *The Bachelder Papers*, 3 vols. Dayton, OH: Morningside Press, 1994.

Livermore, Mary A. *My Story of the War: A Woman's Narrative of Four Years Personal Experience*. Hartford, CT: A. D. Worthington and Co., 1889.

Locke, William Henry. *The Story of the Regiment*. Philadelphia: J. B. Lippincott & Co., 1868.

Marcus, Edward, *A New Canaan Private in the Civil War: Letters of Justus M. Silliman, Seventeenth Connecticut Volunteers*. New Canaan, CT: New Canaan Historical Society, 1984.

Massachusetts Adjutant-General's Office. Annual Report of the Adjutant General, December 31, 1863. Boston: Wright & Potter, State Printers, 1864.

Massachusetts Adjutant-General's Office. Annual Report of the Adjutant General, 1861-1866. Boston: Wright & Potter, State Printers, 1867.

McCalmont, Robert, ed., *Extracts From Letters Written by Alfred B. McCalmont, From the Front During the War of the Rebellion*. Stroudsburg, PA: Daily Record, 1901.

Mills, George H. *History of the Sixteenth North Carolina Regiment*. Privately printed, 1901.

Monument Commission. *Illinois Monuments at Gettysburg*. Springfield, IL: W. W. Rokker, State Printer, 1892.

Moore, John W. *Roster of North Carolina Troops in the War Between the States*, 4 vols. Raleigh: Ashe & Gatling, State Printers, 1882.

Morse, William Lowry. *Grandad and the Civil War*. Privately printed, 1994.

Moyer, Henry P. *History of the Seventeenth Regiment Pennsylvania Volunteer Cavalry*. Lebanon, PA: Sowers Printing Co., n.d.

Myers, Frank M. *The Comanches: A History of White's Battalion. Virginia Cavalry, Laurel Brig., Hampton Div., A.N.V., C. S.A.* Baltimore: Piet & Co., 1871.

Nesbit, John W., comp. *General History of Company D, 149th Pennsylvania Volunteers*. Oakdale, PA: Oakdale Publishing & Printing Co., 1908.

Nevins, Allan, ed. *A Diary of Battle: The Personal Journals of Colonel Charles S. Wainwright, 1862-1865*. New York: Da Capo Press, 1998.

Newcomer, C. Armour. *Cole's Cavalry or Three Years in the Saddle in the Shenandoah Valley*. Baltimore: Cushing & Company, 1895.

New York Monuments Commission, *New York at Gettysburg: Final Report of the Battlefield of Gettysburg*, 3 vols. Albany: J. B. Lyon, Co., 1900-1902.

Nicholson, John, ed. *Pennsylvania at Gettysburg*, 3 vols. Harrisburg: E. K. Meyers, State Printer, 1893.

Nolan, Alan T. *The Iron Brigade: A Military History*. Bloomington: Indiana University Press, 1994.

Norton, Henry. *Deeds of Daring or History of the Eighth N. Y. Volunteer Cavalry*. Norwich, NY: Chenango Telegraph Printing House, 1889.

Park, Robert E. *Sketch of the Twelfth Alabama Infantry*. Richmond: Wm. Ellis Jones, Book and Job Printer, 1906.

Priest, John Michael, ed. *John T. McMahon's Diary of the 136th New York, 1861-1864*. Shippensburg, PA: White Mane Publishing, 1993.

Quiner, E. B. *The Military History of Wisconsin*. Chicago: Clarke & Co., Publishers, 1866.

Reece, Jasper N. *Report of the Adjutant General of the State of Illinois*, 9 vols. (vol. 8). Springfield, IL: Journal Co., 1901.

Reynolds Memorial; Addresses Delivered Before The Historical Society of Pennsylvania Upon the Presentation of a Portrait of Maj.-Gen. John F. Reynolds, March, 8, 1880. Philadelphia: J. B. Lippincott and Co.,1880.

Schurz, Carl. *The Reminiscences of Carl Schurz*, 3 vols. New York: The McClure Co., 1908.

Small, Abner R. *The Sixteenth Maine Regiment in the War of the Rebellion, 1861-1865*. Portland, ME: B. Thurston & Co., 1886.

Smith, A. P. *History of the Seventy-Sixth Regiment New York Volunteers; What It Endured And Accomplished*. Cortland, NY: Truair, Smith & Myers, 1867.

Stevenson, David. *Indiana's Roll of Honor*, 2 vols. Indianapolis: A. D. Streight, Publisher, 1864.

Stine, James Henry, *History of the Army of the Potomac*, Philadelphia, PA: J. B. Rodgers Printing Co., 1892.

Survivors' Association. *History of the 121st Regiment, Pennsylvania Volunteers: "An Account From The Ranks."* Philadelphia: Catholic Standard Press and Times, 1906.

Tevis, C. V. and D. R. Marquis, comps. *The History of the Fighting Fourteenth*. Brooklyn, NY: Eagle Press, 1911.

The Ladies' and Gentlemen's Fulton Aid Society. *Life in Southern Prisons; from the Diary of Corporal Charles Smedley, of Company G, 90th Regiment Penn'a Volunteers*. Lancaster, PA: Pearsol & Geist, 1865.

The Union Army: A History of Military Affairs in the Loyal States, 1861-1865, 8 vols. Madison, WI: Federal Publishing Co., 1908.

Thomas, Mary Warner and Richard A. Sauers, eds. *The Civil War Letters of First Lieutenant James B. Thomas, Adjutant, 107th Pennsylvania Volunteers*. Baltimore: Butternut and Blue, 1995.

Thomson, Orville. *Narrative of the Service of the Seventh Indiana Infantry in the War for the Union*. Self-published, n.d.

Todd, William, ed. *History of the Ninth Regiment N.Y.S.M.-N.G.S.N.Y. (Eighty-Third N. Y. Volunteers)*. New York: Veterans of the Regiment, 1889.

Tompkins, Daniel A., and A. S. *Company K, Fourteenth South Carolina Volunteers*. Charlotte, NC: Observer Printing and Publishing House, 1897.

Tomasak, Peter, ed. *Avery Harris Civil War Journal*. Luzerne, PA: Luzerne National Bank, 2000.

Tremain. Henry Edwin. *Two Days of War, A Gettysburg Narrative and Other Excursions*. New York: Bonnell, Silver, and Bowers, 1905.

Underwood, Adin B. *The Three Years' Service of the Thirty-Third Mass. Infantry Regiment, 1862-1865*. Boston: A. Williams & Co., 1881.

United States Surgeon-General's Office. *Medical and Surgical History of the War of the Rebellion*, 3 vols./6 books. Washington, D.C.: U.S. Government Printing Office, 1870-88.

United States War Department. *The War of the Rebellion: A Compilation of the Official Records of the Union and Confederate Armies*, 128 vols. Washington, D.C.: U.S. Government Printing Office, 1880-1901.

Vail, Enos B. *Reminiscences of a Boy in the Civil War*. Brooklyn, NY: Privately printed, 1915.

Vautier, John D. *History of the 88th Pennsylvania Volunteers in the War for the Union, 1861-1865*. Philadelphia: J. B. Lippincott Co., 1894.

Warren, Horatio N. *Two Reunions of the 142d Regiment, Pa. Vols.* Buffalo: The Courier Co., 1890.

Weld, Stephen M. *War Diary and Letters of Stephen Minot Weld*. Boston: The Riverside Press, 1912.

Drill Manuals

Andrews, Richard Snowden. *Andrews' Mounted Artillery Drill; Compiled According to the Latest Regulations From Standard Military Authority*. Charleston, SC: Ebans and Cogswell, 1863.

Casey, Silas. *Infantry Tactics For the Instruction, Exercise, Manoeuvres of the Soldier, A Company, Line of Skirmishers or Corps D'Armee*, 2 vols. New York: D. Van Nostrand, 1863.

Cooke, Phillip St. George. *Cavalry Tactics or, Regulations for the Instruction, Formations, and Movements of the Cavalry of the Army and Volunteers of the United States*, 2 vols. Philadelphia: J. B. Lippincott & Co., 1862.

Craighill, William P. *The Army Officer's Pocket Companion; Principally Designed for Staff Officers*. New York: D. Van Nostrand, 1862.

Hardee, William J. *Rifle and Light Infantry Tactics for the Exercise and Manoeuvres of Troops When Acting as Light Infantry or Riflemen*, 2 vols. Philadelphia: J. B. Lippincott & Co., 1861.

McClellan, George B. *Regulations and Instructions for the Field Service of the U.S. Cavalry in Time of War*. Philadelphia: J. B. Lippincott & Co., 1862.

Published Secondary Sources

Magazines

Coddington, Ronald S. "Three Bullets at Gettysburg: Medal of Honor Recipients," *Military Images*, vol. 35, no. 3 (Summer 2017), 3.

Dougherty, James J. "?We Have Come to Stay!': The 143rd Regiment Pennsylvania Volunteer Infantry and the Fight for McPherson's Ridge," *Gettysburg Magazine*, no. 24, 38-55.

Herdegen, Lance J. "Old Soldiers And War Talk," *Gettysburg Magazine*, January 1, 1990, 15-24.

Herdegen, Lance J. "The Lieutenant Who Arrested a General," *Gettysburg Magazine*, January 1, 1991, 25-32.

Krumwiede, John F. "A July Afternoon on McPherson's Ridge," *Gettysburg Magazine*, no. 21, 21-44.

Reinsberg, Mark. "General Stone's Elevated Railroad: Portrait of an Inventor, Part III," *The Western Pennsylvania Historical Magazine*, vol. 50, no. 1 (January 1967), 7-21.

Books

Busey, John W. and David G. Martin. *Regimental Strengths and Losses at Gettysburg*, 4th ed. Hightsown, NJ: Longstreet House, 2005.

Busey, Travis W. and John W. Busey. *Confederate Casualties at Gettysburg: A Comprehensive Record*, 4 vols. Jefferson, NC: McFarland & Co., Inc., 2011.

The Catholic Church in the United States of America, 2 vols. New York: Catholic Editing Co., 1914.

The Civil War Commission, Greater Waynesboro Chamber of Commerce. *Fifteen Days Under the Confederate Flag*. Waynesboro, PA, 1963.

Divine, John E. *35th Battalion, Virginia Cavalry*. Lynchburg, VA: H. E. Howard, 1985.

Ernsberger, Don. *Also For Glory, Muster: The Story of the Pettigrew, Trimble Charge at Gettysburg*. Bloomington, IN: Xlibris Corp., 2008.

Gragg, Rod. *Covered With Glory: The 26th North Carolina Infantry at Gettysburg*. New York: Harper Collins Publishers, 2000.

Griffith, Paddy. *Battle in the Civil War*. Camberley, Surrey, UK: Fieldbooks, 1986.

Gottfried, Bradley M. *The Maps of Gettysburg: An Atlas of the Gettysburg Campaign, June 3-July 13, 1863*. El Dorado Hills, CA: Savas Beatie, 2007.

Herdegen, Lance J. *The Iron Brigade in Civil War and Memory*. El Dorado Hills: Savas Beatie, 2012.

Herdegen, Lance J. and William J. K. Beaudot. *In the Bloody Railroad Cut at Gettysburg: The 6th Wisconsin of the Iron Brigade and Its Famous Charge*. El Dorado Hills: Savas Beatie, 2015.

Jordan, Weymouth T., Jr., ed., *North Carolina Troops, 1861-1865, A Roster*, 18 vols. Raleigh, NC: Division of Archives and History, 1987-2004.

Krick, Robert E. L. *Staff Officers In Gray: A Biographical Register of the Staff Officers in the Army of Northern Virginia*. Chapel Hill, NC: The University of North Carolina Press, 2003.

Krumwiede, John F., *Disgrace at Gettysburg: The Arrest and Court- Martial of Brigadier General Thomas A. Rowley, USA*. Jefferson, NC: McFarland & Co., 2006.

Martin, David G. *Confederate Monuments at Gettysburg: The Gettysburg Battle Monuments*, vol. 1. Hightstown, NJ: Longstreet House, 1986.

McKeever, C. [Chauncey], comp. *Civil War Battle Flags of the Union Army and Order of Battle*. New York: Knickerbocker Press, 1997.

McLean, James. *Cutler's Brigade at Gettysburg*. Baltimore and El Dorado Hills, 1995 and 2023.

Raus, Jr., Edmund J. *A Generation on the March: The Union Army at Gettysburg*. Lynchburg, VA: H E. Howard, Inc., 1987.

Reily, John T. *History and Directory of the Boroughs of Gettysburg, Oxford, Littlestown, York Springs, Berwick, and East Berlin, Adams County, Pa. with Historical Collections*. Gettysburg, PA: J. E. Wible, Printer, 1880.

Thomas, Sara Sites, *et al. Fairfield in the Civil War*. Gettysburg, PA: Thomas Publications, 2011.

Venner, William Thomas. *The 11th North Carolina Infantry in the Civil War: A History and Roster*. Jefferson, NC: McFarland & Company, 2015, Kindle edition.

Venner, William Thomas. *The 7th Tennessee Infantry in the Civil War: A History and Roster*. Jefferson, NC: McFarland & Company, 2013.

Wittenberg, Eric J., *The Devil's to Pay," John Buford at Gettysburg: A History and Walking Tour*, El Dorado Hills, CA: Savas Beatie LLC, 2014.

Index

About the Author

A retired high school history teacher, John Michael Priest has been interested in Civil War history since an early age. He is a graduate of Loyola College in Baltimore and Hood College in Frederick, Maryland. Legendary historian Edwin C. Bearss praised Mike's grassroots level of history and viewpoint and called him the "Ernie Pyle" of the Civil War soldier.

Mike appeared on the Discovery Channel's "Unsolved History: Pickett's Charge" (2002), and has written extensively about the Civil War. His most recent book was *Stand To It and Give Them Hell: Gettysburg as the Soldiers Experienced it From Cemetery Ridge to Little Round Top, July 2, 1863* (2016).

He and his wife live in Clear Spring, Maryland.